EVANS'
AMERICAN BIBLIOGRAPHY

1639 - - 1820 A. D.

AMERICAN BIBLIOGRAPHY

BY

CHARLES EVANS

A CHRONOLOGICAL DICTIONARY

OF ALL

BOOKS PAMPHLETS AND PERIODICAL PUBLICATIONS

PRINTED IN THE

UNITED STATES OF AMERICA

FROM THE GENESIS OF PRINTING IN 1639
DOWN TO AND INCLUDING THE YEAR 1820

WITH BIBLIOGRAPHICAL AND BIOGRAPHICAL NOTES

VOLUME 8
1790-1792

Ye shades of ancient heroes, ye who toil'd
Through long successive ages to build up
A labouring plan of state, behold at once
The wonder done!
— *James Thomson*

NEW YORK
PETER SMITH
1941

FIRST PUBLISHED 1914
REPRINTED 1941

PRINTED IN THE UNITED STATES OF AMERICA

TO

THE FOUNDERS

AND

COMMITTEE OF MANAGEMENT

OF THE

JOHN CARTER BROWN LIBRARY
BROWN UNIVERSITY
PROVIDENCE RHODE ISLAND

WHO HAVE SO ADMIRABLY SHOWN HOW PRIVATE
WEALTH INTELLIGENTLY DIRECTED AND ADMINISTERED
CAN AID THE HIGHER SCHOLARSHIP OF THE COUNTRY

This Volume is Dedicated

BY THE AUTHOR

The following supplemental list of Subscribers to this work, received since the publication of the preceding volumes, is here recorded with a deep sense of obligation for their practical assistance in its publication :

BIBLIOTHEQUE DE L'UNIVERSITÉ de Nancy, France.
M. PAUL CHARLES DUMONT, Bibliothècaire en Chef.
BOWDOIN COLLEGE LIBRARY, Brunswick, Maine.
DR. GEORGE THOMAS LITTLE, Librarian.
CITY LIBRARY, Manchester, New Hampshire.
MISS F. MABEL WINCHELL, Librarian.
FREE PUBLIC LIBRARY, Louisville, Kentucky.
MR. GEORGE THOMAS SETTLE, Librarian.
JOHN JERMAIN MEMORIAL LIBRARY, Sag Harbor, New York.
MR. SYLVANUS PIERSON JERMAIN, Secretary.
McGILL UNIVERSITY LIBRARY, Montreal, Canada.
MR. CHARLES HENRY GOULD, Librarian.
MASSACHUSETTS HISTORICAL SOCIETY, Boston, Massachusetts.
MR. WORTHINGTON CHAUNCEY FORD, Editor of Publications.
MEADVILLE THEOLOGICAL SCHOOL LIBRARY, Meadville, Pennsylvania.
WALTER C. GREEN, S. T. B. Librarian.
MECHANICS'-MERCANTILE LIBRARY, San Francisco, California.
MR. FRANCIS BARNUM GRAVES, Librarian.
MITCHELL LIBRARY, Glasgow, Scotland.
MR. FRANCIS T. BARRETT, Librarian.
PHILIPPINE LIBRARY, Manila, Philippine Islands.
MR. JAMES A. ROBERTSON, Librarian.
PUBLIC LIBRARY, Riverside, California.
MR. JOSEPH F. DANIELS, Librarian.
PUBLIC LIBRARY, Rockford, Illinois.
MISS JANE P. HUBBELL, Librarian.
WASHINGTON UNIVERSITY LIBRARY, St. Louis, Missouri.
MR. WINTHROP HOLT CHENERY, Librarian.
ARCHER MILTON HUNTINGTON, ESQUIRE, New York City.
JAMES COMLY McCOY, ESQUIRE, Nayatt Point, Rhode Island.
HAROLD PEIRCE, ESQUIRE, Philadelphia, Pennsylvania.
EDWARD WHEELOCK, M. D., Rochester, New York.
DR. ESTANISLAO S. ZEBALLOS, Buenos Aires, Argentina.
CHAS. FRED. HEARTMAN, 36 Lexington Avenue, New York City.
GEORGE A. JACKSON, 8 Pemberton Square, Boston.
MARTINUS NIJHOFF, Lange Voorhout 9, 'S Gravenhage, Holland.
MARION O'SHAUGHNESSY, Merwin Sales Company, New York City.
THEODORE E. SCHULTE, 132 East 23d Street, New York City.

AMERICAN BIBLIOGRAPHY

1639 - - 1820 A. D.

1790

22298   ADDRESS TO THE INHABITANTS OF ALEXANDRIA, AND OTHER SEA-PORTS IN THE UNITED STATES OF AMERICA. FROM A PROPRIETOR OF LANDS ON THE SCIOTO.
Printed in the year 1790. pp. 15. 8vo.   NYHS.

22299   ADGATE, ANDREW
RUDIMENTS OF MUSIC, ON A NEW AND IMPROVED PLAN. BY ANDREW ADGATE, P. U. A.
Philadelphia: Printed by John M'Culloch, 1790.
10th Pennsylvania District Copyright, issued to Andrew Adgate, as Author, 18 November, 1790.

22300   ÆSOPUS.   619 – 564 B. C.
THE SELECT FABLES OF ÆSOP AND OTHER FABULISTS, IN THREE BOOKS: CONTAINING: I. FABLES FROM THE ANCIENTS. II. FABLES FROM THE MODERNS. III. ORIGINAL FABLES, NEWLY INVENTED. BY ROBERT DODSLEY.
Philadelphia: Printed by William Spotswood, 1790.

22301   THE ALBANY GAZETTE. VOL. VI. NUMB. 325. MONDAY, JANUARY 4, [—VOL. VII. NUMB. 428. THURSDAY, DECEMBER 30, 1790.]
Printed every Monday and Thursday by Charles R. and George Webster, No. 46 (on the north side of) State-Street, corner of Middle-Lane. 1790. fol. AAS.
In July, the Printing-Office was removed to "No. 46, (on the north side of) State-Street, corner of Middle-Alley [Middle-Lane.]"

22302   THE ALBANY REGISTER. VOL. II. NUMB. 65. MONDAY, JANUARY 4, [—VOL. III. NUMB. 129. MONDAY, DECEMBER 27, 1790.]
Printed and published (every Monday at 12s. per ann.) by Robert Barber & Co. Maiden-Lane, four doors west of the Market. 1790. fol.

22303   ALLEN, JOHN
A CONCISE DISCANT [*sic*] UPON THE MAJESTY, EXCELLENCY AND PRECIOUSNESS OF THE SCRIPTURES: IN A LETTER TO A FRIEND.
Boston: Re-printed by Benjamin Edes and Sons. M,DCC,XC. pp. 8.
16mo.   AAS.

22304 THE AMERICAN HERALD, AND THE WASHINGTON GAZETTE. VOL. I. NO. 8. MON-
DAY, AUGUST 30, [—No. 24. MONDAY, DECEMBER 27, 1790.]
Boston [Commonwealth of Massachusetts]: Printed and published by Ed-
ward Eveleth Powars, opposite the new Court-House, in Court-Street. 1790. fol.
In continuation of *The Saturday Evening Herald, and the Washington*
Gazette.

22305 THE AMERICAN [U. S. ARMS] MERCURY. VOL. VI. NUMB. 287. MONDAY, JAN-
UARY 4, [—NUMB. 338. MONDAY, DECEMBER 27, 1790.]
Hartford: Printed by Elisha Babcock. 1790. fol. AAS. CHS. YC.

22306 —— THE CARRIER OF THE AMERICAN MERCURY, PRESENTS THE FOLLOWING TO
HIS CUSTOMERS, WISHING THEM A HAPPY NEW YEAR.
[Hartford: Printed by Elisha Babcock, 1790.] Broadside.

22307 THE AMERICAN MUSEUM, OR REPOSITORY OF ANCIENT AND MODERN FUGITIVE
PIECES, PROSE AND POETICAL FOR JANUARY 1787. [Two lines of verse.] VOL. I.
NO. I. THE THIRD EDITION.
Philadelphia: Carey, Stewart & Co. M.DCC.XC. AAS.

22308 —— THE AMERICAN MUSEUM, OR REPOSITORY OF ANCIENT AND MODERN FUGITIVE
PIECES, PROSE AND POETICAL FOR APRIL, 1788. [Three lines of quotation.] VOL.
III. NO. IV. THE SECOND EDITION.
Philadelphia: Carey, Stewart & Co. M.DCC.XC. AAS. LOC.

22309 —— THE AMERICAN MUSEUM, OR, UNIVERSAL MAGAZINE: CONTAINING ESSAYS ON
AGRICULTURE—COMMERCE—MANUFACTURE — POLITICS—MORALS—AND MANNERS.
SKETCHES OF NATIONAL CHARACTERS—NATURAL AND CIVIL HISTORY—AND BIOG-
RAPHY. LAW INFORMATION—PUBLIC PAPERS—PROCEEDINGS OF CONGRESS—IN-
TELLIGENCE; MORAL TALES—ANCIENT AND MODERN POETRY, &C., &C. VOL. VII,
FROM JANUARY TO JUNE, 1790.
Philadelphia: Carey, Stewart, and Co. M.DCC.XC. pp. 344, 44, 44,
44, 40, (4). 8vo. AAS. BA. HC. LOC. NYHS.

22310 —— THE AMERICAN MUSEUM, OR, UNIVERSAL MAGAZINE: CONTAINING ESSAYS ON
AGRICULTURE—COMMERCE—MANUFACTURES—POLITICS—MORALS—AND MANNERS.
SKETCHES OF NATIONAL CHARACTERS—NATURAL AND CIVIL HISTORY—AND BIOG-
RAPHY. LAW INFORMATION—PUBLIC PAPERS—PROCEEDINGS OF CONGRESS—IN-
TELLIGENCE; MORAL TALES—ANCIENT AND MODERN POETRY, &C., &C. VOL. VIII.
FROM JULY TO DECEMBER, 1790.
Philadelphia: Carey, Stewart & Co. M.DCC.XC. pp. 288, 40, 80, 20,
52. 8vo. AAS. BA. HC. LOC. NYHS.

22311 THE AMERICAN SONGSTER, BEING A COLLECTION OF THE MOST CELEBRATED
ANCIENT AND MODERN SONGS.
Portsmouth: Printed by John Melcher, 1790.

22312 AMERICANISCHER STADT UND LAND KALENDER AUF DAS 1791STE JAHR CHRISTI,
WELCHES EIN GEMEINES JAHR IST VON 365 TAGEN.
Philadelphia: Gedruckt und zu haben bey Carl Cist, in der Zweyten-
strasse, nah am Eck der Rehs-strasse. [1790.] pp. (44). 4to. AAS. LOC.

22313 AMES, PHILOMATH N. pseudonym.
THE AMERICAN ALMANACK, FOR THE YEAR OF OUR LORD M.DCC.XCI. [Twenty lines.]
BY PHILOMATH N. AMES, ESQ. PROFESSOR OF ASTRONOMY AND NATURAL PHILOS-
OPHY IN THE COLLEGE OF BERLIN. CALCULATED FOR THE MERIDIAN OF LITCH-
FIELD, LAT. 41 DEG. 45 MIN. NORTH.
Litchfield: Printed by T. Collier. [1790.] pp. [24.] 12mo. NYPL.

22314   ANDREWS, JOHN   1746 – 1813
A SERMON ON THE IMPORTANCE OF MUTUAL KINDNESS: PREACHED AT ST. JAMES'S BRISTOL, DECEMBER 27, 1789, BEING THE ANNIVERSARY OF ST. JOHN THE EVANGELIST BEFORE THE BRETHREN OF LODGE NO. 25. BY THE REVEREND JOHN ANDREWS, D. D. RECTOR OF ST. JAMES'S BRISTOL, AND PROFESSOR OF RHETORICK AND BELLES LETTRES IN THE COLLEGE AND ACADEMY OF PHILADELPHIA.
Philadelphia: Printed by William Young, 1790.

22315   ANDREWS, ROBERT
THE VIRGINIA ALMANACK, FOR THE YEAR OF OUR LORD, 1791. BEING THE THIRD AFTER BISSEXTILE OR LEAP YEAR, AND THE FIFTEENTH YEAR OF AMERICAN INDEPENDENCE. [Three lines.] BY ROBERT ANDREWS, PHILO. [Three lines of verse.]
Richmond: Printed and sold by John Dixon, Printer to this Commonwealth. [1790.] pp. (32). 16mo.   LOC.

22316   —— THE VIRGINIA ALMANACK, FOR THE YEAR OF OUR LORD, 1791. BEING THE THIRD AFTER LEAP YEAR, AND THE FIFTEENTH OF AMERICAN INDEPENDENCE. BY ROBERT ANDREWS, PHILO. [Thirteen lines.]
Richmond: Printed and sold by Thomas Nicolson. [1790.] pp. (40). 16mo.

22317   —— THE VIRGINIA ALMANACK FOR THE YEAR OF OUR LORD, 1791.
Richmond: Printed and sold by Aug. Davis. [1790.]

22318   THE ARMINIAN MAGAZINE: CONSISTING OF EXTRACTS AND ORIGINAL TREATISES ON GENERAL REDEMPTION. VOL. II. FOR THE YEAR 1790.
Printed in Philadelphia, by Prichard & Hall, in Market-Street, and sold by John Dickins, in Fourth-Street (east side) near the corner of Race-Street.
M.DCC.XC. pp. 620, (4). 8vo.   BA. LOC.

22319   ARMSTRONG, JOHN   1709 – 1779
ART OF PRESERVING HEALTH. A POEM, IN FOUR BOOKS.
New-Haven: Printed and sold by Isaac Beers, 1790.

22320   ASHBURN, REBECCA
THREE REMARKABLE DREAMS, BY MRS. REBECCA ASHBURN, OF PHILADELPHIA.
[Philadelphia: 1790.]

22321   AUSTIN, SAMUEL   1760 – 1830
THE NATURE AND HAPPINESS, OF THAT HABITUAL PREPARATION FOR DEATH, WHICH THE UNCERTAINTY OF LIFE DEMANDS, ILLUSTRATED AND URGED. A FUNERAL SERMON, DELIVERED AT EXETER, ON THE TENTH OF APRIL, SEVENTEEN HUNDRED AND NINETY, AT A RELIGIOUS IMPROVEMENT OF A SINGULAR AND VERY AFFLICTIVE PROVIDENCE, WHICH REMOVED BY DEATH TWO YOUNG PERSONS, BENJAMIN SMITH, JUN. AND MARY SMITH, A SON AND DAUGHTER OF MAJOR BENJAMIN SMITH, OF EXETER, WHO BOTH DIED OF A CONSUMPTION ON THE MORNING OF APRIL 8TH, 1790. BY SAMUEL AUSTIN, A. M. [Two lines of quotations.]
Exeter: Printed by J. Lamson, and sold at his office. M,DCC,XC. pp. 29. 8vo.   AAS.

22322   BACKUS, ISAAC   1724 – 1806
THE LIBERAL SUPPORT OF GOSPEL MINISTERS, OPENED AND INCULCATED. BY ISAAC BACKUS, PASTOR OF A CHURCH IN MIDDLEBOROUGH. [One line from] I TIM. v. 18.
Boston: Printed by Samuel Hall, at No. 53, in Cornhill. 1790. pp. 36. 12mo.   JCB. LOC.

22323   THE BALLOON Almanac [cut] for the year of our Lord, 1791.
Lancaster: Printed and sold by J. Bailey. [1790.]

22324   BALTIMORE. Maryland. Carpenters Society.
Constitution, rules, regulations of the Carpenters Society of Baltimore.
Baltimore: Printed by John Hayes? 1790.

22325   BANCROFT, Aaron   1755 – 1839
A Discourse delivered at Windsor, in the State of Vermont, on the 23rd of June, MDCCXC. At the ordination of the Rev. Samuel Shuttlesworth, to the pastoral care of the Catholick Christian Church and Society in that place. By Aaron Bancroft, a. m. pastor of the Second Church, in Worcester.
Printed at Worcester, Massachusetts, by Isaiah Thomas. MDCCXC. pp. 24. 8vo.   AAS. BM. LOC. HC. JCB. MHS. NYPL.

22326   BARRY, John
The American spelling book, arranged upon a plan entirely new, adapted to the capacities of children, and designed as an immediate improvement in spelling and reading the English language. The whole being recommended by several eminent teachers, as the most useful performance to expedite the instruction of youth. By John Barry, master of the Free School of the Protestant Episcopal Church.
Philadelphia: Printed by Carey, Stewart and Co? 1790.
The *Philadelphia* spelling book, with otherwise the same title, is the 1st Pennsylvania District Copyright, issued to John Barry, as Author, 9 June, 1790.

22327   BARTLET, J.
The Gentleman's pocket farrier; shewing how to use your horse on a journey; and what remedies are proper for common accidents, that may befall him on the road. With a copperplate, shewing the age of a horse by his teeth.
Middletown: Printed and sold by Moses H. Woodward. 1790

22328   BARTRAM, Moses
Exercitatio med. in aug. de victu.
Philadelphiæ, E typis Thomæ Lang. 1790. pp. (2), (2), 28. 8vo.   SGO.

22329   BARTRAM, William   1739 – 1823
Proposals for printing by subscription, on a fine paper, with a new and elegant American letter, cast by John Baine & Co. Travels through North and South Carolina, Georgia, East and West-Florida, the Cherokee Nation and through the extensive territories of the Muscogulges or Creek Confederacy, and the country of the Chactaws: containing an account of the soil and natural productions of those regions together with observations on the manners and customs of the Indians. By William Barton, botanist, of Philadelphia, who was employed from 1773 to 1777, by the celebrated Doctor Fothergill, of London, to explore the extensive countries above mentioned. Conditions. . . .
[Philadelphia: Printed by James and Johnson, 1790.] pp. (3). 4to. NYPL.

22330   BAXTER, RICHARD   1615 – 1691
BAXTER'S DIRECTIONS TO SLAVEHOLDERS REVIVED. . . . TO WHICH IS SUB-
JOINED A LETTER FROM THE WORTHY ANTHONY BENEZET, TO THE CELEBRATED
ABBE RAYNAL. WITH HIS ANSWER.
Philadelphia: Printed by Francis Bailey. MDCCLXXXX. pp. 8; 16; 12.
24mo.

22331   1615 – 1691
——— THE SAINTS EVERLASTING REST: OR, A TREATISE OF THE BLESSED STATE OF
THE SAINTS IN THEIR ENJOYMENT OF GOD IN GLORY: EXTRACTED FROM THE
WORKS OF MR. RICHARD BAXTER, BY JOHN WESLEY, M. A. LATE FELLOW OF
LINCOLN COLLEGE, OXFORD.
*Philadelphia: Printed by Prichard & Hall, in Market-Street, and sold by
John Dickins, on Fourth-Street, No. 43, near Race-Street.* M.DCC.XC. pp. 399,
(1). 8vo.   AAS. JCB. LOC.

22332   BEERS, ANDREW   1749 – 1824
BEERS'S ALMANACK AND EPHEMERIS OF THE MOTION OF THE SUN AND MOON; THE
TRUE PLACES AND ASPECTS OF THE PLANETS; THE RISING, SETTING AND SOUTHING
OF THE MOON, FOR THE YEAR OF OUR LORD, 1791: BEING THE THIRD AFTER
BISSEXTILE OR LEAP YEAR, AND THE FIFTEENTH OF AMERICAN INDEPENDENCE.
[Nine lines.] BY ANDREW BEERS, PHILOM. [Twelve lines of verse.]
Hartford: Printed by Hudson and Goodwin. [1790.] pp. (24). 12mo.
                             AAS. CHS. LOC.

22333   ——— SHEET ALMANACK FOR THE YEAR 1791.
Hartford: Printed by Hudson and Goodwin, 1790. Broadside. fol.

22334   ——— GREENLEAF'S NEW-YORK, CONNECTICUT, & NEW-JERSEY ALMANACK, OR
DIARY, WITH AN EPHEMERIS; FOR THE YEAR OF OUR LORD, 1791.
Printed at New-York—By Thomas Greenleaf, for 1791. [1790.]

22335   BELKNAP, JEREMY   1744 – 1798
THE SUBSCRIBER, BEING ENGAGED IN CONTINUING THE HISTORY OF NEW HAMP-
SHIRE, AND INTENDING TO GIVE A TOPOGRAPHICAL DESCRIPTION OF THE COUNTRY,
AND A PARTICULAR ACCOUNT OF EVERY OCCURRENCE, WHICH MAY DESERVE THE
PUBLICK NOTICE, TAKES THIS METHOD OF APPLYING TO THE MINISTERS AND
OTHER GENTLEMEN OF NOTE, IN THE STATE, AND BEGS THE FAVOUR OF THEM
TO COLLECT AND TRANSMIT TO HIM SUCH INFORMATION AS CAN BE OBTAINED ON
THE FOLLOWING HEADS . . . JEREMY BELKNAP, SUMMER STREET, BOSTON.
MARCH 1, 1790.
[Boston: Printed by Isaiah Thomas and E. T. Andrews, 1790.] Broadside.
8vo.   BM. NYPL.

22336   ——— PROPOSAL, FOR PRINTING BY SUBSCRIPTION, THE SECOND AND THIRD VOL-
UMES OF THE HISTORY OF NEW-HAMPSHIRE. BY JEREMY BELKNAP, A. M.
. . . CONDITIONS. . . .
[Boston: Printed by I. Thomas and E. T. Andrews, 1790.] Broadside.
fol.   NYHS.

22337   BELSHAM, WILLIAM   1753 – 1827
AN ESSAY ON THE AFRICAN SLAVE TRADE.
*Philadelphia: Printed by Daniel Humphreys, in Front-Street, near the
Drawbridge.* M.DCC.XC. pp. [15.] 8vo.   AAS. JCB. LOC.

22338   BEND, JOSEPH GROVE JOHN   1762 – 1812
A DISCOURSE DELIVERED IN ST. PAUL'S CHURCH, PHILADELPHIA, SUNDAY, JULY 25TH, 1790, ON OCCASION OF THE DEATH OF MRS. LUCIA MAGAW, WIFE OF THE REV. SAMUEL MAGAW, D. D.: AND NOW PUBLISHED AT HIS REQUEST. BY JOSEPH BEND, A. M. ASSISTANT MINISTER OF CHRIST-CHURCH AND ST. PETER'S.
Philadelphia: Printed by William Young, M,DCC,XC. pp. 24. 8vo.   BA.

22339   BENEDICT, NOAH
PREPARATION FOR DEATH. A SERMON, DELIVERED AT THE FUNERAL OF THE REVEREND JOSEPH BELLAMY, D. D. OF BETHLEM, MARCH IXTH, 1790. BY NOAH BENEDICT, A. M. PASTOR OF THE CHURCH IN WOODBURY. TO WHICH IS ADDED, AN APPENDIX, CONTAINING SOME MEMOIRS OF THE DOCTOR'S LIFE. [Two lines of Scripture texts.]
New-Haven: Printed by Thomas and Samuel Green. M.DCC.XC. pp. 45.
8vo.   AAS. BM. JCB. LOC. MHS.
Reprinted in the first volume of Dr. Bellamy's Works.

22340   BENHAM, ASAHEL
FEDERAL HARMONY; CONTAINING, IN A FAMILIAR MANNER, THE RUDIMENTS OF PSALMODY; WITH A COLLECTION OF CHURCH MUSIC. (MOST OF WHICH ARE ENTIRELY NEW.)
New-Haven: Printed and sold by Abel Morse. 1790. pp. 12, 36. obl.8vo.
Connecticut District Copyright, issued to Asahel Benham, as Author and Proprietor, 17 September, 1791. For sale by Elisha Whittelsey, junior, in Wallingford, in 1791.

22341   BENTLEY, WILLIAM   1758 – 1819
A COLLECTION OF PSALMS AND HYMNS FOR PUBLIC WORSHIP.
Salem: Printed by Dabney and Cushing. [1789.] pp. 166. 12mo.   BA.

22342   1758 – 1819
—— A SERMON, PREACHED AT THE STONE CHAPEL IN BOSTON, SEPTEMBER 12, 1790. BY WILLIAM BENTLEY, A. M. PASTOR OF THE SECOND CONGREGATIONAL CHURCH IN SALEM. · PUBLISHED AT THE REQUEST OF THE HEARERS.
Boston: Printed by Samuel Hall, at No. 53, Cornhill. MDCCXC. pp. [24.]
8vo.   AAS. BA. BM. BPL. HC. JCB. LOC. MHS.

22343   THE BERKSHIRE [cut] CHRONICLE AND THE MASSACHUSETTS INTELLIGENCER. [Motto.] VOL. II. NUM. 28. THURSDAY, JANUARY 7, [— VOL. III. NUM. 13. THURSDAY, SEPTEMBER 30, 1790.]
Pittsfield, Published by Roger Storrs, near the Meeting-House. 1790.
fol.   AAS.
How long the Chronicle was published after the above date is not know, but publication certainly ceased before the close of this year.

22344   BERQUIN, ARNAUD   1750 – 1791
THE CHILDREN'S FRIEND, AND YOUTH'S MONITOR. CONSISTING OF TALES AND STORIES, EQUALLY ADAPTED FOR INSTRUCTION AND ENTERTAINMENT. TRANSLATED FROM THE FRENCH OF M. BERQUIN. VOL. III. [— IV.]
Boston: Printed by John W. Folsom, for E. Larkin, jun. No. 50 Cornhill. 1790. 2 vols.

22345   BIBLIA.

THE HOLY BIBLE, CONTAINING THE OLD AND NEW TESTAMENTS: TRANSLATED OUT OF THE ORIGINAL TONGUES; AND WITH THE FORMER TRANSLATIONS DILIGENTLY COMPARED AND REVISED.

     Philadelphia: Printed by William Young, Bookseller, No. 52, Second-Street, the corner of Chesnut-Street. M,DCC,XC. Unpaged. Signatures A-Ll in twelves. 12mo.   AAS. NYPL.

Second title: THE NEW TESTAMENT OF OUR LORD AND SAVIOUR JESUS CHRIST, TRANSLATED OUT OF THE ORIGINAL GREEK; AND WITH THE FORMER TRANSLATIONS DILIGENTLY COMPARED AND REVISED.

     Philadelphia: Printed by W. Young, Bookseller and Stationer, the corner of Second and Chesnut-Streets. M,DCC,XC. Unpaged.

     This edition was published in 1789, although dated 1790, in two states: "Some on fine paper." The Publisher's advertisement also states: "It has two strong recommendations to preference—it is cheaper than any imported edition; and it is composed entirely of American manufacture." "He has also put to press a twenty-four mo edition." As follows:

22346   —— THE HOLY BIBLE, CONTAINING THE OLD AND NEW TESTAMENTS: TRANSLATED OUT OF THE ORIGINAL TONGUES; AND WITH THE FORMER TRANSLATIONS DILIGENTLY COMPARED AND REVISED.

     Philadelphia: Printed by William Young, Bookseller, No. 52, Second-Street, the corner of Chesnut-Street. M,DCC,XC. Unpaged. Signatures A-Ll. 24mo.

Second title: THE NEW TESTAMENT OF OUR LORD AND SAVIOUR JESUS CHRIST, TRANSLATED OUT OF THE ORIGINAL GREEK; AND WITH THE FORMER TRANSLATIONS DILIGENTLY COMPARED AND REVISED.

     Philadelphia: Printed by W. Young, Bookseller and Stationer, the corner of Second and Chesnut Streets. M,DCC,XC. Unpaged.

Third title: THE PSALMS OF DAVID IN METRE: TRANSLATED AND DILIGENTLY COMPARED WITH THE ORIGINAL TEXT AND FORMER TRANSLATIONS. BEING THE VERSION APPROVED BY THE CHURCH OF SCOTLAND.

     Philadelphia: Printed by William Young, Bookseller, No 52, Second-Street, the corner of Chesnut-Street. M,DCC,XC. Unpaged. Signatures A-F in sixes.   AAS.

22347   —— THE CHRISTIAN'S NEW AND COMPLETE FAMILY BIBLE: OR UNIVERSAL LIBRARY OF DIVINE KNOWLEDGE: BEING A CLEAR, FULL, AND COMPREHENSIVE EXPOSITION AND COMMENTARY ON THE HOLY SCRIPTURES, CONTAINING THE SACRED TEXTS OF THE OLD AND NEW TESTAMENTS, WITH THE APOCRYPHA AT LARGE: ILLUSTRATED WITH ANNOTATIONS AND COMMENTARIES: WHEREIN OBSCURE PASSAGES ARE MADE CLEAR AND FAMILIAR, SEEMING CONTRADICTIONS RECONCILED; MIS-TRANSLATIONS RECTIFIED; IMPORTANT TRUTHS CONFIRMED, AND DEISM AND INFIDELITY FULLY CONFUTED. TOGETHER WITH PRACTICAL REFLECTIONS ON EACH CHAPTER, AND NOTES, HISTORICAL, CHRONOLOGICAL, BIOGRAPHICAL, MORAL AND DIVINE. BY THOSE EMINENT WRITERS, HENRY, DODDRIDGE, GILL, BROWN, STACKHOUSE, BURKITT, OSTERVALD, &C. &C. THE WHOLE FORMING A COMPLETE BODY OF CHRISTIAN DIVINITY, CALCULATED TO ENLIGHTEN THE UNDERSTANDING, PURIFY THE HEART; PROMOTE THE CAUSE OF HOLINESS; AND MAKE MEN WISE UNTO SALVATION. No. —, [—No. 80.]

     Philadelphia: Published by W. Woodhouse, Bookseller, Front-Street, next door to the Coffee-House. 1790.

     Publication was completed this year. Printed in folio, with new type, on fine demy paper. Completed in eighty numbers — a number every Saturday morning. The Apocrypha at large, with notes, completing the Family Bible, was published October 5th 1790 — the last number containing a list of subscribers.

BIBLIA, continued.

22348 —— THE SELF-INTERPRETING BIBLE: CONTAINING THE SACRED TEXT OF THE OLD
AND NEW TESTAMENTS. TRANSLATED FROM THE ORIGINAL TONGUES, AND WITH
THE FORMER TRANSLATIONS DILIGENTLY COMPARED AND REVISED. TO WHICH
ARE ANNEXED, MARGINAL REFERENCES AND ILLUSTRATIONS, AN EXACT SUMMARY
OF THE SEVERAL BOOKS, A PARAPHRASE ON THE MOST OBSCURE OR IMPORTANT
PARTS, AN ANALYSIS OF THE CONTENTS OF EACH CHAPTER, EXPLANATORY NOTES,
AND EVANGELICAL REFLECTIONS. BY THE REVEREND JOHN BROWN, MINISTER OF
THE GOSPEL AT HADDINGTON. [Five lines of Scripture texts.] [PARTS I-XIII.]
  New-York: Printed by Hodge, Allen & Campbell, 1790.

Advertised as an American edition of the Self-interpreting folio family
Bible: (being the only American edition ever published) Containing the
Old and New Testaments, with the books of the Apocrypha: illustrated with notes and annotations, theological, historical, geographical, systematical, chronological, biographical, practical, critical, explanatory, moral and divine. The whole forming a complete system
of the Christian religion, with practical reflections at the end of each
chapter, calculated to improve the understanding, purify the heart,
promote the cause of virtue, and guide the reader to the mansions of
eternal bliss. By the late reverend John Brown, minister of the Gospel
at Haddington. The third edition. Greatly improved by the addition
of many thousand marginal references and illustrations, carefully corrected by the Author for the press, before his death. It was first seri-
ally published by subscription, in numbers, issued every fortnight.
The completed work to consist of forty numbers, "any surplus to be
given gratis." It was two years in passing through the press and
was printed in large folio, on fine paper of American manufacture,
with a large and new type cast for the work. Every other number
was embellished with an engraving executed by an American artist,
illustrative of some incident of Holy Scripture. And a frontispiece,
title-page, introduction, etc., and a list of subscriber's names, were to
be given at the conclusion of the work.

22349 —— THE HOLY BIBLE, TRANSLATED FROM THE LATIN VULGATE: DILIGENTLY COM-
PARED WITH THE HEBREW, GREEK, AND OTHER EDITIONS IN DIVERS LANGUAGES;
AND FIRST PUBLISHED BY THE ENGLISH COLLEGE AT DOWAY, ANNO 1609. NEWLY
REVISED, AND CORRECTED, ACCORDING TO THE CLEMENTINE EDITION OF THE
SCRIPTURES. WITH ANNOTATIONS FOR ELUCIDATING THE PRINCIPAL DIFFICUL-
TIES OF HOLY WRIT. [One line of Latin from] ISAIAH XII. 3.
  Philadelphia: Printed and sold by Carey, Stewart, and Co. M.DCC.XC.
2 vols. in one. pp. 990. 4to.

The first American edition of the Doway translation of the Vulgate
Bible, and the first Bible, in quarto, published in English in the United
States.

22350 —— THE HOLY BIBLE ABRIDGED: OR, THE HISTORY OF THE OLD AND NEW TEST-
AMENT. ILLUSTRATED WITH NOTES, AND ADORNED WITH CUTS. FOR THE USE OF
CHILDREN. TO WHICH IS ADDED, A COMPLEAT ABSTRACT OF THE OLD AND NEW
TESTAMENT, WITH THE APOCRYPHA, IN EASY VERSE. [Two lines from] LUKE
XVIII, 16.
  *New-York. Printed by Hodge, Allen, and Campbell and sold at their res-
pective Book-Stores.* M,DCC,XC. pp. 180. 32mo.   NYPL.

Second title: COMPLEAT ABSTRACT OF THE HOLY BIBLE IN EASY VERSE; CON-
TAINING THE OLD AND NEW TESTAMENTS, WITH THE APOCRYPHA. [Four lines
of verse.] pp. (135)-180.

22351 | BIBLIA. OLD TESTAMENT. PSALMS.
A NEW VERSION OF THE PSALMS OF DAVID, FITTED TO THE TUNES USED IN CHUR-
CHES. BY N. BRADY, D. D. LATE CHAPLAIN IN ORDINARY, AND N. TATE, ESQ;
LATE POET LAURET [sic] TO THE KING OF ENGLAND.
> Boston (State of Massachusetts) Printed by Joseph Bumstead, for David
> West, No. 36, Marlborough-Street, and E. Larkin, jun. No. 50, Cornhill. MDCC-
> XC. pp. 358, (2). 12mo.   NYPL.

22352 | —— DOCTOR WATTS'S IMITATION OF THE PSALMS OF DAVID, CORRECTED AND EN-
LARGED, BY JOEL BARLOW. TO WHICH IS ADDED A COLLECTION OF HYMNS; THE
WHOLE APPLIED TO THE STATE OF THE CHRISTIAN CHURCH IN GENERAL. THE
THIRD EDITION. LUKE XXIV. [Two lines.]
> Hartford: Printed by Nathaniel Patten. [With the privilege of copy-
> right.] [1790.] pp. 269, (18), 289 – 332. 12mo.   NYPL.

22353 | —— — DOCTOR WATTS'S IMITATION OF THE PSALMS OF DAVID, CORRECTED AND EN-
LARGED, BY JOEL BARLOW. ADAPTED TO THE STATE OF THE CHRISTIAN CHURCH
IN GENERAL.
> New-York: Printed by W. Durell, MDCCXC.

22354 | —— PSALMS, CAREFULLY SUITED TO THE CHRISTIAN WORSHIP IN THE UNITED STATES
OF AMERICA: BEING AN IMPROVEMENT OF THE OLD REVISIONS OF THE PSALMS OF
DAVID. ALLOWED BY THE REVEREND SYNOD OF NEW-YORK AND PHILADELPHIA
TO BE USED IN CHURCHES AND PRIVATE FAMILIES. [Three line quotation.]
> New-York: Printed by Hodge, Allen and Campbell, and sold at their res-
> pective Book-Stores, 1790. pp. (2), (10), (25) – 306, (6). 24mo.   AAS. BU. NYPL.

22355 | —— THE PSALMS OF DAVID IN METRE: TRANSLATED, AND DILIGENTLY COMPARED
WITH THE ORIGINAL TEXT, AND FORMER TRANSLATIONS. BEING THE VERSION
APPROVED BY THE CHURCH OF SCOTLAND.
> Philadelphia: Printed by William Young, Bookseller, No. 52 Second-
> Street, the corner of Chesnut-Street. M,DCC,XC. pp. (71). 12mo.   JCB

22356 | —— THE WHOLE BOOK OF PSALMS IN METRE; WITH HYMNS SUITED TO THE FEASTS
AND FASTS OF THE CHURCH, AND OTHER OCCASIONS OF PUBLIC WORSHIP.
> Philadelphia: Printed by Hall and Sellers, in Market-Street. 1790. pp.
> 221, (3). 12mo.   JCB. LOC.
Usually found bound with the Book of Common Prayer of this date.

22357 | —— DER PSALTER DES KÖNIGS UND PROPHETEN DAVIDS, VERDEUTSCHET VON DR.
MARTIN LUTHER, MIT KURZEN SUMMARIEN ODER INHALT JEDES PSALMEN. UND
MIT VIELEN PARALLELEN ODER GLEICHEN SCHRIFT-STELLEN. DIE ZWEYTE
AUFLAGE.
> Germantaun: Gedruckt bey Michael Billmeyer. 1790. pp. 252. 18mo.   NYPL.

22358 | BIBLIA. NEW TESTAMENT.
THE NEW TESTAMENT OF OUR LORD AND SAVIOR JESUS CHRIST, TRANSLATED
OUT OF THE ORIGINAL GREEK: AND WITH THE FORMER TRANSLATIONS DILIGENTLY
COMPARED AND REVISED BY HIS MAJESTY'S SPECIAL COMMAND. APPOINTED TO
BE READ IN CHURCHES.
> New-Haven: Printed by A. Morse. M.DCC.XC. Unpaged. 12mo.
O'Callaghan notes a long list of errors to be found in this edition.

22359   BIBLIA. NEW TESTAMENT, continued.
—— THE NEW TESTAMENT OF OUR LORD AND SAVIOUR JESUS CHRIST, NEWLY TRANS-
LATED OUT OF THE ORIGINAL GREEK: AND WITH THE FORMER TRANSLATIONS
DILIGENTLY COMPARED AND REVISED. APPOINTED TO BE READ IN CHURCHES.
[Publisher's monogram.]
> *New-York: Printed and sold by Hugh Gaine, at his Book-Store and
> Printing-Office, at the Bible, in Hanover-Square.* M,DCC,XC. Signature A – O in
> twelves. 12mo.   NYPL.

The following errors have been noted: Acts VIII. 9. sorcercy, for sor-
cery. Phil. IV. 15. begginning, for beginning.

22360   BICKERSTAFFE, ISAAC   1735 – 1787
THE MAID OF THE MILL. A COMIC OPERA.
> *Philadelphia: Printed by William Spotswood,* 1790.

22361   BIDDLE, OWEN
A PLAN FOR A SCHOOL AND AN ESTABLISHMENT SIMILAR TO THAT OF ACKWORTH,
IN YORKSHIRE, GREAT-BRITAIN, VARIED TO SUIT THE CIRCUMSTANCES OF THE
YOUTH WITHIN THE LIMITS OF THE YEARLY MEETING FOR PENNSYLVANIA AND
NEW-JERSEY, INTRODUCED WITH THE SENSE OF FRIENDS IN NEW-ENGLAND ON
THE SUBJECT OF EDUCATION; AND AN ACCOUNT OF SOME SCHOOLS IN GREAT-
BRITAIN: TO WHICH IS ADDED OBSERVATIONS AND REMARKS, INTENDED FOR
THE CONSIDERATION OF FRIENDS.
> *Philadelphia: Printed by Joseph Crukshank.* M.DCC.XC. pp. 53. 8vo.
>   AAS. JCB. LCP.

22362   BILLINGS, WILLIAM   1746 – 1800
THE BIRD AND THE LARK. THE AUTHOR SUPPOSES THE AIRS TO BE ORIGINAL.
BY WILLIAM BILLINGS.
> *Boston: Published by the Author,* 1790.

22363   BINGHAM, CALEB   1757 – 1819
THE YOUNG LADY'S ACCIDENCE: OR, A SHORT AND EASY INTRODUCTION TO ENGLISH
GRAMMAR. DESIGNED, PRINCIPALLY, FOR THE USE OF YOUNG LEARNERS, MORE
ESPECIALLY THOSE OF THE FAIR SEX, THOUGH PROPER FOR EITHER. BY CALEB
BINGHAM, A. M. [Two lines of quotation.] THE FOURTH EDITION, CORRECTED.
(PUBLISHED ACCORDING TO ACT.)
> *Printed at Boston. By Thomas and Andrews. At Faust's Statue, No.* 45.
> *Newbury-Street.* MDCCXC. pp. 57. 24mo.   AAS.

8th Massachusetts District Copyright, issued to Caleb Bingham, as
Author, 15 November, 1790.

22364   BLACK, JOHN   1750 – 1802
THE DUTY OF CHRISTIANS IN SINGING THE PRAISES OF GOD. A SERMON.
> *Carlisle: Printed by Kline and Reynolds.* 1790.

22265   BLACKSTONE, Sir WILLIAM   1723 – 1780
COMMENTARIES ON THE LAWS OF ENGLAND. IN FOUR BOOKS. BY SIR WILLIAM
BLACKSTONE, KNT. [Two lines.] IN FOUR VOLUMES. THE FIRST WORCESTER
EDITION, CAREFULLY REPRINTED FROM THE LAST LONDON EDITION. [Six lines.]
> *Printed at Worcester, Massachusetts, by Isaiah Thomas,* MDCCXC. 4 vols.
> pp. 12, 485; vii. 520, xix; vi, 455, xxvii; vi. 443, vii, (52). 12mo.   AAS.

22366   BLAIR, HUGH   1718 – 1800
SERMONS. BY HUGH BLAIR, D. D. F. R. S. ONE OF THE MINISTERS OF THE HIGH CHURCH, AND PROFESSOR OF RHETORIC AND BELLES LETTRES IN THE UNIVERSITY OF EDINBURGH. [Publishers' monogram.]
New-York: Printed by Hodge, Allen, and Campbell, and sold at their several Book-Stores; also, by Robert Campbell, Philadelphia. M.DCC.XC. pp. 292. 8vo.   AAS.

22367   BLIGH, WILLIAM   1754 – 1817
A NARRATIVE OF THE MUTINY, ON BOARD HIS BRITANNIC MAJESTY'S SHIP BOUNTY; AND THE SUBSEQUENT VOYAGE OF PART OF THE CREW, IN THE SHIP'S BOAT, FROM TOFOA, ONE OF THE FRIENDLY ISLANDS, TO TIMOR, A DUTCH SETTLEMENT IN THE EAST-INDIES. WRITTEN BY LIEUT. WILLIAM BLIGH.
Philadelphia: Printed by William Spotswood, MDCCXC. pp. (2), 70. 12mo.   BA. JCB.

22368   BORDLEY, JOHN BEALE   1727 – 1804
A SUPPLEMENT TO THE ESSAY ON MONIES, COINS, &C. PROPOSED FOR THE UNITED STATES OF AMERICA. [Signed, B.]
Philadelphia: Printed by Daniel Humphreys, Front-Street, near the Drawbridge. M.DCC.XC. pp. (2), [7.] 8vo.   BA. NYPL.

22369   BOSTON. MASSACHUSETTS. SOCIETY FOR PROPAGATING THE GOSPEL.
A BRIEF ACCOUNT OF THE PRESENT STATE OF THE SOCIETY FOR PROPAGATING THE GOSPEL AMONG THE INDIANS AND OTHERS IN NORTH-AMERICA,—WITH A SKETCH OF THE MANNER IN WHICH THEY MEAN TO PURSUE THE OBJECTS OF THEIR INSTITUTION. PRESENT STATE OF THE SOCIETY, &C. . . . LETTER FROM THE REV. MR. LITTLE, TO THE SECRETARY OF THE SOCIETY. WELLS, NOVEMBER 24, 1790. . . . LETTER FROM OLIVER WOOD, ESQ. TO THE SECRETARY OF THE SOCIETY. NORRIDGEWALK, AUGUST 9, 1790. . . . [Colophon:]
[Boston:] Published by order of the Society—Peter Thacher, secretary. [1790.] pp. [4.] fol.   AAS. NYPL.

22370   THE BOSTON [cut] GAZETTE, AND THE COUNTRY JOURNAL, CONTAINING THE LATEST OCCURRENCES, FOREIGN AND DOMESTIC. [Motto.] No. 1840. MONDAY, JANUARY 4, [—No. 1891. MONDAY, DECEMBER 27, 1790.]
Printed by Benjamin Edes and Son, No. 7, State-Street, Boston. 1790. fol.   AAS. LOC. MHS.

22371   BOSTWICK, DAVID   1720 – 1763
A FAIR AND RATIONAL VINDICATION OF THE RIGHT OF INFANTS TO THE ORDINANCE OF BAPTISM: BEING THE SUBSTANCE OF SEVERAL DISCOURSES FROM ACTS XI, 39. CONTAINING: I. THE SCRIPTURE GROUND, ON WHICH THE RIGHT OF INFANTS TO BAPTISM IS FOUNDED. II. THE EVIDENCE BY WHICH IT IS SUPPORTED. III. A SOLUTION OF THE MOST MATERIAL OBJECTIONS. . . .
New-Brunswick: Printed by Abraham Blauvelt? 1790. pp. 63. 8vo.

22372   BOWDOINHAM. MAINE. BAPTIST ASSOCIATION.
MINUTES OF THE BOWDOINHAM ASSOCIATION, HELD AT HARPSWELL, 1790.
Boston: 1790.

22373   BROWN, or BRUNO, JOHN   1735 – 1788
THE ELEMENTS OF MEDICINE; OR, A TRANSLATION OF THE ELEMENTA MEDICINÆ BRUNONIS. WITH LARGE NOTES, ILLUSTRATIONS, AND COMMENTS. BY THE AUTHOR OF THE ORIGINAL WORK. A NEW EDITION.
Philadelphia: Printed by T. Dobson at the Stone-house No. 41, Second-Street. MDCCXC. pp. (2), xiii, 390, (8), plate. 8vo.   AAS. JCB. SGO.

22374 THE BRUNSWICK GAZETTE AND WEEKLY MONITOR. [Motto.]
NUMB. 171. TUESDAY, JANUARY 5, [— NUMB. 222, TUESDAY, DECEMBER 28,
1790.]
New-Brunswick: Printed by Abraham Blauvelt. 1790. fol.

22375 BRYANT, ——
TO THE CURIOUS AND BENEVOLENT. A DWARF CHILD. MR. BRYANT RESPECTFULLY
INFORMS THE LADIES AND GENTLEMEN OF NEWBURYPORT, THAT THE DWARF
CHILD WILL BE EXHIBITED ON THIS DAY, AUGUST 3, FROM 9 O'CLOCK A. M., TILL 1,
AND FROM 2 TILL 5 P. M. AT UNION-HALL. ☞ POSITIVELY FOR THE LAST TIME.
THIS CHILD HAS LATELY BEEN EXHIBITED AT MR. BOWEN'S ASSEMBLY-HALL,
BOSTON, WHERE HE WAS ALLOWED TO BE THE GREATEST NATURAL CURIOSITY
EVER SEEN. HE HAS THERE ASSUMED THE NAME OF TOM THUMB, JUN. AS HE IS THE
SMALLEST BOY OF HIS AGE EVER KNOWN. HE IS SIX YEARS OLD, 26 INCHES HIGH,
AND WEIGHS ONLY 12 POUNDS. HE IS VERY HANDSOME, AND WELL PROPORTIONED,
ALSO VERY ACTIVE AND MANLY. THIS SURPRISING LITTLE GENIUS WAS BORN IN
BRIDGEWATER, WHERE HIS PARENTS NOW LIVE; THEY BEING IN LOW CIRCUM-
STANCES, WISH TO MAKE A COLLECTION FOR THE MAINTENANCE AND EDUCATION
OF THEIR CHILD. ADMITTANCE, 1S, 6D; HALF PRICE FOR CHILDREN.
[Newburyport: Printed by John Mycall, 1790.] Broadside. fol.   NYPL.

22376 BUCHAN, WILLIAM   1729 – 1805
DOMESTIC MEDICINE, OR, THE FAMILY PHYSICIAN; BEING AN ATTEMPT TO RENDER
THE MEDICAL ART MORE GENERALLY USEFUL, BY SHEWING PEOPLE WHAT IS IN
THEIR OWN POWER, BOTH WITH RESPECT TO THE PREVENTION AND CURE OF DIS-
EASES. CHIEFLY CALCULATED TO RECOMMEND A PROPER ATTENTION TO REGIMEN
AND SIMPLE MEDICINES. WITH AN APPENDIX, CONTAINING A DISPENSATORY FOR
THE USE OF PRIVATE PRACTITIONERS.
Philadelphia: Printed by R. Aitken & Son, in Market Street. 1790.

22377 BUCKNER, SAMUEL
THE AMERICAN SAILOR: A TREATISE ON PRACTICAL SEAMANSHIP, WITH HINTS AND
REMARKS RELATING THERETO. DESIGNED TO CONTRIBUTE TOWARDS MAKING
NAVIGATION IN GENERAL MORE PERFECT, AND OF CONSEQUENCE, LESS DESTRUCT-
IVE TO HEALTH, LIVES AND PROPERTY. BY SAMUEL BUCKNER.
Newport: Printed and sold by Peter Edes. 1790. pp. (8), 96. 8vo.   JCB.
Rhode Island District Copyright, issued to Peter Edes, as Proprietor,
26 August, 1790.

22378 BULLARD, SAMUEL
AN ALMANACK, FOR THE YEAR OF CHRISTIAN ÆRA, 1791. BEING THE THIRD YEAR
AFTER BISSEXTILE, OR LEAP YEAR; AND THE 15TH OF THE INDEPENDENCE OF
AMERICA. [Fourteen lines.] BY SAMUEL BULLARD. [Four lines of verse.]
*Boston: Printed and sold by J. White and C. Cambridge, near Charles-
River Bridge. [1790.]* pp. (24). 12mo.   AAS. LOC.

22379 BUNYAN, JOHN   1628 – 1688
SOLOMON'S TEMPLE SPIRITUALIZED: OR, GOSPEL-LIGHT BROUGHT OUT OF THE TEM-
PLE AT JERUSALEM, TO LET US MORE EASILY INTO THE GLORY OF NEW-TESTA-
MENT TRUTHS. BY JOHN BUNYAN. THE FIRST ALBANY EDITION.
Albany: Printed by C. R. & G. Webster. 1790. pp. 192. 16mo.   LOC.

22380   BURGES, BARTHOLOMEW
A SERIES OF INDOSTAN LETTERS BY BAR W BURGES CONTAINING, A STRIKING AC-
COUNT OF THE MANNERS & CUSTOMS OF THE GENTOO NATIONS, & OF THE MOGULS
& OTHER MAHOMEDAN TRIBES IN INDOSTAN, WITH OTHER POLEMICAL EAST INDIA
TRACTS BOTH AMUSING, INTERESTING, & PERFECTLY ORIGINAL.
     N. York: Printed & published for the Author by W. Ross. [1790.] pp.
xxv, (1), 168, frontispiece. 12mo.   AAS. BA. BM. LOC. NYHS. NYPL.
     The title-page, and frontispiece engraved by Rollinson. Contains a
twelve-page list of subscriber's names, headed by George Washington, and John Adams.

22381   BURGH, JAMES   1714 – 1775
THE ART OF SPEAKING. CONTAINING I. AN ESSAY; IN WHICH ARE GIVEN RULES
FOR EXPRESSING PROPERLY THE PRINCIPAL PASSIONS AND HUMOURS, WHICH OCCUR
IN READING OR PUBLIC SPEAKING; AND II. LESSONS TAKEN FROM THE ANTIENTS
AND MODERNS, WITH ADDITIONS AND ALTERATIONS WHERE THOUGHT USEFUL; EX-
HIBITING A VARIETY OF MATTER FOR PRACTICE; THE EMPHATICAL WORDS PRINTED
IN ITALICS, WITH NOTES OF DIRECTION REFERRING TO THE ESSAY. TO WHICH
ARE ADDED, A TABLE OF THE LESSONS, AND AN INDEX OF THE VARIOUS PASSIONS
AND HUMOURS IN THE ESSAY AND LESSONS.
     New-York: Printed and sold by Hugh Gaine, 1790.

22382   BURGOYNE, Sir JOHN   1722 – 1791
THE LORD OF THE MANOR. A COMIC OPERA. AS IT IS PERFORMED AT THE THE-
ATRE ROYAL, DRURY-LANE. WITH A PREFACE BY THE AUTHOR.
     Philadelphia: Printed by William Spotswood, Front-Street. M.DCC.XC.
pp. 71. 12mo.   AAS.

22383   THE BURLINGTON ADVERTISER, OR AGRICULTURAL AND POLITICAL INTELLIGENCER.
VOL. I. NUMB. 1. TUESDAY, APRIL 13, [—NUMB. XXXVIII. TUESDAY, DECEM-
BER 28, 1790.]
     *Burlington: Printed by Neale and Lawrence, nearly opposite James
Sterling's Store.* 1790. fol.   NYPL.
     Established by Isaac Neale and Daniel Lawrence. The imprint was
changed in Numb. II. to read: "Printed and published, weekly, by
I. Neale & D. Lawrence, by whom subscriptions, at twelve shillings
specie per annum, essays, articles of intelligence &c. are thankfully
received. Advertisements inserted on the following conditions: those
of no more length than breadth, at three shillings the first week,
and eighteen-pence for every continuance. Those exceeding a square,
in the same proportion." With the issue for April 12th, 1791, at the
end of the first year, Daniel Lawrence withdrew; but the partnership
of Neale and Lawrence was not dissolved until July 7, 1791.
Isaac Neale continued publication as sole printer and publisher to
December 13, 1791, with which issue publication was suspended owing
to the small number of subscribers; the publisher stating that upon
sufficient encouragement he would re-commence its publication on an
improved plan. This encouragement was never given.

22384   THE BURLINGTON ALMANAC, FOR THE YEAR OF OUR LORD, 1791.
     Burlington: Printed and sold by I. Neale & D. Lawrence. [1790.]

22385 BURNET, Matthias   1749 – 1806
A Sermon, preached the second Lord's day after the death of his amiable
and excellent wife, Mrs. Ann Burnet, who died in child-bed, July 7th,
1789, in the xxxv th year of her age. By Matthias Burnet, a. m. pastor
of the first church in Norwalk, Connecticut. [Five lines of Scripture
texts.]
New-Haven: Printed by Thomas and Samuel Green. MDCCXC. pp. (24).
4to.   AAS. BA. LOC. NYPL.

22386 CAMP, John   1753 – 1821
A Sermon, delivered at the ordination of the rev. Winslow Paige, in
Stephentown, March 17th, A. D. 1790. By John Camp, a. m. pastor of the
church in Canaan.
Pittsfield: Printed by Roger Storrs. M,DCC,XC. pp. 16. 4to.   JCB.

22387 CAMPBELL, George   1719 – 1796
A Dissertation of miracles: containing an examination of principles ad-
vanced by David Hume, esq.; in an essay on miracles. By George Campbell, d. d. principal of the Marischal College, and one of the ministers,
of Aberdeen. [Two lines from] John x. 25. The third edition, with additions and corrections.
*Philadelphia: Printed by Thomas Dobson, at the Stone House, in Second
Street.* MDCCXC. pp. xi, 173, (3). 16mo.   AAS. JCB.
Contains a list of Books printed for and sold by Thomas Dobson.

22388 CAMPBELL, Robert
A Catalogue of books, sold by Robert Campbell, at his new book & stationary [*sic*] store, on the west side of Second-street, below the market,
and five doors above Chesnut-street.
[*Philadelphia: Printed for Robert Campbell,* 1790.] Broadside. fol. LOC.

22389 CAMPE, Joachim Heinrich von   1746 – 1818
The New Robinson Crusoe: an instructive and entertaining history. For
the use of children of both sexes. Translated from the French.
*Printed at Boston, by Thomas and Andrews, at Faust's Statue. Sold at
their Bookstore, No. 45, Newbury-Street, and by said Thomas at his Bookstore
in Worcester. Also by J. Boyle and D. West, in Marlborough Street, and B.
Guild, B. Larkin, and E. Larkin, jun. in Cornhill, Boston.* MDCCXC. pp.
270, frontispiece. 16mo.   AAS. LOC.

22390 CAREY, Mathew   1760 – 1839
Information for Europeans who are disposed to migrate to the United
States. In a letter from a citizen of Pennsylvania, to his friend in
Great-Britain.
*Philadelphia: [Printed by] Carey Stewart & Co. [Price one eighth of a
dollar.]* [1790.] pp. (16). 16mo.   JCB. LOC. MHS.

22391 CARLETON, Osgood   1742 – 1816
An Astronomical diary: or, an Almanack, for the year of our Lord, 1791,
[Fourteen lines.] By Osgood Carleton, teacher of mathematicks, in Bos-
ton. [Eight lines of verse.]
*Boston: Printed and sold by Samuel Hall, at No. 53, Cornhill: also, by
Thomas C. Cushing, at his Printing-Office, in Salem.* [1790.] pp. [32.] 12mo.
                                                    AAS. LOC. NYPL.
In this issue is begun the Memoirs of Captain John Smith. Compiled
chiefly from the genuine writings of Capt. Smith himself, and of
his intimate friend Mr. Purchas, by a Rev. Gentleman, eminent for his
literary abilities and historical researches. In his preface, dated,
Boston, May 1, 1789, Carleton says, that he has determined to lay
aside obscure signatures, and publish under his own name. Several
of his Almanacs appeared under fictitious names before this.

22392 THE CARLISLE Gazette, and the western repository of knowledge. Vol. v. No. 231. Wednesday, January 6, [—No. 282. Wednesday, December 29, 1790.]
Carlisle: (State of Pennsylvania) Printed by Kline & Reynolds. 1790. fol.

22393 CATALOGUE of a choice and valuable collection of modern books; among which are, elegant folio Family Bibles, several valuable medical publications, divinity, history, voyages, travels, &c. and a curious assortment of beautiful maps and prints, to be sold on the 2d day of December, 1790, at a large and commodious room in mr. Daniel Peters's tavern, at the sign of the Emperor of Germany, in Gay-street, five doors from Market-street.
Baltimore: Printed by W. Goddard and J. Angell, 1790.

22394 CATALOGUE of a valuable collection of books, in divinity, history, physic, novels, miscellanies, philosophy, navigation, geography, dictionaries, &c. &c. Will be sold by public auction, on Friday, the 30th of April instant, at the shop of mr. Samuel Bayley near the Ferry-way in Newburyport.
Newburyport: Printed by John Mycall. 1790.

22395 CEBES.   5th century b. c.
THE Circuit of human life: a vision. In which are allegorically described, the virtues and vices. Taken from the tablature of Cebes, a disciple of Socrates. For the instruction of youth. The third edition, corrected.
Philadelphia: Printed by Joseph Crukshank, in Market-Street, between Second and Third-Streets. MDCCXC. pp. 88. 18mo.   LOC.

22396 CEBRA, James
James Cebra, respectfully offers his services to such as may think them useful, particularly in the collection of debts. . . . New-York, June 23, 1790. [Colophon:]
[New-York:] Printed by Francis Childs and John Swaine. [1790.]
Broadside. fol.   NYHS.

22397 CHALKLEY, Thomas   1675 – 1741
A Collection of the works of Thomas Chalkley. In two parts. [Five lines from] Psalm i. 1, 2.
Philadelphia: Printed by James & Johnson. M.DCC.XC. pp. [viii], 336; (2), (2), 341–605, (3). 8vo.   AAS. JCB. NYPL.
Second title: A Journal or historical account of the life, travels and christian experiences of the antient, faithful servant of Jesus Christ, Thomas Chalkley, who departed this life in the Island of Tortola, the fourth day of the month 1741. The fifth edition.
Philadelphia: Printed by James & Johnson. M.DCC.XC. pp. (2), (2), 341–605, (3).

22398 CHAMBERLAIN, Thomas   – 1784
Ninth edition. [Cut of minister preaching in pulpit.] The Minister preaching his own funeral sermon: being a warning from Heaven to all vile sinners on earth. With a particular relation of many wonderful things seen by the Rev. Thomas Chamberlain, in a vision just before his decease, the precise time of which was shewn unto him.
Boston: Printed and sold by E. Russell, next Liberty-Stump, by wholesale or retail, cheap. 1790. pp. 15, (1). 16mo.   JCB.

22399   CHANDLER, Thomas Bradbury   1726 – 1790
        Sale catalogue of the books, belonging to the library of the late Rev.
        Dr. Chandler.
            Elizabeth-Town : Printed by Shepard Kollock. 1790.

22400   THE CHARMER: being a select collection of English, Scotch and American
        songs, including the modern; with a selection of favourite toasts and
        sentiments.
            *Philadelphia : Printed and sold by W. Spotswood, Front-Street, between
        Market and Chesnut-Streets.* 1790. pp. — frontispiece. 18mo.

22401   DIE CHESNUTHILLER Wochenschrift.   Num. 1.   Mittwoch, October 6,
        [— Num. 13. Mittwoch, December 29, 1790.]
            *Diese Zeitung wird wöchentlich, nemlich Mittwochs, herausgegeben von
        Samuel Saur.   Buchdrucker auf Chesnuthill, nahe bey dem 10ten meilstein allwo
        die Readinger und Nordwelscher Strasse Zusammenkommen.* 1790.' 4to.
        Established by Samuel Saur, the youngest of Christopher Saur's ten
        children, and continued by him to April, 1794, when he removed to
        Philadelphia, and altered the title to: *Das Philadelphier Wochenblat,*
        which was discontinued, in the same year, upon his removal to Balti-
        more, where he resided until his death, 12 October, 1820, and where
        he was prominent as a printer, publisher, and type founder.

22402   CHETWOOD, William Rufus   – 1766
        The Voyages and adventures of captain Robert Boyle, in several parts of
        the world.   Intermixed with the story of Mrs. Villars, an English
        lady, with whom he made his surprizing escape from Barbary.   Like-
        wise including, the History of an Italian captive, and the Life of Don
        Pedro Aguilo, &c.   Full of various and amazing turns of fortune.
            *Boston : Printed and sold by John West Folsom, No. 30, Union-Street, and
        E. Larkin, jun. No. 50, Cornhill.* 1790.
        A fictitious narrative, frequently reprinted. George Steevens embalmed
        the author's memory, in the liquid amber of his remarks, by calling him,
        "a blockhead, and a measureless and bungling liar."   Also, wrongly
        attributed to Benjamin Victor.

22403   THE CHRISTIAN œconomy.   Translated from the original Greek of an
        old manuscript found in the Island of Patmos where St. John wrote his
        book of the Revelation.
            Albany : Printed by C. R. & G. Webster. 1790. pp. 30. 8vo.   JCB.

22404   —— The Christian œconomy.   Translated from the original Greek of an
        old manuscript found in the Island of Patmos where St. John wrote his
        book of the Revelation.
            Concord : Printed by George Hough. 1790.

22405   THE CHRISTIAN'S, scholar's, and farmer's magazine; calculated, in an emi-
        nent degree, to promote religion; to disseminate useful knowledge; to
        afford literary pleasure and amusement, and to advance the interests
        of agriculture.   By a Number of gentlemen.   [Seven lines of quotations.]
        No. 1. of Vol. ii. for April and May, 1790.   [—No. 6. for February and
        March, 1791.]
            Elizabeth-Town : Printed and sold by Shepard Kollock. M.DCC.XC.
        pp. 736, (6), (2). 8vo.   AAS. BA. LOC.
        Discontinued from want of leisure, on the part of the Editors, to con-
        tinue it.

22406   CHURCHMAN, JOHN   1753 – 1805
AN EXPLANATION OF THE MAGNETIC ATLAS, OR VARIATION CHART, HEREUNTO AN-
NEXED; PROJECTED ON A PLAN ENTIRELY NEW, BY WHICH THE MAGNETIC VARIA-
TION ON ANY PART OF THE GLOBE MAY BE PRECISELY DETERMINED, FOR ANY
TIME PAST, PRESENT, OR FUTURE: AND THE VARIATION AND LATITUDE BEING AC-
CURATELY KNOWN, THE LONGITUDE IS OF CONSEQUENCE TRULY DETERMINED. BY
JOHN CHURCHMAN, LATE LAND SURVEYOR FOR THE DISTRICT OF THE COUNTIES OF
DELAWARE AND CHESTER, AND FOR PART OF LANCASTER AND BERKS, PENNSYL-
VANIA.

> *Philadelphia: Printed by James & Johnson, on the north side of Market-*
> *Street, between Third and Fourth-Streets.* M,DCC,XC. pp. 46, (5), (1), chart,
> 2 tables, 8vo.   AAS. BA. BM. JCB. LOC. MHS.

Title of chart: TO GEORGE WASHINGTON, PRESIDENT OF THE UNITED STATES
OF AMERICA, THIS MAGNETIC ATLAS OR VARIATION CHART, IS HUMBLY INSCRIBED
BY JOHN CHURCHMAN.

> Contains a five-page list of subscriber's names. 3rd Pennsylvania
> District Copyright, issued to John Churchman, as Author, 17 June, 1790.

22407   THE CITY [seal] GAZETTE, OR THE DAILY ADVERTISER. [Motto.] VOL. VIII. NUMB.
1362. FRIDAY, JANUARY 1, [— NUMB. 1663. FRIDAY, DECEMBER 31, 1790.]

> *Charleston: Printed by Markland & M'Iver, Printers to the City, No.* 47,
> *Bay.* 1790. fol.

22408   COGSWELL, JAMES   1720 – 1807
A FUNERAL SERMON, DELIVERED AT BROOKLYN, ON THE 29TH OCTOBER, 1789.
AT THE INTERMENT OF MRS. LOIS WHITNEY, CONSORT OF THE REV. JOSIAH WHIT-
NEY.

> *Norwich: Printed by John Trumbull.* 1790. pp. 22. 8vo.   UTS. YC.

22409   THE COLUMBIAN ALMANACK, AND EPHEMERIS OF THE MOTION OF THE SUN AND
MOON; THE TRUE PLACES AND ASPECTS OF THE PLANETS; THE RISING AND SETTING
OF THE SUN; THE RISING, SETTING, AND SOUTHING OF THE MOON, FOR THE YEAR
OF OUR LORD 1791: BEING THE THIRD AFTER BISSEXTILE, OR LEAP-YEAR, AND
THE FIFTEENTH OF AMERICAN INDEPENDENCE. CALCULATED FOR THE MERIDIAN
OF THE MIDDLE STATES, PARTICULARLY NEW-YORK. [Six lines.] AGREEABLE
TO THE PLAN OF THE LATE J. N. HUTCHINS.

> *New-York: Printed by Samuel Loudon: No.* 5, *Water-Street.* [1790.]
> pp. (32). 12mo.   NYHS.

22410   THE COLUMBIAN ALMANACK, FOR THE YEAR OF OUR LORD, 1791: BEING THE
THIRD AFTER LEAP-YEAR. [Eighteen lines.] ALSO, THE CONSTITUTION OF THE
COMMONWEALTH OF PENNSYLVANIA.

> *Philadelphia: Printed and sold by Peter Stewart, N°.* 34, *in Second, be-*
> *tween Market and Chesnut-Streets.* [1790.] pp. (36), (12). 12mo.   LOC.

22411   THE COLUMBIAN ALMANAC; OR, THE NORTH-AMERICAN CALENDAR, FOR THE
YEAR OF OUR LORD, 1791. BEING THE THIRD AFTER LEAP-YEAR. [U. S. Arms.]

> *Wilmington: Printed and sold by Andrews, Craig, and Brynberg, at the*
> *Post-Office, in Market-Street.* [1790.] pp. (48). 12mo.   NYHS.

22412   THE COLUMBIAN POCKET ALMANACK FOR THE YEAR 1791; BEING THE THIRD
AFTER LEAP-YEAR. [Eighteen lines.

> *Wilmington: Printed and sold by Andrews, Craig, and Brynberg, at the*
> *Post-Office, Market-Street.* [1790.] pp. (24). 24mo.   LOC.

22413 COLUMBIAN [U. S. A.] CENTINEL. No. 27 OF VOL. XIII. WHOLE No. 651. WED-
NESDAY, JUNE 16, [—No. 31 OF VOL. XIV. WHOLE No. 707. WEDNESDAY, DEC-
EMBER 29, 1790.]

> *Printed and published on Wednesdays and Saturdays, by Benjamin Rus-*
> *sell, in State-Street, Boston, Massachusetts.* 1790. fol. AAS. LOC. NYPL.

In continuation of *The Massachusetts Centinel.*

22414 THE COLUMBIAN HERALD, OR THE INDEPENDENT COURIER OF NORTH-AMERICA.
JANUARY - DECEMBER, 1790.

> *Charleston: Printed by T. B. Bowen.* 1790. fol.

22415 THE COLUMBIAN MAGAZINE, OR MONTHLY MISCELLANY. CONTAINING A VIEW OF
THE HISTORY, LITERATURE, MANNERS & CHARACTERS OF THE YEAR 1790. E MOL-
LIT MORES. VOL. 4. [JANUARY - FEBRUARY, 1790.] [Cut.]

> *Philadelphia: Printed for the Proprietors [by William Spotswood,* 1790.]
> pp. (2), 390, (2), (4), 6 plates. 8vo. AAS. BA. HC. JCB. LOC.

In March, the magazine was "transferred to new proprietors, between
whom and the gentlemen, who sometime ago published proposals for
the" Philadelphia Magazine and Universal Asylum," an agreement to
unite the two, has taken place. The joint-proprietors, have, therefore,
resolved to continue the Columbian Magazine, on an enlarged and improved plan, under the title of *The Universal Asylum, and Columbian
Magazine.* By a Society of gentlemen." With this change in name
the magazine was printed by William Young.

22416 THE CONCORD HERALD, AND NEWHAMPSHIRE INTELLIGENCER. THE PRESS IS
THE CRADLE OF SCIENCE, THE NURSE OF GENIUS, AND THE CHILD OF LIBERTY.
VOL. I. No. 1. WEDNESDAY, JANUARY 6, [—No. 52. WEDNESDAY, DECEM-
BER 29, 1790.]

> *Printed at Concord, (Newhampshire) by George Hough.* 1790. fol.

Established by George Hough, and continued by him to 30 October,
1805. With the beginning of the second volume, in January, 1791,
the title was altered to *Hough's Concord Herald,* up to March 9th, when
it was changed to *Concord Herald,* under which name it was published
to the end of the fifth volume, in January, 1795, when the title was
again altered to *Courier of New-Hampshire,* until its publication ceased
in 1805.

22417 CONGREGATIONAL CHURCH IN MASSACHUSETTS.
A RECOMMENDATION FROM THE CONVENTION OF THE CONGREGATIONAL MINISTERS,
AT BOSTON, MAY 26, 1790. [That only properly qualified members of regular
associations be asked to discharge the ministerial office.] SIMEON HOWARD,
MODERATOR OF THE CONVENTION.

> *[Boston:* 1790.] Broadside. fol. JCB.

22418 CONNECTICUT. STATE.
[Seal.] ACTS AND LAWS, MADE AND PASSED BY THE GENERAL COURT OR AS-
SEMBLY OF THE STATE OF CONNECTICUT, IN AMERICA, HOLDEN AT HARTFORD,
(IN SAID STATE) ON THE SECOND THURSDAY OF MAY, ANNO DOMINI, 1790.

> *[New-Haven: Printed by Thomas and Samuel Green.* 1790.] pp. 389-
> -394. fol. PL. WU. YC.

22419 —— — [Seal.] ACTS AND LAWS, MADE AND PASSED, BY THE GENERAL COURT OR
ASSEMBLY OF THE STATE OF CONNECTICUT, IN AMERICA, HOLDEN AT HARTFORD,
(IN SAID STATE) ON THE SECOND THURSDAY OF MAY, ANNO DOMINI, 1790.

> *[New-London: Printed by Timothy Green and Son.* 1790.] pp. 389-394.
> fol. WU.

CONNECTICUT, continued.

22420 —— — [Seal.] ACTS AND LAWS, MADE AND PASSED, BY THE GENERAL COURT OR ASSEMBLY OF THE STATE OF CONNECTICUT, IN AMERICA, HOLDEN AT HARTFORD, (IN SAID STATE) ON THE SECOND THURSDAY OF MAY, ANNO DOMINI, 1790. [Colophon:]
Hartford: Printed by Elisha Babcock. [1790.] pp. 390-396. fol.   CHS.

22421 —— — [Seal.] ACTS AND LAWS, MADE AND PASSED, BY THE GENERAL COURT OR ASSEMBLY OF THE STATE OF CONNECTICUT, IN AMERICA, HOLDEN AT HARTFORD, (IN SAID STATE) ON THE SECOND THURSDAY OF MAY, ANNO DOMINI, 1790. [Colophon:]
Hartford: Printed by Elisha Babcock. [1790.] pp. 391-397. 8vo.   CHS.

22422 —— — [Seal.] ACTS AND LAWS. MADE AND PASSED, BY THE GENERAL COURT OR ASSEMBLY OF THE STATE OF CONNECTICUT, IN AMERICA, HOLDEN AT HARTFORD, (IN SAID STATE) ON THE SECOND THURSDAY OF MAY, ANNO DOMINI, 1790. [Colophon:]
Hartford: Printed by Nathaniel Patten. [1790.] pp. 390-396. fol.   CHS.

22423 —— — [Seal.] ACTS AND LAWS, MADE AND PASSED BY THE GENERAL COURT OR ASSEMBLY OF THE STATE OF CONNECTICUT, IN AMERICA, HOLDEN AT NEW-HAVEN, (IN SAID STATE) ON THE SECOND THURSDAY OF OCTOBER, ANNO DOMINI, 1790. [Colophon:]
Hartford: Printed by Hudson and Goodwin. [1790.] pp. 399-400. fol.   CHS. PL. YC.
This is the official issue.

22424 —— — [Seal.] ACTS AND LAWS, MADE AND PASSED BY THE GENERAL COURT OR ASSEMBLY OF THE STATE OF CONNECTICUT, IN AMERICA, HOLDEN AT NEW-HAVEN, IN SAID STATE, ON THE SECOND THURSDAY OF OCTOBER, ANNO DOMINI, 1790.
[New-London: Printed by Timothy Green and Son. 1790.] pp. 399-400. fol.   NYBA. BSP. WU.

22425 —— — [Seal.] ACTS AND LAWS, MADE AND PASSED BY THE GENERAL COURT OR ASSEMBLY OF THE STATE OF CONNECTICUT, IN AMERICA, HOLDEN AT NEW HAVEN, IN SAID STATE, ON THE SECOND THURSDAY OF OCTOBER, ANNO DOMINI, 1790. [Colophon:]
Hartford: Printed by Elisha Babcock. [1790.] pp. 399-400. 8vo.   CHS.

22426 —— — [Seal.] ACTS AND LAWS, MADE AND PASSED BY THE GENERAL COURT OR ASSEMBLY OF THE STATE OF CONNECTICUT, IN AMERICA, HOLDEN AT NEW-HAVEN, IN SAID STATE, ON THE SECOND THURSDAY OF OCTOBER, ANNO DOMINI, 1790.
[Hartford: Printed by Nathaniel Patten. 1790.] pp. 403-404. fol.   CHS.
Apparently an error in pagination.

22427 —— BY HIS EXCELLENCY SAMUEL HUNTINGTON, ESQUIRE, GOVERNOR AND COMMANDER IN CHIEF IN AND OVER THE STATE OF CONNECTICUT. A PROCLAMATION. [Appointing Thursday, the eleventh day of November, a day of Thanksgiving.]
New-London: Printed by Timothy Green, and Son. 1790. Broadside. fol.

22428 THE CONNECTICUT COURANT, AND WEEKLY INTELLIGENCER. NUMBER 1302. THURSDAY, JANUARY 7, [— NUMBER 1353. MONDAY, DECEMBER 27, 1790.]
Hartford: Printed by Hudson and Goodwin, near the Bridge. 1790. fol.   AAS. CHS. LOC. YC.

22429 —— THE NEWS-BOY'S ADDRESS TO HIS CUSTOMERS.
[Hartford: Printed by Hudson and Goodwin, 1790.] Broadside. nar. fol.

22430 THE CONNECTICUT GAZETTE. VOL. XXVII. NO. 1364. FRIDAY, JANUARY 1, [—
VOL. XXVIII. NO. 1416. FRIDAY, DECEMBER 31, 1790.]
*New-London: Printed by Timothy Green and Son, at the northwest corner
of the Parade.* 1790. fol. **AAS. CHS. NYPL. YC.**

22431 THE CONNECTICUT JOURNAL. NO. 1158. WEDNESDAY, JANUARY 6, [—No. 1209.
WEDNESDAY, DECEMBER 29, 1790.]
*New-Haven: Printed by Thomas and Samuel Green, opposite the Post-
Office.* 1790. fol. **AAS. LOC. YC.**

22432 CONSIDERATIONS ON THE NATURE OF A FUNDED DEBT, TENDING TO SHEW THAT
IT CAN NEVER BE CONSIDERED AS A CIRCULATING MEDIUM; AND THAT THE INTER-
EST OF THE UNITED STATES RENDERS IT ESSENTIALLY NECESSARY TO FUND IT
AGREEABLY TO THE TERMS OF THE ORIGINAL CONTRACT AT THIS TIME, AND NOT
TO ADOPT THE DEBTS OF THE RESPECTIVE STATES.
New-York. M,DCC,XC. pp. (13). 8vo. **AAS. BA. LOC.**
Apparently others were to follow as it concludes: [End of Letter first.]

22433 CRABBE, GEORGE 1754 – 1832
THE VILLAGE, A POEM. IN TWO BOOKS.
New-York: Printed for Berry and Rogers, 1790.

22434 CRAWFORD, CHARLES
OBSERVATIONS UPON NEGRO-SLAVERY. [Eight lines of Scripture texts.] A NEW
EDITION. BY CHARLES CRAWFORD, ESQ.
*Philadelphia: Printed and sold by Eleazer Oswald, in Market-Street,
between Fourth and Fifth-Streets.* M,DCC,XC. pp. 125, (1). 12mo. **AAS. BU. LCP.**

22435 CULLEN, WILLIAM 1712 – 1790
FIRST LINES OF THE PRACTICE OF PHYSIC. BY WILLIAM CULLEN, M. D. [Five
lines.] A NEW EDITION. FROM THE LAST BRITISH EDITION, REVISED, COR-
RECTED AND ENLARGED, BY THE AUTHOR. IN THREE VOLUMES.
Printed at Worcester, Massachusetts, by Isaiah Thomas. MDCCXC. 3 vols.
pp. (2), 368; (2), vii-396; 406. 12mo. **AAS. SGO.**

22436 CUMBERLAND GAZETTE. MONDAY, JANUARY 4, 1789 [*sic* 1790.] [— MONDAY,
DECEMBER 27, 1790.]
*Printed and published by Thomas B. Wait, opposite the Haymarket, Port-
land.* 1790. fol. **AAS. NYHS.**
Notice was given February 15th, that "Preparations are now making
at the Printing-Office in Portland, to carry on the Book Binding business in all its branches. Those who shall be pleased to favor us with
their commands, may depend on their being seasonably, neatly, and
cheaply executed."

22437 CUMSTOCK, ABEL
A NEW-YEAR-GIFT; SHEWING THE INVALIDITY OF INFANT BAPTISM. BY ABEL CUM-
STOCK, OF WARREN.
Litchfield: Printed by Thomas Collier, in the Court-House. M,DCC,XC.
pp. (47). 8vo. **NYPL.**

22438 CUSHING, JOHN – 1823
CHRISTIANS MOURN NOT FOR THEIR FRIENDS WHO SLEEP IN JESUS, AS OTHERS WHO
HAVE NO HOPE. THE SUBSTANCE OF TWO SERMONS, DELIVERED AT ASHBURNHAM,
JULY 31, MDCCXC. BEING LORD'S DAY AFTER THE SUDDEN DEATH OF MRS. DORO-
THY WILDER, CONSORT OF SAMUEL WILDER. ESQ. IN THE 41ST YEAR OF HER AGE.
BY JOHN CUSHING, A. M. PASTOR OF THE CHURCH IN ASHBURNHAM. [Two lines
of Scripture texts.]
Printed at Worcester, Massachusetts, by Isaiah Thomas. MDCCXC. pp. 26.
8vo. **AAS. JCB. LOC.**

22439   DABOLL, Nathan   1750 – 1818
The New-England Almanack, and gentlemen & ladies diary, for the
year of our Lord Christ, 1791: [Ten lines.] By Edmund Freebetter.
     New-London: Printed and sold by T. Green & Son. [1790.] pp. (24).
12mo.   AAS. CHS.

22440   —— Sheet Almanack for the year 1791.
     New-London: Printed by T. Green and Son, 1790. Broadside. fol.

22441   DAGGETT, David   1764 – 1851
Sketches of the life of Joseph Mountain, a negro, who was executed at
New-Haven, on the 20th day of October instant, for a rape, committed
on the 26th day of May last, to be sold at this office. [The writer of
this history has directed that the money arising from the sales thereof, after deducting the expense of printing, &c. be given to the unhappy
girl whose life is rendered wretched by the crime of the malefactor.
     New-Haven: Printed and sold by T. and S. Green, 1790. pp. 20. 8vo. chs.

22442   —— The Life and extraordinary adventures of Joseph Mountain, a negro,
who was executed at New-Haven, on the 20th [October, 1790] ult. for a
rape committed in May last.
     *Philadelphia: Printed by John Dunlap and David C. Claypoole. Sold by
the Hawkers.* 1790.

22443   —— The Life and adventures of Joseph Mountain, a negro, who was executed at New-Haven (Connecticut) on the 20th of October, 1790, for a
rape committed on May last. To which are added, the Adventures of
Isaac Coombs.
     Philadelphia: Printed and sold by William Woodhouse. 1790.

22444   THE DAILY Advertiser. Vol. vi. No. 1519. Friday, January 1, [— No.
1830. Friday, December 31, 1790.]
     *[New-York:] Printed by Francis Childs and John Swaine, No. 190
Water-Street, corner of King-Street.* 1790. fol.   AAS. LOC. NYHS. NYPL.
Beginning with the issue of January 28th, "Printers to the State of
New-York, at their office" followed the firm name in the imprint. On
May 1st. the Printing-Office was removed to, "No. 189. Water-Street,
near King-Street." With the issue for December 14th, the paper
appeared with a new fanciful script heading, with the New York State
Arms dividing the title.

22445   DALLAS, Alexander James   1759 – 1817
Reports of cases, ruled and adjudged in the courts of Pennsylvania, before
and since the Revolution. By A. J. Dallas, esquire. Vol. i. [Five lines
of Latin from] Grotius.
     Philadelphia: Printed for the Reporter, by T. Bradford. MDCCXC. pp. x,
494, xxiv, (1). 8vo.   JCB. LCP.
4th Pennsylvania District Copyright, issued to A. J. Dallas, esquire,
as Author, 22 June, 1790. A second volume was issued in 1798.

22446   DANA, James   1735 – 1812
The Intent of capital punishment. A discourse delivered in the city of
New-Haven, October 20, 1790, being the day of the execution of Joseph
Mountain, for a rape. By James Dana, D. D. pastor of the first church
in said city.
     New-Haven; Printed by T. and S. Green. [1790.] pp. (28). 8vo.   NYPL.

22447   DANBURY. CONNECTICUT. BAPTIST ASSOCIATION.
MINUTES OF THE DANBURY ASSOCIATION HELD IN DANBURY, SEPTEMBER, 1790, WITH THE SENTIMENTS AND PLAN OF THE SAID ASSOCIATION.
Danbury: Printed by Douglas and Ely, 1790.

22448   DAVIDSON, ROBERT   1750 – 1812
GEOGRAPHY EPITOMIZED, OR A TOUR ROUND THE WORLD. BEING A SHORT BUT COMPREHENSIVE DESCRIPTION OF THE TERRAQUEOUS GLOBE; ATTEMPTED IN VERSE (FOR THE SAKE OF THE MEMORY:) AND PRINCIPALLY DESIGNED FOR THE USE OF SCHOOLS. BY AN AMERICAN.
Philadelphia: Printed and sold by Joseph Crukshank. 1790.

22449   DAY, JEREMIAH   1737 – 1806
THE DIVINE RIGHT OF INFANT BAPTISM, CONCISELY PROVED FROM THE HOLY SCRIPTURES; AND OBJECTIONS ANSWERED. A SERMON, DELIVERED BY JEREMIAH DAY, A. M. PASTOR OF THE CHURCH OF NEW-PRESTON. (PUBLISHED BY REQUEST.)
Litchfield: Printed by Thomas Collier, in the south end of the Court-House. 1790. pp. 43. 8vo.   BM. CHS. HC. UTS. YC.

22450   DEANE, SAMUEL   1733 – 1814
THE NEW-ENGLAND FARMER; OR, GEORGICAL DICTIONARY: CONTAINING A COMPENDIOUS ACCOUNT OF THE WAYS AND METHODS IN WHICH THE MOST IMPORTANT ART OF HUSBANDRY, IN ALL ITS VARIOUS BRANCHES, IS, OR MAY BE, PRACTISED TO THE GREATEST ADVANTAGE IN THIS COUNTRY. BY SAMUEL DEANE, A. M. FELLOW OF THE AMERICAN ACADEMY OF ARTS AND SCIENCES. [Three lines of Latin from] VIRGIL.
Printed at Worcester, Massachusetts. By Isaiah Thomas. Sold by him and Company in Boston. MDCCXC. pp. viii, 335. 8vo.   AAS. BA. BM. JCB. LOC.
3rd Massachusetts District Copyright, issued to Isaiah Thomas, as Proprietor, 13 September, 1790. Contains a list of subscribers' names with addresses. A second edition was printed in Worcester in 1797; and a third edition in Boston in 1822.

22451   THE DEATH OF CAIN, IN FIVE BOOKS; AFTER THE MANNER OF THE DEATH OF ABEL. BY A LADY. [Two lines from] MILTON.
*Philadelphia: Printed and sold by William Spotswood.*M,DCC,XC. pp. iv, 103. 24mo.   AAS. JCB.

22452   DELAWARE. STATE.
LAWS OF THE DELAWARE STATE, PASSED AT A SESSION OF THE GENERAL ASSEMBLY, COMMENCED AT DOVER, ON THE 20TH DAY OF OCTOBER, 1789. [Arms.]
Wilmington: Printed by Frederick Craig and Co. 1790. pp. 5. fol.   LOC.

22453   —— — LAWS OF THE DELAWARE STATE, PASSED AT A SESSION OF THE GENERAL ASSEMBLY, COMMENCED AT DOVER, ON THE FOURTH DAY OF JANUARY, 1790. [Arms.]
Wilmington: Printed by Frederick Craig and Co. 1790. pp. 19. fol. LOC.

22454   —— — LAWS OF THE DELAWARE STATE, PASSED AT A SESSION OF THE GENERAL ASSEMBLY COMMENCED AT DOVER ON THE TWENTIETH DAY OF OCTOBER, 1790. [Arms.]
Wilmington, Printed by James Adams, M,DCC,XC. pp. 13. fol.   LOC.

22455   DELAWARE, continued.
—— VOTES AND PROCEEDINGS OF THE HOUSE OF ASSEMBLY OF THE DELAWARE STATE, OCTOBER, 1789.
Wilmington: Printed by Frederick Craig and Co. 1790.

22456   —— — VOTES AND PROCEEDINGS OF THE HOUSE OF ASSEMBLY OF THE DELAWARE STATE, JANUARY, 1790.
Wilmington: Printed by Frederick Craig and Co. 1790.

22457   —— — VOTES AND PROCEEDINGS OF THE HOUSE OF ASSEMBLY OF THE DELAWARE STATE, OCTOBER, 1790.
Wilmington: Printed by James Adams. 1790.

22458   THE DELAWARE GAZETTE, AND GENERAL ADVERTISER. VOL. V. NO. 249. SATURDAY, JANUARY 2, [—VOL. VI. NO. 300. SATURDAY, DECEMBER 25, 1790.]
Wilmington: Printed and published by Frederick Craig and Co. 1790. fol.

22459   DELL, WILLIAM   – 1664
PRÜFUNG DER GEISTER SOWOHL IN DEN LEHRERN ALS IN DEN ZUHÖRERN, U. S. W.
Philadelphia: Gedruckt bey Carl Cist. 1790. pp. 80. 16mo.

22460   DE ROSSET, ARMAND JOHN   1767 – 1859
DE FEBRIBUS INTERMITTENTIBUS.
Philadelphiæ: Typis T. Dobson, 1790. pp. 34. 12mo.   SGO.

22461   DILWORTH, THOMAS   – 1780
THE SCHOOLMASTERS ASSISTANT: BEING A COMPENDIUM OF ARITHMETIC, BOTH PRACTICAL AND THEORETICAL. IN FIVE PARTS. CONTAINING, I. ARITHMETIC IN WHOLE NUMBERS, WHEREIN ALL THE COMMON RULES, HAVING EACH OF THEM A SUFFICIENT NUMBER OF QUESTIONS, WITH THEIR ANSWERS, ARE METHODICALLY AND BRIEFLY HANDLED. II. VULGAR FRACTIONS, WHEREIN SEVERAL THINGS, NOT COMMONLY MET WITH, ARE THERE DISTINCTLY TREATED OF, AND LAID DOWN IN THE MOST PLAIN AND EASY MANNER. III. DECIMALS, IN WHICH, AMONG OTHER THINGS, ARE CONSIDERED THE EXTRACTION OF ROOTS; INTEREST BOTH SIMPLE AND COMPOUND; ANNUITIES, REBATE, AND EQUATION OF PAYMENTS. IV. A LARGE COLLECTION OF QUESTIONS, WITH THEIR ANSWERS, SERVING TO EXERCISE THE FOREGOING RULES; TOGETHER WITH A FEW OTHERS, BOTH PLEASANT AND DIVERTING. V. DUODECIMALS, COMMONLY CALLED CROSS MULTIPLICATION; WHEREIN THAT SORT OF ARITHMETIC IS THOROUGHLY CONSIDERED, AND RENDERED VERY PLAIN AND EASY; TOGETHER WITH THE METHOD OF PROVING ALL THE FOREGOING OPERATIONS AT ONCE BY DIVISION OF SEVERAL DENOMINATIONS, WITHOUT REDUCING THEM TO THE LOWEST TERM MENTIONED. THE WHOLE BEING DELIVERED IN THE MOST FAMILIAR WAY OF QUESTION AND ANSWER, IS RECOMMENDED BY SEVERAL EMINENT MATHEMATICIANS, ACCOMPTANTS, AND SCHOOLMASTERS, AS NECESSARY TO BE USED IN SCHOOLS BY ALL TEACHERS, WHO WOULD HAVE THEIR SCHOLARS THOROUGHLY UNDERSTAND, AND MAKE A QUICK PROGRESS IN ARITHMETIC. TO WHICH IS PREFIXT, AN ESSAY ON THE EDUCATION OF YOUTH; HUMBLY OFFERED TO THE CONSIDERATION OF PARENTS. BY THOMAS DILWORTH, AUTHOR OF THE NEW GUIDE TO THE ENGLISH TONGUE; YOUNG BOOK-KEEPER'S ASSISTANT, &c. &c. AND SCHOOLMASTER IN WAPPING. [Four lines of quotations.]
Philadelphia: Printed and sold by Joseph Crukshank, Market-Street, between Second and Third-Streets. MDCCXC. pp. xiv, (10), 192, portrait. 12mo.
                    AAS. JCB.

22462

DILWORTH, Thomas, continued.

—— A New guide to the English tongue: in five parts. Containing, i. Words both common and proper; . . . ii. A large and useful table of words, that are the same in sound, but different in signification; . . . iii. A short but comprehensive grammar of the English tongue, delivered in the most familiar and instructive method of question and answer; . . . iv. An useful collection of sentences, in prose and verse, divine, moral and historical; . . . And v. Forms of prayer for children, on several occasions. The whole being recommended by several clergymen and eminent schoolmasters. By Thomas Dilworth.

New-York: Printed and sold by Samuel Loudon, 1790.

22463

—— — A New guide to the English tongue: in five parts. Containing, i. Words both common and proper; . . . ii. A large and useful table of words, that are the same in sound, but different in signification; . . . iii. A short but comprehensive grammar of the English tongue, delivered in the most familiar and instructive method of question and answer; . . . iv. An useful collection of sentences, in prose and verse, divine, moral and historical; . . . And v. Forms of prayer for children on several occasions. The whole being recommended by several clergymen and eminent schoolmasters. By Thomas Dilworth.

Philadelphia: Printed for Robert Campbell, 1790.

22464

DILWORTH, W. H.

The Complete letter-writer. Containing familiar letters on the most common occasions in life. Also, a variety of elegant letters for the direction and embellishment of style. On business, duty, amusement, love, courtship, marriage, friendship, & other subjects. In four parts. With directions for writing letters, and the proper forms of address. To which is added, forms of message cards. Second edition, with amendments and additions.

Boston: Printed and sold by John West Folsom, No. 30, Union-Street. MDCCXC. pp. 216. 12mo. AAS.

22465

DODDRIDGE, Philip   1702 – 1751

A Plain and serious address to the master of a family, on the important subject of family – religion. By Philip Doddridge, D. D.

London, Printed: Portsmouth, (N. H.) Re-printed, and to be sold, by George J. Osborne, jun'r. M.DCC.XC. pp. 28. 8vo. AAS.

22466

—— The Rise and progress of religion in the soul, illustrated in a course of serious and practical addresses, suited to persons of every character and circumstance, with a devout meditation and prayer to each chapter. To all which are subjoined a funeral sermon on the one thing needful. By Philip Doddridge, D. D.

New-York: Printed and sold by Samuel Loudon. 1790.

22467

—— Sermons on the religious education of children; preached at Northampton. By Philip Doddridge, D. D.

London, Printed: Portsmouth (N. H.) Re-printed, and to be sold by George Jerry Osborne, jun'r. M,DCC,XC. pp. [111.] 16mo. AAS. BA. BM. JCB. LOC.

22468

—— — Sermons on the religious education of children; preached at Northampton. By Philip Doddridge, D. D.

Newbury Port: Printed by John Mycall, 1790. pp. 111. 16mo.

22469   DODSLEY, ROBERT   1703 – 1764
THE ŒCONOMY OF HUMAN LIFE. COMPLETE, IN TWO PARTS. TRANSLATED FROM AN INDIAN MANUSCRIPT, WRITTEN BY AN ANCIENT BRAMIN. TO WHICH IS PRE-FIXED, AN ACCOUNT OF THE MANNER IN WHICH THE SAID MANUSCRIPT WAS DIS-COVERED; IN A LETTER FROM AN ENGLISH GENTLEMAN RESIDING IN CHINA TO THE EARL OF *******.
New-York: Printed by Hugh Gaine, at the Bible, in Hanover-Square. 1790. pp. 84. 12mo.

22470   —— — THE ŒCONOMY OF HUMAN LIFE, COMPLETE, IN TWO PARTS; TRANSLATED FROM AN INDIAN MANUSCRIPT, WRITTEN BY AN ANCIENT BRAMIN. TO WHICH IS PREFIXED, AN ACCOUNT OF THE MANNER IN WHICH THE SAID MANUSCRIPT WAS DISCOVERED; IN A LETTER FROM AN ENGLISH GENTLEMAN RESIDING IN CHINA, TO THE EARL OF *******.
Philadelphia: Printed for Joseph James. M.DCC.XC. pp.140. 18mo.AAS.JCB.
Contains a two-page list of Books just published, and to be sold by James and Johnson.

22471   DOVER. DELAWARE. BAPTIST ASSOCIATION.
MINUTES OF THE DOVER BAPTIST ASSOCIATION, MET AT THE DIAMOND MEETING-HOUSE, IN ESSEX COUNTY, VIRGINIA, OCTOBER, 1790.
Richmond: Printed by Thomas Nicolson. 1790.

22472   DOWNAME, JOHN   – 1644
A BRIEF CONCORDANCE OR TABLE TO THE BIBLE OF THE LAST TRANSLATION: SERV-ING FOR THE MORE EASY FINDING OUT OF THE MOST USEFUL PLACES THEREIN CONTAINED. CAREFULLY PERUSED AND ENLARGED BY JOHN DOWNAME, B. A. [One line from] PSALM CXIX. 105.
Trenton: Printed and sold by Isaac Collins. M.DCC.XC. pp. (2), 70. 4to.
Sometimes found bound with Isaac Collins' quarto edition of the Bible, printed in 1791.

22473   DUKE, WILLIAM   1757 – 1840
HYMNS AND POEMS, ON VARIOUS OCCASIONS. BY A MEMBER OF THE PROTESTANT EPISCOPAL CHURCH.
Baltimore: Printed by Samuel and John Adams, in Market-Street. M,DCC,XC. pp. 90. 18mo.   BU.

22474   DURELL, WILLIAM
PROPOSALS BY WILLIAM DURELL, No. 198, QUEEN-STREET, FOR PRINTING BY SUB-SCRIPTION AN ESSAY ON THE KINGDOM OF CHRIST. BY THE REV. MR. ABRAHAM BOOTH. CONDITIONS. [Sixteen lines.]
New-York, [Printed by William Durell] October, 1790. Broadside. 4to.
                                              AAS. BU.

22475   DYER, WILLIAM   1636 – 1696
CHRIST'S FAMOUS TITLES, AND A BELIEVER'S GOLDEN CHAIN, HANDLED IN DIVERS SERMONS. . . .
Newbury Port: Printed by John Mycall. 1790.

22476   EDWARDS, JONATHAN   1703 – 1758
A CAREFUL AND STRICT INQUIRY INTO THE MODERN PREVAILING NOTIONS OF THAT FREEDOM OF WILL, WHICH IS SUPPOSED TO BE ESSENTIAL TO MORAL AGENCY, VIR-TUE AND VICE, REWARD AND PUNISHMENT, PRAISE AND BLAME. BY THE LATE REVEREND AND LEARNED JONATHAN EDWARDS, A. M. PRESIDENT OF THE COL-LEGE OF NEW-JERSEY. [One line from] ROM. IX. 16. THE FOURTH EDITION.
Wilmington, (Delaware) Printed and sold by James Adams, in High-Street. M.DCC.XC. pp. xi, 299; (13). 8vo.   AAS. JCB. LOC.

EDWARDS, JONATHAN, continued.

Second heading: REMARKS ON THE ESSAYS ON THE PRINCIPLES OF MORALITY
AND NATURAL RELIGION, IN A LETTER TO A MINISTER OF THE CHURCH OF SCOT-
LAND: BY THE REVEREND MR. JONATHAN EDWARDS, PRESIDENT OF THE COLLEGE
OF NEW-JERSEY, AND AUTHOR OF THE LATE INQUIRY INTO THE MODERN NOTIONS
OF THE FREEDOM OF WILL. [Signed, J. Edwards, Stockbridge, July 25, 1757.]

22477 —— A FAITHFUL NARRATIVE OF THE SURPRISING WORK OF GOD IN THE CONVER-
SION OF MANY HUNDRED SOULS IN NORTHAMPTON, AND THE NEIGHBOURING
TOWNS AND VILLAGES OF NEW-HAMPSHIRE AND NEW-ENGLAND. IN A LETTER
TO REV. DR. BENJAMIN COLMAN OF BOSTON. BY THE REV. MR. EDWARDS,
MINISTER OF NORTHAMPTON. AND PUBLISHED WITH A LARGE PREFACE, BY DR.
WATTS AND DR. GUYSE. TO WHICH IS ADDED, TRUE GRACE, DISTINGUISHED FROM
THE EXPERIENCE OF DEVILS; IN A SERMON PREACHED BEFORE THE SYNOD OF
NEW-YORK. A NEW AMERICAN EDITION.

Elizabeth-Town: Printed by Shepard Kollock. M,DCC,XC. pp. 125; 48-
12mo. AAS. JCB.

Second title: TRUE GRACE, DISTINGUISHED FROM THE EXPERIENCE OF DEVILS;
IN A SERMON, PREACHED BEFORE THE SYNOD OF NEW-YORK, CONVENED AT NEW-
ARK, IN NEW-JERSEY, ON SEPTEMBER 28, N. S. 1752. [PRINTED BY DESIRE OF
THE SYNOD.] BY JONATHAN EDWARDS, A. M. PASTOR OF THE CHURCH OF CHRIST
IN STOCKBRIDGE IN NEW-ENGLAND. [Five lines from] 2 CORINTHIANS. XI. 3.14.
Elizabethtown: Printed by Shepard Kollock. M.DCC.XCI. pp. 43.

22478 EDWARDS, JONATHAN 1745 – 1801
THE SALVATION OF ALL MEN STRICTLY EXAMINED; AND THE ENDLESS PUNISHMENT
OF THOSE WHO DIE IMPENITENT, ARGUED AND DEFENDED AGAINST THE OBJECT-
IONS AND REASONINGS OF THE LATE REV. DOCTOR CHAUNCY, OF BOSTON, IN HIS
BOOK ENTITLED "THE SALVATION OF ALL MEN," &c.
New-Haven: Printed by A. Morse, M,DCC,XC. pp. vi, 331, (3). 8vo.
AAS. BA. BM. HC. JCB. MHS.

Preface dated June 29, 1789. Contains a sixteen-page list of subscribers. At the end the printer makes the following announcement: "Said
Morse dresses his own leather, attends to every part of his business
himself, is emulous to excel in his profession, and the public may depend upon being served by him with the utmost punctuality. Country produce, or clean cotton and linen rags and sheep's pelts will be
taken in payment."

22479 EFFUSIONS OF FEMALE FANCY. BY A YOUNG AMERICAN LADY. CONSISTING OF
ELEGIES AND OTHER ORIGINAL POETIC ESSAYS.
New-York: Printed by Thomas Greenleaf, 1790.

22480 AN ELEGY TO THE MEMORY OF MISS SARAH HART, DAUGHTER OF REV. WILLIAM
HART, OF SAYBROOK; WHO DEPARTED THIS LIFE, JUNE 24, 1788.
Hartford: Printed by Hudson & Goodwin. 1790. pp. 7. 8vo. MHS.

22481 THE ELEMENTS OF GESTURE, ILLUSTRATED BY FOUR ELEGANT COPPER-PLATES;
TOGETHER WITH RULES FOR EXPRESSING WITH PROPRIETY, THE VARIOUS PASSIONS
AND EMOTIONS OF THE MIND.
*Philadelphia: Printed by William Young, Bookseller, the corner of Second
and Chesnut-Streets.* M,DCC,XC. pp. 52, (2), 4 plates. 12mo.

22482 ELLICOTT, ANDREW   1754 – 1820
ELLICOTT'S MARYLAND AND VIRGINIA ALMANAC, AND EPHEMERIS, FOR THE YEAR
OF OUR LORD, 1791; BEING THE THIRD AFTER BISSIXTILE, OR LEAP-YEAR, AND
THE FIFTEENTH YEAR OF AMERICAN INDEPENDENCE. [Seventeen lines.]
  Baltimore: Printed and sold, wholesale and retail, by John Hayes, Market-
Street. [1790.] pp. (48). 12mo.   LOC. MHS.

22483 ELY, ZEBULON   1759 – 1824
THE FRAILTY OF ALL FLESH, AND THE STABILITY OF THE WORD OF THE LORD. A
SERMON, DELIVERED IN THE FIRST SOCIETY IN LEBANON THE SABBATH AFTER
THE DEATH OF MR. JONATHAN L. LEECH, WHO DEPARTED THIS LIFE . . . JAN-
UARY 12, 1790, IN THE 22ND YEAR OF HIS AGE.
  Norwich: Printed by John Trumbull, 1790. pp. 24. 8vo. AAS. BPL.

22484 EMLYN, THOMAS   1663 – 1743
EXTRACTS FROM AN HUMBLE INQUIRY INTO THE SCRIPTURE ACCOUNT OF JESUS
CHRIST; [TOGETHER WITH OTHER EXTRACTS; PROVING THAT THE DOCTRINE OF
THE TRINITY HAS NO SOLID FOUNDATION IN SCRIPTURE.] BY THOMAS EMLYN.
[Three lines from] I COR. VIII. 5.
  Boston: Printed and sold by Samuel Hall, at his Printing - Office, No. 53,
Cornhill. MDCCXC. pp. 47. 8vo. AAS. BA. BM. CHS. HC. JCB. LOC. MHS. NYPL.

22485 EMMONS, NATHANAEL   1745 – 1840
A DISCOURSE, DELIVERED NOVEMBER 7, 1790, AT THE PARTICULAR REQUEST OF
A NUMBER OF RESPECTABLE MEN IN FRANKLIN, WHO WERE FORMING A SOCIETY
FOR THE REFORMATION OF MORALS. AND, NOW PUBLISHED AT THE DESIRE OF
THE HEARERS. BY NATHANAEL EMMONS, A. M. PASTOR OF THE CHURCH IN
FRANKLIN. [Printer's monogram.]
  Printed at Providence, by Bennett Wheeler, Westminster-Street. [1790.]
pp. [32.] 8vo.   AAS. BPL. HC. NYHS. RIHS. YC.

22486 ENCYCLOPÆDIA; OR, A DICTIONARY OF ARTS, SCIENCES, AND MISCELLANEOUS LITER-
ATURE; CONSTRUCTED ON A PLAN, BY WHICH THE DIFFERENT SCIENCES AND ARTS
ARE DIGESTED INTO THE FORM OF DISTINCT TREATISES OR SYSTEMS, COMPREHEND-
ING THE HISTORY, THEORY, AND PRACTICE, OF EACH, ACCORDING TO THE LATEST
DISCOVERIES AND IMPROVEMENTS; AND FULL EXPLANATIONS GIVEN OF THE VARI-
OUS DETACHED PARTS OF KNOWLEDGE, WHETHER RELATING TO NATURAL AND ARTI-
FICIAL OBJECTS, OR TO MATTERS ECCLESIASTICAL, CIVIL, MILITARY, COMMERCIAL,
&C. INCLUDING ELUCIDATIONS OF THE MOST IMPORTANT TOPICS RELATIVE TO
RELIGION, MORALS, MANNERS, AND THE OECONOMY OF LIFE: TOGETHER WITH A
DESCRIPTION OF ALL THE COUNTRIES, CITIES, PRINCIPAL MOUNTAINS, SEAS, RIV-
ERS, &C. THROUGHOUT THE WORLD; A GENERAL HISTORY, ANCIENT AND MODERN,
OF THE DIFFERENT EMPIRES, KINGDOMS, AND STATES; AND AN ACCOUNT OF THE
LIVES OF THE MOST EMINENT PERSONS IN EVERY NATION, FROM THE EARLIEST
AGES DOWN TO THE PRESENT TIMES. COMPILED FROM THE WRITINGS OF THE
BEST AUTHORS, IN SEVERAL LANGUAGES; THE MOST APPROVED DICTIONARIES, AS
WELL OF GENERAL SCIENCE AS OF ITS PARTICULAR BRANCHES; THE TRANSACTIONS,
JOURNALS, AND MEMOIRS, OF VARIOUS LEARNED SOCIETIES, THE MS. LECTURES OF
EMINENT PROFESSORS ON DIFFERENT SCIENCES; AND A VARIETY OF ORIGINAL MA-
TERIALS, FURNISHED BY AN EXTENSIVE CORRESPONDENCE. THE FIRST AMERICAN
EDITION, IN EIGHTEEN VOLUMES, GREATLY IMPROVED. ILLUSTRATED WITH FIVE
HUNDRED AND FORTY-TWO COPPER-PLATES. VOL. I. A—ANG. [—VOL. II. ANG.—
BAR.] INDOCTI DISCANT, ET AMENT MEMINISSE PERITI.
  Philadelphia: Printed by Thomas Dobson, at the Stone House, No. 41,
South Second Street. M.DCC.XCVIII. [1790.] 2 vols. pp. 799, 31 plates; 799,
60 plates (32-91). 4to. AAS. APS. LCP. LOC. MHS. NYHS. NYPL. WC.

ENCYCLOPÆDIA, continued.

This American edition is something more than a reprint of the third edition of the Encyclopædia Britannica, on which it is based, as it contains much original matter, and some of the longer articles are written anew, "by gentlemen eminent in the respective sciences in this country." The article "America," was entirely rewritten by Jedidiah Morse; and as published in separate form, in 1790, makes a duodecimo volume of two hundred and fifty pages, with two maps. The article "Anatomy," was also entirely rewritten, and, as published separately in 1792, forms an octavo volume of four hundred and thirty-eight pages, with twelve plates. The article "Chemistry" was also rewritten and published separately in 1791, as "A System of Chemistry; comprehending the history, theory and practice of the science, according to the latest discoveries and improvements." That the scholars of this country could critically review and correct the scientific authorities of Great Britain in these, and other important branches of study, is significant of a high standard of scholarship. Five hundred and forty-three finely executed copperplates, illustrating the work, are by the American engravers: Scott, Thackara, Valance, Trenchard, Allardice, Smither, Seymour, and others. In this, as well as in other departments of mechanical execution, the publisher spared no expense. The paper, of superfine quality, was manufactured in Pennsylvania. And the types were cast on purpose for this work, by Baine and Company, of Philadelphia. Significant, also, of public interest, was the publisher's announcement, on the completion of the first volume, that "the patronage of a liberal subscription made it necessary to print double the number originally intended." Notwithstanding this, from various causes, chief among which were, its irregular manner of publication, and the period of years required in its printing, copies of the work are uncommonly found even in the older and larger libraries, and all have some peculiarities or defects. The original plan of subscription called for weekly numbers beginning 2 January, 1790, and this arrangement continued up to March. The first ten numbers were then combined to form Part one, and the weekly issue ceased. Part two, completing the first volume, was published in June, 1790. The plan of publication was then changed to a half volume every ten weeks, or a volume every twenty weeks, bound in boards, optional with a subscription of ten dollars at the time of subscribing and payment for the half volumes or volumes on delivery; and, under this arrangement, three volumes were issued each year until the work was completed in eighteen quarto volumes in 1797—in the same year, and in the same format, and number of volumes, with the completion of the Edinburgh edition. The irregular manner of publication did not allow for title-pages, and proper title-pages for all the volumes, together with an engraved frontispiece, dedication, and preface for the first volume, were furnished subscribers at the close of publication, all bearing the date of M.DCC.XCVIII, as if the work were issued in that year. While the tenth volume was printing, in September, 1793, a fire destroyed a great quantity of the printing material, and melted into a mass the figures of the tables of logarithms, which could not be replaced in time to form a part of that volume. When the risks of publication are considered, the courageous and admirable manner in which the publisher carried out the work to a conclusion, gives the name of Thomas Dobson, of Philadelphia, a high rank in the book-publishing annals of this country. In 1800, Dobson began the publication of a Supplement, in the same manner, which was completed in 1803—the three volumes of which bear the date of 1803 as the year of publication.

22487 | ERASMUS, DESIDERIUS 1465 – 1536
A COLLECTION OF THE WISE AND WITTY SAYINGS OF KINGS, CONSULS, GENERALS, PHILOSOPHERS, AND ORATORS OF ANTIQUITY. TRANSLATED FROM ERASMUS.
Hartford: Printed by Hudson & Goodwin, [1790.] pp. 52. 12mo.

22488 | ERRA PATER, pseudonym.
THE BOOK OF KNOWLEDGE: TREATING OF THE WISDOM OF THE ANCIENTS. IN FOUR PARTS. I. SHEWING THE VARIOUS AND WONDERFUL OPERATIONS OF THE SIGNS AND PLANETS, AND OTHER CELESTIAL CONSTELLATIONS, ON THE BODIES OF MEN, &C. II. PROGNOSTICATIONS FOR EVER NECESSARY TO KEEP THE BODY IN HEALTH; WITH SEVERAL CHOICE RECEIPTS IN PHYSIC AND SURGERY. III. AN ABSTRACT OF THE ART OF PHYSIOGNOMY AND PALMISTRY, TOGETHER WITH THE SIGNIFICATION OF MOLES, AND THE INTERPRETATION OF DREAMS, &C. IV. THE FARMER'S CALENDAR, CONTAINING, 1ST. PERPETUAL PROGNOSTICATIONS FOR WEATHER. 2D. THE WHOLE MYSTERY OF HUSBANDRY. 3D. THE COMPLETE AND EXPERIENCED FARRIER AND COWLEECH, &C. WRITTEN BY ERRA PATER, A JEW DOCTOR IN ASTRONOMY AND PHYSIC, BORN IN BETHANY, NEAR MOUNT OLIVET, IN JUDEA. MADE ENGLISH BY W. LILLY, STUDENT IN PHYSIC AND ASTROLOGY. TO WHICH IS ADDED, THE TRUE FORMS OF ALL SORTS OF BILLS, BONDS, COUNTER-BONDS, INDENTURES, LETTERS OF ATTORNEY AND LICENCE, DEEDS OF GIFT, BILLS OF EXCHANGE, &C.
Haverhill: Printed by Peter Edes, MDCCXC. pp. 118, frontispiece. 12mo. AAS.

22489 | —— — THE BOOK OF KNOWLEDGE TREATING OF THE WISDOM OF THE ANCIENTS. IN THREE PARTS. I. SHEWING THE WONDERFUL OPERATION OF THE SIGNS & PLANETS, AND OTHER CELESTIAL CONSTELLATIONS, ON THE BODIES OF MEN, &C. II. AN ABSTRACT OF THE ART OF PHYSIOGNOMY AND PALMISTRY TOGETHER WITH SIGNIFICATION OF MOLES, AND THE INTERPRETATION OF DREAMS, &C. III. THE FARMER'S CALENDAR, &C. PERPETUAL PROGNOSTICATIONS FOR WEATHER—THE MYSTERY OF HUSBANDRY—THE EXPERIENCED FARRIER, &C. WRITTEN BY ERRA PATER, A JEW DOCTOR IN ASTRONOMY AND PHYSIC, BORN IN BETHANY, NEAR MOUNT OLIVET, JUDEA. TO WHICH IS ADDED, THE WHEEL OF FORTUNE.
[Printed and] Sold by J. White and C. Cambridge near Charles River Bridge, Boston. [1790.] pp. 82, frontispiece. 24mo. JCB.

22490 | ERSKINE, RALPH 1685 – 1752
GOSPEL SONNETS: OR, SPIRITUAL SONGS.
Boston: Printed for Ebenezer Larkin, jun. 1790.

22491 | AN ESSAY ON THE CULTURE OF SILK AND RAISING WHITE MULBERRY TREES. . . . BY A CITIZEN OF PHILADELPHIA.
Philadelphia: Printed [by William Spotswood,] for the Author, 1790. pp. 8. 8vo.

22492 | THE ESSEX JOURNAL & NEW-HAMPSHIRE PACKET. NUMB. 288. WEDNESDAY, JANUARY 6, [—NUMB. 339. WEDNESDAY, DECEMBER 29, 1790.]
Newbury-Port: Printed by John Mycall, in Merrimack-Street a little below the Ferry-way, . . . 1790. fol. AAS. LOC.

22493 | ETLICHE CHRISTLICHE GEBÄTE.
Germantaun: Gedruckt bey Michael Billmeyer. 1790. pp. 163. 12mo.

22494 | EVANGELICAL LUTHERAN CHURCH IN NORTH AMERICA.
HOCH-DEUTSCHES LUTHERISCHES A. B. C. UND NAMENBÜCHLEIN.
Germantaun: Gedruckt bey Peter Leibert, 1790.

22495 EVANGELICAL LUTHERAN CHURCH, continued.
ANHANG ZU DEM GESANGBUCH DER VEREINIGTEN EVANGELISCH-LUTHERISCHEN
GEMEINEN IN NORD AMERIKA. ENTHALTEND DEN KLEINEN KATECHISMUS-
LUTHERI, EVANGELIEN, UND EPISTELN AUF ALLE SONNTAGE, WIE DURCH AUF
DIE HOHEN FESTE DURCH GANZE JAHR MIT KIRCHENGEBATEN.
Germantaun: Gedruckt bey Michael Billmeyer. 1790. pp. 80. 8vo. AAS. BU.

22496 FALLACY DETECTED, BY THE EVIDENCE OF FACTS; OR, CONSIDERATIONS ON THE IM-
POLICY AND INJUSTICE A COMPULSORY REDUCTION OF THE INTEREST OF THE PUB-
LICK DEBT. IN A LETTER TO A MEMBER OF CONGRESS.
[Philadelphia:] Printed in the year, M,DCC,XC. pp. (44). 8vo. AAS. LOC.

22497 THE FARMER'S JOURNAL. VOL. I. NO. 1. THURSDAY, MARCH 18, [— NO. 42.
TUESDAY, DECEMBER 28, 1790.]
*Published in Danbury, by Nathan Douglas and Edwards Ely, near the
Court-House.* 1790. fol. AAS. LOC. NYHS.
Established, as a weekly publication, by Nathan Douglas and Edwards
Ely. In January 1793, the partnership was dissolved, Edwards Ely
continuing publication alone to the issue for June 3, 1793, when it was
discontinued. On June 17, 1793, Ely established in continuation the
Farmers Chronicle.

22498 THE FEDERAL ALMANACK, FOR THE YEAR OF OUR LORD, 1791. BEING THE THIRD
AFTER BISSEXTILE OR LEAP-YEAR, AND THE FIFTEENTH OF AMERICAN INDEPEND-
ENCE. [Cut of George Washington.]
Boston: Printed [by Joseph Bumstead,] for and sold by the Booksellers.
[1790.] pp. (24). 12mo. LOC.

22499 THE FEDERAL GAZETTE AND PHILADELPHIA EVENING POST. [Motto.] VOL. III.
TOTAL NO. 391. FRIDAY, 1ST JANUARY, [— VOL. V. TOTAL NO. 700. FRIDAY,
DECEMBER 31, 1790.]
*Philadelphia: Printed and published, daily, by Andrew Brown, at Wash-
ington's Head, Chesnut-Street, opposite the Post-Office.* 1790. 4to. AAS. LCP. LOC.
With the issue for March 8th, the motto was dropped, and its place in
the heading taken by the imprint: Published daily by Andrew Brown,
at Washington's Head, Chesnut-Street, Philadelphia. In April. the
size of the paper was enlarged to folio, and the title altered to: *The
Federal Gazette and Philadelphia Daily Advertiser.* Printed and published by Andrew Brown, in Chesnut-Street, near Front-Street.

22500 —— THE ADDRESS OF THE CARRIERS OF THE FEDERAL GAZETTE TO THEIR CUSTO-
MERS, ON THE COMMENCEMENT OF THE YEAR 1790.
Philadelphia: Printed by Andrew Brown, 1790. Broadside.

22501 THE FEDERAL HERALD. [Motto.] VOL. III. NO. 99. MONDAY, JANUARY 4,
[— VOL. IV. NO. 1. TOTAL NO. 121. MONDAY. JUNE 7, 1790.]
*Lansingburgh: Printed every Monday, by Baboock & Hickok, cor-
ner of King and Hoosack-Streets.* 1790. fol. AAS.
The issue for June 7th, gives the following notice: "The Printers request that all persons who are indebted to them would make immediate payment; and who have demands are desired to present them for
settlement . . . In order that this business may be brought to a close
without procrastination, the publication of the Herald will, for the
present, cease."

22502   FISH, ELISHA   1719 – 1795
THE BAPTISM OF JESUS CHRIST *not* TO BE IMITATED BY CHRISTIANS: CONSIDERED
AND ILLUSTRATED IN AN ESSAY. BY THE REV. ELISHA FISH, OF UPTON. AND
THE REV. JOHN CRANE, OF NORTHBRIDGE. [Three lines from] JESUS CHRIST.
*Boston: Printed and sold by Joseph Bumstead, at his Printing-Office, No.
20, Union-Street.* [1790.] pp. (22). 8vo.   AAS. BM. JCB.
"Printed from new type, but few copies remain for sale."

22503   FLEET, THOMAS, and JOHN
FLEETS' POCKET ALMANACK FOR THE YEAR OF OUR LORD, 1791. BEING THE
THIRD AFTER LEAP YEAR, AND FIFTEENTH OF AMERICAN INDEPENDENCE. CAL-
CULATED CHIEFLY FOR THE USE OF THE COMMONWEALTH OF MASSACHUSETTS,
BOSTON, THE METROPOLIS, BEING IN LATITUDE 42 DEG. 25 MIN. NORTH. LONGI-
TUDE 71 DEG. 4 MIN. WEST FROM THE ROYAL OBSERVATORY AT GREENWICH.
TO WHICH IS ANNEXED, THE MASSACHUSETTS REGISTER, &C.
*Boston: Printed and sold by T. & J. Fleet at the Bible and Heart in
Cornhill.* [1790.] pp. [24], [132.] 24mo.   AAS. BA. HC. LOC. MHS. NYPL.
9th Massachusetts District Copyright, issued to Thomas and John
Fleet, as Proprietors, 13 December, 1790.

22504   FORBES, ELI   1726 – 1804
SORROW BALANCED WITH JOY. A SERMON, PREACHED ON THE TENTH OF MAY,
MDCCXC, AT THE FUNERAL OF THE REV. BENJAMIN TAPPAN, A. M. PASTOR OF
THE CHURCH IN MANCHESTER; WHO DEPARTED THIS LIFE MAY 6, 1790, IN THE
70TH YEAR OF HIS AGE, AND 45TH OF HIS MINISTRY. BY ELI FORBES, A. M. PAS-
TOR OF THE FIRST CHURCH IN GLOUCESTER. PUBLISHED AT THE DESIRE OF THE
BEREAVED FAMILY, CHURCH AND PEOPLE; TO WHOM IT IS MOST RESPECTFULLY
INSCRIBED, BY THEIR FRIEND AND SERVANT — THE AUTHOR.
Printed at Salem, by Thomas C. Cushing. [1790.] pp. 15. 8vo. BA. JCB.

22505   FOSTER, DANIEL   1748 – 1810
AN ELECTION SERMON; DELIVERED BEFORE THE HONORABLE LEGISLATURE OF THE
STATE OF VERMONT; CONVENED AT WESTMINSTER, OCTOBER 8TH, 1789. BY DAN
FOSTER, A. M.
Printed in Windsor, by Alden Spooner. MDCCXC. pp. 26. 4to. BA. HC.

22506   FOSTER, DANIEL   1751 – 1795
A SERMON PREACHED BEFORE HIS EXCELLENCY JOHN HANCOCK, ESQ. GOVERNOUR;
HIS HONOUR SAMUEL ADAMS, ESQ. LIEUTENANT-GOVERNOUR, THE HONOURABLE THE
COUNCIL, SENATE, AND HOUSE OF REPRESENTATIVES, OF THE COMMONWEALTH
OF MASSACHUSETTS, MAY 26, 1790. BEING THE DAY OF GENERAL ELECTION. BY
DANIEL FOSTER, A. M. PASTOR OF THE CHURCH IN NEW-BRAINTREE.
*Boston, Massachusetts: Printed by Thomas Adams, Printer to the honour-
able the General Court.* M,DCC,XC. pp. 35. 8vo. AAS. BA. BM. JCB. LOC. NYHS.

22507   FOX, THOMAS
THE WILMINGTON ALMANACK OR EPHEMERIS, FOR THE YEAR OF OUR LORD, 1791.
Wilmington: Printed and sold by James Adams. [1790.]

22508   FRANKLIN, BENJAMIN   1706 – 1790
THE WAY TO WEALTH; AS CLEARLY SHEWN IN THE PREFACE OF AN OLD PUB-
LICATION, ENTITLED, "POOR RICHARD IMPROVED." BY BENJAMIN FRANKLIN,
L. L. D.
*Printed at Worcester, Massachusetts, by Isaiah Thomas. Sold at his Book-
store in Worcester, and by him and Company in Boston.* MDCCXC. pp. 21,
12mo.   AAS. LOC.

FRANKLIN, BENJAMIN, continued.

22509 —— REMARKS UPON THE NAVIGATION FROM NEWFOUNDLAND TO NEW-YORK, IN OR-
DER TO AVOID THE GULF STREAM ON ONE HAND, AND ON THE OTHER, THE SHOALS
THAT LIE TEN LEAGUES DUE SOUTH OF NANTUCKET, AND SOUTH WEST OF THE
SHOALEST GROUND ON ST. GEORGE'S BANKS, TWENTY-EIGHT LEAGUES. BY DR.
FRANKLIN. . . . DIRECTIONS FOR SAILING BETWEEN THE MIDDLE GROUND
AND THE HORSE SHOE, AT THE ENTRANCE OF CAPE-HENRY. . . . DIRECTIONS
FOR SAILING ON THE COAST OF NORTH CAROLINA. . . . SETTING OF THE
TIDES WITHIN THE CAPES OF DELAWARE BAY.
[Boston: Printed by Benjamin Edes and Son, 1790.] Broadside. fol. NYHS.
Forming page 3 of the issue of 11th October, 1790, of the Boston
Gazette. "A few copies in single sheets may be had of the Printers."

22510 FREE AND ACCEPTED MASONS. GRAND LODGE OF STATE OF NEW JERSEY.
GENERAL REGULATIONS FOR THE GOVERNMENT OF THE GRAND LODGE OF NEW-
JERSEY.
[Trenton: Printed by Isaac Collins? 1790.] pp. 24. 8vo.   NYHS.

22511 FREEMAN, SAMUEL   1743 – 1831
THE COLUMBIAN PRIMER, OR THE SCHOOL MISTRESSES' GUIDE TO CHILDREN IN THEIR
FIRST STEPS TO LEARNING. PART I. CONTAINING WORDS OF ONE AND TWO SYLLA-
BLES. WITH AN APPENDIX, CONTAINING SUNDRY MATTERS WHICH CHILDREN MAY
BE TAUGHT TO SAY BY HEART. BY SAMUEL FREEMAN, ESQUIRE.
*[Boston: Printed by Benjamin Russell? Published and to be sold by
Samuel Freeman, esq. of Portland; and by Mr. Joshua Thomas, opposite the Treas-
ury-Office, Boston. 1790.]*
"A Second part is ready for the Press." First Maine District Copyright
issued to Samuel Freeman, as Author, 14 August, 1790.

22512 —— A CURIOUS ALMANACK, CALCULATED FOR A WATCH-CASE, CONTAINED IN QUAR-
TERLY CIRCLES, WITH THE EXPLANATION, &C. THE CALCULATIONS BY SAMUEL
FREEMAN, WARRANTED FOR THESE [New-England] STATES. ENGRAVED BY
JOSIAH FLAGG.
Boston: Sold by Josiah Flagg, 1790.

22513 THE FREEMAN'S [cut] JOURNAL: OR THE NORTH-AMERICAN INTELLIGENCER.
OPEN TO ALL PARTIES, BUT INFLUENCED BY NONE. VOL. IX. NUMB. CCCCLV. WED-
NESDAY, JANUARY 6, [— NUMB. DVI. WEDNESDAY, DECEMBER 29, 1790.]
*Philadelphia: Printed by Francis Bailey, at Yorick's Head, in Market-
Street. 1790. fol.*   AAS.

22514 FRENEAU, PHILIP   1752 – 1832
A POEM, ON THE RISING GLORY OF AMERICA; BEING AN EXERCISE DELIVERED AT
THE PUBLIC COMMENCEMENT AT NASSAU-HALL, SEPTEMBER 25, 1771.
Philadelphia: Printed by R. Aitken & Son, in Market Street. 1790.

22515 FRIENDS, SOCIETY OF
THE EPISTLE FROM THE YEARLY-MEETING, HELD IN LONDON, BY ADJOURNMENTS,
FROM THE 17TH TO THE 25TH OF THE FIFTH MONTH, 1790, INCLUSIVE. TO THE
QUARTERLY AND MONTHLY MEETINGS OF FRIENDS IN GREAT-BRITAIN, IRELAND,
AND ELSEWHERE.
[Philadelphia? 1790.] pp. (4). fol.

22516 —— FROM OUR YEARLY-MEETING HELD IN LONDON, FROM THE 17TH TO THE 25TH
OF THE FIFTH MONTH, 1790, INCLUSIVE, TO THE YEARLY-MEETING OF FRIENDS, TO
BE HELD AT PHILADELPHIA, FOR PENNSYLVANIA, &C.
[Philadelphia: 1790.] pp. (2). fol.   AAS.

FRIENDS, SOCIETY OF, continued.

22517 —— TO THE PRESIDENT, SENATE, AND HOUSE OF REPRESENTATIVES OF THE UNITED STATES, &C. THE ADDRESS AND MEMORIAL OF THE PEOPLE CALLED QUAKERS, CONVENED AT THEIR YEARLY MEETING FOR PENNSYLVANIA &C. [Regarding national defence.]
[Philadelphia: 1790.] fol.

22518 GAY, EBENEZER   1766 – 1837
AN ORATION ON AMERICAN INDEPENDENCE, JULY 5, 1790.
Hartford: Printed by Hudson and Goodwin? 1790.

22519 GAZETTE [U. S. ARMS] OF MAINE. VOL. I. NO. I. FRIDAY, OCTOBER 8, [—No. 13. THURSDAY, DECEMBER 30, 1790.]
Portland (Massachusetts): Printed and published by Benjamin Titcomb, jun. 1790. fol.   AAS. NYHS.

Established by Benjamin Titcomb, junior, in opposition to Wait's Cumberland Gazette, and continued by him to September, 1796, when he sold it to John Keler Baker, who also purchased Wait's paper, and consolidated the two under the name of *Eastern Herald & Gazette of Maine*, as a semi-weekly, which was continued to 1804, when it was merged with the *Portland Gazette*. In 1819, the name was revived in the weekly edition of the Portland Advertiser.

22520 *General title:* THE GAZETTE OF THE UNITED STATES. A NATIONAL PAPER, PUBLISHED AT THE SEAT OF GOVERNMENT: CONTAINING, A HISTORY OF THE PROCEEDINGS OF THE LEGISLATURE OF THE UNITED STATES, UNDER THE *new* CONSTITUTION, FROM THE FOURTH MARCH 1789, TO THE 14TH APRIL, 1790: THE LAWS AND RESOLUTIONS OF CONGRESS, PASSED DURING THAT PERIOD, AND SKETCHES OF DEBATES IN THE HOUSE OF REPRESENTATIVES. ALSO, THE ADDRESSES TO THE PRESIDENT, OF THE UNITED STATES, WITH HIS ANSWERS TO THE SAME: A SERIES OF ORIGINAL ESSAYS, UPON THE MOST INTERESTING SUBJECTS OF LIFE, MANNERS, AND POLITICS, AGRICULTURE, MANUFACTURES, COMMERCE, AND SCIENCE. DOMESTIC AND FOREIGN INTELLIGENCE, &C. &C. VOLUME FIRST. U S A.
New-York: Published by the Editor (John Fenno) at his Office, [No. 41, *Broad-Street,] near the Exchange..* 1790. pp. (2), (2), 416. fol. AAS. BM. HC. LOC.
Heading: GAZETTE OF THE UNITED STATES. NO. LXXVI. SATURDAY, JANUARY 2, [—No. 70 OF VOL. II. WHOLE No. 174. WEDNESDAY, DECEMBER 29, 1790.]
Published [Wednesdays and Saturdays] by John Fenno, No. 9 *Maiden-Lane, near the Oswego-Market, New-York.* 1790. pp. 301-416; 1-688. fol.
                                            AAS. BM. HC. LOC.
In November, agreeable to his original plan of publishing a national paper at the seat of the national government, when Congress changed its place of meeting, Fenno removed his Office from New York to Philadelphia; the issue for November 3rd, bearing this notice: "This day is published in this city, Philadelphia, No. 54 of the second volume of the Gazette of the United States. Published by John Fenno, at his house, No. 69 Market-Street, north side between Second and Third Streets.

22521 GEMEINNÜTZIGE PHILADELPHISCHE CORRESPONDENZ. NUM. 454. DIENSTAGS DEN 5 JANUAR, [—NUM. 492 (?). DIENSTAG DEN 28 SEPTEMBER (?) 1790.]
Diese Zeitung wird Dienstag nachmittags heraus gegeben von Melchior Steiner, Buchdrucker in der Rees-Strasse, zwischen der Zweyten-und Dritten-Strasse, zu Philadelphia; . . . 1790. fol.   HSP.
Beginning in October, the title was changed to: *Neue Philadelphische Correspondenz*, published semi-weekly on Tuesdays and Fridays, under new editorship, and with a new numbering.

22522   THE GENERAL Advertiser, and political, commercial, agricultural and literary journal. Truth, decency, utility. Weekly No. 1. Daily No. 1. Friday, October 1, This no. gratis. [—Daily No. 79. Friday, December 31, 1790.]

> *Published daily, by Benj. Franklin Bache, up Franklin Court, in Market, between Third and Fourth-Streets, Philadelphia.* 1790. fol.   AAS. HC.

The Tuesday issue constituted the weekly issue. An Index broadside, forms part of the issue for December 30th. Established by Benjamin Franklin Bache, a grandson of Benjamin Franklin, and continued by him until his death, from yellow fever, on the 10th of September, 1798. In August, 1791, the sub-title was dropped from the heading. Beginning with the issue for November 8th, 1794, it was issued as No. 1. *The Aurora,* and continued as *Aurora and general advertiser.* Publication was suspended, on the death of the founder, from September 10th, to October 31st, and was resumed, November 1st, 1798, by his widow, Margaret H. Bache, assisted by William Duane, as editor, to November 13th, after which it was "Published for the heirs of Benj. Franklin Bache," under Duane's editorship, to March, 1800. In January, 1799, the name was altered to *Bache's Philadelphia Aurora;* and from August 30th, to October 19th, 1799, was published tri-weekly, at Bristol. In March, 1800, William Duane, whose marriage to Mrs. Bache had given control, changed the name to *Philadelphia Aurora,* and conducted it to 1822. For a part of the time prior to 1820, the old title of *Aurora and general advertiser* was revived; and a *Weekly Aurora* was also issued. In 1822, Richard Penn Smith purchased the Aurora, and conducted it to November, 1824, when a consolidation was effected with the Franklin Gazette, under the title of *Aurora and Franklin Gazette,* with John Norvell, publisher of the Gazette, as editor. Smith retired in 1827; and Norvell in 1828, after the Aurora was merged, in April, into the Pennsylvania Gazette, as the *Aurora and Pennsylvania Gazette,* published by George Taylor and Company.

22523   DER GENERAL-Postbothe an die Deutsche Nation in Amerika. Num. 1. Dienstags, den 5 Januar, [—No. 48. Dienstags, den 22 Junius, 1790.]

> *Dieser General-Post-bothe wird woechentlich zweymal naemlich Dienstags und Freytags morgens heraus gegeben. Der Jahr gang kostet zwey Thaler, von denen der sine beym einschreiben, der andere aber am Ende des Jahres bezahlet werden. Er ist zu haben bey Melchior Steiner, in seiner Druckerey, in der Rees-strasse, und bey dem Herausgeber C. C. Reiche, in der Vierten-strasse, das naechste Haus and den sieben Sternen, an der Rees-Strassen Ecke, in Philadelphia,* 1790. pp. [192.] 4to.   AAS. LOC.

Discontinued at the above date.

22524   GENEVIÈVE, of Brabant, countess palatine of Offtendinck.
HISTORIE VON DER UNSCHULDIGEN HEILIGEN PFALZGRÄFIN GENOVEVA.
> *Lancaster: Gedruckt bey Jacob Bailey,* 1790.

22525   GENLIS, Stéphanie Félicité Brulart Ducrest de St. Aubin, comtesse de.
The Child of nature, a dramatic piece, in four acts. From the French of madame the marchioness of Sillery, formerly countess of Genlis.
> *Philadelphia: Printed and sold by William Spotswood.* 1790. pp. 68, (4). 12mo.   BM.

22526   THE GENTLEMEN AND LADIES TOWN AND COUNTRY MAGAZINE: CONSISTING OF LIT-
ERATURE, HISTORY, POLITICS, ARTS, MANNERS AND AMUSEMENTS, WITH VARIOUS
OTHER MATTER. [VOL. I.] FOR FEBRUARY, 1789, [—JANUARY, 1790.]
> *Boston: Printed and sold by Nathaniel Coverly at the corner of Back-
Street, leading to Charles River-Bridge.* 1790. pp. 658, 12 plates, printed wrap-
pers. 8vo.   AAS. LOC.

22527   —— THE GENTLEMEN AND LADIES TOWN AND COUNTRY MAGAZINE: CONSISTING OF
LITERATURE, HISTORY, POLITICS, ARTS, MANNERS, AND AMUSEMENTS, WITH VARIOUS
OTHER MATTER. [VOL. II.] FOR FEBRUARY, 1790, [—AUGUST, 1790.]
> *Boston: Printed and sold by Nathaniel Coverly, at the corner of Back-Street,
leading to Charles River-Bridge.* [1790.] pp. 384, 5 plates. 8vo.   AAS. LOC.
>> In July, and August, it was Printed and sold by Nathaniel Coverly, at
the sign of the Grand-Turk. The August issue being the last number
published.

22528   THE GEORGE-TOWN WEEKLY LEDGER. VOL. I. No. 1. SATURDAY, APRIL 17,
[—No. 37, SATURDAY, DECEMBER 25, 1790.]
> *George-Town:* [*Potomack*] *Printed and published by M. Day and W.
Hancock, for the Proprietor.* 1790. fol.
>> Established by M. Day and W. Hancock, for the Proprietor, and con-
tinued, weekly, to October 5, 1793—the last number. In August,
1791, Day and Hancock were succeeded, as printers, by Alexander
Doyle; and, in the spring of 1792, the latter was succeeded by James
Doyle, until publication ceased.

22529   GEORGIA. STATE.
ACTS OF THE GENERAL ASSEMBLY OF THE STATE OF GEORGIA. [1783.—23 DE-
CEMBER, 1789.]
> *[Augusta: Printed by John E. Smith, Printer to the State,* 1790.] pp. (9)
-[30.] 4to.   LOC.

22530   GEORGIA. THE AUGUSTA CHRONICLE AND GAZETTE OF THE STATE. [Motto.] VOL.
IV. No. CLXX. SATURDAY, JANUARY 9, [—No. CCXX. SATURDAY, DECEMBER 25,
1790].
> *Augusta: Printed by John E. Smith, Printer to the State . . .* 1790.
fol.   GHS.
>> The motto, from the Constitution of Georgia, reads: "Freedom of the
press, and trial by jury, shall remain inviolate."

22531   THE GEORGIA GAZETTE. No. 363. THURSDAY, JANUARY 7, [—No. 414. THURS-
DAY, DECEMBER 30, 1790.]
> *Savannah: Printed by James and Nicholas Johnston, Broughton-Street,*
1790. fol.   GHS. LOC.
>> With the issue for January 7th, Nicholas Johnston was admitted to
partnership.

22532   THE GERMAN ALMANAC, OR THE NORTH AMERICAN CALENDAR. BEING A COM-
PLEAT GERMAN CALENDAR, FOR THE YEAR 1791.
> *Philadelphia: Printed and sold by Francis Bailey, No. 116, Market-
Street.* [1790.]

22533   DIE GERMANTAUNER ZEITUNG. JANUARY [—NUMB. 24. DIENSTAG, DEN 28TEN
DECEMBER, 1790.]
> *Germantaun: Gedruckt bey Michael Billmeyer.* 1790. fol. and 4to.   HSP.
>> The bi-monthly publication of the Zeitung, in folio, was changed, with
the issue for July 20th, to a weekly publication, in quarto, with a new
numbering, issued on Tuesdays.

22534   GERMANTOWN. PENNSYLVANIA. SOCIETY FOR PROMOTING MANUFACTURES.
THE CONSTITUTION OF THE GERMANTOWN SOCIETY FOR PROMOTING DOMESTIC
MANUFACTURES.
     *Philadelphia: Printed by Eleazer Oswald, in Market - Street, between
Fourth and Fifth Streets.* M,DCC,XC. pp. 7. 8vo.   LOC. NYPL.

22535   GESNER, SALOMON   1730 – 1788
THE DEATH OF ABEL. IN FIVE BOOKS. ATTEMPTED FROM THE GERMAN OF MR.
GESSNER. [By Mary Collyer.]
     Philadelphia: Printed and sold by Joseph Crukshank. 1790.

22536   EIN GESPRÄCH ZWISCHEN DEM KLEINEN GÖRGEL, EINEM ARMEN MANN; UND
EINEM GEWISSEN VORNEHMEN HERRN, DEM DER NAME PERIANDER BEYGELEGET
WORDEN. AUFS NEUE REVIDIRT. [Ornament.]
     Reading: Gedruckt von Barton u. Jungmann, Im Jahr unsers Herrn. 1790.
pp. 34. 12mo.   JCB.

22537   GLEASON, EZRA
THOMAS'S MASSACHUSETTS, CONNECTICUT, RHODE-ISLAND, NEWHAMPSHIRE & VER-
MONT ALMANACK, WITH AN EPHEMERIS, FOR THE YEAR OF OUR LORD 1791: BEING
THE THIRD YEAR AFTER BISSEXTILE, OR LEAP YEAR, AND FIFTEENTH OF THE IN-
DEPENDENCE OF UNITED STATES. FROM CREATION, ACCORDING TO THE SCRIP-
TURES, 5753. [Six lines. Cut. Four lines of verse.]
     Printed at Worcester, by Isaiah Thomas . . . [1790.] pp. [40.] 8vo.
                                           AAS. LOC. NYPL. YC.
Contains, The Way to wealth. [By Benjamin Franklin, L. L. D.]

22538   GOODRICH, ELIZUR   1734 – 1797
A SERMON, DELIVERED AT THE ORDINATION OF THE REVEREND MATTHEW NOYES,
A. M. TO THE PASTORAL CHARGE OF THE CHURCH OF CHRIST IN NORTHFORD, AUG-
UST 18, 1790. BY ELIZUR GOODRICH, D. D. PASTOR OF THE CHURCH IN DURHAM.
     New-Haven: Printed by A. Morse. M.DCC.XC. pp. [31]. 8vo.
                                 AAS. CHS. JCB. MHS. NYPL. YC.

22539   THE GOSHEN REPOSITORY, AND WEEKLY INTELLIGENCER. VOL. I. No. 51.
TUESDAY, JANUARY 5, [—VOL. II. No. 102. TUESDAY, DECEMBER 28, 1790.]
     Goshen: Printed by David Mandeville, near the Court-House. 1790. fol.
     In this year the following motto was added to the heading: "With
gen'rous freedom for our constant guide, We scorn controul and print
on ev'ry side." In November, the imprint reads: Printed and published by David Mandeville and David M. Westcott, at the Academy.

22540   GRAFTON, JOSEPH   1757 – 1836
STRICTURES UPON AN ESSAY [by Elisha Fish, and John Crane] INTITLED, "THE
BAPTISM OF JESUS CHRIST NOT TO BE IMITATED BY CHRISTIANS, &C." BY JOSEPH
GRAFTON, PASTOR OF THE BAPTIST CHURCH IN NEWTON. [Two lines of Scrip-
ture texts.]
     *Boston: Printed by Benjamin Edes & Son. [Sold by Mr. Richard Everett,
of Watertown.]* M.DCC.XC. pp. 28. 8vo.   AAS. BM. JCB.

22541   GRAY, EDWARD   1764 – 1810
AN ORATION, DELIVERED JULY 5, 1790. AT THE REQUEST OF THE INHABITANTS OF
THE TOWN OF BOSTON, IN CELEBRATION OF THE ANNIVERSARY OF AMERICAN IN-
DEPENDENCE. BY EDWARD GRAY, ESQ. [Two lines of Latin from] CICERO PRO-
LEGE MANILIA, SECT. 15.
     Boston: Printed and sold by Samuel Hall, at No. 53, Cornhill. MDCC-
XC. pp. 16. 8vo.   AAS. BA. BM. JCB. LOC. MHS.

22542 GREEN, ASHBEL 1762 – 1848
A SERMON PREACHED AT THE FUNERAL OF THE REVEREND GEORGE DUFFIELD, D. D.
LATE PASTOR OF THE THIRD PRESBYTERIAN CONGREGATION IN THE CITY OF PHIL-
ADELPHIA; WHO DIED FEBRUARY 2D, 1790. BY ASHBEL GREEN, A. M.
Philadelphia : Printed by Daniel Humphreys, Front-Street, near the Draw-
bridge. M.DCC.XC. pp. [24.] 8vo. AAS. BPL. LOC. MHS.

22543 GREEN, THOMAS – 1814
A SERMON, DELIVERED OCTOBER 24, 1790; TO THE BAPTIST CHURCH AND CONGRE-
GATION, IN CAMBRIDGE, AT THE ADMINISTRATION OF THE ORDINANCE OF BAP-
TISM. BY THOMAS GREEN, V. D. M. [Three lines of Scripture texts.]
Boston : Printed by Nathaniel Coverly, MDCCXC. pp. 26. 8vo. AAS. JCB.

22544 GREEN, TIMOTHY
GREEN'S REGISTER, FOR THE STATE OF CONNECTICUT: WITH AN ALMANACK FOR THE
YEAR OF OUR LORD 1791, CALCULATED BY NATHAN DABOLL, FOR THE MERIDIAN
OF NEW-LONDON. LAT. 41. 25. NORTH.
New-London : Printed by T. Green & Son. [1790.] pp. 95. 32mo. CHS. YC.

22545 GUILD, BENJAMIN
A CATALOGUE OF A LARGE ASSORTMENT OF BOOKS CONSISTING OF THE MOST CELE-
BRATED AUTHORS IN HISTORY VOYAGES TRAVELS GEOGRAPHY ANTIQUITIES PHILOS-
OPHY NOVELS DIVINITY PHYSICK SURGERY ANATOMY ARTS SCIENCES HUSBANDRY
ARCHITECTURE NAVIGATION MATHEMATICKS LAW PERIODICAL PUBLICATIONS POET-
RY PLAYS MUSICK, &C. &C. TO BE SOLD BY BENJAMIN GUILD AT THE BOSTON BOOK-
STORE, NO. 59 CORNHILL, BOSTON.
[Boston : Printed for Benjamin Guild, 1790.] pp. 32. 8vo. JCB.

22546 HABERMANN *[Latin AVENARIUS]*, JOHANN 1520 – 1590
CHRISTLICHE MORGEN-UND ABEND-GEBÄTER, AUF ALLE TAGE IN DER WOCHEN,
DURCH D. JOHANN HABERMANN.
Germantaun : Gedruckt bey Peter Leibert, 1790. pp. 216. 18mo.

22547 HAGAR IN THE DESERT. [Ornament.] TRANSLATED FROM THE FRENCH, FOR THE
USE OF CHILDREN.
Newbury-Port : Printed and sold by John Mycall. [1790?] pp. 24. 12mo. BU.

22548 HALE, SIR MATTHEW 1609 – 1676
SIR MATTHEW HALE'S AFFECTIONATE EPISTLES TO HIS CHILDREN. WITH DIRECTIONS
CONCERNING THE RELIGIOUS OBSERVATION OF THE LORD'S DAY. TO WHICH IS
PREFIXED THE LIFE OF THE AUTHOR. A NEW EDITION.
Philadelphia : Printed by William Spotswood. MDCCXC. pp. [xvi,] 80.
24mo. AAS. JCB. LOC.

22549 HALL, AARON 1751 – 1814
A SERMON AGAINST PROFANE SWEARING. DELIVERED AT KEENE, OCTOBER 17,
1790. BY AARON HALL, A. M.
Keene, (New-Hampshire.) Printed by James D. Griffith. 1790.

22550 HALLING, SOLOMON
AN ORATION DELIVERED BEFORE ST. JOHN'S LODGE, NO. 2. OF NEWBERN, ON THE
27TH DECEMBER, IN THE YEAR OF MASONRY 5789. BY MR. SOLOMON HALLING.
Fayetteville, North-Carolina : Printed by Sibley & Howard. 1790.

22551 HAMILTON, ALEXANDER 1739 – 1802
OUTLINES OF THE THEORY AND PRACTICE OF MIDWIFERY. A NEW EDITION.
Philadelphia : Printed by T. Dobson, 1790. pp. xv, 25–317. 12mo. SGO.

22552 THE HAMPSHIRE [cut] CHRONICLE: POLITICAL AND HISTORICAL, MORAL AND EN-
TERTAINING. COMMONWEALTH OF MASSACHUSETTS. [Motto.] VOL. III. NUMBER
CXLIX, WEDNESDAY, JANUARY 6, [—VOL. IV. NUMBER CC. WEDNESDAY, DECEM-
BER 29, 1790.]
*Printed and published by Ezra Waldo Weld, opposite the Court-House in
Springfield. 1790. fol.* AAS.

22553 THE HAMPSHIRE GAZETTE. VOL. IV. NUMB. 175. WEDNESDAY, JANUARY 6,
[—VOL. V. NUMB. 226, WEDNESDAY, DECEMBER 29, 1790.]
Northampton, (Massachusetts). Published by William Butler, 1790. fol.
AAS. MHS.

22554 HAMPTON, SAMUEL
LONGITUDE: OR, THE ART OF MEASURING AT SEA OR LAND MADE EASY; SHEWING BY
PLAIN AND PRACTICAL RULES, TO MEASURE THE DISTANCE OF ONE PLACE TO THAT
OF ANOTHER; WITH NEW TABLES FOR THE EASE OF THE MEASURER. ALSO, A
STANDARD FOR INVARIABLE MEASURES AND WEIGHTS. BY SAMUEL HAMPTON.
Philadelphia? 1790.

22555 HARRIS, RAYMUND
SCRIPTURAL RESEARCHES ON THE LICITNESS OF THE SLAVE-TRADE, SHEWING ITS
CONFORMITY WITH THE PRINCIPLES OF NATURAL AND REVEALED RELIGION, DELIN-
EATED IN THE SACRED WRITINGS OF THE WORD OF GOD. BY THE REV. R. HARRIS.
[Two lines from] JOHN C.5.V.39.
*London: Printed for John Stockdale, opposite Burlington House, Picca-
dilly. 1788. Frederick-Town: (Maryland). Re-printed by John Winter, in Pat-
rick-Street. 1790. pp. 77, (1). 8vo.* JCB.

22556 HARRIS, THADDEUS MASON   1768 – 1842
THE TRIUMPHS OF SUPERSTITION: AN ELEGY. BY A STUDENT OF HARVARD UNI-
VERSITY. [Two lines of quotation.]
*Printed at Boston, by Isaiah Thomas and Ebenezer T. Andrews. At Faust's
Statue, No. 45, Newbury Street. MDCCXC. pp. 16. 4to.* AAS. JCB. MHS.

22557 THE HARRISBURGH [cut] JOURNAL, AND THE WEEKLY ADVERTISER. VOL. I. No.
20. WEDNESDAY, JANUARY 6, [— No. 52? WEDNESDAY, AUGUST 18? 1790.]
*Harrisburgh, (State of Pennsylvania): Printed by T. Roberts & Co . . .
1790. fol.*
It is uncertain how long after the first of this year publication was continued: it is presumed that it was issued to the end of the first volume.

22558 HART, LEVI   1738 – 1808
THE WAR BETWEEN MICHAEL AND THE DRAGON BRIEFLY CONSIDERED, IN A DIS-
COURSE, AT THE ORDINATION OF THE REVEREND JOHN WILDER, TO THE EVANGEL-
ICAL MINISTRY AND PASTORAL OFFICE, OVER THE FIRST CHURCH IN ATTLE-
BOROUGH, JANUARY 27, 1790. BY LEVI HART, A. M. PASTOR OF A CHURCH IN
PRESTON. [Four lines from] 2 TIMOTHY 4. 7,8. [Printer's monogram.]
*Printed at Providence, by Bennett Wheeler, at his office, on the west side the
River. [1790.] pp. [27.] 8vo.* AAS. BM. BPL. HC. JCB. LOC. NYHS. NYPL.

22559 HARVARD UNIVERSITY.
CATALOGUS BIBLIOTHECÆ HARVARDIANÆ CANTABRIGIÆ NOV-ANGLORUM. [COM-
PILED BY ISAAC SMITH.]
Bostoniæ: Typis Thomæ et Johannis Fleet. MDCCXC. pp. (4), iv, 358.
8vo. AAS. BA. BM. JCB. MHS.

22560 —— Illustrissimo Johanni Hancock, armigero, ll. d. gubernatori; honoratissimo, Samueli Adams, armigero, vice-gubernatori; Consiliariis et
Senatoribus Reipublicæ, Massachusettensis; reverendisque ecclesiarum
in oppidis sex vicinis, Presbyteris, Universitatis Harvardianæ curatoribus; reverendo Josepho Willard, s. t. d. præsidi; [Four lines.] Theses
hasce, juvenes in artibus initiati, [Forty-two names.] Humillimè dedicant.
    . . . Habita in comitiis Universitatis Cantabrigiæ, Massachusettensis,
die Julii xxi. Anno salutis mdccxc. Rerumque Publicarum Foederatarum
Americæ summæ potestatis xv. [Colophon:]
Bostoniæ: Typis Josephi Bumstead. [1790.] Broadside. fol. aas. bm. hc.

22561 —— The Laws of Harvard College.
Boston: Printed by Samuel Hall, at No. 53, Cornhill. M.DCC.XC. pp. 66.
8vo.   aas. ba. bm. jcb. loc. mhs. sgo.

22562 —— Quæstiones sub reverendo Josepho Willard, s. t. d. Universitatis Harvardianæ, quæ est Cantabrigiæ, in Republica Massachusettensi, præside, in comitiis publicis, à laureæ magistralis candidatis, pro modulo
discutiendæ. Die Julii xxi, anno salutis mdccxc.
Bostoniæ: Typis Thomæ et Johannis Fleet. [1790.] Broadside. fol. aas.

22563 HAYES, Thomas ?
Concise observations on the nature of our common food, so far as it tends
to promote or injure health. To which are prefixed, general rules
for a course of diet. By a Gentleman of the Faculty. "Salutem hom-
inibus dando." Cicero.
New-York: Printed for Berry and Rogers. 1790.

22564 HENRY, Matthew   1662 – 1714
A Church in the house. A sermon, preached in London, April 16, 1704,
concerning family-religion. By the late reverend mr. Matthew Henry,
minister of the Gospel in Chester, and author of the Commentary on
the Bible.
*Philadelphia: Printed and sold by John M'Culloch, in Third-street, near
Market-street.* 1790. pp. 36. 12mo.   aas.

22565 THE HERALD of freedom, and the federal advertiser. Vol. iii. No. 32.
Friday, January 1, [—Vol. v. Numb. xxxii. Friday, December 31, 1790.]
*Printed at Boston (Massachusetts) every Tuesday and Friday, by Edmund
Freeman, opposite the north-east corner of the State-House [State-Street.]* 1790. fol.
                                    aas. hc. loc. mhs.
In March, the sub-title was dropped, and a more conventional type of
heading adopted. The imprint was also changed to "Published Tues-
days and Fridays, by Edmund Freeman, State Street, Boston."

22566 HERR, Franz
Eine Kurze Erklärung von dem Geschreiben Wort Gottes; wie auch von
der Christlichen Tauffordnung, und von dem friedlichen Reich Christi;
gegen das Volk welches man Quäker nennt.
[Philadelphia?] Gedruckt im Jahr 1790. pp. 48. 8vo.   bm.

22567 HILL, Samuel
A complete set of round hand copies in single lines, for the use of schools.
Engraved by S. Hill.
*Printed for, & sold by Thomas & Andrews, at Faust's Statue, No. 45, New-
bury Street, & David West, No. 36, Marlborough Street, Boston.* MDCCXC. pp.
(32). obl. 64mo.   aas.
Engraved on one side of the leaf, only.

22568　THE HISTORY OF THE HOLY JESUS, CONTAINING A BRIEF AND PLAIN ACCOUNT OF HIS BIRTH, LIFE, DEATH, RESURRECTION AND ASCENSION INTO HEAVEN; AND HIS COMING AGAIN AT THE GREAT AND LAST DAY OF JUDGMENT. BEING A PLEASANT AND PROFITABLE COMPANION FOR CHILDREN; COMPOSED ON PURPOSE FOR THEIR USE. BY A LOVER OF THEIR PRECIOUS SOULS.
Hudson: Printed and sold by Ashbel Stoddard. 1790.

22569　—— THE HISTORY OF THE HOLY JESUS, CONTAINING A BRIEF AND PLAIN ACCOUNT OF HIS BIRTH, LIFE, DEATH, RESURRECTION AND ASCENSION INTO HEAVEN; AND HIS COMING AGAIN AT THE GREAT AND LAST DAY OF JUDGMENT. BEING A PLEASANT AND PROFITABLE COMPANION FOR CHILDREN; COMPOSED ON PURPOSE FOR THEIR USE. BY A LOVER OF THEIR PRECIOUS SOULS.
Middletown: Printed and sold by Moses H. Woodward. 1790.

22570　HITCHCOCK, ENOS　　　　　　　　　　　　　　　1744 – 1803
MEMOIRS OF THE BLOOMSGROVE FAMILY. IN A SERIES OF LETTERS TO A RESPECTABLE CITIZEN OF PHILADELPHIA. CONTAINING SENTIMENTS ON A MODE OF DOMESTIC EDUCATION, SUITED TO THE PRESENT STATE OF SOCIETY, GOVERNMENT, AND MANNERS, IN THE UNITED STATES OF AMERICA: AND ON THE DIGNITY AND IMPORTANCE OF THE FEMALE CHARACTER. INTERSPERSED WITH A VARIETY OF INTERESTING ANECDOTES. BY ENOS HITCHCOCK, D. D.
Boston: Printed by Thomas and Andrews. MDCCXC. 2 vols. pp. 299;
300. 12mo.　　　　　　　　　　　　　　　　AAS. BA. BM. BPL. HC. JCB. LCP.
Rhode Island District Copyright, issued to Enos Hitchcock; D. D., as Author, 9 August, 1790.

22571　DER HOCH-DEUTSCHE AMERICANISCHE CALENDAR, AUF DAS JAHR 1791. . . .
Germantaun, gedruckt und zu finden bey Michael Billmeyer. [1790.]

22572　DER HOCH-DEUTSCHE AMERICANISCHE CALENDAR AUF DAS JAHR 1791. NACH DER GNADENREICHEN GEBURT UNSERS HERRN UND HEYLANDES JESU CHRISTI, WELCHES EIN GEMEIN IST. [Eight lines.] ZUM DRITTEN MAL HERAUS GEGEBEN.
Dieses Calender ist zu haben in Lancaster bey M. Bartgis, und in den Buchdruckereyen in Harrisburg, Friederich Stadt, und in Winchester bey Matthias Bartgis; also auch bey allen auswartigen Kramern, wo des Herrn Sauers Calender vormals zu haben war. [1790.] pp. (36). 4to.　　　　　　　　LOC.

22573　HODGE, ALLEN, and CAMPBELL, publishers.
NEW-YORK, MARCH 1, 1790. BROWN'S SELF-INTERPRETING FOLIO FAMILY BIBLE, EMBELLISHED WITH A VARIETY OF ELEGANT COPPER-PLATES. (BEING A GENUINE AMERICAN EDITION, THE LARGEST AND CHEAPEST EVER PROPOSED TO BE PRINTED IN THE UNITED STATES.) PROPOSALS FOR PRINTING BY SUBSCRIPTION, BY HODGE, ALLEN, AND CAMPBELL, OF NEW-YORK, AND WILL BE PUT TO THE PRESS ON THE 1ST DAY OF JUNE NEXT. THE HOLY BIBLE, CONTAINING THE OLD AND NEW TESTAMENTS, WITH THE BOOK OF THE APOCRYPHA. . . . CONDITIONS OF PUBLICATION. . . . ADDRESS TO THE CITIZENS OF THE UNITED STATES. . . . (SPECIMEN OF THE WORK.) . . . SUBSCRIBERS NAMES. . . .
[New-York: Printed by Hodge, Allen and Campbell, 1790.] pp. 4. fol. NYHS.

22574　HOME, HENRY, lord KAMES　　　　　　　　　　　1696 – 1782
THE BLACK-SMITH'S LETTER TO THE MINISTERS AND ELDERS OF THE CHURCH OF SCOTLAND, IN WHICH THE MANNER OF PUBLIC WORSHIP IN THAT CHURCH IS CONSIDERED, ITS INCONVENIENCES AND DEFECTS POINTED OUT, AND METHODS FOR THE REMOVING OF THEM HUMBLY PROPOSED.
New-York: Printed by Hugh Gaine, 1790.

22575   HOME, John   1724 – 1808
        American edition. Douglas, a tragedy. As performed by the American
        company, at the theatre, in Southwark, Philadelphia. Written by the
        rev. mr. Home. [Publisher's monogram.]
            Philadelphia: Printed and sold by Enoch Story, Second Street. M.DCC.-
        XC. pp. 67, (1), (2). 12mo.   AAS.
        Has added, New publications. For sale by the Printer hereof. pp. (2).

22576   HOMER, Jonathan   1759 – 1843
        The Character and duties of a christian soldier, considered and applied
        in a sermon, preached before the Ancient and Honorable Company of
        Artillery, on Monday June 7, 1790; being the anniversary of the elec-
        tion of officers. By Jonathan Homer, a. m. pastor of the first church
        in Newton.
            Printed in Boston by Benjamin Russell, State-Street. 1790. pp. 21. 8vo.
                                        AAS. BA. BM. HC. JCB. LOC. MHS.

22577   THE HUDSON Weekly Gazette. Vol. v. No. 249. Thursday, January 7,
        [—Vol. vi. No. 300. Thursday, December 30, 1790.]
            Printed by Ashbel Stoddard, near the Market. 1790. fol.   AAS.

22578   HUMPHREYS, David   1752 – 1818
        The Miscellaneous works of Colonel Humphreys. [Publishers monogram.]
            New-York: Printed by Hodge, Allen, and Campbell; and sold at their
        respective Book-stores. M.DCC.XC. *[With Copyright according to law.]* pp.348. 8vo.
                           AAS. BA. BM. HC. JCB. LCP. LOC. NYPL. WL. YC.
        Contains, An Essay on the life of the honorable major-general Israel
        Putnam: addressed to the State Society of the Cincinnati in Connecti-
        icut. pp. 186-348. 9th New York District Copyright, issued to Rob-
        ert Hodge, Thomas Allen, and Samuel Campbell, as Proprietors, 10
        January, 1792. Reprinted in New York, in 1804.

22579   —— A Poem, on the Happiness of America; addressed to the citizens of the
        United States. By D. Humphreys.
            London, Printed, 1786. *Portsmouth: Re-printed by George Jerry Osborne.*
        1790. pp. 45. 8vo.   AAS. BU.

22580   HUTCHINS, Father Abraham, pseudonym.
        Father Hutchins revived; being an Almanac and ephemeris of the motions
        of the sun and moon, the true places and aspects of the planets: the
        rising and setting of the sun; and the rising, setting, and southing of the
        moon; for the year of our Lord, 1791; being the third after bissextile,
        or leap year, and the 15th of American independence, until the 4th of
        July. [Six lines.] By Father Abraham Hutchins, mathematician.
            New-York: Printed by Hodge, Allen, and Campbell, and sold, wholesale and
        retail, at their Book-stores. [1790.] pp. (36). 12mo.   LOC.
        Contains, Congress of the United States: An Act making further pro-
        vision, for the payment of the debts of the United States. Approved
        August 10, 1790.

22581   HUTCHINS, John Nathan
        Hutchins improved: being an Almanack and ephemeris of the motions of
        the sun and moon; the true places and aspects of the planets; the rising
        and setting of the sun; and the rising, setting and southing of the moon,
        for the year of our Lord 1791: being the third after bissextile, or leap
        year, and 15th year of American independence, till 4th July. [Five
        lines.] By John Nathan Hutchins, philom.
            New-York: Printed and sold by H. Gaine, at his Printing Office, at the
        Bible, in Hanover-Square. Where may be had the New-York Pocket Almanack·
        [1790.] pp. (36). 12mo.   LOC. NYHS.

22582   HUTTON, CHARLES   1737 – 1823
A COURSE OF BOOK-KEEPING ACCORDING TO THE METHOD OF SINGLE ENTRY: WITH A DESCRIPTION OF THE BOOKS, AND DIRECTIONS FOR USING THEM; VERY USEFUL FOR ALL WHO ARE NOT ACQUAINTED WITH ACCOUNTS; BUT PARTICULARLY INTENDED FOR THE USE OF SCHOOLS. EXTRACTED FROM THE WORKS OF CHARLES HUTTON, L. L. D. F. R. S. WITH SUNDRY ALTERATIONS AND ADDITIONS, BY THE EDITOR.
Burlington: Printed by I. Neale and D. Lawrence. 1790.

22583   INDEPENDENT [Mass. Arms] CHRONICLE : AND THE UNIVERSAL ADVERTISER. VOL. XXII. NUMBER 1106. THURSDAY, JANUARY 7, [—NUMBER 1157. THURSDAY DECEMBER 30, 1790.]

Printed and published by Thomas Adams, Printer to the honourable the General Court of the Commonwealth of Massachusetts, at his Printing-Office, opposite the new Court-House, Court-Street. 1790. fol.   AAS. LOC. MHS.

John Nourse, the junior editor, died 2 January, 1790. A supplement to the issue for March 25th, is devoted to the Excise Act of 1790.

22584   THE INDEPENDENT GAZETTEER;OR, THE CHRONICLE OF FREEDOM [Mottoes.] VOL. IX. NUMBER 1263. FRIDAY, JANUARY 1, [—NUMBER 1320. SATURDAY, DECEMBER 25, 1790.]

Philadelphia: Printed by Eleazer Oswald, in Market-Street, between Fourth and Fifth-Streets, . . . 1790. fol.   AAS.

On January 9th, appeared this notice to the public: "The ready access to, and known inpartiality of the Independent Gazetteer, since its establishment which have determined several gentlemen, who are about to form a society in Pennsylvania, similar to that of the Oeconomical Society in France . . . to furnish us with a publication on each of these important and interesting subjects, i. e. Government, and Agriculture. The Independent Gazetteer will, in future, be printed on paper of the royal size, adopt the additional title of Agricultural Repository; appear on Saturdays." Under date of January 15th, another notice to the public states that: "Another paper will be published occasionally at this Office, styled The Chronicle of Freedom, and chiefly contain matters of a political nature, so as to answer the views and wishes of the friends of liberty and good government who reside in the city."

22585   IRISH STATE LOTTERY.
SCHEME OF THE IRISH STATE LOTTERY FOR THE YEAR 1790. . . . SIGNED BY ORDER OF THE MANAGERS AND DIRECTORS, C. AND R. DEEY, SEC.
[New-York? 1790.] Broadside. 8vo.   NYHS.

22586   JACK, ROBERT
A LETTER ON PSALMODY. SHOWING THAT HUMAN COMPOSURES OUGHT NOT TO BE USED IN CHRISTIAN WORSHIP, IN SINGING THE PRAISES OF GOD. TO WHICH IS ADDED PART OF A LECTURE FROM THESE WORDS. HEB. XII. 14. . . . ALSO, A BRIEF DESCRIPTION OF THE CHRISTIAN GRACE, HOPE: THAT HOPE THAT DOTH ACCOMPANY AND COMPREHEND SALVATION.
[Philadelphia:] Printed for Robert Jack [by Francis Bailey.] 1790. pp. 48. 12mo.   PHS.

22587   JAY, JOHN   1745 – 1829
[Seal.] THE CHARGE OF CHIEF JUSTICE JAY TO THE GRAND JURIES ON THE EASTERN CIRCUIT: AT THE CIRCUIT COURTS HELD IN THE DISTRICTS OF NEW-YORK, ON THE 4TH, OF CONNECTICUT ON THE 22D DAYS OF APRIL; OF MASSACHUSETTS ON THE 4TH, AND OF NEW-HAMPSHIRE ON THE 20TH DAYS OF MAY, 1790.
Portsmouth, (N. H.) Printed and to be sold by George Jerry Osborne, jr. at his office,Guttenber's [sic] Head, Congress-Street. pp. [15.] 8vo.   LOC.

22588 JOCELYN, SIMEON
       THE CHORISTER'S COMPANION, (2D PART,) CONTAINING, BESIDES THE RULES OF
       PSALMODY, A CHOICE AND VALUABLE COLLECTION OF PSALM TUNES, HYMNS AND
       ANTHEMS, FROM THE MOST CELEBRATED ANCIENT AND MODERN AUTHORS; TO-
       GETHER WITH SEVERAL TUNES NEVER BEFORE PUBLISHED.
            New-Haven: Printed by T. and S. Green, for Simeon Jocelyn, 1790. pp. 8,
       72. obl. 8vo.

22589 JOHNSON, JOHN   1706 – 1791
       THE ADVANTAGES AND DISADVANTAGES OF THE MARRIAGE-STATE AS ENTERED INTO
       WITH RELIGIOUS OR IRRELIGIOUS PERSONS: REPRESENTED UNDER THE SIMILITUDE
       OF A DREAM. BY THE REV. MR. JOHN JOHNSON. THE NINTH EDITION.
            Boston: Printed by B. Edes & Son, No. 7, State-Street. M,DCC,XC. pp.
       (2), 21. 24mo.   AAS.

22590 —— A MATHEMATICAL QUESTION PROPOUNDED BY THE VICEREGENT OF THE WORLD;
       ANSWERED BY THE KING IN GLORY. ENIGMATICALLY REPRESENTED AND DEMON-
       STRATIVELY OPENED. THE FOURTH EDITION, CORRECTED.
            Hartford: Printed by N. Patten, 1790. pp. 72. 12mo.

22591 THE JOLLY HIBERNIAN IN FULL GLEE; OR, COMPLETE IRISH JESTER, AND WITS
       VADE-MECUM. CONTAINING A MORE HUMOROUS VARIETY OF ORIGINAL STORIES, COM-
       ICAL BULLS, WITTY REPARTEES, ENTERTAINING ANECDOTES, JESTS, &C. THAN EVER
       APPEARED IN THE IRISH OR ANY OTHER LANGUAGE: TO WHICH ARE ADDED, THE
       FACETIOUS HISTORY OF JOHN GILPIN, AND A NEW SONG IN PRAISE OF ST. PATRICK.
            Philadelphia: Printed by Henry Taylor, for Robert Campbell. 1790.
       Three hundred copies, in sheets, offered at the sale of Henry Taylor's
       estate, in 1791.

22592 JONES, HENRY   1721 – 1770
       AMERICAN EDITION. THE EARL OF ESSEX. A TRAGEDY. AS PERFORMED BY THE
       OLD AMERICAN COMPANY, AT THE THEATRE IN SOUTHWARK, PHILADELPHIA.
       WRITTEN BY MR. HENRY JONES. [Publisher's monogram.]
            Philadelphia: Printed and sold by Enoch Story, Second Street. M.DCC.-
       XC. pp. 59, (1). 12mo.   AAS.
       Has added, New publications by the Printer hereof. Who has removed
       to Market-Street, between Fifth and Sixth Streets (No. 209) north side.

22593 JONES, SAMUEL   1735 – 1814
       A SELECTION OF PSALMS AND HYMNS, DONE UNDER THE APPOINTMENT OF THE
       PHILADELPHIAN ASSOCIATION. BY SAMUEL JONES, D. D. AND BURGIS ALLISON, A. M.
            Philadelphia: Printed by R. Aitken & Son, at No. 22, Market Street.
       M,DCC,XC. pp. (iv), (16), 362, (8). 18mo.   LCP. NYPL·

22594 JOYCE and SNOWDON,
       [U. S. Arms.] JOYCE AND SNOWDON'S AMERICAN INK POWDER FOR RECORDS,
       EQUAL TO ANY IMPORTED, OR OFFERED FOR SALE IN THE THIRTEEN UNITED
       STATES. SOLD BY MOST STATIONER'S, BOOKSELLER'S, IRONMONGER'S, &C. IN NEW
       YORK, AND IN OTHER PRINCIPAL CITIES AND TOWNS IN AMERICA. ROLLINSON
       SCULPT, NEW YORK.
            [New-York: 1790.] Broadside. 4to.   NYHS.
       With engraved directions in English, and Dutch. Used as a wrapper
       for the powder.

22595 JUDD, EBEN W.
       STODDARD'S DIARY: OR, THE COLUMBIA ALMANACK, FOR THE YEAR OF OUR LORD
       1791: [Thirteen lines.] BY EBEN W. JUDD, PHILOMATH.
            *Printed and sold by Ashbel Stoddard, at his Printing-Office, in the city of
       Hudson.* [1790.] pp. (24). 12mo.   AAS.

JUDD, EBEN W. continued.

22596 —— THE UNITED STATES ALMANAC, FOR THE YEAR OF OUR LORD 1791: BEING THE THIRD AFTER BISSEXTILE OR LEAP YEAR. AND THE FIFTEENTH OF AMERICAN INDEPENDENCE, 'TILL THE 4TH OF JULY. CONTAINING EVERY THING THAT IS USEFUL OR NECESSARY IN AN ALMANAC. ALSO, A VARIETY OF ENTERTAINING MATTER IN PROSE AND VERSE. BY EBEN W. JUDD, MATHEMATICIAN.
Elizabethtown: Printed by Shepard Kollock. [1790.] pp. 36. 12mo. LOC.

22597 —— WEBSTER'S CALENDAR: OR, THE ALBANY, COLUMBIA, WASHINGTON AND MONT-GOMERY ALMANACK, FOR THE YEAR OF OUR LORD 1791; AND OF AMERICAN INDE-PENDENCE [WHICH WAS DECLARED JULY FOURTH, 1776] PART OF THE XVTH & XVITH: BEING THE THIRD AFTER BESSEXTILE OR LEAP-YEAR. CONTAINING, THE USUAL ASTRONOMICAL CALCULATIONS, &C. TOGETHER WITH A GREAT VARIETY OF MATTERS USEFUL, CURIOUS & ENTERTAINING. CALCULATED FOR THE MERIDIAN OF ALBANY, LAT. 42° 30´ N. LONG. 73° 8´ W. - - - FROM THE EQUATOR 2975 MILES. BY EBEN W. JUDD, PHILOMATH. [Four lines from] GENESIS VIII. 22.
Printed in the city of Albany, by Charles R. & George Webster, at their Printing-Office, No. 46, State-street, corner of Middle-lane; where printing in general is executed on the shortest notice and most reasonable terms. [1790.] pp. (36). 12mo. AAS.

22598 JUVENAL, HORATIO, pseudonym.
AN ADDRESS TO THE FREEMEN OF THE STATE OF CONNECTICUT; A POEM. BY HORA-TIO JUVENAL, ESQUIRE.
Hartford: Printed and sold by Hudson and Goodwin? 1790.

22599 —— A SECOND ADDRESS TO THE FREEMEN OF THE STATE OF CONNECTICUT. BY HORATIO JUVENAL, ESQ.
Litchfield: Printed and sold by Thomas Collier? 1790.

22600 KENNA, J. JUNIOR
ANNA'S TOMB. A POEM. WRITTEN BY J. KENNA, JUN.
Fredericksburg: Printed by Timothy Green. 1790.

22601 KENRICK, WILLIAM   1725 – 1779
THE WHOLE DUTY OF WOMAN. BY A LADY. WRITTEN AT THE DESIRE OF A NOBLE LORD. THE SECOND BOSTON EDITION.
Boston: Printed and sold by Samuel Hall, No. 53, Cornhill. 1790. pp. 61. 16mo.

22602 THE KENTUCKY GAZETTE. VOL. III. NUMB. XIX. SATURDAY, JANUARY 2, [—VOL. IV. NUMB. XVIII. SATURDAY, DECEMBER 25, 1790.]
Lexington: Printed by John Bradford, at his Printing - Office in Main Street, . . . 1790. 4to.

22603 KNOX, HUGH   1733 – 1790
THE MORAL AND RELIGIOUS MISCELLANY; OR, SIXTY-ONE APHORETICAL ESSAYS ON SOME OF THE MOST IMPORTANT CHRISTIAN DOCTRINES AND VIRTUES. BY HUGH KNOX, D. D. IN ST. CROIX. [Seven lines of quotations.]
Hartford: Re-Printed by Hudson & Goodwin. M.DCC.XC. pp. 352, (7). 8vo. AAS. BM. JCB.
Contains a seven-page list of names of subscribers.

22604 KURTZGEFASSTES ARZNEY-BÜCHLEIN FÜR MENSCHEN UND VIEH, DARINNEN CXXX ANSERLESENE RECEPTEN.
Ephrata: Klosterpresse. 1790.   HSP.

22605   LAMBERT, Anne Thérèse, marquise de   1647 – 1733
The Fair solitary; or, female hermit. A novel. From the French of the
marchioness of Lambert.
> *Philadelphia: Printed and sold by William Spotswood, Front Street, be-
> tween Market and Chesnut-Streets, 1790.*

22606   LATHROP, Joseph   1731 – 1820
Christ's warning to the churches, to beware of false prophets, who come
as wolves in sheep's clothing, and the marks by which they are known:
illustrated in two discourses. By Joseph Lathrop, a. m. pastor of a
church in West Springfield. . . . [Second edition.]
> *New-York:* 1790. pp. 56. 8vo.   yc.

22607   LA VALINIERE, Pierre Huet de
Curious and interesting dialogue, French and English; in which every one
is furnished with arguments to defend his religion against all false assertions whatsoever. By the rev. Peter Huet de La Valiniere.
Dialogue curieux et interessant, en François et en Anglois; ou l'on peut
aisément trouver des armes pour defendre sa religion contre toutes
les faussetées inventeÈ contre elle. Par le rev. Pierre de LaValiniere.
> *New-York: Printed by Thomas Greenleaf, for the Author, 1790.*

22608   LAVATER, Johann Caspar   1741 – 1801
Aphorisms on man. Translated from the original manuscript of the rev.
John Casper Lavater; citizen of Zuric. Author of Essays on physiognomy. [Two lines from] Pope.
> *Philadelphia: Printed by William Spotswood.* MDCCXC. pp. viii, 100.
24mo.   aas. jcb.

22609   —— — Aphorisms on man. Translated from the original manuscript of
the rev. John Casper Lavater, citizen of Zuric. [One line from] Juv.
Sat. ix. Third edition. [Printer's monogram.]
> *London: Printed. New-York: Re-printed by T. and J. Swords, for Berry
> and Rogers, Hanover-Square.* M,DCC,XC. pp. 114, (2), frontispiece. 16mo. aas.
Printed on fine writing paper. Contains a List of books, medicines and
household articles for sale by Berry & Rogers.

22610   —— — Aphorisms on man. Translated from the original manuscript of
the rev. John Casper Lavater, citizen of Zuric. [One line from Juvenal.]
Fourth edition.
> *Printed at Boston, by I. Thomas and E. T. Andrews. At Faust's Statue,
> No. 45, Newbury-Street. Sold by them at their Book-store, by D. West, in Marl-
> borough Street, by E. Larkin, jun. in Cornhill, and by I. Thomas, in Worcester.*
MDCCXC. pp. 112, plate. 16mo.   aas.

22611   LAWRENCE, Effingham
Inspected store of drugs and medicines. As good and genuine medicines
are of great consequence to the community at large,—the following
certificate will shew, that the public may depend on being supplied
with such, wholesale and retail, at the store of the subscriber. Effingham Lawrence. [Certificate of the Medical Society of the State of New-York.
Signed by John Charlton. Samuel Bard. John R. B. Rogers. New-York, June
29, 1790.]
> *[New-York:* 1790.] Broadside. 12mo.   nyhs.

22612 LEAMING, JEREMIAH   1717 – 1804
THE EVIDENCES FOR THE TRUTH OF CHRISTIANITY, IN A SERMON, WITH AN APPEN-
DIX. PREACHED AND PUBLISHED BY JEREMIAH LEAMING, D. D. LATE RECTOR OF
THE EPISCOPAL CHURCH AT STRATFORD, IN THE STATE OF CONNECTICUT.
*New-York: Printed by Hugh Gaine, at his Book-Store and Printing Office,
at the Bible, in Hanover-Square.* M,DCC,XC. pp. 28. 8vo.   JCB. YC.

22613 DAS LEBEN EINES JUNGEN HERTZOG'S WELCHER 300 JAHR IN PARADISE,   . . .
Ephrata: Klosterpresse. 1790.

22614 LEE, ANDREW   1745 – 1832
THE DUTY OF GOSPEL MINISTERS, ILLUSTRATED AND URGED, IN A DISCOURSE PREACH-
ED AT THE ORDINATION OF THE REV. JONATHAN ELLIS, TO THE PASTORAL OFFICE
IN THE CHURCH AT TOPSHAM, MASSACHUSETTS, SEPTEMBER 16TH, A. D. 1789. BY
ANDREW LEE, A. M. PASTOR OF A CHURCH AT LISBON, IN CONNECTICUT. [One
line from] ST. PAUL.
Portland: Printed by Thomas Baker Wait. 1790. pp. 32. 8vo. AAS. JCB.

22615 LEE, THOMAS, JUNIOR
SACRED HARMONY, OR A COLLECTION OF PSALM TUNES, ANCIENT AND MODERN. CON-
TAINING A GREAT VARIETY OF THE MOST APPROVED PLAIN AND SIMPLE AIRS TAKEN
FROM THE MASSACHUSETTS HARMONY, WORCESTER COLLECTION, LAWS, ETC. TO
WHICH IS ADDED, SEVERAL NEW TUNES, NEVER BEFORE PUBLISHED, TOGETHER
WITH AN INTRODUCTION TO THE ART OF SINGING. BY R. HARRISON, LONDON.
Boston: Printed and sold by C. Cambridge, near the Boston Stone. [1790.]
pp. 12, 99. obl. 18mo.

22616 LELAND, JOHN   1754 – 1841
THE VIRGINIA CHRONICLE: WITH JUDICIOUS AND CRITICAL REMARKS UNDER XXIV
HEADS. BY JOHN LELAND. [Three lines of quotations.]
Norfolk: Printed by Prentis and Baxter. M,DCC,XC. pp.45,(3). 16mo.
AAS.

22617 ——   — THE VIRGINIA CHRONICLE: WITH JUDICIOUS AND CRITICAL REMARKS, UNDER
XXIV HEADS.
Fredericksburg: Printed by Timothy Green. 1790. pp. 46, (2). 8vo. JCB.

22618 LELAND, JOSEPH
THE FARMER'S DIARY: OR THE UNITED STATES ALMANACK, FOR THE YEAR OF OUR
LORD CHRIST, 1791. BEING THE THIRD AFTER BISSEXTILE, OR LEAP-YEAR. CAL-
CULATED FOR THE MERIDIAN OF DANBURY, IN THE STATE OF CONNECTICUT, LAT
41° 56' NORTH, LONG. 72° 54' WEST; BUT MAY SERVE INDIFFERENTLY FOR ANY
OF THE ADJACENT STATES. CONTAINING, ALL THINGS NECESSARY FOR SUCH A
COMPOSITION. BY JOSEPH LELAND, PHILOM.
Danbury: Printed by Nathan Douglas and Edwards Ely. [1790.]

22619 LE SAGE, ALAIN RENÉ   1668 – 1747
THE COMICAL ADVENTURES OF GIL BLAS OF SANTILLANE. AND THE CHILD OF NA-
TURE, A DRAMATIC NOVEL.
Philadelphia: Printed and sold by William Spotswood. M,DCC,XC. pp.
166; 68, (4). 12mo.   AAS. BM.
Second title: CHILD OF NATURE. A DRAMATIC PIECE, IN FOUR ACTS. FROM
THE FRENCH OF MADAME THE MARCHIONESS OF SILLERY, FORMERLY THE COUNT-
ESS OF GENLIS.
Philadelphia: Printed and sold by William Spotswood. MDCCXC. pp.
68, (4).
Both works have separate signatures, and the latter is sometimes found
separate as a complete work.

22620   THE LIFE OF CASSEM, THE SON OF HAMID, A NOBLE ARABIAN. TRANSLATED FROM AN ORIENTAL MANUSCRIPT.
Salem: Printed and sold by Thomas C. Cushing. 1790.

22621   LIVINGSTON, WILLIAM   1723 – 1790
POEMS. PHILOSOPHIC SOLITUDE, OR THE CHOICE OF A RURAL LIFE. SUPPOSED TO HAVE BEEN WRITTEN BY HIS EXCELLENCY WILLIAM LIVINGSTON, ESQ. PRESENT GOVERNOR OF THE STATE OF NEW-JERSEY. THE THIRTEENTH [*sic*] EDITION. THE PROGRESS OF SCIENCE. SPOKEN AT HARVARD UNIVERSITY, 1788 [*sic* 1780.] BY SAMUEL DEXTER, THEN A. B. NOW A. M. AND PROFESSOR OF BOTANY, AT SAID UNIVERSITY. NEVER BEFORE PUBLISHED [*sic.*]
New-York, Printed by Tho's Greenleaf. M,DCC,XC. pp. 19. 8vo. BU. NYHS.

22622   LOCKE, JOHN   1632 – 1704
A LETTER CONCERNING TOLERATION. BY JOHN LOCKE, GENT.
Stockbridge, (Massachusetts) Printed by Loring Andrews. 1790.

22623   LOW, NATHANAEL   1740 – 1808
AN ASTRONOMICAL DIARY: OR ALMANACK FOR THE YEAR OF CHRISTIAN 1791. [Nine lines, with cut of eclipse of the sun of April 3, 1791, in centre.] BY NATHANAEL LOW.
Printed and sold by T. & J. Fleet, in Boston. [The only proprietors of Dr. Low's copy right.] Where may be had their Pocket Almanack and Register, for 1791. [1790.] pp. [24.] 12mo.   AAS. LOC. NYPL. YC.
10th Massachusetts District Copyright, issued to Thomas & John Fleet, as Proprietors, 13 December, 1790.

22624   LOW, SAMUEL   1765 –
FELLOW-CRAFT HYMN, FOR THE USE OF HOLLAND LODGE. COMPOSED BY BROTHER LOW. [Seven four-line verses.]
[New-York: Printed by Harrisson and Purdy, 1790.] Broadside. fol. NYHS.

22625   —— ODE, FOR ST. JOHN'S DAY, JUNE 24, 5790, PERFORMED AT THE CONSECRATION OF THE NEW BUILDING FOR THE USE OF HOLLAND LODGE, AND THE WASHINGTON CHAPTER OF ROYAL-ARCH MASONS. [COMPOSED BY BROTHER LOW, OF HOLLAND LODGE.] RECITATIVE. [Eight lines.] AIR. [Six four-line verses.] CHORUS. [Four lines.] [Colophon:]
[New-York:] [Printed by Harrisson & Purdy.] [1790.] Broadside.fol.NYHS.

22626   LYMAN, GERSHOM CLARK   1753 – 1813
A SERMON PREACHED AT WILMINGTON, AT THE FUNERAL OF JESSE COOK, ESQUIRE. FEBRUARY 16TH, 1790. BY GERSHOM C. LYMAN, PASTOR OF THE CHURCH IN MARLBOROUGH.
Printed at Bennington, (Vermont) by Haswell & Russell, 1790. pp. 36.
12mo.   JCB.

22627   LYON, JAMES   1735 – 1801
PROPOSALS FOR PRINTING BY SUBSCRIPTION. THE SAINT'S DAILY ASSISTANT, OR MEDITATIONS FOR MORNING AND EVENING, FOR EVERY DAY IN A MONTH: EACH FOUNDED ON A PARTICULAR TEXT OF SCRIPTURE. ADAPTED TO THE DEVOTION OF THE FAMILY AND CLOSET. BY JAMES LYON, A. M. PASTOR OF THE CHURCH AT MACHIAS. CONDITIONS. . . .
[Newbury-Port: Printed by John Mycall, October 13, 1790.] Broadside. 4to.

22628 MC CLURE, DAVID   1748 – 1820
A SERMON, PREACHED AT THE ORDINATION OF THE REVEREND STANLEY GRISWOLD,
A. M. COLLEAGUE PASTOR OF THE FIRST CHURCH AND CONGREGATION IN NEW MIL-
FORD, ON THE TWENTIETH OF JANUARY, M.D.C.C.XC. BY DAVID MCCLURE, A. M.
MINISTER OF THE FIRST CHURCH IN EAST WINDSOR.
    Danbury: Printed by Nathan Douglas and Edwards Ely. M.D.CC.XC.
pp. 24. 12mo.   CHS. JCB. YC.

22629 MACGOWAN, JOHN   1726 – 1780
THE LIFE OF JOSEPH, THE SON OF ISRAEL, IN EIGHT BOOKS. CHIEFLY DESIGNED
FOR THE USE OF YOUTH.
    Stockbridge (Massachusetts): Printed by Loring Andrews, 1790.

22630 MACKLIN, CHARLES   1699 – 1797
LOVE A LA-MODE. . A COMEDY, IN TWO ACTS.
    Philadelphia: Printed by William Spotswood, 1790.

22631 MCKNIGHT, JOHN   1754 – 1823
SIX SERMONS UPON FAITH. BY THE REVEREND MR. JOHN M'KNIGHT, A. M. ONE OF
THE MINISTERS OF THE UNITED PRESBYTERIAN CHURCHES IN NEW-YORK. THESE
SERMONS ARE PUBLISHED AT THE REQUEST OF A NUMBER OF THOSE WHO HEARD
THEM DELIVERED; AND BY THE ADVICE OF SEVERAL RESPECTABLE CHARACTERS
IN THE MINISTRY, TO WHOSE INSPECTION THEY WERE SUBMITTED.
    New-York – Printed by Thomas Greenleaf. M,DCC,XC. pp. [163.] 12mo.
                                                   AAS. NYPL.

22632 MC MAHON, SIMON CREA
THE LIFE AND ADVENTURES OF SIMON CREA MCMAHON, WITH MISCELLANEOUS
PIECES, IN PROSE AND VERSE. PART THE FIRST. ENCOURAGE GENIUS TO HUMAN-
IZE THE GLOWING HEART.
    Richmond: Printed for the Author, 1790.
1st Virginia District Copyright.

22633 MACPHERSON, JAMES   1736 – 1796
THE POEMS OF OSSIAN, THE SON OF FINGAL. TRANSLATED BY JAMES MACPHERSON,
ESQ. A NEW EDITION, CAREFULLY CORRECTED, AND GREATLY IMPROVED. [One
line from] BLAIR.
    Philadelphia: Printed by Thomas Lang, No. 21, Church-Alley. MDCC-
XC. pp. (4), 502. 8vo.   AAS. JCB. LOC.
Second heading: A CRITICAL DISSERTATION ON THE POEMS OF OSSIAN, THE SON
OF FINGAL. BY HUGH BLAIR, D. D. ONE OF THE MINISTERS OF THE HIGH
CHURCH, AND PROFESSOR OF RHETORICK AND BELLES-LETTRES, IN THE UNIVER-
SITY OF EDINBURGH. pp. 415-502.

22634 MAGAW, SAMUEL   1740 – 1812
NOTES ON THE LAST ILLNESS, AND DEATH, OF A MOST BELOVED FRIEND. [Mrs.
Lucia Magaw.]
    *Philadelphia: Printed by William Young, Bookseller, the corner of Second
and Chesnut-Streets.* M.DCC.XC. pp. (36). 12mo.   AAS. BA. NYPL.

22635 MANSFIELD, RICHARD   1723 – 1820
A DISCOURSE CONCERNING THE GRACE OF GOD, IN THE DISPENSATION OF THE GOS-
PEL, AND THE OBLIGATIONS WE ARE UNDER TO MAKE A GOOD IMPROVEMENT OF
IT. A SUMMARY, LIKEWISE, OF SOME OF MANY IRREFRAGABLE PROOFS OF THE
TRUTHS OF CHRISTIANITY, AND CAUTIONS AGAINST ERROR.
    New-Haven: Printed by T. and S. Green. [1790.] pp. 37. 8vo. BA. CHS. YC.

22636   MARIA CECILIA: OR, LIFE AND ADVENTURES OF THE DAUGHTER OF ACHMET III, EMPEROR OF THE TURKS. FROM THE FRENCH.
Philadelphia: Printed by William Spotswood. M.DCC.XC. pp. 247, v. 12mo.   AAS. JCB. LÇP.
Contains a five-page list of books for sale by William Spotswood.

22637   MARIUS, JOHN
ADVICE CONCERNING BILS [*sic*] OF EXCHANGE, WHEREIN IS SET FORTH THE NATURE OF EXCHANGE OF MONIES, THE SEVERAL KINDS OF EXCHANGE IN DIFFERENT COUNTRIES, DIVERS CASES PROPOUNDED AND RESOLVED, OBJECTIONS ANSWERED, &C. WITH TWO EXACT TABLES OF OLD AND NEW STILE. BY IOHN MARIUS, NOTARY PUBLIKE. THE SECOND EDITION, LONDON, ANNO 1654.
Philadelphia: Re-printed by D. Humphreys, Front-Street, near the Drawbridge. M.DCC.XC. pp. vii, 96. 8vo.   AAS.

22638   MARKOE, PETER   1735 – 1792
THE RECONCILIATION; OR THE TRIUMPH OF NATURE. A COMIC OPERA, IN TWO ACTS. BY PETER MARKOE.
Philadelphia: Printed and sold by Prichard & Hall, in Market-Street, between Front and Second Streets. 1790. pp. 48. 12mo.   BA. BU. LCP. LOC. $12

22639   MARTIN, FRANÇOIS XAVIER   1762 – 1846
A FUNERAL ORATION ON THE DEATH OF GENERAL RICHARD CASWELL, WHO DIED AT FAYETTEVILLE, NORTH-CAROLINA, NOVEMBER 20, 1789. BY F. X. MARTIN.
Fayetteville: Printed by Sibley & Howard. 1790.

22640   MARYLAND. STATE.
LAWS OF MARYLAND, MADE AND PASSED AT A SESSION OF ASSEMBLY, BEGUN AND HELD AT THE CITY OF ANNAPOLIS ON MONDAY THE SECOND OF NOVEMBER, IN THE YEAR OF OUR LORD ONE THOUSAND SEVEN HUNDRED AND EIGHTY-NINE. [— 26 December, 1789,] [Arms.]
Annapolis: Printed by Frederick Green, Printer to the State. [1790.] pp. (2), (84). fol.   AAS. LOC. NYPL.

22641   —— VOTES AND PROCEEDINGS OF THE HOUSE OF DELEGATES OF THE STATE OF MARYLAND, NOVEMBER SESSION, 1789. BEING THE FIRST SESSION OF THIS ASSEMBLY. [6 November, — 25 December, 1789.]
[Annapolis: Printed by Frederick Green, 1790.] pp. 119. fol. LOC. NYPL.

22642   —— VOTES AND PROCEEDINGS OF THE SENATE OF THE STATE OF MARYLAND. NOVEMBER SESSION. 1789. BEING THE SIXTH SESSION OF THE THIRD SENATE. [2 November, — 25 December, 1789.]
[Annapolis: Printed by Frederick Green, 1790.] pp. 46. fol.   LOC.

22643   THE MARYLAND GAZETTE. XLVTH YEAR. No. 2243. THURSDAY, JANUARY 7, [— XLVITH YEAR. No. 2294. THURSDAY, DECEMBER 30, 1790.]
Annapolis: Printed by Frederick and Samuel Green. 1790. fol. AAS. MDHS.

22644   THE MARYLAND GAZETTE, AND FREDERICK WEEKLY ADVERTISER. VOL. I. No. 1. SATURDAY, FEBRUARY 20, [— No. 45. SATURDAY, DECEMBER 25, 1790.]
Frederick-Town: Printed by John Winter, at the Printing-Office in Patrick-Street, . . . 1790. fol.
Established by John Winter, and, apparently, continued by him into the year 1793; being succeeded by his *Rights of Man*, in 1794.

22645 THE MARYLAND GAZETTE; OR, THE BALTIMORE ADVERTISER. PUBLISHED EVERY
TUESDAY AND FRIDAY. VOL. VII. No. 547. FRIDAY, JANUARY 1, [— VOL. VIII.
No. 651. FRIDAY, DECEMBER 31, 1790.]
*Baltimore: Printed and published by John Hayes, the corner of Market and
Calvert Streets, where all kinds of printing-work are performed with care and dis-
patch, on the most reasonable terms.* ☞*A letter-box, for the reception af literary
productions, is affixed on the back of the door fronting on Market-Street.* 1790. fol.
NYPL.

22646 THE MARYLAND HERALD, AND EASTERN SHORE INTELLIGENCER. VOL. I. No. 1.
TUESDAY, MAY 11, [—No. 33. TUESDAY, DECEMBER 28, 1790.]
Easton: Printed by James Cowan. 1792. fol. AAS.
Established by James Cowan, and continued to 1804.

22647 THE MARYLAND JOURNAL AND BALTIMORE ADVERTISER. No. 1. OF VOL. XVII.
No. 1208. FRIDAY, JANUARY 1, [—No. 105 OF VOL. XVII. No. 1311. FRIDAY, DE-
CEMBER 31, 1790.]
Baltimore: Printed by W. Goddard, and James Angell, Market-Street.
1790. fol. AAS. MdHS.

22648 MASON, BENJAMIN
LIGHT RISING OUT OF OBSCURITY. OR, A REPLY TO FRANCIS HERR'S PAMPHLET,
INTITLED, A SHORT EXPLICATION OF THE WRITTEN WORD OF GOD; LIKEWISE, OF
THE CHRISTIAN BAPTISM, AND THE PEACEABLE KINGDOM OF CHRIST, AGAINST THE
PEOPLE CALLED QUAKERS. BY BENJAMIN MASON. [Two lines from] I. PETER.
*Philadelphia: Printed by Joseph Crukshank, in Market-Street, between Sec-
ond and Third-Streets.* M.DCC.XC. pp. (46). 8vo. AAS. JCB. LCP. LOC. NYPL.

22649 MASON, JOHN 1646 – 1694
SPIRITUAL SONGS: OR, SONGS OF PRAISE, WITH PENITENTIAL CRIES TO ALMIGHTY
GOD, UPON SEVERAL OCCASIONS. [By Thomas Shepard.] TOGETHER WITH THE
SONG OF SONGS, WHICH IS SOLOMON'S. FIRST TURNED, THEN PARAPHRASED IN
ENGLISH VERSE. WITH AN ADDITION OF A SACRED POEM OF DIVES AND LAZARUS.
New-York: Printed by W. Durell, & Co. [1790.] pp. (199). 12mo. AAS.

22650 MASSACHUSETTS. STATE.
[Arms.] ACTS AND LAWS, PASSED BY THE GENERAL COURT OF MASSACHUSETTS;
BEGUN AND HELD AT BOSTON, IN THE COUNTY OF SUFFOLK, ON WEDNESDAY THE
TWENTY-SEVENTH DAY OF MAY, ANNO DOMINI, 1789; AND FROM THENCE CON-
TINUED BY ADJOURNMENT TO WEDNESDAY THE THIRTEENTH OF JANUARY FOLLOW-
ING. [Colophon:]
*Boston: Printed by Thomas Adams, Printer to the honourable General
Court.* [1790.] pp. 33-74. fol. AAS. LOC. NYPL.

22651 —— [Arms.] [Perpetual] ACTS AND LAWS, PASSED BY THE GENERAL COURT OF
MASSACHUSETTS: BEGUN AND HELD AT BOSTON, IN THE COUNTY OF SUFFOLK, ON
WEDNESDAY THE TWENTY-SIXTH DAY OF MAY, ANNO DOMINI, 1790. [Colophon:]
*Boston: Printed by Thomas Adams, Printer to the honourable General
Court.* [1790.] pp. 75-87. fol. AAS. LOC. NYPL.

22652 —— COMMONWEALTH OF MASSACHUSETTS. BY HIS EXCELLENCY JOHN HANCOCK,
ESQ; GOVERNOUR OF THE COMMONWEALTH OF MASSACHUSETTS. A PROCLAMATION.
[Appointing Thursday, April eighth, a day of public fasting and prayer.]
[Boston: Printed by Thomas Adams, 1790.] Broadside. fol. AAS. MHS.

22653 —— COMMONWEALTH OF MASSACHUSETTS. BY HIS EXCELLENCY JOHN HANCOCK,
ESQ; GOVERNOUR OF THE COMMONWEALTH OF MASSACHUSETTS. A PROCLAMATION.
[Appointing Thursday, September sixteenth, a day of thanksgiving.]
[Boston: Printed by Thomas Adams, 1790.] Broadside. fol. AAS.

MASSACHUSETTS, continued.

22654 —— COMMONWEALTH OF MASSACHUSETTS. BY HIS EXCELLENCY JOHN HANCOCK, ESQ; GOVERNOUR OF THE COMMONWEALTH OF MASSACHUSETTS. A PROCLAMATION. [Appointing Thursday, November twenty-fifth, a day of thanksgiving.] *[Boston: Printed by Thomas Adams, 1790.]* Broadside. fol. AAS. BPL.

22655 —— COMMONWEALTH OF MASSACHUSETTS. IN SENATE, FEBRUARY 24, 1790. . . . REPORT. THE COMMITTEE OF BOTH HOUSES, APPOINTED TO CONSIDER FURTHER AMENDMENTS IN THE CONSTITUTION OF THE UNITED STATES—REPORT, . . . PUBLISHED BY ORDER OF THE HONORABLE SENATE. [Colophon:] *Boston: Printed by Thomas Adams, Printer to the honorable General Court of the Commonwealth of Massachusetts.* M,DCC,XC. pp. [3.] fol. LOC.

22656 —— RESOLVES OF THE GENERAL COURT OF THE COMMONWEALTH OF MASSACHU- SETTS: TOGETHER WITH THE MESSAGES, &C. OF HIS EXCELLENCY THE GOVERNOUR TO THE SAID COURT: BEGUN AND HELD AT BOSTON, IN THE COUNTY OF SUFFOLK, ON WEDNESDAY THE TWENTY-SEVENTH DAY OF MAY, ANNO DOMINI, 1789; AND FROM THENCE CONTINUED BY ADJOURNMENT TO WEDNESDAY THE THIRTEENTH OF JANUARY FOLLOWING. [—9 March, 1790.] *[Boston: Printed by Adams and Nourse, 1790.]* pp. [43]–93, (8). fol.
AAS. LOC. NYPL.

Page 46 is mispaged 76.

22657 —— —— *General title:* RESOLVES OF THE GENERAL COURT OF THE COMMONWEALTH OF MASSACHUSETTS. BEGUN AND HELD AT BOSTON, IN THE COUNTY OF SUFFOLK, ON WEDNESDAY THE TWENTY-SIXTH DAY OF MAY, ANNO DOMINI, 1790. *Boston: Printed by Thomas Adams, Printer to the honorable General Court.* M,DCC,XC. pp. (2). fol. AAS. LOC. NYPL.

22658 —— —— RESOLVES OF THE GENERAL COURT OF THE COMMONWEALTH OF MASSA- CHUSETTS: TOGETHER WITH MESSAGES, &C. OF HIS EXCELLENCY THE GOVERNOUR TO THE SAID COURT: BEGUN AND HELD AT BOSTON IN THE COUNTY OF SUFFOLK, ON WEDNESDAY THE TWENTY-SIXTH DAY OF MAY, ANNO DOMINI, 1790. [—24 June, 1790.] *[Boston: Printed by Thomas Adams, 1790.]* pp. (3)–30. fol. AAS. LOC. NYPL.

22659 —— —— RESOLVES OF THE GENERAL COURT OF THE COMMONWEALTH OF MASSA- CHUSETTS: TOGETHER WITH THE MESSAGES, &C. OF HIS EXCELLENCY THE GOV- ERNOUR TO THE SAID COURT: BEGUN AND HELD AT BOSTON, IN THE COUNTY OF SUFFOLK, ON WEDNESDAY THE TWENTY-SIXTH DAY OF MAY, ANNO DOMINI, 1790; AND FROM THENCE CONTINUED BY PROROGATION AND ADJOURNMENT TO WEDNES- DAY THE FIFTEENTH OF SEPTEMBER FOLLOWING. [—17 September, 1790.] *Boston: Printed by Thomas Adams, 1790.]* pp. (31)–35. fol. AAS.LOC.NYPL.

22660 —— TAX NO. EIGHT. [Arms.] COMMONWEALTH OF MASSACHUSETTS. IN THE YEAR OF OUR LORD, ONE THOUSAND SEVEN HUNDRED AND NINETY. AN ACT, FOR AP- PORTIONING AND ASSESSING A TAX OF TWENTY-FIVE THOUSAND THREE HUNDRED AND SIXTY POUNDS, THREE SHILLINGS AND FIVE PENCE, TO ANSWER THE EXIGEN- CIES OF GOVERNMENT; AND ALSO FOUR THOUSAND ONE HUNDRED AND FIFTY-FIVE POUNDS TWELVE SHILLINGS, TO RE-PLACE THE SAME SUM DRAWN OUT OF THE TREAS- URY, TO PAY THE MEMBERS OF THE HOUSE OF REPRESENTATIVES, FOR THEIR AT- TENDANCE THE TWO LAST SESSIONS OF THE GENERAL COURT; ALSO FOR ASSESSING A FURTHER SUM OF ELEVEN POUNDS FOURTEEN SHILLINGS, SET TO THE TOWN OF BOWDOIN, AND THE SUM OF THIRTY-SIX POUNDS, NINETEEN SHILLINGS AND EIGHT PENCE, SET ON THE LANDS OF THE HEIRS AND ASSIGNS OF THE LATE BRIGADIER WALDO. [Colophon:] *Boston: Printed by Thomas Adams, Printer to the honorable General Court.* M,DCC,XC. pp. 19. fol. AAS. HSP. LOC.

22661 MASSACHUSETTS MEDICAL SOCIETY.
MEDICAL PAPERS. COMMUNICATED TO THE MASSACHUSETTS MEDICAL SOCIETY. TO
WHICH ARE SUBJOINED, EXTRACTS FROM VARIOUS AUTHORS, CONTAINING SOME OF
THE IMPROVEMENTS WHICH HAVE LATELY BEEN MADE IN PHYSICK AND SURGERY.
PUBLISHED BY THE SOCIETY. NUMBER 1.
Boston: Printed by Samuel Hall? 1790. pp. 128. 8vo. BM. MHS. NYHS.

22662 THE MASSACHUSETTS [cut] CENTINEL. [Motto.] NUMBER 32 OF VOL. XII. SAT-
URDAY, JANUARY 2, [—NUMBER 26 OF VOL.XIII. WHOLE No. 650. SATURDAY,
JUNE 12, 1790.]
*Published, on Wednesdays and Saturdays, by Benjamin Russell, near the
State-House, Boston.* 1790. fol. AAS. LOC. NYPL.
With the issue for June 16th, the paper was enlarged to four columns
and the title changed and continued as the *Columbian Centinel.*

22663 THE MASSACHUSETTS MAGAZINE, OR MONTHLY MUSEUM. CONTAINING THE LIT-
ERATURE, HISTORY, POLITICS, ARTS, MANNERS & AMUSEMENTS OF THE AGE. [One
line of Latin.] VOL. II. FOR [JANUARY-DECEMBER] 1790. [Cut.]
*Printed at Boston, by I. Thomas and E. T. Andrews; at Faust's Statue,
No. 45, Newbury Street.* MDCCXC. pp. (2), iii, (1), 780, 14plates. 8vo.
AAS. BA. HC. JCB. LOC. MHS. NYHS.
Engraved title-page, and plates, by Samuel Hill.

22664 MEACHAM, JOSEPH
A CONCISE STATEMENT OF THE PRINCIPLES OF THE ONLY TRUE CHURCH, ACCORDING
TO THE GOSPEL, OF THE PRESENT APPEARANCE OF CHRIST AS HELD TO AND PRAC-
TICED BY THE FOLLOWERS OF THE LIVING SAVIOUR, AT NEW-LEBANON, &c. TO-
GETHER WITH A LETTER FROM JAMES WHITTAKER, MINISTER OF THE GOSPEL IN
THIS DAY OF CHRIST'S SECOND APPEARANCE, TO HIS NATURAL RELATIONS IN ENG-
LAND. DATED OCTOBER 9TH, 1785.
Printed at Bennington, Vermont, by Haswell & Russell. 1790.

22665 MELLEN, JOHN 1722 – 1807
THE FAITH AND PROFESSION OF THE GOSPEL. DISCOURSE DELIVERED AT HINGHAM,
THE SECOND PARISH, AT AN ASSOCIATION OF THE MINISTERS OF THAT VICINITY,
APRIL 8, 1789. BY JOHN MILLEN, A. M. PASTOR OF THE CHURCH IN HANOVER.
PUBLISHED AT THE DESIRE OF THE HEARERS. [Four lines from] ST. PAUL.
*Boston: Printed by Joseph Bumstead, at his Printing-Office, No. 20, Union-
Street.* MDCCXC. pp. (36). 8vo. BM. NYPL.

22666 METHODIST EPISCOPAL CHURCH IN AMERICA.
A FORM OF DISCIPLINE FOR THE MINISTERS, PREACHERS, AND MEMBERS (NOW COM-
PREHENDING THE PRINCIPLES AND DOCTRINES) OF THE METHODIST EPISCOPAL
CHURCH IN AMERICA, CONSIDERED AND APPROVED AT A CONFERENCE HELD AT
BALTIMORE, IN THE STATE OF MARYLAND, ON MONDAY THE 27TH OF DECEMBER,
1784: IN WHICH THOMAS COKE, AND FRANCIS ASBURY, PRESIDED: ARRANGED
UNDER PROPER HEADS, AND METHODISED IN A MORE ACCEPTABLE AND EASY MAN-
NER. THE SIXTH EDITION.
*Philadelphia: Printed by R. Aitken & Son, No. 22, Market Street, and
sold by John Dickins, No. 43, Fourth Street.* M.DCC.XC. pp. iv, 256.12mo. JCB.
Second title: A TREATISE ON THE NATURE AND SUBJECTS OF CHRISTIAN BAP-
TISM. EXTRACTED FROM A LATE AUTHOR. [Moses Hemmenway.]
*Philadelphia: Printed by Joseph Crukshank. Sold by John Dickins, No.
43, Fourth-Street, near the corner of Race-Street.* MDCCXC. pp. 179-256.

METHODIST EPISCOPAL CHURCH, continued.

22667   —— A POCKET HYMN-BOOK, DESIGNED AS A CONSTANT COMPANION FOR THE PIOUS. COLLECTED FROM VARIOUS AUTHORS. THE TENTH EDITION. PSALM CIV. 33. [Three lines.]

Philadelphia: Printed by Joseph James, 1790.

Approved by the Conference, and signed by Thomas Coke, and Francis Asbury. Twenty editions had been issued before the year 1796.

22668   A METHODIST'S REMONSTRANCE ADDRESSED TO A CERTAIN CLERGYMAN, WITH A REPLY. [By William Duke?]

Baltimore: 1790.

22669   THE MIDDLESEX GAZETTE, OR FŒDERAL ADVISER. VOL. V. NUMB. 218. SATURDAY, JANUARY 2, [— VOL. VI. NUMB. 269. SATURDAY, DECEMBER 25, 1790.]

Middletown: Printed and published by Moses H. Woodward. 1790. fol

AAS. CHS.

22670   MILLIGAN, JACOB
THE CHARLESTON DIRECTORY; AND REVENUE SYSTEM OF THE UNITED STATES.

Charleston: Printed by T. B. Bowen. [1790.] pp. 56. 8vo.   HC.

22671   MILTON, JOHN   1608 – 1674
PARADISE REGAIN'D: A POEM IN FOUR BOOKS. BY JOHN MILTON. FROM THE TEXT OF DR. NEWTON. [Eight lines from] ADDISON.

Philadelphia: Printed by W. Young, Bookseller, the corner of Second and Chesnut Street. M,DCC,XC. pp. 80, (4). 12mo.   AAS. LCP.

Has added, a list of American editions sold by William Young.

22672   THE MONITOR; OR A POEM ON DANCING. ADDRESSED TO LADIES AND GENTLEMEN OF THE FAYETTEVILLE ASSEMBLY.

Fayetteville: Printed by Sibley & Howard. 1790.

22673   MONRO, JOHN
A COLLECTION OF ABOUT FIFTY RELIGIOUS LETTERS EXPRESSING THE VARIOUS DUTIES AND EXERCISES OF, AND CROSSES, TRIALS AND DISCOURAGEMENTS IN THE WORLD, THE GRACES, ABILITIES AND CONSOLATIONS IN CHRIST ATTENDING THE CHRISTIAN IN THIS LIFE. WRITTEN TO DIVERS . . . MINISTERS. . . . WITH AN EPISTLE RECOMMENDATORY BY ONE OF THESE MINISTERS. . . .

Philadelphia: Printed by Peter Stewart, 1790.

22674   MONTAGUE, ——
A NEW SYSTEMATICAL COMPENDIUM OF GEOGRAPHY, ON THE FACE OF 52 CARDS. THE FOUR ACES GIVE A GENERAL DESCRIPTION OF THE FOUR QUARTERS OF THE WORLD, WHICH ARE THUS ARRANGED; ASIA UNDER SPADES; AFRICA UNDER CLUBS; EUROPE UNDER HEARTS; AND AMERICA UNDER DIAMONDS. THE FOUR KINGS CONTAIN ALL THE KINGDOMS OF THE WORLD; THEIR LENGTH, BREADTH, &C. ON THE LOWER CARDS OF THE SUIT, EACH KINGDOM IS DESCRIBED WITH ITS BOUNDARIES, DISTANCE FROM LONDON; MOUNTAINS, RIVERS, CLIMATE, SOIL, PRODUCTIONS, MANNERS, CUSTOMS, TRADE, MANUFACTURES, RELIGION, GOVERNMENT, IMPROVEMENTS IN ARTS AND SCIENCES, CURIOSITIES, &C.

Boston: Printed for, and sold by Benjamin Larkin, at Shakespeare's-Head, No. 46, Cornhill. 1790.

12th Massachusetts District Copyright, issued to —— Montague, as Author, 29 December, 1790.

22675 MOORE, EDWARD   1712 – 1757
AMERICAN EDITION. THE GAMESTER, A TRAGEDY. AS PERFORMED BY THE OLD
AMERICAN COMPANY, AT THE THEATRE, IN SOUTHWARK: PHILADELPHIA. WRIT-
TEN BY MR. EDWARD MOORE. [Publisher's monogram.]
*Philadelphia. Printed and sold by E, Story, in Second Street, fifth door
above Arch Street, the east side.* [1790.] pp. 80, (4). 12mo.   AAS.
Has added, New publications. For sale by the Printer hereof. pp. (2).
Seven hundred and fifty copies, in sheets, were offered at the sale of
the estate of Henry Taylor, printer, in 1791.

22676 MOORE, JOHN HAMILTON   – 1807
THE YOUNG GENTLEMAN AND LADY'S MONITOR AND ENGLISH TEACHER'S ASSISTANT;
BEING A COLLECTION OF SELECT PIECES FROM OUR BEST MODERN WRITERS: CAL-
CULATED TO ERADICATE VULGAR PREJUDICES AND RUSTICITY OF MANNERS; IM-
PROVE THE UNDERSTANDING; RECTIFY THE WILL; PURIFY THE PASSIONS; DIRECT
THE MINDS OF YOUTH TO THE PURSUIT OF PROPER OBJECTS; AND TO FACILITATE
THEIR READING, WRITING, AND SPEAKING THE ENGLISH LANGUAGE, WITH ELE-
GANCE AND PROPRIETY. PARTICULARLY ADAPTED FOR THE USE OF OUR EMINENT
SCHOOLS AND ACADEMIES, AS WELL AS PRIVATE PERSONS, WHO HAVE NOT AN OP-
PORTUNITY OF PERUSING THE WORKS OF THOSE CELEBRATED AUTHORS, FROM
WHENCE THIS COLLECTION IS MADE. DIVIDED INTO SMALL PORTIONS FOR THE
EASE OF READING IN CLASSES. THE SIXTH EDITION. BY J. HAMILTON MOORE,
AUTHOR OF THE PRACTICAL NAVIGATOR AND SEAMAN'S NEW DAILY ASSISTANT.
*London: Printed. New-York: Reprinted by Hugh Gaine, at the Bible, in
Hanover-Square.* 1790. pp. vi, 378, [34], 4 plates. 12mo.   LOC.

22677 —— THE YOUNG GENTLEMAN AND LADY'S MONITOR AND ENGLISH TEACHER'S
ASSISTANT; BEING A COLLECTION OF SELECT PIECES FROM OUR BEST MODERN
WRITERS: CALCULATED TO ERADICATE VULGAR PREJUDICES AND RUSTICITY OF
MANNERS; IMPROVE THE UNDERSTANDING; RECTIFY THE WILL; PURIFY THE PAS-
SIONS; DIRECT THE MINDS OF YOUTH TO THE PURSUIT OF PROPER OBJECTS; AND
TO FACILITATE THEIR READING, WRITING, AND SPEAKING THE ENGLISH LANGUAGE,
WITH ELEGANCE AND PROPRIETY. PARTICULARLY ADAPTED FOR THE USE OF OUR
EMINENT SCHOOLS AND ACADEMIES, AS WELL AS PRIVATE PERSONS, WHO HAVE NOT
AN OPPORTUNITY OF PERUSING THE WORKS OF THOSE CELEBRATED AUTHORS,
FROM WHENCE THIS COLLECTION IS MADE. DIVIDED INTO SMALL PORTIONS FOR
THE EASE OF READING IN CLASSES. THE SIXTH EDITION. BY J. HAMILTON
MOORE, AUTHOR OF THE PRACTICAL NAVIGATOR AND SEAMAN'S NEW DAILY AS-
SISTANT.
*New-York: Printed by Hodge, Allen & Campbell, and sold at their res-
pective Book Stores.* 1790, pp. 336, 12mo.   NYPL.

22678 MOORE, THOMAS, pseudonym.
GAINE'S NEW-YORK POCKET ALMANACK, FOR THE YEAR 1791: BEING THE THIRD
AFTER LEAP YEAR, AND 15TH OF AMERICAN INDEPENDENCE, 'TILL 4TH JULY.
CALCULATED FOR THIS AND THE NEIGHBOURING STATES. BY THOMAS MOORE,
PHILO.
New-York: Printed by H. Gaine, at the Bible, in Hanover-Square.
[1790.] pp. (72), 24mo.

22679 —— GAINE'S UNIVERSAL SHEET ALMANACK, FOR THE YEAR OF OUR LORD, 1790.
[New-York: Printed by Hugh Gaine, 1790.] Broadside, fol.
Thirty pages imposed on a single sheet.

22680 THE MORNING POST, AND DAILY ADVERTISER. No. 1712. FRIDAY, JANUARY 1,
[—No. 1959. FRIDAY, DECEMBER 31, 1790.]
*New-York: Printed and published by William Morton, at the Printing-
Office, No. 231, Queen-Street.* 1790. fol.   AAS.

22681   MORSE, JEDIDIAH   1761 – 1826
GEOGRAPHY MADE EASY: BEING AN ABRIDGEMENT OF THE AMERICAN GEOGRAPHY.
CONTAINING, ASTRONOMICAL GEOGRAPHY—DISCOVERY AND GENERAL DESCRIPTION
OF AMERICA—GENERAL VIEW OF THE UNITED STATES—PARTICULAR ACCOUNTS OF
THE THIRTEEN UNITED STATES OF AMERICA, IN REGARD TO THEIR BOUNDARIES,
EXTENT, RIVERS, LAKES, MOUNTAINS, PRODUCTIONS, POPULATION, CHARACTER, GOV-
ERNMENT, TRADE, MANUFACTURES, CURIOSITIES. HISTORY, &C. TO WHICH IS
ADDED, A GEOGRAPHICAL ACCOUNT OF THE EUROPEAN SETTLEMENTS IN AMERICA,
AND OF EUROPE, ASIA AND AFRICA. ILLUSTRATED WITH EIGHT NEAT MAPS AND
CUTS. CALCULATED PARTICULARLY FOR THE USE AND IMPROVEMENT OF SCHOOLS
IN THE UNITED STATES. BY JEDIDIAH MORSE, A. M. MINISTER OF THE CONGRE-
GATION IN CHARLESTOWN, NEAR BOSTON. SECOND EDITION. ABRIDGED BY THE
AUTHOR. [Five lines of quotations.]
> *Printed at Boston, by Isaiah Thomas & Ebenezer T. Andrews.* MDCCXC.
pp. 322, 8 maps. 12mo.   AAS. BM. YC.

     2d Massachusetts District Copyright, issued to Jedidiah Morse, as
Author, 10 July, 1790.

22682   —— THE HISTORY OF AMERICA. IN TWO BOOKS. CONTAINING, I. A GENERAL
HISTORY OF AMERICA, II. A CONCISE HISTORY OF THE LATE REVOLUTION. EX-
TRACTED FROM THE AMERICAN EDITION OF THE ENCYCLOPÆDIA; NOW PUBLISHING.
> *By Thomas Dobson, at the Stone-House, in Second-Street, Philadelphia.*
April, MDCCXC. pp. viii, 260, (4), 2 maps. 12mo.   AAS. LOC.

     In two states: printed on fine, and on common paper. Has added, a
four-page list of Books printed and sold by Thomas Dobson.

22683   —— A SERMON PREACHED LORD'S DAY, FEBRUARY 28, 1790, UPON THE DEATH OF
RICHARD CARY, ESQ., OF CHARLESTOWN WHO DIED FEBRUARY 7. ÆTAT 73. . . .
> *Printed by Samuel Hall, Boston.* MDCCXC. pp. 27. 4to.

                   AAS. BA. BM. IIC. JCB. MHS.

22684   MORTON, SARAH WENTWORTH APTHORP   1759 – 1846
OUÂBI: OR THE VIRTUES OF NATURE. AN INDIAN TALE. IN FOUR CANTOS. BY
PHILENIA, A LADY OF BOSTON. [One line from] SPENSER'S FAIRY QUEEN.
[Ornament.]
> *Printed at Boston, by I. Thomas and E. T. Andrews, at Faust's Statue,*
No. 45, Newbury Street, MDCCXC. pp. 51, (1), frontispiece. 8vo.

               AAS. BA. BM. HC. JCB. LOC. MHS. NYPL.

22685   MOTT, SAMUEL
AN ALMANACK AND EPHEMERIS, FOR THE YEAR OF OUR LORD, 1791; BEING THE
THIRD AFTER LEAP YEAR, AND THE FIFTEENTH OF THE AMERICAN INDEPENDENCE,
UNTIL THE FOURTH OF JULY. [Eleven lines.] BY SAMUEL MOTT.
> *State of New-York: Printed by Nicholas Power, at Poughkeepsie, in the*
County of Dutchess. [1790.] pp. (36). 12mo.   AAS.

     "The first work of the kind ever published in this place" Contains,
The Vision of Theodore.

22686   MURRAY, LINDLEY   1745 – 1826
THE POWER OF RELIGION ON THE MIND, IN RETIREMENT, SICKNESS, AND AT DEATH;
EXEMPLIFIED IN THE TESTIMONIES AND EXPERIENCE OF MEN DISTINGUISHED BY
THEIR GREATNESS, LEARNING, OR VIRTUE. A NEW EDITION.
> *Philadelphia: Printed and sold by Joseph Crukshank, in Market near*
Third Street. MDCCXC. pp. 144. 16mo.   AAS.

     Contains a four-page list of books sold by Joseph Crukshank.

22687 DER NEUE GEMEINNÜTZIGE LANDWIRTHSCHAFTS CALENDER. AUF DAS JAHR NACH DER HEILBRINGENDEN-GEBURT UNSERES HERRN JESU CHRISTI 1791. ZUM VIERTEN MAL HERAUSGEGEBEN.

Lancaster: Gedruckt und zu haben bey Johann Albrecht & Comp. [1790.]

22688 DER NEUE HOCH DEUTSCHE AMERICANISCHE CALENDER AUF DAS JAHR CHRISTI 1791. ZUM ERSTENMAL HERAUS GEGEBEN.

Chesnut Hill: Gedruckt bey Samuel Saur. [1790.]

22689 NEUE PHILADELPHISCHE CORRESPONDENZ. NUM. 1. FREYTAG, DEN 1TEN OCTOBER, [— NUM. 27. FREYTAG, DEN 31TEN DECEMBER, 1790.]

Diese Zeitung wird alle Dienstag und Freytag herausgegeben von Melchior Steiner, Buchdrucker, in der Rees-Strasse, zwischen der Zweyten-und Dritten-Strasse, No. 71; fuer zwey Thaler des Jahrs. Ein Thaler wird beym Einschrieben bezahlb, 1790. fol.

In continuation of, *Gemeinnuetzige Philadelphische Correspondenz.*

22690 NEUE UNPARTHEYISCHE LANCÄSTER ZEITUNG, UND ANZEIGS-NACHRICHTEN. NUM. 127. MITTWOCHS DEN 6 JENNER, [— NUM. 178. MITTWOCHS, DEN 29 DECEMBER, 1790.]

Diese Zeitung wird alle Mittwochs Morgens herausgegeben von Albrecht und Lahn, in den Neuen Buchdruckerey zu Lancaster, . . . 1790. fol.   LOC.

Following the issue for March 17th, the Zeitung was published by ⌐⌐⌐ Johann Albrecht und Comp.—Jacob Lahn retiring.

22691 NEUE UNPARTHEYISCHE READINGER ZEITUNG UND ANZEIGS-NACHRICHTEN. JANUARY – DECEMBER, 1790.

Reading: Gedruckt bey Barton und Jungmann. 1790. fol.

22692 THE NEW-ENGLAND PRIMER, ENLARGED AND IMPROVED: OR, AN EASY AND PLEASANT GUIDE TO THE ART OF READING. ADORNED WITH CUTS. ALSO, THE CATECHISM.

Newburyport: Printed and sold by John Mycall. [1790.] pp.(80). 32mo. BM.

22693 —— THE NEW-ENGLAND PRIMER, ENLARGED AND IMPROVED: OR, AN EASY AND PLEASANT GUIDE TO THE ART OF READING. ADORNED WITH CUTS. ALSO, THE CATECHISM.

Newburyport: Printed and sold by John Mycall; Sold also by Isaiah Thomas at his shops in Boston and Worcester. [1790.] pp. (80). 32mo.   AAS. BM. $15

22694 —— THE NEW-ENGLAND PRIMER, ENLARGED AND IMPROVED: OR, AN EASY AND PLEASANT GUIDE TO THE ART OF READING. ADORNED WITH CUTS. ALSO, THE CATECHISM.

Newburyport: Printed by John Mycall, for John Boyle, Marlborough Street, Boston. [1790.] pp. (80). 32mo. $15

22695 —— THE NEW-ENGLAND PRIMER IMPROVED, FOR THE MORE EASY ATTAINING THE TRUE READING OF ENGLISH. ADORNED WITH CUTTS. TO WHICH IS ADDED, THE ASSEMBLY OF DIVINES CATECHISM.

Boston: Printed by Joseph Bumstead, and sold at his Printing Office, No. 20, Union-Street. 1790. pp. (64). 32mo.

22696 —— THE NEW-ENGLAND PRIMER, MUCH IMPROVED, CONTAINING A VARIETY OF EASY LESSONS FOR ATTAINING THE TRUE READING OF ENGLISH.

Philadelphia: Printed by John M'Culloch, for Robert Campbell, 1790.

22697   —— The New-England Primer improved. For the more easy attaining the true reading of English. To which is added, The Assembly of Divines and mr. Cotton's Catechism.
Providence: Printed and sold by Bennett Wheeler.[1790.] pp. (80). 32mo.

22698   A new general Chart of the West-Indies, from the latest marine journals and surveys. Carefully examined and found to be an accurate copy of a London publication, agreeable to an Act of Parliament. By Osgood Carleton, teacher of navigation, and other branches of the mathematics.
Boston: Published by J. Norman, engraver, at his Office, No. 75, Newbury-Street. 1790. 27¼ x 39¼.

22699   New Hampshire. State.
A Journal of the proceedings of the honourable House of Representatives of the State of New-Hampshire, . . . on Wednesday, the 23d day of December, 1789. [—26 January, 1790.]
Portsmouth, New-Hampshire: Printed by George Jerry Osborne, M,DCC,-XC. pp. 97. 8vo.   NHSL.

22700   —— — A Journal of the proceedings of the honourable House of Representatives of the State of New-Hampshire, . . . on Wednesday, June, 1790.
Portsmouth, New-Hampshire: Printed by George Jerry Osborne. M,DCC,-XC. pp. 82. 8vo.   NHSL.

22701   —— A Journal of the proceedings of the honorable Senate, of the State of New-Hampshire, . . . on Wednesday, December 23d, 1789. [—26 January, 1790.]
Portsmouth: Printed by J. Melcher, M,DCC,XC. pp. 69. 8vo.   NHSL.

22702   —— — A Journal of the proceedings of the honorable Senate, of the State of New-Hampshire, June, 1790.
Portsmouth: Printed by J. Melcher, M,DCC,XC. pp. 51. 8vo.   NHSL.

22703   —— The Public Acts and laws of the State of New-Hampshire, which were enacted at a session of the General Court, begun and held at Portsmouth, on Wednesday the 23d December, 1789.
Exeter: Printed by Henry Ranlet, for the honourable the General Court. A. D. 1790. pp. (2), 255—263. 8vo.   LOC.

22704   —— State of New Hampshire. In the year of our Lord one thousand seven hundred and ninety. An Act directing the mode of choosing representatives to the Congress of the United States. . . . A true copy. Attest, Joseph Pearson, secretary.
[*Exeter: Printed by Henry Ranlet,* 1790.] Broadside. fol.   LOC.

22705   The New-Hampshire Gazette, and the general advertiser. Containing the laws, &c. of the United States, as well as those of this State passed since 1787, with a variety of other matters both useful and entertaining. Vol. xxxiv. No. 1739. Wednesday, January 6, [—Vol. xxxiv [*sic.*] No. 5757 [*sic* 1790.] Wednesday, December 25, 1790.]
Portsmouth: Printed by John Melcher, at his Office in Congress-Street, at nine shillings per annum. 1790. fol.   AAS.
The issue for March 31st, is misnumbered 5751, and the error continued to October 14th, which is again misnumbered 5774, this second error is continued to October 21st, which is again misnumbered 5748, and this third error continued to December 25th, which is numbered 5757, instead of 1790, which it should be.

22706 THE NEWHAMPSHIRE Gazetteer. [Motto.] Vol. iv. No. 178, Saturday, January 2, [—Vol. v. No. 229. Saturday, December 25, 1790.]
Published by H. Ranlet, in the Main Street, Exeter, . . . 1790. fol. **aas.**
In June, the motto was dropped from the heading. From April 24th to October 1st, Friday was the day of publication.

22707 THE NEW-HAMPSHIRE [U. S. Arms] Recorder, and the weekly advertiser. Vol. iii. No. 1. Thursday, March 18, [—No. 32, Thursday, December 16? 1790.]
Keene: (State of New-Hampshire) Printed and published by James Davenport Griffith, in the Main-Street. 1790. fol. **aas.**
A "Recorder Extraordinary," besides the regular issue, was printed on March 18th.

22708 NEW HAVEN. Connecticut.
Bye laws of the city of New-Haven, in Connecticut. As revised, passed and approved since the ninth day of May, A. D. one thousand, seven hundred, and eighty-seven.
New-Haven: Printed by Thomas and Samuel Green. M,DCC,XC. pp. 16. 4to. **hc.**

22709 NEW JERSEY. State.
An Act to ascertain the sum to be raised within this State for the year 1790.
New-Brunswick: Printed by Abraham Blauvelt. 1790.

22710 —— Acts of the fourteenth General Assembly of the State of New-Jersey· At a session begun at Perth-Amboy on the 27th day of October 1789, and continued by adjournments. Being the second sitting. [25 May,—12 June, 1790.]
New-Brunswick: Printed by Abraham Blauvelt, M.DCC.XC. pp. (2),(583)--657. fol. **nypl.**
Second heading: Appendix to the Acts of the fourteenth General Assembly of the State of New-Jersey: containing sundry Acts of the Congress of the United States. Directed to be re-published for the information of the citizens of this State, by a resolution of the Legislature, passed the ninth day of June, one thousand seven hundred and ninety. [1 June, 1789,—26 May, 1790.] pp. (623)—657.

22711 —— — Acts of the fifteenth General Assembly of the State of New-Jersey. At a session begun at Burlington the 26th day of October, 1790, and continued by adjournments. Being the first sitting. [8—26, November, 1790.]
Burlington: Printed by Neale and Lawrence. M.DCC.XC. pp. (2), (661)--716. fol. **nypl.**

22712 —— Journal of the proceedings of Legislative-Council of New-Jersey, at Burlington, from Thursday, May 15th, 1783, to Saturday, June 12th, 1790.
New-Brunswick: Printed by Abraham Blauvelt, 1790. **njsl.**

22713 —— — A Journal of the proceedings of the Legislative-Council of the State of New-Jersey, in General Assembly convened at the city of Burlington, on Tuesday, the 26th day of October, 1790. [—26 November, 1790.]
Burlington: Printed by Neale & Lawrence, 1790.

22714   NEW JERSEY, continued.
—— VOTES AND PROCEEDINGS OF THE GENERAL ASSEMBLY OF THE STATE OF NEW-JERSEY. [27 October,—1 December, 1789.]
New-Brunswick: Printed by Abraham Blauvelt. 1790. pp. 111, (1). fol.

22715   THE NEW-JERSEY JOURNAL, AND POLITICAL INTELLIGENCER. NO. 325. WEDNESDAY, JANUARY 6, [— No. 376. WEDNESDAY, DECEMBER 29, 1790.]
Elizabeth-Town, Printed and published by Shepard Kollock, every Wednesday . . . 1790. fol.   AAS. LOC.

22716   THE NEW-JERSEY, PENNSYLVANIA, DELAWARE, MARYLAND AND VIRGINIA ALMANACK, AND EPHEMERIS, FOR THE YEAR OF OUR LORD, 1791; BEING THE THIRD AFTER BISSEXTILE, OR LEAP-YEAR, THE FIFTEENTH OF AMERICAN INDEPENDENCE, AND THE THIRD YEAR OF OUR FEDERAL GOVERNMENT—WHICH MAY THE GOVERNOR OF THE WORLD PROSPER! [Twenty-two lines.]
Baltimore: Printed and sold by Samuel and John Adams, in Market-Street, between South and Gay-Streets. [1790.] pp. [48.] 12mo.   NYPL.

22717   NEW YORK. STATE.
A CENSUS OF THE ELECTORS AND INHABITANTS IN THE STATE OF NEW-YORK, TAKEN IN THE YEAR 1790, IN PURSUANCE OF A LAW OF THE SAID STATE. . . . [Colophon:]
[New-York:] Printed by Childs and Swaine, Printers to the State. [1790.] Broadside. fol.   LOC. NYPL.

22718   —— JOURNAL OF THE HOUSE OF ASSEMBLY OF THE STATE OF NEW-YORK. THE SECOND MEETING OF THE THIRTEENTH SESSION. [13 January,— 6 April, 1790.] [Arms.]
New-York: Printed by Francis Childs and John Swaine, Printers to the State. —1790. pp. [118.] fol.   LOC. NYHS. NYPL.

22719   —— JOURNAL OF THE SENATE OF THE STATE OF NEW-YORK. THE SECOND MEETING OF THE THIRTEENTH SESSION. [12 January,— 6 April, 1790.] [Arms.]
New-York: Printed by Francis Childs and John Swaine, Printers to the State. —1790. pp. [56.] fol.   NYHS. NYPL.

22720   —— LAWS OF THE STATE OF NEW-YORK. VOLUME THE THIRD. [14 July 1789,— 6 April, 1790.] [Arms.]
New-York: Printed by Francis Childs and John Swaine, Printers to the State.—1790. pp. (2), 48. fol.   LOC. NYHS. NYPL.
A general title-page, covering, only, Laws of the State of New-York, passed at the first [and second] meetings of the thirteenth session of the Legislature of the said State. [14 July, 1789—6 April, 1790.]

22721   NEW YORK. CITY. LOTTERY.
SCHEME OF A LOTTERY, FOR THE PURPOSE OF RAISING SEVEN THOUSAND FIVE HUNDRED POUNDS, AGREEABLE TO AN ACT OF THE LEGISLATURE OF THE STATE OF NEW-YORK, PASSED 8TH OF FEBRUARY, 1790. . . . NEW-YORK, MARCH 6, 1790.
[New-York: Printed by Thomas Greenleaf, 1790.] Broadside. fol. NYHS.

22722   NEW YORK, CITY. THEATRE.
NEW-YORK, MAY 18, 1790. MRS. JOHNSON'S BENEFIT. ON FRIDAY EVENING, THE 20TH OF MAY, WILL BE PRESENTED, A FAVORITE COMEDY, (NEVER PERFORMED HERE) CALLED, FIRST LOVE, OR, THE FRENCH EMIGRANT. [Sixteen lines.] AFTER WHICH A PASTORAL DANCE, CALLED, AULD ROBIN GRAY, OR, JAMIE'S RETURN. [Seven lines.] TO WHICH WILL BE ADDED, A MUSICAL ENTERTAINMENT, (NOT PERFORMED HERE THESE SIX YEARS,) CALLED, THOMAS AND SALLY, OR, THE SAILOR'S RETURN. [Seven lines.] VIVAT RESPUBLICA.
[New-York: 1790.] Broadside. fol.   NYHS.

22723   THE NEW-YORK DAILY GAZETTE. NUMB. 317. FRIDAY, JANUARY 1, [— NUMB.
646. FRIDAY, DECEMBER 31, 1790.]
*Published by Archibald M'Lean, at his Printing-Office, Franklin's Head,
No. 41, Hanover-Square.* 1790. fol.   AAS.

22724   THE NEW-YORK DIRECTORY, AND REGISTER, FOR THE YEAR 1790. ILLUSTRATED
WITH AN ACCURATE AND ELEGANT PLAN OF THE CITY OF NEW-YORK, AND PART OF
LONG-ISLAND, INCLUDING THE SUBURBS, WITH ALL THE STREETS, LANES, PUBLIC
BUILDINGS, WHARVES, &C. EXACTLY LAID DOWN, FROM THE LATEST SURVEY. CON-
TAINING, AN ALPHABETICAL LIST OF THE NAMES, OCCUPATIONS, AND PLACES OF
ABODE OF THE CITIZENS, A REGISTER OF THE CONGRESS OF THE UNITED STATES,
AND THE DIFFERENT DEPARTMENTS OF GOVERNMENT. FOREIGN MINISTERS, GOV-
ERNORS OF THE DIFFERENT STATES. OFFICERS OF THE STATE OF NEW-YORK,
OFFICERS IN CHANCERY, SENATE AND ASSEMBLY, OFFICERS OF CITY & COUNTY,
CHAMBER OF COMMERCE, MARINE SOCIETY, ASSURANCE COMPANY, MINISTERS OF
THE GOSPEL, MEDICAL SOCIETY, THE OTHER SOCIETIES IN THE CITY, ROLL OF
ATTORNIES OF SUPREME COURT, COLUMBIA COLLEGE, LIBRARY SOCIETY, POST
DAYS, STAGES, AND COACH RATES. PRICE — THREE SHILLINGS.
*New-York: Printed by Hodge, Allen, and Campbell, and sold at their sev-
eral Book-Stores.* M,DCC,XC. pp. 144, plan. 12mo.   NYHS. NYPL.

22725   THE NEW-YORK JOURNAL AND DAILY PATRIOTIC REGISTER. [Motto.] NUMB.—
FRIDAY, JANUARY 1, [—NUMB. — FRIDAY, APRIL 30? 1790.]
*New-York: Printed and published by Thomas Greenleaf, at the Printing-
Office, No.* 196, *Water-Street.* 1790. fol.
Publication continued, as a semi-weekly, under the following title:

22726   THE NEW-YORK JOURNAL, & PATRIOTIC REGISTER. [Motto.] NUMB. — TUES-
DAY, MAY 4, [—NUMB. — FRIDAY, DECEMBER 31, 1790.]
*New-York: Printed and published by Thomas Greenleaf, at the Printing-
Office, No.* 196, *Water-Street.* 1790. fol.

22727   THE NEW-YORK JOURNAL, AND WEEKLY REGISTER. [Motto.] NUMBER 1, OF
VOL. xliv. TOTAL NUMB. 2434. THURSDAY, JANUARY 7, [—NUMB. 86, OF VOL.
xliv. TOTAL NUMB. 2520. THURSDAY, DECEMBER 30, 1790.]
*New-York: Printed and published by Thomas Greenleaf, at the Printing-
Office, No.* 196, *Water-Street.* 1790. fol.   AAS. NYPL.
Beginning May 4th, a new plan of publication of twice a week, for both
the daily and weekly, was adopted, under the title of *The New-York
Journal & patriotic register.* Printed and published (on Tuesdays and
Fridays) by Thomas Greenleaf, at his Printing-Office, No. 196 Water
Street.—which was changed to Mondays and Thursdays, beginning
November 1st.

22728   THE NEW-YORK MAGAZINE; OR, LITERARY REPOSITORY. [TO WHICH IS SUBJOINED
THE AMERICAN CHRONOLOGY.] VOLUME I. FOR [JANUARY—DECEMBER,] 1790.
[Two lines of verse.]
*New-York: Printed by Thomas and James Swords, at their Printing-Office,
No.* 44, *Crown-Street [near Smith-Street.]* M.DCC.XC. pp. viii, 730, (4), 54+,
12 plates, map. 8vo.   AAS. HC. LOC. NYHS.

22729   THE NEW-YORK PACKET. [Motto.] No. 1007. SATURDAY, JANUARY 2, [—No. 1162.
THURSDAY, DECEMBER 30, 1790.]
*New-York: Published every Tuesday, Thursday and Saturday, by Samuel
Loudon, No,* 5 *Water-Street, between the Coffee-House and Old-Slip.* 1790. fol.

22730   —— ANNIVERSARY ADDRESS OF THE CARRIERS OF THE NEW-YORK PACKET TO
THEIR GENEROUS PATRONS. [Seven verses.]
[New-York: Printed by Samuel Loudon. 1790.] Broadside. nar. fol.

22731   THE NEW-YORK WEEKLY MUSEUM. NUMBER 86. SATURDAY, JANUARY 2, [—NUM-
BER 131. SATURDAY, NOVEMBER 13? 1790.]
> *New-York: Printed and published by Harrisson and Purdy, at their Print-
ing-Office, No. 3, Peck-Slip; . . . 1790. 4to.*

At about the above date, the title was altered to, *The Weekly Museum.*
Purdy withdrawing from the partnership.

22732   THE NEWPORT HERALD. [Motto.] VOL. IV. No. 150. THURSDAY, JANUARY 7,
[—No. 201. THURSDAY, DECEMBER 30, 1790.]
> *Newport, (Rhode-Island): Published by Peter Edes, in Thames-Street. 1790.*
fol.   AAS.

The issue for June 3d, contains the Ratification of the Constitution of
the United States, by the Convention of the State of Rhode-Island and
Providence Plantations.

22733   THE NEWPORT MERCURY. No. 1449. WEDNESDAY, JANUARY 6, [—No. 1500. MON-
DAY, DECEMBER 27, 1790.]
> *Newport (Rhode - Island): Printed by Henry Barber, at the foot of the
Parade. 1790. fol.*

22734   NEWTON, JOHN   1725 – 1807
OLNEY HYMNS, IN THREE BOOKS. BOOK I. ON SELECT TEXTS OF SCRIPTURE. BOOK
II. ON OCCASIONAL SUBJECTS. BOOK III. ON THE PROGRESS AND CHANGES OF THE
SPIRITUAL LIFE. THE SIXTH EDITION. [Seven lines of quotations.]
> *New-York: Printed by Hodge, Allen, & Campbell, and sold at their respect-
ive Book-stores. M.DCC.XC. pp. 348. 12mo.*   AAS.

Preface signed, John Newton. Olney, Bucks, Feb. 15, 1779.

22735   NICHOLSON, JOHN
ADDRESS TO THE PEOPLE OF PENNSYLVANIA; CONTAINING A NARRATIVE OF THE
PROCEEDINGS AGAINST JOHN NICHOLSON, COMPTROLLER-GENERAL OF THE SAID
COMMONWEALTH.
> *Philadelphia: Printed by Francis Bailey. M.DCC.XC. pp. 56. 8vo.*

22736   NIXON, WILLIAM
AN EASY INTRODUCTION TO THE LATIN PROSODY. PRINTED FOR THE USE OF THE
COLLEGE ACADEMY.
> *Charleston, South-Carolina: Printed by T. B. Bowen? 1790, pp.16.16mo.*

22737   THE NORFOLK AND PORTSMOUTH CHRONICLE. VOL. I. NUMB. 19. SATURDAY,
JANUARY 2, [— VOL. II. NUMB. 70. SATURDAY, DECEMBER 25, 1790.]
> *[Norfolk:] Printed by Prentis & Baxter, near the Borough Tavern.*
1790. fol.

22738   NORTH CAROLINA. STATE.
JOURNAL OF THE CONVENTION OF THE STATE OF NORTH CAROLINA. AT A CON-
VENTION BEGUN AND HELD AT FAYETTEVILLE, ON THE THIRD MONDAY OF NOV-
EMBER, ONE THOUSAND SEVEN HUNDRED AND EIGHTY-NINE, AGREEABLE TO THE
RESOLUTION OF THE LAST GENERAL ASSEMBLY, BEARING DATE THE SEVENTEENTH
OF NOVEMBER, ONE THOUSAND SEVEN HUNDRED AND EIGHTY-EIGHT. . . .
[Colophon:]
> *Edenton: Printed by Hodge & Wills, Printers to the State.* [1790.] pp.16.4to.

A printed copy is with the original minutes in the Office of the Secretary of State of North Carolina. Reprinted in the State Chronicle, of
15 November, 1889.

NORTH CAROLINA, continued.

22739 —— JOURNAL OF THE HOUSE OF COMMONS. STATE OF NORTH-CAROLINA. AT A GENERAL ASSEMBLY, BEGUN AND HELD AT FAYETTEVILLE, ON THE SECOND DAY OF NOVEMBER, IN THE YEAR OF OUR LORD, ONE THOUSAND SEVEN HUNDRED AND EIGHTY-NINE, AND IN THE FOURTEENTH YEAR OF THE INDEPENDENCE OF THE UNITED STATES OF AMERICA: BEING THE FIRST SESSION OF THIS ASSEMBLY. [— 22 December, 1789.] [Colophon:]
Edenton: Printed by Hodge & Wills, Printers to the State. [1790.] pp. 71, (9). fol. LOC. NCSL.

22740 —— JOURNAL OF THE SENATE. STATE OF NORTH-CAROLINA. AT A GENERAL AS-SEMBLY, BEGUN AND HELD AT FAYETTEVILLE, ON THE SECOND DAY OF NOVEMBER, IN THE YEAR OF OUR LORD, ONE THOUSAND SEVEN HUNDRED AND EIGHTY-NINE, AND IN THE FOURTEENTH YEAR OF THE INDEPENDENCE OF THE UNITED STATES OF AMERICA: BEING THE FIRST SESSION OF THIS ASSEMBLY. [— 22 DECEMBER, 1789.]
[Edenton: Printed by Hodge and Wills, 1790.] pp. 52. fol. LOC. NCSL.

22741 —— LAWS OF NORTH-CAROLINA. AT A GENERAL ASSEMBLY, BEGUN AND HELD AT FAYETTEVILLE, ON THE SECOND DAY OF NOVEMBER, IN THE YEAR OF OUR LORD, ONE THOUSAND SEVEN HUNDRED AND EIGHTY-NINE, AND IN THE FOURTEENTH YEAR OF THE INDEPENDENCE OF THE UNITED STATES OF AMERICA: BEING THE FIRST SESSION OF THIS ASSEMBLY. [— 22 December, 1789.] [Colophon:]
Edenton: Printed by Hodge & Wills, Printers to the State. [1790.] pp. 58. fol. NCSL. NCU.

22742 THE NORTH-CAROLINA ALMANAC FOR THE YEAR 1791.
Fayetteville: Printed by George Roulstone, for John Sibley & Co., at Franklin's Head, in Green-Street. [1790.]

22743 THE NORTH-CAROLINA CHRONICLE; OR, FAYETTEVILLE GAZETTE. VOL. I. No. 19. MONDAY, JANUARY 4, [— VOL. II. No. 18. MONDAY, DECEMBER 27, 1790.]
Fayetteville: (North-Carolina) Printed by Sibley & Howard. 1790. 4to.
Before September of this year the imprint was changed to, Printed by George Roulstone, for John Sibley & Co. at Franklin's Head in Green Street.

22744 THE NORTH-CAROLINA GAZETTE. VOL. V. NUMB. 209. THURSDAY, JANUARY 7, [— NUMB. 260. THURSDAY, DECEMBER 30, 1790.]
Newbern: Printed by F. X. Martin. 1790. fol.

22745 THE NORWICH [cut] PACKET. AND THE COUNTRY JOURNAL. VOL. XVI. No. 822. FRIDAY, JANUARY 1, [—VOL. XVII. No. 875. FRIDAY, DECEMBER 24, 1790.]
Norwich: Printed by John Trumbull. 1790. fol. AAS.
February 5th, the cut of a packet was permanently dropped from the heading, which then appeared as, *The Norwich-Packet & Country Journal.* Beginning October 1st, a cut of two figures holding between them a scroll marked *Vox populi. Norwich Packet,* constituted the heading up to the issue for June 9, 1791.

22746 OBSERVATIONS ON UNIVERSAL SALVATION. [Six lines of quotation.]
New-Haven: Printed by A. Morse. M.DCC.XC. pp. 24. 12mo. AAS.

22747   OGDEN, JOHN COSENS   1755 – 1800
A SERMON, DELIVERED BEFORE HIS EXCELLENCY THE PRESIDENT, THE HONOURABLE
SENATE, AND THE HONOURABLE HOUSE OF REPRESENTATIVES, OF THE STATE OF
NEWHAMPSHIRE, AT THE ANNUAL ELECTION, HOLDEN AT CONCORD, ON THE
FIRST WEDNESDAY IN JUNE, M.DCC.XC. BY JOHN C. OGDEN, A. M. RECTOR OF
QUEEN'S CHAPEL IN PORTSMOUTH.
Printed at Concord, by George Hough, for the General Court. M.DCC.XC.
pp. 24. 8vo.   BA. BM. JCB. NYHS.

22748   O'KEEFFE, JOHN   1747 – 1833
THE POOR SOLDIER. A COMIC OPERA, OF TWO ACTS. WITH THE WORDS, SONGS,
DUETS, &C.
Philadelphia: Printed by William Spotswood, 1790.

22749   ——— —— SONGS, DUETS, ETC. IN THE POOR SOLDIER, A COMIC OPERA, AS PERFORMED
WITH UNIVERSAL APPLAUSE AT THE THEATRE, NEW YORK.
New-York: Printed for Berry and Rogers, No. 35, Hanover Square. [1790.]
pp. 24. 12mo.   HSP.

22750   ——— THE PRISONER AT LARGE: A COMEDY IN TWO ACTS. BY THE AUTHOR OF THE
POOR SOLDIER: PERFORMED WITH GREAT APPLAUSE BY THE OLD AMERICAN
COMPANY, PHILADELPHIA.
*Philadelphia: Printed and sold by Enoch Story, Second-Street, five doors
from Arch-Street, the left hand upwards.* 1790.

22751   OSBORNE'S NEW-HAMPSHIRE SPY. A FREE AND IMPARTIAL PAPER. VOL. VII. NO.
XX. SATURDAY, JANUARY 2, [—VOL. IX, NO. XIX. WEDNESDAY, DECEMBER 29,
1790.]
*Published [by George Jerry Osborne] on Wednesdays and Saturdays
- - near the State-House, [Guttemberg's [sic] Head,] Congress-Street, Portsmouth.—Twelve shillings per annum.* 1790. fol.   AAS.

22752   OTTERBEIN, JOHANN DANIEL
JESUS UND DIE KRAFT SEINES BLUTS GANZ BESONDERS VERHERRLICHET AN JOHANN-
JOST WEYGAND EINEM ARMEN SÜNDER DER EINEN MORD BEGANGEN; UND DEN 21
TEN OCTOBER, 1785. AUF DER REICHTSTÄTTE VOR BERLENBURG, MIT DEM
SCHWERD VOM LEBEN ZUM TOD GEBRACHT WORDEN. HERAUSGEGEBEN IN
ZWEY ABSCHITTEN.
*Lancaster, Gedruckt, [bey Johann Albrecht & Comp.] und zu haben in der
Neuen Buchdruckerey, zwischen der Koenig und Dranien-Strasse, in der Prinz-
Strasse,* 1790. pp. 232. 18mo.   HSP. NYPL.

22753   OVIDIUS NASO, PUBLIUS   43 B C–18 A. D.
P. OVIDII NASONIS METAMORPHOSEON LIBRI X. OR TEN SELECT BOOKS OF OVID'S
METAMORPHOSES. WITH AN ENGLISH TRANSLATION, COMPILED FROM THE TWO
FORMER TRANSLATIONS, BY DAVIDSON AND CLARKE; A PROSODY, TABLE AND REF-
ERENCES (AFTER THE MANNER OF MR. STIRLING), POINTING OUT, AT ONE VIEW,
THE SCANNING OF EACH VERSE; AND DAVIDSON'S ENGLISH NOTES.
*Philadelphia: Printed and sold by William Spotswood, Front-Street, be-
tween Market and Chesnut-Streets.* 1790. pp. (44), 328. 8vo. AAS. JCB. LOC. NYHS.

22754   PARKER, JAMES   1714 - 1770
THE CONDUCTOR GENERALIS; OR THE OFFICE, DUTY AND AUTHORITY OF JUSTICES OF
THE PEACE, HIGH-SHERIFFS, UNDER-SHERIFFS, CORONERS, CONSTABLES, GAOLERS,
JURYMEN, AND OVERSEERS OF THE POOR. AS ALSO, THE OFFICE OF CLERKS OF
ASSIZE, AND OF THE PEACE, &C. COMPILED CHIEFLY FROM BURN'S JUSTICE; AND
THE SEVERAL OTHER BOOKS ON THOSE SUBJECTS. BY JAMES PARKER, ESQUIRE,
LATE ONE OF THE JUSTICES OF THE PEACE FOR MIDDLESEX COUNTY IN NEW-
JERSEY; AND NOW REVISED AND ADAPTED TO THE UNITED STATES OF AMERICA.
BY A GENTLEMAN OF THE LAW. THE WHOLE ALPHABETICALLY DIGESTED UNDER
THE SEVERAL TITLES; WITH A TABLE, DIRECTING TO THE READY FINDING OUT THE
PROPER MATTER UNDER THOSE TITLES. TO WHICH ARE ADDED (ABOVE WHAT IS
IN ANY OTHER EDITION OF THE WORK) THE ACT CALLED THE TEN POUND ACT,
AND THE MILITIA LAW OF THE STATE OF NEW-YORK.
> *New-York: Printed by Hugh Gaine,* 1790.

22755   PAYNE, JONAS, and HEARN, PHILIP
A CATALOGUE OF BOOKS TO BE SOLD, AT PAYNE AND HEARN'S BOOK STORE ON THE
BAY, SAVANNAH, FOR CASH AND PRODUCE.
> *[Savannah: Printed by James and Nicholas Johnston,* 1790.] Broadside.
> fol.   LOC.

22756   PEDDLE, Mrs. ——
RUDIMENTS OF TASTE, IN A SERIES OF LETTERS FROM A MOTHER TO HER DAUGHTERS.
TO WHICH ARE ADDED, MAXIMS ADDRESSED TO YOUNG LADIES. BY THE COUNTESS
DOWAGER OF CARLISLE.
> *Philadelphia: Printed by William Spotswood,* MDCCXC. pp. (2), 140.
> 16mo.   JCB.

Second title: MAXIMS ADDRESSED TO YOUNG LADIES ON THEIR FIRST ESTABLISH-
MENT IN THE WORLD. BY THE COUNTESS DOWAGER OF CARLISLE.
> *Philadelphia: Printed by William Spotswood.* M,DCC,XC. pp. 85-140.

22757   PENINGTON, JOHN   1768 - 1793
CHEMICAL AND ECONOMICAL ESSAYS, DESIGNED TO ILLUSTRATE THE CONNECTION BE-
TWEEN THE THEORY AND PRACTICE OF CHEMISTRY, AND THE APPLICATION OF THAT
SCIENCE TO SOME OF THE ARTS AND MANUFACTURES OF THE UNITED STATES OF
AMERICA. BY JOHN PENINGTON. [Two lines of quotation.]
> *Philadelphia: Printed by Joseph James.* M.DCC.XC. pp. viii, 200. 8vo.
> AAS. LOC.

22758   —— AN INAUGURAL DISSERTATION, ON THE PHÆNOMENA, CAUSES, AND EFFECTS OF
FERMENTATION; SUBMITTED TO THE PROVOST, TRUSTEES, AND MEDICAL PROFESSORS
OF THE COLLEGE OF PHILADELPHIA, FOR THE DEGREE OF DOCTOR OF MEDICINE;
JUNE 1790. BY JOHN PENINGTON.
> *Philadelphia: Printed by Joseph James,* 1790. pp. 30. 8vo.   SGO.

22759   PENNSYLVANIA. STATE.
THE CONSTITUTION OF THE COMMONWEALTH OF PENNSYLVANIA. [Ornament.]
> *Philadelphia: Printed by Zachariah Poulson, junior, on the west side of*
> *Fourth-Street, between Market-Street and Arch-Street.* MDCCXC. pp. (29).
> 8vo.   JCB. LOC. NYPL.

22760   —— — THE CONSTITUTION OF THE COMMONWEALTH OF PENNSYLVANIA, AS ALTER-
ED AND AMENDED BY THE CONVENTION FOR THAT PURPOSE FREELY CHOSEN AND
ASSEMBLED, AND BY THEM PROPOSED FOR THE CONSIDERATION OF THEIR CON-
STITUENTS.
> *Philadelphia: Printed by Zachariah Poulson, junior, on the west side of*
> *Fourth-Street, between Market-Street and Arch-Street.* MDCCXC. pp. (28). 8vo.
> AAS. JCB. MHS. NYPL.

PENNSYLVANIA, continued.

22761　—— —— Der Regierungsverfassung der Republik Pennsylvanien, wie sel-
bige, von der zu dem Endzweck frey erwählten und versammelten Convention verändert und verbessert, und ihren Constituenten zur ueber-
legung vorgeleget worden. [Aus dem Englischen übersetzt.]
　　　*Philadelphia: Gedruckt bey Melchior Steiner, in der Rees-strasse zwischen
der Zweyten-und Dritten-Strasse.* 1790. pp. (2), 20, (2). 8vo.　　hc. loc.

22762　—— Laws of the fourteenth General Assembly of the Commonwealth of
Pennsylvania, enacted in the first sitting, which commenced at Phila-
delphia, on Monday the twenty sixth day of October, in the year of our
Lord, one thousand seven hundred and eighty-nine. [— 9 December, 1789.]
　　　[Philadelphia: Printed by Thomas Bradford, 1790,] pp. (205)-[232],(2).
fol.　　　　　　　　　　　　　　　　　　　　　　　　　hsp. loc.

22763　—— —— Laws of the fourteenth General Assembly of the Commonwealth
of Pennsylvania, enacted in the second sitting, which commenced at
Philadelphia, on Tuesday the second day of February, in the year of
our Lord, one thousand seven hundred and ninety. [— 6 April, 1790.]
[Colophon:]
　　　[Philadelphia: Printed by Thomas Bradford. 1790.] pp. (233)-[317.]
fol.　　　　　　　　　　　　　　　　　　　　　　　　　hsp. loc.
　　　The last session under the Constitution of 1776.

22764　—— Minutes of the Convention of the Commonwealth of Pennsylvania,
which commenced at Philadelphia, on Tuesday the twenty-fourth day of
November, in the year of our Lord, one thousand seven hundred and
eighty-nine, for the purpose of reviewing, and if they see occasion, altering and amending, the Constitution of this State.
　　　Philadelphia: Printed by Zachariah Poulson, jun . . . MDCCLXXXIX.
[1790.] pp. 146. fol.　　　　　　　　jcb. lcp. loc. nyhs.　　　$12

22765　—— —— Minutes of the second session of the Convention of the Commonwealth of Pennsylvania, which commenced at Philadelphia, on Tuesday,
the twenty-fourth day of November, in the year of our Lord, one
thousand seven hundred and eighty-nine, for the purpose of reviewing,
and if they see occasion, altering and amending, the Constitution of this
State.
　　　[Philadelphia: Printed by Zachariah Poulson, jun. 1790.] pp. 147-222.
fol.　　　　　　　　　　　　　　　　　　　lcp. loc. nyhs.

22766　—— —— Minutes of the grand committee of the whole Convention of the
Commonwealth of Pennsylvania, which commenced at Philadelphia, on
Tuesday, the twenty-fourth day of November, in the year of our Lord,
one thousand seven hundred and eighty-nine, for the purpose of
reviewing, and if they see occasion, altering and amending, the Constitution of this State.
　　　Philadelphia: Printed by Zachariah Poulson, jun. . . . [1790.] pp. 101.
fol.　　　　　　　　　　　　　　　hsp. jcb. lcp. loc. nyhs.　　　$12
　　　The Convention directed the printing of two thousand copies of the
Minutes of the Convention, and a like number of the Committee of
the whole. And Melchior Steiner, official printer in the German language, was directed to print one thousand copies of each, in that language.

22767　—— State of the accounts of fees, received by the secretary of the Supreme Executive Council, from 26th June, 1786, till the 23d January,
1790.
　　　*Philadelphia: Printed by Eleazer Oswald, in Market-Street, between Fourth
and Fifth-Streets.* M,DCC,XC. pp. [11.] 8vo.　　　　nypl.

PENNSYLVANIA, continued.

22768 —— State of the accounts of David Rittenhouse, esq. treasurer of Pennsylvania. From January 1785, till January 1786. [Ornament.]
Philadelphia: Printed by Eleazer Oswald, No. 156, *Market-Street, between Fourth and Fifth-Streets.* M,DCC,XC. pp. [52.] 8vo.   NYPL.

22769 —— State of the account of David Rittenhouse, esq. treasurer of the Commonwealth of Pennsylvania: from January, 1786, till January, 1787.
Philadelphia: Printed by Francis Bailey, at Yorick's Head, in Market-Street. MDCCXC. pp. (64). 8vo.   NYPL.

22770 —— State of the accounts of David Rittenhouse, esq. treasurer of Pennsylvania, from 1st November, 1787. Including his Continental and State money accounts for the year 1786.
Philadelphia: Printed by R. Aitken & Son, No. 22, *Market Street.* M.-DCC.XC. pp. (70). 8vo.   NYPL.

22771 —— Accounts of the taxes of Chester County. [Ornament.]
Philadelphia: Printed by Francis Bailey, at Yorick's-Head, in Market-street. M,DCC,XC. pp. [35.] 8vo.   NYPL.

22772 —— State of the accounts of Andrew Forrest, collector, of Dauphin County, April, 1785, to August, 1787.
Philadelphia: Printed by Robert Aitken & Son? 1790.

22773 —— State of the accounts of E. Douglas, treasurer of Fayette County, 1785 – 1790.
Philadelphia: Printed by R. Aitken & Son. 1790. pp. 5. 8vo.

22774 —— State of the accounts of George Clingan, esquire, treasurer, of Franklin County, from the time the County was erected until 1st June, 1788.
Philadelphia: Printed by R. Aitken & Son, in Market Street. M.DCC.XC. pp. 12. 8vo.   AAS.

22775 —— Accounts of the taxes of Huntingdon County.
Philadelphia: Printed by Eleazer Oswald, 1790. pp. 4. 8vo.

22776 —— State of the accounts of J. Auld, collector, of Montgomery County, September, 1787—April, 1789.
Philadelphia: Printed by Robert Aitken & Son? 1790. pp. 9. 8vo.

22777 —— State of the account of the taxes of Northampton County.
Philadelphia: Printed by Francis Bailey, at Yorick's-Head, No. 116, *Market-Street* M,DCC,XC. pp. (88). 8vo.   NYPL.

22778 —— State of the account of the taxes of Washington County. [Ornament.]
Philadelphia: Printed by Francis Bailey, at Yorick's Head, in Market-Street. M,DCC,XC. pp. [6.] 8vo.   NYPL.

22779 —— Tagebuch der General Assembly der Republik Pennsylvanien. 1789 – 1790. (Officielle Deutsche Uebersetzung.)
Germantaun: Gedruckt bey Michael Billmeyer, 1790.

22780 THE PENNSYLVANIA Gazette. Numb. 3110. Wednesday, January 6, [—Numb. 3161. Wednesday, December 29, 1790.]
Philadelphia: Printed by Hall & Sellers, at the New-Printing-Office, near the Market. 1790. fol.   AAS. LOC. NYPL.

22781   THE PENNSYLVANIA HERALD, AND YORK GENERAL ADVERTISER. VOL. I. NO. 1.
WEDNESDAY, JANUARY 21, 1789, [—VOL. II. NO. 50. TOTAL NO. 102. WEDNES-
DAY, DECEMBER 29, 1790.]
> *York: Printed every Wednesday, by John Edie.* 1789-1790. fol.

Established by John Edie, and continued by him certainly to the end
of the seventh volume, in February, 1796.

22782   THE PENNSYLVANIA [cut] JOURNAL, AND THE WEEKLY ADVERTISER. PUBLISHED
EVERY WEDNESDAY.—PRICE FOUR-PENCE. NO. 2390. WEDNESDAY, JANUARY 6,
[—NO. 24084 [*sic*] WEDNESDAY, DECEMBER 29, 1790.]
> *Philadelphia: Printed by Thomas Bradford, . . . at his Printing-Office,*
Laetitia-Court. 1790. fol.   **AAS.**

22783   THE PENNSYLVANIA MERCURY AND UNIVERSAL ADVERTISER. NUMB. 491. SAT-
URDAY, JANUARY 2, [—NUMB. 646. THURSDAY, DECEMBER 30, 1790.]
> *Philadelphia: Printed (on Tuesdays, Thursdays and Saturdays) by Daniel*
Humphreys, at the new Printing-Office in Front-Street, near the Drawbridge, . .
1790. 4to.   **AAS.**

22784   THE PENNSYLVANIA PACKET, AND DAILY ADVERTISER. NO. 3408. FRIDAY, JAN-
UARY 1, [—NO. 3719. FRIDAY, DECEMBER 31, 1790.]
> *Philadelphia: Printed and sold by John Dunlap and David C. Claypoole;*
on the south side of Market-Street, the third house east of Second-Street, 1790. fol.
     AAS. LCP. LOC.

Continued as, *Dunlap's American Daily Advertiser.* In the issue of
December 7th, Claypoole announces the dissolution of partnership on
January 1, 1791; and that he proposes to publish a newspaper (every
evening, Sundays excepted) to be called: The Mail, and new daily advertiser.

22785   THE PENNSYLVANIA POCKET ALMANAC FOR THE YEAR OF OUR LORD, 1791.
> *Philadelphia: Printed by Francis Bailey, No. 116, Market-Street.* [1790.]

22786   PERKINS, NATHAN   1748 – 1838
A SERMON, DELIVERED AT THE ORDINATION OF THE REV. HEZEKIAH N. WOODRUFF,
TO THE PASTORAL OFFICE OVER THE FIRST CHURCH OF CHRIST IN STONINGTON,
JULY 2, 1789. BY NATHAN PERKINS, A. M. PASTOR OF A CHURCH OF CHRIST
IN HARTFORD.
> *New-London: Printed by T. Green & Son.* M,DCC,XC. pp. [30.] 8vo.
     AAS. JCB. LOC. MHS.

22787   A PERPETUAL ALMANACK.
> *Richmond: Printed and sold by Aug. Davis,* 1790.

22788   PERRY, R.
A POEM ON THE DESTRUCTION OF SODOM, BY FIRE; OR THE DAY OF JUDGMENT.
TRANSCRIBED BY R. PERRY.
> *Middletown: Printed by M. H. Woodward.* [1790.] pp. 32. 16mo.

22789   PERRY, WILLIAM
THE ONLY SURE GUIDE TO THE ENGLISH TONGUE: OR, NEW PRONOUNCING SPELLING
BOOK. UPON THE SAME PLAN AS PERRY'S ROYAL STANDARD ENGLISH
DICTIONARY, NOW MADE USE OF IN ALL THE CELEBRATED SCHOOLS IN GREAT-
BRITAIN, IRELAND AND AMERICA. . . .
> *Boston: Printed by Nathaniel Coverly, for Robert Bailey Thomas, at Ster-*
ling, 1790.

An edition of one thousand copies was printed.

22790

PERRY, WILLIAM, continued.

—— — THE ONLY SURE GUIDE TO THE ENGLISH TONGUE: OR, NEW PRONOUNCING SPELLING BOOK. UPON THE SAME PLAN AS PERRY'S ROYAL STANDARD ENGLISH DICTIONARY, NOW MADE USE OF IN ALL THE CELEBRATED SCHOOLS IN GREATBRITAIN, IRELAND AND AMERICA. TO WHICH IS ADDED, A GRAMMAR OF THE ENGLISH LANGUAGE; AND, A SELECT NUMBER OF MORAL TALES AND FABLES, FOR THE INSTRUCTION OF YOUTH. WITH AN APPENDIX. CONTAINING, DIRECTIONS FOR THE DIFFERENT SOUNDS OF THE CONSONANTS BEFORE ALL THE VOWELS, WITH EVERY EXCEPTION THAT IS TO BE MET WITH IN OUR LANGUAGE, FROM SUCH GENERAL RULES: ALSO, A COMPLETE LIST OF ALL THE WORDS IN WHICH E FINAL DOES NOT LENGTHEN THE SYLLABLE: LIKEWISE, SEVERAL VALUABLE APHORISMS RESPECTING THE SOUNDS OF THE VOWELS IN THE LAST SYLLABLE OF WORDS ENDING WITH E. AND, A COMPLETE LIST OF ALL THE WORDS IN THE ENGLISH LANGUAGE, WHICH, THOUGH WRITTEN DIFFERENTLY HAVE A SIMILARITY OF SOUND. OF THOSE SUBSTANTIVES AND VERBS, OF THE SAME ORTHOGRAPHY, BUT OF A DIFFERENT ACCENT. OF THOSE SUBSTANTIVES AND VERBS ALIKE IN ORTHOGRAPHY, BUT DIFFERENTLY ACCENTED. OF THE SUBSTANTIVES AND ADJECTIVES CHANGING THE SEAT OF THE ACCENT. BY W. PERRY, LECTURER ON THE ENGLISH LANGUAGE, IN THE ACADEMY, EDINBURGH. FIFTH WORCESTER EDITION. ILLUSTRATED WITH CUTS. CAREFULLY REVISED BY PERRY'S ROYAL STANDARD ENGLISH DICTIONARY. BY ISAIAH THOMAS, AND CORRECTED OF THE NUMEROUS ERRORS, WHICH ARE IN ALL OTHER EDITIONS BOTH BRITISH AND AMERICAN.

Printed at Worcester, Massachusetts, by Isaiah Thomas. Sold wholesale and retail, at his Bookstore in Worcester, and by him and Company in Boston. MDCCXC. pp. 180, frontispiece. 12mo. AAS.

22791

PHILADELPHIA. PENNSYLVANIA.
THE CONSTITUTION AND ORDINANCES OF THE CITY OF PHILADELPHIA.
Philadelphia: Printed by Hall & Sellers. MDCCXC. pp. xxxii, 87. 12mo. NYHS.

22792

PHILADELPHIA. PENNSYLVANIA. BAPTIST ASSOCIATION.
MINUTES OF THE PHILADELPHIA BAPTIST ASSOCIATION. HELD AT NEW-YORK, OCTOBER 5TH, 6TH, AND 7TH, 1790.
[New-York: Printed by William Durell, No. 198, Queen-Street. 1790.] pp. [13], (1), (1). 4to. AAS. BU.
In addition to the annual Circular letter, by Benjamin Foster, there is a Circular letter on universal salvation, by Samuel Jones.

22793

PHILADELPHIA. PENNSYLVANIA. CHRIST CHURCH.
AN ACCOUNT OF THE BIRTHS AND BURIALS IN THE UNITED CHURCHES OF CHRISTCHURCH AND ST. PETER'S, FROM DECEMBER 24, 1789, TO DECEMBER 24, 1790.
[Philadelphia: 1790.] Broadside. fol.

22794

PHILADELPHIA. PENNSYLVANIA. COLLEGE OF PHYSICIANS.
THE CHARTER, CONSTITUTION, AND BYE-LAWS, OF THE COLLEGE OF PHYSICIANS OF PHILADELPHIA.
Philadelphia: Printed by Zachariah Poulson, jun. 1790. pp. 15. 8vo. BM. MHS. SGO.

22795

PHILADELPHIA. PENNSYLVANIA. PENNSYLVANIA HOSPITAL.
A CATALOGUE OF THE BOOKS BELONGING TO THE MEDICAL LIBRARY IN THE PENNSYLVANIA HOSPITAL. TO WHICH ARE PREFIXED THE RULES TO BE OBSERVED IN THE USE OF THEM.
Philadelphia: Printed by Zachariah Poulson, jun. 1790. pp. 35. 8vo. BM, JCB. LOC. SGO.
Reprinted, with additions, in 1794.

22796   PHILADELPHIA. SOCIETY FOR ALLEVIATING THE MISERIES OF PUBLIC PRISONS. EXTRACTS AND REMARKS ON THE SUBJECT OF PUNISHMENT AND REFORMATION OF CRIMINALS. PUBLISHED BY ORDER OF THE SOCIETY, ESTABLISHED IN PHILADELPHIA, FOR ALLEVIATING THE MISERIES OF PUBLIC PRISONS. [Dated, Philadelphia, February 25, 1790.]
    Philadelphia: Printed by Zachariah Poulson, junior, in Fourth Street, near Market-Street, opposite the gate of the Friends' Burying ground. [1790.] pp. 108, folded chart. 8vo.   AAS. BM. JCB. LOC.

22797   PHILADELPHIA. PENNSYLVANIA. ZION'S CHURCH. LOB UND ANBETUNG DES GOTTMENSCHEN AM TAGE DER EINWEIHUNG EINER NEUEN ORGEL AM 10 OCTOBER 1790.
    Germantaun: Gedruckt bey Michael Billmeyer, 1790.
    The dedication sermon was preached by the pastor, Rev. Justus Heinrich Christian Helmuth.

22798   PHILADELPHIA. COLLEGE OF, now UNIVERSITY OF PENNSYLVANIA. AN EXERCISE, PERFORMED AT THE PUBLIC COMMENCEMENT, IN THE COLLEGE OF PHILADELPHIA, JULY 17, 1790. CONTAINING AN ODE, SET TO MUSIC, SACRED TO THE MEMORY OF DR. FRANKLIN.
    Philadelphia: Printed, and sold by William Young, M,DCC,XC. pp. 11. 12mo.   BA.

22799   PHILADELPHIA JEST BOOK, AND CHEERFUL WITTY COMPANION. BEING A CHOICE COLLECTION OF THE MOST HUMOROUS AND DIVERTING JESTS, STORIES, ANECDOTES, BON-MOTS, REPARTEES, NEW SONGS, AND A CURIOUS VARIETY OF TOASTS, SENTIMENT AND HOB-NOBS.
    Philadelphia: Printed and sold by William Woodhouse, 1790.

22800   PINKNEY, WILLIAM   1764 – 1822
  SPEECH OF WILLIAM PINKNEY, ESQ. IN THE HOUSE OF DELEGATES OF MARYLAND, AT THEIR SESSION IN NOVEMBER, 1789. [On slavery and the slave trade.]
    Philadelphia: Printed by Joseph Crukshank, in Market-Street, between Second and Third-Streets. MDCCXC. pp. (22). 8vo. BM. JCB. LOC. MHS. NYHS.

22801   PITKIN, TIMOTHY   1766 – 1847
  A SERMON, PREACHED AT NEW-CAMBRIDGE, IN BRISTOL, FEBRUARY 12TH, 1789, AT THE FUNERAL OF THE REV. SAMUEL NEWELL, PASTOR OF THE CHURCH THERE. WHO DEPARTED THIS LIFE THE 10TH OF FEBRUARY, 1789, IN THE 75TH YEAR OF HIS AGE, AND 42D OF HIS MINISTRY. BY TIMOTHY PITKIN, A. M. [Two lines from Young's Night thoughts.]
    Hartford: Printed by Hudson and Goodwin. M.DCC.XC. pp. 20. 8vo.   BM. CHS. JCB. UTS. YC.

22802   THE PITTSBURGH [cut] GAZETTE. VOL. IV. NO. CLXXX. SATURDAY, JANUARY 2, [—No. 225? SATURDAY, DECEMBER 25, 1790.]
    Pittsburgh: Printed and sold by John Scull, at his Printing-Office in Water Street, near Comsby's Ferry, . . . 1790. fol.

22803   A POCKET ALMANAC, FOR 1791: CONTAINING (BESIDES THE ASTRONOMICAL CALCULATIONS) A VARIETY OF USEFUL LISTS AND TABLES.
    Philadelphia: Printed and sold by John M'Culloch, in Third Street, No. 1, above Market Street. [1790.]

22804   A POCKET MAP OF THE STATE OF PENNSYLVANIA.
    Philadelphia: Printed by William Spotswood, 1790. 11x21.   HC. LOC.
  Re-published from The Columbian Magazine, for 1788.

22805 | PÖLLNITZ, F. C. H. B.
ESSAY ON AGRICULTURE. BY F. C. H. B. POELLNITZ.
New-York: Printed by Francis Childs and John Swaine, MDCCXC. pp. 24, 4 folded plates. 8vo.
BA.

22806 | A POETICAL EPISTLE TO THE ENSLAVED AFRICANS, IN THE CHARACTER OF AN ANCIENT NEGRO, BORN A SLAVE IN PENNSYLVANIA; BUT LIBERATED SOME YEARS SINCE AND INSTRUCTED IN USEFUL LEARNING, AND THE GREAT TRUTHS OF CHRISTIANITY. WITH A BRIEF HISTORICAL INTRODUCTION AND BIOGRAPHICAL NOTICES OF SOME OF THE EARLIEST ADVOCATES FOR THAT OPPRESSED CLASS OF OUR FELLOW-CREATURES. . . .
Philadelphia: Printed by Joseph Crukshank. MDCCXC. pp. 24. 12mo.
BA. BU. JCB.

22807 | THE POLITICAL AND SENTIMENTAL REPOSITORY, OR STRAFFORD REGISTER. VOL. I. No. 1. MONDAY, JULY 12, [—No. 25. MONDAY, DECEMBER 27, 1790.]
Dover: Printed by Eliphalet Ladd. 1790. fol.
Established by Eliphalet Ladd. In a few months the title was changed to, *The Political Repository and Strafford Recorder,* under which name it was continued to January 11, 1792. On January 14th, the Printing Office was destroyed by fire, and beginning with January 25, 1792, Ladd established, with a continuous numbering, *The Pheniz,* which he continued to March, 1794, when he sold his interests to Samuel Bragg, junior, who continued publication to 29 August, 1795, when it was discontinued. Beginning 5 September, 1795, Bragg established in continuation, with a new numbering, *The Sun,* changing this title in November to, *The Sun, Dover Gazette, and County Advertiser,* under which he continued publication into December 1811, when the Printing Office was completely destroyed by fire. Bragg, himself, dying soon after, in the same month. Beginning 4 July, 1812, John Mann resurrected publication, as, *The Dover Sun,* and continued it under this title to 18 August, 1818, at which date he changed the name to *The Strafford Register,* under which it was published to 17 December, 1822, when he again altered its title to, *The New-Hampshire Republican,* which was continued up to 30 October, 1829, when publication ceased.

22808 | POOR ROBIN, pseudonym.
POOR ROBIN ALMANACK & THE MARYLAND EPHEMERIS FOR THE YEAR OF OUR LORD 1790.
George-Town: Printed by Charles Fierer. [1789.]

22809 | POPE, ALEXANDER 1688 – 1744
AN ESSAY ON MAN, IN FOUR EPISTLES: TO HENRY ST. JOHN LORD BOLINGBROKE. BY ALEXANDER POPE, ESQ.
Lansingburgh: Printed by Babcock & Hickok. MDCCLXL [1790.] pp. 44. 16mo.
AAS.

22810 | —— — AN ESSAY ON MAN: [Four lines.] TO WHICH IS ADDED, THE UNIVERSAL PRAYER. BY ALEXANDER POPE, ESQ.
Printed at Worcester, Massachusetts: by Isaiah Thomas, MDCCXC. pp. 48. 12mo.
AAS. JCB.

22811 | THE POTOWMAC GUARDIAN, AND BERKELEY ADVERTISER. VOL. I. NUMBER 1. MONDAY, NOVEMBER 22, [—NUMBER 6. MONDAY, DECEMBER 27, 1790.]
Martinsburg, Virginia: Printed and published every Monday, by N. Willis, at his Printing-Office, in Burke-Street, near the Court-House. 1790. fol.
Established by Nathaniel Willis, and continued by him into the year 1796.

22812 THE POUGHKEEPSIE JOURNAL. VOL. V. NUMB. 231. TUESDAY, JANUARY 5, [— NUMB. 282. SATURDAY, DECEMBER 25, 1790.]
> *Poughkeepsie, Dutchess County: Printed by Nicholas Power, near the Court-House.* 1790. fol.   AAS.
> In the issue for September 25th, announcement is made that "It is the intention of the printer to carry on his business more extensively than merely publishing a news-paper, if possible—therefore begs all persons indebted to make a settlement by the second Tuesday in October, (Court week)."

22813 POWER, ALEXANDER
COPY OF A PETITION WITH SOME OBSERVATIONS, AND A STATEMENT OF FACTS, RELATIVE TO THE CLAIM OF THE OFFICERS OF THE ARTILLERY ARTIFICERS, UNDER THE COMMAND OF THE LATE COLONEL BENJAMIN FLOWER; WHEREBY IS PROVED, THAT THE SAID OFFICERS ARE ENTITLED TO HALF-PAY AND COMMUTATION. ALEXANDER POWER, FOR HIMSELF, AND AS ATTORNEY IN FACT FOR SAID OFFICERS.
> *[Philadelphia: June 10, 1790.]* pp. (12). 4to.   LOC.

22814 PRICE, RICHARD   1723 – 1791
A DISCOURSE ON THE LOVE OF OUR COUNTRY, DELIVERED ON NOV. 4, 1789, AT THE MEETING-HOUSE IN THE OLD JEWRY, TO THE SOCIETY FOR COMMEMORATING THE REVOLUTION IN GREAT BRITAIN. BY RICHARD PRICE, D. D. LL. D. F. R. S. AND FELLOW OF THE AMERICAN PHILOSOPHICAL SOCIETIES AT PHILADELPHIA AND BOSTON.
> *London, Printed: Boston, Reprinted: by Edward E. Powars, Court Street.*
> M.DCC.XC. pp. 40. 8vo.   AAS. BA. BM. JCB.

22815 PRICHARD, WILLIAM
CATALOGUE OF A SALE OF BOOKS, BY AUCTION, WILL COMMENCE TOMORROW EVENING, THE 18TH [MARCH,] INSTANT, AT THE STORE WHERE THE POST-OFFICE WAS LATELY KEPT, IN CHESNUT-STREET, A FEW DOORS ABOVE FRONT-STREET.
> *Philadelphia: Printed for William Prichard,* 1790.
> William Prichard also advertised auction sales of books, on March 25th, the Library of the late Rev'd Dr. Duffield; and on March 31, 1790.

22816 PRINCE, WILLIAM   1766 – 1842
TO BE SOLD, BY WILLIAM PRINCE, AT FLUSHING LANDING, ON LONG-ISLAND, NEAR NEW-YORK, A LARGE COLLECTION, AS FOLLOW, OF FRUIT TREES AND SHRUBS. . . . [Colophon:]
> *New-York, October,* 1790. . . . *Printed by Hugh Gaine, at the Bible, in Hanover-Square.* Broadside. fol.   LCP. LOC.

22817 THE PRODIGAL DAUGHTER.
> *Stockbridge (Massachusetts). Printed and sold by Loring Andrews.* 1790.

22818 PROTESTANT EPISCOPAL CHURCH IN MASSACHUSETTS.
AT A CONVENTION OF CLERGY AND LAY-DEPUTIES OF THE PROTESTANT EPISCOPAL CHURCHES HEREAFTER NAMED, HOLDEN AT SALEM, IN THE COUNTY OF ESSEX, AND COMMONWEALTH OF MASSACHUSETTS, OCTOBER THE FIFTH AND SIXTH, 1790, VIZ. ST. PAUL'S CHURCH, NEWBURYPORT, CHRIST-CHURCH, BOSTON, ST. THOMAS' CHURCH, TAUNTON, ST. ANDREW'S CHURCH, SCITUATE, TRINITY CHURCH, MARSHFIELD, ST. PETER'S CHURCH, SALEM, TRINITY CHURCH, BOSTON, ST. MICHAEL'S CHURCH, MARBLEHEAD, IN THE COMMONWEALTH OF MASSACHUSETTS, AND QUEEN'S CHAPEL, PORTSMOUTH, IN THE STATE OF NEW-HAMPSHIRE. A PLAN OF AN ECCLESIASTICAL CONSTITUTION WAS READ, AND CONSIDERED BY PARAGRAPHS, AND, AFTER SUNDRY AMENDMENTS, WAS UNANIMOUSLY APPROVED, AND IS AS FOLLOWS, VIZ.——AN ECCLESIASTICAL CONSTITUTION FOR THE GOVERNMENT OF THE EPISCOPAL CHURCHES IN THIS COMMON-WEALTH, AND SUCH OTHER CHURCHES AS MAY BE ADMITTED AND ACCEDE TO THE SAME. . . . [Colophon:]
> *Printed by John Mycall in Newburyport.* [1790.] Broadside. fol. AAS. JCB.
> Reproduced, in facsimile, in Currier's History of Newburyport.

AUCTION
VALUES

22819   PROTESTANT EPISCOPAL CHURCH IN PENNSYLVANIA.
JOURNAL OF THE MEETINGS, WHICH LED TO THE INSTITUTION OF A CONVENTION OF
THE PROTESTANT EPISCOPAL CHURCH IN THE STATE OF PENNSYLVANIA: WITH
JOURNALS OF THE FIRST SIX CONVENTIONS.
Philadelphia: Printed by Hall & Sellers. 1790. pp. 26. 8vo.   MHS.

22820   PROTESTANT EPISCOPAL CHURCH IN THE CAROLINAS.
A PASTORAL LETTER FROM THE SYNOD OF THE CAROLINAS TO THE CHURCHES UNDER
THEIR CARE.
Fayetteville: Printed by Sibley & Howard. 1790.

22821   PROTESTANT EPISCOPAL CHURCH IN THE UNITED STATES OF AMERICA.
THE BOOK OF COMMON PRAYER, AND ADMINISTRATION OF THE SACRAMENTS, AND
OTHER RITES AND CEREMONIES OF THE CHURCH, ACCORDING TO THE USE OF THE
PROTESTANT EPISCOPAL CHURCH IN THE UNITED STATES OF AMERICA: TOGETHER
WITH THE PSALTER, OR PSALMS OF DAVID.
Philadelphia: Printed by Hall & Sellers, in Market-Street. MDCCXC.
pp. [327.] 8vo.   AAS. BM. JCB. LCP. LOC.
The first standard Prayer Book for the use of the Protestant Episcopal
Church in the United States. Ratified 16 October, 1789. In general
use 1 October, 1790. 6th Pennsylvania District Copyright, issued to
William Hall, as Proprietor, 7 August. 1790.

$80

22822   —— JOURNAL OF THE PROCEEDINGS OF THE BISHOPS, CLERGY AND LAITY OF THE
PROTESTANT EPISCOPAL CHURCH IN THE UNITED STATES OF AMERICA, IN A CON-
VENTION HELD IN THE CITY OF PHILADELPHIA, FROM . . . SEPTEMBER 29TH,
TO . . . OCTOBER 16TH, ONE THOUSAND SEVEN HUNDRED AND EIGHTY-NINE.
Philadelphia: Printed by Hall and Sellers. M,DCC,XC. pp. 43. 8vo.
AAS. BA. HC. JCB. MHS.

22823   PROUDFIT, JACOB
DE PLEURITIDE VERA.
Philadelphiæ, Impensis R. Aitken et fil. 1790. pp. 29. 8vo.   SGO.

22824   PROVIDENCE. RHODE ISLAND.
[ORDER OF PROCESSION] TO BE OBSERVED ON THE ARRIVAL OF THE PRESIDENT
OF THE UNITED STATES. [Forty-eight lines.]
Providence, [Printed by John Carter.]August 17,1790.Broadside.fol. RIHS.

22825   PROVIDENCE, MARCH 31, 1790. GENTLEMEN, NO PROX FOR THE GENERAL OFFICERS
OF THIS STATE FOR THE YEAR ENSUING HAVING BEEN RECOMMENDED TO THE GOV-
ERNOR, AGREEABLE TO THE CUSTOM OF FORMER TIMES, [Calling a meeting to
prepare a nomination-list] AT THE COURT-HOUSE IN EAST-GREENWICH, ON
TUESDAY, THE SIXTH OF APRIL NEXT, AT TWO O'CLOCK, P. M. WE REMAIN YOUR
MOST HUMBLE SERVANTS, JOHN BROWN, [and four others.]
[Providence: Printed by John Carter? 1790.] Broadside. 4to.   RIHS.

22826   THE PROVIDENCE GAZETTE AND COUNTRY JOURNAL. NO. 1. OF VOL. XXVII. NO.
1357. SATURDAY, JANUARY 2, [—NO. 52 OF VOL. XXVII. NO, 1408. SATURDAY,
DECEMBER 25, 1790.]
*[Providence:] Published by John Carter, at the Post-Office, near the State-
House.* 1790. fol.   AAS. JCB. NYPL. RIHS.

22827   RALLING, JOHN
MISCELLANIES. I. THE TIME-PIECE; OR, AN HONEST SERVANT INSTRUCTING HIS
MASTER IN A LESSON OF THE GREATEST WEIGHT AND IMPORTANCE. II. A HYMN
ON THE MONTH OF MAY, WITH AN ATTEMPT TO ILLUSTRATE SOME OF THE BEAU-
TIES OF THE CREATION. III. AN AFFECTIONATE AND DYING FATHER'S LAST
WORDS; WITH HIS SINCERE AND GODLY ADVICE TO HIS CHILDREN.
Philadelphia: Printed for the Author, by John M'Culloch, M,DCC,XC.
pp. 24. 12mo.   AAS. BU. LCP.

22828   RAMSAY, David   1749 – 1815
A DISSERTATION ON THE MEANS OF PRESERVING HEALTH IN CHARLESTON, AND THE ADJACENT LOW COUNTRY. READ BEFORE THE MEDICAL SOCIETY OF SOUTH CAROLINA, ON THE 29TH OF MAY, 1790.
Charleston: Printed by Markland & McIver, 1790. pp. 32. 8vo. HC. SGO.

22829   READ, Daniel   1757 – 1841
AN INTRODUCTION TO PSALMODY; OR, THE CHILDS INSTRUCTOR IN VOCAL MUSIC. CONTAINING A SERIES OF FAMILIAR DIALOGUES, UNDER THE FOLLOWING HEADS, VIZ. PSALMODY IN GENERAL, STAVE, MUSICAL LETTERS AND CLIFFS, AN EXERCISE FOR THE BASS, AN EXERCISE FOR THE TENOR OR TREBLE, AN EXERCISE FOR THE COUNTER, TONES, SEMITONES, FLATS, SHARPS AND NATURAL, SOLFAING, TRANSPOSITION, &C. THE SEVERAL NOTES AND RESTS, AND THEIR PROPORTION, THE SEVERAL MOODS OF TIME, SEVERAL OTHER CHARACTERS USED IN MUSIC, KEY NOTES, &C. PITCHING TUNES &C. GRACES. (ILLUSTRATED WITH COPPER-PLATES.) BY D. READ. [Two lines from] WATTS.
Printed [by T. and S. Green] for, and sold by the Author, in New-Haven. 1790.

22830   REFORMED (German) CHURCH.
CATECHISMUS, ODER KURZER UNTERRICHT DER CHRISTLICHEN LEHRE FÜR DIE ANGEHENDE JUGEND IN DER CHURFÜRSTLICHEN PFALZ UND ANDERN REFORMIRTEN ORTEN ZU GEBRAUCHEN: SAMT DER HAUS-TAFEL, MIT UND OHNE BIBLISCHEN SPRÜCH-BUCHLEIN. . . .
Philadelphia: Gedruckt bey Carl Cist. 1790. pp. 124. 16mo.   LOC.

22831   THE RELIGIOUS TRADESMAN; OR PLAIN AND SERIOUS HINTS OF ADVICE FOR THE TRADESMAN'S PRUDENT AND PIOUS CONDUCT, FROM HIS ENTRANCE INTO BUSINESS TO LEAVING IT OFF.
Newbury Port: Printed by John Mycall. 1790. pp. 280. 16mo.

22832   REMARKS ON THE MANUFACTURING OF MAPLE SUGAR; WITH DIRECTIONS FOR ITS FURTHER IMPROVEMENT. COLLECTED BY A SOCIETY OF GENTLEMEN, IN PHILADELPHIA, AND PUBLISHED FOR THE GENERAL INFORMATION AND BENEFIT OF THE CITIZENS OF THE UNITED STATES.
Philadelphia: Printed by James & Johnson, M,DCC,XC. pp. 24. 12mo.
BM. JCB.

22833   REMARKS ON THE REPORT OF THE SECRETARY OF THE TREASURY TO THE HOUSE OF REPRESENTATIVES OF THE UNITED STATES. BY A FRIEND TO THE PUBLIC.
Printed, May, A. D. 1790. pp. 31. 8vo.   JCB. LOC. NYPL.

22834   THE RETURNED CAPTIVE. A POEM, FOUNDED ON A LATE FACT.
Norwich: Reprinted by John Trumbull. 1790.

22835   RHODE ISLAND. STATE.
JANUARY, 1790. AT THE GENERAL ASSEMBLY OF THE GOVERNOR AND COMPANY OF THE STATE OF RHODE-ISLAND AND PROVIDENCE-PLANTATIONS, BEGUN AND HELD, BY ADJOURNMENT, AT PROVIDENCE, WITHIN AND FOR THE STATE AFORESAID, ON THE SECOND MONDAY IN JANUARY, IN THE YEAR OF OUR LORD ONE THOUSAND SEVEN HUNDRED AND NINETY, AND IN THE FOURTEENTH YEAR OF INDEPENDENCE. [Colophon:]
[Providence:] Printed by John Carter. [1790.] pp. 16. fol. HSP. JCB. LOC.

22836   —— — MAY, 1790. AT THE GENERAL ASSEMBLY OF THE GOVERNOR AND COMPANY OF THE STATE OF RHODE-ISLAND AND PROVIDENCE-PLANTATIONS, BEGUN AND HOLDEN AT NEWPORT, WITHIN AND FOR THE STATE AFORESAID, ON THE FIRST WEDNESDAY IN MAY, IN THE YEAR OF OUR LORD ONE THOUSAND SEVEN HUNDRED AND NINETY, AND IN THE FOURTEENTH YEAR OF INDEPENDENCE. [Colophon:]
[Providence:] Printed by John Carter. [1790.] pp. 22. fol. HSP. JCB. LOC.

RHODE ISLAND, continued.

22837 — — June, 1790. At the General Assembly of the governor and company of the State of Rhode-Island and Providence-Plantations, begun and held by adjournment at Newport, within and for the State aforesaid, in consequence of warrants issued by his excellency the governor, on Monday the seventh day of June, in the year of our Lord one thousand seven hundred and ninety, and in the fourteenth year of independence.
[Providence: Printed by John Carter, 1790.] pp. 16. fol.   HSP. JCB. LOC.

22838 — — September, 1790. At the General Assembly of the governor and company of the State of Rhode-Island and Providence-Plantations, begun and held by adjournment at Bristol, within and for the State aforesaid, on the first Monday in September, in the year of our Lord one thousand seven hundred and ninety, and in the fifteenth year of independence. [Colophon:]
[Providence:] Printed by J. Carter. [1790.] pp. 20. fol.   JCB. LOC.

22839 — — October, 1790. At the General Assembly of the governor and company of the State of Rhode-Island and Providence-Plantations, begun and held at Providence, within and for the State aforesaid on the last Monday in October, in the year of our Lord, one thousand seven hundred and ninety, and in the fifteenth year of independence. [Colophon:]
[Providence:] Printed by J. Carter. [1790.] pp. 20. fol.   HSP. JCB. LOC.

22840 — — State of Rhode-Island and Providence - Plantations. In General Assembly. January session a. d. 1790. An Act for calling a convention, to take into consideration the Constitution proposed for the United States, passed on the 17th of September, a. d. 1787, by the general convention held at Philadelphia. [Thirty-one lines.] A true copy: witness, Henry Ward, sec'ry. [Colophon:]
[Providence:] Printed by J. Carter. [1790.] Broadside. fol.   LOC. RIHS.

22841 — — State of Rhode-Island and Providence-Plantations. In General Assembly. June session, a. d. 1790. An Act prescribing the mode of electing senators, and a representative, to represent this State in the Congress of the United States of America, and the times and places of holding the elections. [Two columns.] A true copy: witness, Henry Ward, sec'ry. [Colophon:]
[Providence:] Printed by J. Carter. [1790.] Broadside. fol.   RIHS.

22842 — — State of Rhode-Island and Providence-Plantations. In General Assembly. June session, 1790. An Act to incorporate certain persons by the name of the Providence Society for promoting the abolition of slavery, for the relief of persons unlawfully held in bondage, and for improving the conditions of the African race. [Colophon:]
[Providence:] Printed by J. Carter. [1790.] pp. 4. fol.   RIHS.

22843 — — State of Rhode-Island and Providence-Plantations. In General Assembly. September session, a. d. 1790. It is voted and resolved, That a Representative, qualified agreeably to the Constitution of the United States, to represent this State, in the Congress of the United States, for two years next following the third day of March next, be elected by the freemen of this State, in town-meetings legally assembled, on the third Monday in October next: [Nine lines.] A true copy: witness, Henry Ward, sec'ry. [Colophon:]
[Providence:] Printed by J. Carter. [1790.] Broadside. 4to.   RIHS.

RHODE ISLAND, continued.

22844   —— BY HIS EXCELLENCY ARTHUR FENNER, ESQ, GOVERNOR, CAPTAIN-GENERAL, AND COMMANDER IN CHIEF, OF AND OVER THE STATE OF RHODE-ISLAND AND PROVIDENCE-PLANTATIONS. A PROCLAMATION. WHEREAS THE SIXTH ARTICLE OF THE CONSTITUTION OF THE UNITED STATES OF AMERICA REQUIRES, THAT "THE MEMBERS OF THE SEVERAL STATE LEGISLATURES, AND ALL EXECUTIVE AND JUDICIAL OFFICERS, BOTH OF THE UNITED STATES AND OF THE SEVERAL STATES, SHALL BE BOUND BY OATH OR AFFIRMATION TO SUPPORT THIS CONSTITUTION:" [Notifying all executive and judicial officers of the State, that they may qualify themselves for the execution of their respective offices.] GIVEN UNDER MY HAND, AT PROVIDENCE, THIS FOURTEENTH DAY OF JUNE, IN THE YEAR OF OUR LORD, ONE THOUSAND SEVEN HUNDRED AND NINETY, AND IN THE FOURTEENTH YEAR OF INDEPENDENCE. ARTHUR FENNER. BY HIS EXCELLENCY'S COMMAND, HENRY WARD, SEC'RY. GOD SAVE THE UNITED STATES OF AMERICA. [Colophon:]
Providence: Printed by John Carter. [1790.] Broadside. fol.   RIHS.

22845   —— THE BILL OF RIGHTS, AND AMENDMENTS TO THE CONSTITUTION OF THE UNITED STATES, AS AGREED TO BY THE CONVENTION OF THE STATE OF RHODE-ISLAND AND PROVIDENCE-PLANTATIONS, AT SOUTH-KINGSTOWN, IN THE COUNTY OF WASHINGTON, ON THE FIRST MONDAY OF MARCH, A. D. 1790. [Three columns.] THE FOREGOING IS A TRUE COPY: BY ORDER OF THE CONVENTION, DANIEL UPDIKE, SECRETARY.
[Newport: Printed by Peter Edes, 1790.] Broadside. fol.   RIHS.

22846   —— PROVIDENCE, MONDAY, MAY 31, 1790. SATURDAY NIGHT, AT 11 O'CLOCK, AN EXPRESS ARRIVED IN TOWN FROM NEWPORT, WITH THE IMPORTANT INTELLIGENCE, THAT THE CONVENTION OF THIS STATE HAD RATIFIED THE CONSTITUTION OF THE UNITED STATES. THE QUESTION, "SHALL THE CONSTITUTION BE ADOPTED, OR NOT WAS TAKEN ON SATURDAY, ABOUT 5 O'CLOCK, P. M. WHEN THE AFFIRMATIVE WAS CARRIED BY A MAJORITY OF TWO, — 34 MEMBERS VOTING FOR, AND 32 AGAINST IT. THIS PLEASING AND MOST INTERESTING EVENT WAS IMMEDIATELY ANNOUNCED HERE, BY THE RINGING OF BELLS, AND FIRING TWO FEDERAL SALUTES —ONE FROM THE ARTILLERY ON FEDERAL HILL—AND ANOTHER FROM THE SHIP WARREN, CAPT. SHELDON, LATELY ARRIVED FROM INDIA. RATIFICATION OF THE CONSTITUTION OF THE UNITED STATES, BY THE CONVENTION OF THE STATE OF RHODE-ISLAND AND PROVIDENCE-PLANTATIONS. . . .
[Providence: Printed by John Carter, 1790.] Broadside. fol.   AAS.

22847   —— — RHODE-ISLAND AND PROVIDENCE-PLANTATIONS UNITED TO THE GREAT AMERICAN FAMILY. PROVIDENCE, MONDAY MAY 31, 1790. [Two columns. A variant of the preceding.] [Colophon:]
[Providence:] [Printed by J. Carter.] [1790.] Broadside. fol.   RIHS.

22848   —— RATIFICATION OF THE CONSTITUTION OF THE UNITED STATES BY THE CONVENTION OF THE STATE OF RHODE-ISLAND AND PROVIDENCE-PLANTATIONS. [TWO columns.] THE FOREGOING IS A TRUE COPY. BY ORDER OF THE CONVENTION, DANIEL UPDIKE, SECRETARY.
[Newport: Printed by Peter Edes, 1790.] Broadside. fol.   AAS. RIHS.

22849   —— — RATIFICATION OF THE CONSTITUTION OF THE UNITED STATES BY THE CONVENTION OF THE STATE OF RHODE-ISLAND AND PROVIDENCE-PLANTATIONS. . . . DONE IN CONVENTION, AT NEWPORT, IN THE COUNTY OF NEWPORT, IN THE STATE OF RHODE-ISLAND AND PROVIDENCE-PLANTATIONS, THE 29TH DAY OF MAY, IN THE YEAR OF OUR LORD ONE THOUSAND SEVEN HUNDRED AND NINETY. [Two columns. Ratification of Constitution; Bill of Rights; proposed Amendments.]
[Newport: Printed by Henry Barber? 1790.] Broadside. fol.   AAS.

22850   RHODE ISLAND. COLLEGE OF, NOW BROWN UNIVERSITY.
HONORATISSIMO JABEZ BOWEN, ARMIGERO, COLLEGII RHOD. INSULÆ QUOD PROVI-
DENTIÆ EST CANCELLARIO; REVERENDO ÆQUÈ AC HONORANDO JACOBO MANNING,
S. T. D. PRÆSIDI, [Five lines.] HÆC PHILOSOPHEMATA, JUVENES IN ARTIBUS IN-
ITIATI, [Twenty-two names] HUMILLIMÈ DEDICANT. THESES [Three columns.]
[Colophon:]
     *Habita in solennibus Academicis Providentiæ, in Rep. Ins. Rhod. et Prov.
Plant. kalendis Septembris, A. D.* M,DCC,XC. *Rerumpublicarum Fœderatarum
Americæ summæ potestatis* XV. *Providentiæ: Typis Bennett Wheeler.* Broadside.
fol.   AAS. BU.

22851   —— THE REVEREND PERES FOBES, PROFESSOR OF NATURAL AND EXPERIMENTAL
PHILOSOPHY, IN RHODE-ISLAND COLLEGE, PROPOSES TO EXHIBIT A COURSE OF
LECTURES UPON NATURAL PHILOSOPHY AND ASTRONOMY, VIZ. [Fourteen lines.]
     [Providence: Printed by John Carter.] June 24, 1790. Broadside. 4to. BU.

22852   RICHARDSON, SAMUEL   1689 – 1761
THE HISTORY OF SIR CHARLES GRANDISON. ABRIDGED FROM THE WORKS OF SAMUEL
RICHARDSON, ESQ. AUTHOR OF PAMELA, AND CLARISSA.
     Philadelphia: Printed by M. Carey, 1790.

22853   RIGG, EDWARD
THE NEW AMERICAN LATIN GRAMMAR: OR, A COMPLETE INTRODUCTION TO THE
LATIN TONGUE. FORMED FROM THE MOST APPROVED WRITINGS IN THIS KIND.
BY THE LATE PRESIDENTS BURR, FINLEY AND OTHERS: AND NOW CAREFULLY RE-
VISED AND REFORMED BY A GREAT VARIETY OF AMENDMENTS, CORRECTIONS, AND
USEFUL REMARKS, MOST OF WHICH ARE ENTIRELY NEW; WITH THE DEFINITIONS
OF ALL THE GRAMMATICAL TERMS, IN THEIR PROPER PLACES. THE WHOLE REN-
DERED MUCH MORE USEFUL THAN ANY OF THE KIND YET PUBLISHED. BY EDWARD
RIGG, LATE TEACHER OF A GRAMMAR SCHOOL IN THE CITY OF NEW-YORK.
     New-York: Printed and sold by Hugh Gaine, 1790.

22854   RILEY, GEORGE
CHOICE EMBLEMS, NATURAL, HISTORICAL, FABULOUS, MORAL, AND DIVINE, FOR THE
IMPROVEMENT AND PASTIME OF YOUTH: ORNAMENTED WITH NEAR FIFTY HAND-
SOME ALLEGORICAL ENGRAVINGS, DESIGNED ON PURPOSE FOR THIS WORK. WITH
PLEASING AND FAMILIAR DESCRIPTIONS TO EACH, IN PROSE AND VERSE, SERVING
TO DISPLAY THE BEAUTIES AND MORALS OF THE ANCIENT FABULISTS. THE WHOLE
CALCULATED TO CONVEY THE GOLDEN LESSONS OF INSTRUCTION UNDER A NEW AND
MORE DELIGHTFUL DRESS. [Four lines from] GOLDSMITH.
     *Philadelphia: Printed and sold by Joseph Crukshank, in Market near
Third-Street.* MDCCXC. pp. xii, 166. 18mo.   AAS.

22855   ROBERTS, DANIEL   1658 – 1726
SOME MEMOIRS OF THE LIFE OF JOHN ROBERTS. WRITTEN BY HIS SON DANIEL
ROBERTS. THE SEVENTH EDITION. [Three lines from] PSALM XXXVII. 23, 39.
     *Philadelphia: Printed and sold by Joseph Crukshank, in Market-Street,
between Second and Third-Streets.* MDCCXC. pp. [66], (6), 12mo. AAS. NYPL.
     Appended is a six-page list of Books printed and sold by J. Crukshank.

22856   ROBERTSON, JOHN   1712 – 1776
TABLES OF DIFFERENCE OF LATITUDE AND DEPARTURE· CONSTRUCTED TO EVERY
QUARTER OF A DEGREE OF THE QUADRANT, AND CONTINUED FROM ONE, TO THE
DISTANCE OF ONE HUNDRED MILES OR CHAINS. [Ornament.]
     *Philadelphia: Printed and sold by Joseph Crukshank, in Market-Street.
between Second and Third-Streets.* MDCCXC. pp. (2), 90. 8vo.   AAS.
     Also found bound with the 1792 edition of Robert Gibson's Treatise
of practical surveying.

22857   ROLLINSON, WILLIAM
(NO. 33, SMITH-STREET.) TO THE INHABITANTS OF NEW-YORK. LADIES AND
GENTLEMEN, THE ARTIST WHO HAD THE HONOUR OF TAKING HIS EXCELLENCY THE
PRESIDENT'S LIKENESS, AND EXECUTING IT AS A MEDAL, TAKES THE MOST CORRECT
AND EXPRESSIVE LIKENESS IN FOUR MINUTES—FINISHES THEM AS MINIATURE IN
HAIR—PAINTING OR CRAYONS, FROM ONE DOLLAR TO THREE GUINEAS, EITHER AS
PROFILE, THREE QUARTER OR FULL FACES. . . . NEW-YORK, MAY 13, 1790.
[New-York: 1790.] Broadside. 16mo.   NYHS.
Probably refers to the J. Manly Medal, executed in Philadelphia, from
drawings by Joseph Wright,—the first Washington Medal executed in
this country.

22858   ROOSEN, GERHARD   1612–1711
CHRISTLICHES GEMÜTHS-GESPRÄCH VON DEM GEISTLICHEN UND SELIGMACHENDEN
GLAUBEN, UND ERKÄNTNUSS DER WARHEIT, SO ZU DER GOTTSELIGKEIT FÜHRET
IN DER HOFFNUNG DES EWIGEN LEBENS, TIT. I. L. ANS LICHT GEGEBEN IN FRAG
UND ANTWORT FÜR DIE ANKOMMENDE JUGEND WODURCH DIESELBE ZU EINER
HEILSAMEN LEBENS-UEBUNG MÖCHTE GERETSZT UND GEBRACHT WERDEN, DER
WARHEIT ZUM BESTEN.
Germantown: Gedruckt bey Michael Billmeyer, 1790.pp.241. 16mo. AAS.LCP.

22859   ROSS, ROBERT   –1799
THE NEW PRIMER, OR LITTLE BOY AND GIRL'S SPELLING-BOOK.
Middletown: Printed and sold by Woodward and Green. 1790.

22860   ROWE, ELIZABETH SINGER   1674–1737
DEVOUT EXERCISES OF THE HEART, IN MEDITATION AND SOLILOQUY, PRAYER AND
PRAISE. BY THE LATE PIOUS AND INGENIOUS MRS. ROWE. REVIEWED AND PUB-
LISHED AT HER REQUEST, BY I. WATTS, D. D.
Boston: Printed and sold by Samuel Hall. MDCCXC. pp.139, (2.)16mo.AAS.

22861   —— FRIENDSHIP IN DEATH; IN TWENTY LETTERS FROM THE DEAD TO THE LIVING.
TO WHICH ARE ADDED, LETTERS MORAL AND ENTERTAINING, IN PROSE AND VERSE.
IN THREE PARTS.
Printed at Boston, by Joseph Bumstead, for E. Larkin, jun. 1790.

22862   RUSH, BENJAMIN   1745–1813
AN EULOGIUM IN HONOR OF THE LATE DR. WILLIAM CULLEN, PROFESSOR OF THE
PRACTICE OF PHYSIC IN THE UNIVERSITY OF EDINBURGH; DELIVERED BEFORE
THE COLLEGE OF PHYSICIANS OF PHILADELPHIA, ON THE 9TH OF JULY; AGREE-
ABLY TO THEIR VOTE OF THE 4TH OF MAY, 1790. BY BENJAMIN RUSH, M. D.
PROFESSOR OF THE THEORY AND PRACTICE OF MEDICINE, IN THE COLLEGE OF
PHILADELPHIA. PUBLISHED BY ORDER OF THE COLLEGE OF PHYSICIANS.
*Philadelphia: Printed by Thomas Dobson, Bookseller, at the Stone House
in Second Street.* M,DCC,XC. pp. (30), (1). 8vo. BA. BPL. LOC. NYHS. RIMS. SGO.
5th Pennsylvania District Copyright, issued to Thomas Dobson, as Pro-
prietor, 30 July, 1790.

22863   —— — AN EULOGEUM [*sic*] IN HONOR OF THE LATE DR. WILLIAM CULLEN, PROFESSOR
OF THE PRACTICE OF PHYSIC IN THE UNIVERSITY OF EDENBURGH [*sic*] DELIVERED
BEFORE THE COLLEGE OF PHYSICIANS OF PHILADELPHIA ON THE 9TH OF JULY,
1790. BY BENJAMIN RUSH, M. D.
New-York: Printed by W. Durell, No. 196, Queen-Street. 1790.   NYHS.

22864   —— AN INQUIRY INTO THE EFFECTS OF SPIRITUOUS LIQUORS ON THE HUMAN BODY.
TO WHICH IS ADDED, A MORAL AND PHYSICAL THERMOMETER. BY BENJAMIN
RUSH, M. D. PROFESSOR OF THE THEORY AND PRACTICE OF MEDICINE IN THE UNI-
VERSITY OF PHILADELPHIA.
Printed at Boston, by Thomas and Andrews. At Faust's Statue, No. 45,
Newbury Street. MDCCXC. pp, 12. 12mo.   AAS. BPL. HC. LOC. RIMS. SGO.

RUSH, BENJAMIN, continued.

22865 —— —— AN INQUIRY INTO THE EFFECTS OF SPIRITUOUS LIQUORS UPON THE HUMAN BODY, AND THEIR INFLUENCE UPON THE HAPPINESS OF SOCIETY. BY BENJAMIN RUSH, M. D. PROFESSOR OF THE THEORY AND PRACTICE OF MEDICINE IN THE COLLEGE OF PHILADELPHIA. THE THIRD EDITION WITH ADDITIONS.

> *Philadelphia: Printed by Thomas Bradford,* [1790.]
> Reprinted in Edinburgh in 1791.

22866 —— THOUGHTS UPON THE AMUSEMENTS AND PUNISHMENTS WHICH ARE PROPER FOR SCHOOLS. ADDRESSED TO GEORGE CLYMER, BY BENJAMIN RUSH.

> *Philadelphia:* 1790.

22867 RUSSELL, JONATHAN   1771 – 1832
A TRIBUTE TO THE MEMORY OF NATHAN HAYWARD, A JUNIOR SOPHISTER IN RHODE-ISLAND COLLEGE, WHO DIED SEPTEMBER 25, 1789. AETAT. 19. PRONOUNCED IN THE COLLEGE-HALL, MARCH 10, 1790. BY JONATHAN RUSSELL, CLASS-MATE OF THE DECEASED. PUBLISHED AT THE REQUEST OF THE STUDENTS.

> *Printed at Providence, by Bennett Wheeler,* MDCCXC. pp. 14. 8vo.
> > BA. BU. LOC. PPL.

22868 SALEM. MASSACHUSETTS. MARINE SOCIETY.
LAWS OF THE MARINE SOCIETY AT SALEM, IN THE COMMONWEALTH OF MASSACHUSETTS, AS AMENDED AND AGREED UPON, AT AN ADJOURNMENT, NOV. 4, 1790. TO WHICH ARE ANNEXED, THE SEVERAL ACTS OF THE GENERAL COURT, RELATING TO THE SOCIETY.

> *Printed by T. C. Cushing, in Salem.* [1790.] pp. 20. 8vo.   HC.

22869 THE SALEM GAZETTE. NO. 1, IN 1790. TUESDAY, JANUARY 5, [— NUMBER 52, IN 1790. TUESDAY, DECEMBER 28, 1790.]

> *Published by Thomas C. Cushing, No. 8, Paved-Street, near Court and Washington Streets, Salem.* 1790. fol.   AAS. LOC.

> Established by Thomas C. Cushing, in continuation of *The Salem Mercury.* The first number was called *The American Eagle,* and the second, *The Salem Gazette,* under which title it has had a continuous publication down to the present day. With the issue for January 4, 1791, Cushing gave to the Gazette the numbering of Volume V, Number 221, in continuation from the first number of The Salem Mercury, with which he thus established a succession. With the issue for October 14, 1794, William Carleton, who was associated with Cushing, in the firm of Cushing & Carleton, Booksellers, became the publisher of the Gazette to July 25, 1797. Beginning in June, 1796, the Gazette was published as a semi-weekly, on Tuesdays and Fridays. With the issue for July 25, 1797, Thomas C. Cushing resumed publication of the Gazette, until the close of the year 1822, when the printing establishment of the Gazette passed into the control of his son, Caleb Cushing, and Ferdinand Andrews. Since which time, with various changes in proprietorship, the Gazette has been continuously published to the present day.

22870 SARJEANT, THOMAS
THE FEDERAL ARITHMETICIAN, OR THE SCIENCE OF NUMBERS IMPROVED, WITH THEIR APPLICATION TO THE FINANCES AND TO THE TRADE AND COMMERCE OF THE UNITED STATES. BY THOMAS SARJEANT, LATE MASTER OF THE MATHEMATICAL SCHOOL, IN THE ACADEMY OF THE PROTESTANT EPISCOPAL CHURCH, IN THE CITY OF PHILADELPHIA.

> *Philadelphia: Printed by Thomas Dobson,* 1790.

22871 THE SATURDAY EVENING HERALD, AND THE WASHINGTON GAZETTE. VOL. I. NO. 1.
SATURDAY, JULY 17, [— NO. 7. SATURDAY, AUGUST, 28, 1790.]
> *Boston [Commonwealth of Massachusetts]: Printed and published by Edward Eveleth Powars, opposite the new Court-House, in Court-Street. 1790. fol.*

Established by Edward Eveleth Powars, and continued by him to the
end of the first volume. Beginning August 30th, the title was altered
to, *The American Herald, and the Washington Gazette,* until publication
ceased.

22872 SAUNDERS, RICHARD, pseudonym.
POOR RICHARD IMPROVED: BEING AN ALMANACK AND EPHEMERIS OF THE MOTIONS
OF THE SUN AND MOON; THE TRUE PLACES AND ASPECTS OF THE PLANETS; THE
RISING AND SETTING OF THE SUN; AND THE RISING, SETTING AND SOUTHING OF THE
MOON, FOR THE YEAR OF OUR LORD 1791: BEING THE THIRD AFTER LEAP-YEAR.
[Eight lines.] BY RICHARD SAUNDERS, PHILOM.
> *Philadelphia: Printed and sold by Hall & Sellers—No. 51—Market st.*
[1790.] pp. (44). 12mo.

Contains, The Constitution of the Commonwealth of Pennsylvania.

22873 SAVANNAH. GEORGIA. DANCING ASSEMBLY.
RULES AND REGULATIONS FOR THE DANCING ASSEMBLY OF SAVANNAH. . . .
[Dated, Savannah, 19th November, 1790.]
> *[Savannah: Printed by James & Nicholas Johnston, 1790.]* Broadside. fol.

22874 SAYRE, FRANCIS BOWES
AN INAUGURAL DISSERTATION ON THE CAUSES WHICH PRODUCE A PREDISPOSITION TO
PHTHISIS PULMONALIS, AND THE METHOD OF OBVIATING THEM; SUBMITTED TO THE
EXAMINATION OF THE REV. WILLIAM SMITH, S. T. P. PROVOST, AND THE MEDICAL
PROFESSORS OF THE COLLEGE OF PHILADELPHIA, FOR THE DEGREE OF DOCTOR OF
MEDICINE, ON THE TWENTY-SECOND DAY OF OCTOBER, 1790. BY FRANCIS BOWES
SAYRE, M. B. SENIOR MEMBER OF THE AMERICAN MEDICAL SOCIETY, AND MEMBER
OF THE MEDICAL SOCIETY OF NEW-JERSEY.
> *Trenton: Printed by Isaac Collins. 1790. pp. 24. 8vo.*   SGO.

22875 THE SCHOOL FOR LOVE; OR, SCHEME TO GAIN HER. A COMEDY, IN FIVE ACTS.
WROTE BY A GENTLEMAN OF PHILADELPHIA.
> *Philadelphia: Printed by Prichard & Hall?* 1790.

22876 THE SCHOOL OF VIRTUE; OR, THE HISTORY OF HENRY HOWARD AND THE HONOR-
ABLE MISS HENRIETTA COLVILLE. A NOVEL, ON A NEW PLAN. TO WHICH IS
ADDED, THE FEMALE HERMIT.
> *Philadelphia: Printed and sold by W. Spotswood, Front - Street, between
Market and Chesnut-Streets. 1790.*

22877 SCHRÖDER, JOHANN GEORG
MERKWÜRDIGE GESCHICHTE VON EINEM MENSCHEN, DER MIT DEM TEUFEL IN
EINEN BUND GETRETEN AUF 18 JAHR UND WIEDER DURCH CHRISTUM EOLÖSET
WORDEN IST. VON JOHANN GEORG SCHRÖDER, D. D. EVANGEL. PREDIGER IN
MARYLAND.
> *Ephrata: Klosterpresse, 1790. pp. 48. 12mo.*

22878 SCHWACHE AUSDRÜCKE DER WEHMUTH ÜBER DEN TOD DR. CASPER DIETRICH
WEYBERGS.
> *Philadelphia: Gedruckt bey Carl Cist, 1790.*

22879   SCOTT, WILLIAM   1750 – 1804
LESSONS IN ELOCUTION, OR, A SELECTION OF PIECES IN PROSE AND VERSE, FOR THE
IMPROVEMENT OF YOUTH IN READING AND SPEAKING. BY WILLIAM SCOTT. THE
SECOND AMERICAN EDITION, FROM THE FIFTH BRITISH EDITION.
> *Philadelphia: Printed by William Young, Bookseller, the corner of Second
> and Chesnut-Streets.* 1790.
Second title: THE ELEMENTS OF GESTURE, ILLUSTRATED BY FOUR ELEGANT COP-
PER-PLATES; TOGETHER WITH RULES FOR EXPRESSING WITH PROPRIETY THE VA-
RIOUS PASSIONS AND EMOTIONS OF THE MIND.
> *Philadelphia: Printed by William Young, Bookseller, the corner of Second
> and Chesnut-Streets.* M,DCC,XC. pp. 52, (2), 4 plates.
The latter was also sold separately.

22880   SEABURY, SAMUEL   1729 – 1796
AN ADDRESS TO THE MINISTERS AND CONGREGATIONS OF THE PRESBYTERIAN AND
INDEPENDENT PERSUASIONS IN THE UNITED STATES OF AMERICA. BY A MEMBER
OF THE EPISCOPAL CHURCH. [Six lines Scripture texts.]
> *[New Haven:] Printed [by T. and S. Green] in the year* M,DCC,XC.
> pp. (55). 12mo.   AAS. BA. JCB. NYHS.

22881   SELBY, WILLIAM   – 1800·
APOLLO AND THE MUSES MUSICAL COMPOSITIONS. BY WILLIAM SELBY, ORGANIST OF
THE STONE CHAPEL, IN BOSTON, MASSACHUSETTS.
> *Boston: Printed for the Author.* 1790.
In six numbers. Dedicated (by permission) to Mrs. S. Mason, of Boston.

22882   —— TWO ANTHEMS, FOR THREE AND FOUR VOICES. COMPOSED . . . BY WILLIAM
SELBY, PROFESSOR OF MUSIC, IN BOSTON.
> *Boston: Printed for the Author.* [1790.] pp. (2), (16). obl. 4to.
Title, and eight leaves of engraved music.

22883   SELECT VERSES FOR LITTLE MASTERS AND MISSES. ORNAMENTED WITH ALPHABET-
ICAL WOODCUTS.
> *New-York: Printed by William Durell,* 1790.

22884   A SELECTION OF SACRED HARMONY, CONTAINING LESSONS EXPLAINING THE GAMUT,
KEYS AND CHARACTERS USED IN VOCAL MUSIC.
> *Philadelphia: Printed by William Young.* 1790.

22885   A SERMON IN PRAISE OF SWEARING. DEUT. VI. 13. THE LATTER PART OF THE
VERSE. AND SHALL SWEAR BY HIS NAME.
> *Salem: Printed by Thomas C. Cushing? Sold by William Carleton.* 1790.

22886   SEWALL, DANIEL   1755 – 1842
AN ASTRONOMICAL DIARY, OR ALMANACK, FOR THE YEAR OF CHRISTIAN ÆRA, 1791:
BEING 3RD AFTER BISSEXTILE OR LEAP YEAR. CALCULATED FOR THE MERIDIAN
OF PORTSMOUTH, NEW-HAMPSHIRE, LAT. 43 DEG. 5 MIN. NORTH: BUT WILL SERVE
FOR ANY OF THE NEW-ENGLAND STATES; CONTAINING EVERY THING NECESSARY
FOR SUCH A WORK, WITH A VARIETY OF OTHER USEFUL MATTERS. BY DANIEL
SEWALL. [Ten lines of verse.]
> *Portsmouth: ·New-Hampshire, Printed and sold (wholesale and retail very
> cheap) by John Melcher, at his Printing-Office in Market-Street. Sold also by most
> of the Shopkeepers in town and country.* [1790.] pp. (24). 12mo.   LOC. NYPL.

SEWALL, DANIEL, continued.

22887　—— THE CONCORD CALENDAR: OR, NEW-HAMPSHIRE ALMANACK, FOR THE YEAR
OF OUR REDEMPTION 1791: [Twelve lines.] BY ELIJAH BICKERSTAFF, JUN.
PHILOMATHEMATICIAN. [Four lines of verse.]
*Printed at Concord, by Geo. Hough—Sold at his Office by the gross, dozen, or
single. With great allowance to those who take a large quantity.* [1790.] pp. (24).
12mo.　　　　　　　　　　　　　　　　　　　　　　　　　　AAS.
Allibone says that Daniel Sewall, sometimes called himself Isaac (Elijah?)
Bickerstaff, jr.

22888　SEWARD, ANNA　　　　　　　　　　　　　　　　　1747 – 1809
MONODY ON MAJOR ANDRE, (WHO WAS EXECUTED AT TAPPAN, NOVEMBER — 1780.)
BY MISS SEWARD. TO WHICH ARE ADDED, MAJOR ANDRE'S LETTERS ADDRESSED
TO MISS SEWARD, WHEN AT HIS 18 YEAR.
*Philadelphia: Printed and sold by Enoch Story, in Third-Street, third
door from Chesnut-Street.* [1790?] [pp. 56.] 8vo.　　　　　　NYHS.　　　　$23
[To which is added, Edmund of the Vale. A hermit's tale, recorded
by his own hand and found in his cell. This tale is the production of
Miss Sophia Lee, a lady to whom the public have been obliged for several very ingenious and elegant performances. Critical Rev.] From
the imprint this would appear to be Story's first edition, which would
make the year 1788 a more probable date of publication.

22889　SHAFTSBURY. VERMONT. BAPTIST ASSOCIATION.
MINUTES OF THE SHAFTSBURY ASSOCIATION, AT THEIR ANNUAL CONVENTION, HELD
IN ADAMS, 1790.
Bennington: Printed by Haswell and Russell? 1790.

22890　A SHORT INTRODUCTION TO LATIN GRAMMAR, FOR THE USE OF THE UNIVERSITY AND
ACADEMY OF PENNSYLVANIA, IN PHILADELPHIA. [Two lines from HORACE.]
FOURTH [FIFTH] EDITION, CAREFULLY REVISED.
Boston: Printed and sold by John W. Folsom, No. 30, Union - Street.
MDCCXC. pp. iv, 127, (1). 16mo.　　　　　　　　　　　　AAS.
A reprint of the fourth Philadelphia edition. "Lately been in-
troduced to other public seminaries in New-Hampshire and Massachu-
setts." Has added, a one-page list of "Books sold by John W. Folsom."

22891　SMITH, WILLIAM　　　　　　　　　　　　　　　　1727 – 1803
A SERMON, ON TEMPORAL AND SPIRITUAL SALVATION : DELIVERED IN CHRIST-CHURCH,
PHILADELPHIA, BEFORE THE PENNSYLVANIA SOCIETY OF THE CINCINNATI. BY
WILLIAM SMITH, D. D. PROVOST OF THE COLLEGE AND ACADEMY OF PHILADEL-
PHIA. PREPARED AND PUBLISHED AT THE REQUEST OF THE SOCIETY.
Philadelphia: From the Press of T. Dobson, M,DCC,XC. pp. (2), (2), 25,
(3). 8vo.　　　　　　　　　　　　AAS. BA. JCB. NYHS. NYPL.

22892　SMITH, WILLIAM　　　　　　　　　　　　　　　　1754 – 1821
A DISCOURSE AT THE OPENING OF THE CONVENTION OF CLERICAL AND LAY DELE-
GATES OF THE CHURCH, IN THE STATE OF RHODE-ISLAND, DELIVERED IN TRINITY
CHURCH, NEWPORT, THURSDAY, THE 8TH OF NOVEMBER, 1790. [With Appendix.]
[Four lines.] BY WILLIAM SMITH, A. M. RECTOR OF TRINITY-CHURCH, NEWPORT.
Providence: Printed by J. Carter. [1790.] pp. 19, xii. 8vo.BU.HC.LOC.RIHS.

22893　SOCIETY OF THE CINCINNATI.
PROCEEDINGS OF THE THIRD GENERAL-MEETING OF THE SOCIETY OF THE CINCIN-
NATI, AT PHILADELPHIA, MAY, 1790.
New-York: 1790. pp. 7. fol.

22894   SONGS FOR THE AMUSEMENT OF CHILDREN.
      Middletown: Printed by M. H. Woodward, 1790.

22895   SOUTH CAROLINA. STATE.
      ACTS AND ORDINANCES OF THE GENERAL ASSEMBLY OF THE STATE OF SOUTH-CARO-
      LINA: PASSED FEBRUARY 20TH, 1790. [Arms.]
        Charleston: Printed for A. Timothy, Printer to the State. 1790. pp. (2),
      18. fol.   BM. JCB. LOC.

22896   —— THE CONSTITUTION OF THE STATE OF SOUTH-CAROLINA. RATIFIED SEPTEM-
      BER 3, 1790.
        Charleston: Printed for A. Timothy, Printer to the State. M,DCC,-
      LXXXX. pp. [12.] 4to.   NYPL.

22897   —— THE PUBLIC LAWS OF THE STATE OF SOUTH-CAROLINA, FROM ITS FIRST ESTAB-
      LISHMENT AS A BRITISH PROVINCE DOWN TO THE YEAR 1790, INCLUSIVE, IN
      WHICH IS COMPREHENDED SUCH OF THE STATUTES OF GREAT BRITAIN AS WERE
      MADE OF FORCE BY THE ACT OF ASSEMBLY OF 1712, WITH AN APPENDIX CONTAIN-
      ING SUCH OTHER STATUTES AS HAVE BEEN ENACTED OR DECLARED TO BE OF FORCE
      IN THIS STATE, EITHER VIRTUALLY OR EXPRESSLY, TO WHICH IS ADDED THE TITLES
      OF ALL THE LAWS (WITH THEIR RESPECTIVE DATES) WHICH HAVE BEEN PASSED IN
      SOUTH-CAROLINA DOWN TO THE PRESENT TIME, ALSO THE CONSTITUTION OF THE
      UNITED STATES WITH THE AMENDMENTS THERETO, AND LIKEWISE THE NEWLY ADOPT-
      ED CONSTITUTION OF THE STATE OF SOUTH-CAROLINA, TOGETHER WITH A COPIOUS
      INDEX TO THE WHOLE. BY THE HONORABLE JOHN FAUCHERAUD GRIMKÉ, ESQ.
      A. B. & L. L. D AND ONE OF THE ASSOCIATE JUDGES OF THE SUPERIOR COURTS IN THE
      STATE OF SOUTH-CAROLINA. [One line of Latin from] 4 INST. 246, 332.
        Philadelphia: Printed by R. Aitken & Son, in Market-Street. M.DCC.XC-
      pp. lxxvii, 504, 43, (58). 4to.   BM. HSP. JCB. LOC. NYHS. NYPL.

22898   —— STATE OF SOUTH-CAROLINA. AN ORDINANCE, PRESCRIBING, ON THE PART OF
      THIS STATE, THE TIMES, PLACES, AND MANNER OF HOLDING ELECTIONS FOR REP-
      RESENTATIVES IN CONGRESS. . . . IN THE SENATE HOUSE, THE 20TH DAY OF
      JANUARY, 1790. . . .
        [*Charleston: Printed for A. Timothy, 1790.*] Broadside. 4to.   NYPL.

22899   THE SOUTH CAROLINA GAZETTE AND GENERAL ADVERTISER. JANUARY–DEC-
      EMBER, 1790.
        Charleston: Printed by John Miller. 1790. fol.

22900   SPIERIN, GEORGE HARTWELL
      A SERMON DELIVERED AT NEWBURGH, BEFORE THE FRATERNITY OF LODGE NO. 18
      OF FREE AND ACCEPTED MASONS, JUNE 24, 1790.
        Goshen: Printed by David Mandeville, 1790.   NYHS.

22901   SPRING, SAMUEL   1746 – 1819
      THREE SERMONS TO LITTLE CHILDREN: ON THE NATURE AND BEAUTY OF THE DUTI-
      FUL TEMPER. TO WHICH IS ADDED, SEVERAL FORMS OF PRAYER, FOR LITTLE
      CHILDREN. WITH EXTRACTS FROM VARIOUS AUTHORS. BY SAMUEL SPRING, A. M.
      PASTOR OF A CHURCH IN NEWBURY-PORT.
        New-York: Printed by William Durell. M,DCC,XC. pp. 95, frontispiece.
      24mo.   AAS.

22902   STANDFAST, RICHARD
      A DIALOGUE BETWEEN A BLIND-MAN AND DEATH. BY RICHARD STANDFAST, LATE
      MINISTER OF THE GOSPEL IN BRISTOL. [Cut.]
        *London; Printed: Boston; Re-printed, (at the earnest request of a number
      of well-disposed christians) by E. Russell, next Liberty-Stump, for J. Plumer,
      trader, in Newbury.[Price six pence single.]*☞* May be had, The Tragedy of Louis
      Capet, and sundry other new pieces.* [1790.] pp. 16. 16mo.   BU.

22903   STATE GAZETTE OF NORTH-CAROLINA. VOL. V. NO. 207. FRIDAY, JANUARY 1, [— No. 259. FRIDAY, DECEMBER 31, 1790.]
>>> *Edenton: Printed by Hodge & Wills.* 1790. fol.

22904   THE STATE [S. C. arms] GAZETTE OF SOUTH-CAROLINA. JANUARY–DECEMBER, 1790.
>>> *Charleston: Printed for A. Timothy, Printed to the State.* 1790. fol.

22905   STEARNS, JOSIAH   1732 – 1788
SERMONS ON THE DIVINE CHARACTER; DELIVERED NOVEMBER 4TH, 1787, AT EXETER, IN NEW-HAMPSHIRE. . . .
>>> *Exeter: Printed by Henry Ranlet,* M,DCC,XC, *and sold at his Office.* pp. (64). 8vo.   JCB. LOC.

22906   STEARNS, SAMUEL   1747 – 1819
THE UNIVERSAL CALENDER AND NORTH AMERICAN ALMANACK, FOR THE YEAR OF OUR LORD 1791. AND FROM THE CREATION OF THE WORLD, ACCORDING TO SACRED WRIT, 5753. BEING THE THIRD AFTER BISSEXTILE OR LEAP YEAR, AND THE FIFTEENTH OF THE INDEPENDENCE OF THE STATE OF VERMONT AND AMERICA. CALCULATED FOR THE LATITUDE AND LONGITUDE OF THE STATE OF VERMONT. BY SAMUEL STEARNES [*sic.*] PROFESSOR OF THE MATHEMATICS, NATURAL PHILOSOPHY, AND PHYSIC.
>>> *Printed at Bennington, by Anthony Haswell. Sold by him wholesale and retail.* [1790.] pp. (24). 12mo.
>>> Contains, J. Read, Esq'rs much-approved method of raising hemp.

22907   —— — THE UNIVERSAL CALENDAR, AND NORTH-AMERICAN ALMANACK, FOR THE YEAR OF OUR LORD 1791. AND OF THE CREATION, ACCORDING TO THE SCRIPTURES, 5753: BEING THE THIRD AFTER BISSEXTILE, OR LEAP YEAR; AND THE FIFTEENTH OF THE INDEPENDENCE OF AMERICA. [Ten lines.] CALCULATED FOR THE LATITUDE AND LONGITUDE OF THE TOWN OF BOSTON, IN THE COMMONWEALTH OF MASSACHUSETTS. BY SAMUEL STEARNS, PROFESSOR OF THE MATHEMATICS, NATURAL PHILOSOPHY & PHYSIC.
>>> *Boston: Printed by Edes & Son, No. 7, State-Street.* [1790.] pp. (28). 12mo.   NYHS.
>>> The Author's Preface, dated, London, June 2. 1790, says: "Two and twenty years have revolved since I first published astronomical calculations." Contains, The Author's Philosophical contemplations, &c. in verse. And Read's much-approved method of raising hemp.

22908   STERNE, LAURENCE   1713 – 1768
THE BEAUTIES OF STERNE: INCLUDING ALL HIS PATHETIC TALES, AND MOST DISTINGUISHED OBSERVATIONS ON LIFE. SELECTED FOR THE HEART OF SENSIBILITY. TO WHICH IS ADDED, THE LIFE OF MR. STERNE. [Four lines of quotation.]
>>> *Philadelphia: Printed by T. Seddon, in Market-Street, between Front and Second-Streets.* MDCCXC. pp. 191. 16mo.   AAS.

22909   —— A SENTIMENTAL JOURNEY THROUGH FRANCE AND ITALY, BY MR. YORICK. IN TWO VOLUMES. VOL. I. [— II.]
>>> *Philadelphia: Printed by T. Seddon, in Market-Street, between Front and Second-Streets.* MDCCXC. 2 vols. in one. pp. 156. 12mo.   AAS.

22910   STERRY, CONSIDER, and JOHN   1766 – 1823
THE AMERICAN YOUTH: BEING A NEW AND COMPLETE COURSE OF INTRODUCTORY
MATHEMATICS: DESIGNED FOR THE USE OF PRIVATE STUDENTS. BY CONSIDER and
JOHN STERRY. VOL. I. [Three lines.]
> *Printed at Providence, by Bennett Wheeler, for the Authors,* 1790. pp. 387,
> (1). 8vo.   AAS. BU. HC. LOC. RIHS. YC.

Proposals, dated Preston, May 31, 1788, for printing, by subscription,
the first volume of The American youth, "to be published if a sufficient
number of subscriptions are taken," were printed in the Connecticut
Gazette of June 20, 1788. The manuscript was approved by Jared
Mansfield, of New-Haven, and Joseph Huntington, of Dartmouth College. Volume one was all that was published.

22911   STONINGTON. CONNECTICUT. BAPTIST ASSOCIATION.
MINUTES OF THE STONINGTON ASSOCIATION HELD AT ELDER SIMEON BROWN'S
MEETING-HOUSE IN STONINGTON, 1790.
> *New-London: Printed by T. Green & Son,* 1790.   BM.

22912   STOVER, WILLIAM LILLY
THE COLUMBIAN ALMANACK, AND MAGAZINE OF KNOWLEDGE AND FUN, FOR,
THE YEAR OF OUR LORD SEVENTEEN HUNDRED AND NINETY-ONE. BEING THE
THIRD AFTER BISSEXTILE OR LEAP YEAR, AND THE FIFTEENTH AND SIXTEENTH
OF AMERICAN INDEPENDENCE. [Twelve lines.] BY WILLIAM LILLY STOVER,
PROFESSOR OF ASTRONOMY AND ASTROLOGY. CALCULATED AT NEWPORT, LATI-
TUDE 41° 25'N.
> *Newport (Rhode-Island): Printed and sold by P. Edes.* [1790.] pp. (24).
> 12mo.   LOC. NHS. NYHS. RIHS.

22913   STRONG, NATHAN   1748 – 1816
A SERMON, DELIVERED IN PRESENCE OF HIS EXCELLENCY SAMUEL HUNTINGTON,
ESQ. L. L. D. GOVERNOR, AND THE HONORABLE THE GENERAL ASSEMBLY OF THE
STATE OF CONNECTICUT, CONVENED AT HARTFORD, ON THE DAY OF THE ANNIVER-
SARY ELECTION, MAY 13TH, 1790. BY NATHAN STRONG, A. M. PASTOR OF THE
FIRST CHURCH IN HARTFORD. [Publishers' monogram.]
> *Hartford: Printed by Hudson and Goodwin.* M.DCC.XC. pp. 32. 8vo.
>   AAS. BA. CHS. JCB. LOC. MHS. NYHS. NYPL. UTS. YC.

22914   STRONG, NEHEMIAH   1729 – 1807
AN ASTRONOMICAL DIARY, KALENDAR, OR ALMANACK, FOR THE YEAR OF OUR LORD
1791. [Eleven lines.] BY N. STRONG, LATE PROFESSOR OF MATHEMATICKS, AND
NATURAL PHYLOSOPHY IN YALE-COLLEGE. [Four lines of verse.]
> *Hartford: Printed for Nathaniel Patten.* 1790. pp. (24.) 12mo. AAS. CHS.
Apparently the same as West's Bickerstaff Astronomical diary, etc. for
1791, printed by Patten, this year.

22915   —— —— AN ASTRONOMICAL DIARY, KALENDER, OR ALMANACK, FOR THE YEAR OF
OUR LORD 1791. . . . BY N. STRONG.
> *Hartford: Printed by Elisha Babcock.* [1790.] pp. (24). 12mo. CHS. YC.

22916   —— THE MIDDLESEX ALMANACK, OR LADY AND GENTLEMAN'S DIARY, FOR THE YEAR
OF OUR LORD CHRIST, 1791: . . .
> *Middletown: Printed and sold by Moses H. Woodward.* [1790.] pp. (24).
> 12mo.   CHS.

STRONG, NEHEMIAH, continued.

22917 —— STAFFORD'S ALMANACK, FOR THE YEAR OF OUR LORD, 1791: AND FROM THE
CREATION OF THE WORLD, 5740. AND THE 15TH OF AMERICAN INDEPENDENCE,
JULY 4TH. BEING THE THIRD AFTER BISSEXTILE OR LEAP-YEAR. [Eight lines.]
THE ASTRONOMICAL CALCULATIONS BY N. STRONG, A. M. [Six lines of verse.]
New-Haven: Printed and sold by Thomas & Samuel Green. [1790.]
pp. (24). 12mo.   AAS. BPL. LOC. YC.

22918 SUMNER, CLEMENT
AN ORATION, DELIVERED BEFORE THE MOST ANCIENT AND HONORABLE SOCIETY OF
FREE AND ACCEPTED MASONS, OF THE RISING SUN LODGE, IN KEENE, ON JUNE
24, 5789. BY BROTHER CLEMENT SUMNER, M. M. AND A MEMBER OF SAID LODGE.
Keene: (State of New-Hampshire) Printed by Brother James D. Griffith.
1790.

22919 SWAN, TIMOTHY   1758 – 1842
THE FEDERAL HARMONY: IN THREE PARTS. CONTAINING, I. AN INTRODUCTION TO
THE GROUNDS OF MUSICK. II. A LARGE COLLECTION OF CELEBRATED PSALM AND
HYMN TUNES FROM THE MOST APPROVED ANCIENT AND MODERN AUTHORS: TO-
GETHER WITH SEVERAL NEW ONES, NEVER BEFORE PUBLISHED: SUITED TO ALL
METRES USUALLY SUNG IN CHURCHES. III. SELECT ANTHEMS, &C. &C. COMPILED
FOR THE USE OF SCHOOLS AND SINGING SOCIETIES. [One line from] PSALM CXL X.
*Boston: Printed and sold by John Norman at his office No. 75, Newbury-
street.* MDCCXC. pp. 128. obl. 8vo.   RIHS.
Title enclosed in an ornamental border. "A new edition. With large
additions, corrected and revised, with great attention and accuracy."

22920 SWORDS, THOMAS, and JAMES
NEW-YORK, JULY 5, 1790. PROPOSALS FOR PRINTING BY SUBSCRIPTION, IN
TWELVE VOLUMES, SIXTEENS. THE CHILDREN'S FRIEND. TRANSLATED FROM THE
THE FRENCH OF THE CELEBRATED MR. BERQUIN. . . .
[New-York: Printed by T. and J. Swords, 1790.] Broadside. fol. NYHS.

22921 A TABLE; CALCULATED TO SHEW THE CONTENTS OF ANY SLED OR CART LOAD OF WOOD.
Boston: Printed and sold by Benjamin Edes and Son. 1790.

22922 A TABLE SHEWING THE DISTANCE FROM ONE POST TOWN TO ANOTHER IN THE UNITED
STATES OF AMERICA, MAY 1, 1790, WITH EXPLANATION.
Philadelphia, Printed and sold by B. Towne, in Church Alley. [1790.]
Broadside. fol.

22923 TATE, JAMES
MAJOR EST VERITAS, & PRÆVALEBIT. A MODERN VINDICATION OF INFANT BAPTISM,
EXTRACTED FROM SACRED SCRIPTURE, FROM RATIONAL ARGUMENT, AND FROM
CHURCH HISTORY. PRESENTED TO THE CANDID PUBLICK BY THEIR HUMBLE SER-
VANT, JAMES TATE, A. M.
Savannah: Printed by James and Nicholas Johnston. M.DCC.XC. pp.
[16.] 8vo.   BA.

22924 TATHAM, WILLIAM   1752 – 1819
PROPOSALS FOR PUBLISHING A LARGE AND COMPREHENSIVE MAP OF THE SOUTHERN
DIVISION OF THE UNITED STATES OF AMERICA. BY SUBSCRIPTION ONLY. BY
WILLIAM TATHAM. RICHMOND IN VIRGINIA, SEPTEMBER 30, 1790.
Richmond: 1790. Broadside. fol.
With Power of attorney to Francis Thornton, esq. to collect subscrip-
tions, attached.

22925 THACHER, PETER   1752 – 1802
A SERMON, PREACHED AT EXETER, IN NEWHAMPSHIRE, JUNE 2, 1790, AT THE OR-
DINATION OF THE REV. MR. WILLIAM FREDERICK ROWLAND, TO THE PASTORAL
CARE OF THE FIRST CHURCH, IN THAT TOWN. BY PETER THACHER, A. M. PASTOR
OF A CHURCH IN BOSTON. [Ornament.]
Exeter: Printed by Henry Ranlet, M,DCC,XC, and sold at his Office. pp.
(44.) 8vo.   AAS. BA. HC. JCB. MHS. NYHS. NYPL.

22926 THAYER, ELIHU   1747 – 1812
THE FAITHFUL WATCHMAN. A SERMON PREACHED AT THE ORDINATION OF THE
REVEREND PETER SANBORN, A. M. PASTOR OF THE THIRD CHURCH, IN READING,
JUNE 9, 1790. BY ELIHU THAYER, PASTOR OF THE FIRST CHURCH IN KINGSTON.
[Ornament.]
Newbury Port: Printed and sold by John Mycall. M,DCC,XC. pp. (37).
8vo.   AAS. BM. JCB. LOC. NYPL.

22927 THOMAS'S MASSACHUSETTS SPY; OR THE WORCESTER GAZETTE. VOL. XVIII. NO.
874. THURSDAY, JANUARY 7, [— VOL. XIX. NO. 926. THURSDAY, DECEMBER 30,
1790.]
Printed at Worcester, Massachusetts, by Isaiah Thomas, . . 1790.fol. AAS.

22928 THOMPSON, ABRAHAM
POEMS ON THE MOST SOLEMN SUBJECTS. WRITTEN BY ABRAHAM THOMPSON.
*Printed [by T. and S. Green] for the Author; and sold by him at his house
in Broad-way, New-Haven.* 1790.

22929 THOMPSON, JOHN
THE LOST AND UNDONE SON OF PERDITION: OR THE BIRTH, LIFE, AND CHARACTER
OF JUDAS ISCARIOT. FAITHFULLY COLLECTED FROM SEVERAL ANCIENT AUTHORS
OF UNDOUBTED CREDIT. BY J. THOMPSON.
Danbury: Printed by Douglas and Ely? [1790.]

22930 THOMSON, JAMES   1700 – 1748
THE SEASONS: CONTAINING SPRING. SUMMER. AUTUMN. WINTER. BY JAMES
THOMSON. FIRST AMERICAN EDITION.
*Newburyport: Printed by John Mycall, for the Proprietor of the Boston
Bookstore, No. 59 Cornhill, Boston.* [1790.] 12mo.

22931 —— — THE SEASONS: CONTAINING SPRING. SUMMER. AUTUMN. WINTER. BY
JAMES THOMSON. WITH THE LIFE OF THE AUTHOR, BY DR. SAMUEL JOHNSON.
*Philadelphia: Printed by H. Taylor, for R. Campbell, north-east corner
of Second and Chesnut Streets.* M,DCC,XC. pp. xix, (21)-190. 16mo. AAS. LOC.

22932 THORNTON, ELISHA
THE RHODE-ISLAND ALMANACK, FOR THE YEAR OF OUR LORD 1791. [BEING THIRD
AFTER LEAP-YEAR, AND FIFTEENTH OF AMERICAN INDEPENDENCE. CALCULATED
FOR THE MERIDIAN OF NEWPORT, LATITUDE 41, 25, N, AND LONGITUDE 71, 15, W, AND
MAY SERVE THE ADJACENT STATES. THE ASTRONOMICAL CALCULATIONS BY E.
THORNTON. [Eight lines of verse.]
Newport (Rhode-Island) Printed and sold by P. Edes. [1790.] pp. [20.]
12mo.   AAS. NYPL. RIHS.
In his Preface the Author states: "The Printer having for three years
past condescended to print my Almanack in the plain and friendly
style, which style though adapted and agreeable to me and my friends,
is not adapted nor so agreeable to his friends and customers in general; . . . I have sold my calculations to him, with my name sub-
scribed as per title page, and he is to publish said Almanack to his
liking. . . ."

22933   THORNTON, THOMAS
      TRUE AND AUTHENTIC HISTORY OF HIS EXCELLENCY GEORGE WASHINGTON. . . .
        Philadelphia: 1790.

22934   THOUGHTS ON THE DOCTRINE OF UNIVERSAL SALVATION. AS PREACHED, MAIN-
      TAINED AND PROPAGATED BY MR. JOHN MURRAY, AND OTHERS OF THE PEOPLE
      CALLED UNIVERSAL BAPTISTS. BY A YOUTH OF THIS CITY. [Three lines from]
      ELIHU.
        Philadelphia: Printed for the Author, (by Prichard and Hall,) and sold by
      the Booksellers in Philadelphia, New-York, and Boston. 1790. (Price one-eighth
      of a dollar). pp. 24. 12mo.   BM. JCB.

22935   THE [cut] TIMES. AND THE PATOWMACK PACKET. [Motto.] VOL. I. No. 47,
      WEDNESDAY, JANUARY 6, [— VOL. II. No. 98. WEDNESDAY, DECEMBER 29, 1790.]
        George-Town: Printed by Charles Fierer and Thomas W. Fosdick. 1790.
      fol.

22936   TO THE FREE ELECTORS OF THE CITY OF NEW-YORK. FELLOW CITIZENS, YOUR
      TOO GREAT SECURITY MAY DISAPPOINT YOUR WISHES. IT IS EVIDENT THAT YOU
      GENERALLY APPROVE THE CONDUCT OF YOUR REPRESENTATIVE IN CONGRESS, AND
      INTEND THAT HE SHALL BE RE-ELECTED: BUT TAKING IT FOR GRANTED THERE IS
      NO OPPOSITION, VERY FEW OF YOU GO TO THE POLLS. IT IS SAID THAT SCARCELY
      A HUNDRED VOTES HAVE BEEN HITHERTO GIVEN IN THIS CITY FOR REPRESENTA-
      TIVE, . . . [Urging the re-election of John Lawrance.] A FAST FRIEND.
      THURSDAY, APRIL 29, 1790.
        [New-York: 1790.] Broadside. fol.   NYHS.

22937   TO THE FREEMEN OF THE STATE OF RHODE-ISLAND. [In support of Governor
      Arthur Fenner, with his acknowledgment.]
        [Providence: Printed by John Carter, 1790.] Broadside. fol.

22938   TO THE HONORABLE THE REPRESENTATIVES OF THE FREEMEN OF THE COMMON-
      WEALTH OF PENNSYLVANIA, IN GENERAL ASSEMBLY MET. THE PETITION OF THE
      SUBSCRIBERS, RESPECTFULLY SHEWETH, THAT IN THE EARLY STAGES OF THE INDE-
      PENDENCE OF THE UNITED STATES, IT WAS THOUGHT ADVISEABLE BY THE LEGIS-
      LATURE OF THIS COMMONWEALTH, TO IMPOSE A TEST OF ABJURATION AND ALLEGI-
      ANCE ON THE INHABITANTS OF THIS STATE, IN ORDER TO SECURE THEIR FIDELITY
      TO THE CAUSE OF AMERICA. [Praying that a law be passed abolishing the tests.]
        [Philadelphia: 1790.] Broadside. fol.   LCP.

22939   TO THE VOTERS OF MARYLAND. ON MONDAY NEXT, YOU ARE TO ELECT SIX REPRE-
      SENTATIVES IN CONGRESS; . . . [Signed, a Citizen. October 1, 1790.]
        Baltimore: Printed by William Goddard and James Angell, 1790.] Broad-
      side. fol.   LOC.

22940   TOBLER, JOHN
      THE SOUTH-CAROLINA AND GEORGIA ALMANAC, FOR THE YEAR OF OUR LORD 1791:
      BEING THE THIRD AFTER LEAP YEAR, AND (TILL 4TH OF JULY) THE FIFTEENTH
      YEAR OF AMERICAN INDEPENDENCE. [Five lines.] BY JOHN TOBLER, ESQ.
      [Eleven lines.]
        Charleston: Printed by Markland & M'Iver, No. 47, Bay. [1790.] pp. (44).
      12mo.   LOC.
        Contains, The Constitution of the State of South-Carolina. And Duties
      payable on goods, wares and merchandizes, imported into the United
      States, according to Act of Congress, passed 10th August, 1790, and
      which is to be in force from and after 1st January, 1790.

22941   TODD, WILLIAM
AN ORATION, DELIVERED BEFORE THE MOST ANCIENT AND HONORABLE SOCIETY OF
FREE AND ACCEPTED MASONS, OF THE RISING SUN LODGE, IN KEENE, ON THE
FESTIVAL OF ST. JOHN THE EVANGELIST, DECEMBER 27, 5789. BY BROTHER
WILLIAM TODD, M. M. AND A MEMBER OF SAID LODGE. [Four lines of verse.]
    Keene: (State of New-Hampshire) Printed by brother James D. Griffith.
[1790.] pp. 23. 8vo.
                                                  AAS. BA.

22942   TOPHAM, EDWARD   1751 – 1820
THE LIFE OF JOHN ELWES, ESQUIRE, MEMBER OF THREE SUCCESSIVE BRITISH PAR-
LIAMENTS FOR BERKSHIRE. BY EDWARD TOPHAM.
    London, printed ; New-York: Re-printed for Berry and Rogers, 1790. pp.
95. 12mo.
                                                  LOC.

22943   THE TRAGEDY OF LOUIS CAPET.
    Boston: Printed by E. Russell, next Liberty-Stump. 1790.

22944   A TREATISE ON THE NATURE AND SUBJECTS OF CHRISTIAN BAPTISM. EXTRACTS
FROM A LATE AUTHOR. [Moses Hemmenway.]
    *Philadelphia: Printed by Joseph Crukshank. Sold by John Dickins, No.
43, Fourth-Street, near the corner of Race-Street.* MDCCXC, pp. (2), (71). 12mo.
                                              AAS. NYPL.

22945   TRUMBULL, BENJAMIN   1735 – 1820
A SERMON, DELIVERED AT THE ORDINATION OF THE REV. THOMAS HOLT, A. M. TO
THE PASTORAL CHARGE OF THE CHURCH IN HARDWICK. JUNE 25TH, MDCCXC.
BY BENJAMIN TRUMBULL, A. M. PASTOR OF THE CHURCH IN NORTH-HAVEN.
    Printed at Worcester, Massachusetts, by Isaiah Thomas. MDCCXC. pp.
36. 12mo.
                              AAS. CHS. JCB. NYPL. UTS. YC.

22946   TRUMBULL, JOHN   1756 – 1843
PROPOSALS BY JOHN TRUMBULL FOR PUBLISHING BY SUBSCRIPTION TWO PRINTS
FROM ORIGINAL PICTURES PAINTED BY HIMSELF, REPRESENTING THE DEATH OF
GENERAL WARREN AT THE BATTLE OF BUNKER HILL, AND THE DEATH OF GEN-
ERAL MONTGOMERY IN THE ATTACK OF QUEBEC.
    New-York: 1790. pp. 4. 4to.

22947   TUDOR, WILLIAM   1750 – 1819
A GRATULATORY ADDRESS, DELIVERED JULY 5TH, 1790, BEFORE THE SOCIETY OF
THE CINCINNATI, OF THE COMMONWEALTH OF MASSACHUSETTS. PUBLISHED BY
THEIR ORDER. [Ornament.]
    Printed in Boston, by Benjamin Russell, near the State-House. M,DCC,XC.
pp. 14. 4to.
                                AAS. BA. BM. JCB. LOC. MHS. NYPL.

22948   TYLER, ROYALL   1757 – 1826
THE CONTRAST, A COMEDY; IN FIVE ACTS: WRITTEN BY A CITIZEN OF THE UNITED
STATES; PERFORMED WITH APPLAUSE AT THE THEATRES IN NEW-YORK, PHILA-
DELPHIA, AND MARYLAND; AND PUBLISHED (UNDER AN ASSIGNMENT OF THE
COPYRIGHT) BY THOMAS WIGNELL. PRIMUS EGO IN PATRIAM AONIO—DEDUXI
VERTICE MUSAS. VIRGIL. (IMITATED.) FIRST ON OUR SHORES I TRY THALIA'S
POWERS, AND BID THE LAUGHING, USEFUL MAID BE OURS.
    *Philadelphia: From the Press of Prichard & Hall, in Market-Street, be-
tween Second and Front-Streets.* M.DCC.XC. pp. (xxiv), 79, (1), frontispiece.
8vo.
                                       AAS. BA. BPL. HSP. LCP. LOC.
    Contains, a thirteen-page list of subscribers. Reprinted, in an edition
of one hundred and seventy-five copies, in New York, in 1887. 2nd.
Pennsylvania District Copyright, issued to Thomas Wignell, as Proprietor, 15 June, 1790. This is the first American play successfully
acted upon the American stage, being first produced at the Theatre in
New York, 16 April, 1789.

$25

22949   UNITED STATES OF AMERICA.
ACTS PASSED AT A CONGRESS OF THE UNITED STATES OF AMERICA, BEGUN AND
HELD AT THE CITY OF NEW-YORK, ON WEDNESDAY THE FOURTH OF MARCH [—29
September], IN THE YEAR M,DCC,LXXXIX. AND OF THE INDEPENDENCE OF THE UN-
ITED STATES, THE THIRTEENTH. BEING THE ACTS PASSED AT THE FIRST SESSION
OF THE FIRST CONGRESS OF THE UNITED STATES, TO WIT, NEW-HAMPSHIRE,
MASSACHUSETTS, CONNECTICUT, NEW-YORK, NEW-JERSEY, PENNSYLVANIA, DEL-
AWARE, MARYLAND, VIRGINIA, SOUTH-CAROLINA, AND GEORGIA; WHICH ELEVEN
STATES RATIFIED THE CONSTITUTION OF GOVERNMENT FOR THE UNITED STATES,
PROPOSED BY THE FEDERAL CONVENTION, HELD IN PHILADELPHIA, ON THE SEVEN-
TEENTH OF SEPTEMBER, ONE THOUSAND SEVEN HUNDRED AND EIGHTY-SEVEN.
[Two lines.]

> *New-York: Printed by Francis Childs and John Swaine, Printers to the
> United States.* [1790?] pp. [93,] (1). fol.   BA. NYPL.

By Resolution of both Houses of Congress, a correct copy of the Constitution of the United States preceded the Acts of this session.

22950   —— — ACTS PASSED AT A CONGRESS OF THE UNITED STATES OF AMERICA, BEGUN
AND HELD AT THE CITY OF NEW-YORK, ON WEDNESDAY, THE FOURTH OF MARCH,
[—29 September], IN THE YEAR M,DCC,LXXXIX, AND OF THE INDEPENDENCE OF
THE UNITED STATES, THE THIRTEENTH. BEING THE ACTS PASSED AT THE FIRST
SESSION OF THE FIRST CONGRESS OF THE UNITED STATES, TO WIT, NEW-HAMP-
SHIRE, MASSACHUSETTS, CONNECTICUT, NEW-YORK, NEW-JERSEY, PENNSYLVANIA,
DELAWARE, MARYLAND, VIRGINIA, SOUTH-CAROLINA, AND GEORGIA; WHICH
ELEVEN STATES RESPECTIVELY RATIFIED THE CONSTITUTION OF GOVERNMENT
FOR THE UNITED STATES, PROPOSED BY THE FEDERAL CONVENTION, HELD IN
PHILADELPHIA, ON THE SEVENTEENTH OF SEPTEMBER, ONE THOUSAND SEVEN-
HUNDRED AND EIGHTY-SEVEN. [Ornament.]

> *Richmond: Printed by Augustine Davis, for the Gneneral [sic] Assembly
> of Virginia.* [1790.] pp. [79], (1). fol.   LOC. NYPL.

By Resolution of both Houses of Congress, a correct copy of the Constitution of the United States is prefixed. "Reprinted by Resolution
of the last General Assembly of this State for the use of the Counties."

22951   —— — THE CONSTITUTION AND LAWS OF THE UNITED STATES.

> *America: Portsmouth, (New-Hampshire) Printed by George Jerry Osborne,
> junior, and to be sold by him at his Office, Guttemberg's [sic]Head, Congress-Street.*
> M.DCC.XC. pp. 157. 8vo.   AAS.

22952   —— ACTS PASSED AT THE SECOND SESSION OF THE CONGRESS OF THE UNITED STATES
OF AMERICA, BEGUN AND HELD AT THE CITY OF NEW-YORK, ON MONDAY THE
FOURTH OF JANUARY [—12 August], IN THE YEAR M,DCC,XC: AND OF THE INDE-
PENDENCE OF THE UNITED STATES, THE FOURTEENTH. PUBLISHED BY AUTHORITY.

> *New-York: Printed by Francis Childs and John Swaine, Printers to the
> Congress of the United States.* [1790.] pp. [226.] [—ccxxviii.] fol.
>   BA. BU. LOC. NYPL. RIHS.

Contains the Treaties and Conventions ratified with the several countries of Europe, and with the Indian tribes.

22953   —— AMENDMENTS PROPOSED TO BE ADDED TO THE FEDERAL CONSTITUTION, BY
THE CONGRESS OF THE UNITED STATES OF AMERICA, BEGUN AND HELD AT THE
CITY OF NEW-YORK, ON WEDNESDAY, THE FOURTH DAY OF MARCH, IN THE YEAR
M,DCC,LXXXIX.

> *Printed at Boston, Massachusetts, by Thomas Adams, Printer to the hon-
> ourable the General Court.* M,DCC,XC. pp. 8. 8vo.   AAS. MHS.

UNITED STATES, continued.

22954 —— THE COMMITTEE, APPOINTED TO EXAMINE INTO THE MEASURES TAKEN BY CONGRESS AND THE STATE OF VIRGINIA, RESPECTING THE LANDS RESERVED FOR THE USE OF THE OFFICERS AND SOLDIERS OF THE SAID STATE, ON CONTINENTAL AND STATE ESTABLISHMENTS, IN THE CESSION MADE BY THE SAID STATE TO THE UNITED STATES, OF THE TERRITORY NORTH-WEST OF THE RIVER OHIO, AND TO REPORT THE SAME TO THE HOUSE. REPORT. . . . [Colophon.]

[New-York, Printed by Thomas Greenleaf.] [1790.] pp. [6.] fol.   NYPL.

22955 —— CONGRESS OF THE UNITED STATES: AT THE SECOND SESSION, BEGUN AND HELD AT THE CITY OF NEW-YORK, ON MONDAY, THE FOURTH OF JANUARY, ONE THOUSAND SEVEN HUNDRED AND NINETY. AN ACT AUTHORIZING THE SECRETARY OF THE TREASURY TO FINISH THE LIGHT-HOUSE, ON PORTLAND-HEAD, IN THE DISTRICT OF MAINE. APPROVED, AUGUST THE TENTH, 1790.

[New-York: Printed by Francis Childs and John Swaine, 1790.] Broadside. fol.   NYPL. RIHS.

22956 —— CONGRESS OF THE UNITED STATES, AT THE SECOND SESSION, BEGUN AND HELD AT THE CITY OF NEW-YORK, ON MONDAY, THE FOURTH OF JANUARY, ONE THOUSAND SEVEN HUNDRED AND NINETY. AN ACT FOR GIVING EFFECT TO THE SEVERAL ACTS THEREIN MENTIONED, IN RESPECT TO THE STATE OF NORTH-CAROLINA, AND OTHER PURPOSES. . . .

[New-York: Printed by Francis Childs and John Swaine, 1790.] pp. (3). fol.   JCB.

22957 —— CONGRESS OF THE UNITED STATES: AT THE SECOND SESSION BEGUN AND HELD AT THE CITY OF NEW-YORK, ON MONDAY THE FOURTH OF JANUARY, ONE THOUSAND SEVEN HUNDRED AND NINETY. AN ACT FOR GIVING EFFECT TO THE SEVERAL ACTS THEREIN MENTIONED, IN RESPECT TO THE STATE OF RHODE-ISLAND AND PROVIDENCE PLANTATIONS. . . .

[New-York: Printed by Francis Childs and John Swaine, 1790.] pp. (2). fol.   LOC. RIHS.

22958 —— CONGRESS OF THE UNITED STATES: AT THE SECOND SESSION, BEGUN AND HELD AT THE CITY OF NEW-YORK ON MONDAY THE FOURTH OF JANUARY, ONE THOUSAND SEVEN HUNDRED AND NINETY. AN ACT FOR REGULATING THE MILITARY ESTABLISHMENT OF THE UNITED STATES. . . . APPROVED, APRIL 30TH, 1790. GEORGE WASHINGTON, PRESIDENT OF THE UNITED STATES. [Colophon:]

[New-York:] Printed by Francis Childs and John Swaine. [1790.] pp. [3.] fol.   NYPL.

22959 —— CONGRESS OF THE UNITED STATES: AT THE SECOND SESSION, BEGUN AND HELD AT THE CITY OF NEW-YORK, ON MONDAY THE FOURTH OF JANUARY, ONE THOUSAND SEVEN HUNDRED AND NINETY. AN ACT FOR THE GOVERNMENT AND REGULATION OF SEAMEN IN THE MERCHANTS SERVICE. APPROVED, JULY THE TWENTIETH, 1790.

[New-York: Printed by Francis Childs and John Swaine. 1790.] pp. [4.] fol.   LOC. NYPL.

22960 —— CONGRESS OF THE UNITED STATES: AT THE SECOND SESSION, BEGUN AND HELD AT THE CITY OF NEW-YORK, ON MONDAY THE FOURTH OF JANUARY, ONE THOUSAND SEVEN HUNDRED AND NINETY. AN ACT FOR THE GOVERNMENT OF THE TERRITORY OF THE UNITED STATES, SOUTH OF THE RIVER OHIO. . . . APPROVED, MAY TWENTY-SIXTH, 1790. GEORGE WASHINGTON, PRESIDENT OF THE UNITED STATES.

[New-York: Printed by Francis Childs and John Swaine, 1790.] Broadside. fol.   AAS. NYPL.

UNITED STATES, continued.

22961 —— CONGRESS OF THE UNITED STATES: AT THE SECOND SESSION, BEGUN AND HELD AT THE CITY OF NEW-YORK, ON MONDAY THE FOURTH OF JANUARY, ONE THOUS-AND SEVEN HUNDRED AND NINETY. AN ACT FOR THE RELIEF OF JOHN STEWART AND JOHN DAVIDSON.

[New-York: Printed by Francis Childs and John Swaine, 1790.] Broadside. fol.
NYPL.

22962 —— CONGRESS OF THE UNITED STATES: AT THE SECOND SESSION BEGUN AND HELD AT THE CITY OF NEW-YORK, ON MONDAY THE FOURTH OF JANUARY, ONE THOUS-AND SEVEN HUNDRED AND NINETY. AN ACT FURTHER TO, SUSPEND PART OF AN ACT, ENTITULED, "AN ACT TO REGULATE THE ,COLLECTION OF THE DUTIES IM-POSED BY LAW ON THE TONNAGE OF SHIPS OR VESSELS, AND ON GOODS, WARES AND MERCHANDIZES IMPORTED INTO THE UNITED STATES," AND TO AMEND THE SAID ACT. [Nineteen lines.] APPROVED, THE 15TH OF.APRIL, 1790. GEORGE WASH-INGTON, PRESIDENT OF THE UNITED STATES. [Colophon:]

[New-York:] Printed by Francis Childs and John Swaine, 1790.] Broadside. fol.
RIHS.

22963 —— CONGRESS OF THE UNITED STATES: AT THE SECOND SESSION, BEGUN AND HELD AT THE CITY OF NEW-YORK ON MONDAY THE FOURTH OF JANUARY, ONE THOUS-AND SEVEN HUNDRED AND NINETY. AN ACT IMPOSING DUTIES ON THE TONNAGE OF SHIPS OR VESSELS. APPROVED, JULY THE TWENTIETH, 1790.

[New-York: Printed by Francis Childs and John Swaine, 1790.] Broadside. fol.
NYPL. RIHS.

22964 —— — AN ACT IMPOSING DUTIES ON THE TONNAGE OF SHIPS OR VESSELS. . . . 1790, JUNE THE 24TH – – READ THE THIRD TIME, AND PASSED THE HOUSE OF REPRESENTATIVES. [Colophon.]

[New-York: Printed by Francis Childs and John Swaine, 1790.] Broadside. fol.
AAS.

22965 —— CONGRESS OF THE UNITED STATES: AT THE SECOND SESSION, BEGUN AND HELD AT THE CITY OF NEW-YORK, ON MONDAY THE FOURTH OF JANUARY, ONE THOUS-AND SEVEN HUNDRED AND NINETY. AN ACT MAKING FURTHER PROVISION FOR THE PAYMENT OF THE DEBTS OF THE UNITED STATES. APPROVED, AUGUST THE TENTH, 1790.

[New-York: Printed by Francis Childs and John Swaine, 1790.] Broadside. fol.
AAS. LOC. NYPL. RIHS.

22966 —— CONGRESS OF THE UNITED STATES: AT THE SECOND SESSION, BEGUN AND HELD AT THE CITY OF NEW-YORK, ON MONDAY, THE FOURTH OF JANUARY, ONE THOUS-AND SEVEN HUNDRED AND NINETY. AN ACT PROVIDING FOR HOLDING A TREATY OR TREATIES TO ESTABLISH PEACE WITH CERTAIN INDIAN TRIBES. [Fifteen lines.] APPROVED, JULY THE TWENTY-SECOND, 1790. GEORGE WASHINGTON, PRESIDENT OF THE UNITED STATES. (TRUE COPY.) [Signed, Th: Jefferson.] SECRETARY OF STATE.

[New-York: Printed by Francis Childs and John Swaine, 1790.] Broadside. fol.
RIHS.

22967 —— CONGRESS OF THE UNITED STATES: AT THE SECOND SESSION, BEGUN AND HELD AT THE CITY OF NEW-YORK, ON MONDAY THE FOURTH OF JANUARY, ONE THOUS-AND SEVEN HUNDRED AND NINETY. AN ACT TO AMEND THE ACT FOR THE ESTAB-LISHMENT AND SUPPORT OF LIGHT-HOUSES, BEACONS, BUOYS, AND PUBLIC PIERS. APPROVED, JULY THE TWENTY-SECOND, 1790.

[New-York: Printed by Francis Childs and John Swaine, 1790.] Broadside. fol.
NYPL. RIHS.

UNITED STATES, continued.

22968 —— CONGRESS OF THE UNITED STATES: AT THE SECOND SESSION, BEGUN AND HELD AT THE CITY OF NEW-YORK ON MONDAY THE FOURTH OF JANUARY, ONE THOUSAND SEVEN HUNDRED AND NINETY. AN ACT TO PRESCRIBE THE MODE IN WHICH THE PUBLIC ACTS, RECORDS AND JUDICIAL PROCEEDINGS IN EACH STATE, SHALL BE AUTHENTICATED SO AS TO TAKE EFFECT IN EVERY OTHER STATE. . . . APPROVED, MAY TWENTY-SIXTH, 1790. GEORGE WASHINGTON, PRESIDENT OF THE UNITED STATES.
[New-York: Printed by Francis Childs and John Swaine, 1790.] Broadside. fol.   NYPL.

22969 —— CONGRESS OF THE UNITED STATES: AT THE SECOND SESSION, BEGUN AND HELD AT THE CITY OF NEW-YORK, ON MONDAY, THE FOURTH OF JANUARY, ONE THOUSAND SEVEN HUNDRED AND NINETY. AN ACT TO PROVIDE FOR THE SETTLEMENT OF ACCOUNTS BETWEEN THE UNITED STATES AND INDIVIDUAL STATES. . . . APPROVED, AUGUST 5, 1790. GEORGE WASHINGTON, PRESIDENT OF THE UNITED STATES. JOHN ADAMS, VICE-PRESIDENT. TRUE COPY. [Signed, Th: Jefferson.] SECRETARY OF STATE.
[New-York: Printed by Francis Childs and John Swaine. 1790.] pp. (2). fol.

22970 —— CONGRESS OF THE UNITED STATES: AT THE SECOND SESSION, BEGUN AND HELD AT THE CITY OF NEW-YORK, ON MONDAY, THE FOURTH OF JANUARY, ONE THOUSAND SEVEN HUNDRED AND NINETY. AN ACT TO PROVIDE FOR MORE EFFECTUALLY FOR THE COLLECTION OF THE DUTIES IMPOSED BY LAW ON GOODS, WARES AND MERCHANDIZE, IMPORTED INTO THE UNITED STATES, AND ON THE TONNAGE OF SHIPS OR VESSELS. . . . APPROVED, AUGUST THE FOURTH, 1790.
[New-York: Printed by Francis Childs and John Swaine, 1790.] pp. 41. fol.   RIHS.

22971 —— —— CONGRESS OF THE UNITED STATES. AN ACT TO REGULATE THE COLLECTION OF THE DUTIES IMPOSED BY LAW ON THE TONNAGE OF SHIPS OR VESSELS, AND ON GOODS, WARES, AND MERCHANDISES, IMPORTED INTO THE UNITED STATES.
Savannah: Printed by James and Nicholas Johnston, 1790.

22972 —— CONGRESS OF THE UNITED STATES: AT THE SECOND SESSION, BEGUN AND HELD AT THE CITY OF NEW-YORK, ON MONDAY, THE FOURTH OF JANUARY, ONE THOUSAND SEVEN HUNDRED AND NINETY. AN ACT TO REGULATE TRADE AND INTERCOURSE WITH THE INDIAN TRIBES. APPROVED, JULY THE TWENTY-SECOND, 1790.
[New-York: Printed by Francis Childs and John Swaine, 1790.] pp. (2). fol.   LOC. NYPL.
All the separate broadside Acts of Congress from 1789-1791, in the New York Public Library, are printed on writing paper, and have the words "[True copy]" or "Deposited among the rolls in the office of the Secretary of State," with space before the words, "Secretary of State" containing the autographed signature of Thomas Jefferson.

22973 —— THE CONGRESSIONAL REGISTER; OR, HISTORY OF THE PROCEEDINGS AND DEBATES OF THE FIRST HOUSE OF REPRESENTATIVES OF THE UNITED STATES OF AMERICA: NAMELY, NEW-HAMPSHIRE, MASSACHUSETTS, CONNECTICUT, NEW-YORK, NEW-JERSEY, PENNSYLVANIA, DELAWARE, MARYLAND, VIRGINIA, SOUTH-CAROLINA AND GEORGIA. BEING THE ELEVEN STATES THAT HAVE RATIFIED THE CONSTITUTION OF THE GOVERNMENT OF THE UNITED STATES. CONTAINING AN IMPARTIAL ACCOUNT OF THE MOST INTERESTING SPEECHES AND MOTIONS; AND ACCURATE COPIES OF REMARKABLE PAPERS LAID BEFORE AND OFFERED TO THE HOUSE. TAKEN IN SHORT HAND, BY THOMAS LLOYD. THE SECOND EDITION. VOLUME II.
New-York: Printed by Hodge, Allen, and Campbell, and for T. Lloyd, the Proprietors. M,DCC,XC. pp. 449. 8vo.   AAS. BA. BU. HC. NYPL.

UNITED STATES, continued.

22974 —— — THE CONGRESSIONAL REGISTER; OR, HISTORY OF THE PROCEEDINGS AND
DEBATES OF THE FIRST HOUSE OF REPRESENTATIVES OF THE UNITED STATES OF
AMERICA: NAMELY, NEW-HAMPSHIRE, MASSACHUSETTS, CONNECTICUT, NEW-
YORK, NEW-JERSEY, PENNSYLVANIA, DELAWARE, MARYLAND, VIRGINIA, SOUTH-
CAROLINA, AND GEORGIA; BEING THE ELEVEN STATES THAT HAVE RATIFIED THE
CONSTITUTION OF THE GOVERNMENT OF THE UNITED STATES. CONTAINING AN
IMPARTIAL ACCOUNT OF THE MOST INTERESTING SPEECHES AND MOTIONS; AND AC-
CURATE COPIES OF REMARKABLE PAPERS LAID BEFORE AND OFFERED TO THE
HOUSE. TAKEN IN SHORT HAND, BY THOMAS LLOYD. VOLUME III.

*New-York: Printed by Hodge, Allen, and Campbell, and for T. Lloyd, the
Proprietors.* M.DCC.XC. pp. 502. 8vo.   AAS. BA. BU. HC. NYPL.

22975 —— — THE CONGRESSIONAL REGISTER; OR, HISTORY OF THE PROCEEDINGS AND
DEBATES OF THE FIRST HOUSE OF REPRESENTATIVES OF THE UNITED STATES OF
AMERICA: NAMELY, NEW-HAMPSHIRE, MASSACHUSETTS, CONNECTICUT, NEW-
YORK, NEW-JERSEY, PENNSYLVANIA, DELAWARE, MARYLAND, VIRGINIA, NORTH-
CAROLINA, SOUTH-CAROLINA, AND GEORGIA. BEING THE TWELVE STATES THAT
HAVE RATIFIED THE CONSTITUTION OF THE GOVERNMENT OF THE UNITED STATES.
CONTAINING, AN IMPARTIAL ACCOUNT OF THE MOST INTERESTING SPEECHES AND
MOTIONS; AND ACCURATE COPIES OF REMARKABLE PAPERS LAID BEFORE AND OF-
FERED TO THE HOUSE. TAKEN IN SHORT-HAND BY THOMAS LLOYD. VOLUME
IV. [NO. I–V.]

*New-York: Printed by Hodge, Allen, and Campbell, and for T. Lloyd, the
Proprietors.* M,DCC,XC. pp. 190.+ 8vo.   AAS. BA. HC. NYPL. RIHS.

Second title: ACTS PASSED AT THE SECOND SESSION OF THE FIRST CONGRESS OF
THE UNITED STATES OF AMERICA, BEGUN AND HELD AT THE CITY OF NEW-YORK,
ON MONDAY, THE FOURTH OF JANUARY, 1790. AND OF THE INDEPENDENCE OF
THE UNITED STATES, THE FOURTEENTH. VOL. II.

*New-York: Printed by Hodge, Allen, and Campbell, and sold at their respect-
ive Book-Stores; also, by T. Lloyd.* M.DCC.XC. pp. (24)+ 8vo.   NYPL.

Given as an addenda to The Congressional Register, as issued in numbers. The numbers end somewhat abruptly, with Number v, of Volume IV. Total No. XXXVII, for May 14, 1790.

22976 —— CONSTITUTION OF THE UNITED STATES OF AMERICA. WE, THE PEOPLE OF THE
UNITED STATES, IN ORDER TO FORM A MORE PERFECT UNION, TO ESTABLISH JUS-
TICE, INSURE DOMESTIC TRANQUILITY, PROVIDE FOR THE COMMON DEFENSE, PRO-
MOTE THE GENERAL WELFARE, AND SECURE THE BLESSINGS OF LIBERTY TO OUR-
SELVES AND OUR POSTERITY, DO ORDAIN AND ESTABLISH THIS CONSTITUTION FOR
THE UNITED STATES OF AMERICA. . . . RATIFICATION OF THE CONSTITUTION
OF THE UNITED STATES BY THE CONVENTION OF THE STATE OF RHODE-ISLAND
AND PROVIDENCE PLANTATIONS. WE, THE DELEGATES OF THE PEOPLE OF THE
STATE OF RHODE-ISLAND AND PROVIDENCE PLANTATIONS . . . HAVING MATURE-
LY CONSIDERED THE CONSTITUTION FOR THE UNITED STATES OF AMERICA, . . .
DO, BY THESE PRESENTS, ASSENT TO AND RATIFY THE SAID CONSTITUTION. . . .
DONE IN CONVENTION AT NEWPORT, . . . THE 29TH DAY OF MAY, 1790.
[Double columns.]

[Providence: Printed by John Carter. 1790.] pp. (3). fol.

22977 —— THE CONSTITUTION OF THE UNITED STATES OF AMERICA. AS AGREED UPON
BY THEIR DELEGATES IN THE CONVENTION, SEPTEMBER 17TH, 1787. TOGETHER
WITH THE ARTICLES OF AMENDMENT, AS ADOPTED BY THE CONGRESS OF THE SAID
STATES, IN THE YEAR 1789.

Windsor: Re-printed by Alden Spooner. 1790. pp. 23. 4to.   AAS. LOC.

UNITED STATES, continued.

22978 —— GENERAL POST-OFFICE, NEW-YORK, JANUARY 20, 1790. SIR, IN OBEDIENCE TO THE ORDERS OF THE SUPREME EXECUTIVE, I HAVE THE HONOR OF LAYING BEFORE YOU SUCH REMARKS AND OBSERVATIONS AS HAVE OCCURRED TO ME, IN ATTENDING TO THE DEPARTMENT OF THE POST-OFFICE; . . . SAMUEL OSGOOD. THE HON. ALEXANDER HAMILTON, ESQ. SECRETARY OF THE TREASURY.
[*New-York: Printed by Francis Childs and John Swaine. 1790.*] pp. [7.]
fol. LOC. RIHS.

22979 —— IN CONGRESS AT NEW-YORK, MONDAY, THE 9TH OF AUGUST, 1790. SIR IN OBEDIENCE TO A RESOLUTION OF THE HOUSE—TRANSMIT RESOLUTION OF —18 MAY RESPECTING THE TERMS FOR WHICH THE MEMBERS OF THE PRESENT CONGRESS WERE CHOSEN.
[*New-York: Printed by Francis Childs and John Swaine*, 1790.] pp. (4).
4to. RISL.

22980 —— JOURNAL OF THE HOUSE OF REPRESENTATIVES OF THE UNITED STATES. ANNO MDCCLXXXIX, AND OF THE INDEPENDENCE OF THE UNITED STATES, THE THIRTEENTH. [4 March, —29 September, 1789.]
Richmond: Printed by Augustine Davis, for the General Assembly of Virginia. [1790.] pp. 145. fol.

22981 —— JOURNAL OF THE HOUSE OF REPRESENTATIVES OF THE UNITED STATES. ANNO M,DCC,XC, AND OF THE INDEPENDENCE OF THE UNITED STATES THE FOURTEENTH. [4 January,—12 August, 1790.]
New-York: Printed by Francis Childs and John Swaine. M,DCC,XC.
pp. 261. fol. AAS. BA. BU. LCP. LOC. NYPL.

22982 —— JOURNAL OF THE SECOND SESSION OF THE SENATE OF THE UNITED STATES OF AMERICA, BEGUN AND HELD AT THE CITY OF NEW-YORK, JANUARY 4TH, [—12 August] 1790; AND IN THE FOURTEENTH YEAR OF THE INDEPENDENCE OF THE SAID STATES.
New-York: Printed by John Fenno. in Maiden-Lane, M,DCC,XC. pp.
(224). fol. AAS. BA. BU. LOC. NYPL. RIHS.
Pages 222, 223, 224, are misnumbered 122, 123, 124.

22983 —— THE MEMORIAL AND REMONSTRANCE OF THE PUBLIC CREDITORS, WHO ARE CITIZENS OF THE COMMONWEALTH OF PENNSYLVANIA, BY THEIR COMMITTEE, DULY APPOINTED, INSTRUCTED, AND AUTHORIZED. . . . TO THE HONORABLE THE SENATE AND HOUSE OF REPRESENTATIVES OF THE UNITED STATES OF AMERICA, IN CONGRESS ASSEMBLED. [By Alexander James Dallas.]
Philadelphia: Printed by Zachariah Poulson, jun. MDCCXC. pp. (28).
8vo. CLS. JCB.

22984 —— THE MEMORIAL OF THE PUBLICK CREDITORS, CITIZENS OF THE STATE OF NEW-JERSEY.
Trenton: Printed by Isaac Collins. M.DCC.XC. pp. 16. 8vo. BA.

22985 —— ORDER OF CONGRESS ON THE TREASURY FOR THE PAYMENT OF ARREARS DUE TO THE TROOPS OF VIRGINIA AND NORTH-CAROLINA.
[*New-York: Printed by Francis Childs and John Swaine*, June 7, 1790.]
Broadside. fol.

UNITED STATES, continued.

22986　—— PHILADELPHIA, WEDNESDAY, JUNE 2. [1790.] CONGRESS. HOUSE OF REPRE-
SENTATIVES, MONDAY, MAY 21. THE HOUSE TOOK UP THE RESOLUTION PROPOSED
BY MR. FITZSIMONS, THAT CONGRESS SHOULD MEET AND HOLD THEIR NEXT SESSION
AT THE CITY OF PHILADELPHIA. THIS MOTION PRODUCED MUCH DEBATE, AND
FINALLY WAS AGREED TO . . . FOR IT 38, AGAINST IT 22. NEW-YORK, JUNE 1,
ADOPTION OF THE CONSTITUTION BY RHODE-ISLAND. [Eleven lines.] [Colophon:]
　　　Philadelphia: Printed by Dunlap and Claypoole. [1790.] Broadside.
fol.　　　　　　　　　　　　　　　　　　　　　　　　　　　RIHS.

22987　—— A PLAN FOR THE GENERAL ARRANGEMENT OF THE MILITIA OF THE UNITED
STATES. [By Henry Knox.] PUBLISHED BY ORDER OF THE HOUSE OF REPRE-
SENTATIVES.
　　　New-York: Printed by Francis Childs and John Swaine. M,DCC,XC.
pp. (1), (1), [3.] fol.　　　　　　　　　　　　　BA. HC. NYPL.
Copies of this, without the title-page, and Knox's letter of transmittal,
have the following heading:

22988　—— —— A PLAN FOR THE GENERAL ARRANGEMENT OF THE MILITIA OF THE UNITED
STATES. [By Henry Knox.] PUBLISHED BY ORDER OF THE HOUSE OF REPRE-
SENTATIVES.
　　　New-York: Printed by Francis Childs and John Swaine. M,DCC,XC.
pp. [26.] fol.　　　　　　　　　BPL. HC. LOC. NYPL. RIHS.
Three hundred copies ordered printed.

22989　—— [PROCLAMATION OF THE PRESIDENT OF THE TREATY WITH THE CREEK INDIANS.
NEW YORK. AUGUST 14. 1790.
　　　New-York: Printed by Francis Childs and John Swaine, 1790.] Broad-
side. fol.

22990　—— REGULATIONS FOR THE ORDER AND DISCIPLINE OF THE TROOPS OF THE UNITED
STATES.
　　　*Boston: Printed and sold by T. & J. Fleet, at the Bible and Heart in Corn-
hill.* 1790.

22991　—— —— REGULATIONS FOR THE ORDER AND DISCIPLINE OF THE TROOPS OF THE
UNITED STATES. PART I.
　　　Fayetteville: Re-printed by Howard and Roulstone, for John Sibley and Co.
MDCCXC. pp. 72. 12mo.　　　　　　　　　　　　　NCU.

22992　—— —— REGULATIONS FOR THE ORDER AND DISCIPLINE OF THE TROOPS OF THE
UNITED STATES. BY BARON STEUBEN, LATE MAJOR-GENERAL AND INSPECTOR-
GENERAL IN THE ARMY OF THE UNITED STATES. ILLUSTRATED WITH ALL THE
NECESSARY COPPER PLATES.
　　　New-York: Printed by Hugh Gaine, 1790.

22993　—— REPORT OF THE REGISTER OF THE TREASURY, TO THE HOUSE OF REPRESENTA-
TIVES, ON THE ACCOUNTS OF ROBERT MORRIS, WHILE SUPERINTENDENT OF FI-
NANCE, 1781, TO HIS RESIGNATION IN 1784. . . . JOSEPH NOURSE.
　　　[*New-York: Printed by Francis Childs and John Swaine,* March 4, 1790.]
pp. (2). fol.

22994　—— REPORT OF THE SECRETARY OF STATE, ON THE SUBJECT OF ESTABLISHING A
UNIFORMITY IN THE WEIGHTS, MEASURES AND COINS OF THE UNITED STATES.
PUBLISHED BY ORDER OF THE HOUSE OF REPRESENTATIVES. [First impression.]
　　　New-York: Printed by Francis Childs and John Swaine. MDCCXC.
pp. [21.] fol.　　　　　　　　　　　　　　　　　LOC.

UNITED STATES, continued.

22995 —— — REPORT OF THE SECRETARY OF STATE, ON THE SUBJECT OF ESTABLISHING
A UNIFORMITY IN THE WEIGHTS, MEASURES AND COINS OF THE UNITED STATES.
PUBLISHED BY ORDER OF THE HOUSE OF REPRESENTATIVES. [Second impres-
sion.]
New-York: Printed by Francis Childs and John Swaine. MDCCXC.
pp. [21], blank, [21]–[22.] fol. LOC.

22996 —— — REPORT OF THE SECRETARY OF STATE, ON THE SUBJECT OF ESTABLISHING
A UNIFORMITY IN THE WEIGHTS, MEASURES AND COINS OF THE UNITED STATES.
PUBLISHED BY ORDER OF THE HOUSE OF REPRESENTATIVES. [Third impression.]
New-York: Printed by Francis Childs and John Swaine. MDCCXC.
pp. [22], [21], blank. fol. LOC.

22997 —— — REPORT OF THE SECRETARY OF STATE, ON THE SUBJECT OF ESTABLISHING
A UNIFORMITY IN THE WEIGHTS, MEASURES AND COINS OF THE UNITED STATES.
PUBLISHED BY ORDER OF THE HOUSE OF REPRESENTATIVES. [Fourth impres-
sion.]
New-York: Printed by F. Childs and J. Swaine. M,DCC,XC. pp. [49.]
8vo. AAS. BA. BM. JCB. LCP. LOC. MHS. NYHS. NYPL.

22998 —— REPORT OF THE SECRETARY OF THE TREASURY TO THE HOUSE OF REPRESENT-
ATIVES, RELATIVE TO A PROVISION FOR THE SUPPORT OF THE PUBLIC CREDIT OF
THE UNITED STATES, IN CONFORMITY TO A RESOLUTION OF THE TWENTY-FIRST DAY
OF SEPTEMBER, 1789. PRESENTED TO THE HOUSE ON THURSDAY, THE 14TH DAY
OF JANUARY, 1790. PUBLISHED BY ORDER OF THE HOUSE OF REPRESENTATIVES.
New-York; Printed by Francis Childs and John Swaine. M,DCC,XC.
pp. [51.] fol. AAS. BA. PPL. JCB. LOC. NYHS. NYPL. RIHS.

22999 —— RICHMOND, MARCH 26, 1790. IT HAVING BEEN PROVIDED BY AN ACT OF THE
PRESENT SESSION OF CONGRESS, THAT THE MARSHALS OF THE SEVERAL DISTRICTS
OF THE UNITED STATES, SHALL CAUSE THE NUMBER OF INHABITANTS WITHIN THEIR
RESPECTIVE DISTRICTS TO BE TAKEN, . . . EDWARD CARRINGTON, MARSHAL, FOR
THE DISTRICT OF VIRGINIA.
[Richmond: Printed by John Dixon, 1790.] Broadside. fol. LOC.

23000 —— RULES AND ARTICLES FOR THE BETTER GOVERNMENT OF THE TROOPS RAISED
OR TO BE RAISED AND KEPT IN PAY BY AND AT THE EXPENCE OF THE UNITED
STATES OF AMERICA.
Printed at Philadelphia, 1790. pp. 39. 8vo.

23001 —— THE SECRETARY OF STATE, TO WHOM WAS REFERRED BY THE HOUSE OF REPRE-
SENTATIVES THE LETTER OF JOHN H. MITCHELL, RECITING CERTAIN PROPOSALS,
FOR SUPPLYING THE UNITED STATES WITH COPPER COINAGE, HAS HAD THE SAME
UNDER CONSIDERATION, ACCORDING TO INSTRUCTIONS, AND BEGS LEAVE TO REPORT
THEREON AS FOLLOWS. . . . THOMAS JEFFERSON. APRIL 14, 1790.
[New-York: Printed by Francis Childs and John Swaine, 1790.] pp.
(2). fol. LOC. RIHS.

23002 —— TREASURY DEPARTMENT, MARCH 1, 1790. PURSUANT TO THE ACT FOR ESTAB-
LISHING THE TREASURY DEPARTMENT, THE SECRETARY OF THE TREASURY RES-
PECTFULLY REPORTS TO THE HOUSE OF REPRESENTATIVES . . . ESTIMATE OF
EXTRAORDINARIES, TO MAKE GOOD DEFICIENCIES IN THE FORMER ESTIMATE OF
THE CIVIL LIST FOR THE YEAR 1789, . . . [Colophon:]
New-York: Printed by Francis Childs and John Swaine. [1790.] pp.[10.]
fol. BA. LOC. RIHS.

UNITED STATES, continued.

23003 —— TREASURY DEPARTMENT, MARCH 4, 1790. IN OBEDIENCE TO THE ORDER OF THE HOUSE OF REPRESENTATIVES, OF THE SECOND INSTANT, THE SECRETARY OF THE TREASURY, RESPECTFULLY REPORTS, THAT IN HIS OPINION THE FUNDS IN THE FIRST INSTANCE REQUISITE TOWARDS THE PAYMENT OF INTEREST ON THE DEBTS OF THE INDIVIDUAL STATES, ACCORDING TO THE MODIFICATIONS PROPOSED BY HIM IN HIS REPORT OF THE NINTH OF JANUARY PAST; MAY BE OBTAINED FROM THE FOLLOWING OBJECTS. . . . [Colophon:]
New-York: Printed by Francis Childs and John Swaine. [1790.] pp. [3.] fol.   LOC. RLHS.

23004 —— TREASURY DEPARTMENT, JULY 20TH, 1790. IN OBEDIENCE TO THE ORDER OF THE HOUSE OF REPRESENTATIVES, OF THE TWENTIETH OF JANUARY LAST, THE SECRETARY OF THE TREASURY RESPECTFULLY REPORTS, THAT IN THE FORMATION OF A PLAN FOR THE DISPOSITION OF THE VACANT LANDS OF THE UNITED STATES. ALL WHICH IS HUMBLY SUBMITTED, ALEXANDER HAMILTON, SECRETARY OF THE TREASURY. [Colophon:]
[New-York:] Printed by Francis Childs and John Swaine. [1790.] pp. [4.] fol.   LOC. NYPL. RIHS.

23005 —— TREASURY DEPARTMENT, DECEMEBR 13, 1790 IN OBEDIENCE TO THE ORDER OF THE HOUSE OF REPRESENTATIVES, OF THE NINTH DAY OF AUGUST LAST, RE-QUIRING THE SECRETARY OF THE TREASURY TO PREPARE AND REPORT, ON THIS DAY, SUCH FURTHER PROVISION AS MAY, IN HIS OPINION, BE NECESSARY FOR ES-TABLISHING THE PUBLIC CREDIT—THE SAID SECRETARY RESPECTFULLY REPORTS, [On funds, for paying accruing interest.] [Colophon:]
[New-York:] Printed by Francis Childs and John Swaine. [1790.] pp. [7.] fol.   BA. LOC. NYPL.

23006 —— — TREASURY DEPARTMENT, DECEMBER 13, 1790. IN OBEDIENCE TO THE ORDER OF THE HOUSE OF REPRESENTATIVES, OF THE NINTH DAY OF AUGUST LAST, REQUIRING THE SECRETARY OF THE TREASURY TO PREPARE AND REPORT, ON THIS DAY, SUCH FURTHER PROVISION AS MAY, IN HIS OPINION, BE NECESSARY FOR ESTABLISHING THE PUBLIC CREDIT—THE SAID SECRETARY FURTHER RESPECT-FULLY REPORTS, [On a National Bank.] [Colophon:]
[New-York:] Printed by Francis Childs and John Swaine. [1790.] pp. [22.] fol.   LOC. NYPL.

23007 [U. S. arms.] THE UNITED STATES CHRONICLE: POLITICAL, COMMERCIAL, AND HISTORICAL. [R. I. arms.] VOL. VII. NUMB. 315. THURSDAY, JANUARY 7, [—NUMB. 366. THURSDAY, DECEMBER 30, 1790.]
Printed and published by Bennett Wheeler in Westminster-Street, Providence. 1790. fol.   AAS.

23008 THE UNIVERSAL ASYLUM AND COLUMBIAN MAGAZINE FOR [MARCH–DECEMBER,] 1790. VOL. V. [Cut.]
Philadelphia: Printed for the Proprietors by W. Young Bookseller No. 52 Second Street. [1790.] pp. (2), 422, (2), (8), 2 plates. 8vo. AAS. BA. HC. LOC.
The engraved title, is the work of Thackara & Vallance. The cut by C. W. Peale, del'r. In continuation, from February, 1790, of *The Columbian magazine, or monthly miscellany.*

23009 UNIVERSALIST CHURCH.
ARTICLES OF FAITH, AND PLAN OF CHURCH GOVERNMENT, COMPOSED AND ADOPTED BY THE CHURCHES BELIEVING IN THE SALVATION OF ALL MEN, MET IN PHILA-DELPHIA ON THE 25TH OF MAY, 1790. TO WHICH ARE ADDED, SUNDRY RECOM-MENDATIONS, AND A CIRCULAR LETTER, ADDRESSED TO THE CHURCHES IN THE UNITED STATES BELIEVING THE SAME DOCTRINE.
Philadelphia: Printed by Thomas Dobson, at the Stone-House, in Second-Street. 1790.   BA.

23010   USSHER, George Neville
THE ELEMENTS OF ENGLISH GRAMMAR, METHODICALLY ARRANGED FOR THE ASSIST-
ANCE OF YOUNG PERSONS WHO STUDY THE ENGLISH LANGUAGE GRAMMATICALLY:
TO WHICH IS ADDED, A CONCISE TREATISE OF RHETORIC. DESIGNED PARTICULARLY
FOR THE USE OF LADIES BOARDING SCHOOLS. BY G. NEVILLE USSHER.
Portsmouth: Printed by John Melcher, 1790.

23011   VAN CUELEN, Jacobus
THE DELAWARE ALMANAC, OR EASTERN-SHORE CALENDAR, FOR THE YEAR OF OUR
LORD, 1791: BEING THE THIRD AFTER LEAP YEAR. BY JACOBUS VAN CUELEN.
[Cut.]
*Wilmington: Printed and sold by Andrews, Craig and Brynberg, at the
Post-Office in Market street.* [1790.] pp. (36). 12mo.   LOC.

23012   DER VERBESSERTE Hoch Deutsche Americanische Land und Staats Calen-
DER. AUF DAS JAHR. . . . 1791. ZUM SIEBENTEN MAL HERAUSGEGEBEN.
Friedrich Stadt, Maryland: Gedruckt bey Matthias Bartgis. [1790.]

23013   VERMONT. State.
ACTS AND LAWS, PASSED BY THE LEGISLATURE OF THE STATE OF VERMONT, AT THEIR
SESSION AT CASTLETON, THE SECOND THURSDAY OF OCTOBER, 1790.
[Windsor: Printed by Alden Spooner. 1790.] pp. 11. 4to.   LOC.

23014   —— BY HIS EXCELLENCY MOSES ROBINSON, ESQUIRE, GOVERNOR AND COMMAND-
ER IN CHIEF IN AND OVER THE STATE OF VERMONT, A PROCLAMATION.
[Appointing Wednesday, the 28th of April, a day of public humiliation, fasting
and prayer.] ALL SERVILE LABOUR AND RECREATION IS FORBIDDEN ON SAID
DAY. GIVEN AT THE COUNCIL CHAMBER IN BENNINGTON, THE 31ST DAY OF
MARCH, IN THE YEAR OF OUR LORD 1790, AND IN THE 14TH YEAR OF THE INDE-
PENDENCE OF VERMONT. MOSES ROBINSON. BY HIS EXCELLENCY'S COMMAND.
JOSEPH FAY, SECRETARY. GOD SAVE THE PEOPLE.
[Bennington: Printed by Haswell & Russell, 1790.] Broadside fol. NYHS.

23015   [Vt. arms.] THE VERMONT Gazette. [U. S. arms.] [Motto.] VOL. VII. NUMB.
32. MONDAY, JANUARY 4, [— VOL. VIII. NUMB. 31. MONDAY, DECEMBER 27,
1790.]
*Printed and published (every Monday) by Haswell & Russell, at their
Office a few rods south of the Courthouse, Bennington. 1790. fol.*   AAS.
With the issue for October 25th, David Russell withdrew from the
partnership. From November 1st, the name of Anthony Haswell
alone appears as printer and publisher.

23016   THE VERMONT [cut] JOURNAL, AND THE UNIVERSAL ADVERTISER. VOL. VII. No.
336. WEDNESDAY, JANUARY 6, [— VOL. VIII. No. 387. TUESDAY, DECEMBER 28,
1790.]
Windsor: Printed by Alden Spooner. 1790. fol.   AAS.
The cut was omitted in the issue for June 2d.

23017   VIRGINIA. State.
ACTS PASSED AT A GENERAL ASSEMBLY, OF THE COMMONWEALTH OF VIRGINIA,
BEGUN AND HELD AT THE CAPITOL, IN THE CITY OF RICHMOND, ON MONDAY, THE
NINETEENTH OF OCTOBER, IN THE YEAR OF OUR LORD, ONE THOUSAND SEVEN
HUNDRED AND EIGHTY-NINE [— 19 December, 1789.] [Ornament.]
Richmond: Printed by John Dixon, Printer to this Commonwealth. [1790.]
pp. 50. fol.   LOC. VSL.

VIRGINIA, continued.

23018　——— Journal of the House of Delegates of the Commonwealth of Virginia, begun and held at the capitol in the city of Richmond on Monday, the nineteenth of October, in the year of our Lord one thousand seven hundred and eighty-nine, and of the Commonwealth the fourteenth [— 19 December, 1789.] [Ornament.]
Richmond: Printed by John Dixon, Printer to this Commonwealth. [1790.] pp. [120.] fol.　　　　　　　　　　　　　　　　LOC. VSL.

23019　——— Journal of the Senate of the Commonwealth of Virginia; begun and held in the city of Richmond, on Monday, the 19th day of October, in the year of our Lord 1789, and in the fourteenth year of the Commonwealth. [— 19 December, 1789.]
[Richmond: Printed by John Dixon, 1790.]
Reprinted in Richmond, in 1828.

23020　——— A List of balances due from the several counties for taxes from the year 1782 to the year 1790 inclusive.
Richmond: Printed by John Dixon. 1790. pp. 4. fol.　　　　LCP.

23021　THE VIRGINIA [U. S. arms] Centinel; or, the Winchester Mercury. [Motto.] Vol. ii. No. 93. Wednesday, January 6, [— Vol. iii. No. 144. Wednesday, December 29, 1790.]
Winchester: Printed by Richard Bowen and Co. 1790. fol.

23022　THE VIRGINIA Gazette and Alexandria Advertiser. Vol. i. No. 24. Thursday, January 7, [— Vol. ii. No. 75. Thursday, December 30, 1790.]
Alexandria: Printed by Hanson and Bond. 1790. fol.　　　AAS.
Beginning with the issue for October 21st, the following motto was added to the heading: "Oh! Thou, by whose almighty nod the scale Of empire rises, or, alternate, falls, Send forth the SAVING VIRTUES round this land!"

23023　THE VIRGINIA Gazette, and general advertiser. Vol. v. Numb. 212. Wednesday, August 25, [— Numb. 230. Wednesday, December 29, 1790.]
Richmond: Printed by Aug. Davis. 1790. fol.　　　　　LOC.
In continuation of *The Virginia Independent Chronicle.*

23024　THE VIRGINIA Gazette, and Petersburg Intelligencer. [Motto.] Vol. iv. No. 184. Thursday, January 7, [— Vol. v. No. 235. Thursday, December 30, 1790.]
Petersburg: Printed by William Prentis, 1790. fol.

23025　THE VIRGINIA Gazette, and weekly advertiser. No. 389. Thursday, January 7, [— No. 440. Thursday, December 30. 1790.]
Richmond: Printed by Thomas Nicolson. 1790. fol.

23026　THE VIRGINIA Herald, and Fredericksburg advertiser. [Motto.] Vol. ii. Numb. 136. Thursday, January 7, [— Numb. 187. Thursday, December 30, 1790.]
Fredericksburg: Printed by Timothy Green. 1790. fol.

23027   THE VIRGINIA INDEPENDENT CHRONICLE, AND GENERAL ADVERTISER. VOL. V. NUMB. 179. WEDNESDAY, JANUARY 6, [— NUMB. 211. WEDNESDAY, AUGUST 18, 1790.]

[Richmond:] Printed by Aug. Davis. 1790. fol.   LOC.
Continued as, *The Virginia Gazette, and general advertiser.*

23028   THE VOCAL REMEMBRANCER: BEING A CHOICE SELECTION OF THE MOST ADMIRED SONGS, INCLUDING THE MODERN. EMBELLISHED WITH AN ELEGANT PASTORAL SCENE.

Philadelphia: Printed by William Spotswood? 1790. pp. viii,184. 12mo.LCP.

23029   WALKER, ROBERT   1716 – 1783
SERMONS ON PRACTICAL SUBJECTS BY ROBERT WALKER, ONE OF THE MINISTERS OF THE HIGH CHURCH OF EDINBURGH. [Six lines of Scripture texts.] THE THIRD EDITION.

Philadelphia: Printed by R. Aitken & Son, in Market Street. M.DCC.XC. pp. iv, 295, (1). 12mo.   AAS.

23030   WARD, BENJAMIN M.
AN ESSAY ON RELIGION, AND THE PLAIN WAY TO HEAVEN. BY BENJAMIN M. WARD, PHILOM.

Baltimore: Printed by Samuel and John Adams, for the Author, Talbot County (at the place known by the name of The Trap). 1790.

23031   WARING, WILLIAM
THE NEW-JERSEY ALMANACK, FOR THE YEAR OF OUR LORD 1791; BEING THE THIRD AFTER BISSEXTILE OR LEAP-YEAR, AND THE SIXTEENTH YEAR OF AMERICAN INDEPENDENCE, AFTER THE 4TH OF JULY, NEXT. . . . CAREFULLY CALCULAT-ED FOR THE MERIDIAN OF PHILADELPHIA, BY WILLIAM WARING.

Trenton: Printed and sold by Isaac Collins. [1790.] pp. (40). 16mo. AAS.

23032   —— POOR WILL'S ALMANACK, FOR THE YEAR OF OUR LORD, 1791. [Twenty lines.] THE ASTRONOMICAL CALCULATIONS BY WILLIAM WARING.

Philadelphia; Printed and sold by Joseph Crukshank, in Market-Street, between Second and Third Streets. [1790.] pp. (44). 12mo.   AAS.

23033   —— POOR WILL'S POCKET ALMANACK, FOR THE YEAR 1791. [Nineteen lines.]
Philadelphia: Printed and sold by Joseph Crukshank, in Market-Street. [1790.] pp. [40.] 32mo.   NYPL.

23034   —— POULSON'S TOWN AND COUNTRY ALMANAC, FOR THE YEAR OF OUR LORD, 1791; BEING THE THIRD AFTER LEAP-YEAR. [Thirty lines.] THE ASTRONOMICAL CAL-CULATIONS BY WILLIAM WARING.

Philadelphia: Printed and sold by Zachariah Poulson, junior, in Fourth-street, near Market-street, opposite the Friend's Burying ground. [1790.] pp. (36). 12mo.   LOC.

23035   WARREN, MERCY OTIS   1728 – 1814
POEMS, DRAMATIC AND MISCELLANEOUS. BY MRS. M. WARREN. [Two lines from] POPE. [Ornament.]

Printed at Boston, by I. Thomas and E. T. Andrews. At Faust's Statue, No. 45, Newbury Street. MDCCXC. pp. 252. 12mo. AAS. BA. BM. BU. HC. NYPL.
7th Massachusetts District Copyright, issued to Mrs. M. Warren, as Author, 23d October, 1790.

23036   WARREN. RHODE ISLAND. WARREN ASSOCIATION.
MINUTES OF THE WARREN ASSOCIATION, HELD AT THE BAPTIST-MEETING-HOUSE IN HARVARD, M,DCC,XC.

Boston: Printed by Samuel Hall, at No. 53, *Cornhill,* 1790. pp.12. 12mo.
AAS. JCB.

23037   THE WASHINGTON SPY. VOL. I. NO. 1. THURSDAY, AUGUST 12, [— NO. 21. THURSDAY, DECEMBER 30, 1790.]

Elizabeth (Hager's) Town, Printed by Stewart Herbert. 1790. fol.
Established by Stewart Herbert; and continued by him until his death in 1796, when his widow, Phebe Herbert, was associated with John D. Cary, administrator of his estate, in continuing its publication up to June 1, 1796, when this arrangement was dissolved by mutual consent, Mrs. Herbert continuing publication. In March, 1797, Thomas Grieves, attorney for John D. Cary, administrator of the estate of Stewart Herbert, deceased, established, in continuation, *The Maryland Herald, and Elizabeth-Town Advertiser.*

23038   WATERHOUSE, BENJAMIN   1754 – 1846
ON THE PRINCIPLE OF VITALITY. A DISCOURSE DELIVERED IN THE FIRST CHURCH IN BOSTON, TUESDAY, JUNE 8TH, 1790. BEFORE THE HUMANE SOCIETY OF THE COMMONWEALTH OF MASSACHUSETTS. BY B. WATERHOUSE, M. D. PROFESSOR OF THE THEORY AND PRACTICE OF PHYSIC, AND LECTURER ON NATURAL HISTORY IN THE UNIVERSITY OF CAMBRIDGE. OF ALL THE POWERS IN NATURE, HEAT IS THE CHIEF. BACON.

Boston: Printed by Thomas and John Fleet. 1790. pp. (2), (2), 24, (4). 4to.
AAS. BM. HC. JCB. LOC. MHS. NYHS. SGO.

23039   WATSON, ELKANAH   1758 – 1842
A TOUR IN HOLLAND, IN MDCCLXXXIV. BY AN AMERICAN. [Ornament.]

Printed at Worcester, Massachusetts, by Isaiah Thomas. Sold at his Bookstore in Worcester, and by him and Company in Boston. MDCCXC. pp. 191. 8vo. AAS. JCB. LOC. MHS. NYPL.

23040   WATTS, ISAAC   1674 – 1748
DIVINE AND MORAL SONGS FOR THE USE OF CHILDREN.

Bennington: Printed by Haswell and Russell. 1790.

23041   —— HORÆ LYRICÆ. POEMS, CHIEFLY OF THE LYRIC KIND. IN THREE BOOKS. SACRED I. TO DEVOTION AND PIETY. II. TO VIRTUE, HONOUR, AND FRIENDSHIP. III. TO THE MEMORY OF THE DEAD. BY I. WATTS, D. D. [Six lines of Latin, and Greek quotations.]

Boston: Printed by S. Hall, for B. Larkin, in Cornhill; J. White, in Court Street; D. West, in Marlboro'-Street; and E. Larkin, in Cornhill. MDCCXC. pp. xxxviii, 252, portrait, by Hill sc. 12mo. AAS. NYPL.

23042   —— HYMNS AND SPIRITUAL SONGS—IN THREE BOOKS—1. COLLECTED FROM THE SCRIPTURES—2. COMPOSED ON DIVINE SUBJECTS—3. PREPARED FOR THE LORD'S SUPPER. BY I. WATTS, D. D.

Philadelphia: Printed for Robert Campbell. 1790.

23043   WEATHERWISE, ABRAHAM, pseudonym.
THE FEDERAL ALMANACK, FOR THE YEAR OF OUR LORD 1791. . . . BY ABRAHAM WEATHERWISE.

Boston: Printed and sold by J. White and C. Cambridge. [1790.] pp.(24). 12mo. AAS. HC.

WEATHERWISE, ABRAHAM, continued.

23044 —— THE MASSACHUSETTS ALMANACK, FOR THE YEAR OF OUR LORD, 1791, BEING THE THIRD AFTER BISSEXTILE OR LEAP-YEAR, AND FIFTEENTH OF THE INDEPENDENCE OF THE UNITED STATES OF AMERICA. CALCULATED FOR THE MERIDIAN OF BOSTON, BUT WILL SERVE FOR THE NEIGHBOURING STATES WITH LITTLE VARIATION. [Cut.] BY ABRAHAM WEATHERWISE. [Two lines of verse.]
Printed at Boston by Mills & Doyle, for Joseph Hovey, and sold at his Shop, No. 89, Cornhill. [1790.] Broadside. fol.   NYHS.
Seventeen pages, with a large cut of George Washington, imposed on a single sheet.

23045 —— WEATHERWISE'S GENUINE MASSACHUSETTS, RHODEISLAND AND CONNECTICUT ALMANACK, FOR THE YEAR OF OUR LORD 1791: BEING THE THIRD YEAR AFTER BISSEXTILE OR LEAP-YEAR AND FIFTEENTH OF THE INDEPENDENCE OF THE UNITED STATES. [Eight lines. Cut.]
Boston: Printed and sold by N. Coverly, at the Sign of the Grand Turk, Newbury-Street. [1790.] pp. (24). 12mo.   AAS.

23046 —— —— WEATHERWISE'S GENUINE MASSACHUSETTS, RHODEISLAND AND CONNECTICUT ALMANACK, FOR THE YEAR OF OUR LORD, 1791: BEING THE THIRD YEAR AFTER BISSEXTILE OR LEAP-YEAR AND FIFTEENTH OF THE INDEPENDENCE OF THE UNITED STATES. [Eight lines. Cut.]
Boston: Printed [by Nathaniel Coverly] for and sold by the Booksellers in town and country. [1790.] pp. (24). 12mo.   HC. LOC.
There is no difference, but the title, and woodcut, between this and Bickerstaff's Genuine Almanack, printed by Nathaniel Coverly this year.

23047 —— WEATHERWISE'S NEWHAMPSHIRE, MASSACHUSETTS, AND VERMONT ALMANACK, FOR THE YEAR OF OUR LORD, 1791, BEING THE THIRD AFTER BISSEXTILE, OR LEAPYEAR, AND THE FIFTEENTH OF AMERICAN INDEPENDENCE. CALCULATED FOR THE MERIDIAN OF 42 DEG. 23 M. NORTH, AND 71 DEG. 18 M. WEST OF GREENWICH.—FITTING INDIFFERENTLY, NEWHAMPSHIRE, MASSACHUSETTS, RHODE-ISLAND, VERMONT AND NEW-YORK. CONTAINING BESIDES THE USUAL CALCULATIONS, A VARIETY OF CURIOUS, USEFUL AND ENTERTAINING MATTERS. [Six lines of verse.]
Printed at Exeter, by Henry Ranlet, and sold at his Office, by wholesale or retail. [1790.] pp. [24.] 12mo.   NYPL.

23048 —— WEATHERWISE'S TOWN AND COUNTRY ALMANACK, FOR THE YEAR OF OUR LORD 1791. [Eighteen lines.]
Boston: Printed [by Joseph Bumstead] for and sold by the Booksellers. [1790.] pp. (24). 12mo.   AAS.
There is no difference between this Almanac, and Bickerstaff's Genuine Almanack for 1791, printed by Joseph Bumstead, except the titlepage.
At the end is Bumstead's advertisement as printer.

23049 —— —— WEATHERWISE'S TOWN AND COUNTRY ALMANACK, FOR THE YEAR OF OUR LORD, 1791. [Cut of temple, with thirteen columns, thirteen stars over its entrance, and flying angel with trumpet of fame, and staff with liberty cap.]
Boston: Printed [by Joseph Bumstead] for and sold by John W. Folsom, No. 30, Union-Street. Sold also by the Booksellers in town and country. [1790.] pp. (24). 12mo.   NYHS.

23050   WEBSTER, NOAH, JUNIOR   1758 – 1843
AN AMERICAN SELECTION OF LESSONS IN READING AND SPEAKING. CALCULATED TO IMPROVE THE MINDS AND REFINE THE TASTE OF YOUTH. AND ALSO, TO INSTRUCT THEM IN THE GEOGRAPHY, HISTORY, AND POLITICS OF THE UNITED STATES. TO WHICH ARE PREFIXED, RULES IN ELOCUTION, AND DIRECTIONS FOR EXPRESSING THE PRINCIPAL PASSIONS OF THE MIND. BEING THE THIRD PART OF A GRAMMATICAL INSTITUTE OF THE ENGLISH LANGUAGE. BY NOAH WEBSTER, JUN. ESQUIRE. AUTHOR OF "DISSERTATIONS ON THE ENGLISH LANGUAGE." COLLECTION OF ESSAYS AND FUGITIVE WRITINGS," &c. THOMAS AND ANDREWS'S FIRST EDITION. WITH MANY CORRECTIONS AND IMPROVEMENTS, BY THE AUTHOR. [Two lines from] MIRABEAU.

> *Printed at Boston by Isaiah Thomas and Ebenezer T. Andrews. At Faust's Statue, No. 45 Newbury Street. Sold wholesale and retail, at their Bookstore; by said Thomas at his Bookstore in Worcester, and by the Booksellers in town and country.* MDCCXC. pp. 239, (1), portrait. 12mo,   LOC. NYPL.

6th Massachusetts District Copyright, issued to Isaiah Thomas and Ebenezer T. Andrews, as Proprietors, 7 October, 1790. The Publishers advertise: "A new and correct edition of the first, second and third parts of Webster's Grammatical institute of the English language. As said Thomas and Andrews have the Copyright of all the above parts for 14 years, they intend to have their editions uniform, and correct, and page for page with each other that they may be used together in a class."

23051   —— THE AMERICAN SPELLING BOOK: CONTAINING AN EASY STANDARD OF PRONUNCIATION. BEING THE FIRST PART OF A GRAMMATICAL INSTITUTE OF THE ENGLISH LANGUAGE. BY NOAH WEBSTER, JUN. ESQUIRE. THE FIRST CONNECTICUT EDITION.

> *Hartford: Printed by Hudson and Goodwin.* [1790.]

In the "American Mercury," of May 24th, 1790, Nathaniel Patten, Bookseller in Hartford, addressed the citizens of Connecticut as follows: "To the public. A proposal to save three hundred and thirty pounds, six shillings and eight pence annually to the inhabitants of this State. Whereas the Act for the encouragement of literature, in this State, forbids the importation of books from any other in the Union altho the Author has the benefit of the copy, and they are printed by licensed printers, (if there is a copyright sold in this) which prevents a free trade. The consumption of Webster's Spelling-books, is near or quite 20,000 annually; and the price they are commonly selling at is ten shillings per dozen, and fourteen pence single — the monopoly of printing and vending them, being only in one printer, keeps the prices so high — the subscriber can purchase them in New-York, or Philadelphia, of licensed printers, and import into this State, and sell them at six shillings per dozen, and eight pence singly, and get a good profit by them; which, at the rate of 20.000 per year, will save to this State the above sum. Any person who has the sole right of printing and vending them, can find paper and print them, at 2d ¼ each, and they can be bound at 1d. ½ which makes four shillings and three pence per dozen; and to sell them at six shillings makes a profit of more than forty per cent. besides thirty-three and one-third more on those they retail. If the statute law now existing, should this May session be amended and give a free trade thro the United States for those and other books, if bought of licensed printers: the subscriber is ready to come under bonds, that he will supply this State with ten or twenty thousand annually for several years to come, of as well-printed Webster's Spelling books as usual — and at the above prices. Nathaniel Patten. Hartford, May 10, 1790."

WEBSTER, Noah, junior, continued.

23052 —— — The American spelling book: containing an easy standard of pronunciation. Being the first part of a Grammatical institute of the English language. By Noah Webster, jun. esquire. Author of "Dissertations on the English language," "Collection of essays and fugitive writings," &c. Thomas and Andrews's second edition. With additional lessons, corrected by the Author.

Printed at Boston, by Isaiah Thomas and Ebenezer T. Andrews. At Faust's Statue, No. 45, Newbury Street. Sold, wholesale and retail, at their Bookstore; by said Thomas at his Bookstore in Worcester, and by the Booksellers in town and country. MDCCXC. pp. 144, portrait. 12mo. LOC.

4th Massachusetts District Copyright, issued to Isaiah Thomas and Ebenezer T. Andrews, (on all three Parts) as Proprietors, 7 October, 1790. "The reception of our first edition of the American Spelling Book, has been so favourable . . . as to render it almost certain that not only Webster's Spelling Book, but his Grammar, and Selections of lessons for reading and speaking . . . will supersede all other school books of the kind, and come into general use throughout the United States. This very favourable reception has induced us to purchase the exclusive right of printing all the three parts of said Institute in the States of Massachusetts, Newhampshire, and Rhode-Island, for the term of fifteen years."

23053 —— A Collection of essays and fugitiv writings. On moral, historical, political and literary subjects. By Noah Webster, jun. attorney at law. [Three lines of French from] Tableau de Paris. [Ornament.]

Printed at Boston, for the Author, by I. Thomas and E. T. Andrews, At Faust's Statue, No. 45, Newbury Street. MDCCXC. pp. xvi, 414. 8vo.

AAS. BA. BM. HC. JCB. LCP. LOC. MHS. NL. NYHS. NYPL. YC.

Contains an interesting list of subscribers.

23054 —— A Grammatical institute of the English language; comprising an easy, concise and systematic method of education. Designed for the use of English schools in America. In three parts. Part second. Containing a plain and comprehensive grammar, grounded on the true principles and idioms of the language. By Noah Webster, jun. esquire. Author of "Dissertations on the English language," "Collection of essays and fugitive writings," &c. Thomas and Andrews's first edition. With many corrections and improvements, by the Author.

Printed at Boston, by Isaiah Thomas and Ebenezer T. Andrews. At Faust's Statue, No. 45, Newbury Street. Sold, wholesale and retail, at their Bookstore; by said Thomas at his Bookstore in Worcester and by the Booksellers in town and country. MDCCXC. pp. 125, incl. portrait. 12mo. AAS. HC. LOC. NYPL.

5th Massachusetts District Copyright, for rights in Rhode Island, Massachusetts, and New Hampshire, issued to Isaiah Thomas and Ebenezer T. Andrews, 7 October, 1790.

23055 —— — A Grammatical institute of the English language; comprising an easy, concise and systematic method of education. Designed for the use of English schools in America. In three parts. Part second. Containing a plain and comprehensive grammar, grounded on the true principles and idioms of the language. By Noah Webster, jun. esquire. Author of "Dissertations on the English language." "Collection of essays and fugitive writings," &c. The first Connecticut edition.

Printed at Hartford, by Hudson and Goodwin. MDCCXC.

WEBSTER, NOAH, JUNIOR, continued.

23056   ——— THE LITTLE READER'S ASSISTANT. CONTAINING, I. A NUMBER OF STORIES, MOSTLY TAKEN FROM THE HISTORY OF AMERICA, AND ADORNED WITH CUTS. II. RUDIMENTS OF ENGLISH GRAMMAR. III. A FEDERAL CATECHISM; BEING A SHORT AND EASY EXPLANATION OF THE CONSTITUTION OF THE UNITED STATES. IV. GENERAL PRINCIPLES OF GOVERNMENT AND COMMERCE. ALL ADAPTED TO THE CAPACITIES OF CHILDREN. BY NOAH WEBSTER, JUN.

Hartford: Printed by Elisha Babcock. M.DCC.XC. pp. 48; 80; 13. 16mo.

Second title: RUDIMENTS OF ENGLISH GRAMMAR; BEING AN INTRODUCTION TO THE SECOND PART OF THE GRAMMATICAL INSTITUTE OF THE ENGLISH LANGUAGE. . . . TO WHICH IS ADDED, A FEDERAL CATECHISM.

Hartford: Printed by Elisha Babcock. M.DCC.XC. pp. 80.

Third title: A FEDERAL CATECHIZM; BEING A SHORT AND EASY EXPLANATION OF THE CONSTITUTION OF THE UNITED STATES. pp. 52 – 78.

Fourth title: THE FARMER'S CATECHIZM; CONTAINING PLAIN RULES OF HUSBANDRY AND CALCULATED FOR THE USE OF SCHOOLS.

[*Hartford: Printed by Elisha Babcock*, 1790.] pp. 13. AAS. BM, CHS. NYPL.

23057   ——— RUDIMENTS OF ENGLISH GRAMMAR; BEING AN INTRODUCTION TO THE SECOND PART OF THE GRAMMATICAL INSTITUTE OF THE ENGLISH LANGUAGE: COMPILED AT THE REQUEST OF THE COMMITTEE OF THE GRAMMAR SCHOOL IN HARTFORD. TO WHICH IS ADDED A FEDERAL CATECHIZM, BEING AN EASY EXPLANATION OF THE PRINCIPLES OF OUR NATIONAL GOVERNMENT, MONEY AND COMMERCE; CALCULATED FOR SCHOOLS, AND PROPER FOR PRIVATE FAMILIES AS WELL AS CHILDREN. [TWO lines from] MIDDLETON. BY NOAH WEBSTER, JUN. ESQ.

Hartford: Printed by Elisha Babcock. M,DCC,XC. pp. 80. 16mo.

AAS. BM. CHS. NYPL.

23058   ——— — RUDIMENTS OF ENGLISH GRAMMAR. BEING AN INTRODUCTION TO THE SECOND PART OF THE GRAMMATICAL INSTITUTE. COMPILED AT THE DESIRE OF THE COMMITTEE OF THE GRAMMAR SCHOOL IN HARTFORD. BY NOAH WEBSTER, JUN. TO WHICH IS ADDED A FEDERAL CATECHISM.

Albany: Printed and sold by Charles R. and George Webster. 1790.

23059   ——— — RUDIMENTS OF ENGLISH GRAMMAR; BEING AN INTRODUCTION TO THE SECOND PART OF THE GRAMMATICAL INSTITUTE OF THE ENGLISH LANGUAGE: COMPILED AT THE DESIRE OF THE COMMITTEE OF THE GRAMMAR SCHOOL IN HARTFORD. BY NOAH WEBSTER, JUN. ESQUIRE. TO WHICH IS ANNEXED, A FEDERAL CATECHISM; CONTAINING A SHORT EXPLANATION OF THE CONSTITUTION OF THE UNITED STATES. FOR THE USE OF SCHOOLS.

Boston: Printed by Benjamin Russell, and sold by Benjamin Guild, at the Boston Book-Store, No. 59, Cornhill. 1790.

23060   WEBSTER, PELATIAH   1725 – 1795

A PLEA FOR THE POOR SOLDIERS; OR AN ESSAY, TO DEMONSTRATE THAT THE SOLDIERS AND OTHER PUBLIC CREDITORS, WHO REALLY AND ACTUALLY SUPPORTED THE BURDEN OF THE LATE WAR, HAVE NOT BEEN PAID! OUGHT TO BE PAID! CAN BE PAID! AND MUST BE PAID! BY A CITIZEN OF PHILADELPHIA.

Philadelphia: Printed by Francis Bailey, at Yorick's Head, in Market-Street. M,DCC,LXC. [*sic* 1790.] pp. [39.] 8vo.   AAS. BA. JCB. LOC. MHS. NYPL.

To which is added as a Preface, a brief history of the South Sea Company, and particulars of the fatal scheme in 1720.

WEBSTER, PELATIAH, continued.

23061 —— — A PLEA FOR THE POOR SOLDIERS; OR AN ESSAY TO DEMONSTRATE THAT THE SOLDIERS AND OTHER PUBLIC CREDITORS, WHO REALLY AND ACTUALLY SUPPORTED THE BURDEN OF THE LATE WAR, HAVE NOT BEEN PAID! OUGHT TO BE PAID! CAN BE PAID! AND MUST BE PAID! BY A CITIZEN OF PHILADELPHIA.
New-Haven: Re-printed, 1790. pp. 33. 18mo. BA. JCB. NYHS.

23062 WEEKLY [U. S. arms] MONITOR. VOL. V. NUMB. 237. TUESDAY, JANUARY 5, [— VOL. VI. NUMB. 3. TOTAL NO. 285. SATURDAY, DECEMBER 25, 1790.]
Litchfield: Published by Thomas Collier, in the lower room [south end] of the Court-House. 1790. fol. AAS. YC.
With the issue for May 15th, the old cut with the motto "Venerate the plough," is substituted for the cut of the United States arms. The issue for November 29th, contains this notice: "The next number of this paper, which commences Volume VI. will not be published till Saturday, December 11." When it appeared as the *Litchfield-County* [cut] *Monitor.* — the word "County" being dropped, in January, 1791.

23063 THE WEEKLY MUSEUM. [Motto.] NUMBER 132. SATURDAY, NOVEMBER 20, [— NUMBER 137. SATURDAY, DECEMBER 25, 1790.]
New-York: Printed and published by John Harrisson, at his Printing-Office, No. 3, Peck-Slip. 1790. 4to.
In continuation of, *The New-York Weekly Museum.* The motto reads: "Here Justice with her balance sits, and weighs impartially the deeds of men."

23064 WESLEY, CHARLES   1708 – 1788
AN EPISTLE TO THE REVEREND MR. GEORGE WHITEFIELD [in verse]: WRITTEN IN THE YEAR 1755. BY CHARLES WESTLEY [*sic*] A. M. LATE STUDENT OF CHRIST-CHURCH, OXFORD.
London: Printed—Baltimore: Re-printed and sold by Samuel and John Adams. MDCCXC. pp. [7.] 8vo. NYPL.

23065 WEST, BENJAMIN   1730 – 1813
AN ASTRONOMICAL DIARY, KALENDAR, OR ALMANACK, FOR THE YEAR OF OUR LORD 1791. [Eleven lines.] BY ISAAC BICKERSTAFF, ESQ. [Four lines of verse.]
Hartford: Printed by Nathaniel Patten. [1790.] pp. (24), 12mo. AAS.CHS.
Apparently the same as Strong's Astronomical diary, for 1791, also published by Patten.

23066 —— — BICKERSTAFF'S BOSTON ALMANACK, OR, FEDERAL CALENDAR, FOR 1791. THIRD AFTER LEAP-YEAR; AND FIFTEENTH OF INDEPENDENCY. CONTAINING, BESIDES WHAT IS USUAL, A TRUE NARRATIVE OF THE SHOCKING CAPTIVITY OF ROBERT WHITE, AMONG THE ALGERINES. [Cut.]
[Boston:] Printed by E. Russell, cheap to travelling-traders, &c. [1790.] pp. (24). 12mo. AAS.

23067 —— — BICKERSTAFF'S BOSTON ALMANACK, OR, FEDERAL CALENDAR, FOR 1791. . . . SIXTH [*sic* second] EDITION.
[Boston:] Printed by E. Russell, [1790.] pp. (24). 12mo.

23068 —— BICKERSTAFF'S CONNECTICUT ALMANACK, FOR THE YEAR OF OUR LORD, 1791. BEING THE THIRD AFTER BISSEXTILE, OR LEAP YEAR, AND FIFTEENTH OF THE INDEPENDENCE OF UNITED AMERICA. FROM CREATION, ACCORDING TO THE SCRIPTURES, 5753. CONTAINING, BESIDES THE USUAL ASTRONOMICAL CALCULATIONS, GREAT VARIETY OF MATTERS, CURIOUS, USEFUL AND ENTERTAINING. [Four lines of verse.]
Norwich: Printed by J. Trumbull, and sold by the gross, dozen or single. ☞ *Where cash is given for rags.* [1790.] pp. [24.] 12mo. CHS. NYPL.

WEST, BENJAMIN, continued.

23069 —— BICKERSTAFF'S GENUINE ALMANACK, FOR THE YEAR OF OUR LORD 1791. BEING THE THIRD AFTER BISSEXTILE OR LEAP-YEAR, AND THE FIFTEENTH OF AMERICAN INDEPENDENCE. [Sixteen lines.]
Boston: Printed and sold by Joseph Bumstead, at his Printing Office, No. 20, Union-Street. Sold also by the Booksellers. [1790.] pp. (24).12mo. AAS. LOC.
There is no difference between this Almanac and Weatherwise's Town and country Almanack for 1791, except the title page.

23070 —— BICKERSTAFF'S. GENUINE MASSACHUSETTS, RHODEISLAND AND CONNECTICUT ALMANACK, FOR THE YEAR OF OUR LORD 1791: BEING THE THIRD YEAR AFTER BISSEXTILE OR LEAP YEAR AND FIFTEENTH OF THE INDEPENDENCE OF THE UNITED STATES. [Eight lines. Cut.]
Boston: Printed [by Nathaniel Coverly] for and sold by the Booksellers, in town and country. [1790.] pp. (24). 12mo. BPL. LOC.
There is no difference, except the change of name, and the woodcut on the title page, between this and Weatherwise's Genuine Almanack, also printed by Nathaniel Coverly this year.

23071 —— THE NEW-ENGLAND ALMANACK, OR, LADY'S AND GENTLEMAN'S DIARY, FOR THE YEAR OF OUR LORD CHRIST 1791: [Twenty-four lines.] BY ISAAC BICKERSTAFF, ESQ; PHILOM. [Four lines of verse.]
Providence: Printed and sold, wholesale and retail, by John Carter, at the Post-Office, near the State-House. [1790.] pp. (24). 12mo. AAS. RIHS.

23072 —— — THE NEW-ENGLAND ALMANACK, OR, LADY'S AND GENTLEMAN'S DIARY, FOR THE YEAR OF OUR LORD, 1791. BY ISAAC BICKERSTAFF, ESQ.
Providence: Printed by John Carter. Sold by Jacob Richardson, esq. in Newport. [1790.]

23073 —— WHEELER'S NORTH-AMERICAN CALENDAR, OR AN ALMANACK, FOR THE YEAR OF OUR LORD 1791: AND THE FIFTEENTH OF THE INDEPENDENCE OF AMERICA. CONTAINING (BESIDES THE USUAL CALCULATIONS) A VARIETY OF USEFUL AND ENTERTAINING MATTER. TYPE OF THE ECLIPSE, APRIL 3D. [Cut. Four lines of verse.]
Providence: Printed and sold by Bennett Wheeler. [1790.] pp. (24).12mo.
AAS. BU. LOC. RIHS.

23074 WESTERN ADVERTISER AND CHAMBERSBURG WEEKLY NEWSPAPER. VOL. I. NO. 1. JUNE, [—DECEMBER, 1790.]
Chambersburg: Printed by William Davison, 1790. fol.
No copies appear to be extant; and some doubt exists that this newspaper venture was not called The Franklin Minerva. It appears to have been established in June, 1790, by William Davison, and continued by him until his death in July, 1793. He was succeeded by Robert Harper, as editor and proprietor, who changed the name of the paper to, *The Chambersburg Gazette*, beginning, with a new serial numbering, September 12, 1793. In April, 1796, this title was altered to, *The Franklin Repository*, with a new serial numbering, and so continued into the year 1800, when Robert Harper sold the Printing Office to his brother, George Kenton Harper, by whom the Repository was continued into the year 1839, when the latter sold his interests to Joseph Pritts, publisher of the Franklin Whig, who consolidated the two publications as *The Repository and Whig*, in 1840. Joseph Pritts continued publication to 1842; being succeeded by W. H. Downey, to 1844; by John F. Denny, to 1849; and by John W. Boyd, to 1852; when Alexander K. McClure, on becoming proprietor, restored its former title of, *Franklin Repository*, under which, with various editors, it has been continued to the present time.

23075   THE WESTERN [cut] Star. No. 6. Tuesday, January 5, [— No. 57. Tuesday, December 28, 1790.]

     Stockbridge (Massachusetts): Printed and published by Loring Andrews. 1790. fol.   AAS.

23076   WESTMINSTER ASSEMBLY of Divines.

     The Shorter Catechism, agreed upon by the Reverend Assembly of Divines at Westminster, with Scripture Proofs.

     Bennington: Printed by Haswell and Russell. 1790.

23077   WETHERILL, Samuel   1736 – 1816

     A Confutation of the Doctrines of Antinomianism; delivered in the College-Hall, in the city of Philadelphia, on seventh-day evening, June 17, 1790. Together with some observations on the reply made by John Murray, on the second-day evening following. By Samuel Wetherill.

     Philadelphia: Printed and sold by Francis Bailey and Joseph Crukshank, in Market-Street. 1790.

23078   —— Some observations on the doctrines of John Murray, addressed to himself.

     Philadelphia: Printed and sold by Francis Bailey, and Joseph Crukshank, in Market-Street. 1790.

23079   WHITEFIELD, George   1714 – 1770

     Hymn, composed by the late Reverend Mr. George Whitefield, with design to be sung at his own funeral. Now re-published at the request of a number of friends to that truly worthy and pious gentleman. [Adapted to Savanna tune.] [Twelve four-line verses. And] New-England hymn, by the late Reverend Dr. Byles. [Adapted to America tune.] [Three six-line verses.] [Colophon:]

     [Boston:] Printed by E. Russell, next Liberty-Stump. 1790. Broadside. fol.   AAS.

23080   WHITMAN, Samuel   1752 – 1827

     The Doctrine of Christ. A sermon, preached at New-Alstead, New-Hampshire, September 3d, 1789. At the ordination of Mr. Levi Lankton, to the pastoral care of a church in that town. By Samuel Whitman, a. b. pastor of the church in Goshen. . . .

     Northampton: Printed by William Butler, 1790. (*Published at the request of said Church in Alstead.*) pp. 33. 12mo.   AAS. FL. JCB.

23081   WHITNEY, Josiah   1731 – 1824

     A Sermon, occasioned by the death of the Honorable Major-General Israel Putnam, of Brooklyn; who departed this life on Saturday, the 29th day of May, 1790, and delivered at his funeral on the Tuesday following. By Josiah Whitney, a. m. pastor of the first church in Brooklyn. [Seven lines of quotations.]

     Windham: Printed by John Byrne. [1790.] pp. 28. 8vo. chs. jcb. nypl.   **$15**

23082   WHITTAKER, James   1751 – 1787

     A Concise statement of the principles of the only true church, according to the Gospel, of the present appearance of Christ as held to and practiced by the followers of the living saviour, at New Lebanon, &c. Together with a letter from James Whittaker, minister of the Gospel in this day of Christ's second appearing, to his natural relations in England. Dated October 9th, 1785.

     Printed at Bennington, Vermont, by Haswell and Russell, 1790. Reprinted in the United Society, New Gloucester, Maine, in 1847.

23083 WHITTINGTON, Sir RICHARD·   – 1423
THE FAMOUS HISTORY OF WHITTINGTON AND HIS CAT. ADORNED WITH CUTS.
Middletown : Printed and sold by Moses H. Woodward. 1790. pp. 26. 32mo.

23084 WILDER, JOHN   1759 – 1836
THE BLESSEDNESS OF DEPARTED SAINTS. A DISCOURSE, DELIVERED THE NEXT
SABBATH AFTER THE INTERMENT OF DEACON EBENEZER LANE, WHO DIED MAY
12, 1790, IN THE 78TH YEAR OF HIS AGE. BY JOHN WILDER, A. M. PASTOR OF
THE FIRST CHURCH IN ATTLEBOROUGH. PUBLISHED BY THE REQUEST OF THE
MOURNERS. [Two lines.]
        Printed at Providence, by Bennett Wheeler, in Westminster-Street. [1790.]
        pp. 30. 8vo.   BPL. JCB. NYHS. RIHS.

23085 WILLARD, JOSEPH   1738 – 1804
A SERMON, DELIVERED MAY 13, 1790, AT THE FUNERAL OF THE REVEREND TIMO-
THY HILLIARD, A. M. PASTOR OF THE FIRST CHURCH IN CAMBRIDGE, WHO DE-
PARTED THIS LIFE ON LORD'S-DAY, MAY 9, 1790, IN THE 44TH YEAR OF HIS AGE.
BY JOSEPH WILLARD, D. D. PRESIDENT OF THE UNIVERSITY IN CAMBRIDGE.
PRINTED BY DESIRE OF MANY OF THE HEARERS.
        Boston: Printed by Samuel Hall, at his Printing-Office, No. 53, Cornhill.
        M.DCC.XC. pp. 31. 8vo.   AAS. BA. BM. BPL. HC. JCB. MHS. NYHS.

23086 WINTHROP, JOHN   1587 – 1649
A JOURNAL OF THE TRANSACTIONS AND OCCURRENCES IN THE SETTLEMENT OF
MASSACHUSETTS AND THE OTHER NEW-ENGLAND COLONIES, FROM THE YEAR 1630
TO 1644: WRITTEN BY JOHN WINTHROP, ESQ., FIRST GOVERNOR OF MASSA-
CHUSETTS: AND NOW FIRST PUBLISHED FROM A CORRECT COPY OF THE ORIGINAL
MANUSCRIPT. [Two lines of Latin from] TIT. LIV. PREF. [Publisher's mono-
gram.]
        Hartford: Printed by Elisha Babcock, M,DCC,XC. pp. (2), (2), (2), 364,
        (4). 8vo.   AAS. BA. BM. HC. JCB. LOC. NL. NYHS. NYPL. $10
        Transcribed from the original manuscript during the period of Jonathan
        Trumbull as Governor of Connecticut, by the Governor and his Secre-
        tary, John Porter, and by the latter compared and revised for this
        edition, as attested by the Editor, Noah Webster, junior. The copy in
        the New York Public Library has manuscript notes by the editor. In
        the year 1816, a continuation of the matter of this volume was found,
        in manuscript, in the tower of the Old South Church in Boston, and
        placed in the hands of James Savage, who edited the whole manuscript
        for publication, in two volumes, printed in Boston, in 1825-1826. A
        second edition of this reprint, with additions and corrections, was
        printed, in two volumes, in Boston, in 1853.

23087 WOLCOT, JOHN   1738 – 1819
THE POETICAL WORKS OF PETER PINDAR, ESQ. A DISTANT RELATION TO THE POET
OF THEBES. TO WHICH ARE PREFIXED, MEMOIRS AND ANECDOTES OF THE AUTHOR.
        *Newburyport: Printed by John Mycall, for John Boyle, in Marlborough-
        Street, Boston.* [1790.] pp. viii, 314. 12mo.   AAS.

23088 —— THE POETICAL WORKS OF PETER PINDAR, ESQ. A DISTANT RELATION TO THE
POET OF THEBES. TO WHICH ARE PREFIXED MEMOIRS AND ANECDOTES OF THE
AUTHOR. A NEW EDITION, WITH ADDITIONS. VOL. II.
        Philadelphia: Printed for William Spotswood, and Rice & Co. MDCCXC.
        pp. 402. 12mo.   AAS. MHS.

23089   WOODHULL, JOHN   1744 – 1824
A SERMON, FOR THE DAY OF PUBLICK THANKSGIVING, APPOINTED BY THE PRESI-
DENT, ON ACCOUNT OF THE ESTABLISHMENT OF THE NEW CONSTITUTION, &c. NO-
VEMBER 26, 1789. BY THE REV. JOHN WOODHULL, A. M. PASTOR OF THE FIRST
PRESBYTERIAN CHURCH IN FREEHOLD. [One line from] PSAL. XCVII. I.
       Trenton: Printed by Isaac Collins, M.DCC.XC. pp. 24. 8vo.   JCB.
The recto of the first leaf contains the Resolution for printing the
sermon.

23090   WOOLMAN, JOHN   1720 – 1772
A JOURNAL OF THE LIFE, GOSPEL LABOURS, AND CHRISTIAN EXPERIENCES OF THAT
FAITHFUL MINISTER OF JESUS CHRIST, JOHN WOOLMAN, LATE OF MOUNT-HOLLY,
IN THE PROVINCE OF NEW-JERSEY.
       Philadelphia: Printed and sold by Joseph Crukshank, 1790.

23091   WORKMAN, BENJAMIN
ELEMENTS OF GEOGRAPHY, DESIGNED FOR YOUNG STUDENTS IN THAT SCIENCE. IN
SIX SECTIONS. SECT. I. OF THE SOLAR SYSTEM. SECT. II. OF THE EARTH IN
PARTICULAR. SECT. III. OF MAPS AND GLOBES. THE THREE FOREGOING SEC-
TIONS CONTAIN THE SCIENTIFIC OR ASTRONOMICAL PART OF GEOGRAPHY, DIGESTED
IN A CLEAR AND COMPREHENSIVE MANNER. SECT. IV. OF THE DIFFERENT RE-
LIGIONS, GOVERNMENTS, AND LANGUAGES OF NATIONS. SECT. V. OF THE POLITICAL
DIVISIONS OF THE EARTH, INTO EMPIRES, KINGDOMS, &c. OR THE HISTORICAL PART
OF GEOGRAPHY. SECT. VI. OF NATURAL PHILOSOPHY—OR THE PROPERTIES OF
MATTER, LAWS OF NATION, &c. BY BENJAMIN WORKMAN, A. M. THE SECOND
EDITION. ILLUSTRATED WITH THREE COPPER PLATES, VIZ. A MAP OF THE WORLD;
A PLATE OF THE SOLAR SYSTEM, AND A MAP OF THE UNITED STATES.
       *Philadelphia: Printed and sold by John M' Culloch, in Third-Street, the
third door above Market-Street,* 1790.

23092   —— —— ELEMENTS OF GEOGRAPHY, DESIGNED FOR YOUNG STUDENTS IN THAT
SCIENCE. IN SEVEN SECTIONS. SECT. I. OF THE SOLAR SYSTEM. SECT. II. OF
THE EARTH IN PARTICULAR. SECT. III. OF MAPS AND GLOBES. THE THREE
FOREGOING SECTIONS CONTAIN THE SCIENTIFIC OR ASTRONOMICAL PART OF GEOG-
RAPHY, DIGESTED IN A CLEAR AND COMPREHENSIVE MANNER. SECT. IV. OF THE
DIFFERENT RELIGIONS, GOVERNMENTS, AND LANGUAGES OF NATIONS. SECT. V. OF
THE POLITICAL DIVISIONS OF THE EARTH, INTO EMPIRES, KINGDOMS, &c. OR THE
HISTORICAL PART OF GEOGRAPHY. SECT. VI. OF NATURAL PHILOSOPHY; OR THE
PROPERTIES OF MATTER, &c. SECT. VII. OF CHRONOLOGY. BY BENJAMIN WORK-
MAN, A. M. THE THIRD EDITION. ILLUSTRATED WITH, 1. A MAP OF THE WORLD.
2. A PLATE OF THE SOLAR SYSTEM. 3. A MAP OF NORTH AMERICA. 4. A MAP
OF THE UNITED STATES. 5. A MAP OF SOUTH AMERICA. 6. A MAP OF EUROPE.
7. A MAP OF ASIA. 8. A MAP OF AFRICA.
       *Philadelphia: Printed and sold by John M'Culloch, in Third-Street, No. 1,
above Market-Street.* M,DCC,XC. pp. 148, 8 maps, 18mo.   AAS. JCB.
"It is a little more than a twelvemonth since the Elements of geography were first published, yet so great has been the demand for the book,
that two editions have already sold off." —Preface.

23093   —— FATHER TAMMANY'S ALMANAC, FOR THE YEAR OF OUR LORD, 1791: BEING THE
THIRD AFTER BISSEXTILE OR LEAP-YEAR. CONTAINING, [two columns of contents.] THE ASTRONOMICAL CALCULATIONS BY B. WORKMAN, A. M. [Cut.]
       *Philadelphia: Printed by William Young, Bookseller, No. 54, Second-Street,
the corner of Chesnut-Street.* [1790.] pp. (40). 12mo.   AAS.

WORKMAN, Benjamin, continued.

23094   —— The Pennsylvania, Delaware, Maryland and Virginia Almanack, and
        ephemeris, for the year of our Lord, 1791; being the third after bis-
        sextile, or leap-year, and the fifteenth year of American independence,
        which commenced July 4, 1776. Containing the motions of the sun and
        moon, the true places and aspects of the planets, the rising and setting
        of the sun, and the southing, rising, setting, place and age of the moon,
        &c.—The lunations, conjunctions, eclipses, judgment of the weather,
        festivals, and other remarkable days; days for holding courts in Penn-
        sylvania, Delaware, Maryland, and Virginia. — Also, several useful
        tables, and valuable receipts.—Various selections from the Common-
        place-book of the Kentucky Philosopher, an American sage; with inter-
        esting and entertaining essays, in prose and verse—the whole compris-
        ing a greater, more pleasing, and useful variety, than any work of the
        kind and price in North-America. [Two lines of verse.]
            *Baltimore: Printed and sold, wholesale and retail, by William Goddard and
        James Angell. at their Printing-Office, in Market-Street. Sold also by Messrs.
        Hanson and Bond, Printers, in Alexandria.* [1790.] pp. (48). 12mo.   JCB.

23095   YALE COLLEGE.
        Catalogus senatus Academici et eorum qui munera et officia Academica
        gesserunt, quique aliquovis gradu exornati fuerunt in Collegio Yalensi,
        quod est in Novo-Portu Reipublicæ Connecticuttensis in Nov-Anglia.
            *Novi-Portus: Excudebant Thomas et Samuel Green.   Universitatis Typo-
        graphi.* [1790.] pp. 34. 8vo.   BA. MHS. NYPL. RIHS. YC.

23096   —— Illustrissimo Samueli Huntington, arm. ll. d. Reipublicæ Connecticut-
        ensis gubernatori. honoratissimo Olivero Wolcott, armigero, vice-gub-
        ernatori: clarissimisque proceribus politiæ nostræ civilis: reverendo
        pariter ac honorando Ezræ Stiles, s. t. d. ll. d. Collegii Yalensis præsidi,
        [Five lines.] Hasce Theses quas in comitiis publicis Collegii Yalensis, die
        8vo Septembris, Anno Domini m.dcc.xc. . . .   [Colophon:]
            Habita in Comitiis Academicis Novo Portu Connecticutensium, M,DCC,XC.
        E Typis Thomæ et Samuelis Green Universitatis Typographorum. Broadside.fol.YC.

23097   —— Quæstiones pro modulo discutiendæ sub reverendo D. Ezra Stiles, s. t. d.
        ll. d. Collegii Yalensis, quod est, divinia providentia, Novo-Portu Con-
        necticutensium, præsidi, In comitiis publicis a laureæ magistralis candi-
        datis, m.dcc.xc. . . .
            [*Novi-Portus: E. Typis T. et S. Green,* 1790.] Broadside. fol.

23098   YOUNG, Edward   1684 – 1765
        The Complaint: or night-thoughts on life, death, & immortality, by the late
        Dr. Young. To which is prefixed, the life of the author, and annexed,
        a Paraphrase on part of the Book of Job, notes, and a complete index
        and glossary.
            *Newburyport: Printed by John Mycall, for the Proprietor of the Boston
        Book-Store, No. 59, Cornhill, Boston.* [1790.] pp. 408. 12mo.   AAS. JCB.

23099   —— The Last day. A poem. In three books. By Edward Young.
            Salem: Printed by Thomas C. Cushing, 1790.

1791

23100   A., C.
DER BUSSFERTIGE BEICHT-VATER UND SEEL-SORGER, AARON, PRIESTER IN DER
GROSEN STADT BABEL, WIE ER ZUR ERKENNTNISS SEINER SÜNDE KOMMEN UND
DIESELBE BEREUET U. S. W. VON C. A. EIN UM DIE WAHRHEIT WILLEN VERTRIE-
BENER.
> *Ephrata: Gedruckt auf Kosten der Liebhaber.* 1791. pp.vi. 47. 18vo. HCP.

23101   AN ACCOUNT OF THE SOIL, GROWING TIMBER, AND OTHER PRODUCTIONS OF THE LANDS
IN THE COUNTRIES SITUATE IN THE BACK PARTS OF THE STATES OF NEW-YORK
AND PENNSYLVANIA, IN NORTH AMERICA AND PARTICULARLY THE LANDS IN THE
COUNTY OF ONTARIO, KNOWN BY THE NAME OF THE GENESER TRACT, LATELY LO-
CATED, AND NOW IN THE PROGRESS OF BEING SETTLED.
> *Printed in the year* 1791. pp. (2) 37, 2 maps. 4to. AAS. BA. BM. LOC. NYHS.   **$65**

23102   ADAMS, HANNAH   1755 – 1832
A VIEW OF RELIGIONS, IN TWO PARTS. PART I. CONTAINING AN ALPHABETICAL
COMPENDIUM OF THE VARIOUS RELIGIOUS DENOMINATIONS, WHICH HAVE APPEARED
IN THE WORLD, FROM THE BEGINNING OF THE CHRISTIAN ERA TO THE PRESENT
DAY. PART II. CONTAINING A BRIEF ACCOUNT OF THE DIFFERENT SCHEMES OF
RELIGION NOW EMBRACED AMONG MANKIND. THE WHOLE COLLECTED FROM THE
BEST AUTHORITIES, ANCIENT AND MODERN. BY HANNAH ADAMS. THE SECOND
EDITION, WITH LARGE ADDITIONS. [One line quotation.]
> *Boston: Printed by John West Folsom.* [1791.] pp. 410, (17). 8vo.
> BA. BM. JCB. MHS.

The second edition of her "Alphabetical compendium of sects," published in 1784. 16th Massachusetts District Copyright, issued to Hannah Adams, as Author, 6 July, 1791.

23103   ADAMS, ZABDIEL   1739 – 1801
OUR LAPSE IN ADAM, AND REDEMPTION BY CHRIST CONSIDERED, IN TWO SERMONS,
PREACHED AT STERLING, IN THE COMMONWEALTH OF MASSACHUSETTS, THE 16TH
OF JANUARY, 1791. BY ZABDIEL ADAMS, A. M. PASTOR OF THE CHURCH IN LUNEN-
BURG. PUBLISHED AT THE DESIRE OF MANY WHO HEARD THEM.
> *Printed at Boston, by Isaiah Thomas and Ebenezer T. Andrews, Faust's
> Statue, No. 45, Newbury Street.* MDCCXCI. pp. 35. 12mo.   AAS. JCB.

23104   ADLUM, JOHN
A GEOGRAPHICAL AND HYDROGRAPHICAL MAP, EXHIBITING A GENERAL VIEW OF THE
ROADS AND INLAND NAVIGATION OF PENNSYLVANIA, AND PART OF THE ADJACENT
STATES, WHICH ARE NOW THE OBJECT OF IMPROVEMENT, WITH A VIEW TO BRING
TO MARKET, BY THE MOST EASY LAND & WATER CARRIAGE, THE TRADE OF THE
SUSQUEHANNA AND OHIO WATERS, AND OF THAT EXTENSIVE TERRITORY, BOUND-
ING ON AND CONNECTED WITH THE GREAT LAKES. COMPILED FROM ACTUAL SUR-
VEYS, AT THE PARTICULAR REQUEST OF THE SOCIETY LATELY FORMED IN PENN-
SYLVANIA, FOR PROMOTING THE "IMPROVEMENTS OF ROADS AND INLAND NAVIGA-
TION." HUMBLY INSCRIBED TO HIS EXCELLENCY THOMAS MIFFLIN, GOVERNOR,
AND THE GENERAL ASSEMBLY OF THE COMMONWEALTH OF PENNSYLVANIA. BY
JOHN ADLUM & JOHN WALLIS.
> *Philadelphia:* 1791.

16th Pennsylvania District Copyright, issued to John Adlum, as Author,
23 February, 1791.

23105   AN ADDRESS TO THE NUMEROUS AND RESPECTABLE INHABITANTS OF THE GREAT AND EXTENSIVE DISTRICT OF MAINE. FRIENDS, BRETHREN AND FELLOW-CITIZENS, OF THIS IMPORTANT DISTRICT. THE TIME DRAWETH NIGH, WHEN YE MUST BE, AS THE GOD OF NATURE, INTENDED YE SHOULD BE, A FREE, SOVEREIGN AND INDEPENDENT STATE. . . . . A NUMBER OF YOUR REPRESENTATIVES. MARCH, 1791.
[Portland: Printed by Thomas B. Wait, 1791.] pp. 3. fol. AAS. BA. NYPL.

23106   AITKEN, JOHN
A COMPILATION OF THE LITANIES VESPERS HYMNS & ANTHEMS AS THEY ARE SUNG IN THE CATHOLIC CHURCH.
Philadelphia: Printed and sold by John Aitken, 1791. pp. 181. 4to. JCB.
Engraved title. 27th Pennsylvania Copyright, issued to John Aitken, as Author, 25 November, 1791.

23107   ALBANY. NEW YORK.
LAWS AND ORDINANCES OF THE COMMON COUNCIL OF THE CITY OF ALBANY.
Albany: Printed by C. R. & G. Webster? 1791. 4to.

23108   THE ALBANY GAZETTE. VOL. VII. NUMB. 429. MONDAY, JANUARY 3, [— VOL. VIII. NUMB. 532. THURSDAY, DECEMBER 29, 1791.]
Printed every Monday and Thursday, by Charles R. and George Webster, No. 46 (on the north side of) State-Street, corner of Middle-Lane. 1791. fol. AAS.
In the issue for April 11th, notice is given that "The Printers of The Albany Gazette, having determined to erect a Paper-Mill, near this city, the ensuing summer, find themselves necessitated to call on those indebted to them for a payment."

23109   THE ALBANY REGISTER. VOL. III. NUMB. 130. MONDAY, JANUARY 3, [—VOL. IV. NUMB. 181. MONDAY, DECEMBER 26, 1791.]
Printed and published (at 12s. per ann.) by Robert Barber & Co. No. 53, west side of Market Street, opposite the Market. 1791. fol.

23110   ALEXANDER, CALEB   1755 – 1828
AN ESSAY ON THE REAL DEITY OF JESUS CHRIST. TO WHICH ARE ADDED STRICTURES ON EXTRACTS FROM MR. EMLYN'S HUMBLE INQUIRY CONCERNING THE DEITY OF JESUS CHRIST. BY CALEB ALEXANDER, A. M. PASTOR OF A CONGREGATIONAL CHURCH IN MENDON. [Three lines of Scripture texts.]
Boston: Printed by Joseph Bumstead, at his Printing Office, No. 20, Union Street, 1791. pp. (2), ii, (68), errata, 12mo. AAS. BA. BM. JCB. LOC. MHS. NYPL. YC.

23111   ALLEN, TIMOTHY   1715 – 1806
A SERMON AT THE DEDICATION OF A MEETING-HOUSE IN CHESTERFIELD, MASSACHUSETTS.
[Northampton: Printed by William Butler? 1791.]

23112   THE AMERICAN ALMANAC, FOR THE YEAR OF OUR LORD, 1792. BEING BISSEXTILE OR LEAP-YEAR. [Fourteen lines.]
Philadelphia: Printed and sold by Thomas Bradford, No. 8, South Front-Street. [1791.] pp. (36). 12mo.   LOC.

23113   AMERICAN HERALD, AND THE WASHINGTON GAZETTE. VOL. I. NO. 25. MONDAY, JANUARY 3, [— NO. 52. MONDAY, JULY, 11, 1791.]
Boston [Commonwealth of Massachusetts]: Printed and published by Edward Eveleth Powars, opposite the new Court-House, in Court-Street. 1791. fol.
At the end of the first volume, in July, publication ceased. And, in October, Powars succeeded John Howel as publisher of *The Argus.*

23114   THE AMERICAN JEST-BOOK, CONTAINING A CURIOUS VARIETY OF JESTS, ANECDOTES, BON-MOTS, STORIES, ETC. IN TWO PARTS.
     Philadelphia: From the Press of Mathew Carey, 1791. 2 plates.

23115   THE AMERICAN [U. S. arms] MERCURY. NUMB. 339. MONDAY, JANUARY 3, [— VOL. VIII. NUMB. 390. MONDAY, DECEMBER 26, 1791.]
     Hartford: Printed by Elisha Babcock. 1791. fol.   AAS. CHS. YC.

23116   THE AMERICAN MUSEUM, OR, UNIVERSAL MAGAZINE: CONTAINING ESSAYS ON AGRICULTURE — COMMERCE — MANUFACTURES — POLITICS — MORALS — AND MANNERS. SKETCHES OF NATIONAL CHARACTERS—NATURAL AND CIVIL HISTORY—AND BIOGRAPHY. LAW INFORMATION—PUBLIC PAPERS—PROCEEDINGS OF CONGRESS—INTELLIGENCE; MORAL TALES—ANCIENT AND MODERN POETRY, &C. &C. VOL. IX.— FROM JANUARY TO JUNE, 1791.
     Philadelphia: Carey, Stewart, & Co. M.DCC.XCI pp. 344, 48, 40, 48.
   8vo.   AAS. BA. HC. LOC. NYHS.

23117   —— THE AMERICAN MUSEUM, OR, UNIVERSAL MAGAZINE: CONTAINING ESSAYS ON AGRICULTURE—COMMERCE—MANUFACTURES—POLITICS—MORALS—AND MANNERS. SKETCHES OF NATIONAL CHARACTERS—NATURAL AND CIVIL HISTORY—AND BIOGRAPHY. LAW INFORMATION—PUBLIC PAPERS—PROCEEDINGS OF CONGRESS—INTELLIGENCE; MORAL TALES—ANCIENT AND MODERN POETRY, &C. &C. VOL. X.— FROM JULY TO DECEMBER 1791.
     Philadelphia: Carey, Stewart, and Co. M.DCC.XCI. pp. 308, 36, 48, 44.
   8vo.   AAS. BA. HC. LOC. NYHS.

23118   AMERICAN SPY. VOL. I. NUM. 1. FRIDAY, APRIL 8, [— NUM. 39. FRIDAY, DECEMBER 30, 1791.]
     Lansingburgh: Printed by Silvester Tiffany, (a little south of Douglass' Tavern) at twelve shillings per annum. 1791. fol.   AAS.
     Established by Silvester Tiffany, and continued by him to August, 1792, when William W. Wands was admitted to partnership, as Tiffany and Wands. In a short time Tiffany retired, and Wands continued publication alone into the year 1797, selling his interests before September of that year to Charles R. Webster, of Albany, who continued publication certainly to the end of August, 1798.

23119   THE AMERICAN TUTOR'S ASSISTANT; OR, A COMPENDIOUS SYSTEM OF PRACTICAL ARITHMETIC; CONTAINING THE SEVERAL RULES OF THAT USEFUL SCIENCE, CONCISELY DEFINED, METHODICALLY ARRANGED AND FULLY EXEMPLIFIED. THE WHOLE PARTICULARLY ADAPTED TO THE EASY AND REGULAR INSTRUCTION OF YOUTH IN OUR AMERICAN SCHOOLS:—BY SEVERAL TEACHERS IN AND NEAR PHILADELPHIA.
     Philadelphia: Printed and sold by Zachariah Poulson, 1791.
     23d Pennsylvania District Copyright, issued to Zachariah Poulson, as Proprietor, 22 August, 1791.

23120   AMERICANISCHER STADT UND LAND KALENDER AUF DAS 1792STE JAHR CHRISTI, WELCHES EIN SCHALT-JAHR IST VON 366 TAGEN.
     Philadelphia: Gedruckt und zu haben bey Carl Cist, in der Zweyten-strasse, No. 104. nah am Eck der Rehs-strasse. [1791.] pp. (44). 4to.   LOC.

23121   AMES' ALMANACK FOR THE YEAR OF OUR LORD 1792: CALCULATED FOR THE MERID-
IAN OF PORTSMOUTH, NEW-HAMPSHIRE.

> [*Portsmouth:*] *Printed* [*by Charles Peirce*] *and sold by the Shop-keepers
in the town and country.* [1791.]

> This issue does not belong to the series of Ames Almanacs, and was is-
sued without authority from Nathaniel Ames. On the last leaf is an
advertisement of Charles Peirce, at the Columbian Book Store, No. 5,
Daniel Street, Portsmouth, New Hampshire.

23122   ANALYSIS OF THE REV. DR. SAMUEL STANHOPE SMITH S SERMON ON THE GUILT AND
FOLLY OF BEING ASHAMED OF RELIGION.· TEXT, MARK VIII, 38.

> *Boston:* 1791.

23123   ANDERSON, JOHN   1767 – 1835
A DISCOURSE ON THE DIVINE ORDINANCE OF SINGING PSALMS. INTENDED TO PROVE,
I. THAT THE SINGING OF PSALMS IS A PART OF THAT SOCIAL OR PUBLICK WORSHIP
WHICH GOD HATH APPOINTED IN HIS WORD. II. THAT THERE ARE PARTS OF THE
SACRED SCRIPTURES ADAPTED TO THE PURPOSE OF SINGING, WHICH OUGHT TO BE
USED IN THE PUBLICK WORSHIP OF THE CHURCH, TILL THE END OF TIME. III. THAT
THE SCRIPTURE SONGS ARE THE ONLY FORMS OF PSALMODY WHICH OUGHT TO BE
USED IN THE SOLEMN AND PUBLICK WORSHIP OF THE CHURCH. IV. THAT, IN THE
PUBLICK PRAISES OF THE CHURCH, THE MUSICK, OR OUTWARD PART, OUGHT TO BE
CONDUCTED WITH DECENCY AND SIMPLICITY; AND IN SUBSERVIENCY TO THE SPIRIT-
UAL PART, WHICH IS CHIEFLY TO BE REGARDED. TO WHICH IS ADDED, AN AP-
PENDIX, IN TWO NUMBERS. NO. I. CONTAINS A BRIEF HISTORY OF PSALMODY.
NO. II. CONTAINS A REVIEW OF DR. WATTS'S IMITATION OF THE PSALMS OF
DAVID, AS CORRECTED AND ENLARGED BY JOEL BARLOW. BY JOHN ANDERSON,
MINISTER OF THE GOSPEL, AND MEMBER OF THE ASSOCIATE PRESBYTERY OF
PENNSYLVANIA.

> *Philadelphia: Printed by William Young, Bookseller, No, 52, Second-
Street, the corner of Chesnut-Street.* M,DCC,XCI. pp. 112. 16mo.   AAS.

23124   ANDOVER. MASSACHUSETTS. PHILLIPS ACADEMY.
COPY OF THE ADDRESS DELIVERED TO THE STUDENTS OF PHILLIPS' ACADEMY, IN
ANDOVER, IMMEDIATELY AFTER THE EXAMINATION AND EXHIBITION, ON JULY 18,
1791. [Ornament.]

> *Printed at Exeter, by Henry Ranlet, for the Trustees of said Academy.—*
1791. pp. (8). 8vo.   MHS. NYPL.

23125   ANDREWS, ROBERT
THE VIRGINIA ALMANACK, FOR THE YEAR OF OUR LORD, 1792. BEING BISSEXTILE
OR LEAP YEAR. CALCULATED TO THE MERIDIAN OF VIRGINIA AND NORTH-CARO-
LINA. WHEREIN ARE CONTAINED, THE LUNATIONS, CONJUNCTIONS, ECLIPSES,
JUDGMENT OF THE WEATHER, RISING AND SETTING OF THE SUN, MOON, &C. BY
ROBERT ANDREWS, PHILO.

> *Richmond: Printed by Augustine Davis, Printer for the public.* [1791.] pp.
[40.] 12mo.   GHS. LOC. NYPL.

> The Astronomical calculations, only, are the same in the two Andrews'
Virginia Almanacs of this year.

23126   —— THE VIRGINIA ALMANACK, FOR THE YEAR OF OUR LORD, 1792. BEING BISSEX-
TILE, OR LEAP YEAR. AND THE SIXTEENTH OF AMERICAN INDEPENDENCE. BY
ROBERT ANDREWS, PHILO. [Thirteen lines.]

> *Richmond: Printed by T. Nicolson, two doors above the Eagle-Tavern.*
[1791.] pp. (48). 16mo.   LOC.

> Contains. Journey of John Gilpin, linen-draper and captain of the city
train bands. By William Cowper.

23127   THE ANNUAL REGISTER AND POLITICAL REPOSITORY OF THE UNITED STATES OF
AMERICA.
[Philadelphia: Printed by Andrew Brown. 1791?]
From August to December, Andrew Brown announced that he will
commence the publication of the above at Philadelphia.

23128   THE APOLLO: BEING A COLLECTION OF ENGLISH SONGS; INCLUDING A SELECTION OF
MASONIC SONGS, ANTHEMS, ODES, PRELUDES, PROLOGUES, EPILOGUES, TOASTS, &C.
Philadelphia: Printed by William Spotswood. MDCCXCI. pp. (4), 164.
16mo.   AAS.

23129   THE ARGUS. VOL. VI. NUMBER XXXVI. FRIDAY, JULY 22, [— FRIDAY, DECEMBER
30, 1791.]
*Massachusetts: Boston: Printed and published, Tuesdays and Fridays, by
John Howel, opposite the Court-House, in Court-Street.* 1791. fol.   AAS.
In continuation of *The Herald of Freedom.* Beginning August 16th, a
cut of a peacock was added to the heading. With the issue of October 25th, Edward Eveleth Powars, succeeded John Howel as publisher
of The Argus.

23130   ARMSTRONG, JOHN   1709 – 1779
THE ŒCONOMY OF LOVE: A POETICAL ESSAY.
Philadelphia: Printed by Henry Taylor, 1791.
One thousand copies, in sheets, offered at the sale of Henry Taylor's
estate.

23131   ARNAUD, FRANÇOIS THOMAS MARIE DE BACULARD D'   1718 – 1805
FANNY: OR, THE HAPPY REPENTANCE. FROM THE FRENCH OF M. D'ARNAUD.
[Litchfield: Printed by Thomas Collier, 1791?]

23132   ASPLUND, JOHN   – 1807
THE ANNUAL REGISTER OF THE BAPTIST DENOMINATION, IN NORTH-AMERICA; TO
THE FIRST OF NOVEMBER, 1790. CONTAINING AN ACCOUNT OF THE CHURCHES AND
THEIR CONSTITUTIONS, MINISTERS, MEMBERS, ASSOCIATIONS, THEIR PLAN AND
SENTIMENTS, RULE AND ORDER, PROCEEDINGS AND CORRESPONDENCE. ALSO RE-
MARKS UPON PRACTICAL RELIGION. HUMBLY OFFERED TO THE PUBLIC, BY JOHN
ASPLUND. [Preface signed, John Asplund a Sweed. Southampton County,
Virginia, July 14, 1791.]
[Norfolk: Printed by Prentis & Baxter? 1791.] pp. [57,] [57-67,] [69-
70.] 4to.   AAS. BM. JCB. LOC. NYPL. NYHS.
2nd. Virginia District Copyright. Pages 57 to 67, are usually missing
from copies of this work, and when so found, page 57 ends with index.
The copy in the John Carter Brown Library of Brown University, is
complete, and page 57 is without the index. Pages 69–70, containing
Remarks on the foregoing, were evidently printed by a different press
from the body of the work.

23133   ATKINSON, WILLIAM KING
AN ORATION; DELIVERED AT DOVER, NEW-HAMPSHIRE, ON THE FOURTH OF JULY,
1791. BEING THE FIFTEENTH ANNIVERSARY OF AMERICAN INDEPENDENCE.
[Eight lines of quotations.] BY WILLIAM KING ATKINSON.
Dover, New-Hampshire: Printed by E. Ladd, near the Court House.
MDCC,XCI. pp. (23). 4to.   BA. JCB. LOC. MHS.

23134   AUSTIN, DAVID, editor.   1760 – 1831
THE AMERICAN PREACHER; OR, A COLLECTION OF SERMONS FROM SOME OF THE
MOST EMINENT PREACHERS, NOW LIVING, IN THE UNITED STATES, OF DIFFERENT
DENOMINATIONS IN THE CHRISTIAN CHURCH. NEVER BEFORE PUBLISHED. [Edited
by David Austin.] VOLUME I. [—III.]
> *Elizabeth-Town, (New-Jersey) Printed by Shepard Kollock, for the Editors
> who hold the privilege of Copy-right.* M.DCC.XCI. 3 vols. pp. xiv, (9)–396; 403;
> 416. 8vo.   AAS. BA. BM. JCB. NYHS. NYPL.

New-Jersey District Copyright, issued to David Austin, 22 August,
1791. A fourth volume was printed in New-Haven, in 1793.

23135   AUSTIN, SAMUEL   1760 – 1830
DISINTERESTED LOVE, THE ORNAMENT OF THE CHRISTIAN, AND THE DUTY OF MAN.
A SERMON DELIVERED AT NEW-YORK, JUNE 5, 1790; . . . AND PUBLISHED IN
COMPLIANCE WITH THE REQUEST OF A NUMBER OF THE HEARERS. [Four lines
from] SHAFTSBURY.
> *New-York: Printed by Wm. Durell, No. 198, Queen-Street.* MDCCXCI.
> pp. [32.] 8vo.   AAS. BM. HC. JCB. LOC. YC.

23136   —— THE MANNER IN WHICH THE GOSPEL SHOULD BE HEARD, AND THE IMPORTANCE
OF HEARING IT RIGHTLY, ILLUSTRATED AND URGED, IN A DISCOURSE, PREACHED BY
SAMUEL AUSTIN, M. A. IN WORCESTER, ON THE LORD'S DAY IMMEDIATELY SUC-
CEEDING HIS INSTALLATION SEPTEMBER 29TH, MDCCXC. PUBLISHED IN COMPLI-
ANCE WITH THE REQUEST OF MANY OF THE HEARERS.
> *Printed at Worcester, Massachusetts, by Isaiah Thomas.* MDCCXCI. pp.
> 32. 8vo.   AAS. BA. BM. NYPL. YC.

23137   AVERY, DAVID   1746 – 1818
TWO SERMONS ON THE NATURE AND EVIL OF PROFESSORS OF RELIGION, NOT BRIDLING
THE TONGUE. BY DAVID AVERY, PASTOR OF A CONGREGATIONAL CHURCH IN
WRENTHAM. [Six lines of Scripture texts.]
> *Printed in Boston, by Joseph Bumstead, No. 20, Union-Street.* MDCCXCI.
> pp. (66). 8vo.   BA. BM. HC. JCB. LOC. MHS. NYPL. YC.

23138   THE BACHELOR'S ADDRESS TO MODESTY.
> *Norwich: Printed and sold by John Trumbull.* 1791.

23139   BACKUS, ISAAC   1724 – 1806
AN ANSWER TO MR. WESLEY, ON ELECTION AND FINAL PERSEVERANCE.
> *Boston: Printed and sold by Samuel Hall, No. 53 Cornhill.* 1791.

23140   —— THE INFINITE IMPORTANCE OF THE OBEDIENCE OF FAITH, AND OF A SEPARA-
TION FROM THE WORLD, OPENED AND DEMONSTRATED. BY ISAAC BACKUS, PASTOR
OF A CHURCH IN MIDDLEBOROUGH. [Four lines of Scripture texts.] SECOND
EDITION, CORRECTED AND IMPROVED.
> *Boston: Printed and sold by Samuel Hall, No. 53 Cornhill.* MDCCXCI.
> pp. 31. 8vo.   AAS. JCB. LOC.

"This discourse was first published in 1767, the year in which the law
was made that brought on the American war. It is now revised and
corrected to hold up the living obedience of faith, as our only way of
deliverance and happiness." Middleborough, Feb. 27, 1791.

23141 BACKUS, Charles   1749 – 1803
The Faithful ministers of Jesus Christ rewarded. A sermon, delivered at
the ordination of the rev. Azel Backus, to the pastoral care of the
church in Bethlem April 6, 1791. By Charles Backus, a. m. pastor of the
church in Somers.
Litchfield: Printed by Collier and Buel. [1791.] pp. 26. 8vo.
AAS. BM. CHS. HC. JCB. LOC. NYPL. UTS. YC·

23142 BAKER, Gardiner
Notice. The subscriber takes the liberty to acquaint his friends and the
public, that he intends to offer himself as a candidate at the ensuing
election in September next, for the office of collector to the third
ward of this city, agreeable to the late division. [Eight lines.] Gardiner Baker. Maiden-Lane, No. 13. New-York, May 24, 1791. Boundaries of the third ward. [Ten lines.] [Colophon:]
New-York, Printed by John Harrisson, No. 3; Peck-Slip. [1791.] Broadside. fol.   NYHS.

23143 BALCH, Stephen Bloomer   1747 – 1833
Two sermons, on the certain and final perseverance of the saints. By
Stephen Bloomer Balch, a. m. pastor of the Presbyterian congregation,
George-Town. [Three lines from] Psalm xcii. 12.
George-Town: Printed, for the Author, by M. Day and W. Hancock. M,-
DCC,XCI.   PU.
Reprinted, in 1907, in Balch Genealogica.

23144 THE BALTIMORE Daily Repository. Vol. i. No. 1. Monday, October 24, [—
No. 60. Saturday, December 31, 1791.]
*Baltimore: Printed by David Graham, at the New Printing-Office, in Cal-
vert-Street, between Market-Street and the Court-House;* . . . 1791. 4to. MdHS.
Established by David Graham, as the first daily newspaper published
in Baltimore. In April. 1793, Leonard Yundt, and William Patten
were admitted to a partnership, under their individual names. This
ended in a disagreement, which culminated October 19th, 1793—the
last issue of the Repository. Yundt and Patten, establishing on October
28th, *The Baltimore Daily Intelligencer.*

23145 BANGS, Edward   – 1818
An Oration delivered at Worcester, on the fourth of July, 1791. Being
the anniversary of the independence of the United States. By Edward
Bangs, esq.
Printed at Worcester, Massachusetts, by Isaiah Thomas. MDCCXCI. pp.
16. 4to.   AAS. BM. HC. MHS.
The verso of the title-page contains an Ode, written and delivered by
Oliver Fiske.

23146 BANK OF THE UNITED STATES.
The Acts of incorporation, bye-laws, rules and regulations, of the Bank
of the United States.
[Philadelphia: 1791.] pp. (29). 8vo.   LOC.

23147 ——— [Circular describing in detail the notes to be issued by the Bank,
dated, Philadelphia, December 31, 1791.
Philadelphia: 1791.] Broadside. fol.

23148 | BANNEKER, BENJAMIN   1731 – 1806
BENJAMIN BANNEKER'S PENNSYLVANIA, DELAWARE, MARYLAND AND VIRGINIA
ALMANACK AND EPHEMERIS, FOR THE YEAR OF OUR LORD, 1792; BEING BISSEX-
TILE, OR LEAP-YEAR, AND THE SIXTEENTH YEAR OF AMERICAN INDEPENDENCE,
WHICH COMMENCED JULY 4, 1776. [Thirteen lines.]

*Baltimore: Printed and sold, wholesale and retail, by William Goddard
and James Angell, at their Printing-Office, in Market - Street.—Sold, also, by Mr.
Joseph Crukshank, Printer, in Market-Street, and Mr. Daniel Humphreys, Printer,
in South-Front-Street, Philadelphia—and by Messrs. Hanson and Bond, Printers,
in Alexandria.* [1791.] pp. (48). 12mo.   JCB. LOC. MHS. NYPL.

The first publication of Benjamin Banneker, a free negro, born in Baltimore County, fifty-nine years of age at this performance, which he ac-
complished, unaided, from books loaned to him by the Ellicott family—themselves remarkable for scientific achievement. The Publisher's preface makes clear that in selecting Banneker's calculations for
their Almanac, which they did at the instance of James M'Henry, they
were actuated by a mingled feeling of deference for Mr. M'Henry, and
Mr. David Rittenhouse's opinions, of philanthropy, and for the business effect it would have on the sale of the Almanac.

23149 | BAPTISMAL HYMNS. SOME OF WHICH ARE NEWLY SELECTED.
Boston: Printed by Edes and Son, No. 7, State-Street. 1791.

23150 | BAPTIST CHURCH IN NEW YORK.
MINUTES OF THE BAPTIST CONVENTION MET AT MOUNT PLEASANT, MAY 31 AND
JUNE 1, 1791.
New-York: 1791. 12mo.

23151 | —— MINUTES OF THE PROCEEDINGS OF A CONVENTION OF BAPTIST CHURCHES, IN
NEW-YORK, OCTOBER 19, 20, AND 21, 1791. IN FORMING THE NEW-YORK ASSO-
CIATION. [Twelve lines of verse from] RIPPON'S SELECTION.
New-York: Printed by William Durell, No. 19, Queen-Street. M,DCC,-
XCI. pp. 8. 8vo.   JCB.

23152 | BAPTIST CHURCH IN NORTH CAROLINA.
MINUTES OF THE UNITED BAPTIST ASSOCIATION, FORMERLY CALLED THE KEHUKEE
ASSOCIATION, HOLDEN AT FLAT-SWAMP MEETING-HOUSE, PITT COUNTY, NORTH-
CAROLINA, OCTOBER 1791. [Colophon:]
Edenton: Printed by Hodge & Wills. [1791.] pp. 8. 4to.   JCB.

23153 | BAPTIST CHURCH IN VERMONT.
MINUTES OF THE VERMONT ASSOCIATION, AT THEIR ANNUAL CONVENTION: HOLDEN
AT WALLINGFORD, VERMONT, OCTOBER, 1790.
Printed at Bennington, (Vermont), in the year 1791. *By Anthony Has-
well.* pp. 8. 8vo.   AAS.

23154 | BAPTIST CHURCH IN VIRGINIA.
THE MIDDLE DISTRICT ASSOCIATION MET AT CEDAR-CREEK MEETING-HOUSE, MAY,
1791.
Richmond: Printed by Augustine Davis, Printer for the public. [1791.] 8vo.

23155 | —— MINUTES OF THE BAPTIST COMMITTEE HELD AT NUCKOL'S MEETING-HOUSE, IN
THE COUNTY OF GOOCHLAND, MAY, 1791.
Richmond: Printed by John Dixon. 1791. 8vo.

23156 | BARD, JOHN   1716 – 1799
A LETTER FROM JOHN BARD TO THE AUTHOR OF THOUGHTS ON THE DISPENSARY.
New-York: 1791.   NYHS.

23157   BARTLET, J.
THE GENTLEMAN'S POCKET-FARRIER, SHOWING HOW TO USE YOUR HORSE ON A JOURNEY, AND WHAT REMEDIES ARE PROPER FOR COMMON ACCIDENTS, THAT MAY BEFALL HIM ON THE ROAD, WITH A COPPER-PLATE, SHOWING THE AGE OF A HORSE BY HIS TEETH.—THE REMEDIES THIS LITTLE TRACT PRESCRIBES, ARE SIMPLE, AND EASILY OBTAINED, AND NEVER FAIL OF A CURE, WHEN THE DISORDER IS CURABLE; AND NO MAN WHO VALUES HIS HORSE, SHOULD TRAVEL WITHOUT IT.
Philadelphia: Printed and sold by W. Spotswood, 1791.

23158   BARTON, WILLIAM   1739 – 1823
OBSERVATIONS ON THE PROGRESS OF POPULATION, AND THE PROBABILITIES OF THE DURATION OF HUMAN LIFE, IN THE UNITED STATES OF AMERICA. READ BEFORE THE AMERICAN PHILOSOPHICAL SOCIETY HELD AT PHILADELPHIA, FOR PROMOTING USEFUL KNOWLEDGE. BY WILLIAM BARTON, M. A.
[Philadelphia:] Printed by R. Aitken & Son. M.D.CC.XCI. pp. (2), 38. 4to.   BA. 8GO.

23159   BARTRAM, WILLIAM   1738 – 1823
TRAVELS THROUGH NORTH & SOUTH CAROLINA, GEORGIA, EAST & WEST FLORIDA, THE CHEROKEE COUNTRY, THE EXTENSIVE TERRITORIES OF THE MUSCOGULGES, OR CREEK CONFEDERACY, AND THE COUNTRY OF THE CHACTAWS; CONTAINING AN ACCOUNT OF THE SOIL AND NATURAL PRODUCTIONS OF THOSE REGIONS, TOGETHER WITH OBSERVATIONS ON THE MANNERS OF THE INDIANS. EMBELLISHED WITH COPPER-PLATES. BY WILLIAM BARTRAM.
Philadelphia: Printed by James & Johnson. M,DCC,XCI. pp. (2), xxxiv, 522, portrait of Mico Chlucco, map, 7 plates. 8vo. AAS. BA. BM.JCB. LOC. NYPL.
Second title: AN ACCOUNT OF THE PERSONS, MANNERS, CUSTOMS AND GOVERNMENT OF THE MUSCOGULGES OR CREEKS, CHEROKEES, CHACTAWS, &C. ABORIGINES OF THE CONTINENT OF NORTE AMERICA. BY WILLIAM BARTRAM.
Philadelphia: Printed by James & Johnson. M,DCC,XCI. pp. (2), 483-522.
24th Pennsylvania District Copyright, issued to William Barton, as Author, 26 August, 1791. Reprinted in London in 1792, and 1794; in Dublin in 1793; in a German translation in Berlin in 1793; in a Dutch translation, 1794–7; and, in a French translation, in Paris, in 1799, and in 1801.

23160   —— — TRAVELS THROUGH NORTH AND SOUTH CAROLINA, GEORGIA, EAST AND WEST FLORIDA, THE CHEROKEE COUNTRY, THE EXTENSIVE TERRITORIES OF THE MUSCOGULGES, OR CREEK CONFEDERACY, AND THE COUNTRY OF THE CHACTAWS; CONTAINING AN ACCOUNT OF THE SOIL AND NATURAL PRODUCTIONS OF THOSE REGIONS, TOGETHER WITH OBSERVATIONS ON THE MANNERS OF THE INDIANS. EMBELLISHED WITH COPPER-PLATES. BY WILLIAM BARTRAM.
Philadelphia: Printed by James & Johnson. M,DCC,XCI. pp. (2), xxxiv, 522, portrait of Mico Chlucco, map, 7 plates. 8vo.   NYPL.
Second title: AN ACCOUNT OF THE PERSONS, MANNERS, CUSTOMS AND GOVERNMENT OF THE MUSCOGULGES OR CREEKS, CHEROKEES CHACTAWS, &C. ABORIGINES OF THE CONTINENT OF NORTH AMERICA. BY WILLIAM BARTRAM.
Philadelphia: Printed by James & Johnson. M,DCC,XCI. pp. (2), 483-522.
Except for slight differences in its title-page, and the omission of the notice of Copyright on the verso, this impression is identical with the preceding. It would be interesting to learn of any other copies of this work, with these peculiarities. The reprinted title-page is of a slightly different color and quality of paper, and may be the singular work of some collector, or dealer, to complete a defective copy. This particular copy is from the Library of Theodorus Bailey Myers presented to the New York Public Library by his family in 1899.

23161   BAXTER, RICHARD   1615 – 1691
THE SAINTS EVERLASTING REST: OR, A TREATISE OF THE BLESSED STATE OF THE
SAINTS IN THEIR ENJOYMENT OF GOD IN GLORY: EXTRACTED FROM THE WORKS OF
MR. RICHARD BAXTER, BY JOHN WESLEY, M. A. LATE FELLOW OF LINCOLN COL-
LEGE, OXFORD.
*Philadelphia: Printed by Parry Hall, No. 149, Chesnut Street, and sold
by John Dickins, No. 182, Race Street, near Sixth Street.* M.DCC.XCI. pp. 399,
(1). 16mo.   AAS.

23162   BAYLEY, RICHARD   1745 – 1801
A LETTER TO DR. JOHN BARD, IN ANSWER TO A PART OF HIS LETTER, ADDRESSED
TO THE AUTHOR OF THOUGHTS ON THE DISPENSARY.
New-York: 1791.   NYHS.

23163   BEERS, ANDREW   1749 – 1824
BEERS'S ALMANACK AND EPHEMERIS OF THE MOTION OF THE SUN AND MOON; THE
TRUE PLACES AND ASPECTS OF THE PLANETS; THE RISING, SETTING AND SOUTHING
OF THE MOON, FOR THE YEAR OF OUR LORD 1792: BEING BISSEXTILE OR LEAP
YEAR, AND THE SIXTEENTH OF AMERICAN INDEPENDENCE. [Nine lines.] BY
ANDREW BEERS, PHILOM.
Hartford: Printed by Hudson and Goodwin. [1791.] pp. (36). 12mo.
AAS. CHS. LOC.

23164   —— GLORI GREENLEAF'S NEW-YORK, CONNECTICUT, & NEW-JERSEY ALMANACK,
OR DIARY, WITH AN EPHEMERIS; FOR THE YEAR OF OUR LORD, 1792; [Fourteen
lines, with cut.]
Printed at New-York—By Thomas Greenleaf, for M,DCC,XCII. [1791.]
[*Price* 30s *the gross,* 3s *the dozen, and* 6d *single.*] a *Mundi* pp. [48.] 12mo. NYPL.

23165   BEERS, WILLIAM PITT   1766 – 1810
AN ADDRESS TO THE LEGISLATURE AND PEOPLE OF THE STATE OF CONNECTICUT, ON
THE SUBJECT OF DIVIDING THE STATE, INTO DISTRICTS FOR THE ELECTION OF
REPRESENTATIVES IN CONGRESS. BY A CITIZEN OF CONNECTICUT.
New-Haven: Printed by T. & S. Green, 1791. pp. (37). 8vo.
AAS. LOC. MHS. NYPL. YC.

23166   BELKNAP, JEREMY   1744 – 1798
THE HISTORY OF NEW-HAMPSHIRE. VOLUME II. COMPREHENDING THE EVENTS
OF SEVENTY-FIVE YEARS, FROM MDCCXV TO MDCCXC. ILLUSTRATED BY A MAP. BY
JEREMY BELKNAP, A. M. MEMBER OF THE PHILOSOPHICAL SOCIETY IN PHILA-
DELPHIA, AND OF THE ACADEMY OF ARTS AND SCIENCES IN MASSACHUSETTS.
*Printed at Boston, for the Author, by Isaiah Thomas and Ebenezer T. An-
drews, Faust's Statue, No, 45, Newbury-Street.* MDCCXCI. pp. 493, (1), map.
8vo.   AAS. BA. HC. JCB. LOC. MHS. NYHS. NYPL.
The first volume was printed at Philadelphia in 1784; and the third at
Boston in 1792, when the first was also reprinted. The title of the
map is: A New Map of New-Hampshire, by Jeremy Belknap, 1791.
Engraved by S. Hill. 17th Massachusetts District Copyright, issued
to Jeremy Belknap, as Author, 31 August, 1791.

23167   —— PROPOSAL OF JOSEPH BELKNAP AND ALEXANDER YOUNG FOR PRINTING A
WEEKLY PAPER, TO BE ENTITLED THE AMERICAN APOLLO, CONTAINING THE PUB-
LICATIONS OF THE HISTORICAL SOCIETY. . . .
Boston: 1791. pp. 4, (1). 8vo.

23168   BELL, BENJAMIN   1749 – 1806
A SYSTEM OF SURGERY. BY BENJAMIN BELL. [Four lines.] IN FOUR VOLUMES. ILLUSTRATED WITH ONE HUNDRED COPPER-PLATES. THE FIRST AMERICAN EDITION, CORRECTED. VOL. I.
> *Printed at Worcester, Massachusetts, by Isaiah Thomas.* MDCCXCI. pp. 454, (1), 21 plates. 8vo.   RIMS. SGO.

23169   —— — A SYSTEM OF SURGERY. . . . VOL. II [— IV.]
> *Printed at Boston, by Thomas and Andrews.* 1791. 3 vols. pp. 392, 17 plates; 391, 31 plates; 360, 30 plates. 8vo.   RIMS. SGO.

23170   —— A SYSTEM OF SURGERY. EXTRACTED FROM THE WORKS OF BENJAMIN BELL OF EDINBURGH: BY NICHOLAS B. WATERS, M. D. FELLOW OF THE COLLEGE OF PHYSICIANS OF PHILADELPHIA, AND ONE OF THE PHYSICIANS AND SURGEONS TO THE PHILADELPHIA DISPENSARY. ILLUSTRATED WITH NOTES [by John Jones, M. D.] AND COPPER PLATES.
> *Philadelphia: Printed by Thomas Dobson,* 1791. pp. viii, 570, 29,12 plates. 8vo.   BM. SGO.
> 21st Pennsylvania District Copyright, issued to Thomas Dobson, as Proprietor, 19 August, 1791.

23171   —— A TREATISE ON THE THEORY AND MANAGEMENT OF ULCERS: WITH A DISSERTATION ON WHITE SWELLINGS OF THE JOINTS. TO WHICH IS PREFIXED, AN ESSAY ON THE CHIRURGICAL TREATMENT OF INFLAMMATION AND ITS CONSEQUENCES. BY BENJAMIN BELL, MEMBER OF THE ROYAL COLLEGE OF SURGEONS, ONE OF THE SURGEONS TO THE ROYAL INFIRMARY, FELLOW OF THE ROYAL SOCIETY OF EDINBURGH.
> *Boston: Printed by I. Thomas & E. T. Andrews,* 1791. pp. xv, 17—295, plate. 8vo.   RIMS. SGO.

23172   BELL, BENJAMIN   1752 – 1836
THE NATURE AND IMPORTANCE OF A PURE PEACE ILLUSTRATED; AND THE MEANS BY WHICH IT MAY BE OBTAINED AND CULTIVATED, SHOWN, AND URGED, IN A DISCOURSE ON ROMANS, XIV: 17. DELIVERED BEFORE SEVERAL MEMBERS OF BOTH HOUSES OF THE LEGISLATURE OF THE STATE OF VERMONT, DURING THEIR SESSION IN WINDSOR, OCTOBER, 1791. PUBLISHED AT THEIR PARTICULAR DESIRE. BY BENJAMIN BELL, A. M. PASTOR OF A CHURCH IN WINDSOR AND CORNISH. . . .
> *Printed at Windsor by Alden Spooner.* [1791.] pp. 19. 8vo. AAS. JCB. LOC.
> This is not an official Vermont election sermon.

23173   BEND, JOSEPH GROVE JOHN   1762 – 1812
A DISCOURSE, DELIVERED IN ST. PAUL'S CHURCH, BALTIMORE, ON SUNDAY, JUNE 19TH, 1791. BY JOSEPH BEND, A. M.
> *Baltimore: Printed by David Graham,* 1791.
> Recognizing the relationship subsisting between the congregation and the author; in consequence of his recent election to the office of rector of said church.

23174   —— A VALEDICTORY DISCOURSE, PREACHED IN CHRIST-CHURCH AND ST. PETER'S, PHILADELPHIA, ON SUNDAY, THE THIRD OF JULY, 1791. BY JOSEPH BEND, A. M. LATE ASSISTANT-MINISTER OF THE ABOVE CHURCHES AND NOW RECTOR OF ST. PAUL'S, BALTIMORE.
> *Philadelphia: Printed by Hall and Sellers,* 1791.

23175 BENEZET, ANTHONY　　　　　1713 – 1784
KURZER BERICHT VON DEN LEUTEN, DIE MAN QUÄKER NENNET; IHREM URSPRUNG,
IHRER RELIGIONSGRÜNDEN, UND VON IHRER NEIDERLASSUNG IN AMERICA.
MEISTENTHEILS AUS VERSCHIEDENEN AUTORES ZUSAMMEN GEGOGEN, ZUM UN-
TERRICHT ALLER AUFRICHTIGEN NACHFORSCHER, UND INSONDERHEIT FÜR AUS-
LÄNDER. DURCH ANTON BENEZET. AUS DEM ENGLISCHEN ÜBERSETZT.
*Philadelphia: Gedruckt bey Carl Cist, Num. 104, in der Zweyten-Strasse,
nahe am Eck der Rehs-Strasse. 1791.* pp. [36.] 12mo.　　　AAS. NYPL.

23176 BENNET, JOHN
LETTERS TO A YOUNG LADY, ON A VARIETY OF USEFUL AND INTERESTING SUBJECTS:
CALCULATED TO IMPROVE THE HEART, TO FORM THE MANNERS, AND ENLIGHTEN
THE UNDERSTANDING. "THAT OUR DAUGHTERS MAY BE AS POLISHED CORNERS OF
THE TEMPLE." BY THE REV. JOHN BENNET, AUTHOR OF STRICTURES ON FEMALE
EDUCATION.
Hartford: Printed by Hudson & Goodwin, 1791. 2 vols. in one. 12mo.

23177 BENTLEY, WILLIAM　　　　　1758 – 1819
A SERMON, DELIVERED IN THE EAST MEETING-HOUSE, SALEM, ON SUNDAY MORNING,
MARCH 13: OCCASIONED BY THE DEATH OF JONATHAN GARDNER, ESQ. MASTER OF
THE MARINE SOCIETY IN SALEM; WHO DIED MARCH 2, 1791, AET. 63. BY WIL-
LIAM BENTLEY, A. M. PASTOR OF THE SECOND CONGREGATIONAL CHURCH IN SALEM.
Printed at Salem, by Thomas C. Cushing. MDCCXCI. pp. 32. 8vo.
AAS. BA. BM. HC. JCB. MHS. NYHS.

23178 BERRIDGE, JOHN　　　　　1716 – 1793
THE CHRISTIAN WORLD UNMASKED. PRAY COME AND PEEP. BY JOHN BERRIDGE,
A. M. LATE FELLOW OF CLARE-HALL., CAMBRIDGE; AND CHAPLAIN TO THE RIGHT
HON. THE EARL OF BUCHAN. [Three lines of Scripture texts.]
*Philadelphia: Printed by William Young, Bookseller, No. 52, Second-
street, the corner of Chesnut-street.* M,DCC.XCI. pp. 237, (3). 12mo.　　AAS.
Contains, a list of American editions sold by William Young.

23179 BESCHRIEBUNG EINER UNGEHEMEN GROSSEN SCHLANGE, ANACONDA GENANNT.
Philadelphia: Gedruckt? bey Johann Zeller, 89 Race-Street. 1791.

23180 BIBLIA.
THE HOLY BIBLE, CONTAINING THE OLD AND NEW TESTAMENTS: TRANSLATED OUT
OF THE ORIGINAL TONGUES; AND WITH THE FORMER TRANSLATIONS DILIGENTLY
COMPARED AND REVISED.
New-York: Printed by Hugh Gaine, 1791. 12mo.

23181 —— THE SELF-INTERPRETING BIBLE: CONTAINING THE SACRED TEXT OF THE OLD
AND NEW TESTAMENTS. TRANSLATED FROM THE ORIGINAL TONGUES, AND WITH
THE FORMER TRANSLATIONS DILIGENTLY COMPARED AND REVISED. TO WHICH
ARE ANNEXED, MARGINAL REFERENCES AND ILLUSTRATIONS, AN EXACT SUMMARY
OF THE SEVERAL BOOKS, A PARAPHRASE ON THE MOST OBSCURE OR IMPORTANT
PARTS, AN ANALYSIS OF THE CONTENTS OF EACH CHAPTER, EXPLANATORY NOTES,
AND EVANGELICAL REFLECTIONS. BY THE LATE REVEREND JOHN BROWN, MIN-
ISTER OF THE GOSPEL AT HADDINGTON. [Five lines of Scripture texts.] [Parts
XIV.—XXXIV.]
New-York: Printed by Hodge and Campbell, 1791.

23182 —— THE HOLY BIBLE ABRIDGED: OR, THE HISTORY OF THE OLD AND NEW TESTA-
MENT. ILLUSTRATED WITH NOTES, AND ADORNED WITH CUTS. FOR THE USE OF
CHILDREN.
Sagg-Harbour, Printed by David Frothingham, 1791.
Advertised September 13, 1791, as "Now printing and in a short time
ready for sale."

BIBLIA, continued

23183 —— THE HOLY BIBLE, CONTAINING THE OLD AND NEW TESTAMENTS: TRANSLATED OUT OF THE ORIGINAL TONGUES; AND WITH THE FORMER TRANSLATIONS DILIGENTLY COMPARED AND REVISED. [VOL. I.]
Philadelphia: Printed by W. Young, No. 52, *Second, the corner of Chesnut-Street.* M,DCC,XCI. 2 vols. pp. (1202); (360). 18mo.　　AAS. LCP. NYPL.

Second title: THE HOLY BIBLE, CONTAINING THE OLD AND NEW TESTAMENTS: TRANSLATED OUT OF THE ORIGINAL TONGUES; AND WITH THE FORMER TRANSLATIONS DILIGENTLY COMPARED AND REVISED. [VOL. II.]
Philadelphia: Printed by W. Young, No. 52, *Second, the corner of Chesnut-Street.* M,DCC,XCI. (unpaged).

Following Proverbs, which ends the first volume, and the Tables, which end the second volume, are copies of The Psalms of David in metre, without title, and, unpaged, both with the Colophon: Philadelphia: Printed by William Young, No. 52, Second-Street, the corner of Chesnut-Street. M,DCC,XCIII.

Third title: THE NEW TESTAMENT OF OUR LORD AND SAVIOUR JESUS CHRIST, TRANSLATED OUT OF THE ORIGINAL GREEK; AND WITH THE FORMER TRANSLATIONS DILIGENTLY COMPARED AND REVISED.
Philadelphia: Printed by W. Young, No. 52, *Second, the corner of Chesnut-Street.* M,DCC,XCII. pp. (360).

In two states: "a few copies on fine paper." Unpaged. With successive signatures to the Old Testament of 1791, with which it is found bound. "An accurate American edition, in pocket size, is now in press."

23184 —— THE HOLY BIBLE, CONTAINING THE OLD AND NEW TESTAMENTS: TRANSLATED OUT OF THE ORIGINAL TONGUES: AND WITH THE FORMER TRANSLATIONS DILIGENTLY COMPARED AND REVISED.
Trenton: Printed and sold by Isaac Collins. M.DCC.XCI. pp. (1160). 4to.　　NYPL.

$10

Second title: PRACTICAL OBSERVATIONS, ON THE OLD AND NEW TESTAMENTS, ILLUSTRATING THE CHAPTERS, A VERY FEW EXCEPTED, IN THEIR ORDER, WITH ARGUMENTS TO THE DIFFERENT BOOKS. BY THE REVEREND MR. OSTERVALD, PROFESSOR OF DIVINITY, AND ONE OF THE MINISTERS OF THE CHURCH AT NEUFCHATEL IN SWITZERLAND.
Trenton: Printed and sold by Isaac Collins. M.DCC.XCI. pp. (2), 154.

Third title: THE NEW TESTAMENT OF OUR LORD AND SAVIOUR JESUS CHRIST, TRANSLATED OUT OF THE GREEK: AND WITH THE FORMER TRANSLATIONS DILIGENTLY COMPARED AND REVISED.
Trenton: Printed and sold by Isaac Collins. M.DCC.XCI. unpaged.

Fourth title: A BRIEF CONCORDANCE OR TABLE TO THE BIBLE OF THE LAST TRANSLATION: SERVING FOR THE MORE EASY FINDING OUT OF THE MOST USEFUL PLACES THEREIN CONTAINED. CAREFULLY PERUSED AND ENLARGED BY JOHN DOWNAME, B. A. [One line from] PSALM CXIX. 105.
Trenton: Printed and sold by Isaac Collins. M.DCC.XC. pp. (2). 70.

This "highly creditable specimen of typography," is sometimes found bound in two volumes. Other copies are without Ostervald's Practical observations, which was left out owing to objections by the Baptist Associations. And some copies are without the Apocrypha. The Address to the reader is by John Witherspoon. It is said to contain only two typographical errors—one in Luke's description of the Crucifixion "and there were also two other malefactors led with him."

BIBLIA, continued.

23185   —— The Holy Bible, containing the Old and New Testaments: together with the Apocrypha: translated out of the original tongues, and with the former translations diligently compared and revised, by the special command of King James I, of England. With marginal notes and references. To which are added, an index, and an alphabetical table of all the names in the Old and New Testaments, with their significations.

United States of America. Printed at the Press in Worcester, Massachusetts, by Isaiah Thomas. Sold by him in Worcester; and by him and Company, at Faust's Statue, No. 45, Newbury Street, Boston. MDCCXCI. pp. 1310, 48 plates; 89. 4to.   AAS. LCP. NYPL.

Second title: The Old Testament, translated out of the original Hebrew, and with the former translations diligently compared and revised. Together with the Apocrypha. Done by the special command of his Majesty King James I, of England. [One line of Hebrew text from Genesis II. 17. in ornamental border.]

United States of America. Printed at the Press in Worcester, Massachusetts, by Isaiah Thomas. Sold by him in Worcester. Sold also by said Thomas, and Andrews, at Faust's Statue, No. 45, Newbury Street, Boston. MDCCXCI. pp. (2), (9)—1014, plates.

Colophon: Printed at Worcester, by Isaiah Thomas, MDCCXCI.

Third title: The New Testament of our Lord and Saviour Jesus Christ. Translated out of the original Greek: and with the former translations diligently compared and revised, by the special command of his Majesty King James I, of England. [Two lines of Greek text from I Cor. xv. 22, in ornamental border.]

United States of America. Printed at the Press in Worcester, Massachusetts, by Isaiah Thomas. Sold by him in Worcester. Sold also by said Thomas, and Andrews, at Faust's Statue, No. 45, Newbury Street, Boston. MDCCXCI. pp. (2), (2), (1019)–1276. plates.

Colophon: This royal quarto edition of the Bible, and likewise one in folio, with fifty copper plates, were printed by Isaiah Thomas, at Worcester, Massachusetts, MDCCXCI.

Fourth title: A Brief Concordance to the Holy Scriptures of the Old and New Testaments: by which all, or most, of the principal texts of Scripture may be easily found out. Revised and corrected. By John Brown, late minister of the Gospel at Haddington, in Scotland. [Two lines of Scripture texts.]

Printed at Worcester, Massachusetts, by Isaiah Thomas. Sold at his Bookstore in Worcester, and by him and Company in Boston. MDCCXCI. pp. 89.

The Index, and An Alphabetical table of proper names, occupy pages 1277–1310. When bound in two volumes, the division occurs after page 824. This quarto edition is printed in double columns, with ornamental letters at the beginning of the divisions only; and was supplied to subscribers in three forms: one with forty-eight copper plates, and Concordance; one without plates, but with Concordance; and one without plates, or Concordance. The proof examination was the work of the Reverend Joseph Avery, of Holden, Massachusetts.

BIBLIA, continued.

23186 —— THE HOLY BIBLE, CONTAINING THE OLD AND NEW TESTAMENTS; WITH THE APOCRYPHA. TRANSLATED OUT OF THE ORIGINAL TONGUES, AND WITH THE FORMER TRANSLATIONS DILIGENTLY COMPARED AND REVISED, BY THE SPECIAL COMMAND OF KING JAMES I, OF ENGLAND. WITH AN INDEX. APPOINTED TO BE READ IN CHURCHES. VOL. I. [— II.]

United States of America. Printed at the Press in Worcester, Massachusetts, by Isaiah Thomas. Sold by him in Worcester; and by him and Company, at Faust's Statue, No. 45, Newbury Street, Boston. MDCCXCI. 2 vols. pp. (2), (2), 460, (2), 461–1012, 50 plates. fol.   AAS. BU. HC. NYPL.

$15

Second title: THE HOLY BIBLE, CONTAINING THE OLD AND NEW TESTAMENTS: WITH THE APOCRYPHA. TRANSLATED OUT OF THE ORIGINAL TONGUES, AND WITH THE FORMER TRANSLATIONS DILIGENTLY COMPARED AND REVISED, BY THE SPECIAL COMMAND OF KING JAMES I, OF ENGLAND. WITH AN INDEX. APPOINTED TO BE READ IN CHURCHES. VOL. II.

United States of America. Printed at the Press in Worcester, Massachusetts, by Isaiah Thomas. Sold by him in Worcester; and by him and Company, at Faust's Statue, No. 45, Newbury Street, Boston. MDCCXCI. pp. (2), 461–786.

Colophons: At foot of page 635: The end of the Prophets. Printed at Worcester, Massachusetts, by Isaiah Thomas. MDCCXCI. At foot of page 786: This folio edition of the Bible, and one in royal quarto, were printed by Isaiah Thomas, at Worcester, Massachusetts, in the year MDCCXCI. Both are enclosed in ornamental borders.

Third title: THE NEW TESTAMENT OF OUR LORD AND SAVIOUR JESUS CHRIST, TRANSLATED OUT OF THE ORIGINAL GREEK, AND WITH THE FORMER TRANSLATIONS DILIGENTLY COMPARED AND REVISED, BY THE SPECIAL COMMAND OF KING JAMES I, OF ENGLAND. TOGETHER WITH AN INDEX TO THE HOLY BIBLE. APPOINTED TO BE READ IN CHURCHES.

United States of America. Printed at the Press in Worcester, Massachusetts, by Isaiah Thomas. Sold by him in Worcester; and by him and Company, at Faust's Statue, No. 45, Newbury Street, Boston. MDCCXCI. pp. (2), 789–1012.

There are a number of variants among the issues of these handsome volumes. The copies in two volumes, as above, are printed on handmade paper of heavier quality than the one volume issues, and have three title pages, while the latter have only two—a general title page and the New Testament title—with no directions to the binder or list of plates. In the two volume issues these sometimes follow the title of the first volume, and sometimes are found at the end of the second volume. In some copies of the one volume edition the plates are omitted. In all issues three wood cuts mark the first pages of the Old Testament, the New Testament, and the Apocrypha, with ornamental letters beginning each Book; and the catch word "An" appears at the foot of page 1012—indicating an apparently abandoned intention of following the text, as in the quarto edition, with An Alphabetical table of proper names. The fifty copper plates are all executed by American engravers: Joseph H. Seymour, of Philadelphia; Amos Doolittle, of New Haven; and Samuel Hill, and H. Norman, of Boston. The proof revision was principally made by the Reverend Aaron Bancroft, and the Reverend Samuel Austin, and to insure accuracy, comparison was made with at least eight editions printed at different times and places.

23187   BIBLIA. OLD TESTAMENT. PSALMS.
A NEW VERSION OF THE PSALMS OF DAVID, FITTED TO THE TUNES USED IN CHURCHES. BY N. BRADY, D. D. LATE CHAPLAIN IN ORDINARY, AND N. TATE, ESQ; LATE POET LAUREAT TO HIS MAJESTY. WITH HYMNS.
Boston: Printed and sold by Samuel Hall, MDCCXCI. pp. 358. 12mo. HC.

23188   —— DOCTOR WATTS'S IMITATION OF THE PSALMS OF DAVID, CORRECTED AND ENLARGED. BY JOEL BARLOW. TO WHICH IS ADDED A COLLECTION OF HYMNS; THE WHOLE APPLIED TO THE STATE OF THE CHRISTIAN CHURCH IN GENERAL. THE THIRD EDITION.
Hartford: Printed by Hudson and Goodwin, 1791.

23189   —— — DOCTOR WATTS'S IMITATION OF THE PSALMS OF DAVID, CORRECTED AND ENLARGED, BY JOEL BARLOW. TO WHICH IS ADDED A COLLECTION OF HYMNS; THE WHOLE APPLIED TO THE STATE OF THE CHRISTIAN CHURCH IN GENERAL. THE FOURTH EDITION. LUKE XXIV. [Two lines.]
Hartford: Printed by Nathaniel Patten. [With a privilege of copy-right.]
[1791.] pp. 169 [*sic* 269], (18), 289-332. 24mo.   BM. BU. NYPL.

23190   —— — DOCTOR WATTS'S IMITATION OF THE PSALMS OF DAVID, CORRECTED AND ENLARGED, BY JOEL BARLOW. ADAPTED TO THE STATE OF THE CHRISTIAN CHURCH IN GENERAL. ALSO, HYMNS AND SPIRITUAL SONGS. BY I. WATTS, D. D.
New-York: Printed by W. Durell, M,DCC,XCI. 12mo.

23191   —— THE PSALMS, CAREFULLY SUITED TO THE CHRISTIAN WORSHIP IN THE UNITED STATES OF AMERICA. BEING AN IMPROVEMENT OF THE OLD VERSION OF THE PSALMS OF DAVID. ALLOWED, BY THE REVEREND SYNOD OF NEW YORK AND PHILADELPHIA, TO BE USED IN CHURCHES AND PRIVATE FAMILIES.
Elizabeth-Town: Printed by Shepard Kollock, M.DCC.XCI. pp. 314, (10). 18mo.   LOC.

23192   —— THE PSALMS OF DAVID, IMITATED IN THE LANGUAGE OF THE NEW TESTAMENT, AND APPLIED TO THE CHRISTIAN STATE AND WORSHIP. TOGETHER WITH HYMNS, AND SPIRITUAL SONGS, IN THREE BOOKS. I. COLLECTED FROM THE SCRIPTURES. II. COMPOSED ON DIVINE SUBJECTS. III. PREPARED FOR THE LORD'S SUPPER. WITH INDEXES AND TABLES COMPLETE. BY ISAAC WATTS, D. D. [Six lines of quotations.]
Printed at Boston, by I. Thomas and E. 7. Andrews, Faust's Statue, No. 45, Newbury Street, MDCCXCI. pp. 227, (1). 4to.   JCB. NYPL.

23193   —— — THE PSALMS OF DAVID. IMITATED IN THE LANGUAGE OF THE NEW TESTAMENT, AND APPLIED TO THE CHRISTIAN STATE AND WORSHIP. BY I. WATTS, D. D. [Six lines of Scripture texts.]
Boston: Printed by J. W. Folsom, for D. West, Marlboro'-Street. B. Larkin, and E. Larkin, in Cornhill. MDCCXCI. pp. 300, 252. 12mo.   AAS
A reprint of Mycall's revision of 1781.

Second title: HYMNS AND SPIRITUAL SONGS. IN THREE BOOKS. I. COLLECTED FROM THE SCRIPTURES. II. COMPOSED ON DIVINE SUBJECTS. III. PREPARED FOR THE LORD'S SUPPER. BY I. WATTS, D. D. [Six lines of quotations.]
Boston: Printed by J. W. Folsom, for D. West, Marlborough-Street, and E. Larkin, in Cornhill. MDCCXCI. pp. 252.

BIBLIA, PSALMS, continued.

23194 —— THE PSALMS OF DAVID IN METRE: NEWLY TRANSLATED AND DILIGENTLY COM-PARED WITH THE ORIGINAL TEXT, AND FORMER TRANSLATIONS: MORE PLAIN, SMOOTH, AND AGREEABLE TO THE TEXT, THAN ANY HERETOFORE. ALLOWED BY THE AUTHORITY OF THE GENERAL-ASSEMBLY OF THE KIRK OF SCOTLAND, AND APPOINTED TO BE SUNG IN CONGREGATIONS AND FAMILIES. REPRINTED, AT THE REQUEST OF THE PRESBYTERIAN CONGREGATION OF CARLISLE, AND CAREFULLY COMPARED WITH THE ORIGINAL.
Carlisle: Printed by George Kline, 1791.

23195 —— DER PSALTER DES KÖNIGS UND PROPHETEN DAVIDS, . . .
Lancaster: Gedruckt bey Albrecht & Comp. 1791. pp. 152. 12mo.

23196 —— —— DER PSALTER DES KÖNIGS UND PROPHETEN DAVIDS, U. S. W.
Philadelphia: Gedruckt bey Carl Cist, 1791. pp. 251. 12mo. LCP.

23197 —— DAS KLEINE DAVIDISCHE PSALTERSPIEL DER KINDER ZIONS, VON ALTEN UND NEUEN AUSERLESENEN GEISTES GESÄNGEN, ALLEN WAHREN HEILS—BEGIERIGEN SÄULINGEN DER WEISHEIT, INSONDERHEIT ABER DENEN GEMEINDEN DES HERRN, ZUM DIENST UND GEBRAUCH MIT FLEISS ZUSAMMEN GETRAGEN IN GEGENWÄRTIG-BELIEBIGER FORM UND ORDNUNG. NEBST EINEM DREYFACHEN, DARZU NÜTZ-LICHEN UND DER MATERIEN HALBEN NÖTHIGEN REGISTER. ZUM SECHSTEN MAL ANS LICHT GEGEBEN.
Chesnuthill, gedruckt bey Samuel Saur, 1791. Published as the law directs.
pp. (2), (4), 572, (22). 8vo. AAS. LOC. NYPL.
8th Pennsylvania District Copyright, and 1st German Copyright, issued to Samuel Sower, as Proprietor, 16 September, 1790.

23198 —— DER HUNDERT UND NEUNZEHNTE PSALM, GENAU NACH DER GRUNDSPRACHE ÜBERSETZT, VON JOHANN CHRISTOPH KUNZE.
Philadelphia: Gedruckt bey Melchior Steiner, 1791. 8vo. HC.

23199 BIBLIA. OLD TESTAMENT. APOCRYPHA.
TESTAMENT UND ABSCHRIFT DER ZWÖLF PATRIARCHEN DER SÖHNEN JACOBS, U. S. W.
Lancaster: Gedruckt bey Jacob Bailey, 1791. pp. 113. 12mo.

23200 BIBLIA. NEW TESTAMENT.
THE NEW TESTAMENT OF OUR LORD AND SAVIOUR JESUS CHRIST, NEWLY TRANS-LATED OUT OF THE ORIGINAL GREEK; AND WITH THE FORMER TRANSLATIONS DILI-GENTLY COMPARED AND REVISED. [Ornament.]
Newbury-Port: Printed and sold by John Mycall. [1791.] unpaged. 12mo.
The following error has been noted: 1 Tim. IV. 16. "Take heed unto thyself, and unto *thy* doctrine."

23201 —— THE NEW TESTAMENT OF OUR LORD AND SAVIOUR JESUS CHRIST, NEWLY TRANSLATED OUT OF THE ORIGINAL GREEK; AND WITH THE FORMER TRANSLA-TIONS DILIGENTLY COMPARED AND REVISED.
Philadelphia: Printed by John M'Culloch. [1791.] 12mo.

23202 —— DAS NEUE TESTAMENT UNSERS HERRN UND HEYLANDES JESU CHRISTI, NACH DER DEUTSCHEN UEBERSETZUNG D. MARTIN LUTHERS, MIT KURZEM INHALT EINES JEDEN CAPITELS, UND VOLLSTÄNDIGER ANWEISUNG GLEICHER SCHRIFT-STELLEN. WIE AUCH ALLER SONN-UND FEST-TÄGEN EVANGELIEN UND EPISTELN. ERSTE AUFLAGE.
Philadelphia: Gedruckt bey Carl Cist, Num. 104, in der Zweyten-Strasse.
1791. pp. (4), 525, (3). 12mo. AAS.

23203   BIBLIA. NEW TESTAMENT. APOCRYPHA.
EVANGELIUM NICODEMI, ODER HISTORISCHER BERICHT VON DEM LEBEN JESU CHRISTI WELCHES NICODEMUS, EIN RABBI, U. S. W. BESCHRIEBEN.
Lancaster: Gedruckt bey Jacob Bailey, 1791. pp. 95. 12mo.

23204   BICKERSTAFFE, ISAAC   1735 – 1787
THOMAS AND SALLY; OR, THE SAILOR'S RETURN. A MUSICAL ENTERTAINMENT.
Philadelphia: Printed by Henry Taylor, 1791.
One thousand copies, in sheets, offered at the sale of Henry Taylor's estate.

23205   BIDDLE, CLEMENT
THE PHILADELPHIA DIRECTORY. BY CLEMENT BIDDLE.
Philadelphia: Printed by James & Johnson, No. 147, High-Street, for the Editor. M,DCC,XCI. pp. xviii, (1), 187, (1). 8vo.   AAS. HC. HSP. LCP.
18th Pennsylvania District Copyright, issued to Clement Biddle, as Author, 18 March, 1791. Contains twelve pages of "Information concerning the City of Philadelphia." $11

23206   BINGHAM, CALEB   1757 – 1819
THE YOUNG LADY'S ACCIDENCE: OR, A SHORT AND EASY INTRODUCTION TO ENGLISH GRAMMAR. DESIGNED, PRINCIPALLY, FOR THE USE OF YOUNG LEARNERS, MORE ESPECIALLY THOSE OF THE FAIR SEX, THOUGH PROPER FOR EITHER. BY CALEB BINGHAM, A. M. [Two lines of verse.] THE FIFTH EDITION, CORRECTED. [Published according to Act of Congress.]
Printed at Boston, by I. Thomas and E. T. Andrews, at Faust's Statue, No. 45, Newbury Street. MDCCXCI.

23207   BISHOP, ABRAHAM   1763 – 1844
THE TRIUMPH OF TRUTH. —HISTORY AND VISIONS OF CLIO. BY JOHN PAUL MARTIN, A. M. M. S. S. [Six lines of quotations. Ornament.]
Printed at Boston, by Isaiah Thomas and Ebenezer T. Andrews, Faust's Statue, No. 45 Newbury Street. MDCCXCI. pp. 62. 8vo.
     AAS. BM. BPL. HC. JCB. LOC. NYPL. PPL. YC.

23208   BISSETT, JOHN   1762 – 1810
A SERMON DELIVERED IN ST. PAUL'S CHURCH, BALTIMORE, ON THE 19TH OF JUNE (TRINITY SUNDAY) 1791. WITH AN APPENDIX.
Philadelphia: Printed by T. Dobson, at the Stone-House, No. 41, South Second-Street. M,DCC,XCI. pp. (22), (17). 8vo.   CLS. JCB. NYHS.

23209   BLAIR, HUGH   1718 – 1800
SERMONS, BY HUGH BLAIR, D. D. ONE OF THE MINISTERS OF THE HIGH CHURCH, AND PROFESSOR OF RHETORIC AND BELLES LETTRES IN THE UNIVERSITY OF EDINBURGH. THE FIRST AMERICAN EDITION, FROM THE SEVENTEENTH LONDON EDITION. VOLUME THE FIRST. [—SECOND.]
Philadelphia: Printed by and for W. Spotswood, and Carey, Stewart and Co. M,DCC,XCI. 2 vols. pp. 342, iv, (2); 360. 12mo.   AAS. JCB.
A third volume was published by Mathew Carey, in Philadelphia, 1794.

23210   BLAIR, ROBERT   1699 – 1747
THE GRAVE. A POEM. BY ROBERT BLAIR. [One line from] JOB. TO WHICH IS ADDED, AN ELEGY, WRITTEN IN A COUNTRY CHURCH-YARD. BY MR. GRAY.
Philadelphia: Printed and sold by Henry Taylor. M.DCC.XCI. pp. [32.] 12mo.   AAS. LOC.

23211 | THE BLOODY REGISTER. No. V.
Boston: Printed and sold by E. Russell, near Liberty-stump. 1791.

23212 | BLUNDELL, JAMES
AN INAUGURAL DISSERTATION, ON THE DYSENTERY.
Philadelphia: Printed by T. Dobson, 1791. pp. 34. 8vo.   SGO.

23213 | BOOTH, ABRAHAM   1734 – 1806
AN ESSAY ON THE KINGDOM OF CHRIST. BY ABRAHAM BOOTH. [Two lines from]
PSALM CXLV. II.
New-York: Printed and sold by W. Durell, at his Book-Store and Printing-Office, No. 198, Queen-Street. M,DCC,XCI. pp. 128, (4). 12mo.   AAS. JCB. NYPL.

23214 | BOSTON, DECEMBER 19. MELANCHOLY ACCOUNT RESPECTING THE WESTERN ARMY.
[Six columns.]
[Boston:] Printed by B. Edes & Son. [1791.] Broadside. fol.   AAS.

23215 | BOSTON. MASSACHUSETTS. BOSTON TONTINE ASSOCIATION.
THE CONSTITUTION OF THE BOSTON TONTINE ASSOCIATION.
[Boston: Printed by Benjamin Russell.] MDCCXCI. pp. 19, (1). 12mo.
AAS. BA. JCB. MHS. NYHS.

23216 | THE BOSTON [cut] GAZETTE, AND THE COUNTRY JOURNAL. CONTAINING THE
LATEST OCCURRENCES, FOREIGN AND DOMESTIC. [Motto.] No. 1892. MONDAY,
JANUARY 3, [— No. 1943. MONDAY, DECEMBER 26, 1791.]
Printed by Benjamin Edes and Son, No. 7, State-Street, Boston. 1791.
fol.
AAS. LOC. MHS. NYPL.

23217 | BRADFORD, EBENEZER   1746 – 1801
THE DEPRAVITY OF HUMAN NATURE ILLUSTRATED. A SERMON DELIVERED AT
ROWLEY, JULY 5, 1789, BY EBENEZER BRADFORD, A. M. PASTOR OF THE FIRST
CHURCH OF CHRIST IN ROWLEY. PUBLISHED BY DESIRE.
Newburyport. Printed and sold by John Mycall. MDCCXCI. pp. 24.
8vo,
AAS.

23218 | —— A DISCOURSE, DELIVERED AT THE ORDINATION OF THE REVEREND NATHANIEL
HOWE, TO THE PASTORAL CARE OF THE CHURCH IN HOPKINTON, OCTOBER 5,
1789 [*sic* 1791.] BY EBENEZER BRADFORD, A. M. PASTOR OF THE FIRST CHURCH
IN ROWLEY.
Newburyport: Printed by John Mycall. MDCCXCI. pp. (30). 8vo.
AAS. JCB. NYPL.
The error in date is corrected in a single line of errata on the last page.

23219 | —— THE FAITHFULNESS OF A MINISTER OF JESUS CHRIST ILLUSTRATED. A SER-
MON, DELIVERED AT THE ORDINATION OF THE REVEREND MOSES BRADFORD TO
THE PASTORAL CARE OF THE CHURCH IN FRANCIS-TOWN, SEPTEMBER 8, 1790. BY
EBENEZER BRADFORD, A. M. PASTOR OF THE FIRST CHURCH IN ROWLEY. PUB-
LISHED BY DESIRE.
Newburyport: Printed and sold by John Mycall. MDCCXCI. pp. 32.
8vo.
JCB. NYPL.

23220 | —— THE QUALIFICATIONS, COMMISSION AND WORK OF AN AMBASSADOR FOR CHRIST,
ILLUSTRATED. A SERMON, DELIVERED AT THE ORDINATION OF THE REV. NA-
THANIEL LAMBERT, TO THE PASTORAL CARE OF THE CHURCH OF CHRIST IN NEW-
BURY, IN THE STATE OF VERMONT, NOVEMBER 17TH, 1790. BY EBENEZER
BRADFORD, A. M. PASTOR OF THE FIRST CHURCH IN ROWLY [*sic.*]
Printed at Windsor, Vermont, by Alden Spooner, MDCCXCI. pp.18.8vo.JCB.

23221   BRADMAN, ARTHUR
A NARRATIVE OF THE EXTRAORDINARY SUFFERINGS OF MR. ROBERT FORBES, HIS WIFE, AND FIVE CHILDREN, DURING AN UNFORTUNATE JOURNEY THROUGH THE WILDERNESS, FROM CANADA TO KENNEBECK RIVER IN THE YEAR 1784: IN WHICH THREE OF THEIR CHILDREN WERE STARVED TO DEATH. (TAKEN PARTLY FROM THEIR OWN MOUTHS AND PARTLY FROM AN IMPERFECT JOURNAL; AND PUBLISHED AT THEIR REQUEST.) BY ARTHUR BRADMAN.
Portland: Printed at Thomas Baker Wait's Office. MDCCXCI. *Price nine pence.* pp. 13. 16mo.   AAS.
Reprinted in Windsor, Vermont, in 1792; and in Philadelphia in 1794.

23222   BRISSOT DE WARVILLE, JACQUES PIERRE   1754 – 1793
A DISCOURSE UPON THE QUESTION WHETHER THE KING SHALL BE TRIED? DELIVERED BEFORE THE SOCIETY OF THE FRIENDS OF THE CONSTITUTION AT PARIS, AT A MEETING JULY 10, 1791. BY J. P. BRISSOT DE WARVILLE, MEMBER OF THAT SOCIETY: TRANSLATED BY P. J. G. DE NANCREDE, PRECEPTOR OF THE FRENCH LANGUAGE IN THE UNIVERSITY OF CAMBRIDGE. THE FIRST AMERICAN EDITION.
Printed at Boston, by J. Belknap and A. Young. Sold at their Printing-Office, No. 34, Newbury Street, and by the Booksellers in town and country. MDCCXCI. pp. 34. 12mo.   AAS. BA. BM. HC. LOC. MHS. NYHS.

23223   BROOKE, FRANCES MOORE   1745 – 1789
ROSINA OR, LOVE IN A COTTAGE; A COMIC OPERA IN TWO ACTS. AS PERFORMED WITH UNIVERSAL APPLAUSE, BY THE AMERICAN COMPANY.
Philadelphia: Printed and sold by Henry Taylor. M.DCC.XCI. pp. 36. 18mo.   AAS.

23224   BROOKE, HENRY   1706 – 1783
GUSTAVUS VASA, THE DELIVERER OF HIS COUNTRY. A TRAGEDY, AS IT WAS TO HAVE BEEN ACTED AT THE THEATRE-ROYAL IN DRURY-LANE AND NOW PERFORMED BY THE OLD AMERICAN COMPANY AT THE THEATRE IN SOUTHWARK, PHILADELPHIA. BY HENRY BROOK, ESQ. AUTHOR OF THE FOOL OF QUALITY, &C.
Philadelphia: Printed and sold by Enoch Story, in Second Street. 1791. pp. 84. 12mo.   AAS.

23225   BROWN, JOHN   1722 – 1787
A BRIEF CONCORDANCE TO THE HOLY SCRIPTURES OF THE OLD AND NEW TESTAMENTS: BY WHICH ALL, OR MOST, OF THE PRINCIPAL TEXTS OF SCRIPTURE MAY BE EASILY FOUND OUT. REVISED AND CORRECTED. BY JOHN BROWN, LATE MINISTER OF THE GOSPEL AT HADDINGTON, IN SCOTLAND. [Two lines of Scripture texts.]
Printed at Worcester, Massachusetts, by Isaiah Thomas. Sold at his Book-store in Worcester, and by him and Company in Boston. MDCCXCI. pp. 89. 4to.   AAS.
Also found bound with Isaiah Thomas' quarto edition of the Bible, printed by him this year.

23226   BROWN, or BRUNO, JOHN   1735 – 1788
THE ELEMENTS OF MEDICINE; OR, A TRANSLATION OF THE ELEMENTA MEDICINÆ BRUNONIS. WITH LARGE NOTES, ILLUSTRATIONS, AND COMMENTS. BY THE AUTHOR OF THE ORIGINAL WORK. IN TWO VOLUMES. VOL. I. [—II.]
Philadelphia: Printed by W. Spotswood, for Isaiah Thomas, of Worcester, Massachusetts. MDCCXCI. 2 vols. in one. pp. xv, 295, (8), folded table.8vo. AAS.

23227   BROWNSON, OLIVER
SELECT HARMONY; CONTAINING THE NECESSARY RULES OF PSALMODY: TOGETHER WITH A COLLECTION OF APPROVED PSALM TUNES, HYMNS AND ANTHEMS.
New-Haven: Printed by T. & S. Green, 1791.

23228   BRUCE, JAMES   1730 – 1794
AN INTERESTING NARRATIVE OF THE TRAVELS OF JAMES BRUCE, ESQ; INTO ABYS-
SINIA, TO DISCOVER THE SOURCE OF THE NILE. ABRIDGED BY SAMUEL SHAW.
> *New-York: Printed for Berry and Rogers, No. 35, Hanover-Square. 1791.*

23229   THE BRUNSWICK GAZETTE, AND WEEKLY MONITOR. [Motto.] NUMB. 223. TUES-
DAY, JANUARY 4, [— NUMB. 274, TUESDAY, DECEMBER 27, 1791.]
> *New-Brunswick: Printed by Abraham Blauvelt. 1791. fol.*

23230   BUDD, JOHN
A DISSERTATION ON PORTER, READ BEFORE THE MEDICAL SOCIETY OF SOUTH
CAROLINA, ON THE 28TH OF MAY, 1791. BY DR. BUDD.
> *Charleston: Printed by Markland & McIver, No. 47, Bay.* MDCCXCI.
> pp. 12. 12mo.
>
>   AAS. LOC.

23231   BULLARD, SAMUEL
AN ALMANACK, FOR THE YEAR OF OUR CHRISTIAN ÆRA, 1792: AND OF THE CREA-
TION, ACCORDING TO THE SCRIPTURES, 5754: BEING BISSEXTILE, OR LEAP-YEAR;
AND THE SIXTEENTH OF THE INDEPENDENCE OF AMERICA. [Twelve lines.] BY
SAMUEL BULLARD. [Four lines of verse.]
> *Boston: Printed and sold by J. White and C. Cambridge, near Charles-
> River Bridge.* [1791.] pp. (24). 12mo.   LOC.

23232   BUNYAN, JOHN   1628 – 1688
THE PILGRIM'S PROGRESS FROM THIS WORLD TO THAT WHICH IS TO COME, DELIVER-
ED UNDER THE SIMILITUDE OF A DREAM. COMPLETE IN THREE PARTS. . . .
TO WHICH IS ADDED, THE LIFE AND DEATH OF THE AUTHOR. EMBELLISHED
WITH CUTS. . . . BY JOHN BUNYAN.
> *Printed at Worcester, Massachusetts, by Isaiah Thomas.* MDCCXCI. pp.
> 154, plate; (2), 158-292, plate; (2), 297-404, plate. 12mo.   AAS.
>
> A part of the edition appears to have had the imprint of Thomas and
> Andrews, Boston.

23233   BURGHER, JOHN
GOD'S LOVE TO MANKIND, EXEMPLIFIED IN THE FOLLOWING TREATISE: PROVED AND
ILLUSTRATED BY SCRIPTURE AND REASON, THAT JESUS CHRIST TASTETD [*sic*]
DEATH FOR EVERY MAN, AND CONSEQUENTLY THE WHOLE HUMAN RACE WILL FI-
NALLY BE SAVED. BY A RESIDENT OF NEW-YORK. [Two lines from] HOSEA
XIII. 9.
> *New-York: Printed [by Thomas Greenleaf] for the Author,* M,DCC,XCI.
> pp. 18. 12mo.   AAS.

23234   BURGOYNE, Sir JOHN   1722 – 1792
THE LORD OF THE MANOR, A COMIC OPERA, IN THREE ACTS. AS PERFORMED WITH
UNIVERSAL APPLAUSE BY THE AMERICAN COMPANY.
> *Philadelphia: Printed and sold by Henry Taylor,* M.DCC.XCI. pp 63.
> 12mo.   AAS. LOC.

23235   BURKE, Mrs. —
ELA, OR THE DELUSIONS OF THE HEART. A TALE, FOUNDED ON FACTS. TO WHICH
IS ADDED, HENRY AND EMMA:—A POEM. BY MATTHEW PRIOR. AND, THE DE-
SERTED VILLAGE. BY DR. GOLDSMITH.
> *Boston: Printed by John W. Folsom, and sold by E. Larkin, jun. 1791.*

23236   BURKE, EDMUND   1729 – 1797
         AN APPEAL FROM THE NEW TO THE OLD WHIGS, IN CONSEQUENCE OF SOME LATE
         DISCUSSIONS IN PARLIAMENT, RELATIVE TO THE REFLECTIONS ON THE FRENCH
         REVOLUTION. BY THE RIGHT HONOURABLE EDMUND BURKE.
              *London: printed. New-York: Re-printed by Childs and Swaine. Sold by
              Berry and Rogers, New-York; the principal Booksellers in Philadelphia; Thomas
              and Andrews, Boston; and W. P. Young, Charleston South Carolina.*— 1791 —
              pp. (93), (2). 8vo.   AAS. BA. HC. JCB. LOC. MHS. NYPL.

23237   —— A LETTER FROM MR. BURKE, TO A MEMBER OF THE NATIONAL ASSEMBLY; IN
         ANSWER TO SOME OBJECTIONS TO HIS BOOK ON FRENCH AFFAIRS. THE FOURTH
         EDITION.
              *Paris: Printed. New-York: Re-printed by Hugh Gaine, at the Bible, in
              Hanover-Square.* 1791. pp. 39, (1). 8vo.   AAS. BA. NYHS.

23238   —— REFLECTIONS ON THE REVOLUTION IN FRANCE, AND ON THE PROCEEDINGS IN
         CERTAIN SOCIETIES IN LONDON RELATIVE TO THAT EVENT. IN A LETTER INTEND-
         ED TO HAVE BEEN SENT TO A GENTLEMAN IN PARIS. BY THE RIGHT HONOURABLE
         EDMUND BURKE.
              *London: Printed: New-York: Re-printed by Hugh Gaine, at the Bible in
              Hanover-Square,* M,DCC,XCI. pp. (2), (2), (196). 8vo.   AAS. JCB. LOC. NYPL.

23239   THE BURLINGTON ADVERTISER, OR AGRICULTURAL AND POLITICAL INTELLIGENCER.
         VOL. I. NUMB. XXXIX. TUESDAY, JANUARY 4, [— VOL. II. NUMB. LXXXVIII. TUES-
         DAY, DECEMBER 13, 1791.]
              *Burlington: Printed and published, weekly, by I. Neale and D. Lawrence,
              . . .* 1791. fol.   NYPL.
         With the issue for April 12th, Daniel Lawrence withdrew, and pub-
         lication of the paper, until it ceased December 13th, was continued by
         Isaac Neale, as sole printer and publisher.

23240   —— THE NEWS-CARRIERS' ADDRESS TO THE SUBSCRIBERS TO THE BURLINGTON AD-
         VERTISER. JANUARY 1, 1791.
              [Burlington: Printed by Neale & Lawrence, 1791.] Broadside. fol. NYPL.

23241   THE BURLINGTON ALMANAC FOR THE YEAR OF OUR LORD 1792. CONTAINING,
         BESIDES THE USUAL ASTRONOMICAL CALCULATIONS, A VARIETY OF ENTERTAINING
         PIECES IN PROSE AND VERSE.
              Burlington: Printed and sold by Isaac Neale, [1791.]

23242   BURR, AARON   1714 – 1757
         THE SUPREME DEITY OF OUR LORD JESUS CHRIST, MAINTAINED. IN A LETTER TO
         THE DEDICATOR OF MR. EMLYN'S "INQUIRY INTO THE SCRIPTURE ACCOUNT OF
         JESUS CHRIST." INSCRIBED TO THE REVEREND THE CLERGY OF ALL DENOMINA-
         TIONS IN NEW-ENGLAND. WHEREIN MR. EMLYN'S OBJECTIONS ARE FAIRLY AN-
         SWERED AND SHOWN TO HAVE NO VALIDITY. . . . [Eight lines of Scripture
         texts.]
              Boston: Re-printed: by Edward E. Powars, in Court Street. MDCCXCI,
              pp. (2), 61. 8vo.   AAS. BA. BM. HC. JCB. LOC. MHS.

23243   BURTON, ASA   1752 – 1836
         TO BE GREATEST IN CHRIST'S KINGDOM, A NECESSARY QUALIFICATION IN GOSPEL
         MINISTERS. A SERMON, DELIVERED AT THE INSTALMENT OF THE REV. DANIEL
         BRECK, A. M. TO THE PASTORAL CARE OF THE CHURCH OF CHRIST IN HARTLAND,
         IN THE STATE OF VERMONT, NOVEMBER 11TH, MD.CCLXXX,IX. BY ASA BURTON,
         A. M PASTOR OF THE CHURCH OF CHRIST IN THETFORD. PUBLISHED BY DESIRE.
              Windsor, Vermont, Printed by Alden Spooner. MDCCXCI. pp. 22. 8vo.
                                                              JCB. LOC.

23244   CAMPBELL, ROBERT

ROBERT CAMPBELL'S SALE CATALOGUE OF BOOKS. TO BE SOLD ON THE MOST REAS-
ONABLE TERMS, AT NO. 54, SOUTH SECOND-STREET, SECOND DOOR, BELOW THE
CORNER OF CHESNUT-STREET, ON THE WEST SIDE, PHILADELPHIA. CATALOGUES
ARE DELIVERED AT THE PLACE OF SALE TO GENTLEMEN WHO PLEASE TO CALL OR
SEND FOR THEM, AND ORDERS FROM THE COUNTRY, EXECUTED WITH THE UTMOST
CARE AND DISPATCH.

     [Philadelphia: Printed for Robert Campbell, 1791.] pp. 48. 12mo.   AAS.

23245   CAREY, JOHN

A CATALOGUE OF SCARCE AND VALUABLE BOOKS.

     Philadelphia: Printed for John Carey, No. 112, *Union-Street.* 1791.

23246   CAREY, MATHEW, editor.   1760 – 1839

THE BEAUTIES OF POETRY, BRITISH AND AMERICAN: CONTAINING SOME OF THE PRO-
DUCTIONS OF WALLER, MILTON, ADDISON, POPE, SHIRLEY, PARNELL, WATTS,
THOMSON, YOUNG, SHENSTONE, AKENSIDE. GRAY, GOLDSMITH, JOHNSON, MOORE,
GARRICK, COWPER, BEATTIE, BURNS, MERRY, COWLEY, WOLCOTT. PALMERSTON,
PENROSE. EVANS, BARLOW, DWIGHT, FRENEAU, HUMPHREYS, LIVINGSTON, J.
SMITH, W. M. SMITH, LADD, BAYARD, HOPKINSON, JAMES, MARKOE, PRICHARD,
FENTHAM, BRADFORD, DAWES, LATHROP, OSBORNE.

     Philadelphia: From the Press of M. Carey, No. 118, *Market-Street.* M.-
DCC.XCI. pp. viii, 244. 12mo.   AAS, JCB. LCP.

   Contains a List of books and pamphlets lately printed and published by
M. Carey.

23247   CAREY, STEWART, and COMPANY,   publishers.

CATALOGUE OF BOOKS, STATIONARY, CUTLERY, &c. FOR SALE AT CAREY, STEWART &
CO'S STORE, NO. 22, NORTH FRONT-STREET, PHILADELPHIA.

     [Philadelphia: Printed by Carey, Stewart, & Co. 1791.] pp. [12.] 12mo.
                                        AAS. NYPL.

23248   CARLETON, OSGOOD   1742 – 1816

AN ASTRONOMICAL DIARY: OR, AN ALMANACK, FOR THE YEAR OF OUR LORD 1792,
[Sixteen lines.] BY OSGOOD CARLETON, TEACHER OF MATHEMATICKS, IN BOSTON.
[Six lines of verse.]

     Boston: Printed and sold by Samuel Hall. No. 53, *Cornhill: Also, by
Thomas C. Cushing, at his Printing-Office, in Salem.* [1791.] pp. (24). 12mo.
                                      AAS. LOC. NYPL.

   To the publick, is dated: Boston, May 1, 1791. The Memoirs of Capt.
John Smith, are continued.

23249   —— CARLETON'S SHEET ALMANACK, FOR THE YEAR 1792.

     Boston: Printed by Samuel Hall, 1791. Broadside.

23250   —— MAP OF THE UNITED STATES. BY OSGOOD CARLETON.

     Boston: 1791.

   Advertised July 4, 1791, as just come to hand, and for sale by Ambrose
Clark, Baltimore, "plain, colored, or framed."

23251   THE CARLISLE GAZETTE, AND THE WESTERN REPOSITORY OF KNOWLEDGE. VOL.
VI. NO. 283. WEDNESDAY, JANUARY 5, [— VOL. VII. NO. 334. WEDNESDAY,
DECEMBER 28, 1791.]

     Carlisle: (State of Pennsylvania) Printed by Kline & Reynolds, . . .
1791. fol.   NYHS.

   In July the partnership was dissolved, George Kline continuing publication as sole publisher until it was discontinued in 1815. The issue
for September 21st has a Supplement Extraordinary.

23252　A CAVEAT AGAINST POPERY. WRITTEN BY A MEMBER OF THE HOLY CATHOLIC CHURCH. [Two lines from] REV. xviii. 4. [Ornament.]
　　　Baltimore: Printed by Samuel and John Adams, in Market-Street, between South and Gay-Streets. M,DCC,XCI. pp. (28). 8vo.　　　BA. MDHS.

23253　CHALLONER, RICHARD　　　1691 – 1781
　　THINK WELL ON'T; OR, REFLECTIONS ON THE GREAT TRUTHS OF THE CHRISTIAN RELIGION FOR EVERY DAY OF THE MONTH. THIRTY-FOURTH EDITION. FIRST AMERICAN EDITION.
　　　Philadelphia: Carey, Stewart & Co. 1791. 18mo.

23254　CHAMBERLAIN, THOMAS　　　– 1784
　　TENTH EDITION. [Cut of minister preaching in pulpit.] THE MINISTER PREACHING HIS OWN FUNERAL SERMON: BEING A WARNING FROM HEAVEN TO ALL VILE SINNERS ON EARTH. WITH A PARTICULAR RELATION OF MANY WONDERFUL THINGS SEEN BY THE REV. MR. THOMAS CHAMBERLAIN, IN A VISION JUST BEFORE HIS DECEASE, THE PRECISE TIME OF WHICH WAS SHEWN UNTO HIM.
　　　[Boston:] Printed [by E. Russell] for the purchaser, 1791. *[Pr. 7d.] Sold by A. Nelson, travelling-trader of Pownalboro; who would be glad to buy 300 wt. of hair, suitable for barbers, for which he will pay the highest price.* ☞*He also sells goods and books.* pp. 15, (1). 8vo.　　　LOC.

23255　CHAPMAN, JEDIDIAH　　　1741 – 1813
　　FOUR SERMONS ON CHRISTIAN BAPTISM; IN WHICH THE PRIVILEGE OF BELIEVERS, UNDER THE GOSPEL, RESPECTING THE MODE AND SUBJECTS OF BAPTISM, IS ESTABLISHED AND ILLUSTRATED. PUBLISHED AT THE REQUEST OF THE HEARERS. BY JEDIDIAH CHAPMAN, V. D. M. PASTOR OF THE CHURCH OF CHRIST AT ORANGE-DALE.
　　　Elizabethtown: Printed for the Author by Shepard Kollock. M,DCC,XCI. pp. 85, (1). 8vo.　　　AAS. BA. HC. UTS.
　　Reprinted in Boston in 1806.

23256　DIE CHESNUTHILLER WOCHENSCHRIFT. NUM. 14. MITTWOCH, JANUARY 5, [— NUMB. 65. MITTWOCH, DECEMBER 28, 1791.]
　　　Chesnuthill: Gedruckt bey Samuel Saur. 1791. 4to.

23257　CHILDS, ISAAC
　　DIE GESCHICHTE DES ISAAC CHEILDS WELCHES ER GESEHEN HAT, BETREFFEND DAS LAND SEINER GEBURT.
　　　Reading: Gedruckt bey Barton und Jungmann, 1791.

23258　THE CHRISTIAN'S DUTY, EXHIBITED IN A SERIES OF HYMNS COLLECTED FROM VARIOUS AUTHORS. DESIGNED FOR THE WORSHIP OF GOD AND FOR THE EDIFICATION OF CHRISTIANS. RECOMMENDED TO THE SERIOUS OF ALL DENOMINATIONS BY THE BAPTISTS OF GERMANTOWN.
　　　Germantown: Printed by Peter Leibert and Son. 1791. pp. (4), 320, (25). 16mo.　　　HSP.
　　A Hymn book for the Dunkers.

23259　THE CHRISTIAN'S, SCHOLAR'S, AND FARMER'S MAGAZINE, FOR DECEMBER AND JANUARY. [—FEBRUARY AND MARCH, 1791.] [Edited by David Austin.]
　　　Elizabeth-Town: Printed and sold by Shepard Kollock. 1791. pp. 505-736, (6), (2). 8vo.　　　AAS. BA. LOC.
　　Discontinued from want of leisure, on the part of Editors, to continue it.

23260   CHURCHMAN, John   1753 – 1805
A DISSERTATION ON GRAVITATION. BY JOHN CHURCHMAN, AUTHOR OF THE MAG-
NETIC ATLAS.
> *Philadelphia:* 1791.

> 17th Pennsylvania District Copyright, issued to John Churchman, as
> Author, 26 February, 1791.

23261   THE CITY [seal] GAZETTE, OR THE DAILY ADVERTISER. [Motto.] VOL. IX. NUMB.
1664. SATURDAY, JANUARY 1, [—NUMB. 1772 [*sic.* 1972] SATURDAY, DECEMBER
31, 1791.]

> *Charleston: Printed by Markland & M'Iver, Printers to the City, No.* 47,
> *Bay,* 1791. fol.

> Number 1902, for October 8th, was misnumbered 1702, and the error
> continued from then on. The oval cut is a view of Charleston, with
> the legend: Ædes mores juraque curat corpus politicum.

23262   CLARK, JAMES
A TREATISE ON THE PREVENTION OF DISEASES INCIDENTAL TO HORSES, FROM BAD
MANAGEMENT IN REGARD TO STABLES, FOOD, WATER, AIR, AND EXERCISE. TO
WHICH ARE SUBJOINED, OBSERVATIONS ON SOME OF THE SURGICAL AND MEDICAL
BRANCHES OF FARRIERY. BY JAMES CLARK, FARRIER TO HIS BRITANNIC MAJES-
TY, HONORARY AND CORRESPONDING MEMBER OF THE SOCIETY OF AGRICULTURE,
&C. AT ODIAM IN HAMPSHIRE. [Two lines from] LUCAN. FROM THE SECOND
EDINBURGH EDITION, CORRECTED AND ENLARGED.

> *Philadelphia: Printed by William Spotswood.* MDCCXCI. pp. xvi, 208,
> (4). 12mo.   AAS.

> Contains a list of "New books, American editions, printed and sold by
> William Spotswood."

23263   CLORIS, PEDRO
GENTEEL & SURPRIZING FEATS OF ACTIVITY AT UNION-HALL, NEWBURYPORT.
DON PEDRO CLORIS, WHO HAS PERFORMED IN PARIS, LYONS, AND SEVERAL OTHER
LARGE CITIES IN FRANCE - - - LIKEWISE IN PHILADELPHIA, NEW-YORK AND
BOSTON, WITH UNIVERSAL APPLAUSE - - - HAS THE HONOR TO INFORM THE CITI-
ZENS OF NEWBURYPORT, THAT ON WEDNESDAY EVENING - - - - AUGUST 17, WILL
BE PERFORMED, CURIOUS FEATS OF ACTIVITY, ON THE SLACK WIRE, AND EX-
TRAORDINARY BALANCING. . . .

> *[Newburyport: Printed by John Mycall,* 1791.] Broadside. fol.   NYPL.

23264   THE COLUMBIAN ALMANAC, FOR THE YEAR OF OUR LORD, 1792; [Ten lines. Two
columns of contents.]

> *Philadelphia: Printed and sold by Peter Stewart, No.* 34, *South Second-
> Street.* [1791.] pp. (36). 12mo.   AAS.

> Contains, a History of the first printing-press in America.

23265   THE COLUMBIAN ALMANAC; OR, THE NORTH-AMERICAN CALENDAR, FOR THE YEAR
OF OUR LORD, 1792.

> *Wilmington (Del): Printed by Brynberg and Andrews.* [1791.] 12mo.

23266   COLUMBIAN U S A CENTINEL. NO. 32, OF VOL. XIV. WHOLE NO. 708. SATUR-
DAY, JANUARY 1, [—NO. 32, OF VOL. XVI. WHOLE NO. 802. SATURDAY, DECEM-
BER 31, 1791.]

> *Printed and published on Wednesdays and Saturdays, by Benjamin Rus-
> sell, in State-Street, Boston, Massachusetts.* 1791. fol.   AAS. LOC. NYPL.

23267   THE COLUMBIAN HERALD, OR THE INDEPENDENT COURIER OF NORTH AMERICA. JANUARY-DECEMBER, 1791.

Charleston: Printed by T. B. Bowen, 1791. fol.

23268   [Two rows of coffins bearing names of thirty-nine officers killed. Cuts of "Maj.-gen. Richard Butler." And, "Bloody Indian battle, fought at Miami Village, Nov. 4, 1791."] THE COLUMBIAN TRAGEDY: CONTAINING A PARTICULAR AND OFFICIAL ACCOUNT OF THE BRAVE AND UNFORTUNATE OFFICERS, AND SOLDIERS, WHO WERE SLAIN AND WOUNDED IN THE EVER-MEMORABLE AND BLOODY INDIAN BATTLE, PERHAPS THE MOST SHOCKING THAT HAS HAPPENED IN AMERICA SINCE ITS FIRST DISCOVERY; WHICH CONTINUED SIX HOURS, WITH THE MOST UNREMITTED FURY AND UNPARALLELED BRAVERY ON BOTH SIDES, HAVING LASTED FROM DAY-BREAK, UNTIL NEAR TEN O'CLOCK ON FRIDAY MORNING, NOV. 4, 1791; BETWEEN TWO THOUSAND AMERICANS, BELONGING TO THE UNITED ARMY, AND NEAR FIVE THOUSAND WILD INDIAN SAVAGES, AT MIAMI VILLAGE, NEAR FORT-WASHINGTON, IN THE OHIO-COUNTRY, IN WHICH TERRIBLE AND DESPERATE BATTLE A MOST SHOCKING SLAUGHTER WAS MADE OF THIRTY-NINE GALLANT AMERICAN OFFICERS AND UPWARDS OF NINE HUNDRED BRAVE YOUTHFUL SOLDIERS, WHO FELL GLORIOUSLY FIGHTING FOR THEIR COUNTRY.—THESE PARTICULARS AND ELEGY ARE NOW PUBLISHED IN THIS SHEET BY THE EARNEST REQUEST OF THE FRIENDS TO THE DECEASED WORTHIES, WHO DIED IN DEFENCE OF THEIR COUNTRY, NOT ONLY AS A TOKEN OF GRATITUDE TO THE DECEASED BRAVE, BUT AS A PERPETUAL MEMORIAL OF THIS IMPORTANT EVENT, ON WHICH, PERHAPS MAY VERY ESSENTIALLY DEPEND THE FUTURE FREEDOM AND GRANDEUR OF FIFTEEN OR TWENTY STATES, THAT MIGHT, AT SOME PERIOD, BE ANNEXED TO THE AMERICAN UNION. [Cut of Indian warrier. And, Death head.] LIST OF KILLED AND WOUNDED OFFICERS. [Fifteen lines.] A FUNERAL ELEGY ON THE OCCASION. [Text from] 2 SAMUEL. CHAP. I. VER. 19. [Forty-one four-line verses.] [Colophon:]

America: Boston; Printed by E. Russell, for Thomas Bassett, of Dunbarton (New-Hamp.)–[Pr. six pence.] ☞ Said Bassett sells Bickerstaff's Almanack, for 1792, as cheap as at this Office. [1791.] Broadside. fol.   NYHS.

23269   [U. S. arms.] CONCORD HERALD. [N. H. arms.] [Motto.] VOL. II. NO. 8. WHOLE NO. 58. WEDNESDAY, MARCH 9, [—VOL. II. NO. 50. WHOLE NO. 100. THURSDAY, DECEMBER 29, 1791.]

A Political State paper: Printed and published by George Hough, at Concord, New-Hampshire. 1791. fol.

In continuation of *Hough's Concord Herald.*

23270   CONGREGATIONAL CHURCH IN NEW HAMPSHIRE.

AN ADDRESS TO THE INHABITANTS OF THE TOWNS AND PARISHES IN THE STATE OF NEW HAMPSHIRE, PARTICULARLY THOSE WHICH ARE VACANT: FROM THE CONVENTION OF MINISTERS AT THEIR ANNUAL MEETING, HOLDEN AT CONCORD, ON THE FIRST WEDNESDAY IN JUNE, 1791.

Concord: Printed by George Hough. M,DCC,XCI. pp. 13. 8vo.   AAS.

23271   CONNECTICUT. STATE.

[Seal.] ACTS AND LAWS, MADE AND PASSED BY THE GENERAL COURT OR ASSEMBLY OF THE STATE OF CONNECTICUT, IN AMERICA, HOLDEN AT NEW-HAVEN, . . . DECEMBER, . . . 1790. [Colophon:]

Hartford: Printed by Elisha Babcock. [1791.] pp. 401-407. fol. CSL. YC.

This is the official issue.

23272   —— —— [Seal.] ACTS AND LAWS, MADE AND PASSED, BY THE GENERAL COURT OR ASSEMBLY OF THE STATE OF CONNECTICUT, IN AMERICA, HOLDEN AT NEW-HAVEN, IN SAID STATE (BY ADJOURNMENT) ON THE TWENTY-NINTH DAY OF DECEMBER, ANNO DOMINI, 1790. [Colophon:]

New-London: Printed by Timothy Green and Son. [1791.] pp. 401-407. fol.   HSP. NYBA. WU.

CONNECTICUT, continued.

23273 —— — [Seal.] ACTS AND LAWS, MADE AND PASSED BY THE GENERAL COURT OR ASSEMBLY OF THE STATE OF CONNECTICUT, IN AMERICA, HOLDEN AT NEW-HAVEN, . . . OCTOBER [DECEMBER,] . . . 1790.
[New-Haven: Printed by Thomas and Samuel Green, 1791.] pp. 395-402.
fol. HCBA. PL. YC.

23274 —— — [Seal.] ACTS AND LAWS, MADE AND PASSED BY THE GENERAL COURT OR ASSEMBLY OF THE STATE OF CONNECTICUT, IN AMERICA, HOLDEN AT NEW-HAVEN, . . . DECEMBER, . . . 1790. [Colophon:]
Hartford: Printed by Elisha Babcock. [1791.] pp. 401-407. 8vo.CHS.HCBA.

23275 —— — [Seal.] ACTS AND LAWS, MADE AND PASSED BY THE GENERAL COURT OR ASSEMBLY OF THE STATE OF CONNECTICUT, IN AMERICA, HOLDEN AT NEW-HAVEN, . . . DECEMBER, . . . 1790. [Colophon:]
Hartford: Printed by Nathaniel Patten. [1791.] pp. 405-411. fol. CHS.CSL.

23276 —— — [Seal.] ACTS AND LAWS, MADE AND PASSED BY THE GENERAL COURT OR ASSEMBLY OF THE STATE OF CONNECTICUT, IN AMERICA, HOLDEN AT HARTFORD, . . . MAY, . . . 1791. [Colophon:]
Hartford: Printed by Elisha Babcock. [1791.] pp. 409-414. fol. CHS. YC.
This is the official issue.

23277 —— — [Seal.] ACTS AND LAWS, MADE AND PASSED BY THE GENERAL COURT OR ASSEMBLY OF THE STATE OF CONNECTICUT, IN AMERICA, HOLDEN AT HARTFORD, IN SAID STATE, ON THE SECOND THURSDAY OF MAY, ANNO DOMINI, 1791.
[New-London: Printed by Timothy Green and Son. 1791.] pp. 409 - 413.
fol. HSP. NYLI.

23278 —— — [Seal.] ACTS AND LAWS, MADE AND PASSED BY THE GENERAL COURT OR ASSEMBLY OF THE STATE OF CONNECTICUT, IN AMERICA, HOLDEN AT HARTFORD, . . . MAY, . . . 1791.
[New-Haven: Printed by Thomas and Samuel Green. 1791.] pp. 403 - 406.
fol. HCBA. PL. YC.

23279 —— — [Seal.] ACTS AND LAWS, MADE AND PASSED BY THE GENERAL COURT OR ASSEMBLY OF THE STATE OF CONNECTICUT, IN AMERICA, HOLDEN AT HARTFORD, . . . MAY, . . . 1791. [Colophon:]
Hartford: Printed by Nathaniel Patten. [1791.] pp. 412-417. fol.CHS. CSL.

23280 —— — [Seal.] ACTS AND LAWS, MADE AND PASSED BY THE GENERAL COURT OR ASSEMBLY OF THE STATE OF CONNECTICUT, IN AMERICA, HOLDEN AT NEW-HAVEN, . . . OCTOBER, . . . 1791. [Colophon:]
Hartford: Printed by Elisha Babcock. [1791.] pp. 415 - 419. fol. CHS. YC.
There is apparently a Table (pp. 7) printed with the Yale College copy.

23281 —— — [Seal.] ACTS AND LAWS, MADE AND PASSED BY THE GENERAL COURT OR ASSEMBLY OF THE STATE OF CONNECTICUT, IN AMERICA, HOLDEN AT NEW-HAVEN, IN SAID STATE, ON THE SECOND THURSDAY OF OCTOBER, ANNO DOMINI, 1791.
[New-London: Printed by Timothy Green and Son. 1791.] pp. 415 - 418.
fol. HSP. NYLI.

23282 —— — [Seal.] ACTS AND LAWS, MADE AND PASSED BY THE GENERAL COURT OR ASSEMBLY OF THE STATE OF CONNECTICUT, IN AMERICA, HOLDEN AT NEW-HAVEN, . . . OCTOBER, . . . 1791.
[New-Haven: Printed by Thomas and Samuel Green. 1791.] pp. 407 - 410.
fol. HCBA. PL. YC.

AUCTION
VALUES

CONNECTICUT, continued.

23283 —— — [Seal.] ACTS AND LAWS, MADE AND PASSED BY THE GENERAL COURT OR ASSEMBLY OF THE STATE OF CONNECTICUT, IN AMERICA, HOLDEN AT NEW-HAVEN, . . . OCTOBER, ANNO DOMINI, 1791. [Colophon:]
Hartford: Printed by Nathaniel Patten. [1791.] pp. 418-422. fol. CHS. CSL.

23284 —— BY HIS EXCELLENCY SAMUEL HUNTINGTON, ESQUIRE, GOVERNOR AND COMMANDER IN CHIEF IN AND OVER THE STATE OF CONNECTICUT. A PROCLAMATION. [Appointing Thursday, the thirty-first of March, a day of fasting and prayer.]
New-London: Printed by Timothy Green, and Son. 1791. Broadside. fol.
CHS. YC.

23285 —— BY HIS EXCELLENCY SAMUEL HUNTINGTON, ESQUIRE, GOVERNOR AND COMMANDER IN CHIEF IN AND OVER THE STATE OF CONNECTICUT. A PROCLAMATION. [Appointing Thursday, the twenty-fourth day of November, a day of thanksgiving.]
New-London: Printed by Timothy Green and Son, 1791. Broadside. fol.
CHS. YC.

23286 THE CONNECTICUT COURANT, AND WEEKLY INTELLIGENCER. NUMBER 1354. MONDAY, JANUARY 3, [— VOL. XXVI. NUMB. 1405. MONDAY, DECEMBER 26, 1791.]
Hartford: Printed by Hudson and Goodwin, near the Bridge. 1791. fol.
AAS. CHS. LOC. YC.
With the issue for March 21st. the sub-title was permanently dropped from the heading.

23287 —— THE ADDRESS OF THE LAD WHO CARRIES THE CONNECTICUT COURANT, TO HIS CUSTOMERS. HARTFORD, JAN. 1. 1791.
[Hartford: Printed by Hudson and Goodwin, 1791.] Broadside.

23288 THE CONNECTICUT GAZETTE. VOL. XXVIII. No. 1417. FRIDAY, JANUARY 7, [— VOL. XXIX. No. 1468. THURSDAY, DECEMBER 29, 1791.]
New-London: Printed by Timothy Green and Son, at the northwest corner of the Parade. 1791. fol. AAS. CHS. NYPL. YC.
On April 7th, the day of issue was changed from Friday to Thursday.

23289 THE CONNECTICUT JOURNAL. No. 1210. WEDNESDAY, JANUARY 5, [— No. 1261. WEDNESDAY, DECEMBER 28, 1791.]
New-Haven: Printed by Thomas and Samuel Green, opposite the Post-Office. 1791. fol. AAS. LOC. YC.

23290 CONOVER, SAMUEL FORMAN
AN INAUGURAL DISSERTATION ON SLEEP AND DREAMS, THEIR EFFECTS ON THE FACULTIES OF THE MIND; AND THE CAUSES OF DREAMS.
[Philadelphia:] Printed by Thomas Lang, 1791. pp. 25. 8vo. SGO.

23291 CORAM, ROBERT
POLITICAL INQUIRIES: TO WHICH IS ADDED, A PLAN FOR THE GENERAL ESTABLISHMENT OF SCHOOLS THROUGHOUT THE UNITED STATES. BY ROBERT CORAM, AUTHOR OF SOME LATE PIECES IN THE DELAWARE GAZETTE, UNDER THE SIGNITURE [*sic*], OF BRUTUS. [Five lines from] RAYNAL.
Wilmington: Printed by Andrews and Brynberg, in Market - Street, MDCCXCI. pp. 107, (1). 8vo. AAS. BA. BM. JCB. LOC.
Delaware District Copyright, issued to Robert Coram, as Author, 8 February, 1791.

23292   CORNARO, Luigi   1467 – 1566
DISCOURSES ON A SOBER AND TEMPERATE LIFE. WHEREIN IS DEMONSTRATED BY
HIS OWN EXAMPLE THE METHOD OF PRESERVING HEALTH TO EXTREME OLD AGE.
TRANSLATED FROM THE ITALIAN ORIGINAL.
> *Philadelphia: Printed by Thomas Dobson*, 1791. 16mo.

23293   COWPER, WILLIAM   1731 – 1800
THE TASK. A POEM. IN SIX BOOKS. TO WHICH IS ADDED, TIROCINIUM: OR, A RE-
VIEW OF SCHOOLS. BY WILLIAM COWPER, OF THE INNER TEMPLE, ESQ.
> *Printed at Boston, by I. Thomas and E. T. Andrews, Faust's Statue, No.*
> *45 Newbury Street. Sold at their Bookstore, by D. West, in Marlborough Street,*
> *E. Larkin, jun. Cornhill, and at Worcester, by I. Thomas.* MDCCXCI. pp. 189;
> 84. 12mo.   AAS. NYPL.

Second title: TIROCINIUM: OR, A REVIEW OF SCHOOLS. BY WILLIAM COWPER.
OF THE INNER TEMPLE, ESQUIRE. [Ornament.]
> *Printed at Boston, by I. Thomas and E. T. Andrews, Faust's Statue, No.*
> *45, Newbury Street. Sold at their Bookstore, by D. West in Marlborough Street,*
> *E. Larkin, jun. Cornhill, and at Worcester, by I. Thomas.* MDCCXCI. pp. 34.

The latter is sometimes found separate from The Task.

23294   COXE, TENCH   1755 – 1824
A BRIEF EXPLANATION OF LORD SHEFFIELD'S OBSERVATIONS ON THE COMMERCE
OF THE UNITED STATES OF AMERICA.
> *Philadelphia: Printed by Carey Stewart, and Co.* M,DCC,XCI. pp. (48).
> 8vo.   LOC.

Six numbers only. Originally printed in the American Museum.

23295   —— — A BRIEF EXAMINATION OF LORD SHEFFIELD'S OBSERVATIONS ON THE COM-
MERCE OF THE UNITED STATES. IN SEVEN NUMBERS. WITH TWO SUPPLEMENT-
ARY NOTES ON AMERICAN MANUFACTURES.
> *Philadelphia: From the Press of M. Carey.* M.DCC.XCI. pp. vii, [135],
> (1). 8vo.   AAS. CLS. JCB. LOC. MHS. NL. NYHS.

Reprinted in London, with a preface by Capel Lofft, of Bury, Suffolk,
in 1792. 26th Pennsylvania District Copyright, issued to Mathew
Carey, as Proprietor, 14 November, 1791.

23296   COZENS, WILLIAM R.
AN INAUGURAL DISSERTATION ON THE CHEMICAL PROPERTIES OF ATMOSPHERIC AIR.
BY WILLIAM R. COZENS, OF NEW-YORK.
> *Philadelphia: Printed by Thomas Dobson*, 1791. pp. 24. 8vo.   SGO.

23297   CRABBE, GEORGE   1754 – 1832
THE VILLAGE: A POEM. IN TWO BOOKS. BY THE REVD. GEORGE CRABBE, CHAP-
LAIN TO HIS GRACE THE LATE DUKE OF RUTLAND, &C. THE FOURTH EDITION.
> *London: Printed. New-York: Re-printed for Berry and Rogers, No. 35,*
> *Hanover-Square; and sold by Thomas and Andrews, Boston,* 1791. pp. 36. 12mo.

23298   CRAFTS, THOMAS, JUNIOR   1767 – 1798
AN ORATION, PRONOUNCED JULY 4TH, 1791, AT THE REQUEST OF THE INHABITANTS
OF THE TOWN OF BOSTON, IN COMMEMORATION OF THE ANNIVERSARY OF AMERI-
CAN INDEPENDENCE. BY THOMAS CRAFTS, JUN. A. M. [Eight lines from] AD-
DISON.
> *Printed by Benjamin Russell, in Boston, Massachusetts.* MDCCXCI. pp.
> 16. 4to.   AAS. BA. BM. MHS.

Printed also in octavo.

23299   CRISP, STEPHEN   1628 – 1692
EINE KURZE BESCHREIBUNG EINER LANGEN REISE AUS BABYLON NACH BETHEL. DRITTE AUFLAGE
Chesnut Hill: Gedruckt bey Samuel Saur, 1791. pp. 24. 12mo.

23300   CROSWELL, WILLIAM   – 1884
TABLES, FOR READILY COMPUTING THE LONGITUDE, BY THE LUNAR OBSERVATIONS. PARTLY NEW, AND PARTLY TAKEN FROM THE REQUISITE TABLES OF DR. MASKELYNE. WITH THEIR APPLICATION, IN A VARIETY OF RULES AND EXAMPLES. BY WILLIAM CROSWELL, A. M. TEACHER OF NAVIGATION.
Printed at Boston, by I. Thomas and E. T. Andrews, Faust's Statue, No. 45, Newbury Street. MDCCXCI. pp. v, (2), 128. 8vo.   AAS. BM. LOC. MHS.
15th Massachusetts District Copyright, issued to William Croswell, as Author, 20 April, 1791

23301   CUDWORTH, WILLIAM
APHORISMS, CONCERNING THE ASSURANCE OF FAITH: DESIGNED TO RECONCILE DIFFERING SENTIMENTS, ON THAT IMPORTANT POINT. TO WHICH IS ADDED FREE SALVATION DEFENDED; AND SEVERAL COMMON OBJECTIONS ANSWERED. [Six lines of quotations.]
Philadelphia: Printed by W. Young, No. 52, Second-Street, the corner of Chesnut-Street. M,DCC,XCI. pp. 60. 24mo.   AAS.

23302   CUMBERLAND GAZETTE. MONDAY, JANUARY 3, 1790 [*sic* 1791] [—MONDAY, DECEMBER 26, 1791.]
Printed and published by Thomas B. Wait, opposite the Haymarket, Portland. 1791. fol.   AAS. NYHS.
Beginning January 2, 1792, the name was changed to *Eastern Herald.*

23303   CUNNINGHAM, WILLIAM   – 1791
WILLIAM CUNNINGHAM'S LIFE, CONFESSION AND LAST DYING WORDS. FORMERLY BRITISH PROVOST MARSHAL OF THE CITY OF NEW-YORK: EXECUTED IN LONDON FOR FORGERY, AUGUST 10, 1791.
[New-York: 1791.] Broadside. fol.

23304   DABNEY, JOHN
CATALOGUE OF BOOKS, FOR SALE OR CIRCULATION, IN TOWN OR COUNTRY, BY JOHN DABNEY, AT HIS BOOK AND STATIONARY STORE, AND CIRCULATING LIBRARY, IN SALEM: CONSISTING OF THE MOST APPROVED AUTHORS IN HISTORY, LIVES, MEMOIRS, NOVELS, ANTIQUITIES, GEOGRAPHY, POETRY, VOYAGES, TRAVELS, DIVINITY, HUSBANDRY, NAVIGATION, MISCELLANIES, ARTS, SCIENCES, &C. INCLUDING MANY OF THE LATEST AND MOST CELEBRATED VOLUMES IN EUROPE AND AMERICA. HERE YOU MAY RANGE THE WORLD FROM POLE TO POLE, INCREASE YOUR KNOWLEDGE, AND DELIGHT YOUR SOUL; TRAVEL ALL NATIONS, AND INFORM YOUR SENSE, WITH EASE AND SAFETY, AT A SMALL EXPENSE.—ANON. ☞ ALL NEW BOOKS, ON EVERY USEFUL AND ENTERTAINING SUBJECT, WITH ALL SUCH AS APPEAR ADVERTISED, FROM TIME TO TIME, RELATING EITHER TO SCHOOLS, AMUSEMENT, NAVIGATION, OR THE GENERAL BUSINESS OF LIFE, ARE OBTAINED AS SOON AS PUBLISHED, FOR SALE OR LOAN, AT THE LOWEST PRICES. *⁎* HANDSOME ASSORTMENT OF STATIONARY, OF EVERY ARTICLE IN GENERAL USE, CONSTANTLY FOR SALE, TO THE SATISFACTION OF THE PURCHASER.
[Salem:] Printed [by Thomas C. Cushing] for J. Dabney. MDCCXCI. pp. 33, (1). 12mo.   JCB.

23305   DABOLL, NATHAN   1750 – 1818
THE NEW-ENGLAND ALMANACK, AND GENTLEMEN & LADIES DIARY, FOR THE YEAR OF OUR LORD CHRIST, 1792. . . . BY EDMUND FREEBETTER.
New-London: Printed and sold by T. Green and Son. [1791.] pp. (24). 12mo.   AAS. CHS.

23306 DABOLL, NATHAN, continued.
—— SHEET ALMANACK FOR THE YEAR 1792.
New-London: Printed by T. Green and Son, 1791. Broadside. fol.

23307 THE DAILY [N. Y. arms] ADVERTISER. VOL. VII. NO. 1831. SATURDAY, JANUARY
1, [—NO. 2143. SATURDAY, DECEMBER 31, 1791.]
*[New-York:] Printed by Francis Childs and John Swaine, Printers to
the State of New-York, No. 189, Water-Street, near King-Street.* 1791. fol.
AAS. LOC. NYHS. NYPL.

23308 DANA, JAMES   1735 – 1812
THE AFRICAN SLAVE TRADE. A DISCOURSE, DELIVERED IN THE CITY OF NEW-
HAVEN, SEPTEMBER 9, 1790, BEFORE THE CONNECTICUT SOCIETY FOR THE PRO-
MOTION OF FREEDOM. BY JAMES DANA, D. D. PASTOR OF THE FIRST CONGREGA-
TIONAL CHURCH IN SAID CITY.
New-Haven: Printed by Thomas and Samuel Green. M,DCC,XCI. pp.(33).
8vo.   AAS. BA. HC. JCB. LCP. LOC. MHS. NYPL.

23309 DANBURY. CONNECTICUT. BAPTIST ASSOCIATION.
THE MINUTES OF THE DANBURY BAPTIST ASSOCIATION, HELD IN DANBURY, SEP-
TEMBER 1790, WITH THE SENTIMENTS AND PLAN OF THE SAID ASSOCIATION.
Danbury, Printed. New-York: Re-printed by W. Durell, 1791.

23310 —— MINUTES OF THE DANBURY ASSOCIATION. HELD AT STRATFIELD, SEPTEMBER
21, 1791. [Seven lines of exercises.]
[Danbury: Printed by Douglas and Ely, 1791.] pp. 7. 8vo.   JCB.

23311 DAVIDSON, ROBERT   1750 – 1812
GEOGRAPHY EPITOMIZED; OR A TOUR ROUND THE WORLD. BEING A SHORT BUT
COMPREHENSIVE DESCRIPTION OF THE TERRAQUEOUS GLOBE, ATTEMPTED IN
VERSE, AND PRINCIPALLY DESIGNED FOR THE USE OF SCHOOLS.
Burlington: Printed and sold by Isaac Neale, 1791.

23312 DAVIES, SAMUEL   1724 – 1761
LITTLE CHILDREN INVITED TO JESUS CHRIST: A SERMON PREACHED IN HANOVER
COUNTY, VIRGINIA, MAY 8, 1757. BY SAMUEL DAVIES, A. M.
Boston: Printed and sold by T. &. J. Fleet, at the Bible and Heart, 1791.

23313 DAVIS, DANIEL   1762 – 1835
AN ADDRESS TO THE INHABITANTS OF THE DISTRICT OF MAINE, UPON THE SUBJECT
OF THEIR SEPARATION FROM THE PRESENT GOVERNMENT OF MASSACHUSETTS. BY
ONE OF THEIR FELLOW CITIZENS.
Printed at Portland by Thomas B. Wait, April, 1791. pp. (54). 4to.
JCB. LOC. MHS. NYPL.

23314 DAVIS, IGNATIUS
THIRTY DOLLARS REWARD. RAN AWAY, ON THE 22D OF AUGUST LAST, A HANDSOME
NEGRO LAD, NAMED ARCH, ABOUT TWENTY YEARS OF AGE—THE PROPERTY OF
THE SUBSCRIBER—[Eleven lines.] IGNATIUS DAVIS, FREDERICK-COUNTY, SEP-
TEMBER 7, 1791. [Colophon:]
Frederick-Town: Printed by John Winter. [1791.] Broadside. 4to.
NYHS. NYPL.
This appears to have been an annual event in Arch's life. He so far suc-
ceeded as to reduce the amount of the reward to ten dollars in 1793.

23315 DAY, THOMAS   1748 – 1789
THE HISTORY OF SANDFORD AND MERTON. A WORK INTENDED FOR THE USE OF
CHILDREN. VOL. III.
Philadelphia: Printed by William Young, 1791. 12mo.
Volumes I-II, published by William Young, in Philadelphia, in 1788.

23316   THE DEATH OF CAIN: IN FIVE BOOKS. AFTER THE MANNER OF THE DEATH OF ABEL. BY A LADY. [Two lines from] MILTON.
New-York: Printed by T. & J. Swords, No. 27, William Street. 1791.

23317   DE BRAHM, JOHN WILLIAM GERAR   1718 –
VII. ARM OF THE TREE OF KNOWLEDGE, BRANCHING SACRED CHRONOLOGY THROUGH THE SIX DIVINE LABORS IN MYSTIC, PHYSIC, LAW, HISTORY, SACRED AND PROPHANE, GOSPEL AND REVELATION.   [Ornament.]
Philadelphia: Printed by Zachariah Poulson, junior. No. 30, North Fourth-Street, near the College. MDCCXCI. pp. (59). 8vo.   AAS. NYPL.

Second title: TIME AN APPARITION OF ETERNITY, MANIFESTED IN ITS GATHERING BY ATTRACTING POWER, AND IN ITS FLUX BY REPELLING VIRTUE, ONCE THROUGH A CIRCLE AND TWICE THROUGH A COCHLEA FINALLY ABSORBS BY THE POWER ATTRACTING INTO ETERNITY'S FOCUS. [Cut of eternity's abyss. Six lines from] REVEL. X. 6. pp. (2), (5) — 59.

This part appears to have preceded in publication Parts I–VI, printed in the following year.

23318   —— — VII. ARM OF THE TREE OF KNOWLEDGE, BRANCHING SACRED CHRONOLOGY, THROUGH THE SIX DIVINE LABORS IN MYSTIC, PHYSIC, LAW, HISTORY, SACRED AND PROPHANE, GOSPEL AND REVELATION.
Philadelphia: Printed by Zachariah Poulson, junior. MDCCXCI. pp. 59, (21). 8vo.   BA.

23319   —— TIME AN APPARITION OF ETERNITY.
Philadelphia: Printed by Zachariah Poulson, jun. No. 30, Fourth-Street, near the College. MDCCXCI. pp. [28.] 8vo.   AAS. BM. JCB. NYPL.

23320   DE FOE, DANIEL   1661 – 1731
THE LIFE AND MOST SUPRISING ADVENTURES OF ROBINSON CRUSOE, OF YORK, MARINER. CONTAINING A FULL AND PARTICULAR ACCOUNT HOW HE LIVED TWENTY-EIGHT YEARS IN AN UNINHABITED ISLAND ON THE COAST OF AMERICA: HOW HIS SHIP WAS LOST IN A STORM, AND ALL HIS COMPANIONS DROWNED; AND HOW HE WAS CAST UPON THE SHORE BY THE WRECK: WITH A TRUE RELATION HOW HE WAS AT LAST MIRACULOUSLY PRESERVED BY PIRATES. FAITHFULLY EPITOMIZED FROM THE THREE VOLUMES.
Philadelphia: Printed and sold by W. Woodhouse, at the Bible, No. 6, South Front-street. 1791.

23321   DELAWARE. STATE.
LAWS OF THE DELAWARE STATE, PASSED AT A SESSION OF THE GENERAL ASSEMBLY, COMMENCED AT DOVER, ON THE FOURTH DAY OF JANUARY, 1791. [Arms.]
Wilmington: Printed by Frederick Craig and Co. 1791. pp. 37, (1). fol. LOC.

23322   —— VOTES AND PROCEEDINGS OF THE HOUSE OF ASSEMBLY OF THE DELAWARE STATE, JANUARY, 1791.
Wilmington: Printed by Frederick Craig and Co. 1791.

23323   THE DELAWARE GAZETTE. NO. 301. SATURDAY, JANUARY 1, [— NO. 353. SATURDAY, DECEMBER 31, 1791.]
Wilmington: Printed and published by Frederick Craig and Co. 1791. fol.
The partnership of Frederick Craig and Company was dissolved by mutual consent March 5, 1791; and the Gazette continued by Craig's late partners, Peter Brynberg and Samuel Andrews. The imprint reading, from April: "Printed and sold by Peter Brynberg and Samuel Andrews, in Market-Street."

23324   DEXTER, SAMUEL   1761–1816
        THOUGHTS UPON SEVERAL PASSAGES OF SCRIPTURE, BOTH IN THE OLD AND NEW
        TESTAMENT, RELATIVE TO JACOB AND ESAU; WITH INCIDENTAL EXCURSIONS. BY
        PHILOTHEORUS. [Four lines of Scripture texts.]
            Printed at Worcester, Massachusetts, by Isaiah Thomas. MDCCXCI. pp.
        60. 12mo.   AAS. BA. MHS. PPL.

                                                              – 1780
23325   DILWORTH, THOMAS
        A NEW GUIDE TO THE ENGLISH TONGUE: IN FIVE PARTS. CONTAINING, I. WORDS
        BOTH COMMON AND PROPER; FROM ONE TO SIX SYLLABLES: THE SEVERAL SORTS OF
        MONOSYLLABLES IN THE COMMON WORDS BEING DISTINGUISHED BY TABLES INTO
        WORDS OF TWO THREE AND FOUR LETTERS, &C. WITH SIX SHORT LESSONS AT
        THE END OF EACH TABLE, NOT EXCEEDING THE ORDER OF SYLLABLES IN THE FORE-
        GOING TABLES.—THE SEVERAL SORTS OF POLYSYLLABLES ALSO, BEING RANGED IN
        PROPER TABLES, HAVE THEIR SYLLABLES DIVIDED, AND DIRECTIONS PLACED AT
        THE HEAD OF EACH TABLE FOR THE ACCENT TO PREVENT FALSE PRONUNCIATION;
        TOGETHER WITH THE LIKE NUMBER OF LESSONS ON THE FOREGOING TABLES PLACED
        AT THE END OF EACH TABLE, AS FAR AS THE WORDS OF FOUR SYLLABLES, FOR THE
        EASIER AND MORE SPEEDY WAY OF TEACHING CHILDREN TO READ. II. A LARGE
        AND USEFUL TABLE OF WORDS, THAT ARE THE SAME IN SOUND, BUT DIFFERENT IN
        SIGNIFICATION; VERY NECESSARY TO PREVENT THE WRITING ONE WORD FOR AN-
        OTHER OF THE SAME SOUND. III. A SHORT BUT COMPREHENSIVE GRAMMAR OF
        THE ENGLISH TONGUE, DELIVERED IN THE MOST FAMILIAR AND INSTRUCTIVE
        METHOD OF QUESTION AND ANSWER; NECESSARY FOR ALL SUCH PERSONS AS HAVE
        THE ADVANTAGE ONLY OF AN ENGLISH EDUCATION. IV. AN USEFUL COLLECTION
        OF SENTENCES, IN PROSE AND VERSE, DIVINE, MORAL AND HISTORICAL; TOGETHER
        WITH A SELECT NUMBER OF FABLES, &C. &C. ADORNED WITH PROPER SCULPTURES,
        FOR THE BETTER IMPROVEMENT OF THE YOUNG BEGINNER. AND V. FORMS OF
        PRAYER FOR CHILDREN, ON SEVERAL OCCASIONS. BY THOMAS DILWORTH.
            Hartford: Printed and sold by Nathaniel Patten, 1791.

23326   ——   THE SCHOOLMASTERS ASSISTANT: BEING A COMPENDIUM OF ARITHMETIC, BOTH
        PRACTICAL AND THEORETICAL. IN FIVE PARTS. CONTAINING, I. ARITHMETIC IN
        WHOLE NUMBERS, WHEREIN ALL THE COMMON RULES, HAVING EACH OF THEM A
        SUFFICIENT NUMBER OF QUESTIONS, WITH THEIR ANSWERS, ARE METHODICALLY
        AND BRIEFLY HANDLED. II. VULGAR FRACTIONS, WHEREIN SEVERAL THINGS, NOT
        COMMONLY MET WITH, ARE THERE DISTINCTLY TREATED OF, AND LAID DOWN IN
        THE MOST PLAIN AND EASY MANNER. III. DECIMALS, IN WHICH, AMONG OTHER
        THINGS ARE CONSIDERED THE EXTRACTION OF ROOTS; INTEREST, BOTH SIMPLE AND
        COMPOUND: ANNUITIES, REBATE, AND EQUATION OF PAYMENTS. IV. A LARGE COL-
        LECTION OF QUESTIONS, WITH THEIR ANSWERS, SERVING TO EXERCISE THE FORE-
        GOING RULES; TOGETHER WITH A FEW OTHERS, BOTH PLEASANT AND DIVERTING.
        V. DUODECIMALS, COMMONLY CALLED CROSS MULTIPLICATION: WHEREIN THAT SORT
        OF ARITHMETIC IS THOROUGHLY CONSIDERED, AND RENDERED VERY PLAIN AND
        EASY; TOGETHER WITH THE METHOD OF PROVING ALL THE FOREGOING OPERATIONS
        AT ONCE, BY DIVISION OF SEVERAL DENOMINATIONS, WITHOUT REDUCING THEM TO
        THE LOWEST TERM MENTIONED. THE WHOLE BEING DELIVERED IN THE MOST
        FAMILIAR WAY OF QUESTION AND ANSWER, IS RECOMMENDED BY SEVERAL EMIN-
        ENT MATHEMATICIANS, ACCOMPTANTS AND SCHOOL-MASTERS, AS NECESSARY TO BE
        USED IN SCHOOLS BY ALL TEACHERS, WHO WOULD HAVE THEIR SCHOLARS THOR-
        OUGHLY UNDERSTAND, AND MAKE A QUICK PROGRESS IN ARITHMETIC. TO WHICH
        IS PREFIXT. AN ESSAY ON THE EDUCATION OF YOUTH; HUMBLY OFFERED TO THE
        CONSIDERATION OF PARENTS. BY THOMAS DILWORTH, AUTHOR OF THE NEW
        GUIDE TO THE ENGLISH TONGUE; YOUNG BOOK-KEEPER'S ASSISTANT, &C. &C. AND
        SCHOOLMASTER IN WAPPING. [Four lines of quotations.]
            *Wilmington: Printed and sold by Andrews, Craig, and Brynberg, in
        Market-Street.* M,DCC,XCI. pp. xiv, (6), (2), (2), 192, folded table, portrait,
        12mo.   AAS.

23326   DILWORTH, W. H.
THE NEW COMPLETE LETTER WRITER: OR, THE ART OF CORRESPONDENCE. CONTAINING, LETTERS ON THE MOST IMPORTANT SUBJECTS, VIZ. BUSINESS, FRIENDSHIP, LOVE AND MARRIAGE, COURTSHIP, POLITENESS, ECONOMY, AFFECTION, AMUSEMENT, DUTY, ADVICE, RELIGION, &C. COMPOSED BY WRITERS EMINENT FOR THEIR PERSPICUITY AND ELEGANCE OF EXPRESSION. TO WHICH ARE ADDED, FORMS OF MESSAGE-CARDS, AND INSTRUCTIONS HOW TO ADDRESS PERSONS OF ALL RANKS. ALSO, THE PRINCIPLES OF POLITENESS, EXTRACTED FROM THE LETTERS OF THE LATE LORD CHESTERFIELD.—THE ECONOMY OF HUMAN LIFE, COMPLETE, IN TWO PARTS.—MORAL MAXIMS AND REFLEXIONS, BY THE LATE DUKE DE LA ROCHEFOUCAULD.—WITH APHORISMS ON MAN, BY THE REV. JOHN CASPER LAVATER.—AND A COPIOUS ENGLISH SPELLING DICTIONARY. A NEW EDITION, WITH ADDITIONS.
Philadelphia: Printed and sold by W. Spotswood, 1791.

23327   —— — A NEW AND COMPLETE LETTER WRITER; OR, THE ART OF CORRESPONDENCE. CONTAINING LETTERS ON THE MOST IMPORTANT SUBJECTS, VIZ. BUSINESS, FRIENDSHIP, LOVE AND MARRIAGE, COURTSHIP, POLITENESS, ECONOMY, AFFECTION, AMUSEMENT, DUTY, ADVICE, RELIGION, &C. COMPOSED BY WRITERS EMINENT FOR THEIR PERSPICUITY, AND ELEGANCE OF EXPRESSION. TO WHICH ARE ADDED, THE PRINCIPLES OF POLITENESS, EXTRACTED FROM THE LETTERS OF THE LATE LORD CHESTERFIELD. ALSO, MORAL MAXIMS AND REFLECTIONS, BY THE LATE DUKE DE LA ROCHEFOUCAULD. WITH FORMS OF MESSAGE CARDS, INSTRUCTIONS HOW TO ADDRESS PERSONS OF ALL RANKS IN THE UNITED STATES OF AMERICA, FRANCE, SPAIN, ITALY, HOLLAND, AND GREAT-BRITAIN. AND A COPIOUS ENGLISH SPELLING DICTIONARY.
Printed at Worcester, Massachusetts, by Isaiah Thomas. 1791. pp. 271.16mo.

23328   DODDRIDGE, PHILIP   1702 – 1751
A PLAIN AND SERIOUS ADDRESS TO THE MASTER OF A FAMILY, ON THE IMPORTANT SUBJECT OF FAMILY RELIGION. BY THE LATE REVEREND PHILIP DODDRIDGE, D. D.
Boston: Re-printed and sold by Samuel Hall, No. 53, Cornhill. MDCCXCI. pp. 30. 8vo.
                           AAS. BA. JCB. MHS.

23329   —— — A PLAIN AND SERIOUS ADDRESS TO THE MASTER OF A FAMILY, ON THE IMPORTANT SUBJECT OF FAMILY RELIGION. BY THE LATE REVEREND PHILIP DODDRIDGE, D. D.
Reprinted in Danbury, by Douglas and Ely, 1791. 12mo.

23330   —— THE RISE AND PROGRESS OF RELIGION IN THE SOUL. ILLUSTRATED IN A COURSE OF SERIOUS AND PRACTICAL ADDRESSES SUITED TO PERSONS OF EVERY CHARACTER AND CIRCUMSTANCE. WITH A DEVOUT MEDITATION AND PRAYER ADDED TO EACH CHAPTER. TO ALL WHICH ARE SUBJOINED, A FUNERAL SERMON, ON THE ONE THING NEEDFUL. BY PHILIP DODDRIDGE, D. D. [Four lines of Scripture texts.]
Philadelphia: Printed for Robert Campbell, Bookseller, Second-Street, No. 53, the corner of Chesnut-Street. M,DCC,XCI. pp. xii, 307. 16mo.   AAS.

23331   DODSLEY, ROBERT   1703 – 1764
CHRONICLE OF THE KINGS OF ENGLAND, FROM THE REIGN OF WILLIAM THE CONQUEROR (FIRST KING OF ENGLAND) DOWN TO HIS PRESENT MAJESTY GEORGE THE THIRD: CONTAINING, A TRUE HISTORY OF THEIR LIVES, AND THE CHARACTER WHICH THEY SEVERALLY SUSTAINED; WHETHER IN CHURCH OR STATE, IN THE FIELD, OR IN PRIVATE LIFE. BY THE LATE DR. FRANKLIN [*sic.*]
Litchfield: Printed by Thomas Collier. 1791.

Advertised by Collier, in the *Litchfield Monitor,* as above. Whether Dr. Franklin was credited with the authorship of this frequently reprinted work, pseudonymously attributed to Nathan Ben Saadi, a priest of the Jews, through misinformation or a desire to create a market for its sale, cannot now be known. The edition is curious from being the only one so credited.

DODSLEY, ROBERT, continued.

23332 —— THE ŒCONOMY OF HUMAN LIFE. COMPLETE, IN TWO PARTS. TRANSLATED FROM AN INDIAN MANUSCRIPT, WRITTEN BY AN ANCIENT BRAMIN. TO WHICH IS PREFIXED, AN ACCOUNT OF THE MANNER IN WHICH THE SAID MANUSCRIPT WAS DISCOVERED; IN A LETTER FROM AN ENGLISH GENTLEMAN RESIDING IN CHINA, TO THE EARL OF * * * * * * * *
Philadelphia: Printed and sold by W. Woodhouse, at the Bible, No. 6, South Front-Street. 1791.

23333 —— —— THE OECONOMY OF HUMAN LIFE, IN TWO PARTS. TRANSLATED FROM AN INDIAN MANUSCRIPT, WRITTEN BY AN ANCIENT BRAMIN. TO WHICH IS PREFIXED, AN ACCOUNT OF THE MANNER IN WHICH THE SAID MANUSCRIPT WAS DISCOVERED; IN A LETTER FROM AN ENGLISH GENTLEMAN RESIDING IN CHINA, TO THE EARL OF * * * *. PART THE FIRST. THE FIFTEENTH AMERICAN EDITION.
Keene: (State of New-Hampshire) Printed and sold by James D. Griffith, Anno Domini, 1791. pp. 154. 12mo.   NYPL.
Second title: THE OECONOMY OF HUMAN LIFE, IN TWO PARTS. TRANSLATED FROM AN INDIAN MANUSCRIPT, FOUND SOON AFTER THAT WHICH CONTAINED THE ORIGINAL OF THE FIRST PART, AND WROTE BY THE SAME HAND. IN A SECOND LETTER FROM AN ENGLISH GENTLEMAN RESIDING IN CHINA, TO THE EARL OF * * * *. PART THE SECOND. pp. (2),(75)—154.
Contains a list of subscribers.

23334 DÖRING, FRIEDRICH CHRISTLIEB
DASS DAS EVANGELIUM VON JESU CHRISTO, NACH RÖMER I.V. 16. NOCH IMMER EINE KRAFT GOTTES SEY, DIE AUCH DIE VERDORBENSTEN HERZEN WIEDER ZURICHTE BRINGEN UND SELIG MACHEN KAN—ERLAUTERT DURCH DAS DAS BEYSPIEL SEINES SIGNEN BRUDERS, AUGUST SALOMON DÖRINGS, UND MACHT DIE IHM WIEDER-FAHRNE GNADE ZUM PREISE GOTTES ÖFFENTLICH BEKANNT FRIEDRICH CHRIST-LIEB DÖRING, DIENEN AM EVANGELIO ZU MAIWALDAU.
Lancaster: Gedruckt und zu haben [bey Johann Albrecht & Comp.] in der Neuen Buch-druckerey, in der Prinz-Strasse, 1791. pp. 65. 12mo.   AAS. NYPL.
First printed in Germany. An English translation was printed by Charles Cist, in Philadelphia, in 1792. A circumstantial account, by his brother, of the life of August Salomon Döring, who, during his confinement for the murder of a child, was converted, and as a repenting, but pardoned sinner, suffered death in Silesia.

23335 DORSEY, NATHAN
A NEW AND COMPLETE SYSTEM OF INSTRUCTIONS FOR THE SAFE AND SUCCESSFUL AD-MINISTRATION OF MEDICINES, IN THOSE DISEASES INCIDENT TO MARINERS. BY DOCTOR NATHAN DORSEY, FELLOW OF THE COLLEGE OF PHYSICIANS OF PHILA-DELPHIA.
Philadelphia: 1791.
15th Pennsylvania District Copyright, issued to Nathan Dorsey, as Author, 23 February, 1791.

23336 DRAMATIC PIECES, CALCULATED TO EXEMPLIFY THE MODE OF CONDUCT WHICH WILL RENDER YOUNG LADIES BOTH AMIABLE AND HAPPY, WHEN THEIR SCHOOL EDUCA-TION IS COMPLETED. IN THREE VOLUMES. VOLUME I. [— III,] CONTAINING THE GOOD MOTHER-IN-LAW, AND THE GOOD DAUGHTER-IN-LAW.
New-Haven: Printed by Abel Morse. M.DCC.XCI. 3 vols. in one. pp. 52: 47; (3), 47, 50; 48, (49)-92. 12mo.   AAS. JCB. NYPL.
Second title: VOLUME II. THE REFORMATION. AND THE MATERNAL SISTER. A DRAMA, IN THREE ACTS. pp. (3), 47; 50.
Third title: VOLUME III. THE TRIUMPH OF REASON. AND THE CONTRAST. [A drama in three acts.] pp. 48; 49-92.
Pages 5, and 6, of Volume III are repeated, and the error continued.
Preface signed, P. I.

23337   DUNCAN, WILLIAM
THE NEW-YORK DIRECTORY AND REGISTER, FOR THE YEAR 1791. ILLUSTRATED WITH
A NEW AND ACCURATE PLAN OF THE CITY, AND PART OF LONG-ISLAND, EXACTLY
LAID DOWN, AGREEABLY TO THE LATEST SURVEY.— CONTAINING—THE NAMES, OC-
CUPATIONS, AND PLACES OF ABODE OF THE CITIZENS, ARRANGED IN ALPHABETICAL
ORDER: A REGISTER OF THE EXECUTIVE, LEGISLATIVE, AND JUDICIAL MAGIS-
TRATES OF THE UNITED STATES, AND OF THE STATE OF NEW-YORK; THE MINIS-
TERIAL AND CONSULAR APPOINTMENTS FROM THE UNITED STATES TO FOREIGN
POWERS, AND FROM FOREIGN POWERS TO THE UNITED STATES; THE GOVERNORS
OF THE DIFFERENT STATES; THE OFFICERS, BOTH CIVIL AND MILITARY, OF THE
CITY AND COUNTY OF NEW-YORK.—ALSO—AN ACCOUNT OF THE DIFFERENT SO-
CIETIES, AND CHARITABLE AND LITERARY INSTITUTIONS IN THE CITY; WITH THE
NAMES OF THEIR OFFICERS.—TO WHICH IS ADDED—AN EXTRACT FROM SUNDRY
LAWS FOR THE REGULATION OF TRADE, &C. BY WILLIAM DUNCAN.

*New-York: Printed for the Editor, by T. and J. Swords, No. 27, William-
Street.--1791.--[Price three shillings.]* pp. vii, 146, (2), 71, plan. 12mo.   NYPL.

"* As this work was rather late, the Editor, in order to accelerate its
publication, committed the first part of it, viz. the Directory, to
Messrs. T. & J. Swords, and the Register to Mr. T. Greenleaf—from
which circumstance it became necessary to page each part separately."

23338   DUNLAP, WILLIAM   1766 – 1839
DARBY'S RETURN: A COMIC SKETCH, AS PERFORMED AT THE NEW YORK AND PHILA-
DELPHIA THEATRES. [The second edition.]

Philadelphia: Printed by Enoch Story, 1791. pp. 12. 12mo.

23339   DUNLAP'S AMERICAN DAILY ADVERTISER. No. 3720. SATURDAY, JANUARY 1, [—
No. 4034. SATURDAY, DECEMBER 31, 1791.]

*Philadelphia: Printed by John Dunlap, at No. 48 Market-Street, opposite
the Jersey-Market.* 1791. fol.   AAS. LOC.

In continuation of, *The Pennsylvania Packet and daily advertiser.*

23340   DURELL, WILLIAM
NEW-YORK, MAY 1ST, 1791. A NEW AND ELEGANT WORK, ENRICHED WITH UP-
WARDS OF 60 ELEGANT COPPER-PLATES, EXCLUSIVE OF MAPS, AND OTHER EMBEL-
LISHMENTS. PROPOSED TO PRINT BY SUBSCRIPTION, BY WILLIAM DURELL, DR.
MAYNARD'S COMPLEAT TRANSLATION OF THE WHOLE WORKS OF JOSEPHUS. ILLUS-
TRATED WITH NOTES AND MARGINAL REFERENCES. TO BE COMPLETED IN ONLY
SIXTY NUMBERS. . . . CONDITIONS OF PUBLICATION. . . . ADDRESS TO THE
PUBLIC. . . . SPECIMEN OF THE TYPE. . . .

[New-York: Printed by William Durell, 1791.] pp. (2). fol.   NYHS.

23341   DWIGHT, TIMOTHY   1752 – 1817
VIRTUOUS RULERS A NATIONAL BLESSING. A SERMON, PREACHED AT THE GENERAL
ELECTION, MAY 12TH, 1791. BY TIMOTHY DWIGHT, D. D. PASTOR OF A CHURCH
IN FAIRFIELD. [Seven lines from] GOVERNOR PATTERSON'S ANSWER TO THE
ADDRESS OF THE PRESBYTERY OF NEW-BRUNSWICK..

Hartford: Printed by Hudson and Goodwin. M,DCC,XCI. pp. 42. 8vo.
          AAS. BM. CHS. HC. JCB. LOC. MHS. NYPL. UTS. YC.

23342   EDWARDS, JONATHAN   1703 – 1758
THE DISTINGUISHING MARKS OF A WORK OF THE SPIRIT OF GOD; EXTRACTED FROM
MR. EDWARDS BY JOHN WESLEY.

*Philadelphia: Printed by Joseph Crukshank(?), and sold by John Dickins,
No. 182, in Race Street, near Sixth Street.* 1791.

23343 EDWARDS, JONATHAN, continued.

—— TRUE GRACE, DISTINGUISHED FROM THE EXPERIENCE OF DEVILS; IN A SERMON, PREACHED BEFORE THE SYNOD OF NEW-YORK, CONVENED AT NEWARK, IN NEW-JERSEY, ON SEPTEMBER 28, N. S. 1752. [PRINTED BY DESIRE OF THE SYNOD.] BY JONATHAN EDWARDS, A. M. PASTOR OF THE CHURCH OF CHRIST IN STOCKBRIDGE IN NEW-ENGLAND. [Five lines from] 2 Corinthians. XI. 3. 14.

Elizabethtown: Printed by Shepard Kollock. M.DCC.XCI. pp. 48. 12mo.

AAS. BM. JCB. NYPL.

Printed for, and usually found bound with, his "Faithful narrative." (Elizabeth Town, 1790.).

23344 —— —— TRUE GRACE DISTINGUISHED FROM THE EXPERIENCE OF DEVILS; IN A SERMON, PREACHED BEFORE THE SYNOD OF NEW-YORK, CONVENED AT NEW-ARK, IN NEW-JERSEY, ON SEPTEMBER 28, N. S. 1752. BY REV. JONATHAN EDWARDS, LATE PRESIDENT OF THE COLLEGE OF NEW-JERSEY.

Stockbridge (Massachusetts) Printed by Loring Andrews. 1791.

23345 —— TWO DISSERTATIONS, I. CONCERNING THE END FOR WHICH GOD CREATED THE WORLD. II. THE NATURE OF TRUE VIRTUE. BY THE LATE REVEREND, LEARNED AND PIOUS JONATHAN EDWARDS, A. M. PRESIDENT OF THE COLLEGE IN NEW-JERSEY.

Philadelphia: Printed and sold by R. Aitken & Son, No. 22, Market Street. M.DCC.XCI. pp. (6), 206. 12mo. AAS. JCB.

23346 EDWARDS, JONATHAN 1745 – 1801

THE INJUSTICE AND IMPOLICY OF THE SLAVE TRADE, AND OF THE SLAVERY OF THE AFRICANS: ILLUSTRATED IN A SERMON PREACHED BEFORE THE CONNECTICUT SOCIETY FOR THE PROMOTION OF FREEDOM, AND FOR THE RELIEF OF PERSONS UNLAWFULLY HOLDEN IN BONDAGE, AT THEIR ANNUAL MEETING IN NEW-HAVEN, SEPTEMBER 15, 1791. BY JONATHAN EDWARDS, D. D. PASTOR OF A CHURCH IN NEW-HAVEN.

[New-Haven:] Printed by Thomas and Samuel Green. M,DCC,XCI. pp. (2). (37). 8vo. AAS. BA. BM. HC. JCB. LOC. NYHS. NYPL.

A second edition was printed in Boston, in 1822; and a third edition in New Haven, in 1833.

23347 ELLICOTT, ANDREW 1754 – 1820

ELLICOTT'S MARYLAND AND VIRGINIA ALMANAC, AND EPHEMERIS, FOR THE YEAR OF OUR LORD, 1792; BEING BISSEXTILE, OR LEAP-YEAR, AND THE SIXTEENTH YEAR OF AMERICAN INDEPENDENCE. AMONG OTHER INTERESTING PARTICULARS, ARE THE MOTIONS OF THE SUN AND MOON, THE TRUE PLACES AND ASPECTS OF THE EIGHT PLANETS, THE RISING AND SETTING OF THE SUN, AND THE RISING, SETTING, SOUTHING AND AGE OF THE MOON, &C.—TO WHICH ARE ADDED, THE LUNATIONS, CONJUNCTIONS, ECLIPSES, JUDGMENT OF THE WEATHER, FESTIVALS, AND OTHER MEMORABLE DAYS, AND DAYS FOR HOLDING COURTS IN MARYLAND AND VIRGINIA:— LIKEWISE, A TABLE REDUCING THE CURRENCY OF PENNSYLVANIA, NEW-JERSEY, DELAWARE, AND MARYLAND, TO THE CURRENCIES OF THE OTHER STATES, AND TO ENGLISH AND IRISH MONEY—ALSO, A TABLE OF DOLLARS AND OTHER COINS, AS THEY NOW PASS IN EACH OF THE UNITED STATES; WITH MANY OTHER USEFUL TABLES AND PHYSICAL RECEIPTS, A LETTER FROM THE ALLEGHANY PHILOSOPHER— AND SEVERAL COMPOSITIONS IN PROSE AND VERSE:—THE WHOLE CALCULATED TO INSTRUCT AND ENTERTAIN OUR READERS. [Two lines of Latin from] OVID.

Baltimore: Printed and sold, wholesale and retail, by John Hayes, Market-Street. [1791.] pp. (43). 12mo. JCB.

23348   ELLIOT, JOHN
THE MEDICAL POCKET-BOOK. CONTAINING A SHORT BUT PLAIN ACCOUNT OF THE
SYMPTOMS, CAUSES, AND METHODS OF CURE, OF THE DISEASES INCIDENT TO THE
HUMAN BODY. INCLUDING SUCH AS REQUIRE SURGICAL TREATMENT: TOGETHER
WITH THE VIRTUES AND DOSES OF MEDICINAL COMPOSITIONS AND SIMPLES. EX-
TRACTED FROM THE BEST AUTHORS, AND DIGESTED INTO ALPHABETICAL ORDER.
THE TENTH EDITION, WITH ADDITIONS AND CORRECTIONS. BY JOHN ELLIOT, M. D.
> *Boston: Printed by Joseph Bumstead, for David West; No. 36, Marl-
> borough-Street, and E. Larkin, jun. No. 50, Cornhill.* 1791. pp. vii, 117, inter-
> leaved. 12mo.   AAS.

23349   EMMONS, NATHANAEL   1745 – 1840
A DISCOURSE CONCERNING THE PROCESS OF THE GENERAL JUDGMENT. IN WHICH
THE MODERN NOTIONS OF UNIVERSAL SALVATION ARE PARTICULARLY CONSIDERED.
. . . [Two lines from] THE SUPREME JUDGE.
> *Philadelphia: Printed by William Young, Bookseller, No. 52. Second-
> Street, the corner of Chesnut-Street.* M,DCC,XCI. pp. [94,] (2). 12mo.
>   AAS. BM. HC. JCB. LOC.

23350   —— A SERMON, PREACHED AT THE ORDINATION OF THE REV. ELIAS DUDLEY, TO
THE PASTORAL CARE OF THE CHURCH IN OXFORD, APRIL 18, 1791. BY NATHAN-
AEL EMMONS, A. M. PASTOR OF THE CHURCH IN FRANKLIN. [Printer's monogram.]
> *Printed at Providence, by Bennett Wheeler, in Westminster-Street.* [1791.]
> pp. [36.] 8vo.   AAS. JCB. LOC. NYPL. YC.

23351   ENCYCLOPÆDIA; OR, A DICTIONARY OF ARTS, SCIENCES, AND MISCELLANEOUS LIT-
ERATURE; CONSTRUCTED ON A PLAN, BY WHICH THE DIFFERENT SCIENCES AND
ARTS ARE DIGESTED INTO THE FORM OF DISTINCT TREATISES ON SYSTEMS, COM-
PREHENDING THE HISTORY, THEORY, AND PRACTICE, OF EACH, ACCORDING TO THE
LATEST DISCOVERIES AND IMPROVEMENTS; AND FULL EXPLANATIONS GIVEN OF THE
VARIOUS DETACHED PARTS OF KNOWLEDGE, WHETHER RELATING TO NATURAL AND
ARTIFICIAL OBJECTS, OR TO MATTERS ECCLESIASTICAL, CIVIL, MILITARY, COMMER-
CIAL, &C. INCLUDING ELUCIDATIONS OF THE MOST IMPORTANT TOPICS RELATIVE
TO RELIGION, MORALS, MANNERS, AND THE OECONOMY OF LIFE: TOGETHER WITH A
DESCRIPTION OF ALL THE COUNTRIES, CITIES, PRINCIPAL MOUNTAINS, SEAS,
RIVERS, &C. THROUGHOUT THE WORLD; A GENERAL HISTORY, ANCIENT AND MOD-
ERN, OF THE DIFFERENT EMPIRES, KINGDOMS, AND STATES; AND AN ACCOUNT OF
THE LIVES OF THE MOST EMINENT PERSONS IN EVERY NATION, FROM THE EARL-
IEST AGES DOWN TO THE PRESENT TIMES. COMPILED FROM THE WRITINGS OF THE
BEST AUTHORS, IN SEVERAL LANGUAGES; THE MOST APPROVED DICTIONARIES, AS
WELL OF GENERAL SCIENCE AS OF ITS PARTICULAR BRANCHES; THE TRANSACTIONS,
JOURNALS, AND MEMOIRS, OF VARIOUS LEARNED SOCIETIES, THE MS. LECTURES OF
EMINENT PROFESSORS ON DIFFERENT SCIENCES; AND A VARIETY OF ORIGINAL MA-
TERIALS, FURNISHED BY AN EXTENSIVE CORRESPONDENCE. THE FIRST AMERICAN
EDITION, IN EIGHTEEN VOLUMES, GREATLY IMPROVED. ILLUSTRATED WITH FIVE
HUNDRED AND FORTY-TWO COPPER PLATES. VOL. III. BAR—BZO. [VOL. IV. CAA
—CIC.] INDOCTI DISCANT ET AMENT MEMINISSE PERITI.
> *Philadelphia: Printed by Thomas Dobson, at the Stone-House, No. 41,
> South Second Street.* M.DCC.XCVIII. [1791.] 2 vols. pp. 806,20 plates, (92–111);
> 793, 26 plates. (112-137). 4to.   AAS. APS. LCP. LOC. MHS. NYHS. NYPL. WC.

23352   ENFIELD, WILLIAM   1741 – 1797
BIOGRAPHICAL SERMONS, OR, A SERIES OF DISCOURSES ON THE PRINCIPAL CHARAC-
TERS IN SCRIPTURE. BY WILLIAM ENFIELD, LL. D. [One line from] CICERO.
> *Philadelphia: Printed by Francis Bailey, No. 116 Market Street, and T.
> Lang, No. 21, Church-Alley.* MDCCXCI. pp. 247. 12mo.   AAS. JCB.

23353   EQUIANO, OLAUDAH
THE INTERESTING NARRATIVE OF THE LIFE OF OLAUDAH EQUIANO, OR GUSTAVUS
VASSA, THE AFRICAN. WRITTEN BY HIMSELF. VOL. I. [—II.] [Five lines from]
ISAIAH XII. 2, 4. FIRST AMERICAN EDITION.
> *New-York: Printed and sold by W. Durell, at his Book-Store and Printing-*
> *Office, No.* 19, *Q. Street.* M.DCC,XCI. 2 vols. pp. (2), (2), (4), [194], portrait;
> (2), [192], plate. 16mo.   AAS. BM. NYPL.

23354   'ESPINASSE, ISAAC
A DIGEST OF THE LAW OF ACTIONS AT NISI PRIUS. IN TWO VOLUMES. VOL. I. [—II.]
BY ISAAC 'ESPINASSE, ESQ. OF GRAY'S INN, BARRISTER AT LAW. [One line from]
JUVENAL.
> *Philadelphia. Printed by J. Crukshank, and W. Young, Booksellers and*
> *Stationers.* M,DCC,XCI. 2 vols. pp. (24), 434, (46); xviii, 518. 12mo. AAS. BM.

23355   THE ESSEX JOURNAL & NEW-HAMPSHIRE PACKET. NUMB. 340. WEDNESDAY, JANU-
ARY 5, [—NUMB. 392. WEDNESDAY, DECEMBER 28, 1791.]
> *Newbury-Port: Printed by John Mycall in Merrimack-Street a little below*
> *the Ferry-way* . . . 1791. fol.   AAS. LOC.

23356   EVANS, DAVID
A LETTER TO THE REV. DOCTOR [Samuel] JONES; CONTAINING SOME REMARKS ON
THE CIRCULAR LETTER OF THE PHILADELPHIA BAPTIST ASSOCIATION, 1791, [*sic*
1790.] WROTE BY HIMSELF. [Signed, David Evans, New Britain, April 17,
1791.] [Colophon:]
> *Boston:—Reprinted by White & Cambridge, and sold at their Shop, near*
> *Charles-River Bridge.* [1791.] pp. 12. 12mo.   AAS.

23357   —— A LETTER TO THE REV'D DOCTOR [Samuel] JONES : CONTAINING, SOME REMARKS
ON THE CIRCULAR LETTER OF THE BAPTIST ASSOCIATION, 1791 [*sic* 1790.] WROTE
BY HIMSELF. BY DAVID EVANS.
> *Philadelphia: Printed by Thomas Dobson, at the Stone-House, No.* 41,
> *South Second-Street.* 1791.

23358   EVANS, ISRAEL   1748 – 1807
A SERMON, DELIVERED AT CONCORD, BEFORE THE HON. GENERAL COURT, OF THE
STATE OF NEWHAMPSHIRE, AT THE ANNUAL ELECTION, HOLDEN ON THE FIRST
WEDNESDAY IN JUNE, M.DCC.XCI. BY THE REV. ISRAEL EVANS, A. M. PASTOR OF
THE CHURCH IN CONCORD.
> *Concord: Printed by George Hough, for the honourable General Court.*
> M.DCC,XCI. pp. 35. 4to.   BA. BM. LOC. MHS. NHSL.

23359   EWING, JOHN   1732 – 1802
SERMON ON THE DEATH OF GEORGE BRYAN. . . .
> *Philadelphia:* 1791. 8vo.

23360   THE EXPERIENCE OF SEVERAL METHODIST PREACHERS. WITH AN ACCOUNT OF
THEIR CALL TO, AND SUCCESS IN THE MINISTRY. IN A SERIES OF LETTERS, WRIT-
TEN BY THEMSELVES, TO THE REV. JOHN WESLEY, A. M.
> *Philadelphia: Printed by Parry Hall, No.* 149, *in Chesnut Street; and*
> *sold by John Dickins, No.* 43, *in Fourth near Race Street.* M,DCC,XCI. pp. 370,
> (1). 12mo.   AAS. JCB.

23361   AN EXTRACT ON INFANT BAPTISM.
> *Philadelphia: Printed by Joseph Crukshank (?) and sold by John Dickins,*
> *No.* 182, *in Race Street, near Sixth Street.* 1791.

23362   THE FARMER'S JOURNAL. VOL. I. No. 43. TUESDAY, JANUARY 4, [— VOL. II.
No. 42. MONDAY, DECEMBER 26, 1791.]

*Published in Danbury, by Nathan Douglas and Edwards Ely, near the
Court-[Meeting-] House.* 1791. fol.   AAS. LOC.

Beginning May 9th, the day of publication was changed to Monday.

23363   FATHER ABRAHAM'S ALMANAC, FOR THE YEAR OF OUR LORD, 1792; BEING BISSEX-
TILE OR LEAP-YEAR. [Twenty-seven lines.]

*Philadelphia: Printed and sold by Peter Stewart, No. 34, South Second-
Street.* [1791.] pp. (36). 12mo.   LOC.

23364   FAUGERES, PETER   − 1798
A TREATISE ON FEBRIS ASTHENICA GRAVIS, OR THE SEVERE ASTHENIC CONTINUED
FEVER.

New-York: Printed by Harrisson & Purdy, 1791. pp.vii, 9-35. 8vo. BA.SGO.

23365   THE FEDERAL GAZETTE AND PHILADELPHIA DAILY ADVERTISER. VOL. V. No.
701. SATURDAY, JANUARY 1, [— VOL. VII. No. 1011. SATURDAY, DECEMBER
31, 1791.]

*Printed and published by Andrew Brown, at Washington's Head, in Ches-
nut-Street, near Front-Street, . . .* 1791. fol   LCP.

23366   FENELON, FRANÇOIS DE SALIGNAC DE LA MOTHE   1651 − 1715
LES AVENTURES DE TÉLÉMAQUE, FILS D'ULYSSE, PAR MESSIRE FRANCOIS DE SAL-
IGNAC DE LA MOTHE FENELON, PRÉCEPTEUR DE MGRS. LES ENFANTS DE FRANCE,
ET DEPUIS ARCHEVÉQUE DE CAMBRAY, &C. NOUVELLE ÉDITION, SOIGNEUSE-
MENT CORREGÉE.

*A Philadelphie, Chez Charles Cist, Imprimeur - Libraire, Seconde Rue
Nord, No. 104.* [1791.] pp. (2), (2). 278. 12mo.   AAS.

23367   FENN, NATHAN   − 1799
A SERMON, DELIVERED AT THE ORDINATION OF THE REV. SYLVESTER SAGE, M. A. TO
THE PASTORAL CHARGE OF THE CHURCH IN WESTMINSTER, OCTOBER, 1790. BY
NATHAN FENN, M. A. PASTOR OF A CHURCH IN BERLIN.

Printed at Bennington, by Anthony Haswell, M,DCC,XCI. pp. 31. 8vo.
     AAS. JCB. VtSL.

The copy in the American Antiquarian Society lacks the half-title, but
has twenty manuscript lines of errata, added by the Author, on the
last page.

23368   FENNO, JENNY
ORIGINAL COMPOSITIONS, IN PROSE AND VERSE. ON SUBJECTS MORAL AND RELIGIOUS.
BY MISS J. FENNO, OF BOSTON.

Printed in Boston, by Joseph Bumstead, at his Office, No. 20, Union-Street.
MDCCXCI. pp. (2), iii, 125. 16mo.   AAS. BM.

Reprinted, in Wrentham, Massachusetts, in 1803.

23369   FIELDING, HENRY   1707 − 1754
THE HISTORY OF THE ADVENTURES OF JOSEPH ANDREWS, AND HIS FRIEND MR.
ABRAHAM ANDREWS. WRITTEN IN IMITATION OF THE MANNER OF CERVANTES,
AUTHOR OF DON QUIXOTE. BY HENRY FIELDING, ESQ. IN TWO VOLUMES. VOL.
I. [—II.]

*Philadelphia: Printed and sold by W. Woodhouse, at the Bible, No. 6,
South Front-Street.* 1791.

23370   —— — THE HISTORY OF THE ADVENTURES OF JOSEPH ANDREWS, AND HIS FRIEND
MR. ABRAHAM ANDREWS. WRITTEN IN IMITATION OF THE MANNER OF CERVAN-
TES, AUTHOR OF DON QUIXOTE. BY HENRY FIELDING, ESQ.. IN TWO VOLUMES.
VOL. I. [—II.]

Philadelphia: Printed by Henry Taylor, for Robert Campbell. 1791. 2 vols.

FIELDING, HENRY, continued.

23371 —— HISTORY OF TOM JONES, A FOUNDLING. BY HENRY FIELDING. [ABRIDGED FOR THE YOUNG.]

Norwich, (Connecticut): Printed by John Trumbull. 1791. pp. 194. 18mo.

23372 FIELDING, SARAH   1714 – 1768

THE GOVERNESS: OR, LITTLE FEMALE ACADEMY. BEING THE HISTORY OF MRS. TEACHUM, AND HER NINE GIRLS. WITH THEIR NINE DAYS AMUSEMENT. CALCULATED FOR THE ENTERTAINMENT AND INSTRUCTION OF YOUNG LADIES IN THEIR EDUCATION. BY THE AUTHOR OF DAVID SIMPLE. A NEW EDITION. [Thirteen lines from] SHAKESP. MIDSUMMER NIGHT'S DREAM.

Philadelphia: Printed by T. Dobson, at the Stone House, No. 41, *Second-Street.* M,DCC,XCI. pp. xii, 228. 24mo.   AAS.

23373 A FINE LADY.

Norwich: Printed and sold by John Trumbull. 1791.

23374 FISH, ELISHA   1719 – 1795

THE BAPTISM OF JESUS CHRIST *not* TO BE IMITATED BY CHRISTIANS: CONSIDERED AND ILLUSTRATED IN AN ESSAY. BY THE REV. ELISHA FISH, OF UPTON, AND THE REV. JOHN CRANE, OF NORTHBRIDGE. [Three lines from] JESUS CHRIST.

Boston, Printed: New-London, Re-printed by T. Green & Son. [1791.] pp. 23. 8vo.   JCB.

23375 —— — THE BAPTISM OF JESUS CHRIST NOT TO BE IMITATED BY CHRISTIANS: CONSIDERED AND ILLUSTRATED IN AN ESSAY. BY THE REV. ELISHA FISH, OF UPTON, AND THE REV. JOHN CRANE, OF NORTHBRIDGE. [Four lines from] JESUS CHRIST.

Printed by George Hough, at Concord, Newhampshire. Sold at his Office, wholesale and retail. M.DCC.XCI. pp. 24. 12mo.   BM. JCB.

23376 FISHER, MIERS   1748 – 1819

BRIEF OF THE TITLES OF ROBERT MORRIS, ESQUIRE, TO A TRACT OF COUNTRY IN THE COUNTY OF ONTARIO, IN THE STATE OF NEW-YORK, ONE OF THE UNITED STATES OF AMERICA. EXTRACTED FROM AUTHENTIC DOCUMENTS, BY MIERS FISHER, COUNSELLOR AT LAW, IN THE SUPREME COURT OF THE UNITED STATES. TO WHICH IS ADDED A SCHEDULE, CONTAINING AUTHENTIC COPIES OF THE PRINCIPAL ACTS AND RESOLVES OF THE GENERAL CONGRESS OF THE UNITED STATES, AND OF THE LEGISLATURES OF THE STATES OF MASSACHUSETTS AND NEW-YORK, AND OF OTHER DEEDS AND EVIDENCES OF TITLE, CITED IN THE BRIEF, FOR THE SATISFACTION OF THOSE WHO MAY WISH TO SEE THEM AT FULL LENGTH.

Philadelphia: Printed by Benj. Franklin Bache, . . . 1791. pp. (2),(45.) 4to.   BA. NYPL.

23377 FLEET, THOMAS, and JOHN

FLEETS' POCKET ALMANACK FOR THE YEAR OF OUR LORD 1792. BEING BISSEXTILE OR LEAP-YEAR, AND SIXTEENTH OF AMERICAN INDEPENDENCE. CALCULATED CHIEFLY FOR THE USE OF THE COMMONWEALTH OF MASSACHUSETTS, BOSTON, THE METROPOLIS, BEING IN LATITUDE 42 DEG. 25 MIN. NORTH. LONGITUDE 71 DEG. 4 MIN. WEST FROM THE ROYAL OBSERVATORY AT GREENWICH. TO WHICH IS ANNEXED, THE MASSACHUSETTS REGISTER, &C.

Boston: Printed and sold by T. & J. Fleet, at the Bible and Heart in Cornhill. [1791.] pp. [24], [156.] 24mo.   AAS. BA. HC. LOC. MHS. NYPL.

18th Massachusetts District Copyright, issued to Thomas and John Fleet, as Proprietors, 19 November, 1791.

23378   FLETCHER, or DE LA FLECHIERE, JOHN WILLIAM   1729 – 1785
THE WORKS OF THE REV. JOHN FLETCHER. VOLUME I. [—II.] THE FIRST AMER-
ICAN EDITION.
> *Philadelphia: Printed by Joseph Crukshank: Sold by John Dickins, No.
> 43, Fourth-Street, near the corner of Race-Street.* 1791. 2 vols. pp. (2), 330; (2),
> 320. 12mo.   AAS.

The third volume was printed in Philadelphia, in 1792.

23379   FLETCHER, MARY
AN ACCOUNT OF THE DEATH OF THE REV. MR. FLETCHER, VICAR OF MADELEY, IN
SHROPSHIRE. [Three lines of quotation.]
> *Bristol, Printed, Richmond: Re-printed by Augustine Davis.* MDCCXCI.
> pp. [16.] 16mo.   AAS.

Signed, M. F. Madeley, Aug. 18, 1785.

23380   FOBES, PERES   1742 – 1812
A SERMON, DELIVERED IN THE BAPTIST MEETING-HOUSE IN PROVIDENCE, JULY 31,
A. D. 1791. OCCASIONED BY THE DEATH OF THE REV. JAMES MANNING, D. D.
PRESIDENT OF RHODE-ISLAND COLLEGE. BY PERES FOBES, A. M. FELLOW OF THE
AMERICAN ACADEMY OF ARTS AND SCIENCES, PROFESSOR OF NATURAL AND EX-
PERIMENTAL PHILOSOPHY IN THE COLLEGE OF RHODE-ISLAND, AND PASTOR OF
THE CHURCH IN RAYNHAM. [Two lines of quotation.]
> *Providence: Printed by J. Carter.* [1791.] pp. 40. 8vo.
>   AAS. BM. HC. JCB. NYHS.

23381   FOSTER, DANIEL   1751 – 1795
A SERMON, PREACHED AT THE ORDINATION OF THE REVEREND JOSHUA CROSBY, TO
THE PASTORAL CARE OF THE CHURCH AND PEOPLE OF GOD, IN GREENWICH, 2D.
SOCIETY. DECEMBER 2D, M,DCC,LXXXIX. BY DANIEL FOSTER, A. M. PASTOR OF
THE CHURCH IN NEW-BRAINTREE.
> *Springfield, Massachusetts: Printed by Ezra W. Weld.* M,DCC,XCI. pp.
> [20.] 8vo.   AAS. JCB. NYPL.

23382   FOX, THOMAS
THE WILMINGTON ALMANACK, OR EPHEMERIS, FOR THE YEAR OF OUR LORD, 1792.
> *Wilmington: Printed by James Adams.* [1791.]

23383   FRANCE. KINGDOM.
THE FRENCH CONSTITUTION, REVISED, AMENDED, AND FINALLY DECREED, BY THE
NATIONAL ASSEMBLY. PRESENTED TO THE KING ON THE 3D, AND ACCEPTED BY
HIM ON THE 13TH OF SEPTEMBER, 1791.
> *Philadelphia: Printed by William Young, No. 52, Second-Street, the cor-
> ner of Chesnut-Street.* M,DCC,XCI. pp. 22. 8vo.   LOC.

23384   —— — THE FRENCH CONSTITUTION, REVISED, AMENDED, AND FINALLY DECREED
BY THE NATIONAL ASSEMBLY. PRESENTED TO THE KING ON THE 3D, AND AC-
CEPTED BY HIM ON THE 13TH SEPTEMBER, 1791, CONFORMABLE TO THE COPY
PRINTED AT PARIS THE 5TH SEPTEMBER, 1791, AND SIGNED BAUDOUIN.
> *Philadelphia: Printed and sold by Peter Stewart, No. 34, South Second
> Street.* 1791.

23385   FRANKLIN. BENJAMIN   1706 – 1790
THE WAY TO WEALTH. BY DR. FRANKLIN.
> *Boston: Printed and sold by Benjamin Russell,* 1791. Broadside. fol.

23386   —— — THE WAY TO WEALTH. BY DR. FRANKLIN.
> *Boston: Printed and sold by Benjamin Russell,* 1791.

This is the broadside edition, "in pages, printed in a neat pamphlet."

23387   FRASER, Donald
The Young gentleman and lady's assistant; partly original, but chiefly compiled from the works of the most celebrated modern authors; calculated to instruct youth in the principles of useful knowledge: in five parts, viz. Geography, natural-history, elocution, poetry—and miscellany. To which is annexed—a short system of practical arithmetic; wherein every example is wrought at large, and the whole, including the money of the United States, rendered easy to the meanest capacity. This work, is divided into small sections for the convenience of schools. By Donald Fraser, school-master, New-York.
    New-York: Printed by Tho's Greenleaf, M,DCC,XCI. pp. xii, 273, (22). 12mo.   AAS. BM. JCB.
    Contains, list of names of subscribers. 1st New York District Copyright, issued to Donald Fraser, as Author, 30 April, 1791. The work had seven hundred subscribers in the City of New York. An edition of two thousand copies was sold in eighteen months.

23388   FREE AND ACCEPTED MASONS. Grand Lodge of the State of New York. The Constitutions of the ancient and honorable fraternity of Free and Accepted Masons, in the State of New-York. Collected and digested by order of the Grand Lodge.
    Albany: Printed by Robert Barber & Co? 1791.
    "To be sold by Elisha Crane."

23389   FREEMAN, Samuel   1743 – 1831
The Town officer; or the power and duty of selectmen, town clerks, town treasurers, overseers of the poor, assessors, constables, collectors of taxes, surveyors of highways, surveyors of lumber, fence reviewers, and other town officers. As contained in the Laws of the Commonwealth of Massachusetts. With a variety of forms for the use of such officers. To which are added, the power and duty of towns, parishes and plantations; and a plain and regular method to keep accounts of the expenditures of monies voted by a town; upon an inspection of which, the state of its finances may at any time be known. By Samuel Freeman, esq. [With the privilege of copyright.]
    Portland: Printed by Benjamin Titcomb, jun. MDCCXCI. pp. 178, (2). 12mo.   AAS.

23390   THE FREEMAN'S [cut] journal; or, the North-American intelligencer. Open to all parties, but influenced by none. Vol. x. Numb. dvii. Wednesday, January 5, [—Vol. xi. Numb. dlviii. Wednesday, December 28, 1791.]
    Philadelphia: Printed by Francis Bailey, at Yorick's Head, in Market-Street. 1791. fol.   AAS. LOC.
    In March, the Printing Office was removed to High-Street.

23391   FRENEAU, Philip   1752 – 1832
Proposals for a Monmouth newspaper. It is proposed by the subscriber, if sufficient encouragement should be afforded, to publish at Mount-Pleasant, near Middletown Point, in East New-Jersey, a weekly newspaper, to be entitled. The Monmouth Gazette, or, general magazine of information and amusement. [Thirty-four lines.] New-York, February 15th, 1791. Philip Freneau. . . .
    [New-York: Printed by Francis Childs and John Swaine, 1791.] Broadside. fol.
    Probably from want of sufficient encouragement this newspaper venture was abandoned, for *The National Gazette,* which Freneau published in Philadelphia from October 31st, of this year.

23392   FRIENDS, SOCIETY OF
THE EPISTLE FROM THE YEARLY-MEETING, HELD IN LONDON, BY ADJOURNMENTS,
FROM THE 16TH TO THE 24TH OF THE FIFTH MONTH, 1791, INCLUSIVE, TO THE
QUARTERLY AND MONTHLY MEETINGS OF FRIENDS IN GREAT-BRITAIN, IRELAND,
AND ELSEWHERE.
[Philadelphia? 1791.] pp. (4). fol.

23393   —— EXTRACTS FROM THE EPISTLE OF THE MEETING FOR SUFFERINGS IN LONDON,
1751, TO THE QUAKERS' MEETING, HELD 1790.
Trenton: Printed by Isaac Collins? 1791. fol.

23394   —— FROM OUR YEARLY-MEETING HELD IN LONDON, BY ADJOURNMENTS FROM THE
16TH TO THE 24TH OF THE FIFTH MONTH, 1791, INCLUSIVE. TO THE YEARLY-
MEETING OF FRIENDS TO BE HELD AT PHILADELPHIA.
[Philadelphia: 1791.] pp. (2). fol.   AAS.

23395   FROTHINGHAM'S LONG-ISLAND HERALD. [Motto.]   VOL. I. NO. I, TUESDAY, MAY
10, [—NO. 34. TUESDAY, DECEMBER 27, 1791.]
Sagg-Harbour, Printed by David Frothingham, near the Landing. 1791.fol.
Established by David Frothingham, with the motto, "Eye Nature's
walks, shoot folly as it flies,—And catch the manners living as they
rise," and continued by him apparently into the year 1802, when Sel-
leck Osborn purchased the Printing-Office, and changed the name to
Suffolk County Herald. In 1804, the Herald passed into the posses-
sion of Alden Spooner, who again changed the name to *Suffolk Gazette,*
under which title he continued its publication into the year 1811,
when it was discontinued.

23396   G., N.
A SCRIPTURAL COMMENT ON THE ATHANASIAN CREED.
Printed by Thomas Lang, Philadelphia. [1791.] pp. 16. 16mo.   BA.
Title from first page of the text. The initials and date "Philadelphia,
February 22d, 1791," are from the note of gift to George Washington.

23397   GAIFER, pseudonym.
AN ACCOUNT OF THE CONVERSION OF A MOHAMETAN TO THE CHRISTIAN RELIGION:
DESCRIBED IN A LETTER FROM GAIFER, IN ENGLAND, TO ALY-BEN HAYTON, HIS
FRIEND IN TURKEY.
Stockbridge (Massachusetts) Printed by Loring Andrews. 1791.

23398   EIN GANZ NEU EINGERICHTETES LUTHERISCHES A. B. C. BUCHSTABIER–UND NAM-
ENBUCH ZUM NÜTZLICHEN GEBRAUCH DEUTSCHER SCHULEN.
Chesnut Hill: Gedruckt bey Samuel Saur, 1791.   HSP.

23399   —— EIN GANZ NEU EINGERICHTETES LUTHERISCHES A. B. C. BUCHSTABIER—UND
NAMENBUCH ZUM NÜTZLICHEN GEBRAUCH DEUTSCHER SCHULEN.
*[Chesnut Hill: Gedruckt bey Samuel Saur, und zu haben bey] David Saur
and Wm. Jones, Buchbinder und Buchhaendler, 73 Race Street, Philadelphia.* 1791.

23400   GARDINER, JOHN
THE WIDOWED MOURNER. [A poem. Signed, J. G.]
[Boston: 1791.] 12mo.
           BPL.

23401   GARRETTSON, FREEBORN   1752 – 1827
THE EXPERIENCE AND TRAVELS OF MR. FREEBORN GARRETTSON, MINISTER OF THE
METHODIST-EPISCOPAL CHURCH IN NORTH-AMERICA. [One line from] I. SAM.
VII. 12.
*Philadelphia: Printed by Joseph Crukshank, No. 91, High Street, near
Sixth Street.* M,DCC,XCI. pp. 252. 24mo.   AAS.

GARRETTSON, Freeborn, continued.

23402 — — THE EXPERIENCE AND TRAVELS OF MR. FREEBORN GARRETTSON, MINISTER OF THE METHODIST-EPISCOPAL CHURCH IN NORTH-AMERICA. [One line from] I. SAM. VII. 12.

Philadelphia: Printed by Parry Hall, No. 149, in Chesnut Street, and sold by John Dickins, No. 43 Fourth Street, near Race Street. M.DCC.XCI. pp. (276). 12mo. NYHS. NYPL.

7th New York District Copyright, issued to Freeborn Garrettson, as Author, 22 November, 1791.

23403 GAZETTE [U. S. arms] OF MAINE. VOL. I. NO. 14. THURSDAY, JANUARY 6, [— VOL. II. NO. 13. THURSDAY, DECEMBER 29, 1791.]

Portland, (Massachusetts) Printed and published by Benjamin Titcomb, jun. 1791. fol. AAS. NYHS.

With the issue for October 7th, (District of Maine) was substituted for "Massachusetts" in the imprint. On December 29th, the cut of the United States Arms was permanently dropped from the heading, when the paper was enlarged from three to four columns.

23404 *General title:* THE GAZETTE OF THE UNITED STATES. PUBLISHED AT THE SEAT OF GOVERNMENT. BEGINNING APRIL 14, 1790,—AND ENDING APRIL 27, 1791; CONTAINING THE LAWS AND RESOLUTIONS OF CONGRESS PASSED DURING THE SECOND AND THIRD SESSIONS, AND SKETCHES OF DEBATES IN THE HOUSE OF REPRESENTATIVES: ALSO A SERIES OF ORIGINAL ESSAYS, UPON THE MOST INTERESTING SUBJECTS OF LIFE, MANNERS, &C. VOL. SECOND. U. S. A.

Philadelphia: Printed by the Editor (John Fenno) at his Office in High-Street. 1790-1791. pp. (4), 301-832. fol. LCP.

Paged and indexed.

Heading: GAZETTE OF THE UNITED STATES. NO. 71, OF VOL. II. WHOLE NO. 175. SATURDAY, JANUARY 1, [— NO. 71, OF VOL. III. WHOLE NO. 279. SATURDAY, DECEMBER 31, 1791.]

Published Wednesdays and Saturdays by John Fenno, No. 69, Market-[High-] Street, between Second and Third-Streets, Philadelphia. 1791. pp. 689-832; 1–284. fol. AAS. LCP. LOC.

23405 THE GENERAL ADVERTISER AND POLITICAL, COMMERCIAL, AGRICULTURAL AND LITERARY JOURNAL. TRUTH. DECENCY, UTILITY. NUMB. 80. SATURDAY, JANUARY 1, [—NUMB. 392. SATURDAY, DECEMBER 31, 1791.]

Published (daily) by Benj. Franklin Bache, up Franklin-Court, in Market, between Third and Fourth-Streets, Philadelphia. 1791. fol. AAS. HC. LCP. PSL.

August 16th, the sub-title was dropped from the heading, and the imprint changed from colophon to the heading.

23406 GENLIS, Stéphanie Félicité Brulart Ducrest de St. Aubin, comtesse de BEAUTIES OF MADAM GENLIS, BEING A SELECT COLLECTION OF THE MOST BEAUTIFUL TALES AND OTHER STRIKING EXTRACTS FROM ADELA AND THEODORE, AND TALES OF THE CASTLE; THE THEATRE OF EDUCATION, AND SACRED DRAMAS.

Philadelphia: 1791.

23407 GEOGRAPHICAL CARDS, FOR THE AGREEABLE IMPROVEMENT OF LADIES AND GENTLEMEN IN THE NECESSARY AND PLEASING STUDY OF GEOGRAPHY—TAKEN FROM THE LATEST AND BEST AUTHORITIES.

Philadelphia: Printed and sold by Eleazer Oswald. 1791.

23408   THE GEORGE-TOWN WEEKLY LEDGER. VOL. I. NO. 38. SATURDAY, JANUARY 1, [— VOL. II. NO. 90. SATURDAY, DECEMBER 31, 1791.]

> *George-Town: Printed by M. Day and W. Hancock, for the Proprietor.* 1791. fol.

> In August, Day and Hancock were succeeded by Alexander Doyle, as publisher.

23409   THE GEORGIA GAZETTE. NO. 415. THURSDAY, JANUARY 6, [—NO. 466, THURSDAY, DECEMBER 29, 1791.]

> *Savannah: Printed by James and Nicholas Johnston, Broughton - Street.* 1791. fol.
>   GHS. LOC.

23410   GEORGIA. THE AUGUSTA CHRONICLE AND GAZETTE OF THE STATE. [Motto.] VOL. IV. NO. CCXXII. SATURDAY, JANUARY 1, [—NO. CCLXXIII. SATURDAY, DECEMBER 31, 1701.]

> *Augusta: Printed by John E. Smith, Printer to the State.* 1791. fol. GHS.

23411   DIE GERMANTAUNER ZEITUNG. NUM. 25. DIENSTAG, DEN 4TEN JANUAR, [— NUM. 76. DIENSTAG, DEN 27TEN DECEMBER, 1791.]

> *Diese Zeitung wird wochentlich Dienstag Nach mittags herausgegeben von Michael Billmeyer, Buchdrucker, zu Germantaun; fur einen halben Thaler des Jahrs. Ein Viertel Thaler wird beym Einschreiben bezahlt.* 1792. 4to.   HSP.

23412   GESNER, SALOMON   1730 – 1788
THE DEATH OF ABEL. IN FIVE BOOKS. ATTEMPTED FROM THE GERMAN OF MR. GESSNER. BY MARY COLLYER. TO WHICH IS ADDED, THE DEATH OF CAIN. IN FIVE BOOKS.

> *Philadelphia: Printed by William Spotswood.* 1791. pp. viii, 172; iv. 68. 24mo.   AAS. JCB.

> *Second title:* THE DEATH OF CAIN, IN FIVE BOOKS; AFTER THE MANNER OF THE DEATH OF ABEL. BY A LADY. [Two lines from] MILTON.
>   *Philadelphia; Printed and sold by William Spotswood.* 1791. pp. iv, 68.

23413   THE GLASS; OR, SPECULATION: A POEM. CONTAINING AN ACCOUNT OF THE ANCIENT, AND GENIUS OF THE MODERN, SPECULATORS. [Four lines of verse.]

> *New-York: Printed for the Author.*—1791.—pp. [12.] 12mo.   BU. NYHS.

23414   GLEASON, EZRA
THOMAS'S MASSACHUSETTS, CONNECTICUT, RHODE-ISLAND, NEWHAMPSHIRE & VERMONT ALMANACK, WITH AN EPHEMERIS, FOR THE YEAR OF OUR LORD 1792; BEING BISSEXTILE, OR LEAPYEAR, AND SIXTEENTH OF THE INDEPENDENCE OF UNITED AMERICA. FROM CREATION, ACCORDING TO THE SCRIPTURES, 5754. [Six lines. Cut. Four lines.]

> *Printed at Worcester, by Isaiah Thomas. [Price 40s per gross. 4s per dozen. Six pence single.]* [1791.] pp. [48.] 8vo.   AAS. LOC. NYPL. YC.

23415   —— — SECOND EDITION. THOMAS'S MASSACHUSETTS, CONNECTICUT, RHODE-ISLAND, NEWHAMPSHIRE & VERMONT ALMANACK, WITH AN EPHEMERIS, FOR THE YEAR OF OUR LORD 1792: [Nine lines. Four lines of verse.]

> *Printed at Worcester, by Isaiah Thomas.* [1791.] pp. (48). 12mo.   AAS.

> Contains, An Inquiry into the effects of spirituous liquors upon the human body. To which is added, a Moral and physical thermometer. By Benjamin Rush.

23416   GOLDSMITH, Oliver   1728 – 1774
POEMS BY DR. GOLDSMITH; VIZ. THE DESERTED VILLAGE, THE TRAVELLER, AND EDWIN AND ANGELINA.
> *Philadelphia: Printed and sold by Henry Taylor.* M.DCC.XCI. pp. 40.
> 16mo.   AAS. JCB. LOC.

23417   —— THE VICAR OF WAKEFIELD. A TALE. SUPPOSED TO BE WRITTEN BY HIMSELF. [One line of Latin.] IN TWO VOLUMES. VOL. I. [— II.]
> *Philadelphia: Printed by William Young, Bookseller, No. 52, Second-street, the corner of Chesnut-street.* M.DCC.XCI. 2 vols. in one. pp. 140; 134, (2).
> 12mo.   AAS.

Contains a list of "Books to be sold by William Young."

23418   THE GOSHEN REPOSITORY, AND WEEKLY INTELLIGENCER. [Motto.] VOL. II. No. 103. TUESDAY, JANUARY 4, [— VOL. III. No. 154. TUESDAY, DECEMBER 27, 1791.]
> *Goshen: Printed and published by David Mandeville and David M. Westcott, at the Academy [Near the Court-House.]* 1791. fol.

23419   GRAHAM, Jacob
DISPUTATIO MEDICA INAUGURALIS DE SCROPHULA.
> *Philadelphia: Apud Gulielmum Young,* 1791. pp. 26. 8vo.   AGO.

23420   GREEN, Timothy
GREEN'S REGISTER, FOR THE STATE OF CONNECTICUT: [ornamental line.] WITH AN ALMANACK, FOR THE YEAR OF OUR LORD, 1792, CALCULATED BY NATHAN DABOLL, FOR THE MERIDIAN OF NEW-LONDON, LAT 41. 25. NORTH. [Line.]
> *New-London: Printed by T. Green & Son.* [1791.] pp. 92; (15). 12mo.
>   CHS. NL. RIHS. YC.

23421   GREENLEAF, Thomas
TO THE PUBLIC. THE JUST OBSERVATION, THAT A GREATER PROPORTION OF HARMONY AND GOOD WILL ALWAYS SUBSISTS IN THAT COMMUNITY, WHOSE INHABITANTS HAVE ACQUIRED A GENERAL KNOWLEDGE OF ITS LAWS, - - - THOMAS GREENLEAF, NEW-YORK, MARCH 1, 1791. PROPOSALS, FOR RE-PRINTING, BY SUBSCRIPTION, A CORRECT EDITION OF THE REVISED LAWS OF THE STATE OF NEW-YORK, WITH THE ADDITION OF ALL THE LAWS WHICH HAVE BEEN ENACTED SINCE THE REVISION TOOK PLACE—COMPRISING THE WHOLE OF THE LAWS OF THIS STATE NOW IN FORCE. CONDITIONS. . . .
> *[New-York: Printed by Thomas Greenleaf,* 1791.] Broadside. fol. NYHS.

23422   GREGORY, John   1724 – 1773
A FATHER'S LEGACY TO HIS DAUGHTERS. BY THE LATE DR. GREGORY, OF EDINBURGH.
> *Boston: Printed and sold by John W. Folsom, No. 30, Union-Street. Sold also by Daniel Brewer of Taunton.* M,DCC,XCI. pp. 62 32mo.   AAS.

23423   GROSVENOR, Benjamin   1675 – 1758
THE MOURNER: OR THE AFFLICTED RELIEVED
> *Philadelphia: Printed by Robert Aitken.* 1791. pp. 81. 18mo.

23424   HAMILTON, Alexander   1757 – 1804
THE ARGUMENT OF THE SECRETARY OF THE TREASURY UPON THE CONSTITUTIONALITY OF A NATIONAL BANK. [Signed, Alexander Hamilton, Philadelphia, Feb. 23, 1791.]
> *[Philadelphia:* 1791.] pp. 40, 8vo.   BA.

23425   THE HAMPSHIRE [cut] CHRONICLE: POLITICAL AND HISTORICAL, MORAL AND EN-
TERTAINING. COMMONWEALTH OF MASSACHUSETTS. [Motto.] VOL. IV. NUMB.
CCI. WEDNESDAY, JANUARY 5, [— VOL. V. NUMB. 252. WEDNESDAY, DECEMBER
28, 1791.

     *Printed and published by Ezra Waldo Weld, opposite the Court-House, in
Springfield. 1791. fol.*   AAS.

With the issue for November 2d, the title was altered to, *Hampshire and
Berkshire Chronicle*.

23426   THE HAMPSHIRE GAZETTE. VOL. V. NUMB. 227. WEDNESDAY, JANUARY 4,
[—VOL. VI. NUMB. 278. WEDNESDAY, DECEMBER 28, 1791.]

     Northampton, (Massachusetts) Published by William Butler, 1791. fol.
               AAS. MHS.

23427   HANDY, HAST
An INAUGURAL DISSERTATION ON OPIUM; SUBMITTED TO THE EXAMINATION OF THE
REV. WILLIAM SMITH, S. T. P. PROVOST; AND TO THE TRUSTEES AND MEDICAL
PROFESSORS OF THE COLLEGE OF PHILADELPHIA; FOR THE DEGREE OF DOCTOR
OF MEDICINE: ON THE TWENTY-THIRD DAY OF JUNE, A. D. 1791. BY HAST HANDY,
OF THE STATE OF MARYLAND.

     Philadelphia: Printed by T. Lang, No. 21, Church-Alley. MDCCXCI.
pp. (28). 8vo.   CLS. SGO.

23428   HART, OLIVER   1723–1795
AMERICA'S REMEMBRANCER, WITH RESPECT TO HER BLESSEDNESS AND DUTY. A
SERMON, DELIVERED IN HOPEWELL, NEW JERSEY, ON THANKSGIVING DAY, NOV-
EMBER 26, 1789. BY OLIVER HART, A. M. [Four lines of quotations.]

     *Philadelphia: Printed by T. Dobson, at the Stone-House, No. 41, South
Second-Street.* M,DCC,XCI. pp. [24.] 8vo.   BA. BM. CLS. JCB. LCP. LOC. YC

23429   —— A GOSPEL CHURCH PORTRAYED, AND HER ORDERLY SERVICE POINTED OUT—A
SERMON, DELIVERED IN THE CITY OF PHILADELPHIA AT THE OPENING OF THE
BAPTIST ASSOCIATION, OCTOBER 4, 1791. BY OLIVER HART, A. M. PASTOR OF
THE BAPTIST CHURCH IN HOPEWELL, NEW-JERSEY. [Three lines of Scripture
texts.]

     Trenton: Printed by Isaac Collins. M.DCC.XCI. pp. 38. 8vo.   BA. JCB.

23430   HARVARD UNIVERSITY.
CATALOGUS EORUM QUI IN UNIVERSITATE HARVARDIANA, CANTABRIGIÆ, IN REPUB-
LICA MASSACHUSETTENSI, AB ANNO MDCXLII, AD ANNUM MDCCXCI, ALICUJUS GRA-
DUS LAUREÂ DONATI SUNT. THEOLOGIÆ PROFESSORES ET ECCLESIARUM PAS-
TORES LITERIS ITALICIS EXARANTUR. QUI AD IMUM CLASSIUM À CÆTERIS, LINEÂ
INTERPOSITÂ, SEPARANTUR, ALIBI INSTITUTI FUERUNT, VEL APUD NOS GRADU
HONORARIO DONATI.

     Bostoniæ: Typis Thomæ et Johannis Fleet, Universitatis Typographorum,
MDCCXCI. *Annoque rerum-publicarum Americæ Foederatarum summæ potestatis*
XVI. pp. (39). 8vo.   AAS. BA. HC. JCB. LOC. MHS. NL.

23431   —— ILLUSTRISSIMO JOHANNI HANCOCK, ARMIGERO, LL. D. GUBERNATORI; HONORA-
TISSIMO SAMUELI ADAMS, ARMIGERO, VICE-GUBERNATORI; CONSILIARIIS ET SENA-
TORIBUS REIPUBLICÆ MASSACHUSETTENSIS: REVERENDISQUE ECCLESIARUM IN OP-
PIDIS SEX VICINIS, PRESBYTERIS, UNIVERSITATIS HARVARDIANÆ CURATORIBUS;
REVERENDO JOSEPHO WILLARD, S. T. D. PRÆSIDI; [Four lines.] THESES HASCE,
JUVENES IN ARTIBUS INITIATI, [Twenty-seven names.] HUMILLIMÈ DEDICANT
. . . . *Habita in comitiis Universitatis Cantabrigiae, Massachusettensis.
Die Julii* xx. *Anno salutis* MDCCXCI. RERUMQUE PUBLICARUM FOEDERAT-
ARUM AMERICÆ SUMMÆ POTESTATIS XVI. [Colophon:]

     Bostoniæ: Typis Samuelis Hall. [1791.] Broadside. fol.   AAS. BM. HC.

HARVARD UNIVERSITY, continued.

23432 —— THE ORDER OF THE EXERCISES OF COMMENCEMENT, JULY 20, 1791.
[Boston: Printed by Thomas and John Fleet, 1791.] Broadside. fol.   HC.

23433 —— QUÆSTIONES SUB REVERENDO JOSEPHO WILLARD, S. T. D. UNIVERSITATIS HAR-
VARDIANÆ, QUÆ EST CANTABRIGIÆ, IN REPUBLICA MASSACHUSETTENSI, PRÆSIDE,
IN COMITIIS PUBLICIS, À LAUREÆ MAGISTRALIS CANDIDATIS, PRO MODULO DISCU-
TIENDÆ. DIE JULII XX, ANNO SALUTIS MDCCXCI. [Thirty-six lines.] [Colophon:]
Bostoniæ: Typis Thomæ et Johannis Fleet. [1791.] Broadside. fol. AAS. HC.

23434 HARVEY, JAMES
A LETTER WRITTEN BY THE LATE REVEREND JAMES HARVEY, A. M. TO HIS BROTHER.
Norwich: Printed by Eben. Bushnell, 1791. pp. 7. 4to.

23435 HAVEN, SAMUEL   1727 – 1806
A FUNERAL DISCOURSE, DELIVERED AT THE INTERMENT OF THE REV'D. BENJAMIN
STEVENS, D. D. WHO DEPARTED THIS LIFE MAY 18, 1791. BY SAMUEL HAVEN,
D. D. PASTOR OF THE SOUTH CHURCH IN PORTSMOUTH. [Two lines from] PARA-
BLE OF THE TALENTS.   [Ornamental line.]
Dover: Printed by E. Ladd, at his Office, near the Court-House. M,DCC,-
XCI. pp. 32. 18mo.   BM. JCB.
Reprinted in Newburyport, in 1792.

23436 —— — SERMON OCCASIONED BY THE DEATH OF BENJAMIN STEVENS, OF KITTERY
POINT.   WITH NOTES.
Portsmouth: Printed by John Melcher. 1791. pp. 32. 8vo.   NYHS.

23437 HAYNES, LEMUEL
THE CHARACTER AND WORK OF A SPIRITUAL WATCHMAN DECRIBED [*sic.*]   A SER-
MON, DELIVERED AT HINESBURGH, FEBRUARY 23, 1791. AT THE ORDINATION OF
THE REV. REUBEN PARMERLEE.   BY LEMUEL HAYNES, PASTOR OF A CHURCH IN
RUTLAND.
Litchfield, (Connecticut) Printed by Collier and Buel. [1791.]   pp.   [22.]
12mo.   AAS. JCB.
The Author was an Indian convert.   The copy in the American Anti-
quarian Society contains manuscript corrections by him.

23438 HELLENBROEK, ABRAHAM
SPECIMEN OF DIVINE TRUTHS, FITTED FOR THE USE OF THOSE, OF VARIOUS CAPAC-
ITIES, WHO DESIRE TO PREPARE THEMSELVES FOR A DUE CONFESSION OF THEIR
FAITH.   BY THE REV. MR. A. HELLENBROECK, LATE MINISTER OF THE GOSPEL AT
ROTTERDAM.   TRANSLATED FROM THE DUTCH, FOR THE USE OF THE REFORMED
DUTCH CHURCH IN THE CITY OF NEW-YORK.
New-York: Printed by W. Durell, No. 198, Queen-Street. M,DCC,XCI.
pp. 95.   12mo.   AAS. JCB.
"On fine paper, with a large, new type."

23439 THE HERALD OF FREEDOM. VOL. V. NUMB. XXXIII. TUESDAY, JANUARY 4, [—
VOL. VI. NUMB. XXXV. TUESDAY, JULY 19, 1791.]
*Published Tuesdays and Fridays, by Edmund Freeman, State-Street, Bos-
ton.* 1791.   fol.   AAS.
With the issue for April 5th, Edmund Freeman disposed of all interests
in the Herald to John Howel, by whom it was continued to July
19th, at the Printing-office of the American Herald, in Court-Street,
changing the name, after that date, to *The Argus.*

23440   HERVEY, JAMES   1713 – 1758
MEDITATIONS AND CONTEMPLATIONS: IN TWO VOLUMES. CONTAINING, VOL. I. MED-
ITATIONS AMONG THE TOMBS; REFLECTIONS ON A FLOWER GARDEN; AND A DES-
CANT UPON CREATION. VOL. II. CONTEMPLATIONS ON THE NIGHT; CONTEMPLA-
TIONS ON THE STARRY HEAVENS; AND, A WINTER-PIECE. BY JAMES HERVEY,
A. M. LATE RECTOR OF WESTON-FAVELL, NORTHAMPTONSHIRE. VOL. I.. [—II.]
Philadelphia: Printed and sold by W. Woodhouse, at the Bible, No. 6
South Front-Street. M.DCC.XCI. 2vols. pp. 232; 239, (8). 12mo.   AAS.

23441   HILDROP, JOHN   1725 – 1756
AN ESSAY ON HONOUR, IN NINE LETTERS, BY JOHN HILDROP, D. D. RECTOR OF WATH,
IN YORKSHIRE, ENGLAND. PUBLISHED IN THE WEEKLY MISCELLANY.
Elizabeth-Town, Maryland, Reprinted by Stewart Herbert, 1791. pp. (87),
(4). 8vo.   NYPL.
Contains a list of Subscribers' names.

23442   HITCHCOCK, ENOS   1744 – 1803
A DISCOURSE DELIVERED AT THE ORDINATION OF THE REV. ABEL FLINT, TO
THE MINISTERIAL OFFICE IN A CHRISTIAN CHURCH AT HARTFORD, APRIL 20TH,
1791. BY ENOS HITCHCOCK, D. D. PASTOR OF THE BENEVOLENT CONGREGATIONAL
CHURCH OF CHRIST IN PROVIDENCE.
Hartford: Printed by Elisha Babcock. M,DCC,XCI. pp. 23. 8vo.
           AAS. BA. HC. JCB. NYPL.

23443   HOADLY, BENJAMIN   1706 – 1757
THE SUSPICIOUS HUSBAND. A COMEDY. BY THE RIGHT REVEREND DR. BENJAMIN
HOADLY.
Philadelphia: Printed by William Spotswood. MDCCXCI. pp. (4), 68.
12mo.   JCB.

23444   DER HOCH-DEUTSCHE AMERICANISCHE CALENDER, AUF DAS JAHR 1792, U. S. W.
Germantown: Gedruckt bey Michael Billmeyer. [1791.]

23445   HODGSON, EDWARD
THE TRIAL OF RENWICK WILLIAMS, COMMONLY CALLED THE MONSTER, FOR ASSAULT-
ING AND WOUNDING MISS ANN PORTER. TAKEN IN SHORT HAND BY EDWARD
HODGSON. ORNAMENTED WITH A STRIKING LIKENESS OF THE PRISONER.
New-York: Printed by Thomas Greenleaf. Sold by Andrew Marschalk.
1791.

23446   HOLYOKE, SAMUEL   1771 – 1816
HARMONIA AMERICANA: CONTAINING A CONCISE INTRODUCTION TO THE GROUNDS OF
MUSIC, WITH A VARIETY OF AIRS, SUITABLE FOR DIVINE WORSHIP, AND THE USE OF
MUSICAL SOCIETIES, CONSISTING OF THREE AND FOUR PARTS. BY SAMUEL HOLYOKE,
A. B.
Printed at Boston by I. Thomas and E. T. Andrews, 1791. pp. 120. obl.
8vo.   AAS. NYHS.
Contains, a list of subscribers. 13th Massachusetts District Copyright,
issued to Samuel Holyoke, as Author, 24 January, 1791. Advertised
in the Essex Journal in 1791: Newbury-Port: Printed, for the Author,
by John Mycall.

23447   HOME, JOHN   1724 – 1808
DOUGLAS, A TRAGEDY. AS PERFORMED WITH UNIVERSAL APPLAUSE BY THE AMER-
ICAN COMPANY. WRITTEN BY THE REV. MR. HOME.
Philadelphia: Printed and sold by Henry Taylor. M.DCC.XCI. pp 62,
(1). 16mo.   AAS.

23448   HOPKINS, SAMUEL   1721 – 1803
AN INQUIRY INTO THE NATURE OF TRUE HOLINESS. BY SAMUEL HOPKINS, D. D.
PASTOR OF THE FIRST CONGREGATIONAL CHURCH IN NEWPORT.
*Newport—Printed. New-York: Re-printed for M. Smith and C. Davis, by
William Durell, No. 19, Queen-Street.* MDCCXCI. pp. 218, (2). 16mo.
AAS. BM. JCB.

23449   HOSACK, DAVID   1769 – 1835
AN INAUGURAL DISSERTATION ON CHOLERA MORBUS, SUBMITTED TO THE EXAMINA-
TION OF THE REV. JOHN EWING . . . THE TRUSTEES AND MEDICAL PROFESSORS
OF THE UNIVERSITY OF PENNSYLVANIA; . . . ON THE TWELFTH DAY OF MAY,
. . . 1791.
New-York: Printed by Samuel Campbell. M,DCC,XCI. pp. 32. 8vo. SGO.

23450   [U. S. arms.] HOUGH'S CONCORD HERALD. [N. H. arms.] THE LIBERTY OF THE
PRESS IS ESSENTIAL TO THE SECURITY OF FREEDOM IN A STATE.—CONSTITUTION
OF NEWHAMPSHIRE. VOL. II. NO. 1. WHOLE NO. 53. WEDNESDAY, JANUARY 12,
[— NO. 7. WHOLE NO. 57. WEDNESDAY, MARCH 2, 1791.]
Printed by George Hough, at Concord, Newhampshire. 1791. fol.
Beginning March 9th, the title was changed to *Concord Herald.*

23451   HOWARD, BEZALEEL   1753 – 1837
A SERMON, DELIVERED AT THE ORDINATION OF THE REV. ALLEN PRATT, TO THE
PASTORAL CARE OF THE CHURCH IN WESTMORELAND, OCTOBER 6, 1790. BY
BEZALEEL HOWARD, A. M. PASTOR OF THE FIRST CHURCH IN SPRINGFIELD.
Keene, (New-Hampshire) Printed by James D. Griffith. [1791.] pp. 26.
8vo.
HC. JCB. MHS.

23452   HOWARD, SIMEON   1733 – 1804
A SERMON, PREACHED IN BOSTON, NOVEMBER 18, 1791; AT THE ORDINATION OF
THE REV. THOMAS ADAMS, TO THE WORK OF THE GOSPEL MINISTRY, AND PASTORAL
CARE OF A SOCIETY OF PROTESTANT CHRISTIANS, IN THE TOWN OF CAMDEN, IN
SOUTH-CAROLINA. BY SIMEON HOWARD, D. D. PASTOR OF THE WEST CHURCH IN
BOSTON.
*Printed in Boston, by Joseph Belknap and Alexander Young, north side of
the State-House, State-Street.* 1791. pp. (2), 36. 8vo.
AAS. BA. BM. BPL. HC. JCB. LOC. MHS. NYHS. NYPL.

23453   HOWELL, READING
A MAP OF THE STATE OF PENNSYLVANIA, (ONE OF THE UNITED STATES OF AMERICA.)
INCLUDING THE TRIANGLE LATELY PURCHASED OF CONGRESS AND CONTINUING THE
BOUNDARY LINES OF THE STATE, AS RUN BY THE RESPECTIVE COMMISSIONERS,
WITH PART OF LAKE ERIE, AND PRESQU' ISLE. ALSO, BY ACTUAL SURVEY, THE
RIVERS SUSQUEHANNA, ITS NORTH-EAST AND WEST BRANCHES, TIOGA, SINNAMO-
HONING, JUNIATA, LEHIGH, LECHAWAXEN, SCHUYLKILL, AND THE WESTERN RIV-
ERS OHIO, ALLEGHANEY, CONNOWANGO, PART OF THE CHATAUGHQUE LAKE AND
FRENCH CREEK, AGREEABLY TO THE LATE DISCOVERIES MONONGAHALIA, YOUGHA-
GANIA, AND KISKAMINETUS, AND THE LARGER CREEKS AND MOST OF THE LESSER
STREAMS; MOUNTAINS; THE OLD PRINCIPAL ROADS, WITH THE MANY NEW ONES IN
THE NORTHERN AND WESTERN PARTS OF THE STATE, AND THE PORTAGES AND
COMMUNICATIONS FROM THE LATE SURVEYS BY ORDER OF GOVERNMENT. THE DI-
VISION LINES OF THE RESPECTIVE COUNTIES, AND TOWNSHIPS. DELINEATION OF
THE DISTRICTS OF DEPRECIATION AND DONATION LANDS, WITH ALL THE OTHER
DISTRICTS IN THE NEW PURCHASE. THE SEATS OF JUSTICE IN THE RESPECTIVE
COUNTIES, IRON WORKS, MANUFACTORIES, MINERAL, AND OTHER NOTED PLACES.
BY READING HOWELL.
[Philadelphia: Printed for the Author. 1791.]
12th Pennsylvania District Copyright, issued to Reading Howell, as
Author, 11 January, 1791.

HOWELL, Reading, continued.

23454 —— A Map of Pennsylvania, and the parts connected therewith, relating to the roads and inland navigation, especially as proposed to be improved by the late proceedings of Assembly. Copied from his larger map. By Reading Howell. J. Trenchard, engraver.

Philadelphia: Printed for the Author, north Fifth-Street, No. 88. June 25th, 1791. 30x20.

20th Pennsylvania District Copyright, issued to Reading Howell, as Author, 13 June, 1791,

23455 THE HUDSON Weekly Gazette. Vol. vi. No. 301. Thursday, January 6, [—Vol. vii. No. 352. Thursday, December 29, 1791.]

[Hudson:] Printed by Ashbel Stoddard. 1791. fol.

Continued as *Hudson Gazette.*

23456 HUMMING bird, or collection of fashionable songs.

Philadelphia: Printed by Henry Taylor. 1791.

Advertised in the sale of Henry Taylor's estate, as "one-half finished."

23457 HUNTER, John   1728–1793
A Treatise on the venereal disease. By John Hunter.

Philadelphia: Printed and sold by Parry Hall, No. 149, in Chesnut-Street, near Fourth Street. M.DCC.XCI. pp. (10), (2), 369, (22), 6 plates. 8vo.

AAS. RIMS. SGO.

23458 HUNTINGTON, Enoch   1739–1809
A Discourse, occasioned by the death of the honourable Jabez Hamlin, esq. who departed this life April 25th. 1791, æ. 82. Delivered on the ensuing Lord's day. . . .

Middletown: Printed by M. H. Woodward. M.DCC.XCI. pp. 24. 8vo.

AAS. BPL. JCB.

23459 HUNTINGTON, Joseph   1735–1794
Thoughts on the atonement of Christ, with an address to young ministers and students in divinity: containing a vindication of the doctrines of imputed sin from Adam, and righteousness from Christ, and an examination of the new divinity on those points. By Joseph Huntington, D. D. pastor of the first church in Coventry, State of Connecticut.

Newburyport, Massachusetts. Printed and sold by John Mycall. MDCCXCI. pp. (120). 8vo.   AAS. BA. HC. JCB. NYPL.

23460 HUTCHINS, Father Abraham, pseudonym.
Father Hutchins revived; being an Almanac and ephemeris of the motions of the sun and moon; the true places and aspects of the planets; the rising and setting of the sun; and the rising, setting, and southing of the moon; for the year of our Lord 1792: being bissextile, or leap-year, and the 16th of American independence, until the 4th of July. [Six lines.] By Father Abraham Hutchins, mathematician.

New-York: Printed by Hodge, and Campbell; and sold, wholesale and retail, at their Book-stores. [1791.] pp, (36). 12mo.   LOC.

23461 HUTCHINS, John Nathan
HUTCHINS IMPROVED: BEING AN ALMANACK AND EPHEMERIS OF THE MOTIONS OF
THE SUN AND MOON; THE TRUE PLACES AND ASPECTS OF THE PLANETS; THE RIS-
ING AND SETTING OF THE SUN; AND THE RISING, SETTING AND SOUTHING OF THE
MOON, FOR THE YEAR OF OUR LORD 1792: [Seven lines.] BY JOHN NATHAN
HUTCHINS, PHILOM.
*New-York: Printed and sold by H. Gaine, at his Printing-Office, at the
Bible, in Hanover-Square. Where may be had, the New-York Pocket Almanack.*
[1791.] pp. [36.] 12mo.   LOC. NYHS. NYPL.
Contains, A True and wonderful relation of the appearance of three
angels, (cloathed in white raiment) to a young man in Medford, near
Boston, in New-England, on the 4th of February, 1761, at night: to-
gether with the substance of the Discourse, delivered by one of the angels from the 3d chapter of Colossians, and 4th verse. [Three lines from]
Joel ii, 28. By Ebenezer Adams. And, An Act making further provision for the payment of the debts of the United States.

23462 HUTCHINS, Joseph
AN ABSTRACT OF THE FIRST PRINCIPLES OF ENGLISH GRAMMAR. COMPILED FOR
THE USE OF HIS OWN SCHOOL; BY JOSEPH HUTCHINS, D. D.
Philadelphia: 1791. 24mo.   BM.

23463 IMLAY, William Eugene
OBSERVATIONS ON THE MINUTES AND CIRCULAR LETTER OF THE BAPTIST ASSOCI-
ATION: HELD AT NEW-YORK, OCTOBER 5TH, 6TH, AND 7TH, 1790. BY WILLIAM
EUGENE IMLAY.
*Philadelphia: Printed by Thomas Dobson, at the Stone-House, No. 41,
South Second-Street.* 1791.

23464 INDEPENDENT [Mass. arms] CHRONICLE: AND THE UNIVERSAL ADVERTISER,
VOL. XXIII. NUMBER 1158. THURSDAY, JANUARY 6, [—No. 1209. THURSDAY.
DECEMBER 29, 1791.]
*Boston: Printed and published by Thomas Adams, Printer to the honorable
the General Court of the Commonwealth of Massachusetts, at his Printing-Office,
opposite the Court-House, Court-Street.* 1791. fol.   AAS. MHS.

23465 THE INDEPENDENT GAZETTEER, AND AGRICULTURAL REPOSITORY. [Mottoes.]
NUMBER 1321. SATURDAY, JANUARY 1, [—NUMBER 1373. SATURDAY, DECEMBER
31, 1791.]
*Philadelphia: Printed by Eleazer Oswald, in Market-Street, between Fourth
and Fifth-Streets* . . . 1791. fol.   AAS.

23466 INNES, Thomas   1662–1744
A CATECHISM, OR THE PRINCIPLES OF THE CHRISTIAN RELIGION, EXPLAINED IN A
FAMILIAR AND EASY MANNER, ADAPTED TO THE LOWEST CAPACITIES. BY THE
LATE BISHOP INNES, BUCHIN DIOCESE, ABERDEEN.
Edinburgh Printed. New-Haven: Re-printed by T. & S. Green. 1791. pp.
59. 8vo.
The commendatory preface is signed, Samuel, Bp. Connect.

23467 ISRAEL, Frederick
FEAR GOD. THE MOST FREE AND SINCERE INVESTIGATOR OF TRUTHS; OR, DEVOUT
AND CHEERFUL INQUIRER AFTER ETERNAL LIFE, AND "THE THINGS ACCOMPANY-
ING SALVATION." (IN THE TRUE SPIRIT AND GLORIOUS LIBERTY OF THE GOSPEL.)
—MOTTO.—[Seven lines.] BY FREDERICK ISRAEL, F. R. S. . . . [Signed, Fady
A. B. C?]
[New-York: 1st. November, 1791.] pp. (9). fol.   NYHS.
Curious proposals to print a paper, answering to the above title, three
times a week. All contributions to which, including the editor's, were
to be placed in a wheel, and drawn out, in the manner of a lottery,
sufficient for each number.

23468 JARRATT, Devereux 1733 – 1801
Thoughts on some important subjects in divinity; in a series of letters to a friend. By the rev. Devereux Jarratt, rector of Bath parish, in Dinwiddie County, Virginia.

Richmond: 1791.

Preface dated, Bath, Sept. 3, 1791. Reprinted in Baltimore in 1806.

23469 JENKINS, John – 1823
The Art of writing reduced to a plain and easy system. On a plan entirely new. In seven books. By John Jenkins, writing-master. Book I. Containing a plain, easy and familiar introduction to the art. [Three lines from] Moore. (Published according to Act of Congress).

Printed at Boston, by Isaiah Thomas and Ebenezer T. Andrews, at Faust's Statue, No. 45, Newbury Street. MDCCXCI. pp. 32, 3 plates. 8vo. aas. ba. jcb.

Massachusetts District Copyright, issued to John Jenkins, as Author, 24 December, 1790.

23470 JENYNS, Soame 1704 – 1787
Lectures, delivered by Soame Jenyns, esq. author of A View of the internal evidence of the Christian religion, to a select company of friends. Dedicated to Edward Gibbon, esq. [Ornament.]

New-York: Printed and sold by Samuel Loudon, No. 5, Water-Street, and sold by Berry and Rogers, No. 35, Hanover-Square. M,DCC,XCI. pp. (2), (2), xxvi, 203. 12mo. aas. jcb. nypl.

With a Memoir of his life and writings.

23471 —— A View of the internal evidence of the Christian religion. By Soame Jenyns, esquire.

Stockbridge (Massachusetts) Printed by Loring Andrews. 1791.

23472 JOCELYN, Simeon
The Choristers companion; containing, besides the necessary rules of psalmody, a choice and valuable collection of psalm-tunes, hymns and anthems, from the most celebrated ancient and modern authors. The second edition, corrected and enlarged.

New-Haven: Printed by T. & S. Green. 1791. pp. — 72. obl. 8vo.

The additional music, 72 pages, was also published separately.

23473 JOHNSON, Samuel 1709 – 1784
The Prince of Abissinia. A tale. By Samuel Johnson, ll. d. The two volumes complete in one. Volume the first.

Philadelphia: Printed by Francis Bailey, No. 116, Market-Street, and T. Lang, No. 21, Church-Alley. MDCCXCI. pp. 191; (2), 200. 16mo. aas.

Second title: Dinarbas; a tale: being a continuation of Rasselas, prince of Abissinia. [By Ellis Cornelia Knight.] [Seven lines from] Horace.

Philadelphia: Printed by F. Bailey, No. 116, Market-Street, and T. Lang, No. 21, Church-Alley. 1792. pp. (2), 200.

23474   JOHONNET, JACKSON
THE REMARKABLE ADVENTURES OF JACKSON JOHONNET OF MASSACHUSETTS. WHO
SERVED AS A SOLDIER IN THE WESTERN ARMY, IN THE MASSACHUSETTS LINE, IN
THE EXPEDITION UNDER GENERAL HARMAR, AND THE UNFORTUNATE GENERAL
ST. CLAIR. CONTAINING AN ACCOUNT OF HIS CAPTIVITY, SUFFERINGS, AND ESCAPE
FROM THE KICKAPOO INDIANS. WRITTEN BY HIMSELF, AND PUBLISHED AT THE
EARNEST IMPORTUNITY OF HIS FRIENDS, FOR THE BENEFIT OF AMERICAN YOUTH.

     Printed at Lexington, (Kentucky) by John Bradford.   1791.

23475   JONES, WILLIAM
THE WONDERFUL AND SURPRISING RESURRECTION OF WILLIAM JONES, WHO WAS
EXECUTED THE 6TH OF MAY, AT NEWARK, FOR THE MURDER OF SAMUEL SHOT-
WELL. IN A LETTER FROM HIM TO E - - - W - - -, IN NEW - YORK, DATED
M - - - T - - - -, MAY 13, 1791. [Twenty-seven lines.] WILLIAM JONES.

     [Newark: Printed by John Woods, 1791.]   Broadside. fol.   NYHS.

23476   JUDD, EBEN W.
THE UNITED STATES ALMANAC, FOR THE YEAR OF OUR LORD 1792: BEING BISSEX-
TILE OR LEAP YEAR. AND THE XVITH OF AMERICAN INDEPENDENCE, 'TILL 4TH
JULY. CONTAINING EVERY THING THAT IS USEFUL OR NECESSARY IN AN ALMANAC.
ALSO, A VARIETY OF ENTERTAINING MATTER IN PROSE AND VERSE. BY EBEN W.
JUDD, MATHEMATICIAN.

     Elizabeth Town: Printed by Shepard Kollock.   [1791.] pp. (36). 12mo.
                                                LOC.

23477   JUNIUS, pseudonym.
THE LETTERS OF JUNIUS. COMPLETE IN ONE VOLUME, WITH A COPIOUS INDEX. THE
FIRST AMERICAN EDITION. STAT NOMINIS UMBRA.

     *Philadelphia: Printed and sold by Prichard & Hall, in Market Street be-
tween Front and Second Streets.* M,DCC,XCI. pp. (2), (2), 283, (13). 12mo.
                                         AAS. LOC.

23478   —— — THE LETTERS OF JUNIUS. TOGETHER WITH NOTES, AND AN ADDRESS,
WRITTEN BY HIMSELF, TO THE BRITISH NATION.

     Philadelphia: From the Press of M. Carey, 1791. 12mo.

23479   JUVENILE CORRESPONDENCE; OR, LETTERS SUITED TO CHILDREN FROM FOUR TO
ABOVE TEN YEARS OF AGE, IN THREE SETS.

     New-Haven: Printed by Abel Morse. 1791. pp. 106. 18mo.

23480   KEMPIS, THOMAS (HÄMMERLEIN *Latin* MALLEOLUS) Á   1380–1471
OF THE IMITATION OF CHRIST: IN THREE BOOKS. TRANSLATED FROM THE LATIN
OF THOMAS A KEMPIS. BY JOHN PAYNE.

     *Philadelphia: Printed by Joseph Crukshank (?) and sold by John Dickins,
No. 182 Race-Street, near Sixth-Street.* 1791.

23481   THE KENTUCKY GAZETTE. VOL. IV. NUMB. XIX. SATURDAY, JANUARY 1, [--
VOL. XV. NUMB. XIX. SATURDAY, DECEMBER 31, 1791.]

     *Lexington: Printed by John Bradford, at his Printing-Office in Main
Street.* 1791. 4to.

AUCTION
VALUES

23482   KNOXVILLE Gazette. Vol. I. No. 1. Saturday, November 5, [— No. 5. Saturday, December 31, 1791.]

> *Rogersville, Hawkins County, Tennessee: Printed by George Roulstone.* 1791. fol.

Established by George Roulstone, formerly of Salem, Massachusetts, and Fayetteville, North Carolina, at Hawkins Court House, Rogersville, Tennessee. In November, 1792, he removed his press permanently to Knoxville, when the site was laid out for the capital city of the eastern part of the State, and continued publication there into 1797, when it was suspended. In March, 1799, George Wilson issued proposals, in the Winchester Gazette, for publishing a newspaper, in Knoxville, to be called The Observer. Although no numbers are known to be extant, it is probable that, in June, or July, he began the publication, in Knoxville, of the Impartial Observer. This incited Roulstone to revive the Knoxville Gazette, and No. 1 appeared 3d July, 1799. The futility of publishing two newspapers in Knoxville, at this time, soon led their respective publishers to merge their interests, and on 28 August, 1799, appeared No. 1 of the *Impartial The Knoxville Gazette Observer*, Published by Roulstone and Wilson. The words "The Knoxville Gazette" appearing within an arc of rays in the centre, and above the motto: "Liberty the object, Truth the guide." In November, 1800, the partnership was dissolved, George Wilson removing to Jonesborough, Tennessee, where he established in November, 1801, the Washington Newspaper and Advertiser; and Roulstone continuing publication of the Gazette until his death in 1804, when it was continued by his widow, Elizabeth Roulstone, who also succeeded him as Printer to the State. Upon the death of his former partner, George Wilson returned to Knoxville, and, in 1804, began the publication of Wilson's Gazette, which was merged into the *Knoxville Gazette* later in the year, and the latter continued by Wilson, until he removed to Nashville in 1818.

23483   KURZGEFASSTES Arzney-Büchlein für Menschen und Vieh. Darinnen 128 auserlesene Recepte nebst einer prognostischen Tafel.

> *In Wien gedruckt. In Ephrata nach-gedruckt*, 1791. pp. 24. 12mo.

23484   LADY'S Almanack for the year 1792: calculated for the meridian of Portsmouth, N. H. but serves for all the New-England States. Containing besides everything necessary for a work of the kind, a variety of entertainment. [Cut.]

> *[Portsmouth:] Printed [by John Melcher] for, and sold by the shopkeepers in the town and country.* [1791.] pp. [24.] 12mo.   NYHS.

23485   THE LADY'S astronomical diary, or Almanack, for the year of our Lord, [ornamental border around] 1792: being bissextile or leap-year. Fitted to the meridian of Exeter, Newhampshire. By a young lady of Exeter.

> *Printed at Exeter, by Henry Ranlet, and sold at his Office, wholesale and retail.* ☞ *A good chance to town and country shopkeepers who purchase by the quantity.* [1791.] pp. (24). 12mo.   AAS.

23486 LANGDON, Samuel   1723–1797
OBSERVATIONS ON THE REVELATION OF JESUS CHRIST TO ST. JOHN. WHICH COM-
PREHEND THE MOST APPROVED SENTIMENTS OF THE CELEBRATED MR. MEDE,
MR. LOWMAN, BISHOP NEWTON AND OTHER NOTED WRITERS ON THIS BOOK; AND
CAST MUCH ADDITIONAL LIGHT ON THE MORE OBSCURE PROPHESIES; ESPECIALLY
THOSE WHICH POINT OUT THE TIME OF THE RISE AND FALL OF ANTICHRIST. IN
TWO PARTS. CONTAINING PART 1: GENERAL OBSERVATION ON PROPHECY. THE
FORM, ORDER AND STYLE OF THE REVELATION. THE MONITORY VIEW. PART 2.
THE PROPHETIC VISIONS; WHICH ARE DISTINGUISHED INTO FIVE PROPHECIES, EACH
OF WHICH IS SUBDIVIDED INTO SEVERAL SCENES. BY SAMUEL LANGDON, D. D.
MINISTER OF HAMPTONFALLS, IN THE STATE OF NEWHAMPSHIRE. [Three lines
from] REV. CHAP. 1, VERSE 3.

Printed at Worcester, Massachusetts, by Isaiah Thomas. MDCCXCI. pp.
337. 8vo.   AAS. BA. BM. JCB. NYHS.

1st New Hampshire District Copyright, issued to Samuel Langdon, as
Author, 15 July, 1791.

23487 LANGWORTHY, Edward
A POLITICAL HISTORY OF THE STATE OF GEORGIA, FROM ITS FIRST SETTLEMENT;
WITH MEMOIRS OF THE PRINCIPAL TRANSACTIONS WHICH HAPPENED THEREIN DUR-
ING THE LATE REVOLUTION. BY EDWARD LANGWORTHY, ESQ. [Two lines from]
SHAKESPEARE.

Proposals for printing the above appeared in The Georgia Gazette, of
May 12, 1791, as to be published in two volumes "as soon as there are
subscriptions sufficient to defray the expenses of the same." The
work does not appear to have been published; but the particularity of
title would seem to indicate something more than a prospective stage
for publication, and awakens the hope that the work may still exist in
manuscript.

23488 LATHROP, Joseph   1731–1820
CHRIST'S WARNING TO THE CHURCHES, TO BEWARE OF FALSE PROPHETS, WHO COME
AS WOLVES IN SHEEP'S CLOTHING; AND THE MARKS BY WHICH THEY ARE KNOWN:
ILLUSTRATED IN TWO DISCOURSES. BY JOSEPH LATHROP, A. M. PASTOR OF A
CHURCH IN WEST-SPRINGFIELD. [Three lines from] APOSTLE PETER. SECOND
SPRINGFIELD EDITION, WITH AN APPENDIX AND OTHER ENLARGEMENTS.

Springfield: Printed by Ezra Waldo Webb. M.DCC.XCI. pp. 54. 8vo.
      AAS. BA. JCB. LOC. MHS. NYHS. NYPL.

The twelfth edition, with Memoir, was published in Boston, in 1823.

23489 LATHROP, Samuel   –1846
AN ORATION ON THE DEATH OF SAMUEL WALES, JUN'R. A MEMBER OF YALE-COL-
LEGE, (SON OF THE REV. SAMUEL WALES, D. D. PROFESSOR OF DIVINITY IN SAID
COLLEGE,) WHO DIED NOVEMBER 20TH, 1790, AETAT. 17. BY SAMUEL LATHROP.
[Six lines from] THOMPSON'S [sic] SEASONS.

New-Haven: Printed by A. Morse; M.DCC.XCI. pp. 21. 12mo.   AAS.

23490   LAUS DEO! THE WORCESTER COLLECTION OF SACRED HARMONY. FIRST AND
SECOND PARTS. CONTAINING, I. AN INTRODUCTION TO THE GROUNDS OF MUSICK;
OR, RULES FOR LEARNERS. II. A LARGE NUMBER OF CELEBRATED PSALM AND
HYMN TUNES, FROM THE MOST APPROVED AUTHORS. SUITED TO ALL METRES USU-
ALLY SUNG IN CHURCHES. TO WHICH IS NOW ADDED, AN APPENDIX, CONTAINING
A NUMBER OF EXCELLENT PSALM TUNES, (SEVERAL OF WHICH ARE ENTIRELY NEW)
AND OTHER PIECES OF SACRED VOCAL MUSICK, MANY OF WHICH WERE COMPOSED
BY EMINENT EUROPEAN AUTHORS, AND NEVER BEFORE PUBLISHED IN THIS COUN-
TRY. THE WHOLE COMPILED FOR THE USE OF SCHOOLS AND SINGING SOCIETIES
[One line from] PSALM CXLVII. THE THIRD EDITION, WITH LARGE ADDITIONS.

Printed, typographically, at Boston, by Isaiah Thomas and Ebenezer T. An-
drews, sold by them at Faust's Statue, No. 45, Newbury Street; and by said Thomas
in Worcester. Sold also by the Booksellers in town and country. MDCCXCI. pp.
(4), 143, (1). obl. 12mo.   AAS.

In the signed preface, Isaiah Thomas speaks of himself as the compiler
and editor. 20th Massachusetts District Copyright, issued to Isaiah
Thomas, as Proprietor, 29 July, 1791.

23491   LAW, ANDREW   1748 – 1821
THE RUDIMENTS OF MUSIC; OR A SHORT AND EASY TREATISE ON THE RULES OF PSALM-
ODY; TO WHICH ARE ANNEXED A NUMBER OF PLAIN TUNES AND CHARTS. THE
THIRD EDITION,

[Cheshire, Connecticut: Printed by William Law, 1791.]
Connecticut District Copyright, issued to Andrew Law, as Author, 18
October, 1791.

23492   —— SELECT HARMONY; CONTAINING IN A PLAIN AND CONCISE MANNER, THE RULES
OF SINGING; TOGETHER WITH A COLLECTION OF PSALM TUNES, HYMNS AND
ANTHEMS.

[Cheshire, Connecticut: Printed by William Law, 1791.]
Connecticut District Copyright, issued to Andrew Law, 18 October,
1791.

23493   LAW, WILLIAM   1686 – 1761
THE TRUE GROUNDS OF THE BENEFITS OF JESUS CHRIST, AS HE IS THE SAVIOUR OF
ALL MANKIND. BY WILLIAM LAW, M. A.

Charleston: Printed by Markland & M'Iver, No. 47, Bay. MDCCXCI.
pp. 71, (1). 8vo.   AAS.

23494   LELAND, JOHN   1754 – 1841
MR. LELAND'S CIRCULAR LETTER OF VALEDICTION.

Fredericksburg: Printed by Timothy Green. 1791.

23495   —— THE RIGHTS OF CONSCIENCE INALIENABLE; AND THEREFORE RELIGIOUS OPIN-
IONS NOT COGNIZABLE BY LAW: OR, THE HIGH-FLYING CHURCH-MAN STRIPT OF HIS
LEGAL ROBE, APPEARS A YAHO. BY JOHN LELAND. I KNOW NOT TO GIVE FLAT-
TERING TITLES TO MAN. ELIHU.

New-London: Printed by T. Green & Son. M,DCC,XCI. pp. (29), (1).
8vo.   BA. LOC. NYHS.

"The Author of the foregoing pages has a manuscript by him, ready
for the press, entitled, The First rise of sin; neither from a holy nor
sinful cause: unavoidable with God, but avoidable with creatures exhibited in an exposition of the three first chapters of Genesis; in which
a number of conjectures and mathematical calculations are given."
Page 30.

23496   LELAND, JOSEPH
THE FARMER'S DIARY: OR THE UNITED STATES ALMANACK, FOR THE YEAR OF OUR
LORD CHRIST, 1792. . . .   BY JOSEPH LELAND, PHILOM.
Danbury: Printed by Nathan Douglas and Edwards Ely. [1791.]

23497   LE SAGE, ALAIN RENÉ   1668 – 1747
LE DIABLE BOITEUX; OR, THE DEVIL UPON TWO STICKS. TRANSLATED FROM THE
FRENCH OF MONSIEUR LE SAGE, AUTHOR OF THE ADVENTURES OF GIL BLAS. IN
TWO VOLUMES.
Philadelphia: Printed by Henry Taylor, for Robert Campbell. 1791. 2 vols.

23498   —— — LE DIABLE BOITEUX: OR, THE DEVIL UPON TWO STICKS. TRANSLATED
FROM THE FRENCH OF MONSIEUR LE SAGE, AUTHOR OF THE ADVENTURES OF
GIL BLAS. IN TWO VOLUMES.
*Philadelphia: Printed and sold by W. Woodhouse, at the Bible, No. 6,
South-Front-Street.* 1791. 2 vols.

23499   —— THE HISTORY AND ADVENTURES OF GIL BLAS DE SANTILLANE. FROM THE
FRENCH OF M. LE SAGE.
*Philadelphia: Printed and sold by W. Woodhouse, at the Bible, No. 6,
South Front-Street.* 1791.

23500   A LETTER FROM AN EMINENT MINISTER OF THE CHURCH OF SCOTLAND: WRITTEN TO
A MINISTER OF HIS ACQUAINTANCE, AT SOME DISTANCE, IN THE SAME KINGDOM:
GIVING AN ACCOUNT OF HIS CONVERSION AND WONDERFUL CHANGE IN HIS PREACH-
ING, AFTER HE HAD BEEN OF SOME YEARS STANDING IN THE MINISTRY. [Four
lines of Scripture texts.]
Reprinted at Exeter: by Henry Ranlet, 1791. pp. 23. 12mo.   AAS. JCB.

23501   A LETTER FROM MISS S——A TO MRS. R——, WHO, ON HER WAY TO BATH, VISITED
SAINT ROZO VILLOZO! THE MOST CELEBRATED PERSONAGE IN THIS PART OF THE
COUNTRY, AND NOW RESIDING NEAR SHARPSBURG.
Virginia: Shepherd's-Town: Printed by N. Willis. [1791.] pp. 15. 16mo.

23502   A LETTER WRITTEN BY AN UNIVERSALIST TO HIS FRIEND, WITH HIS FRIEND'S AN-
SWER IN OPPOSITION.
Providence: Printed by Bennett Wheeler. 1791.

23503   LEWIS, WILLIAM   1714 – 1781
THE EDINBURGH NEW DISPENSATORY: CONTAINING I. THE ELEMENTS OF PHARMA-
CEUTICAL CHEMISTRY. II. THE MATERIA MEDICA; OR, AN ACCOUNT OF THE NATU-
RAL HISTORY, QUALITIES, OPERATIONS AND USES, OF THE DIFFERENT SUBSTANCES
EMPLOYED IN MEDICINE. III. THE PHARMACEUTICAL PREPARATIONS AND MEDIC-
INAL COMPOSITIONS OF THE NEW EDITIONS OF THE LONDON (1788) AND EDIN-
BURGH (1783) PHARMACOPOEIAS; WITH EXPLANATORY, CRITICAL, AND PRACTICAL
OBSERVATIONS ON EACH: TOGETHER WITH THE ADDITION OF THOSE FORMULAE,
FROM THE BEST FOREIGN PHARMACOPOEIAS, WHICH ARE HELD IN HIGHEST ESTEEM
IN OTHER PARTS OF EUROPE. THE WHOLE INTERSPERSED WITH PRACTICAL CAU-
TIONS AND OBSERVATIONS, AND ENRICHED BY THE LATEST DISCOVERIES IN NATU-
RAL HISTORY, CHEMISTRY, AND MEDICINE; WITH NEW TABLES OF ELECTIVE AT-
TRACTIONS, OF ANTIMONY, OF MERCURY, &C. AND COPPERPLATES OF THE MOST
CONVENIENT FURNACES, AND PRINCIPAL PHARMACEUTICAL INSTRUMENTS. BEING
AN IMPROVEMENT UPON THE NEW DISPENSATORY OF DR. LEWIS. A NEW EDI-
TION; WITH MANY ALTERATIONS, CORRECTIONS, AND ADDITIONS. [By Andrew
Duncan, junior.]
*Philadelphia: Printed by T. Dobson, at the Stone-House, No. 41, in Sec-
ond-Street.* M,DCC,XCI. 8vo.   AAS.

23504   LINN, WILLIAM   1752 – 1808
THE BLESSINGS OF AMERICA. A SERMON, PREACHED IN THE MIDDLE DUTCH CHURCH, ON THE FOURTH JULY, 1791, BEING THE ANNIVERSARY OF THE INDEPENDENCE OF AMERICA: AT THE REQUEST OF THE TAMMANY SOCIETY, OR COLUMBIAN ORDER. BY WILLIAM LINN, D. D.
New-York—Printed by Thomas Greenleaf.—M,DCC,XCI, pp. [39.] 8vo.
               AAS. BA. BM. JCB. LOC. MHS. NYHS. NYPL.
Contains, An Ode, composed for the occasion, at the request of the Society. By Dr. William Pitt Smith. Set to music by Mr. Van Hagen. pp. [37]—[39.] 3d New York District Copyright, issued to Thomas Greenleaf, as Proprietor, 13 July, 1791.

23505   —— SERMONS HISTORICAL AND CHARACTERISTICAL. BY WILLIAM LINN, D. D. ONE OF THE MINISTERS OF THE REFORMED DUTCH CHURCH IN THE CITY OF NEW-YORK.
New-York. Printed by Childs and Swaine. (With the privilege of Copy right). [1791.] pp. xxiii, 360. 12mo.   AAS. BA. BM. JCB. NYHS. PHS.
Contains a long list of subscribers. 2nd New York District Copyright, issued to William Linn, as Author, 1 June, 1791.

23506   LOGAN, GEORGE   1753–1821
FOURTEEN EXPERIMENTS ON AGRICULTURE, (AGREEABLY TO THE ENGLISH MODE OF FARMING) THE RESULT OF SEVEN YEARS CLOSE AND ATTENTIVE OBSERVATION. BY GEORGE LOGAN, OF PHILADELPHIA COUNTY.
Philadelphia: Printed and sold by Eleazer Oswald, 1791.

23507   —— LETTERS ADDRESSED TO THE YEOMANRY OF THE UNITED STATES: SHEWING THE NECESSITY OF CONFINING THE PUBLIC REVENUE TO A FIXED PROPORTION OF THE NET PRODUCE OF THE LAND; AND THE BAD POLICY AND INJUSTICE OF EVERY SPECIES OF INDIRECT TAXATION AND COMMERCIAL REGULATIONS. BY A FARMER.
Philadelphia: Printed by Eleazer Oswald, in Market-Street, No. 156, between Fourth and Fifth-Streets. M,DCC,XCI. pp. [47.] 8vo.   AAS. JCB. LOC.

23508   LOVE, CHRISTOPHER   1618–1651
THE PROPHECIES OF THE REVEREND CHRISTOPHER LOVE, AND HIS LAST WORDS ON THE SCAFFOLD: WHO WAS BEHEADED ON TOWER-HILL, LONDON, ON THE 22D DAY OF AUGUST, 1651.
Norwich: Printed and sold by John Trumbull, 1791.

23509   —— — THE STRANGE AND WONDERFUL PREDICTIONS OF MR. CHRISTOPHER LOVE, MINISTER OF THE GOSPEL AT LAWRENCE-JURY, LONDON, WHO WAS BEHEADED ON TOWER-HILL, ON THE ACCOUNT OF HIS RELIGION. LIKEWISE AN ACCOUNT OF GREAT WARS IN AMERICA IN 1780, WITH THE DESTRUCTION OF POPERY IN THE YEAR 1790: AND IN THE YEAR 1795, RELIGION SHALL FLOURISH OVER ALL THE KING'S DOMAINS. TO WHICH ARE ADDED, TWO LETTERS FROM HIS WIFE, A LITTLE BEFORE HIS DEATH, WITH HIS ANSWER TO HER AGAIN.
Carlisle: Printed by George Kline, 1791.

23510   LOVELASS, PETER
A FULL, CLEAR, AND FAMILIAR EXPLANATION OF THE LAW CONCERNING BILLS OF EXCHANGE, PROMISSORY NOTES. AND THE EVIDENCE ON A TRIAL BY JURY RELATIVE THERETO; WITH A DESCRIPTION OF BANK NOTES, AND THE PRIVILEGE OF ATTORNIES. BY PETER LOVELASS, OF THE INNER TEMPLE, GENT. AUTHOR OF THE LAW'S DISPOSAL. THE THIRD EDITION.
Philadelphia: Printed by Joseph Crukshank, No. 91, High-Street, between Second and Third-Streets. MDCCXCI. pp. x, (135). 8vo.   LOC.
Unpaged. The marginal references giving the pages of the Third English edition, of which it is a reprint.

23511   LOW, NATHANAEL   1740 - 1808
          AN ASTRONOMICAL DIARY: OR ALMANACK FOR THE CHRISTIAN ÆRA 1792. [Fourteen
          lines.] BY NATHANAEL LOW. [Eight lines of verse.]
               Printed and sold by T. & J. Fleet, in Boston. [The only proprietors of Dr.
          Low's Copy right.] Where may be had their Pocket Almanack and Register, for
          1792. [1791.] pp. [24.] 12mo.   AAS. LOC. MHS. NYPL.
               Dr. Low's address to the reader states that this is his thirtieth Almanack
          published. 19th Massachusetts District Copyright, issued to Thomas
          and John Fleet, as Proprietors, 19 November, 1791.

23512   ——— WAIT'S YORK, CUMBERLAND AND LINCOLN ALMANACK FOR THE YEAR OF OUR
          LORD 1792: CALCULATED FOR THE MERIDIAN OF PORTLAND, BUT WILL ANSWER
          FOR ANY OF THE NORTHERN STATES.
               Portland: Printed and sold by Thomas B. Wait. [1791.]
               "It will contain half as much again as any of those published in Boston."

23513   LOWELL, JOHN   1743–1802
          AN EULOGY, ON THE HONOURABLE JAMES BOWDOIN, ESQ. L.L. D. LATE PRESIDENT
          OF THE AMERICAN ACADEMY OF ARTS AND SCIENCES. WHO DIED AT BOSTON,
          NOVEMBER 6, A. D. 1790. DELIVERED BEFORE THE SOCIETY, JANUARY 26, 1791,
          BY JOHN LOWELL, ONE OF THE COUNSELLORS OF THE ACADEMY. [Cut.]
               Printed at Boston, by Isaiah Thomas and Ebenezer T. Andrews, at Faust's
          Statue, No. 45, Newbury Street. MDCCXCI. pp. 24. 4to.
                                               AAS. BA. JCB. LOC. MHS. NYHS. NYPL.
               Reprinted with the second volume of the Memoirs of the American
          Academy of Arts and Sciences, in 1793.

23514   LUTHER, MARTIN   1483 – 1546
          DER KLEINE CATECHISMUS DES SEL D. MARTIN LUTHER, U. S. W.
               Philadelphia: Gedruckt bey Carl Cist, 1791. pp. 128. 16mo.

23515   LYMAN, JOSEPH   1749 – 1828
          LOVE TO CHRIST A LEADING QUALIFICATION OF HIS MINISTERS. A SERMON, PREACHED
          AT THE INTRODUCTION OF THE REVEREND WILLIAM GRAVES, TO THE WORK OF
          THE GOSPEL MINISTRY, IN . . . NORTH-WOODSTOCK, AUGUST 31, 1791.
               Northampton: Printed by William Butler. 1791. pp. 26. 8vo.
                                               AAS. BA. BM. CHS. HC. JCB. UTS.

23516   LYON, JAMES   1735–1801
          THE SAINT'S DAILY ASSISTANT; OR, MEDITATIONS FOR MORNING AND EVENING, FOR
          EVERY DAY IN THE YEAR; EACH FOUNDED ON A PARTICULAR TEXT OF SCRIPTURE.
          ADAPTED TO THE DEVOTIONS OF THE FAMILY AND CLOSET. IN TWELVE NUMBERS.
          BY JAMES LYON, A. M. PASTOR OF THE CHURCH AT MACHIAS. NUMBER 1. [One
          line from] JOHN XXI, 25.
               Newburyport: Printed by John Mycall, for the Author, who has secured
          copyright. [1791.] pp. [131.] 12mo.   AAS. JCB. PPL.
               Number II. was printed in Boston, in 1793. These two numbers were
          all that were published.

23517   MACAULAY, CATHARINE SAWBRIDGE, afterwards GRAHAM   1733–1791
          OBSERVATIONS ON THE REFLECTIONS OF THE RIGHT HON. EDMUND BURKE, ON THE
          REVOLUTION IN FRANCE, IN A LETTER TO THE RIGHT HON. THE EARL OF STANHOPE.
               Printed at Boston, by I. Thomas and E. T. Andrews. Faust's Statue, No.
          45, Newburystreet. MDCCXCI. pp. 39. 8vo.   AAS. BA. BU. LOC. MHS. NYPL.

23518   MAC CLINTOCK, SAMUEL   1732–1804
A DISCOURSE OF SUBMISSION TO THE DIVINE WILL UNDER AFFLICTION, DELIVERED
BY SAMUEL MCCLINTOCK, A. M. MINISTER OF THE GOSPEL AT GREENLAND, AT
THE FUNERAL OF REV. ALPHEUS SPRING, OF KITTERY: WHO DIED JUNE 14TH,
1791, IN THE 52ND YEAR OF HIS AGE: MUCH LAMENTED, AS A GREAT LOSS TO THE
CHURCH OF GOD AND TO THE PUBLIC AS WELL AS TO HIS FAMILY AND PARTICULAR
ACQUAINTANCES.

       Dover, (New Hampshire). Printed by Eliphalet Ladd. M,DCC,XCI. pp.
24. 8vo.
                                           BM. JCB.

23519   —— AN EPISTOLARY CORRESPONDENCE BETWEEN THE REV. JOHN C. OGDEN, REC-
TOR OF ST. JOHN'S CHURCH, AT PORTSMOUTH, NEW-HAMPSHIRE; AND THE REV.
SAMUEL MACCLINTOCK, MINISTER OF THE CONGREGATIONAL SOCIETY IN GREEN-
LAND, ON A VARIETY OF SUBJECTS; PRINCIPALLY THE HIGH POWERS AND PREROG-
ATIVES CLAIMED BY DIOCESAN BISHOPS AS SUCCESSORS TO THE APOSTLES.

       Portsmouth: Printed and sold by J. Melcher, at his Office in Market-Street.
M,DCC,XCI. pp. (38). 8vo.
                             AAS. BA. HC. JCB. NYHS.

23520   M' CORMICK, JAMES
THE WESTERN ALMANAC, FOR THE YEAR OF OUR LORD 1792. BEING BISSEXTILE,
OR LEAP YEAR. ADAPTED TO THE LATITUDE AND MERIDIAN OF CARLISLE. CON-
TAINING, BESIDES THE USUAL ASTRONOMICAL CALCULATIONS, &C. THE FOLLOWING
PIECES, IN PROSE AND VERSE: . . . . THE ASTRONOMICAL CALCULATIONS BY
JAMES M'CORMICK, TEACHER OF MATHEMATICKS IN DICKINSON COLLEGE, CARLISLE.

       Carlisle: Printed by George Kline. [1791.]

23521   M'DONALD, ALEXANDER
THE YOUTH'S ASSISTANT, BEING A PLAIN, EASY AND COMPREHENSIVE GUIDE TO PRAC-
TICAL ARITHMETIC. CONTAINING ALL THE RULES AND EXAMPLES NECESSARY FOR
SUCH A WORK, VIZ. NUMERATION, SIMPLE ADDITION, SUBTRACTION, MULTIPLICA-
TION, AND DIVISION—DIVISION OF WEIGHTS AND MEASURES—REDUCTION OF SEV-
ERAL DENOMINATIONS—THE SINGLE AND DOUBLE RULE OF THREE—TARE AND
TRETT—PRACTICE—SIMPLE INTEREST—ASSURANCE—BROKAGE—COMMISSION—
DISCOUNT—EQUATION OF PAYMENTS—BARTER—LOSS AND GAIN—SINGLE AND DOU-
BLE FELLOWSHIPS—REDUCTION, ADDITION, SUBTRACTION, MULTIPLICATION AND
DIVISION OF VULGAR FRACTIONS—NOTATION, ADDITION, SUBTRACTION, MULTIPLI-
CATION, DIVISION AND REDUCTION OF DECIMAL FRACTIONS—THE RULE OF THREE
—SIMPLE AND COMPOUND INTEREST IN DECIMAL FRACTIONS. BY ALEXANDER
M'DONALD.

       *Providence: Printed by Bennett Wheeler. Sold by Robert Adam, at the head
of the Long-wharff west side the river, Providence.* 1791.

       Rhode Island District Copyright, issued to Robert Adam, as Propri-
etor, 14 April, 1791. In November, Adam disposed of the Copyright
rights in the State of New York to Thomas Greenleaf, but no edition
with a New York imprint is known.

23522   MACGOWAN, JOHN   1726 - 1780
THE LIFE OF JOSEPH, THE SON OF ISRAEL. IN EIGHT BOOKS. CHIEFLY DESIGNED TO
ALLURE YOUNG MINDS TO A LOVE OF THE SACRED SCRIPTURES. BY JOHN MAC-
GOWAN.

       Carlisle: Printed by George Kline, 1791.

23523   —— — THE LIFE OF JOSEPH, THE SON OF ISRAEL: IN EIGHT BOOKS. CHIEFLY
DESIGNED TO ALLURE YOUNG MINDS TO A LOVE OF THE SACRED SCRIPTURES. BY
JOHN MACGOWAN.

       Elizabeth-Town: Printed and sold by Shepard Kollock. 1791.

MACGOWAN, JOHN, continued.

23524 —— —— The Life of Joseph, the son of Israel, in eight books. Chiefly designed to allure young minds to the love of the sacred scriptures. By John Macgowan.
Hartford: Printed by Elisha Babcock, 1791.

23525 —— —— The Life of Joseph, the son of Israel. In eight books. Chiefly designed to allure young minds to a love of the sacred scriptures: By John Macgowan.
Philadelphia: Printed by Thomas Dobson, at the Stone-House, No. 41, Second-Street. 1791.
To the public. Signed, William Rogers, D. D. Philadelphia, Jan. 1, 1791.

23526 —— Priestcraft defended. A sermon occasioned by the expulsion of six young gentlemen from the University of Oxford. For praying, reading and expounding the Scriptures. Humbly dedicated to mr. V—— C——r and the H——ds of H——s. By their humble servant, the Shaver. Supposed to be written by the late Dr. Franklin. . . . The nineteenth edition.
Litchfield: Re-printed by Thomas Collier. [1791.] pp. 30. 16mo.
This is the second instance this year in which the publisher has wrongly made use of the name and fame of Benjamin Franklin to bolster up the sale of pseudonymous works. See Robert Dodsley, passim.

23527 **MACKENZIE, HENRY**   1745 – 1831
The Man of Feeling. A new edition.
Philadelphia: Printed and sold by H. Taylor. M.DCC.XCI. pp. 219.
16mo.   AAS. JCB.

23528 —— —— The Man of Feeling. The third edition.
Litchfield: Re-printed by Thomas Collier, in the Court-House. [1791.] pp. 210. 12mo.   AAS.

23529 **MACPHERSON, JOHN**
Lectures on moral philosophy. By John Macpherson. [Ornament.]
Philadelphia: Printed by Zachariah Poulson, junior, No. 30, North Fourth-Street, near the University. MDCCXCI. pp. (36). 12mo.   BA. NYPL.

23530 **THE MAIL; OR, CLAYPOOLE'S DAILY ADVERTISER.** Number 1. Wednesday, June 1, [— Number 184. Saturday, December 31, 1791.]
Philadelphia: Printed and sold by D. C. Claypoole, at his office, No. 2, South Third-Street, . . . 1791. fol.   AAS.
Established by David C. Claypoole, after the dissolution of his partnership with John Dunlap, and continued by him certainly to the end of September, 1793, when publication was suspended owing to the epidemic of yellow fever in the city. On December 9, 1793, Claypoole resumed his former connection with John Dunlap, as junior editor and publisher of *Dunlap and Claypoole's American Daily Advertiser*, into which The Mail was merged.

23531 **MANSFIELD, ACHILLES**   1751 – 1814
Christianity the wisdom and power of God. A sermon preached November 2, 1791, at the ordination of the Reverend John Elliot, to the pastoral care of the church and society in East-Guilford. By Achilles Mansfield, a. m. pastor of the first church in Killingworth.
Printed by Thomas and Samuel Green, opposite the Post-Office, New-Haven. [1791.] pp. 38. 8vo.   AAS. BM. JCB. YC.

23532 MANSON, ——
MANSON'S PRIMER.
Burlington: Printed and sold by Isaac Neale. 1791.

23533 —— — MANSON'S PRIMER.
Carlisle: Printed and sold by George Kline. 1791.

23534 MARSHALL, WILLIAM
A VINDICATION OF THE ASSOCIATE PRESBYTERY OF PENNSYLVANIA, BEING A REPLY
TO MR. ROBERT ANNAN'S CONCISE AND FAITHFUL NARRATIVE.
Philadelphia: 1791. pp. 132. 12mo.

23535 MARTIN, FRANÇOIS XAVIER   1762 – 1846
THE OFFICE AND AUTHORITY OF A JUSTICE OF THE PEACE, AND OF SHERIFFS, COR-
ONERS, &C. ACCORDING TO THE LAWS OF THE STATE OF NORTH-CAROLINA. BY
FRANÇOIS-XAVIER MARTIN, ESQUIRE, ATTORNEY AT LAW. HAPPY THE COUNTRY
WHERE LAW IS NOT A SCIENCE.
Newbern: [Printed by] Francois-Xavier Martin. 1791. pp. (2), (2), [6],
307, (1), (4). 8vo.   HC. JCB. LOC. NCU. NYPL.
Contains, a four-page list of Subscribers' names.

23536 MARTINET, JOANNES FLORENTIUS   1729 – 1795
THE CATECHISM OF NATURE; FOR THE USE OF CHILDREN. BY DOCTOR MARTINET,
PROFESSOR OF PHILOSOPHY AT ZUTPHEN. TRANSLATED FROM THE DUTCH. [By
John Hall.] [One line from] YOUNG.
Philadelphia: Printed by Thomas Lang. And sold at his House, No. 21,
Church-Alley, and by all the Booksellers. MDCCXCI. pp. 136. 18mo. AAS. LOC.

23537 MARYLAND. STATE.
LAWS OF MARYLAND, MADE AND PASSED AT A SESSION OF ASSEMBLY, BEGUN AND
HELD AT THE CITY OF ANNAPOLIS ON MONDAY THE FIRST OF NOVEMBER, IN THE
YEAR OF OUR LORD ONE THOUSAND SEVEN HUNDRED AND NINETY.   [— 22 Dec-
ember, 1790.] [Arms.]
Annapolis: Printed by Frederick Green, Printer to the State. [1791.] pp.
(2), (93). fol.
AAS. LOC. NYPL.

23538 —— VOTES AND PROCEEDINGS OF THE HOUSE OF DELEGATES OF THE STATE OF
MARYLAND. NOVEMBER SESSION, 1790. BEING THE FIRST SESSION OF THIS
ASSEMBLY. [4 November,—22 December, 1790.]
[*Annapolis: Printed by Frederick Green,* 1791.] pp. 112. fol. LOC. NYPL.

23539 —— VOTES AND PROCEEDINGS OF THE SENATE OF THE STATE OF MARYLAND. NOV-
EMBER SESSION, 1790. BEING THE SEVENTH SESSION OF THE THIRD SENATE.
[1 November,—22 December, 1790.]
[*Annapolis: Printed by Frederick Green,* 1791.] pp. 53. fol. LOC. NYPL.

23540 THE MARYLAND GAZETTE. XLVIITH YEAR. No. 2295. THURSDAY, JANUARY 6,
[— XLVIITH YEAR. No. 2346. THURSDAY, DECEMBER 29, 1791.]
Annapolis: Printed by Frederick and Samuel Green. 1791. fol. AAS. MDHS.

23541 THE MARYLAND GAZETTE, AND FREDERICK WEEKLY ADVERTISER. VOL. I. No.
46. SATURDAY, JANUARY 1, [— VOL. II. No. 98. SATURDAY, DECEMBER 31,
1791.]
*Frederick-Town: Printed by John Winter, at the Printing-Office in Pat-
rick-Street, . . .* 1791. fol.
Apparently continued throughout the year.

23542　THE MARYLAND GAZETTE; OR, THE BALTIMORE ADVERTISER. PUBLISHED EVERY TUESDAY AND FRIDAY. VOL. VIII. No. 652. TUESDAY, JANUARY 4, [— VOL. IX. No. 755. FRIDAY, DECEMBER 30, 1791.]
　　　Baltimore: Printed and published by John Hayes, the corner of Market and Calvert Streets. . . . 1791. fol.　　　　　　　NYPL.

23543　THE MARYLAND HERALD, AND EASTERN SHORE INTELLIGENCER. VOL. I. No. 34. TUESDAY, JANUARY 4, |— VOL. II. No. 83. TUESDAY, DECEMBER 27, 1791.]
　　　Easton: Printed by James Cowan. 1791. fol.　　　　　　AAS.

23544　THE MARYLAND JOURNAL AND BALTIMORE ADVERTISER. No. 1. OF VOL. XVIII. No. 1312. TUESDAY, JANUARY 4, [—No. 104 OF VOL. XVIII. No. 1415. FRIDAY, DECEMBER 30, 1791.]
　　　Baltimore: Printed by W. Goddard and James Angell, Market-Street. 1791. fol.　　　　　　AAS. MdHS.

23545　MASON, BENJAMIN
　　　EIN LICHT DAS AUS DER DUNKELHEIT HERVORLEUCHTET: ODER, EINE ANTWORT AUF EINE KLEINE SCHRIFT VON FRANZ HERR, WELCHE DEN TITEL FÜHRET, KURZE ERKLÄRUNG VON DEM GESCHRIEBENEN WORTE GOTTES; WIE AUCH, VON DER CHRISTLICHEN TAUF-ORDNUNG UND VON DEM FRIEDLICHEN REICHE CHRIST. GEGEN DAS VOLK WELCHES MAN QUAKER NENNET. VON BENJAMIN MASON. [Three lines from] I PETRI.
　　　Philadelphia: Gedruckt bey Carl Cist, num. 104. in der Zweytenstrasse, nah am Eck der Rehsstrasse, 1791. pp. (8), 53. 16mo.　　　AAS HSP.

23546　MASON, JOHN　　　　　　　　　　1646 – 1694
　　　SPIRITUAL SONGS: OR SONGS OF PRAISE, WITH PENITENTIAL CRIES TO ALMIGHTY GOD, UPON SEVERAL OCCASIONS [By Thomas Shepard.] TOGETHER WITH THE SONG OF SONGS, WHICH IS SOLOMON'S. FIRST TURN'D, THEN PARAPHRASED, IN ENGLISH VERSE.
　　　Hartford: Printed by Hudson & Goodwin? 1791.

23547　MASSACHUSETTS. STATE.
　　　[Arms.] ACTS AND LAWS, PASSED BY THE GENERAL COURT OF MASSACHUSETTS: BEGUN AND HELD AT BOSTON, IN THE COUNTY OF SUFFOLK, ON WEDNESDAY THE TWENTY-FIFTH DAY OF MAY, ANNO DOMINI, 1791. [Colophon:]
　　　Boston: Printed by Thomas Adams, Printer to the honorable the General Court, 1791. pp. 107—120. fol.　　　AAS. LOC. NYPL.

23548　——— [Arms.] [Perpetual] ACTS AND LAWS, PASSED BY THE GENERAL COURT OF MASSACHUSETTS: BEGUN AND HELD AT BOSTON, IN THE COUNTY OF SUFFOLK, ON WEDNESDAY THE TWENTY-SIXTH DAY OF MAY, ANNO DOMINI, 1790; AND FROM THENCE CONTINUED BY ADJOURNMENT TO WEDNESDAY THE TWENTY-EIGHTH DAY OF JANUARY FOLLOWING. [Colophon:]
　　　Boston: Printed by Thomas Adams, Printer to the honorable General Court. M,DCC,XCI. pp. 89—105. fol.　　　AAS. LOC. NYPL.

23549　——— COMMONWEALTH OF MASSACHUSETTS. BY HIS EXCELLENCY JOHN HANCOCK, ESQ; GOVERNOUR OF THE COMMONWEALTH OF MASSACHUSETTS. A PROCLAMATION. [Appointing Thursday, March thirty-first, a day of fasting.]
　　　[Boston: Printed by Thomas Adams, 1791.] Broadside. fol.　AAS. BPL.

23550　——— COMMONWEALTH OF MASSACHUSETTS. BY HIS EXCELLENCY JOHN HANCOCK, ESQ; GOVERNOUR OF THE COMMONWEALTH OF MASSACHUSETTS. A PROCLAMATION. [Appointing Thursday, November seventeenth, a day of thanksgiving.]
　　　[Boston: Printed by Thomas Adams, 1791.] Broadside. fol.　AAS. BPL.

MASSACHUSETTS, continued.

23551 —— COMMONWEALTH OF MASSACHUSETTS. GENERAL ORDERS [to the militia of Massachusetts.]
    [*Boston: Printed by Thomas Adams, January 28, 1791.*] Broadside. fol.

23552 —— COMMONWEALTH OF MASSACHUSETTS. GENERAL ORDERS [of General Dennison.]
    [*Boston: Printed by Thomas Adams, April, 1791.*] Broadside. fol.

23553 —— COMMONWEALTH OF MASSACHUSETTS. IN THE HOUSE OF REPRESENTATIVES. FEBRUARY 18, 1791. BILL FOR THE RELIEF OF THE POOR.
    [*Boston: Printed by Thomas Adams, 1791.*] pp. 6. fol.   AAS.

23554 —— RESOLVES OF THE GENERAL COURT OF THE COMMONWEALTH OF MASSACHU-SETTS: TOGETHER WITH THE SPEECHES, &C. OF HIS EXCELLENCY THE GOVERNOUR TO THE SAID COURT: BEGUN AND HELD AT BOSTON, IN THE COUNTY OF SUFFOLK, ON WEDNESDAY THE TWENTY-SIXTH DAY OF MAY, ANNO DOMINI, 1790; AND FROM THENCE CONTINUED BY ADJOURNMENT TO WEDNESDAY THE TWENTY-SIXTH DAY OF JANUARY FOLLOWING. [—11 March, 1791.]
    [*Boston: Printed by Thomas Adams, 1791.*] pp. [36 *sic* 37]—81. Index,— fol.   AAS. NYPL.
    Page 41 omitted to correct error in 37. Page 46 is mispaged 44 and this error continues to the end.

23555 —— —— RESOLVES OF THE GENERAL COURT OF THE COMMONWEALTH OF MASSA-CHUSETTS. BEGUN AND HELD AT BOSTON, IN THE COUNTY OF SUFFOLK, ON WEDNESDAY THE TWENTY-FIFTH DAY OF MAY, ANNO DOMINI, 1791. [18 June, 1791.]
    Boston: Printed by Thomas Adams, Printer to the honourable General Court. M,DCC,XCI. pp. 32. fol.   AAS. LOC. NYPL.

23556 —— TAX NO. NINE. [Arms.] COMMONWEALTH OF MASSACHUSETTS. IN THE YEAR OF OUR LORD, ONE THOUSAND SEVEN HUNDRED AND NINETY-ONE. AN ACT, FOR AP-PORTIONING AND ASSESSING A TAX OF TWENTY-FIVE THOUSAND THREE HUNDRED AND SIXTY-FIVE POUNDS, TWO SHILLINGS AND SEVEN PENCE, TO ANSWER THE EX-IGENCIES OF GOVERNMENT; AND ALSO FOUR THOUSAND ONE HUNDRED AND ELEVEN POUNDS, FOURTEEN SHILLINGS TO RE-PLACE THE SAME SUM DRAWN OUT OF THE TREASURY, TO PAY THE MEMBERS OF THE HOUSE OF REPRESENTATIVES, FOR THEIR ATTENDANCE THE THREE LAST SESSIONS OF THE GENERAL COURT; ALSO FOR ASSESSING A FURTHER SUM OF ELEVEN POUNDS FOURTEEN SHILLINGS, SET TO THE TOWN OF BOWDOIN, AND THE SUM OF THIRTY-SIX POUNDS, NINETEEN SHILL-INGS AND EIGHT PENCE, SET ON THE LANDS OF THE HEIRS AND ASSIGNS OF THE LATE BRIGADIER WALDO. [Colophon:]
    Printed at Boston, (Massachusetts) by Thomas Adams, Printer to the hon. General Court. M,DCC,XCI. pp. 20. fol.   AAS. HSP. LOC.

23557 —— —— COMMONWEALTH [arms] OF MASSACHUSETTS. ALEXANDER HODGDON, ESQ. TREASURER AND RECEIVER-GENERAL OF THE SAID COMMONWEALTH. SPECIE-TAX. NO. 9, GRANTED MARCH 5, 1791. . . . GIVEN UNDER MY HAND AND SEAL AT BOSTON, THE ELEVENTH DAY OF APRIL, IN THE YEAR OF OUR LORD, ONE THOUS-AND SEVEN HUNDRED AND NINETY-ONE.
    [*Boston: Printed by Thomas Adams, 1791.*] Broadside. fol.   LOC.

23558 THE MASSACHUSETTS Magazine, or monthly museum. Containing the literature, history, politics, arts, manners & amusements of the age. [One
line of Latin.] Vol. iii. For [January—December] 1791. [Cut.]

*Printed at Boston, by I. Thomas and E. T. Andrews; at Faust's Statue, No.
45, Newbury Street.* MDCCXCI. pp. (2), iii, (1), 795, 15 plates, engraved title-
page. 8vo.   AAS. BA. HC. JCB. LOC. MHS. NYHS.

23559 MAXCY, Jonathan   1768–1820
The Last enemy destroyed. A funeral sermon, delivered in the Baptist
meeting-house in Providence, July 31, A. D. 1791. Occasioned by the
death of the Rev. James Manning, d. d. president of Rhode-Island College. By Jonathan Maxcy, a. m.

Providence: Printed by John Carter. [1791.] pp. 43. 8vo. BA. JCB. NYHS.

A second edition was printed in Providence, in 1796.

23560 —— Proposals for printing by subscription a Poem, on the "Prospects of
America," with the valedictory addresses subjoined, spoken at the public commencement, in Providence, September 5, 1787. By the author,
Jonathan Maxcy, lately appointed one of the trustees of Rhode-Island
College. To which is added, notes and observations, with an appendix,
by another hand, containing a short topographical and historical account
of the State of Rhode-Island, but more particularly of the town of
Providence: of the College, its regulations and the studies pursued
there, etc. etc.

*[Printed at Providence, by Bennett Wheeler, at his office on the west side of
the River. 1791.]*

23561 —— A Poem on the Prospects of America. To which are subjoined, the
valedictory addresses, delivered on the public commencement at Rhode-
Island College, in Providence, September 5, A. D. 1787. By Jonathan
Maxcy, a. b. [Three lines. Printer's monogram.]

*Printed at Providence, by Bennett Wheeler, at his office on the west side of
the River.* [1791.] pp. 40. 8vo.   BU.

An Appendix, contains a brief topographical and descriptive account
of Rhode Island. The Editor's advertisement announces that it was
his intention "to have subjoined an Appendix, containing a more particular account of the State, Town, and College; but unexpected avo-
cations have prevented," and that it was "now in contemplation to
publish an History of the State on a more comprehensive plan." This
entry is repeated this year as a more probable date of publication than
the year the Poem was delivered. Mr. Maxcy was "appointed one of
the trustees of Rhode-Island College" in 1791, and succeeded Dr.
Manning, who died that year, as President of the College, in 1792.

23562 MELLEN, John, junior   1752–1828
A Sermon, delivered at Harwich, January 21, 1791, at the funeral of the
reverend Isaiah Dunster, pastor of the first church in that town; who
died on the 18th, preceeding, in the 71st year of his age, and 43d of his
ministry. By John Mellen, jun. a. m. pastor of the East Church in
Barnstable. Published at the request of the bereaved society.

Boston: Printed by Samuel Hall, No. 53, Cornhill. MDCCXCI. pp. 22. 8vo.
AAS. BA. HC. JCB. MHS. NYHS.

23563   MERKEL, Lot
LOT MERKEL, No. 31, HANOVER-SQUARE, NEARLY OPPOSITE THE BANK, MANUFACT-
URES AND HAS FOR SALE, A LARGE AND GENERAL ASSORTMENT OF MUFFS AND
TIPPETS. [Twenty-three lines.] NEW-YORK. OCTOBER 20, 1791. [Colophon:]
New-York: Printed by A. M'Lean, Franklin's-Head, Hanover-Square.
[1791.] Broadside. fol.   NYHS.

23564   METHODIST EPISCOPAL CHURCH IN AMERICA.
A FORM OF DISCIPLINE, FOR THE MINISTERS, PREACHERS, AND MEMBERS (NOW COM-
PREHENDING THE PRINCIPLES AND DOCTRINES) OF THE METHODIST EPISCOPAL
CHURCH IN AMERICA, CONSIDERED AND APPROVED AT A CONFERENCE HELD AT
BALTIMORE, IN THE STATE OF MARYLAND, ON MONDAY, THE 27TH OF DECEMBER,
1784: IN WHICH THOMAS COKE, AND FRANCIS ASBURY, PRESIDED: ARRANGED
UNDER PROPER HEADS, AND METHODISED IN A MORE ACCEPTABLE AND EASY MAN-
NER. THE SEVENTH EDITION.
*Philadelphia: Printed by Joseph Crukshank, No. 91, High-Street; and
sold by John Dickins, No. 43, Fourth-Street, near the corner of Race-Street.*
MDCCXCI. pp. iv, 128, 117-222. 12mo.   JCB.

23565   —— MINUTES, TAKEN AT THE SEVERAL CONFERENCES OF THE METHODIST EPISCO-
PAL CHURCH, IN AMERICA. FOR THE YEAR 1791. [PRICE FOUR PENCE.]
*Philadelphia: Printed by Parry Hall, No. 149, in Chesnut Street, near
Fourth Street.* M.DCC.XCI. pp. 16. 16mo.   JCB.

23566   —— A POCKET HYMN-BOOK, DESIGNED AS A CONSTANT COMPANION FOR THE PIOUS.
COLLECTED FROM VARIOUS AUTHORS. THE ELEVENTH? EDITION. PSALM CIV. 33.
[Three lines.]
*Philadelphia: Printed by Parry Hall? and sold by John Dickins, No. 182
Race Street, near Sixth Street.* 1791.

23567   —— —— A POCKET HYMN-BOOK, DESIGNED AS A CONSTANT COMPANION FOR THE
PIOUS. COLLECTED FROM VARIOUS AUTHORS. THE TWELFTH EDITION.
New-York: Printed by William Durell, 1791. pp. 276, (10). 18mo.

23568   THE MIDDLESEX GAZETTE, OR, FŒDERAL ADVERTISER. VOL. VI. NUMB. 270.
SATURDAY, JANUARY 1, [—VOL. VII. NUMB. 322. SATURDAY, DECEMBER 31,
1791.]
Middletown: Printed and published by Moses H. Woodward. 1791.   fol.
                                        AAS. CHS.
Editorial notice is given in the issue for December 10th, that "Moses
H. Woodward has removed all his stock in trade to the store under the
Printing-office: . . . He will be happy to wait on his old customers
at said store, and hopes they will take no exception from the door of
the Printing-office being shut after this date."

23569   MILTON, JOHN   1608 – 1674
PARADISE LOST: A POEM IN TWELVE BOOKS. BY JOHN MILTON. FROM THE TEXT
OF DOCTOR NEWTON. WITH THE LIFE OF THE AUTHOR.
Philadelphia: Printed and sold by Henry Taylor. M.DCC.XCI. pp. 316.
16mo.   AAS. JCB.

23570   —— PARADISE REGAIN'D: A POEM IN FOUR BOOKS. BY JOHN MILTON. FROM THE
TEXT OF DOCTOR NEWTON. TO WHICH ARE ADDED, POEMS ON SEVERAL OCCASIONS.
Philadelphia: Printed and sold by Henry Taylor. M.DCC.XCI. pp. iv,
136. 12mo.   AAS. JCB. LOC.

AUCTION
VALUES

MILTON, John, continued.

23571 —— The Poetical works of John Milton. From the text of doctor Newton. With the life of the Author. In two volumes. Vol. i. [— ii.]
Philadelphia: Printed and sold by Henry Taylor. M.DCC.XCI. 2 vols. in
one. pp. 192; (2), 193–316, 76. 16mo.

23572 —— — The Poetical works of John Milton. From the text of doctor
Newton. With the life of the Author. In two volumes. Vol. i. [—ii.]
*Philadelphia: Printed and sold by W. Woodhouse, at the Bible, No. 6.
South Front-Street.* M.DCC.XCI. 2 vols. in one. pp. 316; (2), 76. 12mo. LOC.

23573 MOORE, Benjamin   1748 – 1816
The Doctrine of regeneration asserted and explained: a sermon, preached
in St. George's chapel, New-York, July 7, 1791. By Benjamin Moore, d. d.
New-York: Printed by Hugh Gaine, in Hanover-Square. 1791. pp. 15. 8vo.

23574 MOORE, Thomas, pseudonym.
Gaine's New-York Pocket Almanack, for the year 1792: being leap year,
and 16th of American independence, 'till 4th of July. Calculated for
this and the neighbouring States. . . . By Thomas Moore, philo.
New-York: Printed by H. Gaine, at the Bible, in Hanover-Square. [1791.]
pp. [72.] 48mo.

23575 MORE, Hannah   1745 – 1833
Search after happiness. A pastoral drama. By miss Hannah More. Per-
formed by some young ladies of Bristol, in England.
Boston: Printed and sold by Edes & Son. 1791.

23576 —— — A Search after happiness: a pastoral drama. By miss Hannah
More. A new edition.
Boston: Printed and sold by T. & J. Fleet, at the Bible and Heart. 1791.

23577 THE MORNING Post, and daily advertiser. No. 1960. Saturday, January 1,
[— No. 2160. Saturday, December 31, 1791.]
*New-York: Printed and published by William Morton, at his Printing-
Office, No. 231. Queen-Street.* 1791. fol.   AAS.
On May 4th, the Printing-office was removed to No. 55, King-Street.

23578 THE MORNING Ray: or, impartial oracle. "The wilderness shall bud and
blossom as the rose!" Vol. i. No. 1. Tuesday, October 25, [—No. 10.
Tuesday, December 27, 1791.]
*Windsor (Vermont)—Published by Hutchins & Spooner, on the Mainstreet,
every Tuesday morning.* 1791. fol.   AAS.
Established by James Reed Hutchins, and Alden Spooner, and continued by them to the end of the first volume, in October, 1792.

23579 MORSE, Jedidiah   1761 – 1826
Geography made easy: being an abridgement of the American geography.
Containing astronomical geography—discovery and general description
of America—general view of the United States—particular accounts
of the thirteen United States of America, in regard to their boundaries,
extent, rivers, lakes, mountains, productions, population, character, government, trade, manufactures, curiosities, history, &c. . . . By Jedidiah Morse, a. m. minister of the congregation in Charlestown, near Boston. Third edition, abridged and corrected by the Author.
Printed at Boston by I. Thomas, and E. T. Andrews. 1791.

23580   THE MOTHER'S GIFT; OR, A PRESENT FOR ALL LITTLE BOYS WHO *wish* TO BE GOOD.
Philadelphia: Printed by W. Spotswood, 1791. 16mo.

23581   MOTT, SAMUEL
AN ALMANACK AND EPHEMERIS, FOR THE YEAR OF OUR LORD, 1792. . . .
Poughkeepsie: Printed and sold by Nicholas Power. [1791.]
"Containing (eight pages more than is common in Almanacks) poetry, recipes, anecdotes, &c. &c."

23582   MURPHY, ARTHUR   1727 – 1805
THE GRECIAN DAUGHTER: A TRAGEDY. AS PERFORMED WITH UNIVERSAL APPLAUSE BY THE AMERICAN COMPANY. WRITTEN BY ARTHUR MURPHY, ESQ.
Philadelphia: Printed and sold by Henry Taylor. M.DCC.XCI. pp. 70.
12mo.   AAS. NYPL.

23583   MURRAY, JOHN   1741 – 1815
SOME HINTS RELATIVE TO THE FORMING OF A CHRISTIAN CHURCH—TO THE RIGHT UNDERSTANDING OF THE SCRIPTURES, AS THE ONLY RULE GIVEN BY THE GREAT HEAD OF THE CHURCH FOR THE DIRECTION THEREOF—TO THE RECTIFYING OF A FEW MISTAKES RESPECTING SOME DOCTRINES PROPAGATED UNDER THE CHRISTIAN NAME. CONCLUDING WITH THE CHARACTER OF A CONSISTENT UNIVERSALIST. IN A LETTER TO A FRIEND. BY JOHN MURRAY. [Five lines of Scripture texts.]
Printed in Boston, by Joseph Bumstead, for Benjamin Larkin, Shakespeare's Head, Cornhill. MDCCXCI. pp. (48). 8vo.   AAS. BA. LOC. MHS. NYPL.

23584   MURRAY, JOHN   1742 – 1793
THE DILIGENT SERVANT EXCITED. A SERMON PREACHED IN THE PRESBYTERIAN CHURCH IN NEWBURY-PORT, JANUARY 23, 1791, THE DAY PRECEDING THE FUNERAL OF THE REV. JOSEPH PRINCE, WHO DEPARTED THIS LIFE ON THE 15TH OF THAT MONTH, ÆTAT 68. PUBLISHED BY REQUEST OF THE MOURNERS. BY JOHN MURRAY, A. M. PASTOR OF SAID CHURCH. [Two lines from] JESUS.
Newburyport: Printed and sold by John Mycall. MDCCXCI. pp. 42, (10),
portrait. 8vo.   AAS. BA. HC. JCB. LOC. MHS. NYPL.
To which is added, an Appendix, containing some curious particulars which occurred during the life of Mr. Prince, who became totally blind at the age of fourteen, written by himself.

23585   —— THE ORIGINAL SIN IMPUTED. OR THREE SERMONS, ON ROMANS V. 18, FIRST CLAUSE. PREACHED IN THE PRESBYTERIAN CHURCH AT NEWBURYPORT, JULY, 1790. PUBLISHED BY REQUEST. . . . [Five lines from] ADAM IN MILTON. I. 10.
Printed by John Mycall in Newburyport, for Edmund Sawyer of Newbury.
MDCCXCI. pp. (94). 8vo.   AAS. BA. LOC.

23586   —— SERMONS. BY JOHN MURRAY, A. M. PASTOR OF THE PRESBYTERIAN CHURCH IN NEWBURYPORT.
Newburyport: Printed by John Mycall. 1791. pp. 613. 12mo.

23587   THE NATIONAL GAZETTE, A PERIODICAL MISCELLANY OF NEWS, POLITICS, HISTORY, AND POLITE LITERATURE. BY PHILIP FRENEAU. NUMB. I. OF VOL. I. MONDAY, OCTOBER 31, [—NUMB. 18. THURSDAY, DECEMBER 29, 1791.]
Printed by Childs and Swaine, at their office No. 209, High-Street near Fifth-Street, Philadelphia. 1791. pp. 1–72. fol.   AAS. HC. LCP. LOC. PSL.
Published by Philip Freneau semi-weekly, as a Jeffersonian, whig paper, until the end of the second volume, October 26, 1793, when its publication ceased, with an intimation that it would be resumed, but this apparently was not done.

23588   NECKER, J. CQUES   1732 – 1804
OF THE IM ORTANCE OF RELIGIOUS OPINIONS. TRANSLATED FROM THE FRENCH OF
MR. NEC KER.

Philadelphia: From the Press of Carey, Stewart & Co. MDCCXCI. pp.
263, (1). 12mo.
AAS. BM.

23589   DER NEUE GEMEINNÜTZIGE LANDWIRTHSCHAFTS CALENDER, AUF DAS JAHR, NACH
DER HEILBRINGENDEN GEBURT UNSERS HERRN JESU CHRISTI, 1792. WELCHES
EIN SCHALT-JAHR VON 366 TAGEN IST. [Nine lines.] ZUM FÜNFTENMAL HERAUS-
GEGEBEN.

*Lancaster, Gedruckt und zu haben bey Johann Albrecht und Comp. in der
Neuen Buchdruckerey, in der Prinz-strasse, das Zweyte Haus, nordwaerts vom
Gesaengniss.* [1791.] pp. (44). 4to.
AAS. LOC.

After the manner common to all the German Almanacs printed in this
country, the cover-title is a full-page woodcut, headed, Neuer Lan-
cästerischer Calender 1792. This general form was continued with
each issue.

23590   DER NEUE HOCH DEUTSCHE AMERICANISCHE CALENDER. AUF DAS JAHR CHRISTI
1792. ZUM ZWEYTENMAL HERAUSGEGEBEN.

Chesnut Hill: Gedruckt bey Samuel Saur. [1791.]

23591   NEUE PHILADELPHISCHE CORRESPONDENZ. NUM. 28. DIENSTAG, DEN 4TEN
JANUAR, [—NUM. 130. FREYTAG, DEN 30 DECEMBER, 1791.]

*Diese Zeitung wird alle Dienstag und Freytag herausgegeben von Melchior
Steiner, Buchdrucker, in der Rees-Strasse, zwischen der Zweyten-und Dritten-
Strasse, No. 71; . . . 1791. fol.*
HSP.

23592   NEUE UNPARTHEYISCHE LANCÄSTER ZEITUNG, UND ANZEIGS-NACHRICHTEN. NUM.
179. MITTWOCHS DEN 5 JANUAR, [—NUM.—MITTWOCHS DEN 28 DECEMBER 1791.]

*Diese Zeitung wird alle Mittwoch Morgen herausgegeben von Johann Albrecht
und Comp. in der Neuen Buchdruckerey zu Lancaester fur einen Thaler des Jahrs.
Ein halben Thaler wird beym Einschreiben bezahlt. 1791. fol.*

23593   NEUE UNPARTHEYISCHE READINGER ZEITUNG UND ANZEIGS-NACHRICHTEN. JAN-
UARY–DECEMBER, 1791.

Reading: Gedruckt bey Barton und Jungmann 1791. fol.

23594   NEW CASTLE COUNTY. DELAWARE.
ORDINANCES, RULES AND BYE-LAWS FOR THE POOR-HOUSE OF NEW-CASTLE COUNTY.
. . . [Colophon:]

Wilmington, Printed by James Adams, M,DCC,XCI. Broadside. fol. LOC.

23595   THE NEW-ENGLAND PRIMER IMPROVED, FOR THE MORE EASY ATTAINING THE
TRUE READING OF ENGLISH. ADORNED WITH CUTTS. TO WHICH IS ADDED, THE
ASSEMBLY OF DIVINES' CATECHISM.

Boston: Printed by Joseph Bumstead, for David West, in Marlboro' Street.
MDCCXCI. pp. [62], *portrait of The President of the United States of America.*
32mo.
LOC.

$14

23596   —— THE NEW-ENGLAND PRIMER IMPROVED, FOR THE MORE EASY ATTAINING THE
TRUE READING OF ENGLISH. TO WHICH IS ADDED, THE ASSEMBLY OF DIVINE'S
CATECHISM.

Boston: Printed and sold by Nathaniel Coverly. MDCCXCI. pp. (64). 32mo.
NYPL.

23597

NEW ENGLAND Primer, continued.
—— The New-England Primer, (enlarged and improved). To which is added, The Assembly's Catechism.

> *Baltimore: Printed and sold by David Graham*, 1791
>
> David Graham, after serving a six years apprenticeship with Hall and Sellers, Philadelphia, opened a Printing-Office in Baltimore, in June, 1791.

23598

THE NEW entertaining Philadelphia jest-book, and chearful witty companion, &c. I love fun——Keep it up! G. A. Stevens.

> *Philadelphia: Printed and sold by W. Woodhouse, at the Bible, No 6, South Front-Street.* 1791.

23599

NEW HAMPSHIRE. State.
A Journal of the proceedings of the honorable House of Representatives of the State of New-Hampshire, begun and holden at Concord, on Wednesday the fifth day of January, 1791. [—18 February, 1791.] [Arms.]

> *Portsmouth: Printed by J. Melcher.* M,DCC,XCI. pp. (175). 8vo.
> LOC. NHSL.

23600

—— *Half-title:* Proceedings of the honorable Senate.
Title: A Journal of the proceedings of the honorable Senate of the State of New-Hampshire, at a session of the General-Court, begun and held at Concord, on Wednesday the 5th day of January, 1791. [—18 February, 1791.] [Arms.]

> *Portsmouth: Printed by J. Melcher.* M,DCC,XCI. pp. (85). 8vo.
> LOC. NHSL. NYPL.

23601

—— *Half-title:* Proceedings of the honorable Senate.
Title: A Journal of the proceedings of the honorable Senate of the State of New-Hampshire, at a session of the General-Court, begun and holden at Concord, on Wednesday the first day of June, 1791, being the day appointed by the Constitution for the annual meeting of the General-Court. [—15 June, 1791.] [Arms.]

> *Portsmouth: Printed by J. Melcher*, 1791. pp. 48. 8vo.　　LOC. NHSL.

23602

—— State of Newhampshire. In Senate, June 13, 1791. Resolved, That the selectmen of every town and place in this State, from whom any certificate or indent taxes are now due, . . . In the House of Representatives, June 15, 1791. The foregoing Resolve was read and concurred. William Plummer, speaker.

> *[Portsmouth: Printed by John Melcher*, 1791.] Broadside. fol. JCB. LOC.

23603

—— State of New-Hampshire. In the House of Representatives, December 29, 1791. Whereas a Resolve passed the General Court, June 13th, 1791, providing for the payment of outstanding taxes, . . . In Senate, December 30, 1791. Read and concurred, Josiah Bartlett, president. [Colophon:]

> *Portsmouth: Printed by George and John Osborne.* [1791.] Broadside. fol.
> JCB. LOC.

23604 THE NEW-HAMPSHIRE Gazette, and the general advertiser. Containing the laws, &c. of the United States, as well as those of this State passed since 1787, with a variety of other matters both useful and entertaining. Vol. xxxiv. No. 5758 [sic] Saturday, January 1, [—Vol. xxxvi. No. 1825. Wednesday, December 28, 1791.]
Portsmouth: Printed by John Melcher, at his office in Market-Street, at nine shillings per annum. 1791. fol. AAS.
The error in numbering is continued from the preceding year, and a correction was made in the issue for January 22d, which is again misnumbered 1761, and this error continues to the end of the year.

23605 THE NEWHAMPSHIRE [U. S. arms] Gazetteer. Vol. 5. No. 22. Saturday, January 1, [—Vol. vi. No. 25. Saturday, December 31, 1791.]
Exeter, (New-Hampshire) Printed and published by Henry Ranlet, at nine shillings per annum. 1791. fol. AAS.

23606 THE NEW-HAMPSHIRE [U. S. arms] Recorder, and the weekly advertiser. Vol. iii. No. 33. Thursday, January 6, [—No. 40. Thursday, February 24, 1791.]
Keene: (State of New-Hampshire) Printed and published by James Davenport Griffith, in the Main-Street. 1791. fol
Discontinued publication sometime this year. In January, 1792, Griffith established *The Cheshire Advertiser.*

23607 THE NEW-HAVEN Gazette. No. 1. Wednesday, January 5, [—No. 26. Wednesday, June 29, 1791.]
[New-Haven:] Printed & published by Abel Morse. 1791. 4to. AAS.
Paged. Discontinued, at the end of six months' publication, on the above date.

23608 NEW JERSEY. State.
Acts of the sixteenth General Assembly of the State of New-Jersey. At a session begun at Trenton the 25th day of October, 1791, and continued by adjournments. Being the first sitting. [5–25 November, 1791.]
Burlington: Printed by Isaac Neale. M.DCC.XCI. pp. (2), (720)–763, (1). fol. NYPL.

23609 —— An Act incorporating the Society for establishing useful manufactures. Passed at Trenton, 22d November, 1791.
Burlington: Printed by Isaac Neale. 1791.

23610 —— Journal of proceedings of Legislative Council of the State of New-Jersey. [25 October,—25 November, 1791.]
Burlington: Printed by Isaac Neale. 1791.

23611 —— Votes and proceedings of the General Assembly of the State of New-Jersey. [25 October,—25 November, 1791.]
Burlington: Printed by Isaac Neale. 1791.

23612 THE NEW-JERSEY Journal, and political intelligencer. No. 377. Wednesday, January 5, [—No. 428. Wednesday. December 28, 1791.]
Elizabeth-Town: Printed and published by Shepard Kollock, every Wednesday. . . . 1791. fol. AAS. LOC.

23613 THE NEW-JERSEY, Pennsylvania, Delaware, Maryland and Virginia Almanac and ephemeris, for the year of our Lord, 1792. . . .
Baltimore: Printed and sold by Samuel and John Adams. [1791.]

23614 NEW YORK. State.
A Census of the electors and inhabitants in the State of New-York, taken
in the year 1790, in pursuance of a law of the said State.
[New-York:] Printed by Childs and Swaine, Printers to the State.
[1791.] Broadside. fol.   NYHS.

23615 —— Journal of the House of Assembly of the State of New-York. Four-
teenth session. [5 January, —24 March, 1791.]
*New-York: Printed by Francis Childs and John Swaine, Printers to the
State.* M,DCC,XCI. pp. [128.] fol.   HC. NYHS. NYPL.

23616 —— Journal of the Senate of the State of New-York. Fourteenth session.
[5 January,—24 March, 1791.] [Arms.]
*New-York: Printed by Francis Childs and John Swaine, Printers to the
State.* M,DCC,XCI. pp. [68.] fol.   AAS. HC. NYHS. NYPL.

23617 —— Laws of the State of New-York. Fourteenth session. [18 January,
—24 March, 1791.] [Arms.]
*New-York: Printed by Francis Childs and John Swaine, Printers to the
State.* M,DCC,XCI. pp. 38, (2). fol.   LOC. NYHS. NYPL.

23618 NEW YORK. City. Society Library. .
Heading: Continuation of the Catalogue [of 1789] of the New-York
Society Library.
[New-York: Printed by Hugh Gaine, 1791.] pp. (81)–(108). 8vo. AAS.

23619 NEW YORK. City. Tammany Society.
American Museum, under the patronage of the Tammany Society or Columbian Order. The Tammany Society has established a museum for the
purpose of collecting and preserving every thing relating to the history of America, likewise, every production of nature or art; for which
purpose part of the funds of the Society are appropriated. Laws and
regulations. . . . New-York. June 1, 1791. [Colophon:]
*Printed by Thomas and James Swords, at their Printing-Office, No. 27,
William-Street.* [1791.] Broadside. fol.   NYPL.

23620 NEW YORK. City. Theatre.
New-York, December 17, 1791. Theatre. By the Old American Company.
On Monday evening, the 19th inst. will be presented, a comedy, called
The Recess: or, the mask'd apparition. [Thirteen lines.] To which will
be added, (the fifth night, by desire,) The Prisoner at large: or, the
humours of Killarney. [Twenty-three lines.] Vivat Respublica.
[New-York: Printed by Hugh Gaine, 1791.] Broadside. fol. NYPL.

23621 NEW YORK. City. Trinity Church.
[The Ballot of Trinity Church corporation, 26 April, 1791 for] Church wardens.
James Duane, Robert Watts. Vestry men. [Twenty names.]
[New-York: Printed by Hugh Gaine, 1791.] Broadside. 12mo. NYHS.

23622 THE NEW-YORK Daily Gazette. Numb. 647. Saturday, January 1, [—Numb.
941. Saturday, December 31, 1791.]
*New-York: Published by Archibald M'Lean, at Franklin's Head, No. 41,
Hanover-Square.* fol.   AAS.

23623 THE NEW-YORK JOURNAL & PATRIOTIC REGISTER. [Motto.] NUMB. 1. OF VOL.
XLV. TOTAL NUMBER 2521. MONDAY, JANUARY 3, [—NUMB. 104. OF VOL. XLV.
TOTAL NUMBER 2624. SATURDAY, DECEMBER 31, 1791.]
*New-York: Printed and published (on Mondays and Thursdays) by Thomas
Greenleaf, at his Printing-Office, No. 196, Water-Street. 1791. fol.* AAS. NYPL.
Paged throughout. Beginning March 26th, the Publisher unable longer
to comply with the inconveniences of a Monday paper changed the is-
sues to Wednesdays and Saturdays.

23624 THE NEW-YORK MAGAZINE; OR, LITERARY REPOSITORY. VOLUME II. [JANUARY
—DECEMBER] 1791. [Two lines of verse.]
*New-York: Printed and sold by Thomas and James Swords, at their office,
No. 27, William-Street. 1791.* pp. viii, 744, 54–,11 plates, map. 8vo.
AAS. BA. HC. LOC. NYHS.

23625 THE NEW-YORK PACKET. [Motto.] No. 1163. SATURDAY, JANUARY 1, [—No.
1218. SATURDAY, DECEMBER 31, 1791.]
*New-York: Published every Tuesday, Thursday and Saturday, by Samuel
Loudon, No. 5, Water-Street, between the Coffee-House and Old-Slip. 1791. fol.*

23626 NEWARK. NEW JERSEY.
CONTRACT FOR ERECTING BRIDGES OVER THE HACKINSACK AND PASSAICK RIVERS, BE-
TWEEN POWLAS-HOOK AND NEWARK, IN THE STATE OF NEW-JERSEY. [Two col-
umns.] NEWARK, STATE OF NEW-JERSEY, APRIL 22, 1791.
[Elizabeth-Town: Printed by Shepard Kollock? 1791.] Broadside. 4to.
NYHS.

23627 NEWMAN, JOHN
A TREATISE ON SCHIRRUS TUMOURS AND CANCERS. BY DR. JOHN NEWMAN, NOW
RESIDENT IN BOSTON.
Boston: Printed by Edes & Son? 1791.

23628 NEWPORT. RHODE ISLAND.
TOWN TAX. WHEREAS THE FREEMEN OF THE TOWN OF NEWPORT, AT A MEETING
LEGALLY HELD ON THE 9TH DAY OF THIS PRESENT MONTH, VOTED AND RESOLVED,
THAT A TAX SHOULD BE IMMEDIATELY ASSESSED ON THE INHABITANTS FOR RAIS-
ING THE SUM OF TWO THOUSAND FIVE HUNDRED POUNDS, LAWFUL MONEY, TOWARDS
PAYING THE DEBTS OF THE TOWN, AND AT THE SAME TIME APPOINTED THE SUB-
SCRIBERS ASSESSORS OF THE SAME: [Notice that rateable estates must be returned
or tax will be apportioned. Signed, John Bours, and twelve others.] NEWPORT,
MAY 18, 1791.
[Newport: Printed by Henry Barber? 1791.] Broadside. fol. NHE.

23629 THE NEWPORT HERALD. [Motto.] VOL. V. No. 202. THURSDAY, JANUARY 6,
[—No. 236. SATURDAY, SEPTEMBER 10, 1791.]
Newport (Rhode-Island) Published by Peter Edes, in Thames-Street. 1791.
fol. AAS.
Publication was discontinued probably in September of this year.

23630 THE NEWPORT MERCURY. No. 1501. THURSDAY, JANUARY 6, [—No. 1550. SAT-
URDAY, DECEMBER 31, 1791.]
*Newport (Rhode-Island) Printed by Henry Barber, at the foot of the Pa-
rade. 1791. fol.*

23631 NEWTON, JOHN   1725 – 1807
       OLNEY HYMNS, IN THREE BOOKS. BOOK I. ON SELECT TEXTS OF SCRIPTURE. BOOK
       II. ON OCCASIONAL SUBJECTS. BOOK III. ON THE PROGRESS AND CHANGES OF THE
       SPIRITUAL LIFE.
             Philadelphia: Printed by William Young, Bookseller, No. 52, Second-Street,
       the corner of Chesnut-Street. 1791. 12mo.

23632 NICHOLS, THOMAS
       HYMNS AND DIVINE SONGS. BY THOMAS NICHOLS, OF COVENTRY. INSPECTED AND
       APPROVED BY THE REV. ISAAC BACKUS, OF MIDDLEBOROUGH.
             Providence: Printed by Bennett Wheeler. 1791. pp. 200. 12mo.

23633 NICOLAS, LEWIS
       THE DIVINITY OF JESUS CHRIST CONSIDERED, FROM SCRIPTURE EVIDENCES. IN
       THREE PARTS. 1. TEXTS OF SCRIPTURE FAVORABLE OR ADVERSE THERETO.
       2. CONJECTURE ON HIS TRUE NATURE, AS COUNTENANCED BY SACRED WRIT.
       3. HIS AGENCY IN CREATION. TO WHICH IS ADDED, AN ATTEMPT TO ACCOUNT
       FOR THE GENERAL DELUGE. BY LEWIS NICOLAS. [Two lines of Latin from] EPIT.
       FOR THE DUKE OF BUCKINGHAM.
             Philadelphia: Sold by the Author at the Debtor's Apartment. Messrs,
       Oswald and Dunlap, in Market-Street, and Mr. Young at the corner of Second and
       Chesnut-Street. 1791.
             22d Pennsylvania District Copyright, issued to Lewis Nicolas, as
       Author, 20 August, 1791.

23634 THE NIGHTINGALE; OR, SONGSTER'S COMPANION. CONSISTING OF AN ELEGANT
       AND POLITE SELECTION OF THE MOST APPROVED ANCIENT AND MODERN SONGS.
       [Two lines of verse.]
             Philadelphia: Printed and sold by W. Woodhouse, at the Bible, No. 6,
       South Front-Street. 1791.

23635 NILES, NATHANIEL   1741 – 1828
       THE PERFECTION OF GOD THE FOUNTAIN OF GOOD. TWO SERMONS, DELIVERED AT
       TORRINGFORD, IN CONNECTICUT, LORD'S DAY, DECEMBER 21ST, 1777, AND PUB-
       LISHED FOR A NUMBER OF THE HEARERS. BY NATHANIEL NILES, A. M. [Orna-
       ment.]
             Norwich, Printed:—Elizabeth Town: Re-printed by S. Kollock. M,DCC,XCI.
       pp. (40). 16mo.   AAS. BA. BM. BU. NYHS. NYPL.

23636 THE NORFOLK AND PORTSMOUTH CHRONICLE. VOL. II. NUMB. 71. SATURDAY, JANU-
       ARY 1, [—VOL. III. NUMB. 123. SATURDAY, DECEMBER 31, 1791.]
             [*Norfolk:*] Printed by Prentis & Baxter. 1791. fol.

23637 NORMAN, JOHN   1748 – 1817
       THE AMERICAN PILOT, CONTAINING THE NAVIGATION OF THE SEA COAST OF NORTH
       AMERICA, FROM THE STREIGHTS OF BELLE ISLE TO CAYENNE, INCLUDING THE ISLAND
       AND BANKS OF NEWFOUNDLAND, THE WEST-INDIA-ISLANDS, AND ALL THE ISLANDS
       ON THE COAST; WITH PARTICULAR DIRECTIONS FOR SAILING TO AND ENTERING THE
       PRINCIPAL HARBOURS, RIVERS, &C. DESCRIBING ALSO THE CAPES, HEADLANDS,
       RIVERS, BAYS, ROADS, HAVENS, HARBOURS, STRAITS, ROCKS, SANDS, SHOALS, BANKS,
       DEPTHS OF WATER AND ANCHORAGE; SHEWING THE COURSES AND DISTANCES FROM
       ONE PLACE TO ANOTHER, THE EBBING OF THE SEA, THE SETTING OF THE TIDE
       AND CURRENTS, &C. WITH MANY OTHER THINGS NECESSARY TO BE KNOWN IN NAV-
       IGATION; LIKEWISE NECESSARY DIRECTIONS FOR THOSE WHO ARE NOT FULLY AC-
       QUAINTED WITH THE USE OF CHARTS.
             Boston: Printed and sold by John Norman. [1791.] 12 charts. fol.   HC.
       Certified by Osgood Carleton, teacher of the mathematics, in Boston, to
       be "as accurate as any of the kind hitherto published."

23638   NORMAN, JOHN, continued.
—— MAP OF THE UNITED STATES OF AMERICA; THE BOUNDARY LINE LAID DOWN AGREEABLE TO THE PEACE OF 1783. CONTAINING THE OHIO COUNTRY, THE GENESEE LANDS, KENNEBECK RIVER, &c. FROM ACTUAL SURVEYS, WITH A VARIETY OF OTHER INFORMATION.
       Boston: Printed and sold by John Norman, at his Office, No. 75, Newbury Street, opposite the Sign of the Lamb, 1791.
       "A large six sheet map." This is probably, the map, by Osgood Carleton, referred to in number 23250, of this volume.

23639   NORTH CAROLINA. STATE.
JOURNAL OF THE HOUSE OF COMMONS OF THE GENERAL ASSEMBLY OF NORTH-CAROLINA, NOVEMBER SESSION, 1790. [Colophon:]
       Edenton: Printed by Hodge & Wills, Printers to the State. 1791. pp. 88–4to.   LOC. NCSL.

23640   —— JOURNAL OF THE SENATE OF THE GENERAL ASSEMBLY OF NORTH-CAROLINA, NOVEMBER SESSION, 1790. [Colophon:]
       Edenton: Printed by Hodge and Wills, Printers to the State. 1791. pp. 60. 4to.   LOC. NCSL.

23641   —— LAWS OF THE STATE OF NORTH-CAROLINA. [A. D. 17 NOVEMBER, 1715,—15 DECEMBER, 1790.] PUBLISHED ACCORDING TO ACT OF ASSEMBLY, BY JAMES IREDELL, NOW ONE OF THE ASSOCIATE JUSTICES OF THE SUPREME COURT OF THE UNITED STATES. [Ornament.]
       Edenton: Printed by Hodge & Wills, Printers to the State of North-Carolina. M,DCC,XCI. pp. iv, 712, xxi, (3). fol.   HC. HSP. JCB. NYHS. NYPL.
       Contains a list of subscribers. $11

23642   —— LAWS OF NORTH-CAROLINA. AT A GENERAL ASSEMBLY, BEGUN AND HELD AT FAYETTEVILLE, ON THE FIRST DAY OF NOVEMBER, IN THE YEAR OF OUR LORD, ONE THOUSAND SEVEN HUNDRED AND NINETY, AND IN THE FIFTEENTH YEAR OF THE INDEPENDENCE OF THE SAID STATE: BEING THE FIRST SESSION OF SAID ASSEMBLY. [—15 December, 1790.] [Colophon:]
       Edenton: Printed by Hodge & Wills, Printers to the State, [1790.] pp. (28). fol.   LOC. NCU. NCSL.

23643   THE NORTH-CAROLINA CHRONICLE: OR, FAYETTEVILLE GAZETTE. VOL. II. No. 19. MONDAY, JANUARY 3, [— No. 28. MONDAY, MARCH 7, 1791.]
       Fayetteville: Printed by George Roulstone for John Sibley & Co. at Franklin's Head in Green-Street, 1791. 4to.
       Discontinued at the above date owing to the expense, and the difficulty of collecting debts to meet it. George Roulstone removed his press to Rogersville, Tennessee, and established there the Knoxville Gazette, in November.

23644   THE NORTH-CAROLINA GAZETTE. VOL. VI. NUMB. 261. THURSDAY, JANUARY 6, [—NUMB. 312. THURSDAY, DECEMBER 29, 1791.]
       Newbern: Printed by F. X. Martin. 1791. fol.

23645   NORTON, ELIJAH
METHODISM EXAMINED. A DISCOURSE, PREACHED UPON JOHN VI: 47. IN WHICH THE DOCTRINES OF FAITH AND FINAL PERSEVERANCE OF ALL BELIEVERS ARE ILLUSTRATED AND PROVEN. IN OPPOSITION TO THE DOCTRINE OF FALLING FROM GRACE, AND OTHER DOCTRINES CONNECTED THEREWITH. BY ELIJAH NORTON, OF WOODSTOCK.
       Printed at Windsor, Vermont. By Alden Spooner. M.DCC.XCI. pp. 24. 8vo.   JCB.

23646   NORTON, NOAH U.
ORATION, DELIVERED AT SOUTHINGTON, MARCH 7, 1791.
Danbury: Printed by Douglas and Ely. 1791. pp. 12. 12mo.

23647   NORWICH PACKET. VOX POPULI.—THE VOICE OF THE PEOPLE. VOL. XVIII. No.
876. FRIDAY, JANUARY 7, [—VOL. XIX. No. 927. THURSDAY, DECEMBER 29,
1791.]
*[Norwich:] Printed and published by John Trumbull, near the Meeting-
House.* 1791. fol.
AAS.
In May, the day of publication was changed to Thursday.

23648   OF COMMERCE AND LUXURY. [Six lines of Latin from] HORAT. L. III. OD. XXIV.
[Monogram.]
*Printed, from the London edition, by T. Lang, No. 21, Church-Alley,
Philadelphia.* M,DCC,XCI. pp. iv, 51. 8vo.   AAS. JCB. LOC. NYPL.

23649   OGDEN, JOHN COSENS   1755 – 1800
AN ADDRESS DELIVERED AT THE OPENING OF PORTSMOUTH ACADEMY, ON EASTER
MONDAY, A. D. 1791. BY THE REVEREND JOHN COSENS OGDEN, RECTOR OF ST.
JOHN'S CHURCH.
· *Printed by George Jerry Osborne, jun. at the Spy Printing-Office, Guttem-
berg's [sic] Head, Congress-Street, Portsmouth.* M,DCC,XCI. pp. 35. 12mo.
AAS. BM. NYHS.

23650   —— LETTERS, OCCASIONED BY THE PUBLICATION OF A PRIVATE EPISTOLARY CORRES-
PONDENCE, BEGUN BY MR. SAMUEL MACCLINTOCK, PREACHER TO A PURITAN CON-
GREGATION, IN GREENLAND, NEW-HAMPSHIRE. BY JOHN COSENS OGDEN, [A
PRESBYTER IN THE PROTESTANT EPISCOPAL CHURCH, IN THE UNITED STATES OF
AMERICA];—DISCOURSE DELIVERED IN ST. JOHN'S CHURCH IN PORTSMOUTH. BY
SAMUEL SEABURY, . . .
*Printed at Boston, by I. Thomas and E. T. Andrews, Faust's Statue, No.
45, Newbury-Street.* MDCCXCI. pp. 60. 12mo.   AAS. BA. HC. JCB. MHS. NYHS.

23651   —— A SERMON PREACHED BEFORE THE COLUMBIAN LODGE, AT NOTTINGHAM, SEP.
7, 1790. IN THE STATE OF NEW-HAMPSHIRE; BY THE REV. JOHN COSENS OGDEN,
RECTOR OF ST. JOHN'S CHURCH, IN PORTSMOUTH, AND CHAPLAIN TO THE GRAND
LODGE OF FREE MASONS, IN SAID STATE.
Portsmouth: New-Hampshire, Printed and sold by John Melcher.
M,DCC,XCI. pp. 23, (1). 8vo.   AAS. JCB. MHS. NYHS.

23652   O'KEEFFE, JOHN   1747 – 1833
PATRICK IN PRUSSIA; OR, LOVE IN CAMP: A COMIC OPERA, IN TWO ACTS; BEING THE
SECOND PART OF THE POOR SOLDIER. WITH ALL THE SONGS, DUETS, &C. PER-
FORMED WITH UNIVERSAL APPLAUSE, BY THE AMERICAN COMPANY. WRITTEN BY
JOHN O'KEEFE, ESQ.
Philadelphia: Printed and sold by Henry Taylor. M.DCC.XCI. pp. 39.
12mo.
BPL. NYPL.

23653   —— THE PRISONER AT LARGE: OR, THE HUMOURS OF KILLARNEY. A COMEDY, IN
TWO ACTS. AS PERFORMED WITH UNIVERSAL APPLAUSE BY THE AMERICAN COM-
PANY. WRITTEN BY JOHN O'KEEFE, ESQ.
Philadelphia: Printed and sold by Henry Taylor. M.DCC.XCI. pp. 35.
12mo.
LOC.
One thousand copies, in sheets, offered at the sale of Henry Taylor's
estate.

23654   OLIPHANT, JAMES   1734 – 1818
A SACRAMENTAL CATECHISM, DESIGNED FOR COMMUNICANTS, OLD AND YOUNG.
Philadelphia: Printed by W. Young, No. 52, Second-Street, the corner of Chesnut-street. 1791.

23655   OSBORNE'S NEW-HAMPSHIRE SPY. A FREE AND IMPARTIAL PAPER. VOL. IX.
NUMB. XIX. SATURDAY, JANUARY 1, [—VOL. XI. NUMB. XIX. WEDNESDAY, DE-
CEMBER 28, 1791.]
☞*Published on Wednesdays and Saturdays—by George and John Osborne—near the State-House, Guttemberg's [sic] Head, Congress-Street, Portsmouth. Twelve shillings per annum. 1791. fol.*

23656   OSTERWALD, JEAN FRÉDÉRIC   1663 – 1747
PRACTICAL OBSERVATIONS, ON THE OLD AND NEW TESTAMENTS, ILLUSTRATING THE
CHAPTERS, A VERY FEW EXCEPTED, IN THEIR ORDER, WITH ARGUMENTS TO THE
DIFFERENT BOOKS. BY THE REVEREND MR. OSTERVALD, PROFESSOR OF DIVINITY,
AND ONE OF THE MINISTERS OF THE CHURCH AT NEUFCHATEL IN SWITZERLAND.
[Ornament.]
Trenton: Printed and sold by Isaac Collins. M.DCC.XCI. pp. (2), 154. 4to.

Usually found bound between the Old, and New Testament, in Collins'
quarto edition of the Bible printed this year. From other copies it
was omitted because of the objections of the Baptist Associations.

23657   PAINE, THOMAS   1736 – 1809
COMMON SENSE; ADDRESSED TO THE INHABITANTS OF AMERICA, ON THE FOLLOWING
INTERESTING SUBJECTS, VIZ. I. OF THE ORIGIN AND DESIGN OF GOVERNMENT IN
GENERAL, WITH CONCISE REMARKS ON THE ENGLISH CONSTITUTION. II. OF MON-
ARCHY AND HEREDITARY SUCCESSION. III. THOUGHTS ON THE PRESENT STATE OF
AMERICAN AFFAIRS. IV. OF THE PRESENT ABILITY OF AMERICA, WITH SOME
MISCELLANEOUS REFLECTIONS. TO WHICH IS ADDED, AN APPENDIX. [Two lines
from] THOMSON.
*Albany: Re-printed by Charles R. and George Webster. M.DCC.XCI. pp.
[60.] 8vo.*   AAS. JCB. NL. NYPL.

23658   —— COMMON SENSE; ADDRESSED TO THE INHABITANTS OF AMERICA, ON THE
FOLLOWING INTERESTING SUBJECTS: I. OF THE ORIGIN AND DESIGN OF GOVERN-
MENT IN GENERAL, WITH CONCISE REMARKS ON THE ENGLISH CONSTITUTION.
II. OF MONARCHY AND HEREDITARY SUCCESSION. III. THOUGHTS ON THE PRESENT
STATE OF AMERICAN AFFAIRS. IV. OF THE PRESENT ABILITY OF AMERICA, WITH
SOME MISCELLANEOUS REFLECTIONS. A NEW EDITION, WITH SEVERAL ADDITIONS
IN THE BODY OF THE WORK. TO WHICH IS ADDED AN APPENDIX, TOGETHER WITH
AN ADDRESS TO THE PEOPLE CALLED QUAKERS. BY THOMAS PAINE, SECRETARY
FOR FOREIGN AFFAIRS TO CONGRESS IN THE AMERICAN WAR, AND AUTHOR OF THE
RIGHTS OF MAN, &C. &C. [Two lines from] THOMSON.
*Philadelphia: Printed and sold by W. and T. Bradford. M,DCC,XCI. pp.
99. 8vo.*   BM. JCB. LOC. NYPL.

23659   —— RIGHTS OF MAN: BEING AN ANSWER TO MR. BURKE'S ATTACK ON THE FRENCH
REVOLUTION. BY THOMAS PAINE, SECRETARY FOR FOREIGN AFFAIRS TO CONGRESS
IN THE AMERICAN WAR, AND AUTHOR OF THE WORK, ENTITLED COMMON SENSE.
*Baltimore: Printed and sold by David Graham, in Calvert-Street, between
Market-Street and the Court-House. M,DCC,XCI. pp. [88.] 8vo.*   LOC.

PAINE, THOMAS, continued.

23660 —— — RIGHTS OF MAN: BEING AN ANSWER TO MR. BURKE'S ATTACK ON THE FRENCH REVOLUTION. BY THOMAS PAINE, SECRETARY FOR FOREIGN AFFAIRS TO CONGRESS IN THE AMERICAN WAR, AND AUTHOR OF THE WORK INTITLED COMMON SENSE.

Reprinted in Bennington, [Vermont,] in the year 1791, by Anthony Haswell. pp. 86–8vo.

NYHS. RIHS.

23661 —— — RIGHTS OF MAN: BEING AN ANSWER TO MR. BURKE'S ATTACK ON THE FRENCH REVOLUTION. BY THOMAS PAINE, SECRETARY FOR FOREIGN AFFAIRS TO CONGRESS IN THE AMERICAN WAR, AND AUTHOR OF THE WORK ENTITLED COMMON SENSE. THIRD EDITION.

Printed at Boston, by I. Thomas and E. T. Andrews, Faust's Statue, No. 45, Newbury Street. MDCCXCI. pp. 79. 8vo.   AAS. BA. HC. JCB. LOC. NYPL.

Dedicated to the President of the United States.

23662 —— — RIGHTS OF MAN: BEING AN ANSWER TO MR. BURKE'S ATTACK ON THE FRENCH REVOLUTION. BY THOMAS PAINE, SECRETARY FOR FOREIGN AFFAIRS TO CONGRESS IN THE AMERICAN WAR, AND AUTHOR OF THE WORK ENTITLED COMMON SENSE. FOURTH AMERICAN EDITION.

Printed at Boston, by I. Thomas and E. T. Andrews, Faust's Statue, No. 45, Newbury Street. MDCCXCI. pp. 79. 8vo.   AAS. BM. JCB. MHS.

23663 —— — RIGHTS OF MAN: BEING AN ANSWER TO MR. BURKE'S ATTACK ON THE FRENCH REVOLUTION. BY THOMAS PAINE, SECRETARY FOR FOREIGN AFFAIRS TO CONGRESS IN THE AMERICAN WAR, AND AUTHOR OF THE WORK ENTITLED COMMON SENSE.

Carlisle: Printed by George Kline, 1791. pp. 90–8vo.

23664 —— — RIGHTS OF MAN: BEING AN ANSWER TO MR. BURKE'S ATTACK ON THE FRENCH REVOLUTION. BY THOMAS PAINE, SECRETARY FOR FOREIGN AFFAIRS TO CONGRESS IN THE AMERICAN WAR, AND AUTHOR OF THE WORK INTITLED COMMON SENSE. SECOND EDITION.

Philadelphia: Re-printed by Samuel Harrison Smith. M.DCC.XCI. pp. [105.] 8vo.

LOC. NYPL.

23665 —— — RIGHTS OF MAN: BEING AN ANSWER TO MR. BURKE'S ATTACK ON THE FRENCH REVOLUTION. BY THOMAS PAINE, AUTHOR OF COMMON SENSE. SECOND PHILADELPHIA EDITION, FROM FOURTH ENGLISH EDITION, CORRECTED AND ENLARGED.

Philadelphia: Re-printed by Samuel Harrison Smith. 1791. pp. (2), 100. 8vo.

LOC.

Contains a preface, by the Author, not in the second edition printed by Smith earlier this year.

23666 PAYSON, SETH   1758 – 1820

MINISTERS CHRIST'S AMBASSADORS. A SERMON, PREACHED AT THE ORDINATION OF THE REV. EBENEZER HILL, TO THE PASTORAL CARE OF THE CHURCH IN MASON, NOVEMBER 3D MDCCXC. BY SETH PAYSON, A. M. PASTOR OF THE CHURCH IN RINDGE.

Printed at Worcester, Massachusetts, by Isaiah Thomas, MDCCXCI. pp. 32. 8vo.

AAS. BA. JCB.

23667   PEALE, REMBRANDT   1778 – 1860
SHADES, OR PROFILES, OF THE PRESIDENT OF THE UNITED STATES. DONE, IN A
NEW METHOD, AND HIS LIKENESS CORRECTLY DELINEATED, BY AN AMERICAN
ARTIST.

     Charleston: 1791.

     July 4, 1791. "Just received from Charleston, and for sale (price one
     dollar) by Rice and Co., in Baltimore."

23668   PELOSI, VINCENT M.
PELOSI'S MARINE LIST AND PRICE CURRENT, CONTAINING THE INWARD AND OUT-
WARD BOUND VESSELS IN EVERY PORT OF THE UNION, WITH OTHER INTERESTING
OCCURRENCES. A COMPENDIOUS PRICE CURRENT, CHIEFLY INTENDED TO ACCOMO-
DATE THE MERCHANT TRADERS AND THEIR FOREIGN CONNECTIONS. NO. 1. MON-
DAY, JULY 11, [—NO. 20. MONDAY, NOVEMBER 21, 1791.]

     Philadelphia: Published every Monday morning at the Merchants and Ex-
     change Coffee House. 1791.   AAS-

     19th Pennsylvania District Copyright, issued to Vincent M. Pelosi, as
     Author, 18 May, 1791.

23669   PENN, WILLIAM   1644 – 1718
FORDERUNG DER CHRISTENHEIT VORS GERICHT. EINE FREUNDLICHE HEIMSUCH-
UNG IN DER LIEBE GOTTES &C. SENDBRIEF AN ALLE DIEJENIGEN, DIE UNTER
DER CHRISTLICHEN CONFESSION UND VON DEN ÄUSSERLICHEN SECTEN UND GE-
MEINEN ODER KIRCHEN ABGESONDERT SIND. SENDBRIEF AN ALLE DIEJENIGEN,
DIE VON DEM TAGE IHRER HEIMSUCHUNG EMPFINDLICH SEYN GEWORDEN. IN
DIE HOCHDEUTSCHE SPRACHE TREULICH TRANSFERIRET.

     Philadelphia: Gedruckt bey Carl Cist, 1791, pp. 9, 119. 16mo. AAS. JCB.

23670   PENNSYLVANIA. STATE.
ACTS OF THE GENERAL ASSEMBLY OF THE COMMONWEALTH OF PENNSYLVANIA,
PASSED AT A SESSION. WHICH WAS BEGUN AND HELD AT THE CITY OF PHILADEL-
PHIA ON TUESDAY, THE SEVENTH DAY OF DECEMBER, IN THE YEAR ONE THOUS-
AND SEVEN HUNDRED AND NINETY, AND OF THE INDEPENDENCE OF THE UNITED
STATES OF AMERICA, THE FIFTEENTH. [—13 April, 1791.] TO WHICH ARE
PREFIXED, THE CONSTITUTION OF THE UNITED STATES, AND THE CONSTITUTION
OF THIS COMMONWEALTH. PUBLISHED BY AUTHORITY.

     Philadelphia: Printed by Hall and Sellers, No. 51, *Market-Street.* M.DCC.-
     XCI. pp. xxxix, 108. fol.   LOC.

23671   —— — ACTS OF THE GENERAL ASSEMBLY OF THE COMMONWEALTH OF PENNSYL-
VANIA, PASSED AT A SESSION, WHICH WAS BEGUN AND HELD AT THE CITY OF PHILA-
DELPHIA ON TUESDAY, THE TWENTY-THIRD DAY OF AUGUST, IN THE YEAR ONE
THOUSAND SEVEN HUNDRED AND NINETY-ONE, AND OF THE INDEPENDENCE OF THE
UNITED STATES OF AMERICA, THE SIXTEENTH. [—30 September, 1791.] PUB-
LISHED BY AUTHORITY.

     Philadelphia: Printed by Hall and Sellers, No. 51, *Market-Street.* M.DCC.-
     XCI. pp. (2), (111)—[174.] fol.   LOC.

23672   —— IN GENERAL ASSEMBLY, MONDAY, MARCH 7, 1791, READ THE FIRST TIME. AN
ACT REPEALING SO MUCH OF ANY ACT OR ACTS OF ASSEMBLY AS AUTHORISED AND
DIRECTS THE ASSESSING LEVYING AND COLLECTING THE TAX THEREIN MENTIONED.
[Twenty-seven lines.]

     [Philadelphia: Printed by Thomas Bradford, 1791.] pp. (2). fol. LOC.

PENNSYLVANIA, continued.

23673 —— In General Assembly, Saturday, March 26, 1791, read the first time. An Act to suspend for the time therein mentioned part of an Act entitled "An Act for furnishing the quota of this State towards paying the annual interest of the debt of the United States and for funding and paying the interest of the debts of this State. [Forty-seven lines.]
[Philadelphia: Printed by Thomas Bradford, 1791.] pp. (2). fol. LOC.

23674 —— In General Assembly, Tuesday, March 29, 1791, read the first time. An Act respecting the creditors of the State. [Forty-nine lines.] [Colophon:]
Philadelphia: Printed by Thomas Bradford. [1791.] pp. (3). fol. LOC.

23675 —— Journal of the first session of the House of Representatives of the Commonwealth of Pennsylvania, which commenced at Philadelphia, on Tuesday, the seventh day of December, in the year of our Lord one thousand seven hundred and ninety. [—13 April, 1791.]
Philadelphia: Printed by Hall and Sellers—No. 51—Market-Street. M,DCC,XC. [1791.] pp. (2), [xii], (3)—[433.] fol. LOC. PSL.

23676 —— —— Journal of the House of Representatives of the Commonwealth of Pennsylvania. [Special session, August 23,—30 September, 1791.]
Philadelphia: Printed by Hall and Sellers, 1791. pp. 434—573; 20; 5. fol. PSL.
The appendix consists of: Report of Register general on public accounts. pp. 20. Report of Comptroller general on public accounts. pp. 5.

23677 —— Journal of the Senate of the Commonwealth of Pennsylvania. Anno MDCCXC, and in the fourteenth year of the independence of the United States of America. [7 December, 1790,—30 September, 1791.]
Philadelphia: Printed by Zachariah Poulson, junior, No. 30, Fourth-Street, between Market-Street and Arch-Street. [1791.] pp. (355). fol. LOC.

23678 —— Copy of a Report from Reading Howell, Frederick Antes and William Dean, esquires, commissioners appointed to explore the head-waters of the Rivers Delaware, Lehigh, and Schuylkill, and the north-east branch of Susquehanna. Also, the Report of the commissioners appointed to examine the western waters of the State of Pennsylvania.
Philadelphia: Printed by Francis Bailey, at Yorick's-Head, No. 116, *Market-Street.* MDCCXCI. pp. (33). 8vo. LCP.

23679 —— Reports of sundry commissioners appointed to view and explore the Rivers Susquehanna and Juniata; the River Delaware; the River Schuylkill, &c. &c. &c.
Philadelphia: Printed by Francis Bailey, at Yorick's-Head, No. 116, *Market-Street.* MDCCXCI. pp. (27). 8vo. LCP.

23680 —— State of the accounts of David Rittenhouse, esq. treasurer of Pennsylvania. For the year 1788.
Philadelphia: Printed by R. Aitken & Son, No. 22, Market-Street. M.DCC.XCI. pp. (56). 8vo. NPYL.

23681 —— —— State of the accounts of David Rittenhouse, esq. treasurer of Pennsylvania. From September 1788, till September 1st, 1789, including his Continental and State money accounts for 1788.
Philadelphia: Printed by R. Aitken & Son, No. 22, Market Street. M.DCC.XCI. pp. (84). 8vo. NYPL.

PENNSYLVANIA, continued.

23682 —— STATE OF THE ACCOUNTS OF BERKS COUNTY, FROM 1776 TILL 1790.
Philadelphia: Printed by R. Aitken, & Son, No. 22, Market Street. 1791.
pp. 36. 8vo.

23683 —— STATE OF THE ACCOUNTS OF THE TAXES OF YORK COUNTY.
Philadelphia: Printed by R. Aitken & Son, No. 22 Market Street.
MDCCXCI. pp. (45). 8vo. NYPL.

23684 —— TAGEBUCH DER GENERAL ASSEMBLY DER REPUBLIK PENNSYLVANIEN, 1790-
1791.
Germantown: Gedruckt bey Michael Billmeyer, 1791.

23685 —— TAGEBUCH DES SENATS DER REPUBLIK PENNSYLVANIEN, 1790-1791.
Germantown: Gedruckt bey Michael Billmeyer, 1791.

23686 THE PENNSYLVANIA GAZETTE. NUMB. 3162. WEDNESDAY, JANUARY 5, [—NUMB.
3213. WEDNESDAY, DECEMBER 28, 1791.]
Philadelphia: Printed by Hall and Sellers, at the New-Printing-Office
near the Market. 1791. fol. AAS. LOC. NYPL.

23687 THE PENNSYLVANIA HERALD, AND YORK GENERAL ADVERTISER. VOL. II. NO.
51. TOTAL NO. 103. WEDNESDAY, JANUARY 5, [—VOL. III. NO. 50. TOTAL NO.
154. WEDNESDAY, DECEMBER 28, 1791.]
York: Printed every Wednesday, by John Edie. 1791. fol.

23688 THE PENNSYLVANIA [cut] JOURNAL, AND THE WEEKLY ADVERTISER. PUBLISHED
EVERY WEDNESDAY.—PRICE FOUR-PENCE. NO. 2391. WEDNESDAY, JANUARY
5, [—NO. 2536. WEDNESDAY, DECEMBER 28, 1791.]
Philadelphia: Printed by Thomas Bradford, . . . at his Printing-Office,
Lætitia-Court. 1791. fol. AAS.

23689 THE PENNSYLVANIA MERCURY AND UNIVERSAL ADVERTISER. NO. 647. SATUR-
DAY, JANUARY 1, [—NO. 800. SATURDAY, DECEMBER 31, 1791.]
Philadelphia: Printed (on Tuesdays, Thursdays and Saturdays) by Daniel
Humphreys, 1791. 4to. AAS.
In July, the title was changed to, *The Pennsylvania Mercury, and Phila-*
delphia Price-current.

23690 PENNSYLVANIA POCKET ALMANAC, FOR THE YEAR OF OUR LORD 1792.
Philadelphia: Printed and sold by Francis Bailey, at Yorick's Head, in
Market-Street. [1791.]

23691 PERKINS, ELIJAH
AN INAUGURAL DISSERTATION ON UNIVERSAL DROPSY.
[Philadelphia:] Printed by P. Stewart, 1791, pp. 43. 8vo. RIHS. SGO.

23692 A PETITION AND REMONSTRANCE TO THE PRESIDENT AND CONGRESS OF THE
UNITED STATES. [Written by a North-Carolina Planter. Four columns of verse,
written in Scottish dialect, on the tax upon liquor.]
[Philadelphia? 1791.] Broadside. fol. NYPL.

23693 PFEIFFER, GEORGE
AN INAUGURAL DISSERTATION ON THE GOUT.
Philadelphia: Printed by T. Dobson. 1791. pp. 50. 8vo. SGO.

23694   THE [cut] PHENIX; OR WINDHAM HERALD. VOL. I. No. 1. SATURDAY, MARCH 12, [—No. 43. SATURDAY, DECEMBER 31, 1791.]
> *Windham: Printed by John Byrne, north of the Court-House.* 1791. fol.
>   AAS. CHS.

> Established by John Byrne, and continuously published weekly, by him up to 29 March, 1811, when his son, Samuel H. Byrne was admitted to partnership, as J. Byrne and Son, and publication continued by them up to the issue for 30 March, 1815, when it was discontinued. Beginning 27 July, 1815, Samuel Green revived its publication, with a continuous numbering; and, on 19 October, 1815, it was "Printed and published by Benjamin G. Willett for Samuel Green" up to 19 September, 1816, when it was finally discontinued. With the issue for 19 April, 1798, the title was shortened to *Windham Herald*, which continued until publication ceased.

23695   PHILADELPHIA. PENNSYLVANIA. BAPTIST ASSOCIATION.
MINUTES OF THE PHILADELPHIAN BAPTIST ASSOCIATION, HELD AT PHILADELPHIA, OCTOBER 4, 5, 6, 1791.
> *[Philadelphia:* 1791.] pp. 10. 4to.
>   BU. JCB.

23696   PHILADELPHIA. PENNSYLVANIA. CHRIST CHURCH.
AN ACCOUNT OF THE BIRTHS AND BURIALS IN THE UNITED CHURCHES OF CHRIST CHURCH AND ST. PETER'S, FROM DECEMBER 24, 1790, TO DECEMBER 24, 1791.
> *[Philadelphia:* 1791.] Broadside. fol.
>   LCP.

23697   PHILADELPHIA. PENNSYLVANIA. EVANGELICAL LUTHERAN CHURCH.
DIE SPUREN DER GÜTE GOTTES IN DER DEUTSCHEN EVANGELISCHEN LUTHERISCHEN GEMEINDE IN PHILADELPHIA.
> *Germantaun: Gedruckt bey Michael Billmeyer,* 1791. pp. 36. 12mo.

23698   PHILADELPHIA. PENNSYLVANIA. ST. ANDREW'S SOCIETY.
THE CONSTITUTION AND RULES OF THE ST. ANDREW'S SOCIETY. . . .
> *Philadelphia: Printed by Hall & Sellers.* MDCCXCI. pp. 12. 12mo.

23699   PILGARLIC, pseudonym.
THE ALBANIAD, AN EPIC POEM, IN THREE CANTOS; BY PILGARLIC.
> *[New-York:] Printed [by Thomas Greenleaf] for the Author,* 1791. pp. (24). 8vo.
>   NYHS. RIHS.

23700   PINKHAM, PAUL
A CHART OF NANTUCKET-SHOALS, SURVEYED BY CAPTAIN PAUL PINKHAM.
> *Boston: Published by John Norman, No. 75, Newbury-Street.* 1791.
> 14th Massachusetts District Copyright, issued to Paul Pinkham, as Author, 24 February, 1791.

23701   THE PITTSBURGH GAZETTE. NUMBER 226. SATURDAY, JANUARY 1, [—NUMBER 278. SATURDAY, DECEMBER 31, 1791.]
> *Pittsburgh: Printed by John Scull.* 1791. fol.

23702   PLAN OF THE BOOK AUCTION TO BE THE FIRST OF JULY NEXT.
> *[Savannah: Printed by James and Nicholas Johnston,* 1791.] Broadside. fol.
>   LOC.

23703 PLOWDEN, CHARLES   1743 – 1821
A SHORT ACCOUNT OF THE ESTABLISHMENT OF THE NEW SEE OF BALTIMORE, MARY-
LAND, AND OF CONSECRATING THE REV. DR. JOHN CARROLL, FIRST BISHOP THERE-
OF, ON THE FEAST OF THE ASSUMPTION, 1790. WITH A DISCOURSE DELIVERED
ON THAT OCCASION, AND THE AUTHORITY FOR CONSECRATING THE BISHOP AND
ERECTING AND ADMINISTERING THE SAID SEE.
> *London Printed. Philadelphia: Reprinted by Carey, Stewart & Co.* 179:
> pp. 20. 8vo.

23704 THE POLITICAL REPOSITORY AND STRAFFORD RECORDER. VOL. I. No. 26. MON-
DAY, JANUARY, 3, [—VOL. II. No. 76. WEDNESDAY, DECEMBER 28, 1791.]
> *Dover: Printed by Eliphalet Ladd.* 1791. fol.

23705 POMFRET, JOHN   1667 – 1703
POEMS UPON SEVERAL OCCASIONS. BY THE REVEREND MR. JOHN POMFRET. TO
WHICH ARE ADDED, HIS REMAINS, WITH SOME ACCOUNT OF HIS LIFE AND WRITINGS.
FROM AN *ACCURATE LONDON EDITION.
> *Philadelphia: Printed and sold by Parry Hall, No. 149. Chesnut Street.*
> M,DCC,XCI. pp. 158, (1). 16mo.   AAS. JCB.

23706 POOR ROBIN, pseudonym.
POOR ROBIN'S ALMANACK FOR THE YEAR 1792.
> *Philadelphia:* [1791.]

23707 POPE, ALEXANDER   1688 – 1744
AN ESSAY ON MAN, IN FOUR EPISTLES: TO HENRY ST. JOHN LORD BOLINGBROKE.
BY ALEXANDER POPE, ESQ.
> *New-London: Printed by T. Green and Son.* 1791.

23708 POPE, AMOS   1771 - 1837
AN ASTRONOMICAL DIARY OR ALMANACK, FOR THE YEAR OF OUR LORD 1792. . . .
> *Boston Printed and sold by John W. Folsom, No. 30, Union Street. Sold*
> *also by the Booksellers in Town and Country.* [1791.] pp. (24). 12mo.   HC.

23709 PORTER, ROBERT
AN ORATION, TO COMMEMORATE THE INDEPENDENCE OF THE UNITED STATES OF
NORTH-AMERICA; DELIVERED AT ZION CHURCH, IN FOURTH-STREET, PHILADEL-
PHIA, JULY 4TH, 1791; AND PUBLISHED AT THE REQUEST OF THE PENNSYLVANIA
SOCIETY OF THE CINCINNATI. BY ROBERT PORTER, A. M.
> *Philadelphia: Printed by T. Dobson, at the Stone House, Second-Street.*
> M,DCC,XCI. pp. (23). 8vo.   JCB. MHS. NYPL.

23710 PORTER, SARAH
THE ROYAL PENITENT. IN THREE PARTS. TO WHICH IS ADDED DAVID'S LAMEN-
TATION OVER SAUL AND JONATHAN. BY MRS. SARAH PORTER, OF PLYMOUTH IN
NEW-HAMPSHIRE.
> *Concord: Printed by George Hough.* 1791. pp. 19. 12mo.   MHS.

23711 THE POTOWMAC GUARDIAN, AND BERKELEY ADVERTISER. VOL. I. NUMBER 7.
MONDAY, JANUARY 3, [—VOL. 2. NUMBER 58. MONDAY, DECEMBER 26, 1791.]
> *Martinsburg, Virginia: Printed and published every Monday by N. Willis,*
> *at his Printing-office, in Burke-Street, near the Court-House.* 1791. fol.

23712 THE POUGHKEEPSIE JOURNAL. NUMB. 283. SATURDAY, JANUARY 1, [—NUMB.
335. THURSDAY, DECEMBER 29, 1791.]
> *Poughkeepsie, Dutchess County: Printed by Nicholas Power, near the*
> *Court-House.* 1791. fol.   AAS.

23713   PRENTICE, CALEB   1746 – 1803
THE TRUTH AND FAITHFULNESS OF GOD, IN THE CALLS OF THE GOSPEL, CONSID-
ERED, IN TWO DISCOURSES, DELIVERED NOVEMBER 21, 1790, IN THE FIRST PAR-
ISH IN READING. BY CALEB PRENTISS, [sic] A. M. PASTOR OF THE FIRST CHURCH
IN READING. [Two lines from] JOB, CHAP. XXXVI. VER. 2 AND 3.
        Boston: Printed and sold by Samuel Hall, No. 53, Cornhill. MDCCXCI.
pp. [30.] 8vo.   AAS.

23714   PRESBYTERIAN CHURCH IN THE UNITED STATES.
ACTS AND PROCEEDINGS OF THE GENERAL ASSEMBLY OF THE PRESBYTERIAN
CHURCH, IN THE UNITED STATES OF AMERICA, A. D. 1790 AND 1791. . . .
        Philadelphia: Printed by R. Aitken & Son. MDCCXCI. pp. 24. 8vo.
                                                        AAS. MHS. PHS. PTS.

23715   A PRESENT TO CHILDREN. CONSISTING OF SEVERAL NEW DIVINE HYMNS AND MORAL
SONGS.
        Norwich: Printed by John Trumbull. 1791.

23716   PRIESTLEY, JOSEPH   1733 – 1804
LETTERS TO THE RIGHT HONOURABLE EDMUND BURKE, OCCASIONED BY HIS REFLEC-
TIONS ON THE REVOLUTION IN FRANCE, &C. THE THIRD EDITION, CORRECTED.
BY JOSEPH PRIESTLEY, L. L. D. F. R. S. AC. IMP. PETROP. R. PARIS. HOLM.
TAURIN. ITAL. HARLEM. AUREL. MED. PARIS. CANTAB. AMERIC. ET PHILAD. SOC.
[Four lines from] MR. BURKE'S REFLECTIONS, PP. 245. 187.
        Birmingham: Printed: New-York: Re-printed by Hugh Gaine, at the
Bible, in Hanover-Square. M,DCC,XCI. pp. vi, 73, (1). 8vo.
                                                AAS. BA. LOC. MHS. NYPL.

23717   PRIME, BENJAMIN YOUNG   1733 – 1791
COLUMBIA'S GLORY, OR BRITISH PRIDE HUMBLED; A POEM ON THE AMERICAN REVO-
LUTION: SOME PART OF IT BEING A PARODY ON AN ODE, ENTITLED BRITAIN'S
GLORY OR GALLIC PRIDE ·HUMBLED; COMPOSED ON THE CAPTURE OF QUEBEC,
A. D. 1759. BY BENJAMIN YOUNG PRIME, M. D. [Eleven lines of Latin from]
HORACE.
        New-York: Printed by Thomas Greenleaf for the Author. M,DCC,XCI.
pp. [vi,] 42. 8vo.   BM. BPL. JCB. LOC. NYHS.
        6th New York District Copyright, issued to Benjamin Young Prime,
as Author, 27 October, 1791.

23718   PROTESTANT EPISCOPAL CHURCH. DIOCESE OF DELAWARE.
JOURNAL OF THE PROCEEDINGS OF A CONVENTION OF THE PROTESTANT EPISCOPAL
CHURCH, IN THE STATE OF DELAWARE, HELD IN DOVER, ON SATURDAY, THE
THIRD DAY OF DECEMBER, 1791.
        New-York: Printed by Hugh Gaine, in Hanover-Square. 1791. pp. (14).
8vo.   NYPL.

23719   PROTESTANT EPISCOPAL CHURCH. DIOCESE OF MARYLAND.
JOURNAL OF THE PROCEEDINGS OF A CONVENTION OF THE PROTESTANT EPISCOPAL
CHURCH IN THE STATE OF MARYLAND, . . . 1791.
        Baltimore: 1791. 8vo.   HC.

23720   PROTESTANT EPISCOPAL CHURCH. DIOCESE OF NEW-JERSEY.
PROCEEDINGS OF A CONVENTION OF THE PROTESTANT EPISCOPAL CHURCH, IN THE
STATE OF NEW-JERSEY, HELD IN TRINITY CHURCH, IN NEWARK, JUNE FIRST,
SECOND, THIRD AND FOURTH, ONE THOUSAND SEVEN HUNDRED AND NINETY-ONE.
        Newark: Printed by John Woods. 1791. pp. 15. 8vo.   NPL.

23721 PROTESTANT EPISCOPAL CHURCH IN THE UNITED STATES OF AMERICA.
THE BOOK OF COMMON PRAYER, AND ADMINISTRATION OF THE SACRAMENTS AND OTHER RITES AND CEREMONIES OF THE CHURCH, ACCORDING TO THE USE OF THE PROTESTANT EPISCOPAL CHURCH IN THE UNITED STATES OF AMERICA: TOGETHER WITH THE PSALTER, OR PSALMS OF DAVID.

> *Philadelphia: Printed by Hall and Sellers, No. 51 Market Street.* MDCC-XCI. pp. [291]; 221, (3). 12mo.   AAS. HC. LOC.

Second title: THE WHOLE BOOK OF PSALMS, IN METRE; WITH HYMNS, SUITED TO THE FEASTS AND FASTS OF THE CHURCH, AND OTHER OCCASIONS OF PUBLIC WORSHIP.

> *Philadelphia: Printed by Hall & Sellers.* MDCCXCI. pp. 221, (3).

The second issue of the standard Book of Common Prayer, of the American Church. Pennsylvania District Copyright, issued to William Hall, 7 August, 1790.

23722 —— CONSTITUTION OF THE PROTESTANT EPISCOPAL CHURCH OF THE UNITED STATES
> *Philadelphia: Printed by Hall & Sellers?* 1791. 12mo.

23723 PROVIDENCE. RHODE ISLAND. BANK.
CONSTITUTION OF THE BANK, ESTABLISHED AT PROVIDENCE, IN THE STATE OF RHODE-ISLAND AND PROVIDENCE PLANTATIONS, ON MONDAY THE THIRD OF OCTOBER, 1791. [Two columns.] [Colophon:]

> *[Providence:] Printed by J. Carter.* [1791.] Broadside. fol. NYHS. RIHS.

Reprinted from the Providence Gazette of October 15, 1791.

23724 —— RULES OBSERVED AT THE BANK IN PROVIDENCE. [Twenty-nine lines.] PROVIDENCE, OCTOBER, 13, 1791. [Colophon:]

> *Printed by J. Carter.* 1791. Broadside. fol.   RIHS.

23725 THE PROVIDENCE GAZETTE AND COUNTRY JOURNAL. NO. 1. OF VOL. XXVIII. NO. 1409. SATURDAY, JANUARY 1, [— NO. 53. OF VOL. XXVIII. NO. 1461. SATURDAY, DECEMBER 31, 1791.]

> *[Providence:] Published by John Carter, at the Post-Office, near the State-House.* 1791. fol.   AAS. JCB. NYPL. RIHS.

23726 RABAUT, called RABAUT DE SAINT-ESTIENNE, JEAN PAUL   1743 – 1793
AN ADDRESS TO THE PEOPLE OF ENGLAND. ON THE SUBJECT OF PEACE. BY M. RABAUT DE ST. ESTIENNE, LATE PRESIDENT OF THE NATIONAL ASSEMBLY OF FRANCE.

> *Boston: Printed by John Howel, and sold by Ebenezer Larkin, jun. No. 50. Cornhill.* 1791.

23727 READ, JOHN K.
THE NEW AHIMON REZON. CONTAINING THE LAWS AND CONSTITUTIONS OF THE GRAND LODGE OF VIRGINIA. TO WHICH IS ADDED, THE HISTORY OF MASONRY, FROM THE CREATION, TO THE DEATH OF QUEEN ELIZABETH. ALSO ILLUSTRATIONS OF THE ROYAL ART: AND A VARIETY OF OTHER MATTER RELATIVE TO THAT INSTITUTION. CAREFULLY COLLATED, FROM THE MOST APPROVED AUTHORS, ANCIENT AS WELL AS MODERN. BY JOHN K. READ, PRESENT DEPUTY GRAND MASTER OF VIRGINIA, AND MEMBER OF THE SUBLIME LODGE OF PERFECTION, OF CHARLESTON. SOUTH-CAROLINA. "CAUSA LATET VIS EST NOTISSIMA.—"OVID MET." L 4. VER. 207. [Ornament.]

> *Richmond: Printed by John Dixon.* MDCC,XCI. pp. (2), xvi, (4), [9], 241, (1). 8vo.   AAS. LOC.

Dedicated to George Washington. Contains, Sanction of the Virginia Grand Lodge for publication. Rules and regulations of the Georgia Grand Lodge. pp. 223—228. A Collection of Masonic songs. pp. 229—241. 3d Virginia District Copyright.

23728 [One line Hebrew.] REASON AND FAITH, OR, PHILOSOPHICAL ABSURDITIES, AND THE NECESSITY OF REVELATION. INTENDED TO PROMOTE FAITH AMONG INFIDELS, AND THE UNBOUNDED EXERCISE OF HUMANITY AMONG ALL RELIGIOUS MEN. BY ONE OF THE SONS OF ABRAHAM TO HIS BRETHREN.
Jamaica Printed, 1788. Philadelphia: Re-printed and sold by Francis Bailey, No. 116, High-Street. MDCCXCI. pp. xii, 9—183. 12mo. AAS. BA. JCB.

23729 REICHE, CARL CHRISTOPH
FIFTEEN DISCOURSES ON THE MARVELLOUS WORKS IN NATURE, DELIVERED BY A FATHER TO HIS CHILDREN; CALCULATED TO MAKE MANKIND FEEL, IN EVERY THING, THE VERY PRESENCE OF A SUPREME BEING, AND TO INFLUENCE THEIR MINDS WITH A PERMANENT DELIGHT IN, AND FIRM RELIANCE UPON, THE DIRECTIONS OF AN ALMIGHTY, ALL-GOOD, AND ALL-WISE CREATOR, AND GOVERNOR. BY CHARLES CHRISTOPHER REICHE, M. A.
Philadelphia: Printed for the Author, by James & Johnson, and to be sold by them, the Author, and all the Booksellers in the City. MDCCXCI. [Three lines of prices.] pp. (2), (2), 180. 12mo.   AAS. BM. JCB. LCP. LOC.
9th Pennsylvania District Copyright, issued to Charles Christopher Reiche, as Author, 15 October, 1790.

23730 RELLY, JAMES   1720 – 1778
HYMNS USED IN THE UNIVERSAL CHURCHES. BY JAMES RELLY. A NEW EDITION.
Boston: Printed for B. Larkin, at Shakespeare's-Head, No. 46, Cornhill. 1791.

23731 REMARKS ON THE MANUFACTURING OF MAPLE SUGAR: WITH DIRECTIONS FOR ITS FURTHER IMPROVEMENT. COLLECTED FROM THE BEST IMPROVEMENTS. BY A SOCIETY OF GENTLEMEN IN PHILADELPHIA, AND PUBLISHED FOR THE BENEFIT AND INFORMATION OF THE CITIZENS OF THE UNITED STATES.
Philadelphia, Printed: New-York, Re-printed by William Morton, No. 231, Queen-Street. 1791. pp. 23. 12mo.   BM. JCB

23732 —— REMARKS ON THE MANUFACTURING OF MAPLE SUGAR; WITH DIRECTIONS FOR ITS FURTHER IMPROVEMENT. BY A SOCIETY OF GENTLEMEN IN PHILADELPHIA.
Albany: Printed by Charles R. and George Webster, 1791.
Recommended by Governor Clinton "to General Assembly now setting." Reprinted in London, in 1791.

23733 RHODE ISLAND. STATE.
FEBRUARY, 1791. AT THE GENERAL ASSEMBLY OF THE GOVERNOR AND COMPANY OF THE STATE OF RHODE-ISLAND AND PROVIDENCE-PLANTATIONS, BEGUN AND HELD BY ADJOURNMENT AT EAST-GREENWICH, WITHIN AND FOR THE STATE AFORESAID, ON THE LAST MONDAY IN FEBRUARY, IN THE YEAR OF OUR LORD ONE THOUSAND SEVEN HUNDRED AND NINETY-ONE, AND IN THE FIFTEENTH YEAR OF INDEPENDENCE.
[Providence: Printed by John Carter, 1791.] pp. 28. fol.   JCB. LOC.

23734 —— — MAY, 1791. AT THE GENERAL ASSEMBLY OF THE GOVERNOR AND COMPANY OF THE STATE OF RHODE-ISLAND AND PROVIDENCE-PLANTATIONS, BEGUN AND HOLDEN AT NEWPORT, WITHIN AND FOR THE STATE AFORESAID, ON THE FIRST WEDNESDAY IN MAY, IN THE YEAR OF OUR LORD ONE THOUSAND SEVEN HUNDRED AND NINETY-ONE, AND IN THE FIFTEENTH YEAR OF INDEPENDENCE.
[Providence: Printed by John Carter, 1791.] pp. 27. fol.   JCB. LOC.

RHODE ISLAND, continued.

23735 — — JUNE, 1791. AT THE GENERAL ASSEMBLY OF THE GOVERNOR AND COMPANY OF THE STATE OF RHODE-ISLAND AND PROVIDENCE-PLANTATIONS, BEGUN AND HOLDEN (BY ADJOURNMENT) AT NEWPORT, WITHIN AND FOR THE STATE AFORESAID, ON THE LAST MONDAY IN JUNE, IN THE YEAR OF OUR LORD ONE THOUSAND SEVEN HUNDRED AND NINETY-ONE, AND IN THE FIFTEENTH YEAR OF INDEPENDENCE. [Colophon:]
Providence: Printed by Bennett Wheeler. [1791.] pp. 33. fol.   JCB. LOC.

23736 — — OCTOBER, 1791. AT THE GENERAL ASSEMBLY OF THE GOVERNOR AND COMPANY OF THE STATE OF RHODE-ISLAND AND PROVIDENCE-PLANTATIONS, BEGUN AND HOLDEN AT SOUTH-KINGSTOWN, WITHIN AND FOR THE STATE AFORESAID, ON THE LAST MONDAY OF OCTOBER, IN THE YEAR OF OUR LORD ONE THOUSAND SEVEN HUNDRED AND NINETY-ONE, AND IN THE SIXTEENTH YEAR OF INDEPENDENCE. [Colophon:]
[Providence:] Printed by J. Carter. [1791.] pp. 41. fol.   JCB. LOC.

23737 — STATE OF RHODE-ISLAND AND PROVIDENCE PLANTATIONS. IN GENERAL ASSEMBLY, JUNE SESSION, 1791. AN ACT FOR GRANTING AND APPORTIONING A TAX OF SIX THOUSAND POUNDS, LAWFUL MONEY, UPON THE INHABITANTS OF THIS STATE. [Two columns.] A TRUE COPY, DULY EXAMINED: WITNESS, HENRY WARD, SEC'RY. [Colophon:]
Providence: Printed by J. Carter. [1791.] Broadside. fol.   RIHS.

23738 — STATE OF RHODE-ISLAND, &C. IN GENERAL ASSEMBLY, OCTOBER SESSION A. D. 1791. WHEREAS THE PRESIDENT AND DIRECTORS OF THE BANK, ESTABLISHED AT PROVIDENCE ON THE THIRD DAY OF OCTOBER LAST, HAVE PETITIONED THIS GENERAL ASSEMBLY FOR AN ACT TO INCORPORATE THE STOCKHOLDERS IN SAID BANK: AND WHEREAS WELL-REGULATED BANKS HAVE PROVED VERY BENEFICIAL IN SEVERAL OF THE UNITED STATES AS WELL AS IN EUROPE: THEREFORE, BE IT ENACTED BY THIS GENERAL ASSEMBLY, [Two columns.] A TRUE COPY, DULY COMPARED: WITNESS, HENRY WARD, SECRETARY. [Colophon:]
[Providence:] Printed by J. Carter. [1791.] Broadside. fol.   RIHS.

23739 RHODE ISLAND. COLLEGE OF, now BROWN UNIVERSITY.
HONORATISSIMO JABEZ BOWEN, ARMIGERO, COLLEGII RHOD. INSULÆ QUOD PROVIDENTIÆ EST CANCELLARIO; [Seven lines.] HÆC PHILOSOPHEMATA, JUVENES IN ARTIBUS INITIATI, [Sixteen names] HUMILLIMÈ DEDICANT. THESES [Three columns.] [Colophon:]
Habita in solennibus Academicis Providentiæ, in Rep, Ins. Rhod. et Prov. Plant. 4° nonas Septembris, A. D. M,DCC,XCI. Rerumpublicarum Fœderatarum Americæ summæ potestatis XVI. Providentiæ: Typis Bennett Wheeler. Broadside. fol.   AAS. BU.

23740 RICHARDSON, SAMUEL   1689 – 1761.
THE PATHS OF VIRTUE DELINEATED; OR, THE HISTORY IN MINIATURE OF THE CELEBRATED CLARISSA HARLOWE, FAMILIARISED AND ADAPTED TO THE CAPACITIES OF YOUTH. [Two lines from] CONGREVE.
Philadelphia: Printed and sold by W. Woodhouse, at the Bible, No. 6, south Front-Street. M.DCC.XCI.

23741 ROBBINS, CHANDLER   1738 – 1799
A SERMON. PREACHED BEFORE HIS EXCELLENCY JONH [*sic*] HANCOCK, ESQ. GOVERNOUR; HIS HONOR SAMUEL ADAMS ESQ. LIEUTENANT-GOVERNOR; THE HONOURABLE THE COUNCIL, AND THE HONOURABLE THE SENATE AND HOUSE OF REPRESENTATIVES, OF THE COMMONWEALTH OF MASSACHUSETTS, MAY 25, 1791. BEING THE DAY OF GENERAL ELECTION. BY CHANDLER ROBBINS, A. M. PASTOR OF THE FIRST CHURCH IN PLYMOUTH.
Boston, Massachusetts: Printed by Thomas Adams, Printer to the honourable the General Court, M,DCC,XCI. pp. 51. 8vo.
AAS. BA. HC. JCB. LOC. MHS. NYHS. NYPL.

23742   RODNEY, Cæsar Augustus   1772-1824
THE ORACLE OF LIBERTY, AND MODE OF ESTABLISHING A FREE GOVERNMENT. [Addressed to the people of Delaware. Signed, Hermes.]
—*Philadelphia—Printed by Parry Hall, No.* 149, *in Chesnut Street, near Fourth Street.* MDCCXCI. pp. [39.] 8vo.   BA. NYPL.

23743   ROWE, Elizabeth Singer   1674 – 1737
DEVOUT EXERCISES OF THE HEART, IN MEDITATION SOLILOQUY, PRAYER AND PRAISE. BY THE LATE PIOUS AND INGENIOUS MRS. ROWE. REVIEWED AND PUBLISHED, AT HER REQUEST BY I. WATTS, D. D.
Philadelphia: Printed & sold by R. Aitken & Son, Market-Street. M.DCC.-XCI. pp. 271. 48mo.   AAS.

23744   —— — DEVOUT EXERCISES OF THE HEART, IN MEDITATION, SOLILOQUY, PRAYER, AND PRAISE. BY THE LATE PIOUS AND INGENIOUS MRS. ROWE. REVIEWED AND PUBLISHED, AT HER REQUEST. BY I. WATTS, D. D.
Philadelphia: Printed by T. Dobson, at the Stone House, No. 41, *South Second-Street.* M,DCC,XCI. pp. 205, (2). 12mo.   AAS.

23745   ROWLANDSON, Mary White
A NARRATIVE OF THE CAPTIVITY, SUFFERINGS AND REMOVES OF MRS. MARY ROWLANDSON, WHO WAS TAKEN PRISONER BY THE INDIANS, WITH SEVERAL OTHERS; AND TREATED IN THE MOST BARBAROUS AND CRUEL MANNER BY THOSE VILE SAVAGES; WITH MANY OTHER REMARKABLE EVENTS DURING HER TRAVELS. WRITTEN BY HER OWN HAND FOR HER PRIVATE USE, AND SINCE MADE PUBLIC AT THE EARNEST DESIRE OF SOME FRIENDS, AND FOR THE BENEFIT OF THE AFFLICTED.
Boston: Re-printed and sold by Thomas and John Fleet, at the Bible and Heart, Cornhill. 1791. pp. 40. 8vo.   BA.

23746   RUM, Sir Richard, pseudonym.
AT A COURT HELD AT PUNCH-HALL, IN THE COUNTY OF BACCHUS. THE INDICTMENT AND TRIAL OF SIR RICHARD RUM, A PERSON OF NOBLE BIRTH AND EXTRACTION, WELL KNOWN BOTH TO RICH AND POOR, THROUGHOUT AMERICA. WHO WAS ACCUSED OF SEVERAL MISDEMEANORS AGAINST HIS MAJESTY'S LIEGE PEOPLE, VIZ: KILLING SOME, WOUNDING OTHERS, BRINGING THOUSANDS TO POVERTY AND MANY GOOD FAMILIES TO UTTER RUIN. IT IS NOT THE USE, BUT THE ABUSE, OF ANY GOOD THING THAT MAKES IT HURTFUL. WITH A PREFACE, AND SONG, COMPOSED BY SIR RICHARD, IMMEDIATELY AFTER HIS DISCHARGE.
Portsmouth: Printed by John Melcher, 1791.

23747   RUSH, Benjamin   1745 – 1813
THOUGHTS UPON FEMALE EDUCATION, ACCOMODATED TO THE PRESENT STATE OF SOCIETY, MANNERS AND GOVERNMENT, IN THE UNITED STATES OF AMERICA. ADDRESSED TO THE VISITORS OF THE YOUNG LADIES' ACADEMY IN PHILADELPHIA. 28 JULY, 1787, AT THE CLOSE OF THE QUARTERLY EXAMINATION. BY BENJAMIN RUSH, M. D. PROFESSOR OF CHEMISTRY IN THE UNIVERSITY OF PENNSYLVANIA.
Boston: Printed and sold by John W. Folsom, No. 30, *Union-Street. Sold also by Daniel Brewer of Taunton.* M,DCC,XCI. pp. 24. 24mo.   AAS.

23748   RUSH, Jacob   1746 – 1820
AN ADDRESS, DELIVERED JULY 8TH, 1790, TO THE JURY IN THE CASE OF THE COMMONWEALTH AGAINST JOHN PURDON AND OTHERS. BY THE HONORABLE JACOB RUSH, ESQUIRE, LATE ONE OF THE JUDGES OF THE SUPREME COURT OF PENNSYLVANIA.
Philadelphia: Printed by William Young, Bookseller, No. 52, *Second-Street, the corner of Chesnut-Street.* 1791. pp. 38. 8vo.

23749   RUSS, D.
          THE URANIAN HARMONY. A COLLECTION OF SACRED MUSIC. BY D. RUSS.
          Philadelphia: Printed by John M' Culloch, 1791. pp. 76—.

23750   ST. JOHN, PETER
          POETICAL RELATION OF THE CAPTURE OF THE CONGREGATION AT MIDDLESEX, [NOW
          DARIEN] CONNECTICUT, (WHO WERE ASSEMBLED FOR DIVINE WORSHIP, JULY 22ND
          1781,) BY A PARTY OF THE ENEMY FROM LONG ISLAND; WITH AN ACCOUNT OF
          THEIR SUFFERINGS, &C., WHILE IN CAPTIVITY. BY PETER ST. JOHN.
              [Danbury?] Printed [by Douglas and Ely?] for the Author. [1791.] 12mo.

23751   SALEM. MASSACHUSETTS.
          ESSEX, SS— TO EITHER OF THE CONSTABLES OF THE TOWN OF SALEM, IN SAID
          COUNTY, GREETING: YOU ARE, IN THE NAME OF THE COMMONWEALTH OF MASS-
          ACHUSETTS, DIRECTED TO WARN AND GIVE NOTICE TO   OF   IN THE
          COUNTY OF   WHO HAS LATELY COME INTO THIS TOWN FOR THE PURPOSE
          OF ABIDING THEREIN, NOT HAVING OBTAINED THE TOWN'S CONSENT THEREFOR,
          THAT HE DEPART THE LIMITS THEREOF, WITH   CHILDREN AND OTHERS UN-
          DER   CARE, WITHIN FIFTEEN DAYS. AND OF THIS PRECEPT, WITH YOUR
          DOINGS THEREON, YOU ARE TO MAKE RETURN INTO THE OFFICE OF THE CLERK OF
          THE TOWN OF SALEM WITHIN TWENTY DAYS NEXT COMING, THAT SUCH PROCEED-
          INGS MAY BE HAD IN THE PREMISES AS THE LAW DIRECTS. GIVEN UNDER OUR
          HANDS AND SEALS, AT SALEM AFORESAID THIS   DAY OF   A. D. 179
              SELECTMEN OF SALEM.
              [Salem: Printed by Thomas C. Cushing, 1791.] Broadside. 4to.   NYBS.

23752   THE SALEM GAZETTE. VOLUME V. NUMBER 221. TUESDAY, JANUARY 4, [—NUM-
          BER 272. TUESDAY, DECEMBER 27, 1791.]
              *Published by Thomas C. Cushing No. 8, Paved-[Main-]Street, near Court
              and Washington Streets, Salem. 1791. fol.*   AAS. LOC.

23753   SAUNDERS, RICHARD, pseudonym.
          POOR RICHARD IMPROVED: BEING AN ALMANACK AND EPHEMERIS OF THE MOTIONS
          OF THE SUN AND MOON; THE TRUE PLACES AND ASPECTS OF THE PLANETS; THE
          RISING AND SETTING OF THE SUN; AND THE RISING SETTING AND SOUTHING OF THE
          MOON, FOR THE YEAR OF OUR LORD 1792: BEING BISSEXTILE, OR LEAP-YEAR.
          [Eight lines.] BY RICHARD SAUNDERS, PHILOM.
              Philadelphia: Printed and sold by Hall & Sellers,—-No. 51—Market-street.
          [1791.] pp. (44). 12mo.   LOC.

23754   SCHEME OF A LOTTERY TO RAISE THE SUM OF FOUR THOUSAND POUNDS, AGREEABLY
          TO AN ACT OF THE LEGISLATURE OF THE STATE OF NEW-JERSEY, PASSED THE
          24TH NOVEMBER, 1790, FOR THE PURPOSE OF LAYING OUT AND IMPROVING THE
          ROADS AND CAUSEWAYS BETWEEN THE TOWN OF NEWARK, IN THE COUNTY OF
          ESSEX, AND PAULES-HOOK FERRY, IN THE COUNTY OF BERGEN, IN SAID STATE.
          . . . NEW-JERSEY, MARCH 8, 1791. [Colophon:]
              Elizabeth-Town, (New-Jersey) Printed by Shepard Kollock. [1791.] Broad-
          side. fol.   NYHS.

23755   SEABURY, SAMUEL   1729 – 1796
          A DISCOURSE, DELIVERED IN ST. JOHN'S CHURCH, IN PORTSMOUTH, NEWHAMPSHIRE,
          AT THE CONFERRING THE ORDER OF PRIESTHOOD ON THE REV. ROBERT FOWLE,
          A. M. OF HOLDERNESS. ON THE FESTIVAL OF ST. PETER, 1791 . . . [Five lines
          of Scripture texts.]
              *Printed at Boston, by Isaiah Thomas and Ebenezer T. Andrews, Faust's
              Statue, No, 45, Newbury Street. For George Jerry Osborne, jun. Printer, in
              Portsmouth.* MDCCXCI. pp. 22. 8vo.   AAS. BA. JCB. LOC. MHS. NYHS.

23756   SERLE, AMBROSE   1742 – 1812
THE CHRISTIAN PARENT: OR SHORT AND PLAIN DISCOURSES CONCERNING GOD, AND THE WORKS AND WORD OF GOD, IN CREATION, REDEMPTION AND SANCTIFICATION: INTENDED ORIGINALLY FOR SOME YOUNG PERSONS IN A FAMILY. [Four lines of Scripture texts.]
New-York: Printed by Samuel Loudon, No. 5, Water-Street. M,DCC,XCI. pp. vi, 158, (2). 16mo.   AAS. BPL.

23757   —— THE CHRISTIAN REMEMBRANCER, OR SHORT REFLECTIONS UPON THE FAITH, LIFE, AND CONDUCT OF A REAL CHRISTIAN. [One line from] 2 TIM. II. 14.
New-York: Printed and sold by Samuel Loudon, No. 5, Water-Street. M,DCC,XCI. pp. iv, 273, (9). 16mo.   AAS.
Contains a List of books for sale by Samuel Louden [*sic.*]

23758   SERMONS TO THE RICH AND STUDIOUS, ON TEMPERANCE AND EXERCISE. WITH A DEDICATION TO DR. CADOGAN. BY A PHYSICIAN. [Seven lines of Latin quotations.]
London Printed: Litchfield: Reprinted by T. Collier. [1791.] pp. 71. 24mo.
     JCB.

23759   SEWALL, DANIEL   1755 – 1842
AN ASTRONOMICAL DIARY, OR ALMANACK, FOR THE YEAR OF CHRISTIAN ÆRA, 1792: BY DANIEL SEWALL. . . .
Portsmouth: New-Hampshire, Printed and sold (wholesale and retail very cheap) by John Melcher, at his Printing-Office in Market-Street: sold also by most of the shopkeepers in town and country. [1791.] pp. [24.] 12mo.

23760   SHAFTSBURY. VERMONT. BAPTIST ASSOCIATION.
MINUTES OF THE SHAFTSBURY ASSOCIATION, AT THEIR ANNUAL CONVENTION, HELD IN STOCKBRIDGE, 1791.
Stockbridge: Printed by Loring Andrews? 1791.

23761   SHEPARD, SAMUEL   1739 – 1846
THREE LETTERS. LETTER FIRST, BEING A SCRIPTURAL ACCOUNT OF WATER BAPTISM; SECOND, A SCRIPTURAL ACCOUNT OF THE COVENANT GOD MADE WITH ABRAHAM. THIRD, A SCRIPTURAL ACCOUNT OF SPIRITUAL BAPTISM. ALSO, A POSTSCRIPT. CONTAINING SOME REMARKS UPON SEVERAL AUTHORS WHO HAVE WRITTEN IN DEFENCE OF INFANT BAPTISM. BY SAMUEL SHEPARD, PREACHER OF THE GOSPEL.
Portsmouth: Printed by George Jerry Osborne. M,DCC,XCI. pp. 72. 12mo.   JCB.

23762   SHERIDAN, THOMAS?
A SHORT, BUT PARTICULAR AND IMPARTIAL, ACCOUNT OF THE TREATMENT OF SLAVES, IN THE ISLAND OF ANTIGUA: WITH ANECDOTES AND NOTES.
Baltimore: Printed by W. Goddard, and James Angell, Market-Street. 1791.
"The Author, a nephew of Thomas Sheridan, A. M. proposes to teach in Baltimore and vicinity."

23763   A SHORT ACCOUNT OF THE APOSTOLIC RITE OF CONFIRMATION, WITH DIRECTIONS TO THOSE WHO WOULD PREPARE THEMSELVES DULY TO RECEIVE IT.
Albany: Printed by Charles R. and George Webster, No. 46, State-Street. 1791.

23764   THE SISTER'S GIFT; OR, THE NAUGHTY BOY REFORMED. PUBLISHED FOR THE ADVANTAGE OF THE RISING GENERATION. [Four lines of quotation.]
Boston: Printed and sold by Samuel Hall, No. 53 Cornhill. 1791. pp. 28. (2). 32mo.

23765   SMART, CHRISTOPHER   1722 – 1770
HYMNS FOR THE AMUSEMENT OF CHILDREN. BY THE REV. CHRISTOPHER SMART,
M. A. TO WHICH ARE ADDED, WATTS'S DIVINE SONGS FOR CHILDREN.
       Philadelphia: Printed by William Spotswood. 1791. pp. iv, 92. 24mo.
                                                 AAS.

23766   SMELLIE, WILLIAM   1740 – 1795
THE PHILOSOPHY OF NATURAL HISTORY. BY WILLIAM SMELLIE, MEMBER OF THE
ANTIQUARIAN AND ROYAL SOCIETIES OF EDINBURGH.
       *Philadelphia: Printed for Robert Campbell, Bookseller, north-east corner of
Second and Chesnut Street.* MDCCXCI. pp. 490, (1). 8vo.   AAS. BM. BPL. JCB.

23767   SMITH, EUNICE
SOME ARGUMENTS AGAINST WORLDLY-MINDEDNESS, AND NEEDLESS CARE AND
TROUBLE. – – WITH SOME OTHER USEFUL INSTRUCTIONS: REPRESENTED BY WAY
OF A DIALOGUE OR DISCOURSE BETWEEN TWO, CALLED BY THE NAMES OF MARY
AND MARTHA.
       Boston: Printed and sold by E. Russell, near the stump of Liberty-Tree.
1791.

23768   SMITH, JOSHUA, and others.
DIVINE HYMNS—OR SPIRITUAL SONGS FOR THE USE OF RELIGIOUS ASSEMBLIES AND
PRIVATE CHRISTIANS. THE THIRD EDITION CORRECTED. WITH AN ADDITION OF
THIRTY-TWO HYMNS.
       Exeter, New-Hampshire, Printed and sold by Henry Ranlet. 1791.

23769   —— — DIVINE HYMNS OR SPIRITUAL SONGS FOR THE USE OF RELIGIOUS ASSEM-
BLIES AND PRIVATE CHRISTIANS. BY JOSHUA SMITH AND OTHERS. CORRECTED
AND ENLARGED.
       Portsmouth: Printed and sold by John Melcher, in Market-Street. 1791.

23770   SMITH, ROBERT   1723 – 1793
THREE SERMONS, ON THE NATURE AND EXCELLENCY OF SAVING FAITH ; DELIVERED
AT PEQUEA, THE 21ST OF AUGUST, AND THE 10TH OF SEPTEMBER, 1791. BY THE
REVEREND ROBERT SMITH, D. D. PASTOR OF THE PRESBYTERIAN CHURCH OF
PEQUEA.
       Lancaster: Printed by Jacob Bailey? 1791.
       Reprinted in Carlisle, in 1792. In Volume IV, Austin's American
preacher. New-Haven, 1793. And in Part two, Select discourses
from the American preacher, in 1796.

23771   SMITH, SAMUEL STANHOPE   1750 – 1819
THREE DISCOURSES, I. ON THE GUILT AND FOLLY OF BEING ASHAMED OF RELIGION.
II. ON THE EVIL OF SLANDER. III. ON THE NATURE AND DANGER OF SMALL
FAULTS. DELIVERED AT BOSTON, IN OCTOBER, MDCCXC. BY THE REVEREND
SAMUEL STANHOPE SMITH, D. D. VICE-PRESIDENT AND PROFESSOR OF MORAL
PHILOSOPHY IN THE UNIVERSITY AT PRINCETON, NEW-JERSEY. PUBLISHED AT
THE REQUEST OF THE HEARERS.   AAS. BA. BM. HC. JCB. LOC. MHS. NYPL.

       Second title: A DISCOURSE ON THE GUILT AND FOLLY OF BEING ASHAMED OF RE-
LIGION. PREACHED AT THE OLD SOUTH CHURCH IN BOSTON, OCTOBER 17TH,
1790. BY THE REVEREND SAMUEL STANHOPE SMITH, D. D. VICE-PRESIDENT AND
PROFESSOR OF MORAL PHILOSOPHY IN THE UNIVERSITY AT PRINCETON, NEW-
JERSEY.
       *Boston: Printed by Joseph Bumstead, at his Printing-Office, No. 20, Union-
Street.* MDCCXCI. pp. (2), (25); [24]; [22.] 8vo.

SMITH, SAMUEL STANHOPE, continued.

Third title: A SERMON ON SLANDER, DELIVERED AT THE CHURCH IN BRATTLE-STREET, BOSTON, OCTOBER 24, 1790. BY THE REVEREND SAMUEL STANHOPE SMITH, D. D. VICE-PRESIDENT AND PROFESSOR OF MORAL PHILOSOPHY IN THE UNIVERSITY AT PRINCETON, NEW-JERSEY.

> *Boston: Printed by Samuel Hall, No. 53, Cornhill.* MDCCXCI. pp. [24.]

Fourth title: A DISCOURSE ON THE NATURE AND DANGER OF SMALL FAULTS, DE-LIVERED AT THE OLD SOUTH CHURCH IN BOSTON, OCTOBER 24, 1790. BY THE REVEREND SAMUEL STANHOPE SMITH, D. D. VICE-PRESIDENT AND PROFESSOR OF MORAL PHILOSOPHY IN THE UNIVERSITY AT PRINCETON, NEW-JERSEY.

> *Boston: Printed by Samuel Hall, No. 53, Cornhill.* MDCCXCI. pp. [22.]

With separate signatures, and sometimes found separate; but should be joined, as given above, by their general title.

23772 —— —— THREE DISCOURSES, I. ON THE GUILT AND FOLLY OF BEING ASHAMED OF RELIGION. II. ON THE EVIL OF SLANDER. III. ON THE NATURE AND DANGER OF SMALL FAULTS. DELIVERED AT BOSTON, IN OCTOBER, 1790. [Ornament.] BY THE REVEREND SAMUEL STANHOPE SMITH, D. D. VICE-PRESIDENT AND PROFESSOR OF MORAL PHILOSOPHY IN THE UNIVERSITY AT PRINCETON, NEW-JERSEY. THE SECOND EDITION.

> *Boston: Printed and sold by Samuel Hall, No. 53, Cornhill.* MDCCXCI. pp. 60. 12mo.   JCB.

23773 SMITH, WILLIAM   1754 – 1821
THE CONFESSION, &C. OF THOMAS MOUNT, WHO WAS EXECUTED AT LITTLE-REST, IN THE STATE OF RHODE-ISLAND, ON FRIDAY THE 27TH OF MAY: 1791, FOR BURG-LARY. [Cut of coffin.] [Colophon:]

> *Printed and sold by Peter Edes in Newport.* [1791.] pp. 21. 8vo. JCB. RIHS.

To the public, is signed, William Smith, Newport, May 20, 1791.

23774 —— —— THE CONFESSION, &C. OF THOMAS MOUNT, WHO WAS EXECUTED AT LITTLE-REST, IN THE STATE OF RHODE-ISLAND, ON FRIDAY THE 27TH OF MAY, 1791, FOR BURGLARY.

> *Newport, Printed. New-Haven: Re-printed by T. & S. Green.* 1791. pp. 22. 8vo.

23775 —— —— [Cut.] THE CONFESSION, &C. OF THOMAS MOUNT, WHO WAS EXECUTED AT LITTLE-REST, IN THE STATE OF RHODE-ISLAND, ON FRIDAY THE 27TH OF MAY, 1791, FOR BURGLARY.

> *Middletown: Re-printed by Moses H. Woodward, for Isaac Riley, & Co.* [1791.] pp. 22. (1). 8vo.   JCB.

"To which is added, a dictionary of the language of the American flash company; the oath administered to a flat on his admission into the flash society; and a number of flash songs."

23776 —— THE CONVICT'S VISITOR; OR, PENITENTIAL OFFICES; CONSISTING OF PRAYERS, LESSONS, AND MEDITATIONS, WITH SUITABLE DEVOTIONS BEFORE, AND AT THE TIME OF EXECUTION. BY WILLIAM SMITH, A. M. RECTOR OF TRINITY CHURCH IN NEWPORT.

> *Newport, (Rhode-Island) Printed by Peter Edes.* [1791.] pp. 85. 8vo. BA. MHS.

SMITH, WILLIAM, continued.

23777 —— A DISCOURSE DELIVERED BEFORE THE GRAND LODGE OF THE MOST ANCIENT AND HONORABLE FRATERNITY OF FREE AND ACCEPTED MASONS, OF THE STATE OF RHODE-ISLAND AND PROVIDENCE-PLANTATIONS, IN TRINITY CHURCH, NEWPORT, ON THE 27TH OF JUNE, 1791, THE DAY BY THEM APPOINTED FOR CELEBRATING THE FESTIVAL OF ST. JOHN THE BAPTIST.
Providence: Printed by Bennett Wheeler. [1791.] pp. 19. 4to. NHS.

23778 —— A DISCOURSE DELIVERED IN CHRIST'S CHURCH AT NORWICH-LANDING. IN THE STATE OF CONNECTICUT, ON WEDNESDAY, THE 24TH DAY OF AUGUST, BEING THE DAY OF INTRODUCING AN ORGAN INTO THAT CHURCH. BY WILLIAM SMITH, A. M. RECTOR OF TRINITY CHURCH, NEWPORT, RHODE-ISLAND STATE. [One line from] PSALM CL. 4.
Norwich: Printed by John Trumbull. M,DCC,XCI. pp. 26. 8vo. AAS. JCB.

23779 SOCIETY FOR USEFUL MANUFACTURES.
SOCIETY FOR USEFUL MANUFACTURES. No.   BE IT KNOWN, THAT   IS A SUBSCRIBER TO THE "SOCIETY FOR ESTABLISHING USEFUL MANUFACTURES" IN THE STATE OF NEW-JERSEY; AND THAT ON THE PAYMENT OF THE SEVERAL INSTALLMENTS, AGREEABLY TO THE ACT INCORPORATING THE SAID SOCIETY, AND THEIR ORDINANCE OF THE TENTH DAY OF DECEMBER ONE THOUSAND SEVEN HUNDRED AND NINETY-ONE   OR   ASSIGNS, WILL BE ENTITLED TO ONE SHARE IN THE STOCK OF SAID SOCIETY   GOVERNOR. COUNTERSIGNED BY   SEC'RY, PRO TEMP. [Colophon:]
New-York: Printed by H[u]g[h Ga[i]n]e. [1791.] Broadside. 4to. NYHS.

23780 THE SOLAR SYSTEM DISPLAYED.
Philadelphia: Printed and sold by John Zeller, at his Printing-Office, No. 89, Race-Street, five doors below Third-Street. 1791.

23781 SOUTH CAROLINA. STATE.
ACTS AND RESOLUTIONS OF THE GENERAL ASSEMBLY OF THE STATE OF SOUTH-CAROLINA, PASSED IN FEBRUARY, 1791.
Charleston: Printed by T. B. Bowen, No. 38, Bay. M.DCC.XCI. pp. (98), (4). fol. BM. LOC.

23782 THE SOUTH CAROLINA GAZETTE AND GENERAL ADVERTISER. JANUARY–DECEMBER, 1791.
Charleston: Printed by John Miller. 1791. fol.

23783 SOUTH CAROLINA YAZOO COMPANY.
AN EXTRACT FROM THE PROCEEDINGS OF THE SOUTH CAROLINA YAZOO COMPANY.
Charleston: Printed for A. Timothy, Printer to the State. MDCCLXXXXI. pp. (2), (2). (2); (2); (2), [44]; (2), [11]; (2), [27], [13], (1). 4to. BA. CLS. HC. LOC.
Second title: AN EXTRACT FROM THE SOUTH-CAROLINA YAZOO COMPANY, CONTAINING AN ACCOUNT OF ITS VIEWS, TRANSACTIONS, AND PRESENT STATE. PUBLISHED BY ORDER OF THE COMPANY. pp. (2), (2).
Third title: A REPORT OF THE SECRETARY OF THE SOUTH-CAROLINA YAZOO COMPANY. 1791. pp. (2).
Fourth title: A REPORT OF THE SECRETARY OF THE SOUTH-CAROLINA YAZOO COMPANY. IN THREE PARTS. PART I. pp. (2), [44.]
Fifth title: A REPORT OF THE SECRETARY OF THE SOUTH-CAROLINA YAZOO COMPANY. IN THREE PARTS. PART II. pp. (2), [11.]
Sixth title: A REPORT OF THE SECRETARY OF THE SOUTH-CAROLINA YAZOO COMPANY. IN THREE PARTS. PART III. pp. (2), [27], [13], (1).
This Report is said to have been drawn up by Robert Goodloe Harper.

23784 SPIERIN, George Hartwell
A Song composed for the fraternity of Steuben Lodge, No. 18. Newburgh, by G . . . H . . . S . . . January 18, 1791. Tune—"God save the King." [Seven, seven-line verses.]
[Goshen: Printed by David Mandeville, and David M. Westcott, 1791.] Broadside. 4to. NYHS.

23785 THE SPORTSMAN'S companion or an essay on shooting: illustriously shewing in what manner to fire at birds of game, in various directions and situations.—And, directions to gentlemen for the treatment and breaking their own pointers and spaniels, and the necessary precautions, to guard against many accidents that attend this pleasant diversion: with several other useful and interesting particulars relative thereto. By a Gentleman who has made shooting his favorite amusement upwards of twenty-six years, in Great-Britain, Ireland, and North-America.
Burlington: Printed by Isaac Neale, 1791.

23786 —— The Sportsman's companion or an essay on shooting: illustriously shewing in what manner to fire at birds of game, in various directions and situations.—And, directions to gentlemen for the treatment and breaking their own pointers and spaniels, and the necessary precautions, to guard against many accidents that attend this pleasant diversion: with several other useful and interesting particulars relative thereto. By a Gentleman, who has made shooting his favorite amusement upwards of twenty-six years, in Great-Britain Ireland, and North-America. Second edition.
Burlington: Printed by Isaac Neale. M,DCC,XCI. pp. [89], (2). 18mo.
LOC. NYPL
Mr. John Singer, Trenton—William Norcross, Bordentown—Joseph Douglas, Croswicks—John Perry & Mr. Zechariah Rossell, Mount-Holly—and Joseph Clunn, Bristol—held subscription papers, and one of them is probably the Author.

23787 SPRING, Samuel 1746 – 1819
The Exemplary pastor. A sermon preached at the ordination of the Rev. Azel Washburn, in Royalton, September 3, M.DCC.LXXX.IX. By Samuel Spring, A. M. pastor of the North church of Newbury-Port. Published by desire.
Printed at Windsor, Vermont, by Alden Spooner. M.DCC.XC.I. pp. 39. 8vo. JCB. NYPL.

23788 STANFORD, John 1754 – 1834
An Essay on the law of God. By John Stanford, M. A. [Two lines from] David.
New-York: Printed by Thomas and James Swords.—1791.—pp. 23. 12mo.
BM. JCB. NYHS.

23789 —— — A Lecture on the excellence of the Gospel of Christ, and its particular influence in supporting the mind under the sufferings of human life. Delivered as introductory to a course of lectures commenced August 7, 1791, under the patronage of a select number of gentlemen in the city of New-York. By John Stanford, M. A.
New-York: Printed by T. and J. Swords, No. 167, William-street. [1791.] pp. 28. 16mo. JCB. NYHS.

23790   STANHOPE, PHILIP DORMER, 4th earl of CHESTERFIELD.   1694 – 1773
PRINCIPLES OF POLITENESS, AND OF KNOWING THE WORLD. BY THE LATE LORD
CHESTERFIELD. METHODISED AND DIGESTED UNDER DISTINCT HEADS, WITH AD-
DITIONS BY THE REV. DR. JOHN TRUSLER: CONTAINING EVERY INSTRUCTION NEC-
ESSARY TO COMPLETE THE GENTLEMAN AND MAN OF FASHION. TO WHICH IS AD-
DED, A FATHER'S LEGACY TO HIS DAUGHTERS; BY THE LATE DR. GREGORY OF
EDINBURGH. ALSO, THOUGHTS ON FEMALE EDUCATION: BY BENJAMIN RUSH, M. D.
THE WHOLE ADMIRABLY CALCULATED FOR THE IMPROVEMENT OF YOUTH.

> *Boston: Printed and sold by John W. Folsom. Sold also by Daniel Brewer*
> *of Taunton.* M,DCC,XCI. pp. 102. 18mo.   AAS. BU

23791   STARKE, MARIANA   1762 – 1838
THE WIDOW OF MALABAR. A TRAGEDY. AS IT IS PERFORMED AT THE THEATRE-
ROYAL, COVENT-GARDEN. WRITTEN BY MARIANA STARKE. [Publisher's mon-
ogram.]

> *Philadelphia: Printed and sold by E. Story, in Fourth, between Market*
> *and Chesnut-streets, (No. 36).* [1791.] pp. (8), 33, (3). 12mo.   AAS.

23792   STATE GAZETTE OF NORTH-CAROLINA. VOL. VI. No. 260. FRIDAY, JANUARY 7,
[— No. 311. FRIDAY, DECEMBER 30, 1791.]

> *Edenton: Printed by Hodge and Wills.* 1791. fol.

23793   THE STATE GAZETTE OF SOUTH-CAROLINA. JANUARY—DECEMBER, 1791.

> *Charleston: Printed for A. Timothy.* 1791. fol.

23794   STEARNS, SAMUEL   1747 – 1819
THE AMERICAN DISPENSATORY. CONTAINING, I. THE MATERIA MEDICA. II. THE
OPERATION OF MEDICINES. III. THE ART AND SCIENCE OF PHARMACY. IV. THE
COMPOSITION OF MEDICINES. V. AN INDEX OF DISEASES AND THEIR REMEDIES.
VI. THE MANUAL OPERATIONS AND BEST REMEDIES USED IN SURGERY. BY THE
HON. SAMUEL STEARNS, ESQR. DOCTOR OF PHYSIC, AND OF THE CANON AND CIVIL
LAWS.

> *New-York:* 1791.

4th New York District Copyright, issued to Samuel Stearns, as Author,
8 September, 1791.

23795   —— THE AMERICAN ORACLE. COMPREHENDING AN ACCOUNT OF RECENT DISCOVER-
IES IN THE ARTS AND SCIENCES, WITH A VARIETY OF RELIGIOUS, POLITICAL, PHYS-
ICAL AND PHILOSOPHICAL SUBJECTS NECESSARY TO BE KNOWN IN ALL FAMILIES,
FOR THE PROMOTION OF THEIR PRESENT FELICITY AND FUTURE HAPPINESS. BY
THE HONOURABLE SAMUEL STEARNS, L. L. D. AND DOCTOR OF PHYSIC; ASTRONOMER
TO THE PROVINCES OF QUEBEC AND NEW-BRUNSWICK; ALSO TO THE COMMON-
WEALTH OF MASSACHUSETTS, AND THE STATE OF VERMONT IN AMERICA. [Two
lines of Latin.]

> *New-York: Printed for, and sold by Hodge and Campbell, Berry and Rogers,*
> *and T. Allen.* M.DCC.XCI. *The Copyright of this Book is secured agreeable to*
> *the Act of Congress.* [*Price two dollars in boards.*] pp. (2), (5), 627, xviii.
> 8vo.   AAS. BM. JCB. NYHS. NYPL.

The body of this edition is identical with the edition printed in London,
with a preface dated, London June 15, 1781 [*sic* 1791], and was evidently printed there. The title-page, and five prefatory pages, dated,
New-York, Sept. 12, 1791, only, were printed in this country. A plate
of the solar system, engraved by J. Robinson, London, should, apparently, face page 90, but is missing from the copy in the New York
Public Library, though always to be found at that page, in the edition
with a London imprint of this year. 5th New York District Copyright,
issued to Samuel Stearns, as Author, 8 September, 1791.

AUCTION
VALUES

STEARNS, Samuel, continued.

23796 —— Dr. Stearns's Tour from London to Paris. Containing, a description of the Kingdom of France. The customs, manners, polity, science, commerce and agriculture of the inhabitants. Its ancient form of government and the new. Particulars concerning the royal family. Causes of the late Revolution. Proceedings and decrees of the National Assembly. An account of the destruction of the Bastille, and of many dreadful commotions which have happened in the Nation. With a minute detail of the late grand proceedings at the Champ de Mars. The whole interspersed with a variety of reflections, humorous, moral, critical, and philosophical. After which is delineated, a new Constitution: with a description of the road to Liberty.

New-Haven: Sold by T. & S. Green, 1791.

Refers, perhaps, to the London, or Dublin, 1790, editions.

23797 —— The Mystery of animal magnetism revealed to the world. Containing philosophical reflections on the publication of a pamphlet entitled, A True and genuine discovery of animal electricity and magnetism, . . .

New-Haven: Sold by Isaac Beers, 1791.

Refers, perhaps, to the London, [1791], edition.

23798 —— The Universal calendar, and the North-American Almanack, for the year of the Christian æra, 1792. [Eight lines.] By the honorable Samuel Stearns, Esq. L. L. D.

Boston: Printed and sold by B. Edes & Son, No. 7, State-Street. pp. (24).
12mo.   AAS.

23799 STERNE, Laurence   1713 – 1768
The Beauties of Sterne: including all his pathetic tales, and most distinguished observations on life. Selected for the heart of sensibility. To which is added, the Life of Mr. Sterne.

Philadelphia; Printed and sold by W. Woodhouse, at the Bible, No. 6, South Front-Street. 1791.

23800 —— A Sentimental journey through France and Italy, by Mr. Yorick. In two volumes.

Philadelphia: Printed and sold by W. Woodhouse, at the Bible, No. 6, South Front-Street. 1791.

23801 STILLMAN, Samuel   1737 – 1807
Apostolic preaching considered in three discourses, delivered November 1790. By Samuel Stillman, D. D. pastor of the first Baptist church in Boston.

Boston: Printed by B. Edes and Son, No. 7, State-Street. M,DCC,XCI.
pp. [75.] 8vo.   AAS. BA. HC. JCB. LOC. MHS.

23802 —— A Sermon, preached May 31, 1791, in Providence, State of Rhode-Island, on the death of Nicholas Brown, esq; who died the 29th preceeding, æt. 62. Published at the desire of the bereaved family. By Samuel Stillman, D. D. pastor of the first Baptist church in Boston, and fellow of R. Island College. [Ornament.]

Providence: Printed by J. Carter. [1791.] pp. [24], (iv). 8vo.
                                  AAS. JCB. NYPL.

23803 STONINGTON. Connecticut. Baptist Association.
Minutes of the Stonington Association. 1791.

New-London: Printed by T. Green and Son? 1791.

23804   STRONG, CYPRIAN   1743 – 1811
A DISCOURSE ON ACTS II. 42. IN WHICH THE PRACTICE OF OWNING THE COVENANT
IS EXAMINED:—THE ARGUMENTS, WHICH HAVE BEEN USED IN ITS FAVOUR ARE
PARTICULARLY CONSIDERED: AND REASONS OFFERED FOR ITS ABOLITION. BY
CYPRIAN STRONG, A. M. PASTOR OF THE FIRST CHURCH IN CHATHAM. [Three lines
of quotations.] THE SECOND EDITION.
       Hartford: Printed by Hudson and Goodwin.   M.DCC.XCI. pp. 56. 4to.
                                          AAS. BM. HC. JCB. LOC. UTS. YC.

23805   STRONG, NEHEMIAH   1729 – 1807
AN ASTRONOMICAL DIARY, KALENDAR, OR ALMANACK, FOR THE YEAR OF OUR LORD
1792. . . . BY NEHEMIAH STRONG.
       Hartford: Printed for Elisha Babcock.   [1791.] pp. (24). 12mo.   CHS.

23806   —— — AN ASTRONOMICAL DIARY, KALENDAR, OR ALMANACK, FOR THE YEAR OF
OUR LORD 1792. [Ten lines.] BY N. STRONG, LATE PROFESSOR OF MATHE-
MATICKS, AND NATURAL PHYLOSOPHY IN YALE-COLLEGE. [Four lines of verse.]
       Hartford: Printed for Nathaniel Patten.   [1791.] pp. (24). 12mo.
                                          AAS. CHS. LOC. YC.

23807   —— — AN ASTRONOMICAL DIARY, CALENDAR, OR ALMANAC, FOR THE YEAR 1792.
ADAPTED TO THE HORIZON AND MERIDIAN OF LITCHFIELD. BY NEHEMIAH
STRONG.
       Litchfield: Printed by T. Collier.   [1791.] pp. (24). 12mo.   CHS.

23808   —— THE MIDDLESEX ALMANACK, OR LADY'S AND GENTLEMAN'S DIARY, FOR THE
YEAR OF OUR LORD CHRIST, 1792: . . .
       Middletown: Printed and sold by Moses H. Woodward.   [1791.] pp. (24).
12mo.
                                                CHS.

23809   —— STAFFORD'S ALMANACK, FOR THE YEAR OF OUR LORD, 1792. [Eleven lines.]
THE SEASONS MORALIZE. [Five four-line verses.]
       New-Haven; Printed by T. and S. Green.   [1791.] pp. (24). 12mo.
                                      AAS. CHS. LOC. NYPL. YC.

23810   —— SHEET ALMANACK FOR THE YEAR 1792.
       New-Haven: Printed by T. and S. Green. [1791.]   Broadside. fol.

23811   STUDDIFORD, PETER
A FUNERAL SERMON, ON THE DEATH OF THE REV. JACOB R. HARDENBERGH, D. D.
PRESIDENT OF QUEEN'S COLLEGE, AND PASTOR OF THE DUTCH CHURCH IN NEW-
BRUNSWICK. BY PETER STUDDIFORD, A. M. TO WHICH IS ADDED, AN ELEGY ON
HIS DEATH, BY A FRIEND.
       New-Brunswick: Printed by Abraham Blauvelt.   1791.

23812   SULLIVAN, JAMES   1744 – 1808
OBSERVATIONS UPON THE GOVERNMENT OF THE UNITED STATES OF AMERICA. BY
JAMES SULLIVAN, ESQ. ATTORNEY-GENERAL OF THE COMMONWEALTH OF MASSA-
CHUSETTS.
       Boston: Printed and sold by Samuel Hall, No. 53, Cornhill.   MDCCXCI.
pp. [55.] 8vo.   AAS. BA. BM. BPL. JCB. LOC. MHS. NL. NYHS. NYPL.

23813   SUMNER, JOSEPH   1740 – 1824
MINISTERS SPIRITUAL BUILDERS OF GOD'S HOUSE. A SERMON, DELIVERED AT
THE ORDINATION OF THE REV. SAMUEL SUMNER, A. M. TO THE PASTORAL CHARGE
OF THE CHURCH IN SOUTHBOROUGH, JUNE 1ST, MDCCXCI. BY JOSEPH SUMNER,
A. M. PASTOR OF THE CHURCH IN SHREWSBURY.
       Printed at Worcester, Massachusetts, by Isaiah Thomas.   MDCCXCI. pp.
30. 8vo.   AAS. JCB.

23814 SWEETING, WHITING   - 1791
THE NARRATIVE OF WHITING SWEETING, WHO WAS EXECUTED AT ALBANY, AUG.
26, 1791. (AND CLOSE PAPERS IN SMALL TYPE.) CONTAINING, AN ACCOUNT OF
HIS TRIAL BEFORE THE SUPREME COURT OF JUDICATURE OF THE STATE OF NEW-
YORK, AT THE JULY TERM, 1791, FOR THE MURDER OF DARIUS QUIMBY; THE
SUBSTANCE OF THE CHARGE OF HIS HONOR THE CHIEF-JUSTICE TO THE JURY, WITH
THE SENTENCE OF DEATH ON THE PRISONER; AN ADDRESS TO THE PUBLIC, ON THE
FATAL CONSEQUENCES OF A LIFE SPENT IN SIN, INSTANCED IN HIS OWN CONDUCT—
SETTING FORTH THE GREAT NECESSITY OF REMEMBERING OUR CREATOR IN THE
DAYS OF OUR YOUTH AND PRACTISING RELIGION AND VIRTUE IN OUR WHOLE LIVES;
AN ADDRESS TO HIS PARENTS; TO HIS BROTHERS AND SISTERS; TO HIS WIFE AND
CHILDREN; WITH A MORAL INSTRUCTION BY WAY OF QUESTION AND ANSWER, PAR-
TICULARLY ADDRESSED TO THEM; AN ADDRESS TO THE PARENTS OF HIS WIFE; TO
HIS BROTHERS AND SISTERS BY MARRIAGE; A FEW LINES ON HIS SENSE OF GRATI-
TUDE TO MR. OSTRANDER THE GOALER [*sic*]; HIS APPEAL TO THE HIGH COURT OF
HEAVEN, FOR THE TRUTH OF HIS DECLARATION "THAT THE MURDER WAS COM-
MITTED WITHOUT MALICE PREPENSE" WITH A SKETCH OF THE PROCEEDINGS WHICH
LED TO HIS BEING TAKEN—THE WARRANT, &C. A FEW WORDS ON THE GREAT IM-
PROPRIETY OF FALSE-SWEARING, OR GIVING A FALSE COLOURING TO TESTIMONY
BEFORE A COURT, IN NOT RELATING THE WHOLE TRUTH; THE REASON FOR HIS ES-
CAPING FROM PRISON; HIS ACKNOWLEDGEMENTS TO THE GENTLEMEN OF THE
CLERGY FOR THEIR ATTENTION TO HIM DURING HIS CONFINEMENT; HIS SENTI-
MENTS OF FREE GRACE, FREE WILL, &C. &C. WRITTEN BY HIMSELF, AND PUB-
LISHED FOR THE BENEFIT OF PRECIOUS SOULS AT HIS PARTICULAR AND DYING RE-
QUEST. TO WHICH ARE ADDED, AN ACCOUNT OF THE BEHAVIOUR OF THE UNHAPPY
SUFFERER FROM HIS CONFINEMENT TO EXECUTION, AND THE SUBSTANCE OF HIS
ADDRESS AT THE GALLOWS. BY ONE WHO HAD FREE ACCESS TO, AND FREQUENT
CONVERSATION WITH HIM. [William Carter.]
        Lansingburgh: Printed and sold by Silvester Tiffany. 1791.
        Extract from the prefatory Advertisement: "The unfortunate Whit-
ing Sweeting, having confidence in my promise, left with me his Nar-
rative for publication; his injunctions have been strictly adhered to,
as will appear on comparing with the copy. No other person has had
his writings, nor an opportunity of transcribing therefrom. Silvester
Tiffany.

23815 —— — THE NARRATIVE OF WHITING SWEETING. WHO WAS EXECUTED AT AL-
BANY, THE 26TH OF AUGUST, 1791. CONTAINING AN ACCOUNT OF HIS TRIAL BE-
FORE THE SUPREME COURT OF JUDICATURE OF THE STATE OF NEW-YORK, AT
THE JULY TERM, 1791, FOR THE MURDER OF DARIUS QUIMBY; THE SUBSTANCE
OF THE CHARGE OF HIS HONOUR THE CHIEF JUSTICE TO THE JURY, WITH THE
SENTENCE OF DEATH ON THE PRISONER; . . . [Same as preceding edition.]
WRITTEN BY HIMSELF, AND PUBLISHED FOR THE BENEFIT OF PRECIOUS SOULS, AT
HIS PARTICULAR AND DYING REQUEST. TO WHICH ARE ADDED, AN ACCOUNT OF
THE BEHAVIOUR OF THE UNHAPPY SUFFERER FROM HIS CONFINEMENT TO EXE-
CUTION, AND THE SUBSTANCE OF HIS ADDRESS AT THE GALLOWS. BY ONE WHO
HAD FREE ACCESS TO, AND FREQUENT CONVERSATION WITH HIM. [William Carter.]
        *Hartford: Printed [by Elisha Babcock] and sold by Hudson and Good-
win.* [1791.] pp. 36. 12mo.

23816 SWIFT, ZEPHANIAH   1759 - 1823
AN ORATION ON DOMESTIC SLAVERY. DELIVERED AT THE NORTH MEETING-HOUSE
IN HARTFORD, ON THE 12TH DAY OF MAY, A. D. 1791. AT THE MEETING OF THE
CONNECTICUT SOCIETY FOR THE PROMOTION OF FREEDOM, AND THE RELIEF OF
PERSONS UNLAWFULLY HOLDEN IN BONDAGE. BY ZEPHANIAH SWIFT, ESQUIRE.
[Publisher's monogram.]
        Hartford: Printed and sold by Hudson and Goodwin, M.DCC.XCI. pp.
[23.] 8vo.
                              AAS. CHS. HC. LOC. MHS. NYPL. UTS. YC.

23817   A SYSTEM OF CHEMISTRY; COMPREHENDING THE HISTORY, THEORY AND PRACTICE OF THE SCIENCE, ACCORDING TO THE LATEST DISCOVERIES AND IMPROVEMENTS. EXTRACTED FROM THE AMERICAN EDITION OF THE ENCYCLOPÆDIA.
Philadelphia: Printed by Thomas Dobson, at the Stone House in Second-Street, between Market and Chesnut Streets. 1791.

23818   A TABLE FOR UNDERSTANDING THE COINS, WEIGHTS AND MEASURES, MENTIONED IN THE BOOKS OF THE OLD AND NEW TESTAMENT.
Norwich: Printed and sold by John Trumbull. 1791.

23819   A TABLE OF INTEREST AT SIX PER CENT.
Norwich: Printed and sold by John Trumbull. 1791.

23820   TATHAM, WILLIAM   1752 – 1819
A TOPOGRAPHICAL ANALYSIS OF THE COMMONWEALTH OF VIRGINIA, COMPILED FOR THE YEARS 1790-1. SHEWING THE EXTENT AND RELATIVE SITUATION OF THE SEVERAL COUNTIES; THEIR DISTANCE FROM THE SEAT OF GOVERNMENT; POPULATION, FORCE, COUNTY LIEUTENANTS, REPRESENTATIVES, &C. ALSO THE DISTRICT, AND COUNTY COURTS, THE CIVIL LIST OF THE COMMONWEALTH, &C. CAREFULLY COLLECTED FROM PUBLIC RECORDS AND OTHER AUTHORITIES. TO BE CONTINUED ANNUALLY. . . . [Colophon:]
Richmond: Printed by Thomas Nicolson exclusive printer for the Author at that place. [1791.] Broadside. fol.   LOC. NYPL.

23821   —— — A TOPOGRAPHICAL ANALYSIS OF THE COMMONWEALTH OF VIRGINIA: COMPILED FOR THE YEARS 1790-1. SHEWING THE EXTENT, AND RELATIVE SITUATION OF THE SEVERAL COUNTIES, THEIR DISTANCE FROM THE SEAT OF GOVERNMENT; POPULATION; FORCE; COUNTY LIEUTENANTS; REPRESENTATIVES, &C. ALSO THE DISTRICT, AND COUNTY COURTS; THE CIVIL LIST OF THE COMMONWEALTH, &C. CAREFULLY COLLECTED FROM PUBLIC RECORDS, AND OTHER AUTHORITIES. TO BE CONTINUED ANNUALLY. . . . [Colophon:]
[Philadelphia: Printed by Charles Cist.] [1791.] Broadside. fol.   JCB.
4th Virginia District Copyright, issued to William Tatham, as Author, 2 August, 1791.

23822   TAYLOR, THOMAS
A SHORT ACCOUNT OF THE LAST SICKNESS AND DEATH OF THAT TRULY GREAT AND EXCELLENT MAN, THE REV. MR. JOHN WESLEY, A. M. TAKEN FROM THE NARRATIVE OF A PERSON WHO WAS PRESENT WHEN HE DIED.
Philadelphia: Printed by Parry Hall? and sold by John Dickins. 1791.

23823   TERSTEEGEN, GERHARD   1697 – 1769
GEISTLICHES BLUMEN-GÄRTLEIN INNIGER SEELEN; ODER KURTZE SCHLUSS-REIMEN, BETRACHTUNGEN UND LIEDER, UEBER ALLERHAND WAHRHEITEN DES INWENDIGEN CHRISTENTHUMS; ZUR ERWECKUNG, STÄRKUNG, UND ERQUICKUNG IN DEM VERBORGENEN LEBEN MIT CHRISTO IN GOTT; NEBST DER FROMMEN LOTTERIE. SIEBENTE UND VERMEHRTE AUFLAGE.
Germantaun Gedruckt und zu finden bey Peter Leibert, 1791. pp. (12), 534, (7). 12mo.   AAS. JCB.

23824   THACHER, PETER   1752 – 1802
A SERMON, PREACHED TO THE SOCIETY IN BRATTLE STREET, BOSTON, NOVEMBER 14, 1790. AND OCCASIONED BY THE DEATH OF THE HON. JAMES BOWDOIN, ESQ. L. L. D. F. R. S. LATELY GOVERNOR OF THE COMMONWEALTH OF MASSACHUSETTS. BY PETER THACHER, A. M. PASTOR OF THE CHURCH IN BRATTLE STREET.
Printed at Boston, by I. Thomas and E. T. Andrews, Faust's Statue, No. 45, Newbury Street. MDCCXCI. pp. 27. 4to.
A different issue from the following:

THACHER, PETER, continued.

23825 —— — A SERMON, PREACHED TO THE SOCIETY IN BRATTLE STREET, BOSTON, NOVEMBER 14, 1790, AND OCCASIONED BY THE DEATH OF THE HON. JAMES BOWDOIN, ESQ. L. L. D. LATELY GOVERNOR OF THE COMMONWEALTH OF MASS-ACHUSETTS. BY PETER THACHER, A. M. PASTOR OF THE CHURCH IN BRATTLE STREET.
Printed at Boston, by I. Thomas and E. T. Andrews, Faust's Statue, No. 45, Newbury Street. MDCCXCI. pp. 31. 8vo. AAS. BA. HC. JCB. LOC. MHS. NYPL.

23826 THOMAS'S MASSACHUSETTS SPY; OR THE WORCESTER GAZETTE. VOL. XIX. NO. 927. THURSDAY, JANUARY 6, [—VOL. XX. NO. 978. THURSDAY, DECEMBER 28, 1791.]
Printed at Worcester, Massachusetts, by Isaiah Thomas. 1791. fol. AAS.

23827 THOMSON, JAMES   1700 – 1748
THE SEASONS: CONTAINING SPRING. SUMMER. AUTUMN. WINTER. BY JAMES THOMSON. WITH THE LIFE OF THE AUTHOR, BY DR. SAMUEL JOHNSON.
Philadelphia: Printed and sold by W. Woodhouse, at the Bible, No. 6, South Front-street. 1791.

23828 THORN, STEPHEN
HASWELL'S VERMONT ALMANAC, FOR THE YEAR OF OUR LORD 1792; AND FROM THE CREATION OF THE WORLD, ACCORDING TO SACRED WRIT, 5754. BEING BISSEX-TILE, OR LEAP YEAR; AND THE 16TH OF AMERICAN INDEPENDENCE. CONTAIN-ING THE USUAL ASTRONOMICAL CALCULATIONS, TOGETHER WITH A VARIETY OF MATTERS, USEFUL AND ENTERTAINING. CALCULATED FOR THE MERIDIAN OF VER-MONT, LAT. 42 DEG. 20 MIN. N. LONG. 4 DEG. 3 MIN. WEST FROM WASHINGTON, IN THE FEDERAL DISTRICT. BY STEPHEN THORN, PHILOM. [Four lines of verse.]
Printed at Bennington, by Anthony Haswell, sold by him wholesale and re-tail. [1791.] pp. (24). 12mo.   NYHS.

23829 —— WEBSTER'S CALENDAR; OR, THE ALBANY ALMANACK, FOR THE YEAR OF OUR LORD 1792; FROM THE CREATION, 5741, AND OF AMERICAN INDEPENDENCE (WHICH WAS DECLARED JULY 4, 1776) PART OF THE XVI AND XVII—BEING BISSEX-TILE OR LEAP-YEAR. [Nineteen lines.] BY STEPHEN THORN, PHILOMATH.
Printed by Charles R. & George Webster, No. 46, State-Street, Albany; where printing in general is performed on reasonable terms. § X § Those who purchase by the quantity will have a generous allowance made them. [1791.] pp. (36). 12mo.   AAS. LOC.
Contains, The Constitution of the State of New-York, established by the Convention, authorised, and empowered for that purpose, April 20, 1777. And, Sketch of the life of Frederic Baron Trenck, with en-graving.

23830 THORNTON, ELISHA
THE RHODE-ISLAND ALMANACK, FOR THE YEAR OF OUR LORD 1792. BEING LEAP YEAR AND SIXTEENTH OF AMERICAN INDEPENDENCE. CALCULATED FOR THE ME-RIDIAN OF NEWPORT, LATITUDE 41 DEG. 25 MIN. N. AND LONGITUDE 71 DEG. 15 MIN. W. AND MAY SERVE THE ADJACENT STATES. THE ASTRONOMICAL CALCULA-TIONS BY E. THORNTON. [Four lines of verse.]
Newport (Rhode-Island) Printed and sold by P. Edes. [1791.] pp. (24). 12mo.   AAS. NYPL. RIHS.

23831 THURSTON, BENJAMIN   1756 – 1804
FOUR SERMONS, DELIVERED BY BENJAMIN THURSTON, A. M. MINISTER OF THE GOS-PEL AT NORTH-HAMPTON, TO THE PEOPLE OF HIS CHARGE THERE: AND PUBLISHED BY THE DESIRE OF MANY OF THE HEARERS.
Portsmouth, (N. H.) Printed and to be sold by George Jerry Osborne, jun'r. at his Office in Congress-Street. M,DCC,XCI. pp. [71.] 8vo. AAS. JCB. LOC. NYHS.

23832   TIFFANY'S [cut] RECORDER. No. 1. TUESDAY, SEPTEMBER 20, [—No. 15. TUES-
DAY, DECEMBER 27, 1791.]
      *Lansingburgh: Printed by Silvester Tiffany, at his Office, over the Store of
Mr. W. Bell.* 1791. fol.
      Established by Silvester Tiffany, and continued by him into the year
1794, when it was sold to George Gardner and   Hill, who continued its publication to August, 1795, as *The Recorder.* In August,
1795, the press was removed to Troy, New York, George Gardner continuing publication of *The Recorder* there, with a continuous serial
numbering, into the year 1796.

23833   THE TIMES, AND PATOWMACK PACKET. [Motto.] VOL. II. No. 99. WEDNESDAY,
JANUARY 5, [—VOL. III. No. 125. WEDNESDAY, JULY 6, 1791.]
      George-Town: Printed by Charles Fierer and Thomas W. Fosdick. 1791.
fol.
      It is not known whether publication was continued after this date.

23834   TO THE PUBLIC. SOME REMARKS ON THE PROCEEDINGS OF THE LATE CONVENTION:
WITH A FEW OBSERVATIONS ON OUR PRESENT GOVERNMENT: ALL WHICH ARE
HUMBLY SUBMITTED—BY THE AUTHOR.
      New-Hampshire: Printed—seventeen hundred and ninety-one. pp. [31,]
(1). 8vo.
                                     AAS. BA. JCB. LOC. NYHS.

23835   TOBLER, JOHN
      THE SOUTH-CAROLINA AND GEORGIA ALMANAC FOR THE YEAR OF OUR LORD 1792:
BEING LEAP YEAR, AND (TILL THE 4TH OF JULY) THE SIXTEENTH OF AMERICAN
INDEPENDENCE. [Four lines.] BY JOHN TOBLER, ESQ. [Six lines. Ornament.]
      Charleston: Printed by Markland & M'Iver, No. 47, Bay. [1791.] pp.
(36). 12mo.
                                              LOC.

23836   —— — THE SOUTH-CAROLINA, NORTH-CAROLINA, AND GEORGIA ALMANACK, FOR
THE YEAR OF OUR LORD 1792: BEING BISSEXTILE, OR LEAP-YEAR, AND (TILL THE
FOURTH OF JULY) THE SIXTEENTH YEAR OF AMERICAN INDEPENDENCE. [Four-
teen lines.] BY JOHN TOBLER, ESQ: "STARS TEACH AS WELL AS SHINE."
      Charleston: Printed by W. P. Harrison. [1791.] pp. (24). 12mo.   LOC.

23837   TOPHAM, EDWARD   1751 – 1820
      A SURPRISING ACCOUNT OF THE LIFE OF THE LATE JOHN ELWES, ESQUIRE. [Two
lines from] SHAFTESBURY'S CHARACT.
      *Philadelphia: Printed and sold by John Zeller, at his Printing-Office, No.
89, Race-Street, five doors below Third-Street.* 1791.

23838   TOWNSEND, SHIPPIE
      SCRIPTURE TRUTHS AND PRECEPTS. A SHORT CATECHISM, WITH PROOFS. DESIGNED
FOR THE ASSISTANCE OF SUCH PERSONS AS WISH TO SEARCH THE SCRIPTURES FOR
A CONSISTENT VIEW OF THE DOCTRINES AND DUTIES CONTAINED IN THEM. WITH
AN APPENDIX, CONCERNING BAPTISM. AND A CONCLUDING REMARK ON THE
LORD'S-SUPPER. [Two lines from] PAUL TO THE CORINTHIANS.
      Boston: Printed and sold by Samuel Hall, No. 53, Cornhill. MDCCXCI.
(*Price 9d.*) pp. 23. 8vo.
                                            AAS. JCB. NYHS.

23839   A TREATISE ON UNIVERSAL REDEMPTION. WHEREIN IS CONTAINED, MANY SCRIPT-
URE PROOFS TO SUPPORT THE SAME. LIKEWISE MANY WEIGHTY AND PRESSING
ARGUMENTS, BOTH FROM SCRIPTURE, REASON AND JUSTICE, TO PROVE THE REALITY
OF THAT DOCTRINE. ALSO—SOME OBSERVATIONS ON THE DIFFERENT OPINIONS OF
THOSE THAT OPPOSE IT. TO WHICH IS ADDED A FEW POETICAL QUERIES TO PROVE
THE SAME.
      Richmond: Printed by Thomas Nicholson? 1791.

AUCTION VALUES

23840   TRUMBULL, BENJAMIN   1735 – 1820
Half-title: MR. TRUMBULL'S SERMON, ON THE IMPORTANCE OF AN IMMMEDIATE CHOICE OF GOD.

Title: ILLUSTRATIONS ON THE NATURE AND IMPORTANCE OF AN IMMEDIATE CHOICE OF GOD. IN A SERMON, DELIVERED AT NORTH-HAVEN, AND SINCE, OCCASIONALLY AT SEVERAL OTHER PLACES. IT IS NOW MADE PUBLIC AT THE PARTICULAR DESIRE, AND EXPENSE, OF AN HONORABLE AND PIOUS FRIEND: WITH A VIEW TO THE AWAKENING AND CONVERSION OF DELAYING SINNERS, AND TO THE INSTRUCTION AND CONSOLATION OF THE SAINTS. BY BENJAMIN TRUMBULL, A. M. PASTOR OF THE CHURCH IN NORTH-HAVEN. [Six lines of Scripture texts.
New-London: Printed by Timothy Green and Son. M,DCC,XCI. pp. [23.] 8vo.   AAS. JCB.

23841   TRUMBULL, JOHN   1750 – 1831
M'FINGAL: AN EPIC POEM. IN FOUR CANTOS. BY JOHN TRUMBULL, ESQ. [Two lines of Latin.] [Ornament.]
Philadelphia: From the Press of Mathew Carey. M.DCC,XCI. pp. (95), (1). 12mo.   AAS. BM. HC. JCB. LCP. NYPL. YC.

23842   UNITED STATES OF AMERICA.
ACTS PASSED AT A CONGRESS OF THE UNITED STATES OF AMERICA, BEGUN AND HELD AT THE CITY OF NEW-YORK, ON WEDNESDAY THE FOURTH OF MARCH, IN THE YEAR M,DCC,LXXXIX: AND OF THE INDEPENDENCE OF THE UNITED STATES, THE THIRTEENTH. PUBLISHED BY AUTHORITY.
Philadelphia: Printed by Francis Childs and John Swaine, Printers to the United States. [1791.] pp. [93]. (1), (1). fol.   LOC.
A reprint of their 1789 edition, printed on fine paper with uncut edges.

23843   —— — ACTS PASSED AT A CONGRESS OF THE UNITED STATES OF AMERICA, BEGUN AND HELD AT THE CITY OF NEW-YORK ON WEDNESDAY THE FOURTH OF MARCH IN THE YEAR M.DCC.LXXXIX, BEING THE ACTS PASSED AT THE FIRST SESSION OF THE FIRST CONGRESS OF THE UNITED STATES, TO WIT, NEW-HAMPSHIRE, MASSACHUSETTS, CONNECTICUT, NEW-YORK, NEW-JERSEY, PENNSYLVANIA, DELAWARE, MARYLAND, VIRGINIA. SOUTH-CAROLINA, AND GEORGIA, WHICH ELEVEN STATES RATIFIED THE CONSTITUTION OF GOVERNMENT FOR THE UNITED STATES.
Hartford: Printed by Hudson and Goodwin. MDCCXCI. pp. 486, (9), 8vo.   BA. BM. JCB. RIHS.

23844   —— — ACTS PASSED AT THE SECOND SESSION OF THE CONGRESS OF THE UNITED STATES OF AMERICA, BEGUN AND HELD AT THE CITY OF NEW-YORK, ON MONDAY, THE FOURTH OF JANUARY, [—12 August,] IN THE YEAR M,DCC,XC: AND OF THE INDEPENDENCE OF THE UNITED STATES, THE FOURTEENTH. PUBLISHED BY AUTHORITY.
Richmond: Printed by Aug. Davis. For the General Assembly of Virginia. [1791.] pp. [112], (2). fol.   LOC. NYPL.

23845   —— — ACTS PASSED AT THE THIRD SESSION OF THE CONGRESS OF THE UNITED STATES OF AMERICA, BEGUN AND HELD AT THE CITY OF PHILADELPHIA ON MONDAY THE SIXTH OF DECEMBER, IN THE YEAR M,DCC.XC [—3 March, 1791]: AND OF THE INDEPENDENCE OF THE UNITED STATES, THE FOURTEENTH. PUBLISHED BY AUTHORITY.
Philadelphia: Printed by Francis Childs and John Swaine, Printers to the Congress of the United States. [1791.] pp. (2), [227] —286, (28), (1). fol.   LOC. NYPL.
This is not the original issue.

UNITED STATES, continued.

23846 —— — ACTS PASSED AT THE THIRD SESSION OF THE CONGRESS OF THE UNITED STATES OF AMERICA, BEGUN AND HELD AT THE CITY OF PHILADELPHIA ON MONDAY THE SIXTH OF DECEMBER, IN THE YEAR M,DCC,XC [—3 March, 1791]: AND OF THE INDEPENDENCE OF THE UNITED STATES THE FOURTEENTH. PUBLISHED BY AUTHORITY.

> *Richmond: Printed by John Dixon. For the General Assembly of Virginia.* [1791.] pp. [41], (1). fol. NYPL.

23847 —— ACTS CONCERNING THE TERRITORY OF COLUMBIA, AND THE CITY OF WASHINGTON. PUBLISHED BY ORDER OF THE HOUSE OF REPRESENTATIVES. [Passed, December, 19, 1791.]

> *[Philadelphia: Printed by Francis Childs and John Swaine. 1791.]* pp. 14. 8vo. AAS. NYPL.

23848 —— A BILL TO AMEND THE ACT, ENTITLED "AN ACT TO PROMOTE THE PROGRESS OF THE USEFUL ARTS."

> *Philadelphia: Printed by Childs and Swaine.* [1790.] pp. 4. fol.

23849 —— CONGRESS OF THE UNITED STATES: AT THE SECOND SESSION, BEGUN AND HELD AT THE CITY OF NEW-YORK, ON MONDAY, THE FOURTH OF JANUARY, ONE THOUSAND SEVEN HUNDRED AND NINETY. AN ACT FOR THE GOVERNMENT & REGULATION OF SEAMEN IN THE MERCHANT SERVICE. [Three columns.] APPROVED JULY 20TH, 1790. GEORGE WASHINGTON, PRESIDENT OF THE UNITED STATES. THOMAS JEFFERSON, SECRETARY OF STATE. (A TRUE COPY.) [With Form of agreement between master and seamen, and blank lined spaces for names, on the verso.]

> *[Boston: Printed by Samuel Hall, No. 53, Cornhill. 1791.]* Broadside. fol. AAS.

23850 —— CONGRESS OF THE UNITED STATES: AT THE THIRD SESSION, BEGUN AND HELD AT THE CITY OF PHILADELPHIA, ON MONDAY THE SIXTH OF DECEMBER, ONE THOUSAND SEVEN HUNDRED AND NINETY. AN ACT DECLARING THE CONSENT OF CONGRESS, THAT A NEW STATE BE FORMED WITH THE JURISDICTION OF THE COMMONWEALTH OF VIRGINIA, AND ADMITTED INTO THE UNION, BY THE NAME OF THE STATE OF KENTUCKY. APPROVED, FEBRUARY 4, 1791.

> *[Philadelphia: Printed by Francis Childs and John Swaine, 1791.]* Broadside. fol. LOC. NYPL.

23851 —— CONGRESS OF THE UNITED STATES: AT THE THIRD SESSION, BEGUN AND HELD AT THE CITY OF PHILADELPHIA, ON MONDAY THE SIXTH OF DECEMBER, ONE THOUSAND SEVEN HUNDRED AND NINETY. AN ACT DECLARING THE CONSENT OF CONGRESS TO A CERTAIN ACT OF THE STATE OF MARYLAND. APPROVED, FEBRUARY 9, 1791.

> *[Philadelphia: Printed by Francis Childs and John Swaine, 1791.]* Broadside. fol. LOC. NYPL.

23852 —— CONGRESS OF THE UNITED STATES: AT THE THIRD SESSION, BEGUN AND HELD AT THE CITY OF PHILADELPHIA, ON MONDAY THE SIXTH OF DECEMBER, ONE THOUSAND SEVEN HUNDRED AND NINETY. AN ACT FIXING THE TIME FOR THE NEXT ANNUAL MEETING OF CONGRESS. APPROVED, MARCH 2, 1791.

> *[Philadelphia: Printed by Francis Childs and John Swaine, 1791.]* Broadside. fol. LOC. NYPL.

UNITED STATES, continued.

23853 —— CONGRESS OF THE UNITED STATES: AT THE THIRD SESSION, BEGUN AND HELD AT THE CITY OF PHILADELPHIA, ON MONDAY THE SIXTH OF DECEMBER, ONE THOUSAND SEVEN HUNDRED AND NINETY. AN ACT FOR GRANTING LANDS TO THE INHABITANTS AND SETTLERS AT VINCENNES AND THE ILLINOIS COUNTRY, IN THE TERRITORY NORTH-WEST OF THE OHIO, AND FOR CONFIRMING THEM IN THEIR POSSESSIONS. APPROVED, MARCH 3, 1791.

[Philadelphia: Printed by Francis Childs and John Swaine, 1791.] pp. (2). fol.
LOC. NYPL.

23854 —— CONGRESS OF THE UNITED STATES: AT THE THIRD SESSION, BEGUN AND HELD AT THE CITY OF PHILADELPHIA, ON MONDAY THE SIXTH OF DECEMBER, ONE THOUSAND SEVEN HUNDRED AND NINETY. AN ACT FOR MAKING COMPENSATIONS TO THE COMMISSIONERS OF LOANS FOR EXTRAORDINARY EXPENSES. APPROVED, MARCH 3, 1791.

[Philadelphia: Printed by Francis Childs and John Swaine, 1791.] Broadside. fol.
LOC. NYPL.

23855 —— CONGRESS OF THE UNITED STATES: AT THE THIRD SESSION, BEGUN AND HELD AT THE CITY OF PHILADELPHIA, ON MONDAY THE SIXTH OF DECEMBER, ONE THOUSAND SEVEN HUNDRED AND NINETY. AN ACT FOR RAISING AND ADDING ANOTHER REGIMENT TO THE MILITARY ESTABLISHMENT OF THE UNITED STATES, AND FOR MAKING FARTHER PROVISIONS FOR THE PROTECTION OF THE FRONTIERS. APPROVED, MARCH 3, 1791.

[Philadelphia: Printed by Francis Childs and John Swaine, 1791.] pp. (4), fol.
LOC. NYPL.

The New York Public Library has a copy of this Act printed on ordinary paper also.

23856 —— CONGRESS OF THE UNITED STATES: AT THE THIRD SESSION, BEGUN AND HELD AT THE CITY OF PHILADELPHIA, ON MONDAY THE SIXTH OF DECEMBER, ONE THOUSAND SEVEN HUNDRED AND NINETY. AN ACT FOR THE ADMISSION OF THE STATE OF VERMONT INTO THIS UNION. APPROVED, FEBRUARY 18, 1791.

[Philadelphia: Printed by Francis Childs and John Swaine, 1791.] Broadside. fol.
LOC. NYPL.

23857 —— CONGRESS OF THE UNITED STATES: AT THE THIRD SESSION, BEGUN AND HELD AT THE CITY OF PHILADELPHIA, ON MONDAY THE SIXTH OF DECEMBER, ONE THOUSAND SEVEN HUNDRED AND NINETY. AN ACT GIVING EFFECT TO THE LAWS OF THE UNITED STATES WITHIN THE STATE OF VERMONT. . . . APPROVED, MARCH THE SECOND, 1791. GEORGE WASHINGTON, PRESIDENT OF THE UNITED STATES.

[Philadelphia: Printed by Francis Childs and John Swaine, 1791.] pp. (2). fol.
LOC. NYPL.

23858 —— CONGRESS OF THE UNITED STATES: AT THE THIRD SESSION, BEGUN AND HELD AT THE CITY OF PHILADELPHIA, ON MONDAY THE SIXTH OF DECEMBER, ONE THOUSAND SEVEN HUNDRED AND NINETY. AN ACT IN ADDITION TO AN ACT, INTITULED, "AN ACT FOR ESTABLISHING THE SALARIES OF THE EXECUTIVE OFFICERS OF GOVERNMENT, WITH THEIR ASSISTANTS AND CLERKS". APPROVED, MARCH 3, 1791.

[Philadelphia: Printed by Francis Childs and John Swaine, 1791.] Broadside. fol.
LOC. NYPL.

UNITED STATES, continued.

23859 —— CONGRESS OF THE UNITED STATES: AT THE THIRD SESSION, BEGUN AND HELD AT THE CITY OF PHILADELPHIA, ON MONDAY THE SIXTH OF DECEMBER, ONE THOUSAND SEVEN HUNDRED AND NINETY. AN ACT MAKING AN APPROPRIATION FOR THE PURPOSE THEREIN MENTIONED. [effecting a recognition of the treaty of the United States and Morocco.] APPROVED, MARCH 3, 1791.

[Philadelphia: Printed by Francis Childs and John Swaine, 1791.] Broadside. fol.
LOC. NYPL.

23860 —— CONGRESS OF THE UNITED STATES: AT THE THIRD SESSION, BEGUN AND HELD AT THE CITY OF PHILADELPHIA, ON MONDAY THE SIXTH OF DECEMBER, ONE THOUSAND SEVEN HUNDRED AND NINETY. AN ACT MAKING APPROPRIATIONS FOR THE SUPPORT OF GOVERNMENT DURING THE YEAR ONE THOUSAND SEVEN HUNDRED AND NINETY, AND FOR OTHER PURPOSES. APPROVED, FEBRUARY 11, 1791.

[Philadelphia: Printed by Francis Childs and John Swaine, 1791.] Broadside. fol.
NYPL.

23861 —— CONGRESS OF THE UNITED STATES: AT THE THIRD SESSION, BEGUN AND HELD AT THE CITY OF PHILADELPHIA, ON MONDAY THE SIXTH OF DECEMBER, ONE THOUSAND SEVEN HUNDRED AND NINETY. AN ACT MAKING FURTHER PROVISION FOR THE COLLECTION OF THE DUTIES BY LAW IMPOSED ON TEAS, AND TO PROLONG THE TERM FOR THE PAYMENT OF THE DUTIES ON WINES. APPROVED, MARCH 3, 1791.

[Philadelphia: Printed by Francis Childs and John Swaine, 1791.] pp. (3). fol.
LOC. NYPL.

23862 —— CONGRESS OF THE UNITED STATES: AT THE THIRD SESSION, BEGUN AND HELD AT THE CITY OF PHILADELPHIA, ON MONDAY THE SIXTH OF DECEMBER, ONE THOUSAND SEVEN HUNDRED AND NINETY. AN ACT PROVIDING COMPENSATIONS FOR THE OFFICERS OF THE JUDICIAL COURTS OF THE UNITED STATES, AND FOR OTHER PURPOSES. APPROVED, MARCH 3, 1791.

[Philadelphia: Printed by Francis Childs and John Swaine, 1791.] pp. (2). fol.
LOC. NYPL.

23863 —— CONGRESS OF THE UNITED STATES: AT THE THIRD SESSION, BEGUN AND HELD AT THE CITY OF PHILADELPHIA, ON MONDAY THE SIXTH OF DECEMBER, ONE THOUSAND SEVEN HUNDRED AND NINETY. AN ACT REGULATING THE NUMBER OF REPRESENTATIVES TO BE CHOSEN BY THE STATES OF KENTUCKY AND VERMONT. APPROVED, FEBRUARY 25, 1791.

[Philadelphia: Printed by Francis Childs and John Swaine, 1791.] Broadside. fol.
LOC. NYPL.

23864 —— CONGRESS OF THE UNITED STATES: AT THE THIRD SESSION, BEGUN AND HELD AT THE CITY OF PHILADELPHIA, ON MONDAY THE SIXTH OF DECEMBER, ONE THOUSAND SEVEN HUNDRED AND NINETY. AN ACT RELATIVE TO THE RIX-DOLLAR OF DENMARK. APPROVED, MARCH 3, 1791.

[Philadelphia: Printed by Francis Childs and John Swaine, 1791.] Broadside. fol.
NYPL. RIHS.

23865 —— CONGRESS OF THE UNITED STATES: AT THE THIRD SESSION, BEGUN AND HELD AT THE CITY OF PHILADELPHIA, ON MONDAY THE SIXTH OF DECEMBER, ONE THOUSAND SEVEN HUNDRED AND NINETY. AN ACT REPEALING, AFTER THE LAST DAY OF JUNE NEXT, THE DUTIES HERETOFORE LAID UPON DISTILLED SPIRITS IMPORTED FROM ABROAD, AND LAYING OTHERS IN THEIR STEAD; AND ALSO UPON SPIRITS DISTILLED WITHIN THE UNITED STATES, AND FOR APPROPRIATING THE SAME. APPROVED, MARCH 3, 1791. [Colophon:]

[Philadelphia:] Printed by Francis Childs and John Swaine. [1791.] pp. [16.] fol.
LOC. NYHS. NYPL. RIHS.

UNITED STATES, continued.

23866 —— CONGRESS OF THE UNITED STATES: AT THE THIRD SESSION, BEGUN AND HELD AT THE CITY OF PHILADELPHIA, ON MONDAY THE SIXTH OF DECEMBER, ONE THOUSAND SEVEN HUNDRED AND NINETY. AN ACT SUPPLEMENTAL TO THE ACT "ESTABLISHING THE TREASURY DEPARTMENT," AND FOR A FARTHER COMPENSATION TO CERTAIN OFFICERS. APPROVED, MARCH 3, 1791.
[Philadelphia: Printed by Francis Childs and John Swaine, 1791.] Broadside. fol.
LOC. NYPL.

23867 —— CONGRESS OF THE UNITED STATES: AT THE THIRD SESSION, BEGUN AND HELD IN THE CITY OF PHILADELPHIA, ON MONDAY THE SIXTH OF DECEMBER, ONE THOUSAND SEVEN HUNDRED AND NINETY. AN ACT SUPPLEMENTARY TO THE ACT, INTITLED, "AN ACT MAKING FURTHER PROVISION FOR THE PAYMENT OF THE DEBTS OF THE UNITED STATES." APPROVED, DECEMBER 27, 1790.
[Philadelphia? Printed by Francis Childs and John Swaine, 1791.] Broadside. fol.
NYPL. RIHS.

23868 —— CONGRESS OF THE UNITED STATES: AT THE THIRD SESSION, BEGUN AND HELD AT THE CITY OF PHILADELPHIA, ON MONDAY THE SIXTH OF DECEMBER, ONE THOUSAND SEVEN HUNDRED AND NINETY. AN ACT SUPPLEMENTARY TO THE ACT MAKING PROVISION FOR THE REDUCTION OF THE PUBLIC DEBT. APPROVED, MARCH 3, 1791.
[Philadelphia: Printed by Francis Childs and John Swaine. 1791.] Broadside. fol.
LOC. NYPL.

23869 —— CONGRESS OF THE UNITED STATES: AT THE THIRD SESSION, BEGUN AND HELD AT THE CITY OF PHILADELPHIA ON MONDAY THE SIXTH OF DECEMBER, ONE THOUSAND SEVEN HUNDRED AND NINETY. AN ACT TO AMEND "AN ACT, FOR ESTABLISHING THE TEMPORARY AND PERMANENT SEAT OF THE GOVERNMENT OF THE UNITED STATES." APPROVED, MARCH 3, 1791.
[Philadelphia: Printed by Francis Childs and John Swaine, 1791.] Broadside. fol.
LOC. NYPL.

23870 —— CONGRESS OF THE UNITED STATES: AT THE THIRD SESSION, BEGUN AND HELD AT THE CITY OF PHILADELPHIA, ON MONDAY THE SIXTH OF DECEMBER, ONE THOUSAND SEVEN HUNDRED AND NINETY. AN ACT TO CONTINUE AN ACT, INTITULED, "AN ACT DECLARING THE ASSENT OF CONGRESS TO CERTAIN ACTS OF THE STATES OF MARYLAND, GEORGIA, AND RHODE-ISLAND AND PROVIDENCE-PLANTATIONS,' SO FAR AS THE SAME RESPECTS THE STATES OF GEORGIA, AND RHODE-ISLAND AND PROVIDENCE-PLANTATIONS. APPROVED, JANUARY 10, 1791.
[Philadelphia: Printed by Francis Childs and John Swaine, 1791.] Broadside. fol.
LOC. NYPL. RIHS.

23871 —— CONGRESS OF THE UNITED STATES: AT THE THIRD SESSION, BEGUN AND HELD AT THE CITY OF PHILADELPHIA, ON MONDAY THE SIXTH OF DECEMBER, ONE THOUSAND SEVEN HUNDRED AND NINETY. AN ACT TO CONTINUE IN FORCE FOR A LIMITED TIME, AN ACT, INTITULED "AN ACT FOR THE TEMPORARY ESTABLISHMENT OF THE POST-OFFICE." APPROVED: MARCH 3, 1791.
[Philadelphia: Printed by Francis Childs and John Swaine, 1791.] Broadside. fol.
LOC. NYPL.

23872 —— CONGRESS OF THE UNITED STATES: AT THE THIRD SESSION, BEGUN AND HELD AT THE CITY OF PHILADELPHIA, ON MONDAY THE SIXTH OF DECEMBER, ONE THOUSAND SEVEN HUNDRED AND NINETY. AN ACT TO CONTINUE IN FORCE, FOR A LIMITED TIME, AN ACT PASSED AT THE FIRST SESSION OF CONGRESS, INTITULED, "AN ACT TO REGULATE PROCESSES IN THE COURTS OF THE UNITED STATES.". APPROVED, FEBRUARY 18, 1791.
[Philadelphia: Printed by Francis Childs and John Swaine, 1791,] Broadside. fol.
LOC. NYPL.

UNITED STATES, continued.

23873 —— CONGRESS OF THE UNITED STATES: AT THE THIRD SESSION, BEGUN AND HELD AT THE CITY OF PHILADELPHIA, ON MONDAY THE SIXTH OF DECEMBER, ONE THOUSAND SEVEN HUNDRED AND NINETY. AN ACT TO CONTINUE IN FORCE THE ACT THEREIN MENTIONED, AND TO MAKE FURTHER PROVISION FOR THE PAYMENT OF PENSIONS TO INVALIDS, AND FOR THE SUPPORT OF LIGHT-HOUSES, BEACONS, BUOYS, AND PUBLIC PIERS. APPROVED, MARCH 3, 1791.

[Philadelphia: Printed by Francis Childs and John Swaine, 1791.] Broadside. fol. LOC. NYPL.

23874 —— CONGRESS OF THE UNITED STATES: AT THE THIRD SESSION, BEGUN AND HELD AT THE CITY OF PHILADELPHIA, ON MONDAY THE SIXTH OF DECEMBER, ONE THOUSAND SEVEN HUNDRED AND NINETY. AN ACT TO EXPLAIN AND AMEND AN ACT, INTITULED "AN ACT MAKING FURTHER PROVISION FOR THE PAYMENT OF THE DEBTS OF THE UNITED STATES." APPROVED, MARCH 2, 1791.

[Philadelphia. Printed by Francis Childs and John Swaine, 1791.] Broadside. fol. LOC. NYPL. RIHS.

23875 —— CONGRESS OF THE UNITED STATES: AT THE THIRD SESSION, BEGUN AND HELD AT THE CITY OF PHILADELPHIA, ON MONDAY THE SIXTH OF DECEMBER, ONE THOUSAND SEVEN HUNDRED AND NINETY AN ACT TO INCORPORATE THE SUB-SCRIBERS TO THE BANK OF THE UNITED STATES. APPROVED, FEBRUARY 25, 1791.

[Philadelphia: Printed by Francis Childs and John Swaine. 1791.] pp. [7.] fol. JCB. LOC. NYPL.

23876 —— CONGRESS OF THE UNITED STATES: AT THE THIRD SESSION, BEGUN AND HELD AT THE CITY OF PHILADELPHIA, ON MONDAY THE SIXTH OF DECEMBER, ONE THOUSAND SEVEN HUNDRED AND NINETY. AN ACT SUPPLEMENTARY TO THE ACT, INTITULED, "AN ACT TO INCORPORATE THE SUBSCRIBERS TO THE BANK OF THE UNITED STATES." APPROVED, MARCH 2, 1791.

[Philadelphia: Printed by Francis Childs and John Swaine, 1791.] Broadside. fol. JCB. NYPL.

23877 —— CONGRESS OF THE UNITED STATES: AT THE THIRD SESSION, BEGUN AND HELD AT THE CITY OF PHILADELPHIA, ON MONDAY THE SIXTH DAY OF DECEMBER, ONE THOUSAND SEVEN HUNDRED AND NINETY. AN ACT TO PROVIDE FOR THE UNLAD-ING OF SHIPS OR VESSELS, IN CASES OF OBSTRUCTION BY ICE. APPROVED, DECEMBER 27, 1790.

[Philadelphia: Printed by Francis Childs and John Swaine, 1791.] Broadside. fol. LOC. NYPL.

23878 —— CONGRESS OF THE UNITED STATES: AT THE THIRD SESSION, BEGUN AND HELD AT THE CITY OF PHILADELPHIA, ON MONDAY THE SIXTH OF DECEMBER, ONE THOUSAND SEVEN HUNDRED AND NINETY. RESOLVED . . . THAT ANDREW BROWN, OR ANY OTHER PRINTER, BE PERMITTED, UNDER THE DIRECTION OF THE SECRETARY OF STATE, TO COLLATE WITH, AND CORRECT BY THE ORIGINAL ROLLS, THE LAWS, RESOLUTIONS AND TREATIES OF THE UNITED STATES, TO BE BY HIM PRINTED.

[Philadelphia: Printed by Francis Childs and John Swaine. 1791.] Broadside. fol. LOC. NYPL.

UNITED STATES, continued.

23879 —— CONGRESS OF THE UNITED STATES: AT THE THIRD SESSION, BEGUN AND HELD AT THE CITY OF PHILADELPHIA, ON MONDAY THE SIXTH OF DECEMBER, ONE THOUSAND SEVEN HUNDRED AND NINETY. RESOLVED . . . THAT THE PRESIDENT TO CAUSE TO BE COMMUNICATED TO THE NATIONAL ASSEMBLY OF FRANCE THE PECULIAR SENSIBILITY OF CONGRESS TO THE TRIBUTE PAID TO THE MEMORY OF BENJAMIN FRANKLIN, BY THE ENLIGHTENED AND FREE REPRESENTATIVES OF A GREAT NATION, IN THEIR DECREE OF THE ELEVENTH OF JUNE, ONE THOUSAND SEVEN HUNDRED AND NINETY. . . . APPROVED, MARCH 2, 1791.
[Philadelphia: Printed by Francis Childs and John Swaine, 1791.] Broadside. fol.
     LOC. NYPL.

23880 —— CONGRESS OF THE UNITED STATES: AT THE THIRD SESSION, BEGUN AND HELD AT THE CITY OF PHILADELPHIA, ON MONDAY THE SIXTH OF DECEMBER, ONE THOUSAND SEVEN HUNDRED AND NINETY. RESOLVED . . . THAT A MINT SHALL BE ESTABLISHED UNDER SUCH REGULATIONS AS SHALL BE DIRECTED BY LAW. APPROVED, MARCH 3, 1791.
[Philadelphia: Printed by Francis Childs and John Swaine, 1791.] Broadside. fol.
     LOC. NYPL.

23881 —— CONGRESS OF THE UNITED STATES: AT THE THIRD SESSION, BEGUN AND HELD AT THE CITY OF PHILADELPHIA, ON MONDAY THE SIXTH OF DECEMBER, ONE THOUSAND SEVEN HUNDRED AND NINETY. [Resolution, authorizing marshals to hire convenient places to serve as temporary jails for the safe-keeping of prisoners in such States as have not complied with their Resolution of 23 September, 1780.] APPROVED, MARCH 3, 1791.
[Philadelphia: Printed by Francis Childs and John Swaine, 1791.] Broadside. fol.
     LOC. NYPL.

23882 —— CONGRESS OF THE UNITED STATES: AT THE THIRD SESSION, BEGUN AND HELD AT THE CITY OF PHILADELPHIA, ON MONDAY THE SIXTH OF DECEMBER, ONE THOUSAND SEVEN HUNDRED AND NINETY. RESOLVED . . . THAT THE PRESIDENT OF THE UNITED STATES BE, AND HE HEREBY IS REQUESTED, TO CAUSE AN ESTIMATE TO BE LAID BEFORE CONGRESS AT THEIR NEXT SESSION, OF THE QUANTITY AND SITUATION OF THE LANDS NOT CLAIMED BY THE INDIANS, NOR GRANTED TO, NOR CLAIMED BY ANY OF THE CITIZENS OF THE UNITED STATES, WITHIN THE TERRITORY CEDED TO THE UNITED STATES, BY THE STATE OF NORTH CAROLINA, AND WITH THE TERRITORY OF THE UNITED STATES NORTH-WEST OF THE RIVER OHIO. APPROVED, MARCH 3, 1791.
[Philadelphia: Printed by Francis Childs and John Swaine, 1791.] Broadside. fol.
     LOC. NYPL.

23883 —— IN THE HOUSE OF REPRESENTATIVES OF THE UNITED STATES, THURSDAY THE THIRD OF MARCH, 1791. ON MOTION, RESOLVED THAT THE CONSIDERATION OF THE AMENDMENTS TO THE CONSTITUTION PROPOSED TO BE MADE, RESPECTING THE JUDICIARY, BE DEFERRED UNTIL THE NEXT SESSION OF CONGRESS, AND THAT ONE HUNDRED COPIES THEREOF BE PRINTED FOR THE USE OF THE MEMBERS OF BOTH. HOUSES. . . . AMENDMENTS TO THE CONSTITUTION OF THE UNITED STATES, TO BE PROPOSED BY CONGRESS TO THE LEGISLATURES OF THE SEVERAL STATES.
[Philadelphia: Printed by Childs and Swaine, 1791.] pp. (2). fol.   LOC.

23884 —— SECOND CONGRESS OF THE UNITED STATES. AT THE FIRST SESSION, BEGUN AND HELD AT THE CITY OF PHILADELPHIA, IN THE STATE OF PENNSYLVANIA, ON MONDAY THE TWENTY-FOURTH OF OCTOBER, ONE THOUSAND SEVEN HUNDRED AND NINETY-ONE. AN ACT FOR THE RELIEF OF DAVID COOK AND THOMAS CAMPBELL. . . . APPROVED, DECEMBER SIXTEENTH, 1791. GO: WASHINGTON, PRESIDENT OF THE UNITED STATES. [Colophon:]
[Philadelphia:] Printed by Childs and Swaine, [1791.] Broadside. fol.
     NYPL.

UNITED STATES, continued.

23885 —— SECOND CONGRESS OF THE UNITED STATES. AT THE FIRST SESSION, BEGUN AND HELD AT THE CITY OF PHILADELPHIA, IN THE STATE OF PENNSYLVANIA, ON MONDAY THE TWENTY-FOURTH OF OCTOBER, ONE THOUSAND SEVEN HUNDRED AND NINETY-ONE. AN ACT GRANTING FURTHER TIME FOR MAKING RETURN OF THE ENUMERATION OF THE INHABITANTS IN THE DISTRICT OF SOUTH-CAROLINA. APPROVED, NOV. 8, 1791.

[Philadelphia: Printed by Francis Childs and John Swaine, 1791.] Broadside. fol. LOC. NYPL.

23886 —— SECOND CONGRESS OF THE UNITED STATES. AT THE FIRST SESSION, BEGUN AND HELD AT THE CITY OF PHILADELPHIA, IN THE STATE OF PENNSYLVANIA, ON MONDAY THE TWENTY-FOURTH OF OCTOBER, ONE THOUSAND SEVEN HUNDRED AND NINETY-ONE. AN ACT MAKING APPROPRIATIONS FOR THE SUPPORT OF GOVERN-MENT FOR THE YEAR ONE THOUSAND SEVEN HUNDRED AND NINETY-TWO. APPROV-ED, DECEMBER 23, 1791. [Colophon:]

[Philadelphia:] Printed by Childs and Swaine, [1791.] pp. (3). fol. NYPL.

All the separate broadside Acts for 1789-1791, in the New York Public Library, are printed on writing paper, and have the words "[True copy]" or "Deposited among the rolls in the office of the Secretary of State," with space before the words" Secretary of State," and have the auto-graphed signature of Thomas Jefferson, not found on copies of ordinary paper.

23887 —— THE CONSTITUTIONS OF THE UNITED STATES, ACCORDING TO THE LATEST AMEND-MENTS: TO WHICH ARE ANNEXED, THE DECLARATION OF INDEPENDENCE; AND THE FEDERAL CONSTITUTION; WITH THE AMENDMENTS THERETO. THIS EDITION CONTAINS THE CONSTITUTION OF VERMONT, NOT IN ANY FORMER ONE.

Philadelphia: From the Press of Carey, Stewart, and Co. M,DCC,XCI. pp. (2), (2), 176. 12mo. AAS. HC. JCB. LOC. NYPL.

23888 —— — THE CONSTITUTION OF THE UNITED STATES, WITH NOTES.

Philadelphia: Printed by John Fenno, 1791. 16mo.

23889 —— AN ABSTRACT OF THE DUTY-LAW OF THE UNITED STATES, ALPHABETICALLY DIGESTED, AND RENDERED VERY CONVENIENT AND USEFUL TO REVENUE-OFFICERS, MERCHANTS, CAPTAINS OF VESSELS, &C.

Baltimore: Printed by W. Goddard and James Angell, 1791.

23890 —— CONTINENTAL IMPOST DUTIES, RATES OF FEES, COINAGE, TONNAGE &C.

Boston: Printed by T. & J. Fleet, 1791. Broadside. fol.

This matter was also furnished folded into size of their Register.

23891 —— — DUTIES PAYABLE ON GOODS, WARES AND MERCHANDIZE, IMPORTED INTO THE UNITED STATES OF AMERICA, AFTER THE 31ST OF DECEMBER, 1790, IN CON-FORMITY TO AN ACT OF CONGRESS: ALSO, RATES OF FEES, COINS AND TONNAGE, BY THE ACT FOR THE COLLECTION OF THE SAID DUTIES, AND BY THE ACT FOR LAYING A DUTY ON THE TONNAGE OF SHIPS OR VESSELS, &C.

Boston: Printed and sold by Thomas Adams, 1791. Broadside. fol.

UNITED STATES, continued.

23892 —— — DUTIES, PAYABLE ON GOODS, WARES, AND MERCHANDIZE, IMPORTED INTO
THE UNITED STATES OF AMERICA, FROM THE FIRST OF JANUARY, 1791, IN CON-
FORMITY TO AN ACT OF CONGRESS, DATED THE 20TH OF AUGUST LAST. ALSO,
RATES OF FEES, COINS, AND TONNAGE, BY THE ACT FOR THE COLLECTION OF THE
SAID DUTIES, AND BY THE ACT FOR LAYING A DUTY ON THE TONNAGE OF SHIPS OR
VESSELS &C.

New York: Printed by Thomas Greenleaf. 1791. Broadside. fol.

"The whole is completely digested upon a large sheet of paper, and
critically explained at the Custom House, in this city, for the convenience of merchants, traders, masters of vessels, &c. throughout the
Union. ☞ Should additional duties take place at this session of Congress, they shall be printed on a strip, and delivered gratis to the purchaser of the sheet, to be annexed to it. January 3, 1791."

23893 —— — DUTIES PAYABLE ON GOODS, WARES AND MERCHANDIZE, IMPORTED INTO
THE UNITED STATES OF AMERICA, FROM AND AFTER THE LAST DAY OF JUNE, 1792.
THE DUTIES OF TONNAGE, AND THE RATES OF COINS, BY WHICH THE DUTIES ARE
TO BE RECEIVED AND ESTIMATED. RATES OF DRAWBACKS, DEBENTURES, FEES, &C.
ALSO THE MODE OF TRANSACTING BUSINESS AT THE CUSTOM-HOUSE FOR THE PORT
OF PHILADELPHIA, WITH EXTRACTS FROM THE REVENUE ACTS, FOR THE DIRECTION
OF MERCHANTS, MASTERS OF VESSELS, AND OTHERS CONCERNED. SUPPLEMENT TO
THE MARINE LIST. [Seven columns.]

[Philadelphia: Published by Vincent M. Pelosi, 1791.] Broadside. fol.
NYHS.

23894 —— — TABLES OF DUTIES, PAYABLE ON GOODS, IMPORTED INTO THE UNITED
STATES OF AMERICA, AFTER THE 31ST DAY OF DECEMBER, 1790, BY ACT OF CONG-
RESS OF THE 10TH OF AUGUST, 1790. ALSO, RATES OF FEES, COINS, AND OF
TONNAGE, BY THE ACT FOR THE COLLECTION OF THE SAID DUTIES, AND BY THE
ACT FOR LAYING A TONNAGE ON VESSELS. LIKEWISE, MODE OF TRANSACTING BUS-
INESS AT THE CUSTOM HOUSES OF THE UNITED STATES, AND EXTRACTS FROM THE
REVENUE ACTS, FOR THE DIRECTION OF MERCHANTS, MASTERS OF VESSELS, AND
OTHERS CONCERNED.

*Wilmington: Printed and sold by Peter Brynberg and Samuel Andrews,
in Market-Street. 1791.*

23895 —— — ESTIMATE OF THE EXPENDITURES FOR THE CIVIL LIST OF THE UNITED STATES,
TOGETHER WITH THE INCIDENTAL AND CONTINGENT EXPENCES [sic] OF THE SEVERAL
DEPARTMENTS AND OFFICES, FOR THE YEAR, 1792. [Dated November 4th, 1791.]
[Colophon:]

[Philadelphia:] Printed by Childs and Swaine, [1791.] pp. [20.] fol.
BA. JCB. LOC. NYPL.

23896 —— — THE EXCISE LAW, OR, "AN ACT REPEALING AFTER THE LAST DAY OF JUNE NEXT,
THE DUTIES HERETOFORE LAID UPON DISTILLED SPIRITS IMPORTED FROM ABROAD,
AND LAYING OTHERS IN THEIR STEAD; AND ALSO UPON SPIRITS DISTILLED WITHIN
THE UNITED STATES, AND FOR APPROPRIATING THE SAME.

*Philadelphia: Printed by Thomas Dobson, at the Stone-House, No. 41,
South Second-Street. 1791.*

UNITED STATES, continued.

23897 —— EXPLANATIONS AND INSTRUCTIONS CONCERNING THE ACT, ENTITLED, "AN ACT REPEALING AFTER THE LAST DAY OF JUNE NEXT, THE DUTIES HERETOFORE LAID UPON DISTILLED SPIRITS IMPORTED FROM ABROAD, AND LAYING OTHERS IN THEIR STEAD; AND ALSO UPON SPIRITS DISTILLED WITHIN THE UNITED STATES; AND FOR APPROPRIATING THE SAME:" PASSED IN THE THIRD SESSION OF CONGRESS, ON THE 2D. OF MARCH, 1791. [*Also*, INSTRUCTIONS CONCERNING THE ACT, ENTITLED, "AN ACT MAKING FURTHER PROVISION FOR THE COLLECTION OF THE DUTIES BY LAW IMPOSED ON TEAS, AND TO PROLONG THE TERM FOR THE PAYMENT OF THE DUTIES ON WINES.]
[Philadelphia: 1791.] pp. (23). 8vo.   LOC. NYHS. NYPL.

23898 —— JOURNAL OF THE HOUSE OF REPRESENTATIVES OF THE UNITED STATES. ANNO MDCCXC, AND OF THE INDEPENDENCE OF THE UNITED STATES THE FOUR-TEENTH. [4 January,—11 August, 1790.]
Richmond: Printed by Augustine Davis, for the General Assembly of Virginia. 1791. pp. 152. fol.
An Appendix, pages 127-152, contains the "Resolves" of nine State Conventions, relative to the ratification of the Constitution of the United States.

23899 —— JOURNAL OF THE HOUSE OF REPRESENTATIVES OF THE UNITED STATES, ANNO M,DCC,XC, AND OF THE INDEPENDENCE OF THE UNITED STATES, THE FIFTEENTH. [6 December, 1790—3 March, 1791.]
Philadelphia: Printed by Francis Childs and John Swaine. M,DCC,CXI [*sic* 1791.] pp. 146. fol.   AAS. BA. LCP. LOC. NYPL. RIHS.
An Appendix contains the Proceedings of the District of Kentucky for admission into the Union.

23900 —— JOURNAL OF THE SECOND SESSION OF THE SENATE OF THE UNITED STATES OF AMERICA, BEGUN AND HELD AT THE CITY OF NEW-YORK, JANUARY 4TH, [—12 AUGUST,] 1790; AND IN THE FOURTEENTH YEAR OF THE INDEPENDENCE OF THE SAID STATES.
Richmond: Printed by Augtstine [*sic*] *Davis, for the General Assembly of Virginia.* M,DCC,XCI. pp. [110.] fol.   NYPL.

23901 —— JOURNAL OF THE THIRD SESSION OF THE SENATE OF THE UNITED STATES OF AMERICA, BEGUN AND HELD AT THE CITY OF PHILADELPHIA, DECEMBER 6TH, 1790 [—3 MARCH, 1791,] AND IN THE FIFTEENTH YEAR OF THE SOVEREIGNTY OF THE SAID UNITED STATES.
Philadelphia: Printed by John Fenno, No. 69, High-Street, a few doors above Second-Street. M,DCC,XCI. pp. 203. fol.
AAS. BA. BU. JCB. LOC. NL. NYPL. RIHS.

23902 —— LAWS OF THE UNITED STATES OF AMERICA. VOLUME I. CONTAINING, THE FEDERAL CONSTITUTION; THE ACTS OF THE THREE SESSIONS OF THE FIRST CONGRESS; THE TREATIES EXISTING BETWEEN THE UNITED STATES AND FOREIGN NATIONS, AND THE SEVERAL INDIAN TRIBES. ALSO, THE DECLARATION OF INDE-PENDENCE, AND SUNDRY RESOLVES AND ORDINANCES OF CONGRESS UNDER THE CONFEDERATION. THE WHOLE COLLATED WITH AND CORRECTED BY, THE ORIG-INAL ROLLS IN THE OFFICE OF THE SECRETARY OF STATE, AGREEABLY TO A RE-SOLVE OF CONGRESS, PASSED FEBRUARY 18, 1791. TO WHICH IS ADDED, A COM-PLETE INDEX.
New-York: Printed and sold by Childs and Swaine. [1791.] pp. vii, 592, 8vo.   AAS. BA. JCB. RIHS.
In two states: printed on large and small paper. "The Index of fifty-six pages, or a complete digest of the Laws, was executed by an eminent law character."

UNITED STATES, continued.

23903 —— — LAWS OF THE UNITED STATES OF AMERICA; COLLATED WITH, AND COR-
RECTED BY, THE ORIGINAL ROLLS IN THE OFFICE OF THE SECRETARY OF STATE,
AGREEABLY TO A RESOLVE OF CONGRESS, PASSED THE 18TH FEBRUARY, ONE
THOUSAND SEVEN HUNDRED AND NINETY-ONE. WITH A COPIOUS INDEX. VOLUME I.
COMPRISING THE FEDERAL CONSTITUTION, THE ACTS OF THE THREE SESSIONS OF
THE FIRST CONGRESS, AND THE TREATIES. TO WHICH IS ADDED, AN APPENDIX,
CONTAINING THE DECLARATION OF INDEPENDENCE, AND SUNDRY ACTS OF CON-
GRESS, UNDER THE CONFEDERATION.

> *Philadelphia: Printed by Andrew Brown.* M,DCC,XCI. pp. (4), 490, (24).
> 8vo.   AAS.

23904 —— TO THE HONORABLE THE SPEAKER AND MEMBERS OF THE HOUSE OF REPRE-
SENTATIVES OF THE UNITED STATES. THE PETITION OF JAMES JACKSON [Con-
testing the election of Anthony Wayne as Representative from Georgia, on the
ground "that an improper and undue return has been made. . . . there being
nine votes more than voters."] THE COMMITTEE TO WHOM WAS REFERRED THE
PETITION OF JAMES JACKSON, WITH INSTRUCTIONS TO REPORT A MODE OF IN-
VESTIGATING AND DECIDING THEREON, RESPECTFULLY SUBMIT, AS THEIR OPINION,
THE FOLLOWING RESOLUTIONS. . . .

> *[Philadelphia: Printed by Francis Childs and John Swaine,* 1791.] pp.
> (2). fol.   LOC.

23905 —— THE PROCEEDINGS OF A COURT OF ENQUIRY, HELD AT THE SPECIAL REQUEST OF
BRIGADIER GENERAL JOSIAH HARMAR, TO INVESTIGATE HIS CONDUCT, AS COM-
MANDING OFFICER OF THE EXPEDITION AGAINST THE MIAMI INDIANS, 1790: THE
SAME HAVING BEEN TRANSMITTED BY MAJOR GENERAL ST. CLAIR, TO THE SECRE-
TARY OF THE UNITED STATES FOR THE DEPARTMENT OF WAR. PUBLISHED BY
AUTHORITY.

> *Philadelphia: Printed by John Fenno,* M.DCC.XCI. pp. (2), (2), (31). fol.
>   BA. LOC. MHS. NYHS. NYPL.

$35

23906 —— PROPOSITIONS RESPECTING THE COINAGE OF GOLD, SILVER, AND COPPER.

> *[Philadelphia: Printed by Francis Childs and John Swaine,* 1791.] pp.
> [12.] fol.   LOC.

23907 —— REGULATIONS FOR THE ORDER AND DISCIPLINE OF THE TROOPS OF THE UNITED
STATES. COMPILED BY FREDERICK WILLIAM STEUBEN, INSPECTOR GENERAL OF
THE ARMIES OF THE UNITED STATES. [Publisher's monogram.]

> *State of Rhode-Island, &c. Printed at Providence, by Bennett Wheeler,*
> 1791. pp. 115, plate 1. 12mo.   RIHS.

"As directed to be practised by the militia of the State of Rhode-Island,
by his excellency the Governor. In this edition several capital errors,
which have appeared in former editions, are corrected."

23908 —— REPORT OF THE ATTORNEY-GENERAL. READ IN THE HOUSE OF REPRESENTA-
TIVES, DECEMBER 31, 1790. [In response to an order of the House to report on
the judiciary system of the United States. Dated, December 27, 1790.] [Colo-
phon:]

> *[Philadelphia:] Printed by Francis Childs and John Swaine.* [1791.]
> pp. [34.] fol.   BA. JCB. LOC. NYPL.

UNITED STATES, continued.

23909 —— —— REPORT OF THE ATTORNEY-GENERAL. READ IN THE HOUSE OF REPRE-
SENTATIVES, DECEMBER 31, 1790. [On the judiciary system of the United
States.] [Second edition.] [Colophon:]
[Philadelphia:] Printed by Francis Childs and John Swaine. [1791.]
pp. [32.] fol. AAS. BA. JCB. LOC. RIHS.

23910 —— REPORT OF THE SECRETARY OF STATE, ON THE SUBJECT OF ESTABLISHING A
UNIFORMITY IN THE WEIGHTS, MEASURES AND COINS OF THE UNITED STATES.
PUBLISHED BY ORDER OF THE HOUSE OF REPRESENTATIVES. [Fifth impression.]
New-York: Printed by F. Childs and J. Swaine. M,DCC,XC [1791.]
pp. [52], (1). 8vo. BA. RIHS.

23911 —— REPORT OF THE SECRETARY OF STATE, ON THE SUBJECT OF THE COD AND
WHALE FISHERIES, MADE CONFORMABLY TO AN ORDER OF THE HOUSE OF REP-
RESENTATIVES OF THE UNITED STATES, REFERRING TO HIM THE REPRESENTATION
OF THE GENERAL COURT OF THE COMMONWEALTH OF MASSACHUSETTS ON THOSE
SUBJECTS; FEBRUARY 1, 1791. [PUBLISHED BY ORDER OF THE HOUSE OF REP-
RESENTATIVES.]
Philadelphia: Printed by Francis Childs and John Swaine, M,DCC,XCI.
pp. [28.] fol. AAS. BA. JCB. LOC. NYPL. RIHS.
In addition to the regular House edition, two hundred copies were
ordered printed by the Senate, as follows:

23912 —— —— REPORT OF THE SECRETARY OF STATE, ON THE SUBJECT OF THE COD AND
WHALE FISHERIES, MADE CONFORMABLY TO AN ORDER OF THE HOUSE OF REP-
RESENTATIVES OF THE UNITED STATES, REFERRING TO HIM THE REPRESENTATION
OF THE GENERAL COURT OF THE COMMONWEALTH OF MASSACHUSETTS ON THOSE
SUBJECTS; FEBRUARY 1ST, 1791. PUBLISHED BY ORDER OF THE SENATE OF THE
UNITED STATES.
Philadelphia: Printed by John Fenno, No. 69, in High-Street. M.DCC.XCI.
pp. (34). fol. BA. JCB. LOC. NYPL.

23913 —— REPORT OF THE SECRETARY OF STATE, TO THE PRESIDENT OF THE UNITED
STATES, OF THE QUANTITY AND SITUATION OF THE LANDS NOT CLAIMED BY THE
INDIANS, NOR GRANTED TO, NOR CLAIMED BY ANY CITIZENS, WITHIN THE TERRITORY
OF THE UNITED STATES. READ IN THE HOUSE OF REPRESENTATIVES, NOV-
EMBER 10, 1791.
[Philadelphia: Printed by Francis Childs and John Swaine, 1791.] pp.
[8.] fol. AAS. BA. JCB. LOC. NYPL. RIHS.

23914 —— REPORT OF THE SECRETARY OF THE TREASURY OF THE UNITED STATES, ON THE
SUBJECT OF MANUFACTURES. PRESENTED TO THE HOUSE OF REPRESENTATIVES,
DECEMBER 5, 1791.
[Philadelphia:] Printed by Childs and Swaine. [1791.] pp. (2), (2), [58.]
fol. AAS. BA. JCB. LOC. NYPL. RIHS.
Reprinted both here and abroad. The sixth edition printed in Philadel-
phia, in 1827.

23915 —— REPORT ON PRIVILEGES AND RESTRICTIONS ON THE COMMERCE OF THE UNITED
STATES, IN FOREIGN COUNTRIES. [14 February, 1791.]
Philadelphia: Printed by Francis Childs and John Swaine. 1791. BA.

UNITED STATES, continued.

23916 —— RETURN OF THE WHOLE NUMBER OF PERSONS WITHIN THE SEVERAL DISTRICTS OF THE UNITED STATES, ACCORDING TO "AN ACT PROVIDING FOR THE ENUMERATION OF THE INHABITANTS OF THE UNITED STATES"; PASSED MARCH THE FIRST, ONE THOUSAND SEVEN HUNDRED AND NINETY-ONE [*sic* 1790.]

Philadelphia: Printed by Childs and Swaine. M,DCC,XCI. pp. [56] + 8vo.   AAS. BA. CLS. HC. JCB. LOC. NYPL. RIHS.

The first published Census of the inhabitants of the United States. Additional matter received during printing, was printed on thin paper for pasting on the blank spaces left for that purpose. The copies in the Library of Congress have additional matter so added under Kentucky, and South Carolina, attested by the autograph of Thomas Jefferson. Reprinted in London, in 1793; and in Washington, in 1802.

23917 —— —— SCHEDULE OF THE WHOLE NUMBER OF PERSONS WITHIN THE SEVERAL DISTRICTS OF THE UNITED STATES, ACCORDING TO AN ACT "PROVIDING FOR THE ENUMERATION OF THE INHABITANTS OF THE UNITED STATES, PASSED MARCH THE 1ST, 1790. OCTOBER 31, 1791.

[Philadelphia: 1791.] Broadside. fol.   NYPL. RIHS.

23918 —— RULES AND ARTICLES FOR THE BETTER GOVERNMENT OF THE TROOPS RAISED, OR TO BE RAISED, AND KEPT IN PAY BY, AND AT THE EXPENCE OF THE UNITED STATES OF AMERICA.

[Philadelphia? 1791.] pp. 44. 8vo.   LOC.

23919 —— THE SECRETARY OF STATE, TO WHOM WAS REFERRED, BY THE HOUSE OF REPRESENTATIVES OF THE UNITED STATES, THE PETITION OF JACOB ISAACKS, OF NEWPORT, IN RHODE-ISLAND, HAS EXAMINED INTO THE TRUTH AND IMPORTANCE OF THE ALLEGATIONS THEREIN SET FORTH, AND MAKES THEREON THE FOLLOWING REPORT. [On converting salt-water into fresh.] TH: JEFFERSON. PHILADELPHIA, [*sic*] NOVEMBER 21ST, 1791.

[Philadelphia: Printed by John Fenno? 1791.] Broadside. fol. LCP. LOC.

23920 —— THE SECRETARY OF THE TREASURY HAVING ATTENTIVELY CONSIDERED THE SUBJECT REFERRED TO HIM BY THE ORDER OF THE HOUSE OF REPRESENTATIVES OF THE FIFTEENTH DAY OF APRIL LAST, RELATIVELY TO THE ESTABLISHMENT OF A MINT MOST RESPECTFULLY SUBMITS THE RESULT OF HIS ENQUIRIES AND REFLECTIONS. . . . ALEXANDER HAMILTON. JANUARY 28, 1791. [Colophon:]

[Philadelphia:] Printed by Francis Childs and John Swaine. [1791.] pp. [22.] fol.   AAS. BA. LOC. NYPL.

23921 —— SPEECH OF THE PRESIDENT OF THE UNITED STATES TO CONGRESS, OCTOBER 25, 1791. [Colophon:]

Philadelphia: Printed by John Fenno. [1791.] Broadside. fol.   AAS.

23922 —— STATEMENTS OF THE RECEIPTS AND EXPENDITURES OF PUBLIC MONIES, DURING THE ADMINISTRATION OF THE FINANCES BY ROBERT MORRIS, ESQUIRE, LATE SUPERINTENDANT; WITH OTHER EXTRACTS AND ACCOUNTS FROM THE PUBLIC RECORDS, MADE OUT BY THE REGISTER OF THE TREASURY, BY DIRECTION OF THE COMMITTEE OF THE HOUSE OF REPRESENTATIVES, APPOINTED BY AN ORDER OF THE HOUSE OF THE 19TH MARCH 1790, UPON THE MEMORIAL OF THE SAID LATE SUPERINTENDANT OF FINANCE. [With Appendix (A). (B).] AUGUST 30, 1790.

[Philadelphia: Printed by Francis Childs and John Swaine, 1791.] pp. (36), (4). (14). fol.   AAS. LOC. NYPL.

UNITED STATES, continued.

23923 —— THE TREASURER OF THE UNITED STATES' ACCOUNTS OF PAYMENTS AND RE-
CEIPTS OF PUBLIC MONIES, FROM 1ST OCTOBER, 1790 TO 30TH JUNE, 1791. PRE-
SENTED TO THE HOUSE OF REPRESENTATIVES, 26TH OCTOBER, 1791. [Colophon:]
[Philadelphia:] Printed by Childs and Swaine. [1791.] pp. 52. fol.
BA. JCB. LOC. NYPL.

23924 —— LETTER FROM THE TREASURER OF THE UNITED STATES WITH ACCOUNTS OF RE-
CEIPTS AND EXPENDITURES OF PUBLIC MONEYS FROM JULY 11 TO SEPT. 30, 1791.
Philadelphia: Printed by Childs and Swaine. [1791.] pp. 52. fol.

23925 —— TREASURY DEPARTMENT JANUARY 6, 1791. SIR I HAVE THE HONOR TO TRANS-
MIT TO YOU A REPORT TO THE HOUSE OF REPRESENTATIVES, RELATIVE TO AP-
PROPRIATIONS OF MONEY, FOR CERTAIN PURPOSES THEREIN MENTIONED. . . .
ALEXANDER HAMILTON.
[Philadelphia: Printed by Francis Childs and John Swaine, 1791.] pp.
[12.] fol.
BA. JCB. LOC. RIHS.

23926 —— TREASURY DEPARTMENT, JANUARY 6, 1791. SIR, I HAVE THE HONOR TO IN-
FORM YOU THAT PRIOR TO THE RECEIPT OF THE ORDER OF THE HOUSE OF REP-
RESENTATIVES OF THE 30TH ULTIMO, THE FORMATION OF SEVERAL RETURNS OF
THE NATURE OF THOSE DESIGNATED IN THEIR RESOLUTION HAD BEEN COMMENCED
AT THE TREASURY. . . . ALEXANDER HAMILTON. A GENERAL ABSTRACT OF
DUTIES ARISING ON THE TONNAGE OF VESSELS ENTERED INTO THE UNITED STATES
FROM THE 1ST OF OCTOBER, 1789, TO THE 30TH OF SEPTEMBER, 1790. . . .
ABSTRACT OF DUTIES ARISING ON GOODS WARES AND MERCHANDIZE IMPORTED INTO
THE UNITED STATES, FROM THE 1ST DAY OF AUGUST, TO THE 30TH OF SEPTEM-
BER, 1789. . . . JOSEPH NOURSE, REGISTER.
[Philadelphia: Printed by Francis Childs and John Swaine, 1791.]
pp. (4), table. fol.
BA. JCB. LOC. NYPL. RIHS.

23927 —— TREASURY DEPARTMENT, FEBRUARY 15, 1791. SIR, I DO MYSELF THE HONOR
TO TRANSMIT THROUGH YOU TO THE HOUSE OF REPRESENTATIVES, A GENERAL
RETURN OF THE EXPORTS OF THE UNITED STATES, ABSTRACTED FROM CUSTOM-
HOUSE RETURNS, COMMENCING ON THE VARIOUS DAYS IN AUGUST, 1789, WHEREON
THEY WERE RESPECTIVELY OPENED, AND ENDING ON THE 30TH OF SEPTEMBER
LAST. . . . ALEXANDER HAMILTON.
[Philadelphia: Printed by John Fenno, 1791.] pp. (4). fol.   LOC. RIHS.

23928 —— TREASURY OF THE UNITED STATES. DECEMBER 5TH, 1791. SIR, PERMIT ME,
THROUGH YOU, TO LAY BEFORE THE HONORABLE HOUSE OF REPRESENTATIVES,
MY SPECIE ACCOUNT, FROM THE 1ST JULY TO THE 30TH SEPTEMBER, AS SETTLED
AT THE TREASURY. . . .   SAMUEL MEREDITH, TREASURER OF THE UNITED
STATES.
[Philadelphia: Printed by Childs and Swaine, 1791.] pp. 14. fol.
AAS. BA. LOC.

23929 [U. S. arms.] THE UNITED STATES CHRONICLE: POLITICAL, COMMERCIAL, AND
HISTORICAL. [R. I. arms.] VOL. VIII. NO. 367. THURSDAY, JANUARY 6, [—NO.
416. THURSDAY, DECEMBER 29, 1791.]
Published by Bennett Wheeler, in Westminster-Street, Providence, 1791.
fol.
AAS. NYPL.

23930 THE UNIVERSAL ASYLUM AND COLUMBIAN MAGAZINE FOR [JANUARY—JUNE,]
1791. VOL. II. [Cut.]
*Philadelphia: Printed for the Proprietors by W. Young Bookseller No.
52 Second Street.* [1791.] pp. (2), 430, (2), 8. 8vo.   AAS. HC. JCB. LOC.

23931 —— THE UNIVERSAL ASYLUM AND COLUMBIAN MAGAZINE FOR [JULY—DECEMBER,] 1791. VOL. III. [Cut.]
Philadelphia: Printed for the Proprietors by W. Young Bookseller No. 52 Second Street. [1791.] pp. 439, (9). 8vo.   AAS. HC. JCB. LOC.

23932 DER VERBESSERTE HOCH-DEUTSCHE AMERICANISCHE LAND UND STAATS CALENDER. AUF DAS JAHR . . . 1792. ZUM ACHTENMAL HERAUSGEGEBEN.
Friedrich Stadt, Maryland: Gedruckt bey Matthias Bärtgis. [1791.]

23933 VERMONT. STATE.
ACTS AND LAWS, PASSED BY THE LEGISLATURE OF THE STATE OF VERMONT, AT THEIR ADJOURNED SESSION AT BENNINGTON, JANUARY, 1791.
Printed at Bennington, by Anthony Haswell, for the honorable General Assembly. [1791.] pp. 28. 8vo.   AAS.

23934 —— —— ACTS AND LAWS, PASSED BY THE LEGISLATURE OF THE STATE OF VERMONT, AT THEIR SESSION AT WINDSOR, OCTOBER, 1791.
Printed at Windsor, by Alden Spooner, for the General Assembly. [1791.] pp. 32. 8vo.

23935 —— BY HIS EXCELLENCY THOMAS CHITTENDEN, ESQUIRE, GOVERNOR, CAPTAIN-GENERAL, AND COMMANDER IN CHIEF IN AND OVER THE STATE OF VERMONT, A PROCLAMATION. [Appointing] THURSDAY THE FIRST DAY OF DECEMBER NEXT, TO BE OBSERVED AS A DAY OF PUBLIC ADORATION, THANKSGIVING, AND PRAISE, THROUGHOUT THIS STATE. . . . IT IS RECOMMENDED, THAT THE SAID DAY BE OBSERVED BY ALL PERSONS WITH DECENT SOLEMNITY. GIVEN UNDER MY HAND, IN THE COUNCIL-CHAMBER IN WINDSOR, THIS 20TH DAY OF OCTOBER, A. D. 1791, IN THE 15TH YEAR OF OUR INDEPENDENCE. THOMAS CHITTENDEN. BY HIS EXCELLENCY'S COMMAND, JOSEPH FAY, SECRETARY. GOD SAVE THE PEOPLE. [Colophon:]
Windsor: Printed by Alden Spooner. [1791.] Broadside. fol.   NYHS.

23936 —— BY HIS EXCELLENCY THOMAS CHITTENDEN, ESQUIRE, GOVERNOR AND COMMANDER IN CHIEF, IN AND OVER THE STATE OF VERMONT. A PROCLAMATION. [Appointing Wednesday, the twenty-seventh day of April next, a day of public humiliation, fasting and prayer.] ☞ ALL SERVILE LABOR AND RECREATION IS FORBIDDEN ON SAID DAY. GIVEN AT THE COUNCIL CHAMBER, AT BENNINGTON, THE TWENTY-SEVENTH DAY OF JANUARY, IN THE YEAR OF OUR LORD, ONE THOUSAND SEVEN HUNDRED, AND NINETY-ONE, AND IN THE FIFTEENTH YEAR OF THE INDEPENDENCE OF VERMONT. THOMAS CHITTENDEN. BY HIS EXCELLENCY'S COMMAND, JOSEPH FAY, SECRETARY. GOD SAVE THE PEOPLE.
[*Bennington: Printed by Anthony Haswell*, 1791.] Broadside. fol. NYHS.

23937 —— A JOURNAL OF THE PROCEEDINGS OF THE GENERAL ASSEMBLY OF THE STATE OF VERMONT, AT THEIR STATED SESSION, HELD AT CASTLETON, ON THE SECOND THURSDAY OF OCTOBER, 1790. [—28 October, 1790.]
Printed at Windsor, Vermont, by Alden Spooner, M,DCC,XCI. pp. 54. 4to.   LOC.

23938 —— A JOURNAL OF THE PROCEEDINGS OF THE GENERAL ASSEMBLY OF THE STATE OF VERMONT, AT THEIR SESSION AT BENNINGTON, JANUARY, 1791.
Printed at Bennington by Anthony Haswell, for the honorable General Assembly, M.DCC.XCI. pp. 85. 8vo.   HC.

VERMONT, continued.

23939 —— STATUTES OF THE STATE OF VERMONT; REVISED AND ESTABLISHED BY AUTHOR-
ITY, IN THE YEAR M,DCC,LXXXVII, INCLUDING THOSE PASSED SINCE THAT PERIOD
UNTIL THE SESSION OF THE ASSEMBLY OF SAID STATE, HOLDEN AT BENNINGTON
IN JANUARY, 1791. LIKEWISE, THE SEVERAL ACTS RESPECTING SALES BY THE
SURVEYOR GENERAL.
> *Printed in Bennington, Vermont, in the year* M,DCC,XCI. *By Anthony
Haswell.* pp. 315, (5). 8vo.   AAS. BM. JCB. LOC. NYHS.

23940 [Vt. arms.] THE VERMONT GAZETTE. [U. S. arms.] [Motto.] VOL. VIII. NUMB.
32. MONDAY, JANUARY 3, [—VOL. IX. NUMB. 31. WHOLE NUMB. 447. MONDAY,
DECEMBER 26, 1791.]
> *Printed and published (every Monday) by Anthony Haswell, at his office, a
few rods south of the Courthouse. Bennington.* 1791. fol.   AAS.

23941 THE VERMONT [cut] JOURNAL AND THE UNIVERSAL ADVERTISER. VOL. VIII. No.
388. TUESDAY, JANUARY 4, [—VOL. IX. No. 439. TUESDAY, DECEMBER 27, 1791.]
> *Windsor: Printed by Alden Spooner.* 1791. fol.   AAS.

With the issue for November 8th, "Printer to the State of Vermont"
is added to the imprint.

23942 VINCENT, THOMAS   1634 – 1678
GOD'S TERRIBLE VOICE IN THE CITY: WHEREIN YOU HAVE I. THE SOUND OF THE
VOICE, IN THE NARRATION OF THE TWO LATE DREADFUL JUDGMENTS OF PLAGUE
AND FIRE, INFLICTED BY THE LORD UPON THE CITY OF LONDON; THE FORMER IN
THE YEAR 1665, THE LATTER IN THE YEAR 1666. II. THE INTERPRETATION
OF THE VOICE . . . BY THOMAS VINCENT.
> *Windham: Printed by John Byrne.* 1790. pp. 46. 8vo.

23943 VIRGINIA. STATE.
ACTS PASSED AT A GENERAL ASSEMBLY, OF THE COMMONWEALTH OF VIRGINIA.
BEGUN AND HELD AT THE CAPITOL, IN THE CITY OF RICHMOND, ON MONDAY, THE
EIGHTEENTH OF OCTOBER, IN THE YEAR OF OUR LORD, ONE THOUSAND SEVEN
HUNDRED AND NINETY. [—29 December, 1790.] [Ornament.]
> *Richmond: Printed by John Dixon, Printer to this Commonwealth.* [1791.]
pp. 66. fol.   HSP. LOC. NYPL. VSL.

23944 —— JOURNAL OF THE HOUSE OF DELEGATES OF THE COMMONWEALTH OF VIRGINIA;
BEGUN AND HOLDEN IN THE CITY OF RICHMOND, IN THE COUNTY OF HENRICO, ON
MONDAY, THE EIGHTEENTH DAY OF OCTOBER, IN THE YEAR OF OUR LORD, ONE
THOUSAND SEVEN HUNDRED AND NINETY. [—29 December, 1790.]
> *[Richmond: Printed by Augustine Davis,* 1791.]

Reprinted in Richmond, in 1828.

23945 —— JOURNAL OF THE SENATE OF THE COMMONWEALTH OF VIRGINIA; BEGUN AND
HELD IN THE CITY OF RICHMOND, ON MONDAY, THE 18TH OF OCTOBER, IN THE
YEAR OF OUR LORD 1790, AND IN THE FIFTEENTH YEAR OF THE COMMONWEALTH.
[—29 December, 1790.]
> *[Richmond: Printed by Augustine Davis,* 1791.]

Reprinted in Richmond, in 1828.

23946 THE VIRGINIA [U. S. arms] CENTINEL; OR, THE WINCHESTER MERCURY. [Motto.]
VOL. III. No. 145. WEDNESDAY, JANUARY 5, [—VOL. IV. No. 196. SATURDAY,
DECEMBER 31, 1791.]
> *Winchester: Printed by Richard Bowen and Co.* 1791. fol.

Continued as, *Bowen's Virginia Centinel & Gazette: or, the Winchester
Political repository.*

23947 THE VIRGINIA GAZETTE AND ALEXANDRIA ADVERTISER. [Motto.] VOL. II. No. 76.
THURSDAY, JANUARY 6, [—VOL. III. No. 127. THURSDAY, DECEMBER 29, 1791.]
Alexandria: Printed by Hanson and Bond. 1791. fol.　　　　　　AAS.

23948 THE VIRGINIA GAZETTE AND GENERAL ADVERTISER. VOL. V. NUMB. 231. WED-
NESDAY, JANUARY 5, [—VOL. VI. NUMB. 312. WEDNESDAY, DECEMBER 28,
1791.]
[Richmond:] Printed by Aug. Davis, Printer for the public. 1791. fol.
In continuation of, *The Virginia Independent Chronicle, and general
advertiser.*

23949 THE VIRGINIA GAZETTE, AND PETERSBURG INTELLIGENCER. VOL. V. No. 236.
THURSDAY, JANUARY 6, [—VOL. VI. No. 287. THURSDAY, DECEMBER 29, 1791.]
Petersburg: Printed by William Prentis. 1791. fol.

23950 THE VIRGINIA GAZETTE, AND WEEKLY ADVERTISER. No. 441. THURSDAY, JAN-
UARY 6, [—No. 478. FRIDAY, DECEMBER 30, 1791.]
*Published by Thomas Nicolson, two doors above the Eagle Tavern, Rich-
mond.* 1791. fol.

23951 THE VIRGINIA HERALD & FREDERICKSBURG ADVERTISER. VOL. IV. NUMB. 188.
THURSDAY, JANUARY 6, [—NUMB. 239. THURSDAY, DECEMBER 29, 1791.]
Fredericksburg: Printed by Timothy Green. 1791. fol.　　　　LOC.

23952 VIVIAN, THOMAS
THREE INSTRUCTIVE DIALOGUES, BETWEEN A TRUE GOSPEL MINISTER AND ONE OF HIS
PARISHONERS, [*sic*] UPON THE CHRISTIAN RELIGION. BY THE REV. ARCHDEACON
VIVIAN, DEVONSHIRE. TENTH EDITION.
*Baltimore: Printed by David Graham, in Calvert-Street, between Market-
Street and the Court-House.* MDCCXCI. pp. 31. 16mo.　　AAS. BA. MdHS.

23953 WALKER, JEREMIAH
THE FOURFOLD FOUNDATION OF CALVINISM EXAMINED AND SHAKEN. BEING THE
SUBSTANCE OF A SERMON PREACHED AT HEBRON, ON THURSDAY THE ELEVENTH
OF SEPTEMBER, ONE THOUSAND SEVEN HUNDRED AND EIGHTY-EIGHT. BY JERE-
MIAH WALKER. [Ornament.] [Two lines of quotations.]
Richmond: Printed by John Dixon, MDCCXCI. pp. viii, [48.] 8vo. LOC.
Preface dated, Georgia, Elbert County, 3d of February, 1791.

23954 WARING, WILLIAM
A JOURNAL FOR LUNAR OBSERVATIONS, BY WHICH THE CALCULATION OF LONGITUDE
IS MUCH EXPEDITED, THE MARINER BEING LED THROUGH THE OPERATION BY A
REGULAR PRINTED FORM IN EACH PAGE, HAVING ONLY TO FILL THE BLANKS FROM
THE NAUTICAL ALMANAC AND PROPER TABLES, AS INDICATED BY THE LEADING
LINES TO THE RESPECTIVE NUMBERS: CONTAINING ALSO, IN THE SAME PAGE,
BLANKS FOR CALCULATING THE LATITUDE FROM THE MOON'S MERIDIONAL ALTI-
TUDE. WITH DIRECTIONS EXEMPLIFIED, &C. BY WILLIAM WARING.
Philadelphia: 1791.
14th Pennsylvania District Copyright, issued to William Waring, as
Author, 22 February, 1791.

23955 —— THE NEW-JERSEY ALMANACK, FOR THE YEAR OF OUR LORD 1792; BEING BIS-
SEXTILE OR LEAP-YEAR, AND THE SEVENTEENTH YEAR OF AMERICAN INDEPEND-
ENCE AFTER THE 4TH OF JULY NEXT. [Fourteen lines.] CAREFULLY CALCU-
LATED FOR THE LATITUDE AND MERIDIAN OF PHILADELPHIA, BY WILLIAM WAR-
ING.
Trenton: Printed and sold by Isaac Collins. [1791.] pp. (44). 12mo.
AAS. LOC.

WARING, WILLIAM, continued.

23956 —— POOR WILL'S ALMANACK, FOR THE YEAR OF OUR LORD, 1792; [Twenty lines.] THE ASTRONOMICAL CALCULATIONS BY WILLIAM WARING.
Philadelphia: Printed and sold by Joseph Crukshank, No. 91, High-Street. [1791.] pp. (48). 12mo. AAS.

23957 —— POOR WILL'S POCKET ALMANACK, FOR THE YEAR 1792; BEING BISSEXTILE OR LEAP-YEAR. [Eighteen lines.]
Philadelphia: Printed and sold by Joseph Crukshank, No. 91, High-Street. [1791.] pp. [44.] 48mo. AAS. HC. LOC.

23958 —— POULSON'S TOWN AND COUNTRY ALMANAC, FOR THE YEAR OF OUR LORD, 1792; BEING BISSEXTILE, OR LEAP-YEAR. [Thirty lines.] THE ASTRONOMICAL CALCULATIONS BY WILLIAM WARING.
Philadelphia: Printed and sold by Zachariah Poulson, junior, No. 30, Fourth-Street, near the College. [1791.] pp. (36). 12mo. AAS. LOC.

23959 WARREN. RHODE ISLAND. WARREN ASSOCIATION.
MINUTES OF THE WARREN ASSOCIATION, HELD AT THE BAPTIST MEETING-HOUSE IN NEW-ROWLEY, MDCCXCI.
Printed in Boston, by Joseph Bumstead, Union-Street. [1791.] pp. 14. 8vo. AAS. BM. JCB.

23960 THE WASHINGTON SPY. VOL. I. NO. 22. THURSDAY, JANUARY 6, [—VOL. II. NO. 73. THURSDAY, DECEMBER 29, 1791.]
Elizabeth (Hager's) Town, Printed by Stewart Herbert. 1791. fol.

23961 WATTS, ISAAC 1674 – 1748
DR. WATTS' PLAIN AND EASY CATECHISMS FOR CHILDREN. THE FIRST EXETER EDITION. [Ornament.]
Printed at Exeter, by Henry Ranlet, and sold at his Office.—1791. [Ornament.] pp. 36. 18mo. AAS.

23962 WEATHERWISE, ABRAHAM, pseudonym.
THE MASSACHUSETTS AND NEW-HAMPSHIRE ALMANACK; FOR THE YEAR OF OUR LORD 1792. . . . BY ABRAHAM WEATHERWISE, PHILOM.
Boston: Printed J. White and C. Cambridge, [1791.] pp. (24). 12mo. AAS. LOC.

23963 —— WEATHERWISE'S GENUINE MASSACHUSETTS, NEW-HAMPSHIRE, VERMONT RHODE-ISLAND, AND CONNECTICUT ALMANACK, FOR THE YEAR OF OUR LORD 1792.
Boston: Printed and sold by Nathaniel Coverly. MDCCXCII [1791.] pp. (24). 12mo. AAS.
"The Printers of this Almanac can assure the public it is entirely free from the infection of the small-pox."

23964 —— WEATHERWISE'S TOWN & COUNTRY ALMANACK FOR THE YEAR OF OUR LORD 1792.
Boston: Printed and sold by John W. Folsom. [1791.]

23965 WEBSTER, NOAH, JUNIOR 1758 – 1843
THE AMERICAN SPELLING BOOK: CONTAINING AN EASY STANDARD OF PRONUNCIATION. BEING THE FIRST PART OF A GRAMMATICAL INSTITUTE OF THE ENGLISH LANGUAGE. BY NOAH WEBSTER, JUN. ESQUIRE. AUTHOR OF "DISSERTATIONS ON THE ENGLISH LANGUAGE," "COLLECTION OF ESSAYS AND FUGITIVE WRITINGS," &C. THOMAS AND ANDREWS'S THIRD EDITION.
Printed at Boston, by Isaiah Thomas and Ebenezer T. Andrews. At Faust's Statue, No. 45, Newbury Street. MDCCXCI.

WEBSTER, NOAH, JUNIOR, continued.

23966 —— A GRAMMATICAL INSTITUTE OF THE ENGLISH LANGUAGE; COMPRISING AN EASY, CONCISE AND SYSTEMATIC METHOD OF EDUCATION. DESIGNED FOR THE USE OF ENGLISH SCHOOLS IN AMERICA. IN THREE PARTS. PART SECOND. CONTAINING A PLAIN AND COMPREHENSIVE GRAMMAR, GROUNDED ON THE TRUE PRINCIPLES AND IDIOMS OF THE LANGUAGE. BY NOAH WEBSTER, JUN. ESQUIRE. AUTHOR OF "DISSERTATIONS ON THE ENGLISH LANGUAGE," "COLLECTION OF ESSAYS AND FUGITIVE WRITINGS," &C. THE SECOND CONNECTICUT EDITION.

Printed at Hartford, by Hudson and Goodwin. MDCCXCI.

23967 —— THE LITTLE READER'S ASSISTANT; CONTAINING I. A NUMBER OF STORIES, MOSTLY TAKEN FROM THE HISTORY OF AMERICA, AND ADORNED WITH CUTS. II. RUDIMENTS OF ENGLISH GRAMMAR. III. A FEDERAL CATECHISM, BEING A SHORT AND EASY EXPLANATION OF THE CONSTITUTION OF THE UNITED STATES. IV. GENERAL PRINCIPLES OF GOVERNMENT AND COMMERCE. V. THE FARMER'S CATECHISM. THE SECOND EDITION.

Hartford: Printed by Elisha Babcock, 1791. pp. 141. 16mo.   AAS. YC.

23968 —— — THE LITTLE READER'S ASSISTANT; CONTAINING I. A NUMBER OF STORIES MOSTLY TAKEN FROM THE HISTORY OF AMERICA, AND ADORNED WITH CUTS. II. RUDIMENTS OF ENGLISH GRAMMAR. III. A FEDERAL CATECHISM, BEING A SHORT AND EASY EXPLANATION OF THE CONSTITUTION OF THE UNITED STATES. IV. GENERAL PRINCIPLES OF GOVERNMENT AND COMMERCE. V. THE FARMER'S CATECHISM. BY NOAH WEBSTER, JUN. ATTORNEY AT LAW. THE THIRD EDITION.

Northampton: Printed by William Butler. M.DCC.XCI. pp. 137. 16mo.
   AAS.

Contains also, On a reform of spelling.

23969 —— THE PROMPTER; OR A COMMENTARY ON COMMON SAYINGS AND SUBJECTS, WHICH ARE FULL OF COMMON SENSE, THE BEST SENSE IN THE WORLD. "TO SEE ALL OTHERS FAULTS AND FEEL OUR OWN."

Hartford: Printed by Hudson and Goodwin. M,DCC,XCI. pp. 94. 12mo.
   BPL. HC. NYPL.

23970 WEBSTER, PELATIAH   1725 – 1795
AN ADDRESS TO THE STOCK-HOLDERS OF THE BANK OF NORTH-AMERICA, ON THE SUBJECT OF THE OLD AND NEW BANKS. BY A CITIZEN OF PHILADELPHIA.

Philadelphia: Printed and sold by Joseph Crukshank, No. 91, *High-Street.* 1791. pp. 8. 8vo.

23971 —— — AN ADDRESS TO THE STOCKHOLDERS OF THE BANK OF NORTH-AMERICA: ON THE SUBJECT OF THE OLD AND NEW BANK. BY A CITIZEN OF PHILADELPHIA. [Colophon:]

Philadelphia: Printed by Joseph Crukshank. MDCCXCI. pp. 16. 8vo.

23972 —— POLITICAL ESSAYS ON THE NATURE AND OPERATION OF MONEY, PUBLIC FINANCES, AND OTHER SUBJECTS: PUBLISHED DURING THE AMERICAN WAR, AND CONTINUED UP TO THE PRESENT YEAR, 1791. BY PELATIAH WEBSTER, A. M.

Philadelphia: Printed and sold by Joseph Crukshank, No. 91, *High-Street.* MDCCXCI. pp. viii, [504.] 8vo.
   AAS. BA. BM. HC. JCB. LCP. LOC. MHS. NYHS. NYPL.

23973 THE WEEKLY MUSEUM. [Motto.] NUMBER 138. SATURDAY, JANUARY 1, [—NUMBER 190. SATURDAY, DECEMBER 31, 1791.]

New-York: Printed and published by John Harrisson, at his Printing-Office, No. 3, *Peck-Slip.* 1791. 4to.

23974

THE WEEKLY Register. Vol. I. No. 1. Tuesday, November 29, [—No. 5. Tuesday, December 27, 1791.]

Norwich: Published by Ebenezer Bushnell, 24 rods west of the Meeting-House. 1791. fol.

Established by Ebenezer Bushnell. On June 7, 1792, Bushnell and his brother-in-law, Thomas Hubbard, "entered a partnership in the Printing and Stocking-weaving business, under the firm of Bushnell and Hubbard." On October 1, 1793, Bushnell withdrew. Thomas Hubbard continued the publication until October, 1796, when he removed to Chelsea Landing, now a part of Norwich, and established *The Chelsea Courier*, in continuation.

23975

WEICHENHAN, Erasmus   – 1594

Christliche Betrachtungen über die Evangelischen Texte, so man pfleget zu lesen an denen Sontagen und hohen Festen. Christlich und aufrichtig gepredigt und beschrieben durch Erasmum Weichenhan. [Vignette.]

Germantown: Gedruckt bey Michael Billmeyer. 1791. pp. 6, 785. 4to.

This work, which was first, posthumously, printed in 1672, reflects the religious views of the Schwenkfelders. In typography, paper and binding, this reprint "at the expense of United Friends" is a very creditable piece of bookmaking. The preface is dated, Montgomery County, February 12, 1791.

23976

WESLEY, John   1703 – 1791

Explanatory Notes upon the New Testament. By John Wesley, M. A. Late Fellow of Lincoln-College, Oxford. Volume the First. The First American Edition.

Philadelphia: Printed by Joseph Crukshank: Sold by John Dickins, No. 43, Fourth-Street, near the corner of Race-Street. MDCCXCI. pp. 416. 8vo.   AAS.

23977

—— Primitive Physic: or an Easy and Natural Method of Curing most Diseases. By John Wesley, m. a. [One line of Latin.] The Twenty-second Edition.

Philadelphia: Printed by Parry Hall, No. 149, Chesnut Street, and sold by John Dickins, in Fourth Street, No. 43, near Race Street. M.DCC.XCI. pp. 191. 12mo.   AAS. SGO.

23978

—— Reasons against a Separation from the Church of England. By John Wesley, A. M.—Printed in London in the year 1758—

[Without Place or Printer. 1791.] pp. (8). 8vo.   NYPL.

23979

WEST, Benjamin   1730 – 1813

Bickerstaff's Genuine Almanack, for the Year of our Lord 1792. Being Bissextile, or Leap-year, and the Sixteenth of American Independence. [Twelve lines.] Calculated for the Meridian and Latitude of Boston, and will serve without any sensible error for any part of New-England.

Boston: Printed for and sold by the Booksellers. [1791.] pp. (24). 12mo.   AAS. NYHS.

This is identical with The Federal Almanack, for 1792, with a different title-page only.

23980

— — Bickerstaff's Genuine Almanack for the Year of our Lord 1792. . . . [Cut of Washington.]

Boston: Printed and sold by Shop-keepers in Town and Country. [1791.]

WEST, Benjamin, continued.

23981 —— — The Federal Almanack, for the year of our Lord, 1792. Being bissextile, or leap-year, and the sixteenth of American independence. [Cut of Washington.]
Boston: Printed for and sold by the Booksellers. [1791.] pp. (24). 12mo.
BPL. NYHS.

23982 —— Bickerstaff's Genuine Boston Almanack, or, federal calendar, for 1792. Being leap-year; and sixteenth of independency: containing, besides what is usual, an account of a most horrid murder, discovered by a faithful dog. [Cut of astronomer taking an observation.]
[Boston:] Printed by E. Russell, in Essex-Street, cheap to travelling-traders, &c. [1791.] pp. (24). 12mo.
LOC. NYPL.

23983 —— — Bickerstaff's Genuine Boston Almanack, or, federal calendar, for 1792. Being leap-year; and sixteenth of independency: containing, besides what is usual, an account of a most horrid murder, discovered by a faithful dog. Second edition.
[Boston:] Printed by E. Russell, in Essex-Street, cheap to travelling-traders, &c. [1791.] pp. (24). 12mo.
AAS.

23984 —— Bickerstaff's Genuine Massachusetts, New-Hampshire, Vermont, Rhode-Island, and Connecticutt [sic] Almanack, for the year of our Lord, 1792: being bissextile or leap year, and sixteenth of the independence of America. [Three lines. Cut. Six lines.]
Boston: Printed and sold by Nathaniel Coverley [sic Coverly.] M,DCC-XCII [1791.] pp. (24). 12mo.
AAS. LOC.

23985 —— — Bickerstaff's Genuine Massachusetts, New-Hampshire, Vermont, Rhode-Island, and Connecticutt [sic] Almanack, for the year of our Lord, 1792: . . .
Boston: Printed and sold by Nathaniel Coverley [sic Coverly.] M,DCC,-XCII [1791.] pp. (24). 12mo.
A variant from the preceding in its illustrations.

23986 —— Bickerstaff's New-England Almanack, for the year of our Lord,1792: being bissextile or leap year, and the sixteenth of the independence of America. Calculated for the meridian of Norwich, but will serve without essential variation for the adjacent states. [Ten lines.]
Printed at Norwich, by J. Trumbull, and sold by the gross, dozen or single. ☞ *Where cash is given for linen rags.* [1791.] pp. (20). 12mo. CHS. NYPL.

23987 —— The New-England Almanack, or, lady's and gentleman's diary, for the year of our Lord Christ 1792: being bissextile, or leap-year, and the sixteenth of American independence, which commenced July 4, 1776. [Twenty-one lines.] By Isaac Bickerstaff, esq. philom. [Three lines from] Milton.
Providence: Printed and sold, wholesale and retail, by John Carter, at the Post-Office, near the State-House. [1791.] pp. (24). 12mo. AAS. LOC. RIHS.

23988 —— — The New-England Almanack, or, lady's and gentleman's diary, for the year of our Lord 1792. By Isaac Bickerstaff, esq.
Providence: Printed by John Carter. Sold by Jacob Richardson, esq; in Newport. [1791.]

WEST, BENJAMIN, continued.

23989 —— WHEELER'S NORTH-AMERICAN CALENDAR, OR AN ALMANACK, FOR THE YEAR OF OUR LORD 1792: BEING BISSEXTILE, OR LEAP-YEAR, AND THE SIXTEENTH OF THE INDEPENDENCE OF AMERICA. CONTAINING (BESIDE THE USUAL CALCULATIONS) A VARIETY OF USEFUL AND ENTERTAINING MATTER. TYPE OF THE ECLIPSE, MARCH 22D. [Cut.]

Providence: Printed and sold by Bennett Wheeler. [1791.] pp. (24). 12mo.
AAS. LOC. RIHS.

23990 WESTERN ADVERTISER AND CHAMBERSBURG WEEKLY newspaper. [JANUARY— DECEMBER, 1791.]

Chambersburg: Printed by William Davison. 1791. fol.

23991 THE WESTERN [cut] STAR. [VOL. II. NO. 6. WHOLE] NO. 58. TUESDAY, JANUARY 4, [—VOL. II. NO. 5. WHOLE NO. 109. TUESDAY, DECEMBER 27, 1791.]

Printed and published by Loring Andrews, Stockbridge (Massachusetts). 1791. fol. AAS.

23992 —— THE NEW-YEAR'S WISH OF THE POST WHO CARRIES THE WESTERN-STAR.

[Stockbridge: Printed by Loring Andrews, 1791.] Broadside.

23993 WETHERILL, SAMUEL 1736 – 1816
THE GROUNDS AND REASON OF INCARNATION AND PROCESS OF CHRIST EXPLAINED; IN WHICH IS SHEWN, THAT HE DID NOT SUFFER IN THE PLACE AND STEAD OF SIN-NERS, AND, CONSEQUENTLY, HIS RIGHTEOUSNESS IS NOT IMPUTED TO MEN. BEING A DEFENCE OF THE DOCTRINES CONTAINED IN A PAMPHLET, ENTITLED, "A CON-FUTATION OF THE DOCTRINES OF ANTINOMIANISM," &C. IN REPLY TO SEVERAL SERMONS PREACHED BY THE REVEREND ASHBEL GREEN. TO WHICH IS ADDED, A FEW SENTIMENTS ON THE DOCTRINE OF UNIVERSAL SALVATION, AS HELD BY THE MISTICK: TOGETHER WITH A SHORT ADDRESS TO THE REVEREND JOSEPH PILMORE. BY SAMUEL WETHERILL.

Philadelphia: Printed and sold by Francis Bailey, on the south side of Market-Street, near Fourth-Street, at the Sign of Yorick's Head, and by Joseph Crukshank on the north side of Market-Street, between Second and Third-Streets. 1791.

23994 WETMORE, IZRAHIAH 1728 – 1798
THE IMPORTANT DUTIES AND QUALIFICATIONS OF GOSPEL MINISTERS, CONSIDERED IN A SERMON PREACHED AT THE ORDINATION OF THE REV. DAVID LEWIS BEEBEE TO THE PASTORAL OFFICE OVER THE FIRST CHURCH OF CHRIST, IN WOODBRIDGE,— FEBRUARY 23, 1791.

New-Haven: Printed by A. Morse. 1791. pp. 22. 8vo.

23995 WHARTON, CHARLES HENRY 1748 – 1833
A SHORT AND CANDID ENQUIRY INTO THE PROOFS OF CHRIST'S DIVINITY, . . . IN A LETTER TO A FRIEND.

Wilmington: Printed by Brynberg & Andrews. 1791. pp. 48. 12mo.

23996 WHEELER, BENNETT
THE YOUNG MASON'S MONITOR; CONTAINING SOME NECESSARY HINTS TO YOUNG BRETHREN—YET NOT BENEATH THE ATTENTION OF ANY. TO WHICH IS ANNEXED, A COLLECTION OF MASONIC SONGS, ODES, &C. MANY OF THEM NEW AND EXCELLENT. COMPILED BY B. WHEELER, SECRETARY OF ST. JOHN'S LODGE, NO. 1. PROVIDENCE. [Cut of masonic emblems.]

Printed at Providence, [by and] for the Editor, in the year of light 5791 [1791.] pp. 46, (1). 12mo. RIHS.

23997

WHEELING, W.

PRICE WOODS'S TOWN AND COUNTRY ALMANAC, AND EPHEMERIS OF THE MOTION OF THE SUN AND MOON—THE TRUE PLACES AND ASPECTS OF THE PLANETS—THE RISING AND SETTING OF THE SUN—THE RISING, SETTING AND SOUTHING OF THE MOON, FOR THE YEAR OF OUR LORD 1792: BEING BESSEXTILE, OR LEAP-YEAR, AND THE SIXTEENTH OF AMERICAN INDEPENDENCE. [Fourteen lines.] ASTRONOMICAL CALCULATIONS BY W. WHEELING.

Newark (N. J.): Printed by John Woods. Six pence. [1791.] pp. (39). 16mo.

JCB.

Contains, The Reconciliation, a dialogue performed by the students at Orange Academy.

23998

WHITEFIELD, GEORGE   1714 – 1770

THE DOCTRINE OF ELECTION DEFENDED AND SUPPORTED. BEING A LETTER FROM THE REV. GEORGE WHITEFIELD, IN ANSWER TO A SERMON, PUBLISHED BY THE REV. JOHN WESLEY, IN FAVOUR OF UNIVERSAL REDEMPTION.

Windham: Printed by John Byrne. [1791.] pp. (28). 8vo.   NYPL.

23999

WHITEHEAD, JOHN   1740 – 1804

A DISCOURSE DELIVERED AT THE NEW CHAPEL IN THE CITY ROAD ON THE NINTH OF MARCH, 1791, AT THE FUNERAL OF THE LATE REV. MR. JOHN WESLEY. . . . BY JOHN WHITEHEAD, M. D.

Philadelphia: Printed by Joseph Crukshank, No. 91, High Street, and sold by John Dickins, No. 182, in Race Street, near Sixth Street. M.DCC.XCI.

24000

——— A DISCOURSE DELIVERED AT THE NEW CHAPEL IN THE CITY ROAD, ON THE NINTH OF MARCH, 1791, AT THE FUNERAL OF THE LATE REV. MR. JOHN WESLEY. [Four lines from] REV. XIV. 13. BY JOHN WHITEHEAD, M. D. THE SECOND EDITION. [PRICE ONE-EIGHTH OF A DOLLAR.]

Philadelphia: Printed by Joseph Crukshank, No. 91, High Street, and sold by John Dickins, No. 182, in Race Street, near Sixth Street. M.DCC.XCI. pp. (69). 12mo.

NYPL.

Second title: SOME ACCOUNT OF THE LAST SICKNESS AND DEATH OF THE REV. JOHN WESLEY, M. A. [Two lines from] PSALM CXII. 6. CXVI. 15.

Philadelphia: Printed by Joseph Crukshank, No. 91, High Street, and sold by John Dickins, No. 182, in Race Street, near Sixth Street. M.DCC.XCI. pp. (2), (51)–(69).

24001

WILLIAMS, DAVID   1738 – 1816

LESSONS TO A YOUNG PRINCE, BY AN OLD STATESMAN, ON THE PRESENT DISPOSITION IN EUROPE TO A GENERAL REVOLUTION. THE SIXTH EDITION. WITH THE ADDITION OF A LESSON ON THE MODE OF STUDYING AND PROFITING BY THE REFLECTIONS ON THE FRENCH REVOLUTION: BY THE RIGHT HONORABLE EDMUND BURKE. EMBELLISHED WITH FIVE COPPERPLATES, DELINEATING FIVE POLITICAL CONSTITUTIONS IN A MODE ENTIRELY NEW. [Three lines of Latin from] CIC, DE DIV. LIB. II. VER. 4.

London—Printed: New-York, Re-printed by Childs and Swaine. Sold by Berry and Rogers, No. 35, Hanover-Square.—1791.—pp. 68, 5 plates. 8vo.

AAS. BA. HC. JCB. LOC. MHS. NYHS. NYPL.

24002

——— — LESSONS TO A YOUNG PRINCE, BY AN OLD STATESMAN, ON THE PRESENT DISPOSITION IN EUROPE, TO A GENERAL REVOLUTION. [THE SIXTH EDITION.] WITH THE ADDITION OF A LESSON, ON THE MODE OF STUDYING AND PROFITING BY THE REFLECTIONS ON THE FRENCH REVOLUTION: BY THE RIGHT HONORABLE EDMUND BURKE, TOGETHER WITH A LESSON ON THE AMERICAN REVOLUTION. EMBELLISHED WITH FIVE COPPERPLATES, DELINEATING FIVE POLITICAL CONSTITUTIONS, IN A MODE ENTIRELY NEW.

Philadelphia: Carey, Stewart & Co. 1791.

24003   WILLIAMS, Helen Maria   1762 – 1827
Letters on the French Revolution, written in France, in the summer of 1790, to a friend in England; containing, various anecdotes relative to that interesting event, and Memoirs of Mons. and Madame Du F——. By Helen Maria Williams. The first American edition. [Volume I.]
> *Printed at Boston, by J. Belknap and A. Young. Sold at their Printing-Office, No. 34, Newbury Street, and by the Book-sellers in Town and Country.* MDCCXCI. pp. 137. 12mo.   AAS. BM. NYPL.

A second volume was printed, in 1792, with the title, Letters from France.

24004   WILLISON, John   1680 – 1750
An Explanation of the Assembly's Shorter Catechism.
> *Philadelphia: Printed by W. Young, No. 52, Second-Street, the corner of Chesnut-street.* 1791. 16mo.

24005   —— The Mother's Catechism, for the young child: or, a preparatory help for the young and ignorant. In order to their easier understanding the Assembly's Shorter Catechism. To which is prefixed, an advice to parents and children.
> *Carlisle: Printed by George Kline*, 1791.

24006   WILSON, James   1742 – 1798
A Charge delivered by the Hon. James Wilson, Esq. one of the associate justices of the Supreme Court of the United States, to the grand jury, impannelled for the Circuit Court of the United States, holden for the middle-circuit at the capitol, in the city of Richmond, and district of Virginia, on Monday, the 23d day of May. 1791.
> *Richmond: Printed by Augustine Davis,* M,DCC,XCI. pp. [29.] 8vo. LOC.

24007   —— An Introductory lecture to a course of law lectures. By James Wilson, L. L. D. To which is added, a Plan of the lectures.
> *Philadelphia: From the Press of T. Dobson.* M,DCC,XCI. pp. (96). 8vo.
>   LCP. NYHS. NYPL.

11th Pennsylvania District Copyright, issued to James Wilson, as Author, 3 January, 1791.

24008   EIN WOHL eingerichtetes Deutsches A. B. C. Buchstaber und Lesebuch zum Gebrauch Deutscher Schulen. Enthaltend: 1. Das A. B. C. nebst einer groesen Menge Buchstabir-und Leseübungen. 2. Das Gebat des Herrn die Gebote, den Glauben, nebst dem 5, 6 und 7ten Capitel aus Matthäo. 3. Einen hinreichenden grundischen und fasslichen Unterricht das Deutsche richtig zu lernen. 4. Eine Anweisung den kindern das Schreiben und Rechnen leichter und begretflicher zu machen. 5. Einige angenehme und moralische Geschichten und Erzählungen für Kinder, mit Kupfern. 7. Eine Erdbescoübung und allgemeine Nachricht von der Erde und den wier Welttheilen Europa, Asia, Africa und Columbia oder America, zum Nutzen der Erwachsenen sowohl als der Kinder.
> *Germantaun, gedruckt und zu haben bey Michael Billmeyer.* 1791.

13th Pennsylvania District Copyright, issued to Michael Billmeyer. as Proprietor, 12 January, 1791.

24009   —— Ein Wohl eingerichtetes Deutsches A. B. C. Buchstaber, und Lesebuch zum Gebrauch Deutscher Schulen.
> *Germantaun, Gedruckt und zu haben bey Michael Billmeyer.* 1791.

25th Pennsylvania District Copyright, issued to Michael Billmeyer, as Proprietor, 17 October, 1791.

24010   WOODS'S Newark Gazette and New-Jersey Advertiser. Vol. i. No. 1. Thursday, May 19, [—No. 33. Thursday, December 29, 1791.]
      Newark, New-Jersey : Printed by John Woods. 1791. fol.

Established by John Woods, and continued by him to November, 1797, when a new serial numbering was begun, and after a few weeks, Woods was succeeded by John H. Williams, who printed the Gazette "for the Proprietors" into the year 1799, when Jacob Halsey became the printer and publisher into the year 1801, when he sold his interests to John Wallis, one of his assistants, who continued its publication to the end of the year 1804, when it was discontinued. In March, 1793, the title was altered to, *Woods's Newark Gazette and Paterson Advertiser*, up to June, 1795, when the old form was reverted to until Woods withdrew, and his name was dropped. Jacob Halsey shortened the title to *The Newark Gazette*, under which name it was continued until publication ceased in December, 1804.

24011   WORCESTER, Noah   1758 – 1837
      A Friendly letter to the reverend Thomas Baldwin, containing an answer to his Brief defence of the practice of the close communionists. In eight parts. . . . [Seven lines of Scripture texts.]
      Printed by Geo. Hough, at his office in Concord. M.DCC.XCI. pp. 48. 8vo.
                                          AAS. BA. JCB. LOC.

24012   —— The Gospel-ministry illustrated. A sermon preached at the ordination of the rev. Thomas Worcester, pastor of the church in Salisbury, Nov. 9, 1791. By Noah Worcester, a. b. pastor of the church in Thornton.
      Newburyport: Printed by John Mycall, for William Hoyt. [1791.] pp. (34). 8vo.
                                AAS. BM. JCB. LOC. NYPL.

24013   WORKMAN, Benjamin
      Elements of geography, designed for young students in that science. In seven sections. Sect. 1. Of the solar system. Sect. 2. Of the earth in particular. Sect. 3. Of maps and globes. The three foregoing sections contain the scientific or astronomical part of geography digested in a clear and comprehensive manner. Sect. 4. Of the different religions, governments and languages of nations. Sect. 5. Of the political divisions of the earth into empires, kingdoms &c. or the historical part of geography. Sect. 6. Of natural philosophy or the properties of matter &c. Sect. 7. Of chronology. By Benjamin Workman, a. m. The third edition. Illustrated with 1. A Map of the World. 2. A part of the solar system. 3. A Map of North America. 4. A Map of the United States. 5. A Map of South America. 6. A Map of Europe. 7. A Map of Asia. 8. A Map of Africa.
      Philadelphia: Printed and sold by John M'Culloch, 1791.

28th Pennsylvania District Copyright, issued to John M'Culloch, as Proprietor, 9 December, 1791.

24014   —— Father Tammany's Almanac, for the year 1792; being bissextile or leap year. Containing, astronomical calculations; with every other thing necessary in an Almanac. [Seventeen lines. Cut.]
      Philadelphia, Printed and sold by John M'Culloch, at No. 1. North Third-Street. [1791.] pp. (36). 12mo.
                                              VSL.

24015   YALE COLLEGE.
CATALOGUE OF BOOKS IN THE LIBRARY OF YALE-COLLEGE, NEW-HAVEN.
[New-Haven:] Printed by T. & S. Green. MDCCXCI. pp. (50), (2). 8vo.
AAS. CHS. LOC. YC.
> The total number of books in the Library is stated to be about twenty-
> seven hundred volumes—only one hundred more than appeared in
> the Catalogue issued in 1743.

24016   —— ILLUSTRISSIMO SAMUELI HUNTINGTON, ARM. LL. D. REIPUBLICÆ CONNECTICUT-
TENSIS GUBERNATORI: HONORATISSIMO OLIVERO WOLCOTT, ARM. VICE-GUBERNA-
TORI: CLARISSIMISQUE PROCERIBUS POLITIÆ NOSTRÆ CIVILIS: REVERENDO PARIT-
ER AC HONORANDO EZRÆ STILES, S. T. D. LL. D. COLLEGII YALENSIS PRÆSIDI,
[Five lines.] HASCE THESES, QUAS IN COMITIIS PUBLICIS COLLEGII YALENSIS,
DIE 14TO SEPTEMBRIS, ANNO DOMINI, M,DCC,XCI. DEFENDERE CONABUNTUR,
JUVENES IN ARTIBUS INITIATI, [Twenty-eight names.] HABITA IN COMITIIS AC-
ADEMICIS NOVO PORTU CONNECTICUTTENSIUM, M,DCC,XCI.
> *[Novo-Portu:] E Typis Thomæ et Samuelis Green, Universitatis Typo-
> graphorum.* [1791.] Broadside. fol.   HC.

24017   YORK COUNTY. MAINE.
THIS IS TO GIVE NOTICE TO THE PROPRIETORS AND OWNERS OF LANDS, IN THE TOWN
OF SHAPLEIGH, IN THE COUNTY OF YORK, THAT THEIR LANDS ARE TAXED BY THE
ASSESSORS OF SAID PROPRIETORS, [Forty-eight lines.] BY ORDER OF SAID PRO-
PRIETORS' COMMITTEE, DANIEL SEWALL, COLLECTOR. YORK, APRIL 6, 1791.
> *[Portsmouth: Printed by John Melcher?* 1791.] Broadside. 4to.   AAS.

24018   YOUNG, EDWARD   1684 – 1765
THE COMPLAINT: OR, NIGHT-THOUGHTS ON LIFE, DEATH, AND IMMORTALITY. TO
WHICH IS ADDED, A PARAPHRASE ON PART OF THE BOOK OF JOB. A NEW EDI-
TION. [One line of Latin from] VIRG. WITH THE LIFE OF DR. EDWARD YOUNG.
> *Philadelphia: Printed by Henry Taylor, for Robert Campbell,* 1791.

24019   —— — THE COMPLAINT: OR, NIGHT-THOUGHTS ON LIFE, DEATH, AND IMMORTAL-
ITY. TO WHICH IS ADDED, A PARAPHRASE ON PART OF THE BOOK OF JOB.
> *Philadelphia: Printed and sold by W. Woodhouse, at the Bible, No. 6,
> South Front-Street.* 1791.

24020   —— RESIGNATION: IN TWO PARTS, AND A POSTSCRIPT TO MRS. B * * * * * * *.
> *Philadelphia:* 1791. 12mo.   BM.

24021   ZEAL FOR THE TRUTH; OR, AN ATTEMPT TO VINDICATE THE CHRISTIAN RELIGION
AGAINST THE ERRORS INTRODUCED BY ANTICHRIST. BY A LOVER OF MANKIND.
> *Philadelphia: Printed and sold by Francis Bailey,* 1791.

1792

24022   ACCOUNT OF THE REMARKABLE CONVERSION OF A LITTLE BOY AND GIRL.
        Dover: Printed by Eliphalet Ladd. 1792.   AAS.

24023   ADAMS, ZABDIEL   1739 – 1801
        THE DUTY OF MINISTERS GIVING THEMSELVES WHOLLY TO THEIR WORK; REPRE-
        SENTED IN A SERMON PREACHED MAY 16TH, 1792. AT THE INSTALLATION OF
        THE REV. MR. JOHN FOSTER. OVER THE CHURCH, AND FIRST CONGREGATIONAL
        SOCIETY IN TAUNTON, COMMONWEALTH OF MASSACHUSETTS. . . . TO WHICH ARE
        ADDED THE CHARGE AND RIGHT-HAND OF FELLOWSHIP, BY THE REVEREND
        DOCTORS HOWARD AND LATHROP, OF BOSTON.
        Boston: Printed by T. & J. Fleet, 1792. pp. (34). 8vo.
                                       AAS. BA. JCB. LOC. MHS. NYHS.

24024   ADDOMS, JONAS SMITH
        AN INAUGURAL DISSERTATION ON THE MALIGNANT FEVER, WHICH PREVAILED IN THE
        CITY OF NEW-YORK DURING THE MONTHS OF AUGUST, SEPTEMBER, AND OCTOBER
        IN THE YEAR 1791.
        New-York: Printed by T. and J. Swords, 1792. pp. 37. 8vo.   SGO.

24025   AN ADDRESS TO THE MEMBERS OF THE PROTESTANT EPISCOPAL CHURCH, IN THE
        UNITED STATES OF AMERICA. [Ornament.] [Signed, An Episcopalian.]
        New-York:—Printed in the year 1792. pp. 12. 12mo.   JCB. NYHS.
        Reprinted in Charleston, in 1795.

24026   ADVICE TO PREVENT POVERTY.
        Windsor: Printed by Alden Spooner, 1792.

24027   ÆSOPUS   619 – 564 B. C.
        SELECT FABLES OF ESOP AND OTHER FABULISTS. IN THREE BOOKS. BY R. DODSLEY.
        [Seven lines from] PARADISE LOST, B. 8. L. 370. A NEW EDITION.
        Printed and sold by Benjamin Johnson, High-Street, Philadelphia.
        M,DCC,XCII. pp. 209, (6). 12mo.   AAS. JCB.

24028   THE ALBANY GAZETTE. VOL. VIII. NUMB. 533. MONDAY, JANUARY 2, [—VOL IX.
        NUMB.   MONDAY, DECEMBER 31, 1792.]
        Printed every Monday and Thursday by Charles R. and George Webster,
        No. 46, (on the north side of) State-Street, corner of Middle-Lane. 1792. fol.

24029   THE ALBANY [N. Y. arms] REGISTER. [Motto.] VOL. IV. NUMB. 182. MONDAY,
        JANUARY 2, [—VOL. V. NUMB. 234. MONDAY, DECEMBER 31, 1792.]
        [Albany:] Printed every Monday, by John Barber and Solomon South-
        wick, No. 48, north side of State-Street. 1792. fol.
        The motto reads: Let party feuds or civil discord rage—Our Press shall
        e'er impartially engage.

24030   ALEXANDER, Caleb   1755 – 1828
A GRAMMATICAL SYSTEM OF THE ENGLISH LANGUAGE; COMPREHENDING A PLAIN AND FAMILIAR SCHEME OF TEACHING YOUNG GENTLEMEN AND LADIES THE ART OF SPEAKING AND WRITING CORRECTLY THEIR NATIVE TONGUE. BY CALEB ALEXANDER, A. M.

> *Boston: Printed and sold by S. Hall, No. 53 Cornhill.* 1792. pp. 96. 12mo.   AAS. BPL.

26th Massachusetts District Copyright, issued to Caleb Alexander, as Author, 28 February, 1792.

24031   ALLEINE, Joseph   1634 – 1668
THE SOLEMN WARNINGS OF THE DEAD. OR, AN ADMONITION TO UNCONVERTED SINNERS; BY JOSEPH ALLEINE. AND, A CALL TO THE UNCONVERTED; BY MR. RICHARD BAXTER. HE BEING DEAD YET SPEAKETH. HEB. XI. 4.

> *Philadelphia: Printed by Parry Hall, No. 149, Chesnut street; and sold by John Dickins, No. 182, Race street, near Sixth street.* M.DCC.XCII. pp. 186, (2). 12mo.   NYPL.

The two supplemental pages contain, "Books, published by John Dickins, for the use of the Methodist Societies in the United States of America." The first published catalogue of what is now the Methodist Book Concern.

24032   ALLEN, Paul, junior   1775 – 1826
AN ORATION, ON THE DEATH OF ROGER WILLIAMS HOWELL, A MEMBER OF THE SENIOR CLASS OF RHODE-ISLAND COLLEGE, WHO DIED OCTOBER 7, 1792, ÆTAT. 20. PRONOUNCED IN THE COLLEGE-CHAPEL, NOVEMBER 22, 1792. BY PAUL ALLEN, JUN. CLASSMATE OF THE DECEASED. PUBLISHED AT THE REQUEST OF THE STUDENTS. [Five lines from] THOMSON.

> *[Providence:] Printed by J. Carter.* [1792.] pp. (11). 8vo.
>   AAS. BA. BM. BU. RIHS.

24033   ALLEN, Thomas
—NEW-YORK-–1792.—THOMAS ALLEN'S SALE CATALOGUE OF BOOKS, CONSISTING OF A VERY EXTENSIVE COLLECTION OF VALUABLE BOOKS IN EVERY BRANCH OF SCIENCE AND POLITE LITERATURE, ANCIENT AND MODERN, WHICH WILL BE DISPOSED OF, WHOLESALE AND RETAIL, ON REASONABLE TERMS, AT HIS BOOK AND STATIONARY STORE, NO. 12, QUEEN-STREET, NEW-YORK. ☞ T. ALLEN PRESENTS HIS SINCERE THANKS TO HIS FRIENDS AND CUSTOMERS, AND TO THE PUBLIC IN GENERAL, FOR THEIR FORMER FAVOURS, AND BEGS LEAVE TO INFORM THEM, THAT HE HAS REMOVED FROM NO. 16, TO NO. 12, QUEEN-STREET; AND IS CONSTANTLY ENLARGING HIS ASSORTMENT BY FRESH IMPORTATIONS OF BOOKS FROM VARIOUS PARTS OF EUROPE. HE FLATTERS HIMSELF THAT AT HIS STORE WILL BE FOUND AS ELEGANT A COLLECTION, AND AT AS LOW PRICES, AS AT ANY PLACE IN THIS CITY. CATALOGUES DELIVERED AT THE PLACE OF SALE, GRATIS.

> *New-York: Printed for Thomas Allen, Bookseller and Stationer, No. 12, Queen-Street.*—1792. pp. 55. 8vo.   AAS. MHS.

24034   ALLEN, Timothy   1715 – 1806
A DISCOURSE, DELIVERED IN CHESTERFIELD, DECEMBER 8, 1791. AT THE DEDICATION OF THE NEW MEETING-HOUSE. BY TIMOTHY ALLEN, A. M. AND PASTOR OF THE CHURCH THERE. AND (PUBLISHED) BY DESIRE OF THOSE WHO HEARD IT.

> *Northampton: Printed by William Butler.*—1792. pp. 19. 8vo.   JCB.

24035   THE AMERICAN APOLLO, CONTAINING THE PUBLICATIONS OF THE HISTORICAL SO-
CIETY, ESSAYS, MORAL, POLITICAL, AND POETICAL, AND THE DAILY OCCURRENCES
IN THE NATURAL, CIVIL, AND COMMERCIAL WORLD. [Cut.] SCIENTIÆ PATER MUS-
ARUM PRINCEPS.   ☞ SUBSCRIPTIONS FOR THE AMERICAN APOLLO, ARE RE-
CEIVED BY THE PUBLISHERS AT THEIR PRINTING-OFFICE, STATE STREET, BOSTON,
AND BY THE FOLLOWING PRINTERS AND BOOKSELLERS—MR. J. DABNEY, AND MR.
W. CARLETON, SALEM—B. EMERSON, ESQ. POSTMASTER, NEWBURY-PORT.—J.
LIBBEY, ESQ. POST-MASTER, PORTSMOUTH—S. FREEMAN, ESQ. POSTMASTER,
PORTLAND—I. THOMAS, ESQ. WORCESTER—MR. E. W. WELD, SPRINGFIELD, T.
HILLDRUP, ESQ. POSTMASTER, HARTFORD, AND BY MANY OTHER GENTLEMEN IN
VARIOUS PARTS OF THE UNITED STATES. [No. 1.—PART II—VOL. 1. FRIDAY,
JANUARY 6,—No. 39—PART II—VOL. I. FRIDAY, SEPTEMBER 28, 1792.]

> *Printed at Boston, by Belknap and Young, State Street.* [1792.] pp. (4)
> 408. 8vo.   AAS. BA. BM. HC. JCB. LOC.

> No dates are given. And it appears that each of the thirty-nine num-
> bers had a similar cover, with the above title, and two pages of adver-
> tisements. Beginning with the first number, and continuing success-
> ively for each of the thirty-nine weekly issues, there was published one
> signature, of usually eight pages, which could be separated from the
> rest, and was called Part I, which contained the Publications of the
> Massachusetts Historical Society. After thirty numbers were issued,
> this was published separately, and the *American Apollo* was published
> in folio newspaper form. 21st Massachusetts District Copyright, is-
> sued to Belknap and Young, as Proprietors, 5 June, 1792.

24036   —— AMERICAN APOLLO. VOL. II. No. 1. FRIDAY, OCTOBER 5, [—VOL. II. No. 13.
WHOLE NO. 52. FRIDAY, DECEMBER 28, 1792.]

> *Printed and published, on Fridays, by Belknap and Young, in State-Street,*
> *Boston.* 1792. fol.   BA.

24037   AMERICAN CHRONOLOGY.

> *Philadelphia: From the Press of Mathew Carey,* 1792.
> Advertised as "in press" January, 1792.

24038   THE AMERICAN GAZETTE, AND NORFOLK AND PORTSMOUTH WEEKLY ADVERTISER.
[Motto.] VOL. I. NUMBER 1. WEDNESDAY, JULY 18, [—NUMBER 24. WEDNESDAY,
DECEMBER 26, 1792.]

> *Norfolk: Printed by C. Willett and W. Davis, near the Market.* 1792. 4to.
> Established by Charles Willett, and William Davis, and continued by
> them into the year 1794, when they established, with a new number-
> ing, in May, 1794, the *American Gazette, and Norfolk and Portsmouth Pub-*
> *lic Advertiser.* In August, 1794, the partnership was dissolved, Charles
> Willett retiring, and in the same month establishing The Herald, and
> Norfolk and Portsmouth Advertiser, at the same Printing-Office, on
> Wednesdays and Saturdays, and William Davis continuing the Ameri-
> can Gazette, changing the days of publication to Tuesdays and Fridays.
> In May, 1796, the title was altered to, *American Gazette & General*
> *Advertiser.*

24039   THE AMERICAN [U. S. arms] MERCURY. VOL. VIII. NUMB. 391. MONDAY, JANUARY
2, [—NUMB. 443. MONDAY, DECEMBER 31, 1792.]

> *Hartford: Printed by Elisha Babcock.* 1792. fol.   AAS. CHS. YC.

24040   THE AMERICAN MUSEUM, OR, REPOSITORY OF ANCIENT AND MODERN FUGITIVE
PIECES, &C. PROSE AND POETICAL FOR MARCH 1787. [Two lines of verse.] VOL. I.
NUMB. III. THE THIRD EDITION.

> *Philadelphia: Printed by Mathew Carey,* M.DCC.XCII.   AAS.

THE AMERICAN MUSEUM, continued.

24041 —— THE AMERICAN MUSEUM, OR REPOSITORY OF ANCIENT AND MODERN FUGITIVE PIECES, &C, PROSE AND POETICAL FOR SEPTEMBER, 1787. [Three lines of quotations.] VOL. II. NO. III. THE SECOND EDITION.
Philadelphia: Printed by Mathew Carey, No. 118, *Market-Street. March* 22, M.DCC.XCII. AAS. LOC.

24042 —— THE AMERICAN MUSEUM: OR REPOSITORY OF ANCIENT AND MODERN FUGITIVE PIECES, &C. PROSE AND POETICAL. FOR OCTOBER, 1787. [Three lines of quotations.] VOL. II. NO. IV. THE SECOND EDITION.
Philadelphia: Printed by Mathew Carey, No. 118, *Market-Street.* M.DCC-XCII. AAS. LOC.

24043 —— THE AMERICAN MUSEUM: OR REPOSITORY OF ANCIENT AND MODERN FUGITIVE PIECES, &C. PROSE AND POETICAL FOR NOVEMBER, 1787. [Three lines of quotations.] VOL. II. NUMB. V. SECOND EDITION.
Philadelphia: Printed by Mathew Carey, June 23, M.DCC.XCII. AAS. LOC.

24044 —— THE AMERICAN MUSEUM: OR REPOSITORY OF ANCIENT AND MODERN FUGITIVE PIECES, &C. PROSE AND POETICAL. FOR MAY, 1788. [Three lines of quotations.] VOL. III. NO. V. THE SECOND EDITION.
Philadelphia: Printed by Mathew Carey, No. 118, *Market-Street. June* 9, M.DCC.XCII. AAS. LOC.

24045 —— THE AMERICAN MUSEUM, OR, UNIVERSAL MAGAZINE: CONTAINING ESSAYS ON AGRICULTURE—COMMERCE—MANUFACTURES—POLITICS—MORALS—AND MANNERS. SKETCHES OF NATIONAL CHARACTERS—NATURAL AND CIVIL HISTORY—AND BIOGRAPHY. LAW INFORMATION—PUBLIC PAPERS—PROCEEDINGS OF CONGRESS—INTELLIGENCE; MORAL TALES—ANCIENT AND MODERN POETRY, &C. &C. [VOL. XI.] FOR THE YEAR 1792. PART I. FROM JANUARY TO JUNE.
Philadelphia: From the Press of M. Carey, No. 118, *Market-Street.* M.DCC.XCII. pp. 308, 36, 92, 48, (4). 8vo. AAS. BA. BM. HC. LOC. NYHS.

24046 —— THE AMERICAN MUSEUM, OR, UNIVERSAL MAGAZINE: CONTAINING ESSAYS ON AGRICULTURE—COMMERCE—MANUFACTURES—POLITICS—MORALS—AND MANNERS. SKETCHES OF NATIONAL CHARACTERS—NATURAL AND CIVIL HISTORY—AND BIOGRAPHY. LAW INFORMATION—PUBLIC PAPERS—PROCEEDINGS OF CONGRESS—INTELLIGENCE; MORAL TALES—ANCIENT AND MODERN POETRY, &C. &C. [VOL. XII.] FOR THE YEAR 1792. PART II. FROM JULY TO DECEMBER.
Philadelphia: From the Press of M. Carey, No. 118, *Market-Street.* M.DCC.XCII. pp. 352, 36, 44, 40. 8vo. AAS. BA. BM. HC. JCB. LOC. NYHS.
Discontinued with the issue for December, owing to the action of the Post Office Department denying magazines the use of the mails. An attempt was made, by the Publisher, to continue its publication in 1798-1799, and a single volume, sometimes called XIII, completed its publication in 1799.

24047 THE AMERICAN POCKET ALMANAC, FOR THE YEAR OF OUR LORD 1793: OF AMERICAN INDEPENDENCE THE SEVENTEENTH. THE FIRST AFTER BISSEXTILE, OR LEAP-YEAR. CONTAINING, (BESIDES EVERY THING THAT IS COMMON IN AN ALMANAC OF THE KIND) THE WHOLE OF THE ACT TO PROVIDE FOR THE NATIONAL DEFENCE, BY ESTABLISHING AN UNIFORM MILITIA THROUGHOUT THE UNITED STATES, AND A GREAT VARIETY OF LISTS, USEFUL TABLES, AND OTHER MATTER.
Philadelphia: Printed and sold by Thomas Lang, No. 21, *Church-Alley.* [1792.] pp. (48). 48mo. LOC.

24048   AMERICAN SPY. VOL. I. NUM. 40. FRIDAY, JANUARY 6, [—VOL. II. NUM. 91. FRI-
DAY, DECEMBER 28, 1792.]

> *Lansingburgh: Printed by Silvester Tiffany, (a little south of Douglass' Tav-*
> *ern) at twelve shillings per annum.* 1792. fol.

With the issue for August 3d, William W. Wands, was admitted to partnership, as Tiffany and Wands.

24049   THE AMERICAN THEATRE. BEING A COLLECTION OF PLAYS, TAKEN FROM BELL'S
THEATRE, AND PERFORMED BY THE OLD AMERICAN COMPANY, PHILADELPHIA.
[Seven lines of verse.] VOL. I. [Publisher's monogram.]

> *[Philadelphia:] Printed and sold by Enoch Story, Fourth street, (No. 36.)*
> *nearly opposite the Indian Queen.* — 1792. pp. (2), 80, (1), 2; 59, (1); 84; (8),
> 33, 3; 67, (1), (2), frontispiece. 12mo.   AAS.

Second title: AMERICAN EDITION. THE GAMESTER, A TRAGEDY, AS PERFORMED
BY THE AMERICAN COMPANY, AT THE THEATRE, IN SOUTHWARK, PHILADELPHIA.
WRITTEN BY MR. EDWARD MOORE. [Publisher's monogram.]

> *Philadelphia: Printed and sold by E. Story, in Second Street, fifth door*
> *above Arch Street, the east side.* [1790.] pp. 80, (1), (2).

Third title: AMERICAN EDITION. THE EARL OF ESSEX. A TRAGEDY. AS PER-
FORMED BY THE OLD AMERICAN COMPANY, AT THE THEATRE IN SOUTHWARK,
PHILADELPHIA. WRITTEN BY HENRY JONES. [Publisher's monogram.]

> *Philadelphia: Printed and sold by Enoch Story, Second Street.* M.DCC.XC.
> pp. 59, (1).

Fourth title: GUSTAVUS VASA, THE DELIVERER OF HIS COUNTRY. A TRAGEDY.
AS IT WAS TO HAVE BEEN ACTED AT THE THEATRE ROYAL IN DRURY LANE, NOW
PERFORMED BY THE OLD AMERICAN COMPANY, AT THE THEATRE, IN SOUTHWARK,
PHILADELPHIA.

> *Philadelphia: Printed and sold by Enoch Story, in Second Street.* 1790.
> pp. 84.

Fifth title: THE WIDOW OF MALABAR. A TRAGEDY. AS IT IS PERFORMED AT
THE THEATRE-ROYAL, COVENT-GARDEN. WRITTEN BY MARIANA STARKE. [Pub-
lisher's monogram.]

> *Philadelphia: Printed and sold by E. Story, in Fourth, between Market*
> *and Chesnut-Streets. (No. 36.)* [1791.] pp. (2), (2), (2), (2), 33, (3).

Sixth title: AMERICAN EDITION. DOUGLAS, A TRAGEDY. AS PERFORMED BY
THE AMERICAN COMPANY, AT THE THEATRE, IN SOUTHWARK, PHILADELPHIA.
WRITTEN BY THE REV. MR. HOME. [Publisher's monogram.]

> *Philadelphia: Printed and sold by Enoch Story, Second Street.* M.DCC.XC.
> pp. 67, (1), (2).

Advertised: VOL. II. THE GRECIAN DAUGHTER. BY ARTHUR MURPHY.—THE
SUSPICIOUS HUSBAND. BY BENJAMIN HOADLY.—THE TRUE-BORN IRISHMAN.
BY CHARLES MACKLIN.—SELIMA AND AZORE. BY JEAN FRANÇOIS MARMONTEL.
—THE FIRST, SECOND AND THIRD PARTS OF THE POOR SOLDIER. BY JOHN
O'KEEFFE.—THE PRISONER AT LARGE. BY JOHN O'KEEFFE.

24050   AMERICANISCHER HAUS UND WIRTHSCHAFTS - CALENDER AUF DAS 1793STE JAHR
CHRISTI. ZUM ZWÖLFTENMAL HERAUSGEGEBEN.

> *Philadelphia: Gedruckt bey Steiner & Kämmerer.* [1792.]

No Almanacs of this series were published for the years 1791 and 1792.

24051 AMERICANISCHER Stadt und Land Kalender Auf das 1793ste Jahr Christi, Welches ein Gemein Jahr ist von 365 Tagen.
   Philadelphia. Gedruckt und zu haben bey Carl Cist, in der Zweyten-strasse, No. 104. nah am Eck der Rehs-strasse. [1792.] pp. (42). 4to.   AAS. LOC.

24052 ANDERSON, James   1680 – 1739
   The Constitutions of the ancient and honourable fraternity of Free and Accepted Masons: containing their history, charges, addresses, &c., collected and digested from their old records, faithful traditions, and lodge-books for the use of Masons. To which are added, the History of Masonry in the Commonwealth of Massachusetts, and the Constitution, laws, and regulations of their Grand Lodge. Together with a large collection of songs, epilogues, &c. By Thaddeus Mason Harris.
   Printed at Worcester, by brother Isaiah Thomas. In the christian era MDCCXCII; *in the year of light* VMDCCXCII. pp. 228, plate. 4to.
                                                 AAS. BA. HC. JCB. MHS.
   41st Massachusetts District Copyright, issued to Isaiah Thomas, as Proprietor, 7 December, 1792.

24053 ANDREWS, Robert
   The Virginia Almanack, for the year of our Lord, 1793. Being the first after leap year. And the seventeenth of American independence. By Robert Andrews, philo. Signs, planets, and aspects. [Twelve lines.]
   Richmond: Printed by T. Nicolson, two doors above the Eagle-Tavern.
   [1792.] pp. (48). 12mo.   GHS. LOC.
   Contains, Bathmendi, a Persian tale.

24054 AN APPENDIX to the Impartial statement of the controversy respecting the decision of the late committee of canvassers.
   New-York: Printed by Childs and Swaine. M,DCC,XCII. pp. [22.] 8vo.
                                                 JCB. NYHS. NYPL.
   This "Appendix" is a separate and distinct publication, answering and controverting the assertions in the "Impartial statement," and supplementary to it, only in that way.

24055 ARABIAN nights entertainments.
   The Oriental moralist, or the beauties of the Arabian nights entertainments.
   New-York: Printed for Berry, Rogers & Berry, No. 35, Hanover-Square.
   1792.

24056 THE [cut] ARGUS. Tuesday, January 3, [— Tuesday, December 25, 1792.]
   Boston:—Printed and published, on Tuesdays and Fridays, by Edward Eveleth Powars, opposite the Court-House, Court-Street. 1792. fol.
   The cut is of a Peacock. No serial volume, or number is given. In October, publication became weekly on Tuesdays, only.

24057 ARISTOTLE, pseudonym.
   Aristotle's Book of problems, with other astronomers, astrologers, philosophers, physicians, &c: wherein are contained divers questions and answers touching the state of man's body. Together with the reasons of divers wonders in the creation; the generation of birds, beasts, fishes, and insects; and many other problems on the most weighty matters, by way of question and answer. A new edition.
   Philadelphia: Printed for the Booksellers. MDCCXCII. pp. 68. 12mo. AAS.

ARISTOTLE, continued.

24058 —— —— ARISTOTLE'S LAST LEGACY, UNFOLDING THE MYSTERIES OF NATURE IN THE [*sic*] GENERATION OF MAN. TREATING, I. OF VIRGINITY, ITS SIGNS AND TOKENS, AND HOW A MAN MAY KNOW WHETHER HE HATH MARRIED A VIRGIN OR NOT. II. OF THE ORGAN OF GENERATION IN WOMEN, WITH A DESCRIPTION OF THE WOMB. III. OF THE USE AND ACTION OF THE GENITALS IN THE WORK OF GENERATION. IV. OF CONCEPTION; AND HOW TO KNOW WHETHER A WOMAN HAS CONCEIVED, AND WHETHER OF A MALE OR FEMALE. V. OF THE PLEASURE AND ADVANTAGE OF MARRIAGE; WITH THE UNHAPPY CONSEQUENCES OF UNEQUAL MATCHES, AND MISERIES OF UNLAWFUL LOVE. VI. OF BARRENNESS, WITH REMEDIES AGAINST IT; AND THE SIGNS OF INSUFFICIENCY BOTH IN MEN AND WOMEN. VII. DIRECTIONS TO BOTH SEXES HOW TO MANAGE THEMSELVES IN THE ACT OF COITION, OR THEIR VENEREAL EMBRACES. VIII. A VADE-MECUM FOR MIDWIVES AND NURSES; CONTAINING PARTICULAR DIRECTIONS FOR THE FAITHFUL DISCHARGE OF THEIR SEVERAL EMPLOYMENTS. IX. EXCELLENT REMEDIES AGAINST ALL DISEASES INCIDENT TO VIRGINS AND CHILD-BEARING WOMEN; FITTED FOR THE USE OF MIDWIVES, &C. A NEW EDITION.

Philadelphia: Printed for the Booksellers. MDCCXCII. pp. 39 [*sic* 34.] 12mo.   AAS.

24059 ASH, JOHN   1724 – 1779
GRAMMATICAL INSTITUTES; OR, AN EASY INTRODUCTION TO DR. LOWTH'S ENGLISH GRAMMAR, DESIGNED FOR THE USE OF SCHOOLS, AND TO LEAD YOUNG GENTLEMEN AND LADIES, INTO THE KNOWLEDGE OF THE FIRST PRINCIPLES OF THE ENGLISH LANGUAGE. . . . WITH AN APPENDIX, CONTAINING, I. THE DECLENSION OF IRREGULAR AND DEFECTIVE VERBS. II. THE APPLICATION OF THE GRAMMATICAL INSTITUTES. III. SOME USEFUL OBSERVATIONS ON THE ELLIPSIS. TO WHICH IS NOW ADDED; SELECT LESSONS TO INSTIL JUST SENTIMENTS OF VIRTUE IN YOUTH. AND A COLLECTION OF BOOKS, PROPER FOR YOUNG GENTLEMEN AND LADIES, TO SHORTEN THE PATH TO KNOWLEDGE.

New-York: Printed by Hugh Gaine, 1792.

24060 ASBURY, FRANCIS   1745 – 1816
AN EXTRACT FROM THE JOURNAL OF FRANCIS ASBURY, BISHOP OF THE METHODIST EPISCOPAL CHURCH IN AMERICA, FROM AUGUST 7, 1771, TO DECEMBER, 29, 1778. VOLUME I.

Philadelphia: Printed by Joseph Crukshank, No. 87, High-Street: Sold by John Dickins, No. 182, in Race-Street, near Sixth-Street. 1792. pp. (2), (2), (356). 12mo.   AAS. NYPL.

All that was published. The first seventy pages were reprinted from the Arminian Magazine.

24061 BACKUS, ISAAC   1724 – 1806
THE KINGDOM OF GOD, DESCRIBED BY HIS WORD, WITH ITS INFINITE BENEFITS TO HUMAN SOCIETY. BY ISAAC BACKUS, PASTOR OF A CHURCH IN MIDDLEBOROUGH. [One line from] PSALM XCVII. 1. [Ornament.]

Boston: Printed and sold by Samuel Hall. MDCCXCII. pp. 24. 8vo.
       BU. NYPL.

24062 —— THE NATURE AND NECESSITY OF AN INTERNAL CALL TO PREACH THE EVERLASTING GOSPEL; WITH MARKS TO DISTINGUISH THE MINISTERS OF CHRIST FROM ALL DECEIVERS. BY ISAAC BACKUS, PASTOR OF A CHURCH IN MIDDLEBOROUGH. [One line from] ROM. X. 15. THE SECOND EDITION, IMPROVED. [Ornament.]

Boston: Printed and sold by Samuel Hall, in Cornhill. MDCCXII [*sic* 1792.] pp. 44. 8vo.   AAS.

First printed in 1754. Preface dated, February 20, 1792.

24063 BAILEY, FRANCIS
BAILEY'S POCKET ALMANAC, FOR THE YEAR OF OUR LORD 1793; AND OF THE EM-
PIRE THE SEVENTEENTH. THE FIRST AFTER BISSEXTILE, OR LEAP-YEAR. [Six
lines of verse. U. S. arms.]
*Philadelphia: Printed and sold by Francis Bailey, at Yorick's Head, in
Market-Street.* [1792.] pp. (48). 48mo.   AAS.
Interleaved. Contains, An Act more effectually to provide for the
national defence, by establishing a uniform militia throughout the
United States.

24064 BALTIMORE. MARYLAND. CARPENTERS SOCIETY.
A PRICE-BOOK, IN ALPHABETICAL ORDER, OF SUNDRY CARPENTERS WORK, COLLECTED,
CALCULATED, AND NOW, BY THE AUTHORITY OF AN ANGRY BLOCK-CORNICE ARCHI-
TECT, DICTATED FOR THE CARPENTERS OF BALTIMORE TOWN; TOGETHER WITH
EXPLANATORY NOTES, &C. &C. AND A NUMBER OF ADDITIONAL PRICES, &C. &C. FOR
CURRIERS GRAIN-BOARDS, SALT-BOLES, BRUSH-HANDLES, WOOD-HORSES, THREE
LEGGED STOOLS, &C. &C. NEVER ATTEMPTED TO BE CALCULATED BY ANY PERSON
HERETOFORE.
*Baltimore: Printed by David Graham. Sold by John Dalrumple, John
Scrogs, Christian Baum, in behalf of themselves and the Carpenters Society.* 1792.

24065 BALTIMORE. MARYLAND. COMMERCIAL FIRE COMPANY.
ARTICLES, FOR THE GOVERNMENT OF THE COMMERCIAL FIRE-COMPANY OF BALTI-
MORE. JANUARY 1, 1792. [Colophon:]
Baltimore: Printed by W. Goddard and J. Angell. [1792.] Broadside.
fol.   MDHS.

24066 THE BALTIMORE COLLECTION OF CHURCH MUSIC.
Baltimore: Published by John Hagerty, Stationer, in Water-Street. 1792.
"Neatly engraved and printed on copper plates, well adapted for the use
of schools."

24067 THE BALTIMORE DAILY REPOSITORY. VOL. I. NO. 61. MONDAY, JANUARY 2,
[—No. 372. MONDAY, DECEMBER 31, 1792.]
*Baltimore: Printed by David Graham, at the New Printing-office, in Cal-
vert-Street, between Market-Street and the Court-House;* . . . 1792. 4to.   MDHS.

24068 —— NEW-YEAR VERSES, ADDRESSED TO THE PATRONS OF THE BALTIMORE DAILY
REPOSITORY, BY THEIR OBEDIENT SERVANTS, THE NEWS-CARRIERS. JANUARY 2,
1792. . . .
[Baltimore: Printed by David Graham, 1792.] Broadside. 4to.   LOC.

24069 THE BALTIMORE EVENING POST; A DAILY, POLITICAL AND COMMERCIAL PAPER.
OPEN TO ALL PARTIES, BUT INFLUENCED BY NONE. NO. 1. FRIDAY, JULY 13,
[—No. 144. MONDAY, DECEMBER 31, 1792.]
*Baltimore: Printed (daily) by Philip Edwards, in Market-Street, seven
doors west of Gay-Street.* 1792. fol.
Established by Philip Edwards. The first number was distributed gratis
as appears from a notice "To the public" in the Baltimore Daily Repository of July 9, 1792, in which Philip Edwards announces his intention to publish The Baltimore Evening Post, as soon as sufficient
number of subscribers are obtained. Beginning October 21st, 1793,
the title was altered to *Edwards's Baltimore Daily Advertiser*, and so
continued to January 1, 1795, when it was consolidated with the
Maryland Journal, as the *Maryland Journal and Baltimore Universal
Daily Advertiser*, printed by Philip Edwards & Co.

24070   BANK OF THE UNITED STATES.
A TABLE FOR RECEIVING AND PAYING GOLD AT THE BANK OF THE UNITED STATES,
SHEWING THE VALUE OF GOLD IN DOLLARS AND CENTS, FROM ONE TO A THOUSAND
PENNYWEIGHTS. ACCORDING TO THE ACT OF CONGRESS, ASCERTAINING THE
STANDARD AND VALUE OF GOLD.
Philadelphia: Printed by John Fenno, 1792.

24071   BANNEKER, BENJAMIN   1731 – 1806
BANNEKER'S ALMANACK, AND EPHEMERIS FOR THE YEAR OF OUR LORD, 1793; BE-
ING THE FIRST AFTER BISSEXTILE OR LEAP-YEAR: CONTAINING THE MOTIONS OF
THE SUN AND MOON; THE TRUE PLACES AND ASPECTS OF THE PLANETS; THE RIS-
ING AND SETTING OF THE SUN; RISING, SETTING, AND SOUTHING OF THE MOON; THE
LUNATIONS, CONJUNCTIONS, AND ECLIPSES; AND THE RISING, SETTING, AND SOUTH-
ING OF THE PLANETS AND NOTED FIXED STARS.
Philadelphia: Printed and sold by Joseph Crukshank, No. 87, *High-Street.*
[1792.] pp. [44.] 12mo.   AAS. LOC. NYPL.
Contains, A Plan of a Peace-office, for the United States.

24072   —— BENJAMIN BANNEKER'S PENNSYLVANIA, DELAWARE, MARYLAND, AND VIRGINIA
ALMANACK, FOR THE YEAR OF OUR LORD 1793. . . .
Baltimore: Printed and sold by William Goddard and James Angell.
[1792.]   JCB.

24073   —— COPY OF A LETTER FROM BENJAMIN BANNEKER, TO THE SECRETARY OF STATE,
WITH HIS ANSWER.
*Philadelphia: Printed and sold by Daniel Lawrence, No. 33, North Fourth-
Street, near Race.* M.DCC.XCII. pp. [12.] 4to.   NYPL.

24074   —— — COPY OF A LETTER FROM BENJAMIN BANNEKER, TO THE SECRETARY OF
STATE, WITH HIS ANSWER. TO WHICH IS ADDED, FOR THE INFORMATION OF THE
PUBLIC, AN ACCOUNT OF BENJAMIN BANNEKER [A FREE NEGRO.]
*Philadelphia: Printed by Joseph Crukshank. Sold by Daniel Lawrence,
No. 33, North Fourth street, and Joseph Crukshank, High street.* 1792. pp. 15.
4to.   AAS. HC. JCB. NYHS.

     $12

24075   BARLOW, JOEL   1754 – 1812
ADVICE TO THE PRIVILEGED ORDERS, IN THE SEVERAL STATES OF EUROPE, RESULT-
ING FROM THE NECESSITY AND PROPRIETY OF A GENERAL REVOLUTION IN THE
PRINCIPLE OF GOVERNMENT. BY JOEL BARLOW, ESQUIRE. PART I.
London—Printed: New-York—-Reprinted by Childs and Swaine. M.DCC.-
XCII. pp. (2), (2), [118.] 12mo.   BA. HC. JCB. LOC. NYHS. YC.
11th New York District Copyright, issued to Joel Barlow, as Author,
11 June, 1792.

24076   BARNES, JOSEPH
TREATISE ON THE JUSTICE, POLICY AND UTILITY OF ESTABLISHING AN EFFECTUAL
SYSTEM FOR PROMOTING THE PROGRESS OF USEFUL ARTS, BY ASSURING PROPERTY
IN THE PRODUCTS OF GENIUS. TO WHICH ARE ADDED, OBSERVATIONS ON THE DE-
FICIENCY OF, AND EXCEPTIONS TO THE BILL REPORTED IN MARCH, 1792. WITH
NOTES, TENDING TO DEMONSTRATE, THAT NO PROPERTY IS SECURED IN THE PROD-
UCTS OF GENIUS, UNDER THE EXISTING PATENT SYSTEM. ALSO, THE PRINCIPLES
UPON WHICH A BILL OUGHT TO BE FORMED, TO BE EFFECTUAL AND EQUITABLE.
BY JOSEPH BARNES.
Philadelphia: Printed by Francis Bailey. MDCCXCII. pp. 34. 12mo.
     BA. RIHS.

24077   BARTGIS'S Maryland Gazette, and Frederick-Town weekly advertiser. No.
1. Tuesday, May 22, [—No. 32. Tuesday, December 25, 1792.]
*Frederick-Town: Printed by Matthias Bartgis, at his English and German
Printing-office. 1792.* 4to   MDHS.
After an interval of two years from the suspension of his *Maryland
Chronicle*, in 1789, Matthias Bartgis established the above, giving notice in July that all persons owing him for their English and German
newspapers and advertisements from 1786 till the year 1790, should
make payment.

24078   BARTLETT, John   – 1844
A Discourse, on the subject of Animation. Delivered before the Humane
Society of the Commonwealth of Massachusetts, June 11, 1792. By John
Bartlett, A. M. Arteria animam accipit e pulmonibus. [Ornament.]
*Printed at Boston, by Isaiah Thomas and Ebenezer T. Andrews, Faust's
Statue, No. 45, Newbury Street.* MDCCXCII. pp. 40. 4to.
   AAS. BA. CLS. HC. JCB. LOC. MHS. NYHS, NYPL. SGO.
With an Appendix, containing, Act of incorporation of the Humane
Society of the Commonwealth of Massachusetts, and the Rules and Reg-
ulations of said Society since their incorporation; with the methods of
treatment in cases of apparent death, Communications, Catalogue of
members, &c. &c.

24079   BARTON, Benjamin Smith   1766 – 1815
An Account of the most effectual means of preventing the deleterious
consequences of the bite of the Crotalus Horridus, or Rattlesnake.
Philadelphia: Printed by R. Aitken & Son, 1792. pp. 19. 4to.   SGO.
Reprinted from the American Philosophical Society Transactions. Vol. 3.

24080   BAXTER, Richard   1615 – 1691
The Causes, evils, and cures, of heart and church divisions; extracted
from the works of Mr. Richard Baxter, and Mr. Jeremiah Burroughs.
[One line from] Ps. xxxiv. 14.
*Philadelphia: Printed by Parry Hall No. 149, Chesnut Street, and sold by
John Dickins No 182, in Race Street near Sixth Street.* MDCCXCII. pp. (136).
12mo.   AAS. NYPL.
Extracted, abridged, and edited, with recommendatory dedication, To
the Ministers and Members of the Methodist Episcopal Church. By
Francis Asbury.

24081   BEATTIE, James   1753 – 1803
Elements of moral science. By James Beattie, LL. D. professor of moral
philosophy and logic in Marischal College, Aberdeen. First volume.
*Philadelphia: From the Press of Mathew Carey, No. 118, Market-Street,
Jan. 28, M,DCC,XCII.* pp. 224, (3). 12mo.   AAS. JCB. LOC.
A second volume was published in 1794. Introduced as a text-book
into the University of Pennsylvania. A slip containing an Extract
from the Critical Review, Vol. 69, Page 628, commending the work,
is pasted in front of the title page.

24082   BEEMAN, Anna
Hymns on various subjects; By Anna Beeman. To which is added a number
of hymns from different authors. [Five lines from] Col. iii. 16.
[Norwich: Printed by John Trumbull. 1792.] pp. 110 + 12mo.   BU.

24083   BEERS, ANDREW   1749 – 1824
BEERS' ALMANACK AND EPHEMERIS OF THE MOTION OF THE SUN AND MOON; THE TRUE PLACES AND ASPECTS OF THE PLANETS; THE RISING AND SETTING OF THE SUN; THE RISING, SETTING AND SOUTHING OF THE MOON, FOR THE YEAR OF OUR LORD 1793: . . . . BY ANDREW BEERS, PHILOM.
> *Hartford: Printed by Hudson and Goodwin.* [1792.] pp. (36). 12mo.
AAS. CHS.

24084   —— GLORI GREENLEAF'S NEW-YORK, CONNECTICUT, & NEW-JERSEY ALMANACK, OR DIARY, WITH AN EPHEMERIS FOR THE YEAR OF OUR LORD 1793; BEING THE FIRST AFTER BISSEXTILE, OR LEAP-YEAR, THE SEVENTEENTH OF THE INDEPENDENCE OF THE U. STATES OF AMERICA, AND FROM CREATION 5742. CALCULATED FOR THE MERIDIAN, AND HORIZON OF NEW-YORK, BUT WILL SERVE WITHOUT ESSENTIAL VARIATION, FOR CONNECTICUT AND NEW-JERSEY. CONTAINING USUAL ASTRONOMICAL CALCULATIONS, AND A GREATER VARIETY OF OTHER MATTER THAN IS COMMON IN AN ALMANACK—ALL OF WHICH IS INSTRUCTIVE—ENTERTAINING —AND CURIOUS.
> *Printed at New-York—by Thomas Greenleaf,* M,DCC,XCIII [1792.] A Mundi. pp. (32). 12mo.
AAS. LOC.

24085   BELKNAP, JEREMY   1744 – 1798
A DISCOURSE, INTENDED TO COMMEMORATE THE DISCOVERY OF AMERICA BY CHRISTOPHER COLUMBUS; DELIVERED AT THE REQUEST OF THE HISTORICAL SOCIETY IN MASSACHUSETTS, ON THE 23D DAY OF OCTOBER, 1792, BEING THE COMPLETION OF THE THIRD CENTURY SINCE THAT MEMORABLE EVENT. TO WHICH ARE ADDED, FOUR DISSERTATIONS, CONNECTED WITH VARIOUS PARTS OF THE DISCOURSE, VIZ. 1. ON THE CIRCUMNAVIGATION OF AFRICA BY THE ANCIENTS. 2. AN EXAMINATION OF THE PRETENTIONS OF MARTIN BEHAIM TO A DISCOVERY OF AMERICA PRIOR TO THAT OF COLUMBUS, WITH A CHRONOLOGICAL DETAIL OF ALL THE DISCOVERIES MADE IN THE 15TH CENTURY. 3. ON THE QUESTION, WHETHER THE HONEY-BEE IS A NATIVE OF AMERICA? 4. ON THE COLOUR OF THE NATIVE AMERICANS AND THE RECENT POPULATION OF THIS CONTINENT. BY JEREMY BELKNAP, D. D. [Six lines of Latin from] SENECA'S MEDEA, WRITTEN IN THE REIGN OF NERO.
> *Printed at the Apollo Press, in Boston, by Belknap and Hall, State Street,* MDCCXCII. pp. 132, (2). 8vo.   AAS. BA. BM. HC. JCB. LOC. MHS. NYHS. NYPL.
39th Massachusetts District Copyright, issued to Jeremy Belknap, as Author, 23 October, 1792.

24086   —— THE FORESTERS, AN AMERICAN TALE: BEING A SEQUEL TO THE HISTORY OF JOHN BULL THE CLOTHIER. IN A SERIES OF LETTERS TO A FRIEND. [Publishers monogram.]
> *Printed at Boston, by I. Thomas and E. T. Andrews, Proprietors of the work, Faust's Statue, No. 45, Newbury Street.* MDCCXCII. pp. 216, frontispiece. 12mo.
AAS. BM. LOC. NYPL.
23d Massachusetts District Copyright, issued to Thomas & Andrews, as Proprietors, 11 February, 1792.

24087   —— THE HISTORY OF NEW-HAMPSHIRE. VOLUME I. COMPREHENDING THE EVENTS OF ONE COMPLETE CENTURY FROM THE DISCOVERY OF THE RIVER PASCATAQUA. BY JEREMY BELKNAP, A. M. MEMBER OF THE AMERICAN PHILOSOPHICAL SOCIETY HELD AT PHILADELPHIA FOR PROMOTING USEFUL KNOWLEDGE. [Four lines of Latin from] OVID.
> *Boston: Re-printed for the Author,* M.DCC.XCII. [*Published according to Act of Congress.*] pp. viii, 362, ciii. 8vo.
HC. JCB. LOC. MHS.
The Preface, dated, Dover, June 1, 1784; the body of the work, pp. 1—362; and Appendix, pp. i—xxxviii, are unchanged from the original issue. The introductory pages viii, and Appendix pages xxxix—ciii, are the only additions made to this second issue.

BELKNAP, JEREMY, continued.

24088 —— — THE HISTORY OF NEW-HAMPSHIRE, VOLUME III. CONTAINING A GEO-
GRAPHICAL DESCRIPTION OF THE STATE; WITH SKETCHES OF ITS NATURAL HISTORY,
PRODUCTIONS, IMPROVEMENTS, AND PRESENT STATE OF SOCIETY AND MANNERS,
LAWS AND GOVERNMENT. BY JEREMY BELKNAP, A. M. MEMBER OF THE PHILO-
SOPHICAL SOCIETY IN PHILADELPHIA, AND OF THE ACADEMY OF ARTS AND SCIENCES
IN MASSACHUSETTS.

> *Printed at Boston, for the Author, By Belknap and Young, State Street.*
MDCCXCII. pp. 480, 7, (1). 8vo. AAS. BA. BM. HC. JCB. LOC. MHS. NYHS. NYPL.

> Contains, A Catalogue of subscribers to this work. The first volume
was printed at Philadelphia in 1784, and reprinted at Boston in this
year, as above. The second volume was printed at Boston, in 1791.

24089 —— JESUS CHRIST THE ONLY FOUNDATION. A SERMON ON I. CORINTHIANS, III.
II. BY JEREMY BELKNAP, A. M. MINISTER OF THE CHURCH IN FEDERAL-STREET,
BOSTON. THE SECOND EDITION. [Ornament.]

> *Boston: Printed by Samuel Hall, in Cornhill.* MDCCXCII. pp. 31. 8vo.
> AAS. BA. BM. JCB. LOC. MHS. NYPL.

> "First printed in 1779. And now reprinted for distribution among the
Indians, by the Missionaries of the Society for propagating the Gospel
among the Indians, by their request."

24090 BELL, BENJAMIN 1752 – 1836
THE FOLLY OF SINNERS, IN EXCUSING THEMSELVES FROM BLAME, WHILE CONTINUING
IN AN IMPENITENT STATE, ILLUSTRATED; IN A DISCOURSE, ON GENESIS III,
12, 13. DELIVERED AT CORNISH, (NEW-HAMPSHIRE) 1792. BY BENJAMIN
BELL, A. M. PASTOR OF A CHURCH OF CHRIST IN WINDSOR AND CORNISH.
[Four lines of Scripture texts.]

> *Windsor, (Vermont) Printed by Alden Spooner.* [1792.] pp. 51. 8vo.
> AAS. BPL. LOC. YC.

24091 BEND, JOSEPH GROVE JOHN 1762 – 1812
A DISCOURSE, DELIVERED IN ST. PAUL'S CHURCH, BALTIMORE, ON SUNDAY, JAN.
15TH, 1792; BEING THE FIRST SUNDAY AFTER THE DEATH OF MISS MARY IRE-
LAND, DAUGHTER OF MR. EDWARD IRELAND, OF BALTIMORE. BY JOSEPH BEND,
A. M. RECTOR OF SAID CHURCH.

> *Baltimore: Printed and sold by David Graham,* 1792.

24092 BENHAM, ASAHEL
FEDERAL HARMONY; CONTAINING, IN A FAMILIAR MANNER, THE RUDIMENTS OF
PSALMODY; WITH A COLLECTION OF CHURCH MUSIC. . . . SECOND EDITION.

> *New-Haven: Printed and sold by A. Morse.* 1792. pp. 58. obl. 8vo.

24093 BENNET, JOHN
LETTERS TO A YOUNG LADY, ON A VARIETY OF USEFUL AND INTERESTING SUBJECTS:
CALCULATED TO IMPROVE THE HEART, FORM THE MANNERS, AND ENLIGHTEN THE
UNDERSTANDING. "THAT OUR DAUGHTERS MAY BE POLISHED CORNERS OF THE
TEMPLE." BY THE REV. JOHN BENNET, AUTHOR OF STRICTURES ON FEMALE ED-
UCATION. IN TWO VOLUMES. VOL. I. [—II.]

> *Newburyport: Printed and sold by John Mycall.* [1792.] pp. 145; 168,
(12). 12mo. AAS.

> Contains a twelve-page list of "Names of the subscribers for re-printing
this valuable work."

24094

BENNET, JOHN, continued.

—— STRICTURES ON FEMALE EDUCATION; CHIEFLY AS IT RELATES TO THE CULTURE OF THE HEART, IN FOUR ESSAYS. BY A CLERGYMAN OF THE CHURCH OF ENGLAND. . . .

Norwich, Printed by E. Bushnell. [1792.] pp. v, (1), 133. 16mo.   LOC.

24095

BERQUIN, ARNAUD   1750 – 1791

THE LOOKING-GLASS FOR THE MIND; OR, INTELLECTUAL MIRROR: BEING AN ELEGANT COLLECTION OF THE MOST DELIGHTFUL LITTLE STORIES AND INTERESTING TALES, CHIEFLY TRANSLATED FROM THAT MUCH ADMIRED WORK L'AMI DES ENFANS. [By Samuel Cooper.]

Boston: 1792.

With seventy-four illustrations by Thomas Bewick.

24096

BIBLIA.

THE HOLY BIBLE, CONTAINING THE OLD AND NEW TESTAMENTS: NEWLY TRANSLATED OUT OF THE ORIGINAL TONGUES, AND WITH THE FORMER TRANSLATIONS DILIGENTLY COMPARED AND REVISED. [Six lines of Scripture texts.]

New-York: Printed by T. Allen, Bookseller & Stationer, No. 186, Pearl Street. 1792. unpaged. 20 plates. 4to.   NYPL.

Second title: THE NEW TESTAMENT OF OUR LORD AND SAVIOUR JESUS CHRIST, NEWLY TRANSLATED OUT OF THE ORIGINAL GREEK; AND WITH THE FORMER TRANSLATIONS DILIGENTLY COMPARED AND REVISED.

New-York: Printed by T. Allen, Bookseller & Stationer, No. 186, Pearl-Street. 1792. unpaged.

With the Apocrypha. An Index to the Holy Bible. A Table of Scripture measures, weights, and coins. And, An Alphabetical table of proper names, &c.

24097

—— THE HOLY BIBLE, CONTAINING THE OLD AND NEW TESTAMENTS: NEWLY TRANSLATED OUT OF THE ORIGINAL TONGUES, AND WITH THE FORMER TRANSLATIONS DILIGENTLY COMPARED AND REVISED. [Six lines of Scripture texts.]

New-York: Printed by Hodge and Campbell, and sold at their respective Book-Stores. M.DCC.XCII. unpaged. 4to.   AAS. NYPL.

Second title: THE NEW TESTAMENT OF OUR LORD AND SAVIOUR JESUS CHRIST, NEWLY TRANSLATED OUT OF THE ORIGINAL GREEK; AND WITH THE FORMER TRANSLATIONS DILIGENTLY COMPARED AND REVISED.

New-York: Printed by Hodge and Campbell, and sold at their respective Book-Stores. M.DCC.XCII. unpaged.

Third heading: THE PSALMS OF DAVID IN METRE. pp. 49.

These two editions, issued after the dissolution of the former firm of Hodge, Allen and Campbell, are the same in format: both are printed with large type upon a good quality of paper. Differences are found in some copies having the Aprocypha, and in others this is omitted. Some have The Psalms of David in metre, added, while in others it is omitted. Copies are found with and without plates. In common, however, all copies have: An Index to the Holy Bible. Tables of Scripture measures, weights, and coins. And, An Alphabetical table of proper names, &c.

BIBLIA, continued.

24098 —— The Holy Bible, containing the Old and New Testaments: translated out of the original tongues; and with the former translations diligently compared and revised. [Publisher's monogram.]
    New-York: Printed and sold by Hugh Gaine, at his Book-Store and Printing-Office, at the Bible, in Hanover-Square. M,DCC,XCII. A-Ll in twelves. 12mo.
                                       AAS. NYPL.   **$10**

Second title: The New Testament of our Lord and Saviour Jesus Christ, newly translated out of the original Greek; and with the former translations diligently compared and revised. [Publisher's monogram.]
    New-York: Printed and sold by Hugh Gaine, at his Book-Store and Printing-Office, at the Bible, in Hanover-Square, M,DCC,XCII. sig. A-O in twelves.

The Ruby types for this edition is said to have been set up in Scotland, and imported, in page-form, ready for printing. The New Testament was also published separately. In 1803, the plates were sold to Mathew Carey of Philadelphia.

24099 —— The Self-interpreting Bible: containing the sacred text of the Old and New Testaments. Translated from the original tongues, and with the former translations diligently compared and revised. To which are annexed, marginal references and illustrations, an exact summary of the several books, a paraphrase on the most obscure or important parts, an analysis of the contents of each chapter, explanatory notes, and evangelical reflections. By the late reverend John Brown, minister of the Gospel at Haddington. [Five lines of Scripture texts.]
    New-York: Printed by Hodge and Campbell, and sold at their respective Book Stores. M.DCC.XCII. unpaged. 19 plates. fol.   AAS. NYPL.   **$15**

Second title: The New Testament of our Lord and Saviour Jesus Christ: to which are annexed, marginal references and illustrations, an exact summary of the several books, a paraphrase on the most obscure or important parts, an analysis of the contents of each chapter, explanatory notes and evangelical reflections. By the late reverend John Brown, minister of the Gospel at Haddington. [Three lines from] Col. II. 17.
    New-York: Printed by Hodge and Campbell, and sold at their respective Book Stores. M.DCC.XCII. unpaged.

The printing of this edition was begun in 1790: Parts xxxv to the end being printed this year. The Apocrypha is printed in smaller type. The completed work also contains: An Alphabetical table of proper names, pp. (4); and a List of the names of over thirteen hundred subscribers, headed by George Washington, President of the United States, which is of unusual interest from their wide geographical distribution, pp. (8). Some copies appear to have the imprint: Printed for T. Allen, and sold at his Bookstore.

24100 —— The Bible, in miniature. Adorned with cuts.
    Philadelphia: 1792.
    25 November, 1792. "Just published and for sale at No. 79, North-Third-Street, Philadelphia."

24101 —— The Pocket Bible. With Psalms.
    New-York: 1792.
    4 September, 1792. "Now in press, ready in September and October next, the first American edition of the Pocket Bible, with Psalms."

24102   BIBLIA. OLD TESTAMENT. PSALMS.

PSALMS, CAREFULLY SUITED TO THE CHRISTIAN WORSHIP IN THE UNITED STATES OF AMERICA: BEING AN IMPROVEMENT ON THE OLD VERSIONS OF THE PSALMS OF DAVID ALLOWED BY THE REVEREND SYNOD OF NEW-YORK AND PHILADELPHIA, TO BE USED IN CHURCHES AND PRIVATE FAMILIES. ALL THINGS WRITTEN IN THE LAW OF MOSES, AND THE PROPHETS, AND THE PSALMS CONCERNING ME, MUST BE FULFILLED.

New-York: Printed by Hodge & Campbell, and sold at their respective Book-Stores. M,DCC,XCII. pp. (2), (2), 318. 16mo.   BU. NYHS. NYPL.

24103   —— — PSALMS, CAREFULLY SUITED TO THE CHRISTIAN WORSHIP IN THE UNITED STATES OF AMERICA. BEING AN IMPROVEMENT OF THE OLD VERSIONS OF THE PSALMS OF DAVID. ALLOWED BY THE REVEREND SYNOD OF NEW-YORK AND PHILADELPHIA, TO BE USED IN CHURCHES AND PRIVATE FAMILIES. [Three lines of Scripture texts.]

New-York: Printed for Berry and Rogers, and John Reid. M.DCC.XCII. pp. 312, (1), (11). 12mo.   BU. NYHS. NYPL.

24104   —— — PSALMS, CAREFULLY SUITED TO THE CHRISTIAN WORSHIP IN THE UNITED STATES OF AMERICA. BEING AN IMPROVEMENT OF THE OLD VERSIONS OF THE PSALMS OF DAVID. ALLOWED, BY THE REVEREND SYNOD OF NEW YORK AND PHILADELPHIA, TO BE USED IN CHURCHES AND PRIVATE FAMILIES.

Philadelphia: Printed by Francis Bailey, No. 116, *High-Street.* M,DCC,-XCII. pp. 285. 24mo.   BU. PHS.

24105   —— THE PSALMS OF DAVID, IMITATED IN THE LANGUAGE OF THE NEW TESTAMENT, AND APPLIED TO THE CHRISTIAN STATE AND WORSHIP. BY ISAAC WATTS, D. D. [Six lines of Scripture texts.]

Boston: From the Press of J. Bumstead. For John Boyle, and David West, Marlborough-Street. M.DCC.XCII. pp. 582. 12mo.   JCB. NYPL.

Second title: HYMNS AND SPIRITUAL SONGS. IN THREE BOOKS. I. COLLECTED FROM THE SCRIPTURES. II. COMPOSED ON DIVINE SUBJECTS. III. PREPARED FOR THE LORD'S SUPPER. BY ISAAC WATTS, D. D. [Five lines of quotations.]

Boston: From the Press of J. Bumstead. For John Boyle, and David West, Marlborough-Street. M.DCC.XCII. pp. (2), (311)–582.

24106   —— THE PSALMS OF DAVID, IMITATED IN THE LANGUAGE OF THE NEW TESTAMENT, AND APPLIED TO THE CHRISTIAN STATE AND WORSHIP. BY ISAAC WATTS, D. D. CORRECTED AND ACCOMODATED TO THE USE OF THE CHURCH OF CHRIST IN AMERICA. [Six lines of Scripture texts.]

Newburyport: Printed and sold by John Mycall. Sold also by Thomas and Andrews, and E. Larkin, in Boston. [1792.] pp. 288; 246, (9), (9). 12mo.   AAS. NYPL.

Mycall's revision of 1781. Printed on thick paper.

Second title: HYMNS AND SPIRITUAL SONGS, IN THREE BOOKS: I. COLLECTED FROM THE SCRIPTURES. II. COMPOSED ON DIVINE SUBJECTS. III. PREPARED FOR THE LORD'S SUPPER. BY ISAAC WATTS, D. D. CORRECTED, AND ACCOMODATED TO THE USE OF THE CHURCH OF CHRIST IN AMERICA. [Six lines of quotations.]

Newburyport: Printed and sold by John Mycall. Sold also by Thomas and Co. E. Larkin, and D. West, in Boston. [1792.] pp. 246, (9), (9).

24107   BIBLIA. PSALMS, continued.
—— THE PSALMS OF DAVID, WITH HYMNS AND SPIRITUAL SONGS. ALSO, THE CATE-
CHISM, CONFESSION OF FAITH AND LITURGY OF THE REFORMED CHURCH IN THE
NETHERLANDS. FOR THE USE OF THE REFORMED DUTCH CHURCH IN NORTH
AMERICA.
    New-York: Printed by Hodge and Campbell, and sold at their respective
Book-Stores. M.DCC.XCII. [*With privilege of Copy Right according to law.*]
pp. (2), (2), (12), 498, (4). 12mo.   LOC.
    8th New York District Copyright, issued to The Minister, Elders and
Deacons of the Reformed Protestant Dutch Church in the City of New-
York, as Proprietors, 30 December, 1791.

24108   —— A SELECTION OF PSALMS, WITH OCCASIONAL HYMNS.
    Charleston: 1792.
    For the use of the Protestant Episcopal Church. Attested as a true
copy. Charleston, Nov. 10, 1792. Reprinted with the Book of common prayer, in Charleston, 1799.

24109   BIBLIA. NEW TESTAMENT.
THE NEW TESTAMENT OF OUR LORD AND SAVIOUR JESUS CHRIST, NEWLY TRANS-
LATED OUT OF THE ORIGINAL GREEK, AND WITH THE FORMER TRANSLATIONS
DILIGENTLY COMPARED AND REVISED.
    Philadelphia: Printed by Benjamin Johnson, M,DCC,XCII. pp, (276).
12mo.   AAS.
    Paragraphs 4, and 5, Chapter IX, of Matthew, are misplaced.

24110   —— THE NEW TESTAMENT OF OUR LORD AND SAVIOUR JESUS CHRIST, TRANSLATED
OUT OF THE ORIGINAL GREEK; AND WITH THE FORMER TRANSLATIONS DILIGENTLY
COMPARED AND REVISED.
    Philadelphia: Printed by W. Young, No. 52, Second, the corner of Chesnut-
Street. M,DCC,XCII. pp. (360). 12mo.   NYPL.
    Unpaged. With successive signatures to the Publisher's edition of the
Old Testament, printed in 1791, and bound with it.

24111   BICKERSTAFFE, ISAAC   1735 – 1787
THE ROMP. A MUSICAL ENTERTAINMENT, IN TWO ACTS. ALTERED FROM LOVE IN
THE CITY, BY MR. BICKERSTAFF. AS NOW PERFORMED WITH GREAT APPLAUSE BY
THE OLD AMERICAN COMPANY AT THE THEATRE IN SOUTHWARK. A NEW EDITION.
    Philadelphia: From the Press of Mathew Carey, Oct. 31, 1792. pp. 33.
12mo.   HSP. LCP.

24112   BINGHAM, CALEB   1757 – 1819
THE CHILD'S COMPANION; BEING A CONCISE SPELLING-BOOK; CONTAINING A SE-
LECTION OF WORDS IN MODERN USE, PROPERLY ARRANGED, AND DIVIDED IN SUCH A
MANNER AS WILL MOST NATURALLY LEAD THE LEARNER TO A RIGHT PRONUNCIA-
TION. TOGETHER WITH A VARIETY OF LESSONS FOR READING, &c. DESIGNED
FOR THE USE OF SCHOOLS. BY CALEB BINGHAM, A. M. AUTHOR OF THE YOUNG
LADY'S ACCIDENCE. "SIMPLICITY IS ALL THE AUTHOR'S AIM." PUBLISHED AC-
CORDING TO ACT OF CONGRESS.
    Boston: Printed by Samuel Hall, No. 53, Cornhill. 1792.
    22d Massachusetts District Copyright, issued to Caleb Bingham, as
Author, 24 January, 1792.

BINGHAM, Caleb, continued.

24113 —— — The Child's companion; being a concise spelling-book, containing a selection of words in modern use, properly arranged, and divided in such a manner as will most naturally lead the learner to a -right pronunciation. Together with a variety of lessons for reading, &c. Designed for the use of schools. By Caleb Bingham, a. m. author of the Young lady's accidence. The second edition.

Boston: Printed by Samuel Hall, No. 53, Cornhill. 1792.

This edition followed the first in a few weeks after its publication.

24114 —— The Young lady's accidence; or, a short and easy introduction to English grammar. Designed, principally, for the use of young learners, more especially those of the fair sex, though proper for either. By Caleb Bingham, a. m. [Two lines of verse.] The sixth edition, corrected. [Published according to Act of Congress.]

Printed at Boston, by I. Thomas and E. T. Andrews, at Faust's Statue, No. 45, Newbury Street. MDCCXCII. pp. 57. 24mo.   AAS. BM.

An edition of four thousand copies was printed.

24115 BIRD, Jonathan   1747 – 1813
The Parable of the unclean spirit opened and applied, in two discourses, on Math. xii. 43-45. By Jonathan Bird, a. m. New-Durham.

Catskill-Landing: Printed by M. Croswell & Co. 1792. 8vo.   BM.

24116 BLACK, John   1750 – 1802
An Examination of the reverend John Anderson's Discourse on the divine ordinance of singing psalms; wherein the inconclusive reasoning, and many inconsistencies of that writer are detected, and the truth vindicated, agreeably to the principles exhibited in a sermon on the subject of psalmody, published by the author hereof, in the year 1790.

York, Pennsylvania: Printed by John Edie. 1792. pp. 115. 12mo.
       PHS. PU.

24117 BLAIR, —
The Life of faith exemplified and recommended:—[In a letter found in the study of the Rev. mr. Blair, late of Doningham, Newingham.—Being an answer to this question.—How to live in this world, so as to live in Heaven.

Wilmington: Printed and sold by James Adams. 1792.

24118 BLAIR, Hugh   1718 – 1800
Sermons, by Hugh Blair, d. d. f. r. s. Ed. One of the ministers of the high church, and professor of rhetoric and belles lettres in the University of Edinburgh. In two volumes. Volume i. [—ii.] [Printers monogram.]

Printed at Boston, by I. Thomas, and E. T. Andrews, for the Proprietor of the Boston Bookstore. MDCCXCII. 2vols. pp. 395; 396. 8vo.   AAS. JCB. LOC.

24119 —— — Sermons, by Hugh Blair, d. d. One of the ministers of the high church, and professor of rhetoric and belles lettres in the University of Edinburgh. In two volumes. The second American edition, from the seventeenth London edition. Volume i. [—ii.]

*New-York: Printed by T. Allen, Bookseller and Stationer, No. 12, Queen-Street.—1792.—*pp. 363, (4); 368, (5). 12mo.   AAS. NYPL.

BLAIR, Hugh, continued.

24120 —— — Sermons, by Hugh Blair, D. D. One of the ministers of the high church, and professor of rhetoric and belles lettres in the University of Edinburgh. To which is prefixed, that admired tract on the Internal evidence of the Christian religion. By Soame Jenyns, of the British Parliament. Volume the first. The sixteenth edition.
London, Printed :—Baltimore: Re-printed, for the Rev. M. L. Weems, by Samuel and John Adams, Book-Printers, in Market-street, between South and Gay-streets. MDCCXCII. pp. 285. 8vo. AAS. BA.
A second volume was printed in Baltimore, in 1793.

24121 —— The Beauties of Blair, being a collection of select sentences from the classical works of that celebrated author.
Philadelphia: From the Press of Mathew Carey, No. 118, *Market-Street,* 1792,

24122 —— — The Beauties of Blair, being a collection of select sentences from the classical works of that celebrated author.
Philadelphia: Printed by Francis Bailey and Thomas Lang. 1792. 18mo.

24123 BLAKE, Joseph, junior 1768 – 1802
An Oration, pronounced July 4th, 1792, at the request of the inhabitants of the town of Boston, in commemoration of the anniversary of American independence. By Joseph Blake, jun. [One line of Latin.]
Printed by Benjamin Russell, in Boston, Massachusetts. MDCCXCII. pp. 16. 4to. AAS. BA. BM. HC. JCB. MHS. NYPL.

24124 BLODGET, William
A New and correct Map of the State of Connecticut one of the United States of North America from actual survey—Humbly dedicated to his excellency Samuel Huntington esquire governor and commander in chief of said State. Joel Allen script. et sculpt.
Printed in Middletown for the Publisher March 1792. 28 x 36.
Joel Allen printed 301 copies of this Map, for William Blodget, March—July, 1792. Another impression, undated, and with slight changes in the title, is dedicated to the Governor, by William Blodget, as follows:

24125 —— — A New and correct Map of the State of Connecticut one of the United States of North America from actual survey—Humbly dedicated by permission to his excellency Samuel Huntington esquire governor and commander in chief of said State. By his most humble servant William Blodget.
[*Norwich? Printed for the Publisher.* 1792.] 27¼ x 35.
Advertised for sale by Thomas Hubbard, in Norwich, September, 1795. Proposals for printing the above, by subscription, were made in the Connecticut Gazette of 5 February, 1790.

24126 BLOOD, Caleb 1754 – 1814
A Sermon preached before the honorable Legislature of the State of Vermont; convened at Rutland, October 11th, 1792. Being the day of general election. Printed by order of the General Assembly. By Caleb Blood, pastor of a Baptist church in Shaftsbury.
Printed at Rutland by Anthony Haswell. [1792.] pp. 38. 8vo. JCB.

24127   THE BOOK OF NATURE; OR, THE TRUE SENSE OF THINGS. EXPLAINED AND MADE EASY TO THE CAPACITIES OF CHILDREN.
> *Philadelphia: Printed by Daniel Lawrence, and sold by the Booksellers* 1792.

24128   BOOTH, ABRAHAM   1734 – 1806
COMMERCE IN THE HUMAN SPECIES, AND THE ENSLAVING OF INNOCENT PERSONS, INIMICAL TO THE LAWS OF MOSES, AND THE GOSPEL OF CHRIST. A SERMON, PREACHED IN LITTLE PRESCOT STREET, GOODMAN'S FIELDS, LONDON, JAN. 29, 1792. BY ABRAHAM BOOTH, A. M. PASTOR OF A BAPTIST CHURCH. [Eight lines of quotations.]
> *London, Printed, Philadelphia: Re-printed and sold by Daniel Lawrence, No. 33, North 4th street, near Race-street.* M.DCC.XCII. pp. (40). 8vo.

                                             AAS. LOC. RIHS.

24129   BORDLEY, JOHN BEALE   1727 – 1804
SKETCHES ON ROTATION OF CROPS.
> *Philadelphia: Printed by Charles Cist.* M,DCC,XCII. pp. (2), 47. 8vo. BA.

24130   BOSTON, THOMAS   1676 – 1732
THE CROOK IN THE LOT: OR, THE SOVEREIGNTY AND WISDOM OF GOD, IN THE AFFLICTIONS OF MEN, DISPLAYED; TOGETHER WITH A CHRISTIAN DEPORTMENT UNDER THEM. BEING THE SUBSTANCE OF SEVERAL SERMONS ON ECCL. VII. 13. PROV. XVI. 19, AND I PET. V. 6. BY THE REVEREND AND LEARNED MR. THOMAS BOSTON, LATE MINISTER OF THE GOSPEL AT ETTRICK. [Two lines from] PSAL. XXIV. 19.
> *Philadelphia: Printed by R. Aitken & Son, No. 22, Market Street.* M.DCC.XCII. pp. 168. 12mo.

                                             AAS.

24131   BOSTON. MASSACHUSETTS.
REPORT CONCERNING THE TOWN GOVERNMENT. BOSTON, JANUARY 13, 1792.
> *[Boston:* 1792.] Broadside.   MHS.

24132   —— REPORT OF THE COMMITTEE RELATIVE TO CARRYING THE BY-LAWS OF THE TOWN INTO EXECUTION, AT A TOWN MEETING IN FANEUIL HALL, MARCH 27, 1792.
> *[Boston:* 1792.] pp. (3).   MHS.

24133   BOSTON. MASSACHUSETTS. MARINE SOCIETY.
CONSTITUTION AND LAWS OF THE BOSTON MARINE SOCIETY, INSTITUTED IN 1742.
> *Boston:* 1792. 12mo.

24134   BOSTON, FEBRUARY 22, 1792. INCORPORATION. AN ANTIQUARIAN, CITIZEN OF BOSTON, IN HIS RESEARCHES LATELY, FOUND THE FOLLOWING ORIGINAL PAPER, WHEREBY IT APPEARS THAT SEVENTY YEARS AGO THE SUBJECT OF INCORPORATION WAS AGITATED BY THE INHABITANTS OF THIS TOWN, . . .
> *[Boston:* 1792.] Broadside. fol.

                                             MHS.

24135   (CIRCULAR.) BOSTON, (MASSACHUSETTS) FEB. 28, 1792. SIR, WE HAVE HAD THE HONOUR TO BE APPOINTED A COMMITTEE, BY THE OFFICERS OF THE MASSACHUSETTS LINE OF THE LATE ARMY, TO ATTEND TO AND PROSECUTE THEIR MEMORIAL TO THE CONGRESS OF THE UNITED STATES, ON THE SUBJECT OF COMPENSATION FOR THE LOSSES SUSTAINED BY THEM AND THE SOLDIERS WHO SERVED DURING THE WAR, IN CONSEQUENCE OF THE SINGULAR MANNER IN WHICH THEIR SERVICES HAVE BEEN ACKNOWLEDGED AND REQUITED BY THE UNITED STATES. [Commending General William Hull, chosen as their agent to represent them before the Congress at Philadelphia.]
> *[Boston:* 1792.] Broadside. fol.   NYHS.

Signed in manuscript by W. Heath, J. Brooks, H. Jackson, W. Eustis, Thos. Edwards, Jos. Crocker. And addressed to John Lamb, esqr. New York.

BOSTON, continued.

24136 —— CIRCULAR LETTER. FROM A COMMITTEE APPOINTED BY THE OFFICERS OF THE MASSACHUSETTS LINE OF THE LATE FEDERAL ARMY, TO THE OFFICERS OF THE DIFFERENT STATES. [Notifying them that they had selected General William Hull to be their agent before Congress, and recommending him to their attention and assistance.] [PETITION OF THE MASSACHUSETTS OFFICERS TO CONGRESS.] . . . B. LINCOLN. MEMORIAL, &c. [of the officers, now residing in the State of New-York, of the late American army, to Congress. Signed,] EBENEZER STEVENS.

[New-York: 1792.] pp. (3). fol. 　　　　　　　　　　　　　LOC.

24137 THE BOSTON [cut] GAZETTE, AND THE COUNTRY JOURNAL, CONTAINING THE LATEST OCCURRENCES, FOREIGN AND DOMESTIC. [Motto.] No. 1944. MONDAY, JANUARY 2, [—No. 1996. MONDAY, DECEMBER 31, 1792.]
　　Printed by Benjamin Edes and Son, No. 7, State-Street, Boston. 1792. fol.
　　　　　　　　　　　　　　　　　　　AAS. LOC. MHS. NYPL.

In April, the Printing-office was removed "to the House next to Col. Colman's, in Kilby-Street." In May, a smaller cut, of the same design, was used, and the descriptive line dropped, reducing the heading correspondingly.

24138 BOURKE, MICHAEL
A REVIEW OF THE SUBJECT OF CANINE MADNESS. BY MICHAEL BOURKE, M. D. [Ornament.]
　　Philadelphia: From the Press of Mathew Carey. May 22,—M.DCC.XCII.
pp. (13). 8vo. 　　　　　　　　　　　　　　　BA. LOC.
The Dedication, to Doctor Benjamin Rush, is dated, Norfolk, Virginia, Feb. 10th, 1792.

24139 BOWDEN, JOHN 　　　　　　　　　　　　　1751 – 1817
AN ADDRESS FROM JOHN BOWDEN, A. M. TO THE MEMBERS OF THE EPISCOPAL CHURCH IN STRATFORD. TO WHICH IS ADDED, A LETTER TO THE REV'D MR. JAMES SAYRE. [Nineteen lines.]
　　New-Haven: Printed by T. and S. Green. [1792.] pp. (39). 8vo.
　　　　　　　　　　　　　　　　　BA. JCB. LOC. NYHS.

24140 BOWDOINHAM. MAINE. BAPTIST ASSOCIATION.
MINUTES OF THE BOWDOINHAM ASSOCIATION; HELD AT BOWDOIN, OCTOBER 3D & 4TH, M,DCC,XCII.
　　Boston, Printed by Edes & Son, M,DCC,XCII. pp. [13.] 8vo. 　　AAS.
With The Circular Letter, by Samuel Flagg.

24141 BOWEN'S VIRGINIA CENTINEL & GAZETTE: OR, THE WINCHESTER POLITICAL REPOSITORY. PATRIA CARA, CARIOR LIBERTAS. VOL. IV. No. 197. SATURDAY, JANUARY 7, [—VOL. V. No. 248. MONDAY, DECEMBER 31, 1792.]
　　Winchester: Printed by Richard Bowen. 1792. fol. 　　　　LOC.
In March, Monday was made the day of publication.

24142 BRACKENRIDGE, HUGH HENRY, formerly HUGH MONTGOMERY 　1748 – 1816
MODERN CHIVALRY: CONTAINING THE ADVENTURES OF CAPTAIN JOHN FARRAGO, AND TEAGUE O'REGAN, HIS SERVANT. VOLUME I. BY H. H. BRACKENRIDGE. [One line of Latin from] JUVENAL.
　　Philadelphia: Printed and sold by John M'Culloch, No. 1. North Third-Street. M.DCC.XCII. *[Entered according to Act of Congress.]* pp. 156. 12mo.
　　　　　　　　　　　　　　　　AAS. JCB. LCP. MHS. NYPL.

BRACKENRIDGE, HUGH HENRY, continued.

24143   —— — MODERN CHIVALRY; CONTAINING THE ADVENTURES OF CAPTAIN JOHN FARRAGO, AND TEAGUE O'REGAN, HIS SERVANT. VOLUME II. BY H. H. BRACKENRIDGE. [One line of Latin from] JUVENAL.

Philadelphia: Printed and sold by John M'Culloch, No. 1. North Third-Street. MDCCXII. [*sic* 1792.] *[Entered according to Act of Congress.]* pp. 156. 12mo.   JCB. LCP. NYPL.

30th Pennsylvania District Copyright, issued to H. H. Brackenridge, as Author, 14 February 1792. The third volume was printed at Pittsburgh, in 1793; and the fourth, and concluding volume, at Philadelphia, in 1797. After the fourth volume was printed the Author entirely re-wrote the work. The New York Public Library posseses the Author's interleaved copy of volumes one, and two, containing his additions, erasures, and corrections made, evidently, with a view to publishing a revised edition—the error in date of publication evaded his scrutiny. The revised edition,—and the one usually found and quoted from, though much toned down and weakened from the earlier editions,— was printed at Pittsburgh, in 1819, after the death of the Author. Later editions, some ten were published before the year 1855, are abridgments of the first and second volumes as originally issued in 1792.

24144   BRADMAN, ARTHUR
A NARRATIVE OF THE EXTRAORDINARY SUFFERINGS OF MR. ROBERT FORBES, HIS WIFE AND FIVE CHILDREN DURING AN UNFORTUNATE JOURNEY THROUGH THE WILDERNESS FROM CANADA TO KENNEBECK RIVER IN THE YEAR 1784. IN WHICH THREE OF THEIR CHILDREN WERE STARVED TO DEATH. TAKEN PARTLY FROM AN IMPERFECT JOURNAL, AND COMPILED AT THEIR REQUEST. BY ARTHUR BRADMAN.

Printed at Windsor, 1792, by Alden Spooner, and sold at his Office. pp. 15. 16mo.

24145   BRIGGS, RICHARD
THE NEW ART OF COOKERY, ACCORDING TO THE PRESENT PRACTICE; BEING A COMPLETE GUIDE TO ALL HOUSEKEEPERS, ON A PLAN ENTIRELY NEW; CONSISTING OF THIRTY-EIGHT CHAPTERS. CONTAINING, PROPER DIRECTIONS FOR MARKETING, AND TRUSSING OF POULTRY. THE MAKING SOUPS AND BROTHS. DRESSING ALL SORTS OF FISH. SAUCES FOR EVERY OCCASION. BOILING AND ROASTING. BAKING, BROILING, AND FRYING. STEWS AND HASHES. MADE DISHES OF EVERY SORT. RAGOUS AND FRICASEES. DIRECTIONS FOR DRESSING ALL SORTS OF ROOTS AND VEGETABLES. ALL SORTS OF AUMLETS AND EGGS. PUDDINGS, PIES, TARTS, &C. PANCAKES AND FRITTERS. CHEESECAKES AND CUSTARDS. BLANCMANGE, JELLIES, AND SYLLABUBS. DIRECTIONS FOR SEAFARING MEN. DIRECTIONS FOR THE SICK. PRESERVING, SYRUPS, AND CONSERVES. DRYING AND CANDYING. ALL SORTS OF CAKES. HOGS PUDDINGS, SAUSAGES, &C. POTTING, AND LITTLE COLD DISHES. THE ART OF CARVING. COLLARING, SALTING, AND SOUSING. PICKLING. TO KEEP GARDEN VEGETABLES, &C. MADE WINES. CORDIAL WATERS. BREWING. ENGLISH AND FRENCH BREAD, &C. BY RICHARD BRIGGS, MANY YEARS COOK AT THE GLOBE TAVERN FLEET-STREET, THE WHITE HART TAVERN, HOLBORN, AND NOW AT THE TEMPLE COFFEE-HOUSE, LONDON.

Philadelphia: Printed for W. Spotswood, R. Campbell, and B. Johnson. M,DCC,XCII. pp. xvi. [*sic* xviii], + 557, (1). 12mo.   AAS. BM.

Page xiv, of the contents is misnumbered xii, and the error continued.

24146 BRISSOT DE WARVILLE, JACQUES PIERRE   1754 – 1793.
NEW TRAVELS IN THE UNITED STATES OF AMERICA. PERFORMED IN 1788. BY
J. P. BRISSOT DE WARVILLE. TRANSLATED FROM THE FRENCH. [Five lines of quotations.]
    *New-York: Printed by T. & J. Swords, for Berry & Rogers, Booksellers
and Stationers, No. 35, Hanover-Square.—1792.—pp. 264, (3), (4). 12mo.*

NYHS. NYPL.

24147 BRODDECK, CHRISTIAN
GEISTIGES WETTER-GLÖCKLEIN, ODER CHRISTLICHE DONNER-UND WETTER-
GEBÄTER AUF ALLERLEY FÄLL, ANDÄCHTIGEN HERZENS MIT FLEISS ZUSAMMEN-
GETRAGEN VON CHRISTIAN BRODDECK.
    Chesnuthill: Gedruckt bey Samuel Saur. 1792.

24148 BROWN, JOHN   1722 – 1787
A BRIEF CONCORDANCE TO THE HOLY SCRIPTURES OF THE OLD AND NEW TESTA-
MENTS: BY WHICH ALL, OR MOST, OF THE PRINCIPAL TEXTS OF SCRIPTURE MAY BE
EASILY FOUND OUT. REVISED AND CORRECTED. BY JOHN BROWN, LATE MINISTER
OF THE GOSPEL AT HADDINGTON, IN SCOTLAND. [Two lines of Scripture texts.]
    *Printed at Worcester, Massachusetts, by Isaiah Thomas and Leonard Wor-
cester, for Isaiah Thomas. Sold at his Bookstore in Worcester, and by him and
Company in Boston.* MDCCXCII. pp. 322. obl. 12mo.   AAS. JCB.

24149 THE BRUNSWICK GAZETTE. NUMB. 275. TUESDAY, JANUARY 3, [—NUMB. 318.
TUESDAY, OCTOBER 30, 1792.]
    New-Brunswick: Printed by Abraham Blauvelt, 1792. fol.
In March, the printer attempted an innovation, the imprint reading:
Brunswic. (New-Jersey): Printed by Abraham Blauvelt. Discontinued
at the above date, and succeeded by *The Guardian; or, New-Brunswick
Advertiser.*

24150 BRYDONE, PATRICK   1743 – 1818
A TOUR THROUGH SICILY AND MALTA. IN A SERIES OF LETTERS TO WILLIAM BECK-
FORD, ESQ. OF SOMERBY, IN SUFFOLK; FROM P. BRYDONE, F. R. S. IN TWO VOL-
UMES [in one.] A NEW EDITION.
    *Boston: Printed by Joseph Bumstead, for John Boyle, David West, and
E. Larkin, jun.* M.DCC.XCII. 2 vols. in one. pp. (2), (2), viii, 363. 12mo.

AAS. LOC.

24151 BUCHAN, WILLIAM   1729 – 1805
DOMESTIC MEDICINE, OR THE FAMILY PHYSICIAN; BEING AN ATTEMPT TO RENDER
THE MEDICAL ART MORE GENERALLY USEFUL, BY SHEWING PEOPLE WHAT IS IN
THEIR OWN POWER, BOTH WITH RESPECT TO THE PREVENTION AND CURE OF DIS-
EASES. CHIEFLY CALCULATED TO RECOMMEND A PROPER ATTENTION TO REGIMEN
AND SIMPLE MEDICINES. WITH AN APPENDIX, CONTAINING A DISPENSATORY FOR
THE USE OF PRIVATE PRACTITIONERS. THE THIRTEENTH EDITION, WITH MANY
ADDITIONS.
    Philadelphia: 1792.

24152 BUCHANAN, GEORGE   1763 – 1807
AN ORATION UPON THE MORAL AND POLITICAL EVIL OF SLAVERY. DELIVERED AT
A PUBLIC MEETING OF THE MARYLAND SOCIETY, FOR PROMOTING THE ABOLITION
OF SLAVERY, AND THE RELIEF OF FREE NEGROES, AND OTHERS UNLAWFULLY HELD
IN BONDAGE. BALTIMORE, JULY 4TH, 1791. BY GEORGE BUCHANAN, M. D. MEM-
BER OF THE AMERICAN PHILOSOPHICAL SOCIETY.
    Baltimore: Printed by Philip Edwards. MDCCXCII. pp. (20). 4to.

LCP. NYPL.

Dedicated to Thomas Jefferson. Another impression, bearing date of
M,DCC,XCIII, was reprinted in W. F. Poole's "Anti-slavery opinions before 1800," printed in Cincinnati, in 1873.

24153   BUCHANAN, JAMES
A REGULAR ENGLISH SYNTAX. WHEREIN IS EXHIBITED THE WHOLE VARIETY OF ENGLISH CONSTRUCTION, PROPERLY EXEMPLIFIED; TO WHICH IS ADDED THE ELEGANT MANNER OF ARRANGING WORDS AND MEMBERS OF SENTENCES. THE WHOLE REDUCED TO PRACTICE. FOR THE USE OF PRIVATE YOUNG GENTLEMEN AND LADIES, AS WELL AS OUR MOST EMINENT SCHOOLS. BY JAMES BUCHANAN. THE FIFTH AMERICAN EDITION.

Philadelphia: Printed by Charles Cist, No. 104, in Second-Street, near the corner of Race-Street. M,DCC,XCII. pp. xxviii, 196. 12mo.   LOC. NYPL.

24154   BUCKLAND, JAMES
A WONDERFUL DISCOVERY OF AN OLD HERMIT, WHO LIVED UPWARDS OF TWO HUNDRED YEARS. [Publisher's monogram.]
Windham, Printed. [By John Bryne.] M,DCC,XCII. pp. (11). 12mo. LOC.

24155   BUELL, SAMUEL   1716 – 1798
THE IMPORT OF THE SAINT'S CONFESSION, THAT THE TIMES OF MEN ARE IN THE HAND OF GOD: EXHIBITED TO VIEW IN AN ANNIVERSARY, EUCHARISTICAL, AND HALF-CENTURY SERMON; DELIVERED AT EAST-HAMPTON, ON THE LORD'S DAY, JANUARY 1, 1792. BY SAMUEL BUELL, D. D. AND PASTOR OF THE CHURCH THERE. [Seven lines of Scripture texts.]
New-London: Printed by T. Green & Son. [1792.] pp. 52, (3). 8vo.
                                          BM. JCB.
Contains a three-page list of subscriber's names.

24156   BULLARD, SAMUEL
AN ALMANACK FOR THE YEAR OF CHRISTIAN ÆRA, 1793. BY SAMUEL BULLARD.
Boston: Printed by B. Edes & Son. [1792.] pp. (24). 12mo.   AAS.

24157   BURKE, EDMUND   1729 – 1797
REFLECTIONS ON THE REVOLUTION IN FRANCE, AND ON THE PROCEEDINGS IN CERTAIN SOCIETIES IN LONDON, RELATIVE TO THAT EVENT. IN A LETTER INTENDED TO HAVE BEEN SENT TO A GENTLEMAN IN PARIS. BY THE RIGHT HONOURABLE EDMUND BURKE.
Philadelphia: Printed by William Young, Bookseller, No. 52, Second-Street, the corner of Chesnut-Street. 1792. pp. 256. 8vo.   AAS. JCB. MHS. NYHS.

24158   BURLAMAQUI, JEAN JACQUES   1694 – 1748
THE PRINCIPLES OF NATURAL AND POLITICAL LAW. TRANSLATED IN ENGLISH BY MR. NUGENT. THE FOURTH EDITION.
Boston: Printed for John Boyle, Marlboro' Street. 1792. pp. 424. 8vo. HC.

24159   BURLINGTON. NEW JERSEY. BURLINGTON LIBRARY.
CATALOGUE OF BURLINGTON LIBRARY.
Burlington: Printed by Isaac Neale. 1792.

24160   BURN, RICHARD   1709 – 1785
BURN'S ABRIDGMENT, OR THE AMERICAN JUSTICE; CONTAINING THE WHOLE PRACTICE, AUTHORITY AND DUTY OF JUSTICES OF THE PEACE; WITH CORRECT FORMS OF PRECEDENTS RELATING THERETO, AND ADAPTED TO THE PRESENT SITUATION OF THE UNITED STATES.
Dover, (New-hampshire.) Printed for, and sold by Eliphalet Ladd, at his Printing-office, near the Court-House. M,DCC,XCII. pp. viii, 484, (1). 8vo. AAS.
Edited by Eliphalet Ladd. 2d New Hampshire District Copyright, issued to Eliphalet Ladd, as Proprietor, 9 February, 1792.

BURN, RICHARD, continued.

24161 —— — BURN'S ABRIDGMENT, OR THE AMERICAN JUSTICE; CONTAINING THE WHOLE PRACTICE, AUTHORITY AND DUTY OF JUSTICES OF THE PEACE; WITH CORRECT FORMS OF PRECEDENTS RELATING THERETO, AND ADAPTED TO THE PRESENT SITUATION OF THE UNITED STATES. THE SECOND EDITION.

Dover, (New-Hampshire): Printed for, and sold by Eliphalet Ladd, at his Printing-office, near the Court-House. 1792. pp. 484. 8vo.   AAS. BM. JCB.

24162 BURROUGHS, STEPHEN   1765 – 1840
A FAITHFUL NARRATIVE OF THE WONDERFUL DEALINGS OF GOD, TOWARDS POLLY DAVIS, OF NEWGRANTHAM, IN THE STATE OF NEWHAMPSHIRE. TAKEN FROM HER OWN MOUTH, AND THE TESTIMONY OF SEVERAL WITNESSES, OF ESTABLISHED AND APPROVED VERACITY, WHO WERE PRESENT WITH HER THROUGH THE SCENES OF DISTRESS, AND THAT SUDDEN AND SURPRISING RECOVERY CONTAINED IN THE FOLLOWING ACCOUNT; TAKEN AS ABOVE, ON THE TWELFTH DAY OF SEPTEMBER, 1792. BY THE REVEREND MR. BURROUGHS, OF HANOVER, AND THE REVEREND MR. ESTERBROOKS, OF NEWGRANTHAM.

Springfield: Printed by Ezra Waldo Weld. 1792. pp. 15. 8vo.

24163 —— — A FAITHFUL NARRATIVE OF THE WONDERFUL DEALINGS OF GOD, TOWARDS POLLY DAVIS, OF NEW-GRANTHAM, IN THE STATE OF NEW-HAMPSHIRE, TAKEN FROM HER OWN MOUTH, SEPTEMBER 12, 1792. BY THE REV. MR. BURROUGHS, OF HANOVER, AND THE REV. MR. EASTERBROOKS, OF NEW-GRANTHAM; BOTH OF THESE GENTLEMEN OF UNDOUBTED VERACITY.

Boston: Printed and sold by S. Hall, No. 53, Cornhill. [1792.] pp. 8. 8vo.
AAS. JCB.

24164 —— — A FAITHFUL NARRATIVE OF THE WONDERFUL DEALINGS OF GOD, TOWARDS POLLY DAVIS, OF NEWGRANTHAM IN THE STATE OF NEW-HAMPSHIRE. TAKEN FROM HER OWN MOUTH, AND THE TESTIMONY OF SEVERAL WITNESSES, OF ESTABLISHED AND APPROVED VERACITY, WHO WERE PRESENT WITH HER THROUGH THE SCENES OF DISTRESS, AND THAT SUDDEN AND SURPRISING RECOVERY, CONTAINED IN THE FOLLOWING ACCOUNT; TAKEN AS ABOVE, ON THE 12TH DAY OF SEPTEMBER, IN THE YEAR OF OUR LORD JESUS CHRIST, 1792. BY THE REVEREND MR. BURROUGHS, OF HANOVER AND THE REVEREND MR. EASTERBROOKS, OF NEWGRANTHAM.

Boston: Printed for, and sold by the Booksellers. [1792.] pp. [8.] 8vo.
AAS.

24165 —— — A FAITHFUL NARRATIVE OF THE WONDERFUL DEALINGS OF GOD, TOWARDS POLLY DAVIS, OF NEWGRANTHAM, IN THE STATE OF NEWHAMPSHIRE. TAKEN FROM HER OWN MOUTH, AND THE TESTIMONY OF SEVERAL WITNESSES, OF ESTABLISHED AND APPROVED VERACITY, WHO WERE PRESENT WITH HER THROUGH THE SCENES OF DISTRESS, AND THAT SUDDEN AND SURPRISING RECOVERY, CONTAINED IN THE ACCOUNT.

Norwich: Printed and sold by John Trumbull. 1792.

24166 —— — A FAITHFUL NARRATIVE OF THE WONDERFUL DEALINGS OF GOD, TOWARDS POLLY DAVIS, OF NEWGRANTHAM, IN THE STATE OF NEW-HAMPSHIRE. TAKEN FROM HER OWN MOUTH, AND THE TESTIMONY OF SEVERAL WITNESSES OF ESTABLISHED AND APPROVED VERACITY, WHO WERE PRESENT WITH HER THROUGH THE SCENES OF DISTRESS, AND THAT SUDDEN AND SURPRISING RECOVERY, CONTAINED IN THE FOLLOWING ACCOUNT; TAKEN AS ABOVE, ON THE 12TH DAY OF SEPTEMBER, 1792. BY THE REVEREND MR. BURROUGHS, OF HANOVER, AND THE REVEREND MR. ESTERBROOKS, OF NEWGRANTHAM.

Springfield, Printed: Litchfield, Re-printed by Collier and Buel. [1792.] pp. 12. 12mo.

24167   BUSHNELL, EBENEZER, and HUBBARD, THOMAS
BUSHNELL & HUBBARD'S NORWICH ALMANACK FOR THE YEAR OF OUR LORD 1793.
BEING THE FIRST AFTER BISSEXTILE OR LEAP YEAR: AND THE 16TH, OF THE IN-
DEPENDENCE OF AMERICA, CALCULATED FOR THE MERIDIAN OF NORWICH.
[Nine lines.]
[Norwich:] Printed by Bushnell and Hubbard. [1792.] pp. (20). 12mo.
NYPL.

24168   —— BUSHNELL & HUBBARD'S SHEET ALMANACK FOR THE YEAR 1793.
[Norwich: Printed by Bushnell and Hubbard. 1792.] Broadside. fol.

24169   BY AN ARRIVAL AT NEW-PORT, WE HAVE RECEIVED THE FOLLOWING GLORIOUS AND
INTERESTING ADVICES. BELFAST, OCTOBER, 10. WE HAVE MORE THAN ONCE
STATED IT WAS OUR OPINION, THAT IRELAND IS DEEPLY INVOLVED IN THE PROG-
RESS OF LIBERTY IN FRANCE; AND NOT ONLY IRELAND BUT THE WHOLE WORLD.
[News of the retreat of the allied armies, under the Duke of Brunswick, and
Dumourier's intention to establish his winter headquarters in Brussels.]
[Philadelphia: Printed by John Dunlap, 1791.] Broadside. fol.

24170   CAMPBELL, DANIEL, or DONALD   1665 – 1722
SACRAMENTAL MEDITATIONS ON THE SUFFERINGS AND DEATH OF CHRIST. IN WHICH
THE HUMILIATION AND SUFFERINGS OF CHRIST, IN HIS BIRTH, IN HIS LIFE, BEFORE,
AT, AND AFTER HIS DEATH, WITH THE END OF HIS SUFFERINGS, AND THE SACRA-
MENTAL PROMISE ARE CONSIDERED. BY THE REV. DANIEL CAMPBELL, MIN-
ISTER OF THE GOSPEL IN KILMICHAEL OF GLASRIE, WITHIN THE PRESBYTERY
AND SYNOD OF ARGYLE. CRUX CHRISTI, NOSTRA CORONA.
*Philadelphia: Printed by Johnston and Justice, at Franklin's Head, No.
41. Chesnut-Street.* M,DCC,XCII. pp. 143, (1). 12mo.   AAS.

24171   CAMPE, JOACHIM HEINRICH   1746 – 1818
THE NEW ROBINSON CRUSOE: AN INSTRUCTIVE AND ENTERTAINING HISTORY. TRANS-
LATED FROM THE FRENCH. IN TWO VOLUMES. VOL. I. [—II.]
*Philadelphia: Printed and sold by W. Woodhouse, at the Bible, No. 6, South
Front-Street.* M.DCC.XCII. 2 vols. pp. 172; 163. 12mo.   AAS.

William Woodhouse appears to have issued an edition this year with
copper plates; but there are no plates in the only copy seen.

24172   CAREY, JOHN
CATALOGUE OF PART OF A PRIVATE LIBRARY, CONSISTING OF A NUMBER OF SCARCE
AND VALUABLE BOOKS, PARTICULARLY THE GREEK AND LATIN CLASSICS.
*Philadelphia: Printed [by Mathew Carey] for John Carey, No. 26, Pear
street.* 1792.

24173   CAREY, MATHEW   1760 – 1839
MATHEW CAREY'S CATALOGUE OF BOOKS, FOR AUGUST, 1792.
[Philadelphia: From the Press of Mathew Carey, 1792.] pp. 12. 12mo.
AAS.

24174   —— [M. CAREY'S CATALOGUE FOR OCTOBER, 1792.] MATHEW CAREY, NO. 118,
MARKET-STREET, PHILADELPHIA, HAS IMPORTED FROM LONDON, DUBLIN, AND
GLASGOW, AN EXTENSIVE ASSORTMENT OF BOOKS, AMONG WHICH ARE THE FOL-
LOWING: . . .
[Philadelphia: From the Press of Mathew Carey, 1792.] pp. 12. 12mo.
AAS.

CAREY, MATHEW, continued.

24175 —— [M. CAREY'S CATALOGUE FOR NOVEMBER, 1792.] MATHEW CAREY, No. 118, MARKET-STREET, PHILADELPHIA, HAS IMPORTED FROM LONDON, DUBLIN, AND GLASGOW, AN EXTENSIVE ASSORTMENT OF BOOKS, AMONG WHICH ARE THE FOLLOWING: . . .

[Philadelphia: From the Press of Mathew Carey, 1792.] pp. 24. 12mo.
AAS.

24176 —— M. CAREY'S CATALOGUE FOR DECEMBER, 1792.

[Philadelphia: From the Press of Mathew Carey, 1792.] pp. 24. 12mo.
AAS.

24177 CARLETON, OSGOOD   1742 – 1816
CARLETON'S ALMANACK, (ENLARGED AND IMPROVED) FOR THE YEAR OF OUR LORD, 1793: BEING THE FIRST YEAR AFTER BISSEXTILE, OR LEAP-YEAR, AND THE SEVENTEENTH OF THE INDEPENDENCE OF THE UNITED STATES OF AMERICA. [Fourteen lines.] BY OSGOOD CARLETON, TEACHER OF MATHEMATICKS, IN BOSTON. [Eight lines of verse.]

Boston: Printed and sold by Samuel Hall, No. 53, Cornhill. . . .
[1792.] pp. (36). 12mo.   AAS. LOC.

24178 CARLISLE. PENNSYLVANIA. TEMPLE PATRICK SOCIETY.
A DEBATE PROPOSED IN THE TEMPLE PATRICK SOCIETY, AND FULLY DISCUSSED BY THE MEMBERS, WHETHER WITCHES, WIZARDS, MAGICIANS, SORCERERS, &C, HAD SUPERNATURAL POWERS.

Carlisle: Printed by George Kline, 1792.

24179 THE CARLISLE GAZETTE, AND WESTERN REPOSITORY OF KNOWLEDGE. VOL. VII. No. 335. WEDNESDAY, JANUARY 4, [—VOL. VIII. No. 386. WEDNESDAY, DECEMBER 26, 1792.]

Carlisle: (State of Pennsylvania) Printed by George Kline, . . . 1792.
fol.   NYHS.

24180 CARTER, SUSANNAH
THE FRUGAL HOUSE-WIFE; OR, COMPLETE WOMAN COOK: WHEREIN THE DRESSING ALL SORTS OF VICTUALS WITH CLEANLINESS, DECENCY AND ELEGANCE, IS EXPLAINED IN FIVE HUNDRED APPROVED RECEIPTS, IN GRAVIES, SAUCES, ROASTING, FRYING, BROILING, STEWS, HASHES, SOUPS, FRICASSES, RAGOOS, PASTES, PIES, TARTS, CAKES, PUDDINGS, SYLLABUBS, CREAMS, FLUMMERY, JELLIES, JAMS AND CUSTARDS. TOGETHER WITH THE BEST METHODS OF POTTING, COLLARING, PRESERVING, DRYING, CANDYING, PICKLING, AND MAKING OF ENGLISH WINES. TO WHICH ARE ADDED, TWELVE NEW PRINTS, EXHIBITING A PROPER ARRANGEMENT OF DINNERS, TWO COURSES FOR EVERY MONTH IN THE YEAR, WITH VARIOUS BILLS OF FARE. BY SUSANNAH CARTER, LONDON.

New-York: Printed for Berry and Rogers, No. 35, Hanover-Square. 1792.

24181 CARVER, JONATHAN   1732 – 1780
THREE YEARS TRAVELS THROUGH THE INTERIOR PARTS OF NORTH-AMERICA, FOR MORE THAN FIVE THOUSAND MILES, CONTAINING AN ACCOUNT OF THE GREAT LAKES, AND ALL THE LAKES, ISLANDS, AND RIVERS, CATARACTS, MOUNTAINS, MINERALS, SOIL AND VEGETABLE PRODUCTIONS OF THE NORTH-WEST REGIONS OF THAT VAST CONTINENT; WITH A DESCRIPTION OF THE BIRDS, BEASTS, REPTILES, INSECTS AND FISHES PECULIAR TO THE COUNTRY. TOGETHER WITH A CONCISE HISTORY OF THE GENIUS, MANNERS, AND CUSTOMS OF THE INDIANS INHABITING THE LANDS THAT LIE ADJACENT TO THE HEADS AND TO THE WESTWARD OF THE GREAT RIVER MISSISSIPPI; AND AN APPENDIX, DESCRIBING THE UNCULTIVATED PARTS OF AMERICA THAT ARE THE MOST PROPER FOR FORMING SETTLEMENTS. BY CAPTAIN JONATHAN CARVER, OF THE PROVINCIAL TROOPS IN AMERICA.

Philadelphia: Printed by Joseph Crukshank, No. 87, High-Street, 1792.
pp. xvi, 282. 12mo..   AAS. NYPL.

24182   CATALOGUE OF ABOUT TWO THOUSAND VOLUMES OF BOOKS, ON VARIOUS SUBJECTS, MANY OF WHICH ARE VERY SCARCE, TO BE SOLD AT MR. STARCK'S TAVERN.
Baltimore: Printed by David Graham, 1792.

24183   CATSKILL [cut] PACKET. VOL. I. NUMB. 1. MONDAY, AUGUST 6, [—NUMB. 22. MONDAY, DECEMBER 31, 1792.]
Printed by M. Croswell & Co. Catskill-Landing. 1792. fol.   NYHS.
Established by Mackay Croswell, and continued by him after the year 1810. In December, 1792, the Printing-Office was "removed into the chamber over the store of Messrs Noah Everest & Co." And again, in June, 1793, removed "next door to G. Ball's Tavern." In August, 1793, at the commencement of the second volume, the size of the paper was enlarged, and the day of publication changed to Tuesday. In 1794, the title was altered to *Catskill Packet, & western mail* ; and, before 1810, this was changed to *Catskill Recorder.*

24184   CHALLONER, RICHARD   1691 – 1781
THE GARDEN OF THE SOUL; OR, A MANUAL OF SPIRITUAL EXERCISES AND DEVOUT INSTRUCTIONS FOR CHRISTIANS, WHO, (LIVING IN THE WORLD), ASPIRE TO DEVOTION. BY BISHOP CHALLENOR [*sic.*]
Philadelphia: From the Press of Mathew Carey, No. 116 Market Street, April 23, M.DCC.XCII. pp. 159. 12mo.

24185   CHAMBERLAIN, THOMAS   – 1784
ELEVENTH? EDITION. [Cut.] THE MINISTER PREACHING HIS OWN FUNERAL SERMON : BEING A WARNING FROM HEAVEN TO ALL VILE SINNERS ON EARTH. WITH A PARTICULAR RELATION OF MANY WONDERFUL THINGS SEEN BY THE REV. MR. THOMAS CHAMBERLAIN, IN A VISION JUST BEFORE HIS DECEASE, THE PRECISE TIME OF WHICH WAS SHEWN UNTO HIM.
[Boston:] Printed and sold by E. Russell, in Essex-Street, next the stump of Liberty-Tree. 1792.

24186   CHARLESTON. SOUTH CAROLINA.
AT A MEETING OF THE INHABITANTS OF CHARLESTON, ON MAY 7TH, A COMMITTEE WAS APPOINTED TO PREPARE A PLAN FOR THE ESTABLISHMENT OF A FUND TO PURCHASE OR TAKE UP SPECIALTIES OR OTHER AUTHENTIC VOUCHERS OF DEBTS DUE FROM THE INHABITANTS OF THIS STATE, WITH THE VIEW OF EXTENDING CREDIT TO THE PERSONS OWING THE SAME, ON THEIR GIVING GOOD AND SUFFICIENT SECURITY FOR THE REPAYMENT THEREOF; WHICH COMMITTEE HAVING REPORTED, THE SAME WAS LAID BEFORE A MEETING OF THE INHABITANTS ON JUNE 11TH, AND AFTER BEING CONSIDERED AND AMENDED, WAS AGREED TO AND IS AS FOLLOWS: A BANKING COMPANY TO BE ESTABLISHED BY THE NAME OF THE "REDEMPTION BANK" . . . PUBLISHED BY ORDER OF THE MEETING, WILLIAM SMITH, CHAIRMAN. CHARLESTON, JUNE 11, 1792.
[Charleston: Printed by Markland and M'Iver. 1792.] Broadside. fol. LOC.

24187   CHASE, AMOS   – 1849
ON FEMALE EXCELLENCE. OR A DISCOURSE, IN WHICH GOOD CHARACTER IN WOMEN IS DESCRIBED; AND THE WORTH AND IMPORTANCE OF SUCH A CHARACTER, CONTEMPLATED, BY AMOS CHASE, A. M. PASTOR OF THE SECOND CHURCH IN LITCHFIELD: OCCASIONED BY THE DEATH OF HIS WIFE. AND DELIVERED AT LITCHFIELD, SOUTH-FARMS, ON LORD'S DAY, MARCH 6TH, 1791. [One line from] SOLOMON.
Litchfield: Printed by Collier and Buel. M.DCC.XCII. pp. 27. 4to. JCB.

24188 THE CHESHIRE ADVERTISER. NUMB. 1. THURSDAY, JANUARY 5, [—NUMB. 52? THURSDAY, DECEMBER 27? 1792.]
  Keene, (New-Hampshire): Printed by James Davenport Griffith. 1792. fol.
  Established by James Davenport Griffith, after the suspension of his *New-Hampshire Recorder*, in 1791, and continued by him into December of this year when publication ceased.

24189 DIE CHESNUTHILLER WOCHENSCHRIFT. NUM. 66. MITTWOCH, JANUARY 4, [—NUM. 117. MITTWOCH, DECEMBER 26, 1792.]
  Chesnuthill: Gedruckt bey Samuel Saur. 1792. 4to.

24190 CHRIST'S LETTER TO KING AGBARUS, &c.
  Boston: Printed and sold by E. Russell, in Essex-Street, next the stump of Liberty-Tree. 1792.

24191 THE CHRISTIAN ECONOMY, TRANSLATED FROM THE ORIGINAL GREEK, OF AN OLD MANUSCRIPT, FOUND IN THE ISLAND OF PATMOS, WHERE ST. JOHN WROTE HIS BOOK OF THE REVELATIONS.
  New-York: Printed for Benjamin Gomez, bookbinder and stationer, No. 32, Maiden-Lane. [1792.] pp. 48. 16mo.
    BA.

24192 —— CHRISTIAN ECONOMY. TRANSLATED FROM A GREEK MANUSCRIPT FOUND IN THE ISLAND OF PATMOS, WHERE ST. JOHN WROTE THE APOCALYPSE.
  Philadelphia: From the Press of Mathew Carey, No. 118, Market-street. Feb. 8, M,DCC,XCII. pp. 44, (4). 16mo.
    AAS. BA. LOC.

24193 THE CITY GAZETTE & [cut] DAILY ADVERTISER. [Motto.] VOL. X. NUMB. 1773. MONDAY, JANUARY 2, [—NUMB. 2068. MONDAY, DECEMBER 31, 1792.]
  Charleston: Printed by Markland & M'Iver, Printers to the City, No. 47, Bay. 1792. fol.
  At the beginning of the year, a new, script, heading was adopted with a smaller cut of Charleston than before.

24194 CLARK, EDWARD
 LETTERS TO A FRIEND: CONTAINING THOUGHTS ON THE BEGINNING OF THE NEW TESTAMENT DISPENSATION, AND CHRISTIAN BAPTISM. OCCASIONED BY A PIECE ENTITLED, THE BAPTISM OF CHRIST NOT TO BE IMITATED BY CHRISTIANS. BY EDWARD CLARK, PREACHER OF THE GOSPEL AT MEDFIELD.
  Printed at Worcester, Massachusetts, by Isaiah Thomas and Leonard Worcester. MDCCXCII. pp. 48. 8vo.
    AAS. BM. JCB.

24195 CLEAVELAND, BENJAMIN, and others.
 HYMNS ON DIFFERENT SPIRITUAL SUBJECTS. IN TWO PARTS. PART FIRST. CONTAINING XXVI HYMNS, ON VARIOUS SUBJECTS, SUITABLE FOR CHRISTIAN WORSHIP. BY BENJAMIN CLEAVELAND. PART SECOND. CONTAINING XXXII HYMNS BY ANNA BEEMAN, OF WARREN IN CONNECTICUT. AND XXIV HYMNS BY AMOS WELLS. TO WHICH IS ADDED A NUMBER OF HYMNS BY DIFFERENT AUTHORS; PARTICULARLY ADAPTED TO THE BAPTIST WORSHIP.
  Norwich: Printed and sold by John Trumbull, 1792.

24196 COE, CURTIS
 A SERIOUS ADDRESS OF A MINISTER TO HIS PEOPLE. THE MEANING OF THE WORD BAPTISM CONSIDERED: SEVERAL REASONS ASSIGNED FOR THE BAPTISM OF INFANTS AND OBJECTIONS ANSWERED. BY CURTIS COE A. M. PASTOR OF THE CHURCH AT DURHAM.
  Portsmouth: Printed by John Melcher, 1792. 12mo.
    BA.
  4th New Hampshire District Copyright, issued to Curtis Coe, as Author, 9 July, 1792.

24197   COGSWELL, JAMES   1720 – 1807
THE BLESSEDNESS OF THE GODLY IN A FUTURE STATE, ESPECIALLY AS IT CONSISTS IN A TOTAL DELIVERANCE FROM ALL EVIL, AND A GRACIOUS REWARD OF THEIR OBEDIENCE AND LOVE TO GOD IN THE PRESENT STATE. ILLUSTRATED IN A SERMON, DELIVERED AT HAMPTON, ON THE 28TH DAY OF JULY, 1791, AT THE INTERMENT OF THE REV. SAMUEL MOSELY, A. M. PASTOR OF THE CHURCH OF CHRIST IN THAT TOWN; WHO DEPARTED THIS LIFE ON THE 26TH OF JULY, IN THE 83D YEAR OF HIS LIFE, AND 57TH OF HIS MINISTRY. BY JAMES COGSWELL, D. D. PASTOR OF THE SECOND CHURCH IN WINDHAM. 2 COR. 4. 17. [Three lines.]
Windham: Printed by John Byrne. 1792. pp. 28. 8vo.   CHS. JCB.

24198   COLESBERRY, HENRY
TENTAMEN MEDICUM INAUGURALE DE EPILEPSIA.
Wilmingtonii: E typis Brynberg et Andrews. 1792. pp. 28. 8vo.   SGO.

24199   A COLLECTION OF LESSONS AND HYMNS, FROM THE HOLY SCRIPTURES; TOGETHER WITH FORMS OF PRAYER. FOR THE USE OF SCHOOLS.
Salem: Printed by Thomas C. Cushing for William Carleton, at the Bible and Heart. 1792.

24200   COLMAN, GEORGE, the younger.   1762 – 1836
INKLE & YARICO, AN OPERA, AS PERFORMED WITH GREAT APPLAUSE, AT THE THEATRE ROYAL, —— LONDON. AND NOW PERFORMED WITH APPLAUSE BY THE NEW AMERICAN COMPANY, PHILADELPHIA. [Printer's monogram.]
Philadelphia: Printed and sold at E. Story's office, in Fourth-Street, nearly opposite the Indian Queen Tavern. [1792.] pp. [66.] 12mo.   AAS.
Printed on writing-paper. The libretto by Samuel Arnold. The story of Inkle and Yarico is from No. 11, of The Spectator.

24201   THE COLUMBIAN ALMANAC, FOR THE YEAR OF OUR LORD, 1793. . . .
Philadelphia: Printed and sold by Stewart & Cochran. [1792.]

24202   THE COLUMBIAN ALMANAC, OR THE NORTH AMERICAN CALENDAR, FOR THE YEAR OF OUR LORD, 1793. . . .
Wilmington: Printed and sold by Brynberg and Andrews. [1792.]

24203   COLUMBIAN U S A CENTINEL. No. 33, OF VOL. XVI. WHOLE NO. 803. WEDNESDAY, JANUARY 4, [—No. 32, OF VOL. XVIII. WHOLE NO. 916. SATURDAY, DECEMBER 29, 1792.]
Printed and published, on Wednesdays and Saturdays by Benjamin Russell, in State-Street, Boston, Massachusetts. 1792. fol.   AAS. LOC. NYPL.
Beginning September 12th, the size of the paper was enlarged.

24204   THE COLUMBIAN HERALD OR THE INDEPENDENT COURIER OF NORTH AMERICA. JANUARY—DECEMBER, 1792.
Charleston: Printed by T. B. Bowen. 1792. fol.

24205   THE COLUMBIAN MIRROR AND ALEXANDRIA GAZETTE. VOL. I. No. 1. WEDNESDAY, NOVEMBER 21, [—No. 12. SATURDAY, DECEMBER 29, 1792.]
Alexandria—Printed, every Wednesday and Saturday, by John Smith and Ellis Price, at the east end of the Market-house. 1792. fol.
Established by John Smith and Ellis Price. In September, 1793, the partnership terminated by mutual consent, Ellis Price continuing publication as sole proprietor. In 1796, Henry Gird junior, was associated with Ellis Price in its publication; and, in 1798, the latter withdrew. Henry Gird junior, continued publication alone up to November, 1800, being succeeded in that month by William Fowler. A tri-weekly publication, on Tuesdays, Thursdays and Saturdays, was begun in 1795, and continued to the end.

24206 | A COMPENDIOUS SYSTEM OF ANATOMY. IN SIX PARTS. PART I. OSTEOLOGY. II. OF THE MUSCLES. III. OF THE ABDOMEN. IV. OF THE THORAX. V. OF THE BRAIN AND NERVES. VI. OF THE SENSES. EXTRACTED FROM THE AMERICAN EDITION OF THE ENCYCLOPÆDIA, NOW PUBLISHING, BY THOMAS DOBSON, PHILADELPHIA.

Philadelphia: Printed by Thomas Dobson, at the Stone House, in Second-Street, between Market and Chesnut-Streets. 1792. pp. 438, 12 plates. 8vo. SGO.

24207 | A COMPLETE GUIDE FOR THE MANAGEMENT OF BEES, THROUGH THE YEAR. BY A FARMER OF MASSACHUSETTS. ILLUSTRATED WITH A COPPERPLATE.

Printed at Worcester, Massachusetts, by Isaiah Thomas & Leonard Worcester, for Isaiah Thomas. Sold at his Bookstore in Worcester, and by said Thomas and Andrews, in Boston. MDCCXCII. pp. 46, plate. 16mo.   AAS. JCB. LOC.

In some copies the plate is crudely engraved. Others have the plate of better workmanship, with "Worcester Published by I. Thomas, 1792." also engraved upon it. The Library of Congress has both forms. 28th Massachusetts District Copyright, issued to Isaiah Thomas, as Proprietor, 30 March, 1792.

24208 | [U. S. arms.] CONCORD HERALD. [N. H. arms.] No. 51. VOL. II. WHOLE NO. 101. THURSDAY, JANUARY 5, [—No. 50. VOL. III. WHOLE NO. 152. THURSDAY, DECEMBER 27, 1792.]

A Political State Paper: Printed and published by George Hough, at Concord, New-Hampshire. 1792. fol.

24209 | THE CONCORD MIRROUR. NUMB. 1. MONDAY, OCTOBER 29, [— NUMB. 10. MONDAY, DECEMBER 31, 1792.]

Concord, New-Hampshire: Printed by Elijah Russell. 1792. fol.

Established by Elijah Russell. In October, 1794, his brother-in-law, Moses Davis, became a partner in its publication. In April, 1795, the paper was enlarged, and the title changed to *The Federal Mirrour.* In November, 1796, Davis established the Republican Gazetteer, this title being altered to Russell & Davis's Republican Gazetteer until its publication was merged into *The Federal Mirrour,* in November, 1797. In April, 1797, Russell & Davis, established the New Star, an octavo periodical, which they issued simultaneously, in two editions, and which was discontinued, after the issue of twenty-five numbers, in October, 1797. The Mirrour was continued by Moses Davis to about August, 1799, in which month Davis established *The Dartmouth Gazette.*

24210 | CONDORCET, MARIE JEAN ANTOINE NICOLAS DE CARITAT, marquis DE. THE LIFE OF VOLTAIRE. BY THE MARQUIS DE CONDORCET. TO WHICH ARE ADDED MEMOIRS OF VOLTAIRE, WRITTEN BY HIMSELF. TRANSLATED FROM THE FRENCH. IN TWO VOLUMES. VOL. I. [—II.]

Philadelphia: Printed by and for W. Spotswood. M,DCC,XCII. 2 vols. in one. pp. 412. 12mo.   AAS. BM. BPL. JCB.

24211 | CONGREGATIONAL CHURCH IN MASSACHUSETTS. REVEREND SIR, AND RESPECTED GENTLEMEN, THE CONVENTION OF CONGREGATIONAL MINISTERS, WITH THE CONGREGATIONAL CHARITABLE SOCIETY, OF THE COMMONWEALTH OF MASSACHUSETTS [Soliciting contributions for the work of the Society.] BOSTON, JULY 25, 1792.

[Boston: 1792.] Broadside. fol.   AAS.

24212   CONNECTICUT. STATE.
[Seal.] ACTS AND LAWS, MADE AND PASSED BY THE GENERAL COURT OR ASSEMBLY OF THE STATE OF CONNECTICUT, IN AMERICA; HOLDEN AT HARTFORD, IN SAID STATE, ON THE SECOND THURSDAY OF MAY, ANNO DOMINI, 1792. [Colophon:]
Hartford: Printed by Elisha Babcock. [1792.] pp. 421–436. fol.

This is the official issue.   CHS. CSL. YC.

24213   —— — [Seal.] ACTS AND LAWS, MADE AND PASSED BY THE GENERAL COURT OR ASSEMBLY OF THE STATE OF CONNECTICUT, IN AMERICA, HOLDEN AT HARTFORD, IN SAID STATE, ON THE SECOND THURSDAY OF MAY, ANNO DOMINI, 1792.
[New-London: Printed by Timothy Green and Son. 1792.] pp. 419–430.
fol.   HSP. NYLI.

24214   —— — [Seal.] ACTS AND LAWS, MADE AND PASSED BY THE GENERAL COURT OR ASSEMBLY OF THE STATE OF CONNECTICUT, IN AMERICA; HOLDEN AT HARTFORD, IN SAID STATE, ON THE SECOND THURSDAY OF MAY, ANNO DOMINI, 1792.
[New-Haven: Printed by Thomas and Samuel Green. 1792.] pp. 411–421.
fol.   HCBA. PL. YC.

24215   —— — [Seal.] ACTS AND LAWS, MADE AND PASSED BY THE GENERAL COURT OR ASSEMBLY OF THE STATE OF CONNECTICUT, IN AMERICA; HOLDEN AT NEW-HAVEN, IN SAID STATE, ON THE SECOND THURSDAY OF OCTOBER, ANNO DOMINI, 1792.
Hartford: Printed by Elisha Babcock. [1792.] pp. 437–460. fol.

This is the official issue.   CHS. CSL. YC.

24216   —— — [Seal.] ACTS AND LAWS, MADE AND PASSED BY THE GENERAL COURT OR ASSEMBLY OF THE STATE OF CONNECTICUT, IN AMERICA, HOLDEN AT NEW-HAVEN, IN SAID STATE, ON THE SECOND THURSDAY OF OCTOBER, ANNO DOMINI, 1792.
[New-London: Printed by Timothy Green and Son. 1792.] pp. 431–447.
fol.   HSP. NYLI.

24217   —— — [Seal.] ACTS AND LAWS, MADE AND PASSED BY THE GENERAL COURT OR ASSEMBLY OF THE STATE OF CONNECTICUT, IN AMERICA, HOLDEN AT NEW-HAVEN, IN SAID STATE, ON THE SECOND THURSDAY OF OCTOBER, ANNO DOMINI, 1792.
[New-Haven: Printed by Thomas and Samuel Green. 1792.] pp. 423–434. fol.
       HCBA. PL. YC.

24218   —— BY HIS EXCELLENCY SAMUEL HUNTINGTON, ESQUIRE, GOVERNOR AND COMMANDER IN CHIEF IN AND OVER THE STATE OF CONNECTICUT. A PROCLAMATION. [Appointing Thursday, the twelfth day of April, a day of fasting and prayer.]
New-London: Printed by T. Green & Son. 1792. Broadside. fol.   CHS.

24219   —— BY HIS EXCELLENCY SAMUEL HUNTINGTON, ESQUIRE, GOVERNOR AND COMMANDER IN CHIEF IN AND OVER THE STATE OF CONNECTICUT. A PROCLAMATION. [Appointing Thursday, th , twenty-ninth day of November, a day of thanksgiving.]
New-London: Printed by T. Green & Son. 1792. Broadside. fol. CHS. YC.

24220 CONNECTICUT SOCIETY FOR THE PROMOTION OF FREEDOM.
THE CONSTITUTION OF THE CONNECTICUT SOCIETY FOR THE PROMOTION OF FREE-
DOM, AND THE RELIEF OF PERSONS UNLAWFULLY HELD IN BONDAGE, AS REVISED
AND ENLARGED ON THE 13TH DAY OF SEPTEMBER, 1792.
NEW-HAVEN, SEPTEMBER 13TH, 1792. AT A MEETING OF THE "CONNECTICUT
SOCIETY FOR THE PROMOTION OF FREEDOM, AND FOR THE RELIEF OF PERSONS
UNLAWFULLY HOLDEN IN BONDAGE, AT NEW-HAVEN ON THE 13TH DAY OF SEP-
TEMBER, A. D. 1792, THE FOREGOING CONSTITUTION WAS APPROVED FOR THE FU-
TURE REGULATION OF SAID SOCIETY—AND THE FOLLOWING OFFICERS WERE
CHOSEN, VIZ. [Two columns.]
[New-Haven: Printed by Thomas and Samuel Green. 1792.] pp. (3). fol.
NYHS.

24221 THE CONNECTICUT COURANT. VOL. XXVII. NUMB. 1406. MONDAY, JANUARY 2,
[—NUMB. 1458. MONDAY, DECEMBER 31, 1792.]
Hartford: Printed by Hudson and Goodwin, near the Bridge. 1792. fol.
AAS. CHS. LOC. YC.

24222 ——— THE NEWS LAD'S ADDRESS TO THE READERS OF THE CONNECTICUT COURANT.
HARTFORD. JANUARY 1, 1792.
[Hartford: Printed by Hudson and Goodwin, 1792.] Broadside.

24223 THE CONNECTICUT GAZETTE. VOL. XXIX. NO. 1469. THURSDAY, JANUARY 5,
[—VOL. XXX. NO. 1520. THURSDAY, DECEMBER 27, 1792.]
*New-London: Printed by Timothy Green and Son, at the north-west corner
of the Parade. 1792. fol.* AAS. CHS. NYPL. YC.

24224 THE CONNECTICUT JOURNAL. NO. 1262. WEDNESDAY, JANUARY 4, [—NO. 1313.
WEDNESDAY, DECEMBER 26, 1792.]
New-Haven: Printed by Thomas and Samuel Green, opposite the Post-office.
1792. fol. AAS. LOC. YC.

24225 THE CONSTITUTION [of Kentucky] SHOWN TO BE CONSISTENT WITH A NEW ELEC-
TION. BY FREE SUFFRAGE.
Lexington: Printed by John Bradford, 1792. 8vo.

24226 THE CONVERSION AND DEATH OF JOSEPH, AN AFFECTING STORY, FOUNDED ON
FACT. EMBELLISHED WITH TWO ELEGANT ENGRAVINGS. PUBLISHED ACCORDING
TO ACT OF CONGRESS.
Hartford: Printed by Elisha Babcock? 1792.
Sold also by William Carleton, Salem; and by Thomas B. Wait, Port-
land, this year.

24227 COOPER, WILLIAM
AN ANTHEM. DESIGNED FOR THANKSGIVING DAY. BUT PROPER FOR ANY PUBLICK
OCCASION. BY WILLIAM COOPER. [Verse.] PUBLISHED ACCORDING TO ACT OF
CONGRESS.
*Printed at Boston, by Isaiah Thomas and Ebenezer T. Andrews, Faust's
Statue, No. 45, Newbury Street.* 1792. pp. 16. obl. 16mo. AAS. LOC.
25th Massachusetts District Copyright, issued to Thomas & Andrews,
as Proprietors, 22 February, 1792.

24228   CORDIER, Mathurin   1479 – 1564
         Corderii Colloquiorum centura selecta: a select century of Corderius's
         Colloquies. With an English translation as literal as possible: de-
         signed for the use of beginners in the Latin tongue. By John Clarke,
         late master of the publick grammar-school in Hull, and author of the
         Introduction to the making of Latin.
                   New-York: Printed by Hugh Gaine, at the Bible, in Hanover-Square.
              1792.

24229   COWPER, William   1731 – 1800
         Poems. By William Cowper.
              Salem: Printed by Thomas C. Cushing. 1792. 2vols. 12mo.

24230   COXE, Tench   1755 – 1824
         Reflexions on the state of the Union. [Two lines of Latin.] [Ornament.]
              Philadelphia: From the Press of Mathew Carey. May 9.—M,DCC,XCII.
              pp. 38. 8vo.
                                                             AAS. LOC.

24231   CRAFTON, William Bell
         An Address to the people of Great Britain, on the propriety of abstain-
         ing from West India sugar & rum. [Eight lines of verse from] Cowper's
         Negro's complaint. The eighth edition.
              London – – Printed, New-York Re-printed by William Durell No. 19,
         Queen Street. M,DCC,XCII. pp. 12. 12mo.   JCB.
         Also attributed to William Fox.

24232   —— —— An Address to the people of Great-Britain, on the propriety of
         abstaining from West-India sugar and rum. [Eight lines of verse from]
         Cowper's Negro's complaint. The ninth edition.
              First printed in London. Re-printed by Samuel Hall, in Boston. 1792.
         pp. [12.] 8vo.
                                                             AAS.

24233   —— —— A Short sketch of the evidence for the abolition of the slave
         trade. Delivered before a committee of the House of Commons. To
         which is added, a recommendation of the subject to the serious atten-
         tion of people in general. [Three lines from] Matt. chap. VII. ver. 12.
              London, Printed, Philadelphia: Re-printed by Daniel Lawrence. M.DCC.-
         XCII. pp. 28; 16, (3). 12mo.   JCB. NYHS.
         Second title: An Address to the people of Great Britain, on the pro-
         priety of abstaining from West India sugar and rum. [Eight lines of verse
         from] Cowper's Negro's complaint. The tenth edition, with additions.
              London, Printed, Philadelphia: Re-printed by Daniel Lawrence. M.DCC.-
         XCII. pp. 16, (3).

24234   CRAIGHEAD, or CRAGHEAD, Robert
         Advice to communicants, for necessary preparation, and profitable im-
         provement of the great and comfortable ordinance of the Lord's Sup-
         per: that therein true spiritual communion with Christ may be ob-
         tained, and the eternal enjoyment of God sealed. By Robert Crag-
         head, minister of the Gospel in L. Derry. [Six lines of Scripture texts.]
              Philadelphia: Printed and sold by Stewart & Cochran, No. 34, *South
         Second Street.* M,DCC,XCII. pp. 137, (2). 12mo.   AAS. JCB.

24235   CRISP, Stephen   1628 – 1692
         Eine kurtze Beschreibung einer langen Reise von Babylon nach Bethel.
              Chesnuthill: Gedruckt bey Samuel Saur. 1792. pp. 24. 12mo.   PSL.

24236   CULLEN, WILLIAM   1712 – 1790
FIRST LINES OF THE PRACTICE OF PHYSIC. BY WILLIAM CULLEN, M. D. WITH
PRACTICAL AND EXPLANATORY NOTES, BY JOHN ROTHERHAM, M. D. OF EDINBURGH.
> *Philadelphia: Printed by Parry Hall, No. 149, Chesnut street, near Fourth
street.* 1792. 2vols. 8vo.

24237   —— SYNOPSIS AND NOSOLOGY, BEING AN ARRANGEMENT AND DEFINITION OF DISEASES,
BY WILLIAM CULLEN, M. D. PROFESSOR OF THE PRACTICE OF PHYSIC IN THE UNI-
VERSITY OF EDINBURGH; FRST [*sic*] PHYSICIAN TO HIS BRITANNIC MAJESTY FOR
SCOTLAND; FELLOW OF THE ROYAL COLLEGE OF PHYSICIANS OF EDINBURGH; OF
THE ROYAL SOCIETIES OF LONDON AND OF EDINBURGH; OF THE ROYAL SOCIETY
OF MEDICINE OF PARIS, &C. &C. &C. THE FIRST TRANSLATION FROM LATIN TO
ENGLISH.
> *Printed at Hartford, by Nathaniel Patten, for Isaiah Thomas, sold by said
Thomas in Worcester, Massachusetts, and by him and Company in Boston.* MDCC-
XCII. pp. xxxix, [80.] 16mo.   AAS. JCB. SGO.

24238   CULVER, NATHAN
THE LATE WONDERFUL AMERICAN VISION; EXHIBITING THE JUDGMENTS THAT MUST
SHORTLY COME TO PASS.
> *New-York?* 1792.
For sale in Providence, 25 July, 1792.

24239   CURRIE, WILLIAM   1754 – 1828
AN HISTORICAL ACCOUNT OF THE CLIMATES AND DISEASES OF THE UNITED STATES
OF AMERICA; AND OF THE REMEDIES AND METHODS OF TREATMENT, WHICH HAVE
BEEN FOUND MOST USEFUL AND EFFICACIOUS, PARTICULARLY IN THOSE DISEASES
WHICH DEPEND UPON CLIMATE AND SITUATION. COLLECTED PRINCIPALLY FROM
PERSONAL OBSERVATION, AND THE COMMUNICATIONS OF PHYSICIANS OF TALENTS AND
EXPERIENCE, RESIDING IN THE SEVERAL STATES. BY WILLIAM CURRIE, FELLOW
OF THE COLLEGE OF PHYSICIANS OF PHILADELPHIA. [One line of Latin from]
HOR.
> *Philadelphia: Printed by T. Dobson, at the Stone-House, No. 41, South
Second-Street.* M,DCC,XCII. pp. (2), (2), (4), (409), v. 8vo.
>   BA. BM. HC. JCB. LOC. SGO.

24240   DABOLL, NATHAN .   1750 – 1818
THE NEW-ENGLAND ALMANACK, AND GENTLEMEN & LADIES DIARY, FOR THE YEAR
OF OUR LORD CHRIST, 1793: BEING THE FIRST YEAR AFTER BISSEXTILE OR LEAP-
YEAR, AND THE 17TH OF AMERICAN INDEPENDENCE. [Seven lines.] BY NATHAN
DABOLL. [Four lines of verse.]
> *New-London: Printed and sold by T. Green & Son.* [1792.] pp. (24).
12mo.   CHS. LOC. NYPL.
"To Mr. Daboll, the public have for many years been indebted for the
correct calculations of Freebetter's Almanack."

24241   —— THE SHEET ALMANACK FOR THE YEAR 1793.
> *New-London: Printed by T. Green & Son.* 1792. Broadside. fol.

24242   DAGGETT, HERMAN   1766 – 1832
THE RIGHTS OF ANIMALS: AN ORATION DELIVERED AT THE COMMENCEMENT OF
PROVIDENCE COLLEGE, SEPTEMBER 7, 1791.
> *Sagg-Harbour: Printed by David Frothingham.* 1792. pp. 14. 8vo.

24243 THE DAILY [N. Y. arms] ADVERTISER. VOL. VIII. NO. 2144. MONDAY, JANUARY 2,
[—NO. 2459. MONDAY, DECEMBER 31, 1792.]
[New-York:] Printed by Francis Childs and John Swaine, Printers to the
State of New-York, No. 189, Water-Street near King-Street. 1792. fol.
AAS. LOC. NYHS. NYPL.
Beginning June 7th, the Printing-Office was at No. 29, corner of Water
and King-Streets; changing, on June 11th, to "Printers to the State, No.
29, Water-Street, corner of King-Street: Enquire at the door in King-
Street."

24244 DANA, JAMES   1735 – 1812
THE DOCTRINE AND MISSION OF JESUS CHRIST. A SERMON PREACHED IN CAMBRIDGE,
IN THE COMMONWEALTH OF MASSACHUSETTS, JANUARY 25, 1792, AT THE INSTAL-
LATION OF THE REVEREND ABIEL HOLMES TO THE PASTORAL CARE OF THE FIRST
CHURCH AND SOCIETY IN THE SAID TOWN. BY JAMES DANA, D. D. PASTOR OF THE
FIRST CONGREGATIONAL CHURCH IN NEW-HAVEN, CONNECTICUTT [*sic.*] [Ornament.]
Printed by Samuel Hall, in Cornhill, Boston. MDCCXCII. pp. [35.] 8vo.
AAS. BA. HC. JCB. MHS. NYPL.

24245 DANA, JOSEPH   1742 – 1827
A NEW AMERICAN SELECTION OF LESSONS IN READING AND SPEAKING; CONSISTING
OF SACRED, MORAL AND HISTORICAL EXTRACTS; HUMOROUS, ENTERTAINING, AND
DESCRIPTIVE PIECES; SELECT SENTENCES AND MAXIMS; POETRY, DIALOGUES, &C.
TO WHICH ARE ADDED, ELEMENTS OF GESTURE, ILLUSTRATED WITH COPPER PLATE
ENGRAVINGS. DESIGNED FOR THE USE OF SCHOOLS. BY JOSEPH DANA, A. B.
Boston: 1792. pp. 300, 4 plates. 12mo.   BM.
33d Massachusetts District Copyright, issued to Joseph Dana, as Author,
4 September, 1792.

24246 DANBURY. CONNECTICUT. BAPTIST ASSOCIATION.
THE MINUTES OF THE DANBURY ASSOCIATION, HELD IN NEW-HARTFORD, SEPT.
19TH, AND 20TH, 1792.
[Danbury: Printed by Nathan Douglas and Edwards Ely. 1792.] pp. 4.
4to.   JCB.

24247 DARTMOUTH COLLEGE.
CATALOGUS EORUM QUI IN COLLEGIO DARTMUTHENSI (A REVERENDO ELEAZARO
WHEELOCK, S. T. D. INSTITUTO) NOVÆ HANTONIÆ, AB ANNO M,DCC,LXXI, AD ANNUM
MD,CC,XCII, ALICUJUS GRADUS LAUREÂ DONATI SUNT. ALUMNORUM NOMINA AL-
PHABETICE DISPORUNTUR. [Six columns.] [Colophon:]
Typis Isaiah Thomas et Ebenezer T. Andrews, Boston, 1792. Broadside.
fol.   AAS. LOC.

24248 DAVIES, SAMUEL   1724 – 1761
SERMONS ON IMPORTANT SUBJECTS, BY THE LATE REVEREND AND PIOUS ·SAMUEL
DAVIES, A. M. SOMETIME PRESIDENT OF THE COLLEGE IN NEW-JERSEY. IN THREE
VOLUMES. THE FIFTH EDITION. TO WHICH ARE NOW ADDED, THREE OCCASIONAL
SERMONS, NOT INCLUDED IN THE FORMER EDITIONS; MEMOIRS AND CHARACTER OF
THE AUTHOR; AND TWO SERMONS ON OCCASION OF HIS DEATH, BY THE REV. DRS.
GIBBONS AND FINLEY. VOL. I. [—III.]
New-York: Printed for T. Allen, Bookseller and Stationer, No. 12, *Queen-*
Street.—1792.—3 vols. pp. (2), (2), (4), 478; (2), (6), 471; (2), (4), 435. 8vo. NYPL.

24249 DAY, THOMAS   1748 – 1789
THE HISTORY OF SANDFORD AND MERTON. ABRIDGED FROM THE ORIGINAL. FOR
THE AMUSEMENT AND INSTRUCTION OF JUVENILE MINDS.
New-York: Printed and sold by William Durell at his Book store and
Printing-office, No, 19, *Queen-Street.* M,DCC,XCII. pp. 133, frontispiece. 24mo.
AAS.

24250   DEARBORN, Benjamin   1755 – 1838
      The Pupil's guide or assistant in writing &c. By Benjamin Dearborn.
        Boston: Printed by B. Edes & Son? 1792.
        40th Massachusetts District Copyright, issued to Benjamin Dearborn,
      as Author, 30 November, 1792.

24251   DE BRAHM, John William Gerar   1718 –
      Voice of the everlasting Gospel. By John William Gerar De Brahm.
        *Philadelphia: Printed by Zachariah Poulson, junior, No. 30, North Fourth-
        Street, near the University.* MDCCXCII. pp. (61); (13); (24); (14); (16); (59); (20);
        (23). 8vo.   AAS. BM. NYPL.

        Second title: The Voice of the everlasting Gospel sounding through eight
      branches of the tree of knowledge, on the fathomless water of the
      church in love near landing on time's flux into eternity. [Cut. Three lines
      from] Hez. xlvii. 1-11.   pp. (2) — (39).

        Third title: ii. Arm of the tree of knowledge of good and evil branching
      forth physic or nature from power attractive and repelling virtue.
      Explanation of the mystic figure: the rays converging into the focus
      represent attracting power; the dotted circles, diverging from and re-
      turning to the focus, represent repelling virtue. [Cut. Three lines from]
      Psalm cxi. 23.   pp. (2), (43)—(61).

        Fourth title: iii. Arm of the tree of knowledge of good and evil branch-
      ing forth the word of God, His Commandments, laws and statutes. [Six
      lines of Scripture. Cut.]   pp. (13).

        Fifth title: iv. Arm of the tree of knowledge of good and evil branching
      forth sacred history and where blended with profane. [Eight lines of
      Scripture. Cut.]   pp. (24).

        Sixth title: v. Arm of the tree of knowledge of good and evil branching
      revelation by apparition and audible voice, by dream and a secret speak-
      ing to the feeling of the mind throughout the time of the everlasting
      Gospel. [Three lines of Scripture. Cut.]   pp. (14).

        Seventh title: vi. Arm of the tree of knowledge of good and evil branch-
      ing forth the ante & post-diluvian, to wit, the state of Eden, which was,
      now Earth, which is. [Five lines of Scripture. Cuts of Garden of Eden, and
      Earth.]   pp. (16).

        Eighth title: vii. Arm of the tree of knowledge, branching sacred chron-
      ology through the six divine labors in mystic, physic, law, history, sacred
      and profane, Gospel and revelation. [Ornament.]
         *Philadelphia: Printed by Zachariah Poulson, junior, No. 30, North
        Fourth-Street, near the College.* MDCCXCI. pp. (59).

        Ninth title: Time an apparition of eternity, manifested in its gathering
      by attracting power, and in its flux by repelling virtue, once through
      a circle and twice through a cochlea finally absorbs by the power at-
      tracting into eternity's focus, [Cut of eternity's abyss. Six lines from]
      Revel. x. 6.   pp. (2), (5)—(59).

        Tenth title: General tables of time's flux.   pp. (20).

        Eleventh title: viii. Arm of the tree of knowledge of good and evil,
      branching forth the natural motion and course of the visible astral
      bodies, collectively—in systems, and abstractedly—in single planets
      and their places. Representation of the orb. [Cut.] Reference to the
      letters in the orb. [Seven lines.] [Signed, J. W. G. de Brahm. Philadel-
      phia, 2nd. 1. month, vulgar 31st iii. month, 1793.]   pp. (23).

24252   DE FOE, DANIEL   1661 – 1731
THE FAMILY-INSTRUCTOR. IN THREE PARTS. RELATING I. TO PARENTS AND CHILD-
REN. II. TO MASTERS AND SERVANTS. III. TO HUSBANDS AND WIVES. AN AMER-
ICAN EDITION.
> *Philadelphia: Printed and sold by Stewart & Cochran, No. 34, South
> Second-Street.* M,DCC,XCII. pp. 319, (1). 12mo.   AAS.

24253   —— THE WONDERFUL LIFE, AND SURPRISING ADVENTURES OF THAT RENOWNED HERO
ROBINSON CRUSOE, WHO LIVED TWENTY-EIGHT YEARS ON AN UNINHABITED ISLAND,
WHICH HE AFTERWARDS COLONISED. [Ornament.]
> *Boston: Printed and sold by J. White and C. Cambridge, near Charles-
> river Bridge.* 1792. pp. [72,] frontispiece, 2 cuts. 24mo.   AAS.

24254   —— — THE WONDERFUL LIFE, AND SURPRISING ADVENTURES OF THAT RENOWNED
HERO ROBINSON CRUSOE.
> *London, Printed; Philadelphia, Reprinted by Charles Cist, No. 104 in
> Second Street,* 1792. pp. 160. 32mo.

24255   DELAWARE. STATE.
LAWS OF THE DELAWARE STATE, PASSED AT A SESSION OF THE GENERAL ASSEMBLY,
COMMENCED AT DOVER, ON THE THIRD DAY OF JANUARY, 1792. [Arms.]
> *Wilmington, Printed by James Adams,* M,DCC,XCII. pp. 31. fol.   LOC.

24256   —— MINUTES OF THE GRAND COMMITTEE OF THE WHOLE CONVENTION OF THE DELA-
WARE STATE, WHICH COMMENCED AT DOVER, ON TUESDAY, THE TWENTY-NINTH
DAY OF NOVEMBER, IN THE YEAR OF OUR LORD ONE THOUSAND SEVEN HUNDRED
AND NINETY-ONE. FOR THE PURPOSE OF REVIEWING, ALTERING, AND AMENDING
THE CONSTITUTION OF THIS STATE; OR, IF THEY SEE OCCASION, FOR FORMING A
NEW ONE IN STEAD THEREOF.
> *Wilmington: Printed by James Adams.* 1792. pp. 80. fol.

24257   —— DRAUGHT OF A CONSTITUTION OF GOVERNMENT: PUBLISHED FOR THE CONSIDER-
ATION OF THE CITIZENS OF THE DELAWARE STATE; PURSUANT TO AN ORDER OF
THE CONVENTION, OF THE 31ST OF DECEMBER, 1791. [Ornament.]
> *Wilmington: Printed by Peter Brynberg and Samuel Andrews, in Market-
> Street.* 1792. pp. (24). 8vo.   LCP. NYPL.

24258   —— MINUTES OF THE CONVENTION OF THE DELAWARE STATE, AT THE SECOND SES-
SION THEREOF, WHICH COMMENCED AT DOVER, ON TUESDAY THE TWENTY-NINTH
DAY OF MAY, IN THE YEAR OF OUR LORD, ONE THOUSAND SEVEN HUNDRED AND
NINETY-TWO, FOR THE PURPOSE OF REVIEWING, ALTERING AND AMENDING THE
CONSTITUTION OF THIS STATE, OR IF THEY SEE OCCASION, FOR FORMING A NEW
ONE INSTEAD THEREOF.
> *Wilmington: Printed by Peter Brynberg and Samuel Andrews.* [1792.]
> pp. 107. fol.

24259   —— THE CONSTITUTION OF THE STATE OF DELAWARE. [Ornaments.]
> *Wilmington: Printed by Brynberg and Andrews in Market-Street.* 1792.
> pp. (42). 8vo.   LOC. NYPL.

24260   THE DELAWARE GAZETTE. NO. 354. SATURDAY, JANUARY 7, [—NO. 405. SATUR-
DAY, DECEMBER 29, 1792.]
> *Wilmington: Printed and sold by Peter Brynberg and Samuel Andrews, in
> Market-street.* . . . 1792. fol.

24261   DELL, WILLIAM   – 1664
LEHRE VON DER TAUFE, DIE VON IHREN ALTEN UND NEUEREN VERFÄLSCHUNGEN
BEFREYET UND NACH IHRER URSPRÜNGLICHEN REINIGKEIT UND WAHRHEIT WIE-
DER HERGESTELLT WIRD. AUS DEM ENGLISCHEN ÜBERSETZT.
> *Philadelphia: Gedruckt bey Carl Cist.* 1792. pp. 63; 32. 16mo.

DELL, WILLIAM, continued.
Second title: ZWEI SENDSCHREIBEN AUS SEWELLS GESCHICHTE DER QUÄKER.
Philadelphia: Gedruckt bey Carl Cist. 1792. pp. 32.

24262 —— PRÜFUNG DER GEISTER SOWOHL IN DEN LEHRERN ALS IN DEN ZUHÖRERN, U. S. W.
Philadelphia: Gedruckt bey Carl Cist. 1792. pp. 80. 8vo.

24263 DE LOLME, JEAN LOUIS   1740 – 1806
THE CONSTITUTION OF ENGLAND; OR, AN ACCOUNT OF THE ENGLISH GOVERNMENT:
IN WHICH IT IS COMPARED, BOTH WITH THE REPUBLICAN FORM OF GOVERNMENT,
AND THE OTHER MONARCHIES IN EUROPE. BY J. L. DE LOLME, ADVOCAT, MEM-
BER OF THE COUNCIL OF THE TWO HUNDRED IN THE REPUBLIC OF GENEVA. A
NEW EDITION, ENLARGED. PONDERIBUS LIBRATA SUIS,— OVID. MET. L. I. 13.
*New-York: Printed by Hodge & Campbell, and sold at their respective
Book-Stores.* M.DCC.XCII. pp. xvi, (25) —376, (8). 8vo.   AAS. LOC.

24264 THE DEVOUT CHRISTIAN'S VADE MECUM: BEING A SUMMARY OF SELECT AND NECES-
SARY DEVOTIONS. CONTAINING AMONG OTHER ARTICLES, THE HYMNS AND PSALMS,
AS SUNG IN ENGLISH, IN THE ROMAN CATHOLIC CHAPELS OF PHILADELPHIA.
Philadelphia: From the Press of Mathew Carey, April 23, MDCCXCII.

24265 DE WITT, SIMEON   1756 – 1834
A MAP OF THE STATE OF NEW YORK. BY SIMEON DE WITT, SURVEYOR-GENERAL.
Albany: 1792. 1st. sheet.   HC.
12th New York District Copyright, issued to Simeon De Witt, as
Author, 26 October, 1792.

24266 THE DIARY; OR, LOUDON'S REGISTER. NO. 1. WEDNESDAY, FEBRUARY 15, [—No.
275. MONDAY, DECEMBER 31, 1792.]
New-York: Published by Samuel Loudon, jun. No. 5, Water-Street; . . .
1792. fol.   NYPL.
Established by Samuel Loudon, junior, as a daily newspaper, in continuation of the *New-York Packet,* published by Samuel Loudon, senior,
from 1776, which suspended publication in January, 1792. In August, 1792, the paper was enlarged to four columns, with a change of
types in the heading, and "junior" was dropped from the publisher's
name. Beginning in January, 1793, the Diary was printed by Samuel
Loudon and Son. In January, 1794, by Loudon and Brower, as *The
Diary; or, evening register.* And, in January, 1795, again by Samuel
Loudon, junior, as *The Diary, & universal daily advertiser*—the word
"daily" was dropped in August. In 1796, *The Diary* was printed by
Cornelius C. Van Allen and Company. In January, 1797, it was print-
ed by Crookes and Saunders, for John I. Johnson; and, after June 17th,
John Crookes, for the Proprietor, as *The Diary and mercantile advertiser.*
In 1799, the title was shortened to, *Mercantile advertiser*—at first,
Printed and published by James Chevalier; and, from October 1st,
by John Crookes, for the Proprietor. Afterwards it was published by
Crookes and Butler; and, by Amos Butler. Continued under this title
after the year 1835.

24267 DICKINSON, JONATHAN   1688 – 1747
FAMILIAR LETTERS TO A GENTLEMAN, UPON A VARIETY OF SEASONABLE AND IMPORT-
ANT SUBJECTS IN RELIGION. BY JONATHAN DICKINSON, A. M. MINISTER OF THE
GOSPEL AT ELIZABETH-TOWN, NEW-JERSEY. [Nine lines of Scripture texts.]
*Philadelphia: Printed for William Young, No. 52, Second-street, the cor-
ner of Chesnut-street.* M.DCC.XCII. pp. iv, [4], 9–455, (1). 12mo.   AAS. JCB.

24268   DILWORTH, Thomas   −1780

A New guide to the English tongue: in five parts. Containing i. Words, both common and proper, from one to six syllables: the several sorts of monosyllables in the common words being distinguished by tables, into words of two, three and four letters, &c. With six short lessons at the end of each table, not exceeding the order of syllables in the foregoing tables. The several sorts of polysyllables, also, being ranged in proper tables, have their syllables divided, and directions placed at the head of each table for the accent to prevent false pronunciation; together with the like number of lessons on the foregoing tables, placed at the end of each table as far as to words of four syllables, for the easier and more speedy way of teaching children to read. ii. A large and useful table of words. that are the same in sound, but different in signification: very necessary to prevent the writing one word for another of the same sound. iii. A short, but comprehensive grammar of the English tongue, delivered in the most familiar and instructive method of question and answer, necessary for all such persons as have the advantage only of an English education. iv. An useful collection of sentences in prose and verse divine, moral and historical.; together with a select number of fables adorned with proper sculptures for the better improvement of the young beginners. And v. Forms of prayer for children on several occasions. The whole, being recommended by several clergymen and eminent schoolmasters, as the most useful performance for the instruction of youth, is designed for the use of schools in Great-Britain, Ireland, and in the several English colonies and plantations abroad. The forty-eighth edition. By Thomas Dilworth, author of the Schoolmaster's assistant; Young book-keeper's assistant, &c.

Hartford: Printed and sold by Nathaniel Patten. MDCCXCII. pp. (2), 150, portrait. 12mo.
                                        NYPL.

24269   ────── The Schoolmasters assistant: being a compendium of arithmetic, both practical and theoretical. In five parts. Containing, i. Arithmetic in whole numbers, wherein all the common rules, having each of them a sufficient number of questions, with their answers, are methodically and briefly handled. ii. Vulgar fractions, wherein several things, not commonly met with, are distinctly treated of, and laid down in the most plain and easy manner. iii. Decimals, in which among other things, are considered the extraction of roots; interest, both simple and compound; annuities: rebate, and equation of payments. iv. A large collection of questions with their answers, serving to exercise the foregoing rules, together with a few others, both pleasant and diverting. v. Duodecimals, commonly called cross multiplication: wherein that sort of arithmetic is thoroughly considered, and rendered very plain and easy; together with the method of proving all the foregoing operations at once, by division of several denominations, without reducing them into the lowest terms mentioned. The whole being delivered in the most familiar way of question and answer, is recommended by several eminent mathematicians, accomptants, and schoolmasters, as necessary to be used in schools by all teachers, who would have their scholars thoroughly understand, and make a quick progress in arithmetic. To which is prefixt, An Essay on the education of youth; humbly offered to the consideration of parents. The twenty-fourth edition. By Thomas Dilworth, author of the New guide to the English tongue; Young book-keeper's assistant, &c. &c. and schoolmaster in Wapping. [Six lines.]

New-York: Printed and sold by Hugh Gaine, Bookseller and Stationer, at the Bible, in Hanover-Square—M,DCC,XCII. pp. xiv, (6), (2), (2), 192, folded table. 12mo.
                                        AAS.

DILWORTH, Thomas, continued.

24270 —— — The Schoolmaster's assistant; being a compendium of arithmetic, both practical and theoretical. In five parts. Containing, I. Arithmetic in whole numbers, . . . II. Vulgar fractions, . . . III. Decimals, . . . IV. A large collection of questions, . . . Duodecimals, . . . The whole being delivered in the most familiar way of question and answer, . . .
Wilmington: Printed by Brynberg and Andrews, in Market-Street. 1792. Portrait. 12mo.

24271 —— A New guide to the English tongue: in five parts. Containing I. Words both common and proper; . . . II. A large and useful table of words, that are the same in sound, but different in signification; . . . III. A short but comprehensive grammar of the English tongue, . . IV. An useful collection of sentences in prose and verse, . . . V. Forms of prayer for children, on several occasions. The whole being recommended by several clergymen, and eminent schoolmasters.
New-York: 1792. 12mo.

24272 DODDRIDGE, Philip 1702 – 1751
Christ formed in the soul, the only foundation of hope for eternity. A sermon, addressed to young persons. By P. Doddridge. Gal. IV. 19. [Two lines.]
Providence: Reprinted by John Carter. M,DCC,XCII. pp. (30), (1). 8vo.
AAS. LOC. NYPL. RIHS.

24273 —— A Sermon, urging the care of the soul, as the one thing needful. By P. Doddridge, D. D.. One thing is needful. Luke x. 42.
Providence: Reprinted by John Carter. M,DCC,XCII. pp. (28). 8vo.
AAS. MHS. NYHS. NYPL. RIHS.

24274 —— Some remarkable passages in the life of the Hon. Col. James Gardiner, who was slain at the battle of Preston Pans, September 21, 1745. To which is added, the Sermon, occasioned by his heroick death. By P. Doddridge, D. D. [Two lines of Latin from] Virg.
Printed at Boston, by I. Thomas and E. T. Andrews, Faust's Statue, No. 45, Newbury Street. M,DCC,XCII. pp. 254. 12mo. AAS. JCB. NYPL.

24275 DODSLEY, Robert 1703 – 1764
The Œconomy of human life. Complete, in two parts: translated from an Indian manuscript, written by an ancient Bramin. To which is prefixed, an account of the manner in which the said manuscript was discovered; in a letter from an English gentleman residing in China, to the Earl of *******.
New-Haven: Printed and sold by Abel Morse, 1792. pp. 102. 12mo.

24276 —— — The Œconomy of human life. Complete, in two parts: translated from an Indian manuscript, written by an ancient Bramin. To which is prefixed, an account of the manner in which the said manuscript was discovered; in a letter from an English gentleman residing in China, to the Earl of *******
New-York: Printed by Hugh Gaine, at the Bible, in Hanover-Square. 1792.

DODSLEY, ROBERT, continued.

24277 —— — THE OECONOMY OF HUMAN LIFE. IN TWO PARTS. TRANSLATED FROM AN INDIAN MANUSCRIPT WRITTEN BY AN ANCIENT BRAMIN. TO WHICH IS PREFIXED AN ACCOUNT OF THE MANNER IN WHICH THE SAID MANUSCRIPT WAS DISCOVERED. IN A LETTER FROM AN ENGLISH GENTLEMAN, RESIDING IN CHINA, TO THE EARL OF * * *

Norwich: Printed by John Trumbull, M,D,CC,XCII. pp. 136. 16mo. AAS.

24278 —— — THE OECONOMY OF HUMAN LIFE. IN TWO PARTS. TRANSLATED FROM AN INDIAN MANUSCRIPT, WRITTEN BY AN ANCIENT BRAMIN. TO WHICH IS PREFIXED, AN ACCOUNT OF THE MANNER IN WHICH THE SAID MANUSCRIPT WAS DISCOVERED. IN A LETTER FROM AN ENGLISH GENTLEMAN IN CHINA, TO THE EARL OF —— .

Windsor: Printed by Alden Spooner. 1792.

24279 DÖRING, FRIEDRICH CHRISTLIEB
THAT THE GOSPEL OF JESUS CHRIST, ACCORDING TO ROM. I. 16. CONTINUES TO PROVE ITSELF AS THE POWER OF GOD UNTO SALVATION, ABLE TO RECLAIM AND SAVE THE MOST DEPRAVED HEARTS, IS ILLUSTRATED BY THE EXAMPLE OF AUGUST SOLOMON DŒRING, HAVING EXPERIENCED GRACE; THE NARRATIVE OF WHICH IS NOW PUBLISHED TO THE HONOUR AND GLORY OF GOD, BY HIS OWN BROTHER FREDERICK CHRISTLIEB DŒRING, MINISTER OF THE GOSPEL AT MAIWALDAW, IN SILESIA. TRANSLATED FROM THE GERMAN.

Philadelphia: Printed by Charles Cist:—and to be sold by Tobias Hirte, No. 118, North Second-Street, [next door to Widow Rasor], M,DCC,XCII. pp. (2), [70.] 12mo.
AAS.

A printed slip pasted on the cover reads: This Book is to be had at the following places, viz. Philadelphia, of Jacob Ritter, in Front-street 3d door below Arch-street. Baltimore, Nicholas Tshudy, in Market-street. Fredericktown, Jacob Steiner. Hagarstown, Peter Hœfly. Yorktown, Ernst Schlosser and John Morris. Lancaster, Matthæus Hehl. Readingtown, Erhard Roos and Gottlob Youngman. Germantown, Peter Leibert and Justus Fox. Hope, Frederick Peter.

24280 DUNCAN, WILLIAM   1717 – 1760
THE ELEMENTS OF LOGIC. IN FOUR BOOKS. BOOK I. OF THE ORIGINAL OF OUR IDEAS, THEIR VARIOUS DIVISIONS, AND THE MANNER IN WHICH THEY CONTRIBUTE TO THE INCREASE OF KNOWLEDGE; WITH A PHILOSOPHICAL ACCOUNT OF THE RISE, PROGRESS, AND NATURE OF HUMAN LANGUAGE. BOOK II. OF THE GROUNDS OF HUMAN JUDGMENT, THE DOCTRINE OF PROPOSITIONS, THEIR USE IN REASONING, AND DIVISION INTO SELF EVIDENT AND DEMONSTRABLE. BOOK III. OF REASONING, AND DEMONSTRATION, WITH THEIR APPLICATION TO THE INVESTIGATION OF KNOWLEDGE, AND THE COMMON AFFAIRS OF LIFE. BOOK IV. OF THE METHODS OF INVENTION AND SCIENCE, WHEN THE SEVERAL DEGREES OF EVIDENCE ARE EXAMINED, THE NOTION OF CERTAINTY IS FIXED AND STATED, AND THE PARTS OF KNOWLEDGE IN WHICH IT MAY BE ATTAINED, DEMONSTRATED AT LARGE. DESIGNED PARTICULARLY FOR YOUNG GENTLEMEN AT THE UNIVERSITY, AND TO PREPARE THE WAY TO THE STUDY OF PHILOSOPHY AND THE MATHEMATICS. BY WILLIAM DUNCAN, PROFESSOR OF PHILOSOPHY IN MARISCHAL COLLEGE, ABERDEEN. [Two lines of Latin from] HOR. THE FIRST AMERICAN EDITION.

Philadelphia: From the Press of Mathew Carey. August 10,—M,DCC,-XCII. pp. 239, (1). 12mo.
AAS. JCB.

24281   DUNCAN, WILLIAM
THE NEW-YORK DIRECTORY, AND REGISTER, FOR THE [sic] YEAR 1792. ILLUSTRA-
TED WITH A NEW AND ACCURATE PLAN OF THE CITY, AND PART OF LONG-ISLAND,
EXACTLY LAID DOWN, AGREEABLY TO THE LATEST SURVEY.—CONTAINING—THE
NAMES, OCCUPATIONS, AND PLACES OF ABODE OF THE CITIZENS, ARRANGED IN
ALPHABETICAL ORDER; A LIST OF ENGINEERS AND FIREMEN OF THE CITY OF NEW-
YORK; A REGISTER OF THE EXECUTIVE, LEGISLATIVE, AND JUDICIAL MAGISTRATES
OF THE UNITED STATES, AND OF THE STATE OF NEW-YORK; THE MINISTERIAL
AND CONSULAR APPOINTMENTS FROM THE UNITED STATES TO FOREIGN POWERS,
AND FROM FOREIGN POWERS TO THE UNITED STATES; THE GOVERNORS OF THE
DIFFERENT STATES; THE OFFICERS BOTH CIVIL AND MILITARY, OF THE CITY
AND COUNTY OF NEW-YORK.—ALSO—AN ACCOUNT OF THE DIFFERENT SOCIETIES,
AND CHARITABLE AND LITERARY INSTITUTIONS IN THE CITY; WITH THE NAMES OF
THEIR OFFICERS.—TO WHICH IS ADDED—A LIST OF DUTIES PAYABLE ON GOODS,
WARES AND MERCHANDIZE, IMPORTED INTO THE UNITED STATES.—AND—A CHRON-
OLOGICAL TABLE OF REMARKABLE EVENTS WHICH HAVE HAPPENED SINCE THE
FIRST DISCOVERY OF AMERICA. BY WILLIAM DUNCAN.

*New-York: Printed for the Editor, by T. and J. Swords, No. 27, William-
Street.—1792.—[Price three shillings and six pence.]* pp. viii, 230, plan. 12mo.
NYPL.

24282   DUNLAP'S AMERICAN DAILY ADVERTISER. No. 4035. MONDAY, JANUARY 1, [—No.
4347. MONDAY, DECEMBER 31, 1792.]

*Philadelphia: Printed by John Dunlap, at No. 48, Market-Street, op-
posite the Jersey-Market.* 1792. fol.   AAS. LOC.

24283   DUTCH, EBENEZER
A DISCOURSE DELIVERED BEFORE THE ASSOCIATION, AT THE DEDICATION OF A NEW
MEETING-HOUSE, AUGUST 9, 1791. BY EBENEZER DUTCH, A. M. PASTOR OF THE
SECOND CHURCH IN BRADFORD.

Newburyport: Printed and sold by John Mycall. MDCCXCII. pp. 48.
8vo.   AAS. BPL. JCB. LOC.

24284   DWIGHT, THEODORE   1764 – 1846
AN ORATION, SPOKEN BEFORE THE SOCIETY OF THE CINCINNATI, OF THE STATE OF
CONNECTICUT, MET IN HARTFORD, ON THE 4TH OF JULY, 1792. BY THEODORE
DWIGHT, ESQUIRE. [Publishers monogram.]

Printed at Hartford, by Hudson and Goodwin. MDCCXCII. pp. 18. 8vo.
AAS. HC. LOC.

24285   EAMES, JONATHAN   1730 – 1800
WALKING WITH GOD, CONSIDERED AND IMPROVED, IN A SERMON, DELIVERED AT
NEWBURY, APRIL 29, 1792. OCCASIONED BY THE DECEASE OF THE REV. JOHN
TUCKER, D. D. PASTOR OF THE FIRST CHURCH THERE. WHO DEPARTED THIS
LIFE, MARCH 22, 1792. BY JONATHAN EAMES, A. M. PASTOR OF A CHURCH IN
NEWTOWN, NEW-HAMPSHIRE.

Newburyport: Printed and sold by John Mycall, 1792. pp. (48). 8vo.
AAS. BA. BM. BPL. JCB. MHS. NYHS. NYPL.

24286   EASTERN HERALD. MONDAY, JANUARY 2, [—MONDAY, DECEMBER 31, 1792.]

*Printed and published by Thomas B. Wait, opposite the Haymarket, Port-
land.* 1792. fol.

In continuation of the *Cumberland Gazette.*

24287　ECKLEY, JOSEPH　　　　　　　　　　　　　1750 – 1811
A SERMON, PREACHED AT THE REQUEST OF THE ANCIENT AND HONOURABLE AR-
TILLERY COMPANY, JUNE 4, 1792: BEING THE ANNIVERSARY OF THEIR ELECTION
OF OFFICERS. BY JOSEPH ECKLEY, A. M. MINISTER OF THE OLD SOUTH CHURCH
IN BOSTON. [Ornament.]
　　　Boston: Printed by Samuel Hall.　MDCCXCII. pp. [30.] 8vo.
　　　　　　　　　　　　　　　　　　　AAS. BA. BM. HC. JCB. LOC.

24288　EDWARDS, JONATHAN　　　　　　　　　　　1703 – 1758
A HISTORY OF THE WORK OF REDEMPTION. CONTAINING THE OUTLINES OF A BODY
OF DIVINITY, IN A METHOD ENTIRELY NEW. BY THE LATE REVEREND MR. JONA-
THAN EDWARDS. THE THIRD AMERICAN EDITION.
　　　*Printed at Worcester, Massachusetts, by Isaiah Thomas & Leonard Worces-
ter, for Isaiah Thomas.*　MDCCXCII. pp. 355. 8vo.　　　AAS.

24289　—— AN HUMBLE INQUIRY INTO THE RULES OF THE WORD OF GOD, CONCERNING THE
QUALIFICATIONS REQUISITE TO A COMPLETE STANDING AND FULL COMMUNION IN
THE VISIBLE CHRISTIAN CHURCH. BY THE LATE JONATHAN EDWARDS, A. M.
　　　Wilmington: Printed by James Adams, sen.　1792.

24290　EDWARDS, JONATHAN　　　　　　　　　　　1745 – 1801
ALL DIVINE TRUTH PROFITABLE: ILLUSTRATED IN A SERMON PREACHED AT HAMDEN
[sic], JANUARY 11TH, 1792. AT THE ORDINATION OF THE REV. DAN BRADLEY,
TO THE PASTORAL CHARGE OF THE FIRST CHURCH IN WHITES-TOWN, IN THE STATE
OF NEW-YORK. BY JONATHAN EDWARDS, D. D. PASTOR OF A CHURCH IN NEW-
HAVEN.
　　　New-Haven: Printed by A. Morse.　MDCCXCII. pp. (42). 8vo.
　　　　　　　　　　　　　　　　　AAS. JCB. NYHS. NYPL.

24291　—— FAITH, AND A GOOD CONSCIENCE, ILLUSTRATED IN A SERMON, DELIVERED AT THE
ORDINATION OF THE REVEREND WILLIAM BROWN, TO THE PASTORAL OFFICE IN
THE FIRST CHURCH IN GLASTENBURY, ON THE 27TH. OF JUNE, 1792; AND PRINTED
AT THE REQUEST OF THE HEARERS. BY JONATHAN EDWARDS, D. D. PASTOR OF A
CHURCH IN NEW-HAVEN.
　　　New-Haven: Printed by A. Morse.　MDCCXII [sic 1792.] pp. (33). 4to.
　　　　　　　　　　　　　　　　AAS. BM. CHS. JCB. NYPL.

24292　—— THE INJUSTICE AND IMPOLICY OF THE SLAVE TRADE, AND OF THE SLAVERY OF
THE AFRICANS: ILLUSTRATED IN A SERMON PREACHED BEFORE THE CONNECTICUT
SOCIETY FOR THE PROMOTION OF FREEDOM, AND FOR THE RELIEF OF PERSONS
UNLAWFULLY HOLDEN IN BONDAGE, AT THEIR ANNUAL MEETING IN NEW-HAVEN,
SEPTEMBER 15, 1791. BY JONATHAN EDWARDS, D. D. PASTOR OF A CHURCH IN
NEW-HAVEN. TO WHICH IS ADDED, A SHORT SKETCH OF THE EVIDENCE FOR THE
ABOLITION OF THE SLAVE TRADE, DELIVERED BEFORE A COMMITTEE OF THE BRIT-
ISH HOUSE OF COMMONS. [Signed, W. B. C. i. e. William Bell Crafton.]
　　　Providence: Printed by John Carter.　M,DCC,XCII. pp. (60). 8vo.
　　　　　　　　　　　　　　　　AAS. JCB. LOC. MHS. RIHS.

24293　—— THE MARRIAGE OF A WIFE'S SISTER CONSIDERED IN A SERMON DELIVERED IN
THE CHAPEL OF YALE-COLLEGE, IN THE EVENING AFTER THE COMMENCEMENT,
SEPTEMBER 12, A. D. 1792; BEING THE ANNIVERSARY CONCIO AD CLERUM. BY
JONATHAN EDWARDS, D. D. PASTOR OF A CHURCH IN NEW-HAVEN.
　　　Printed at New-Haven, by T. and S. Green.　[1792.] pp. (27). 8vo.
　　　　　　　　　　　　　　　　AAS. BA. BM. JCB. NYPL.

•24294   EDWARDS, Morgan   1722 – 1795
MATERIALS TOWARDS A HISTORY OF THE BAPTISTS IN JERSEY; DISTINGUISHED INTO FIRSTDAY BAPTISTS, SEVENTHDAY BAPTISTS, TUNCKER BAPTISTS, ROGERENE BAPTISTS. VOL. II. BY MORGAN EDWARDS, A. M. AND QUONDAM FELLOW OF R. I. COLLEGE. . . .

> *Philadelphia: Printed by Thomas Dobson, at the Stone-House, in Second-Street.* MDCCXCII. pp. vii, 155, (1). 12mo.   AAS. HSP. JCB.

The first volume was published in 1770.

24295   ELLICOTT, Andrew   1754 – 1820
ELLICOTT'S VIRGINIA, MARYLAND, AND PENNSYLVANIA ALMANAC, AND EPHEMERIS, FOR THE YEAR OF OUR LORD, 1793.

> *Baltimore: Printed and sold by John Hayes.* [1792.]

24296   —— A PLAN OF THE CITY OF WASHINGTON, IN THE TERRITORY OF COLUMBIA, CEDED BY THE STATES OF VIRGINIA AND MARYLAND TO THE UNITED STATES OF AMERICA, AND BY THEM ESTABLISHED, AS THE SEAT OF THEIR GOVERNMENT, AFTER THE YEAR 1800.

> *Philadelphia: 1792.*   BM.

Andrew Ellicott completed the Plan begun by L'Enfant, and his improved Plan was engraved in Philadelphia, and Boston, in 1792.

24297   ELLWOOD, Thomas   1639 – 1713
DAVIDEIS. THE LIFE OF DAVID, KING OF ISRAEL. A SACRED POEM. BY THOMAS ELLWOOD. THE SIXTH EDITION.

> *Dover, (New-Hampshire), Re-printed by Eliphalet Ladd,* 1792. 4to. MHS.

24298   ELY, John
THE CHILD'S INSTRUCTOR CONSISTING OF EASY LESSONS FOR CHILDREN ON SUBJECTS WHICH ARE FAMILIAR TO THEM IN LANGUAGE ADAPTED TO THEIR CAPACITIES. BY A TEACHER OF LITTLE CHILDREN IN PHILADELPHIA. [One line from] ST. PAUL. VOLUME I.

> *Philadelphia: 1792.*

35th Pennsylvania District Copyright, issued to John Ely, as Author, 24 September, 1792.

24299   EMERSON, John   1745 – 1826
ALL THE WORKS OF CHRIST IN CREATION AND PROVIDENCE, EXECUTED BY INFINITE WISDOM AND GOODNESS: ILLUSTRATED IN A FUNERAL SERMON. ON THE DEATH OF MRS. SARAH LEAVITT, THE VIRTUOUS AND AMIABLE CONSORT OF THE REV. MR. JONATHAN LEAVITT, WHO DIED SUDDENLY, AT HEATH, OCTOBER 11TH, IN THE 49TH YEAR OF HER AGE. BY JOHN EMERSON, A. M. PASTOR OF THE CHURCH IN CONWAY. [Four lines of Scripture texts.]

> *Printed at Greenfield, Massachusetts, by Thomas Dickman.* MDCCXCII. pp. 26. 8vo.   AAS. BA. JCB.

24300   ENCYCLOPÆDIA; OR, A DICTIONARY OF ARTS, SCIENCES, AND MISCELLANEOUS LIT-
ERATURE; CONSTRUCTED ON A PLAN, BY WHICH THE DIFFERENT SCIENCES AND
ARTS ARE DIGESTED INTO THE FORM OF DISTINCT TREATISES ON SYSTEMS, COM-
PREHENDING THE HISTORY, THEORY, AND PRACTICE, OF EACH, ACCORDING TO THE
LATEST DISCOVERIES AND IMPROVEMENTS; AND FULL EXPLANATIONS GIVEN OF THE
VARIOUS DETACHED PARTS OF KNOWLEDGE, WHETHER RELATING TO NATURAL AND
ARTIFICIAL OBJECTS, OR TO MATTERS ECCLESIASTICAL, CIVIL, MILITARY, COM-
MERCIAL, &C. INCLUDING ELUCIDATIONS OF THE MOST IMPORTANT TOPICS RELA-
TIVE TO RELIGION, MORALS, MANNERS, AND THE OECONOMY OF LIFE: TOGETHER
WITH A DESCRIPTION OF ALL THE COUNTRIES, CITIES, PRINCIPAL MOUNTAINS, SEAS,
RIVERS, &C. THROUGHOUT THE WORLD; A GENERAL HISTORY, ANCIENT AND MOD-
ERN, OF THE DIFFERENT EMPIRES, KINGDOMS, AND STATES; AND AN ACCOUNT OF
THE LIVES OF THE MOST EMINENT PERSONS IN EVERY NATION, FROM THE EARL-
IEST AGES DOWN TO THE PRESENT TIMES. COMPILED FROM THE WRITINGS OF THE
BEST AUTHORS, IN SEVERAL LANGUAGES; THE MOST APPROVED DICTIONARIES, AS
WELL OF GENERAL SCIENCE AS OF ITS PARTICULAR BRANCHES; THE TRANSAC-
TIONS, JOURNALS, AND MEMOIRS OF VARIOUS LEARNED SOCIETIES, THE MS. LEC-
TURES OF EMINENT PROFESSORS ON DIFFERENT SCIENCES; AND A VARIETY OF
ORIGINAL MATERIALS, FURNISHED BY AN EXTENSIVE CORRESPONDENCE. THE
FIRST AMERICAN EDITION, IN EIGHTEEN VOLUMES, GREATLY IMPROVED. ILLUS-
TRATED WITH FIVE HUNDRED AND FORTY-TWO COPPERPLATES. VOL. V. CIC—
DIA. [VOL. VI. DIA—ETH. VII. ETM—GOA.] INDOCTI DISCANT ET AMENT MEM-
INISSE PERITI.

> *Philadelphia: Printed by Thomas Dobson, at the Stone House, No.* 41,
> *South Second Street.* [1792.] 3vols. pp. 807, (1), 24 plates (138–161); 794, 22
> plates (162–183); 797, (1), 38 plates (184–221). 4to.

AAS. APS. LCP. LOC. MHS. NYHS. NYPL. WC.

24301   ENGLAND. CHURCH OF
     A CATECHISM OR AN INTRODUCTION TO BE LEARNED BY EVERY PERSON BEFORE HE
BE BROUGHT TO BE CONFIRMED BY THE BISHOP.

> *Richmond: Printed by Thomas Nicolson,* 1792.

24302   EPICTETUS   60 –
     [*Greek title.*] [EPICTETI ENCHIRIDION.] EX EDITIONE JOANNIS UPTON ACCURATE
EXPRESSUM.

> *Philadelphiæ: Impensis Mathæi Carey.* MDCCXCII. pp. 22; 23. 24mo.

AAS. LOC.

24303   ERSKINE, EBENEZER   1680 – 1754
     SERMONS UPON THE MOST IMPORTANT AND INTERESTING SUBJECTS. BY THE LATE
REVEREND EBENEZER ERSKINE, MINISTER OF THE GOSPEL AT STIRLING. THE
FIRST AMERICAN EDITION.

> *Philadelphia: Printed by John M'Culloch, No.* 1, *North Third-street.*
> M.DCC.XCII. pp. 511, (2). 12mo.   AAS. JCB.

     Contains an eight-page list of Subscribers' names.

24304   THE ESSEX JOURNAL & NEW-HAMPSHIRE PACKET. NUMB. 393. WEDNESDAY, JAN-
UARY 4, [—NUMB. 445. WEDNESDAY, DECEMBER 26, 1792.]

> *Newburyport: Printed by John Mycall, in Merrimack-Street, a little below
> the Ferry-way,* . . . 1792. fol.   AAS. LOC. NYHS.

24305   AN EULOGIUM AND VINDICATION OF MASONRY. SELECTED AND IMPROVED FROM
VARIOUS WRITERS.

> *Philadelphia: Printed by William Woodhouse,* 1792. pp. 29. 8vo.

24306   EXTRACT FROM AN ESSAY ON THE CULTURE OF SILK.

> *Burlington: Printed by Isaac Neale.* 1792.

24307   THE FARMER AND CITIZEN: DIALOGUE.
[Philadelphia: 1792.] Broadside.

24308   THE FARMER'S JOURNAL. VOL. II. No. 43. MONDAY, JANUARY 2, [—VOL. III. No. 43. SATURDAY, DECEMBER 29, 1792.]
Published in Danbury, (Connecticut) by Douglas and Ely. 1792. fol. AAS.
Beginning July 7th, the day of publication was changed to Saturday.

24309   THE FARMER'S REGISTER. VOL. I. No. 1. SATURDAY, SEPTEMBER 29, [—No. 14. SATURDAY, DECEMBER 29, 1792.]
Kingston, (Ulster County) Printed by Nicholas Power and William Copp. 1792. fol.
Established by Nicholas Power and William Copp. In September, 1793, at the close of the first volume, Nicholas Power withdrew, and William Copp established, with a new serial numbering, the *Rising Sun*, associating Samuel Freer with him in its publication. This arrangement apparently continued into the year 1798, when, in May, Samuel Freer and Son established, with a new serial numbering, the *Ulster and Delaware Gazette*, changing its title, in the following year, to *Ulster Gazette*, under which name it was continued after the year 1810, being published in that year by Samuel S. Freer.

24310   A FATHER'S ADVICE TO HIS CHILD; OR THE MAIDEN'S BEST ADORNING.
Exeter: Printed by Henry Ranlet—1792. [Ornament.] pp. 8. 16mo. BU.

24311   FATHER ABRAHAM'S ALMANACK, FOR THE YEAR OF OUR LORD 1793. CONTAINING (BESIDES ASTRONOMICAL CALCULATIONS) VARIETY OF USEFUL AND ENTERTAINING MATTER.
Philadelphia: Printed by Stewart and Cochran, No. 34, South Second-Street. [1792.]

24312   FATHER NICHOLAS; AN ENTERTAINING STORY, EXEMPLIFYING THE POWER OF CORRUPT SOCIETY AND FALSE SHAME, OVER THE NATURAL FEELINGS OF VIRTUE.
Printed by M. Croswell, & Co. Catskill-Landing. 1792.

24313   THE FEDERAL GAZETTE AND PHILADELPHIA DAILY ADVERTISER. VOL. VIII. No. 1012. MONDAY, 2D JANUARY, [—VOL. IX. No. 1321. MONDAY, 31 DECEMBER, 1792.]
Printed and published by Andrew Brown, at Washington's Head, in Chesnut-Street, near Front-Street, . . . 1792. fol. LCP.
Beginning September 1st, the paper was enlarged to royal folio.

24314   THE FEDERAL SPY. VOL. I. No. 1. TUESDAY. DECEMBER 18, [—No. 2. TUESDAY, DECEMBER 25, 1792.]
Springfield—(Massachusetts)—Published by James R. Hutchins, at the corner of the entrance to the Court-House. 1793. fol. AAS.
Established by James Reed Hutchins and continued by him into the year 1794, when he quit publication. In December, 1794, John Worthington Hooker and Francis Stebbins, continued its publication into the year 1796, when Hooker withdrew in May of that year, and Stebbins continued publication alone into the year 1800, being succeeded by Timothy Ashley, Ashley & Brewer, and Henry Brewer, until publication ceased in the year 1805. Beginning with the issue for 29 January, 1793, the title was changed to *Federal Spy and Springfield Advertiser*; and, on 24 December, 1793, to *Federal Spy and Springfield Weekly Advertiser*, changing again, in 1794, to *The Federal Spy*, which was continued to the end.

24315   FEDERAL TONTINE ASSOCIATION.
        CONSTITUTION OF THE FEDERAL TONTINE ASSOCIATION.
            Philadelphia: 1792. pp. 15. 8vo.
                                                            MHS.

24316   FENNING, DANIEL
        THE READY RECKONER: OR TRADERS USEFUL ASSISTANT, IN BUYING AND SELLING
        ALL SORTS OF COMMODITIES, EITHER WHOLESALE OR RETAIL. SHEWING AT ONE
        VIEW THE AMOUNT OR VALUE OF ANY NUMBER OR QUANTITY OF GOODS OR MER-
        CHANDISE, FROM HALF A FARTHING TO TWENTY SHILLINGS, EITHER BY THE LONG
        OR SHORT HUNDRED, HALF HUNDRED OR QUARTER, POUND OR OUNCE, ELL OR YARD,
        &C. &C. IN SO PLAIN AND EASY A MANNER, THAT PERSONS QUITE UNACQUAINTED
        WITH ARITHMETICK MAY HEREBY ASCERTAIN THE VALUE OF ANY NUMBER OF HUN-
        DREDS, POUNDS, OUNCES, ELLS OR YARDS, &C. AT ANY PRICE WHATEVER: AND TO
        THE MOST READY IN FIGURES, IT WILL BE EQUALLY USEFUL, BY SAVING MUCH TIME
        IN CASTING UP WHAT IS HERE CORRECTLY DONE TO THEIR HAND. TO WHICH IS
        ADDED, A TABLE OF SIMPLE AND COMPOUND INTEREST. BY DANIEL FENNING.
            Printed for Isaiah Thomas. Sold at his Bookstore in Worcester, Massachu-
        setts, and by him and Company in Boston. MDCCXCII. pp. (2), (2), 166. nar.
        8vo.
                                                            AAS.

24317   FIELDING, HENRY   1707 – 1754
        THE BEAUTIES OF FIELDING: CAREFULLY SELECTED FROM THE WORKS OF THAT EMI-
        NENT WRITER. TO WHICH IS ADDED, SOME ACCOUNT OF HIS LIFE. FIRST AMERI-
        CAN EDITION.
            Philadelphia: From the Press of M. Carey, Oct. 27, M.DCC.XCII. pp. (vi),
        143. 24mo.
                                                            AAS.

24318   —— THE HISTORY OF TOM JONES, A FOUNDLING.
            Philadelphia: Printed and sold by W. Woodhouse, at the Bible, No. 6,
        South Front-street. 1792.

24319   THE FIRST PRINCIPLES OF PRACTICAL CHRISTIANITY, LAID DOWN IN QUESTION AND
        ANSWER, FOR THE MOST PART EXPRESSED IN THE VERY WORDS OF SCRIPTURE.
            Lancaster: Printed by William Dickson, in King Street. 1792.

24320   FLEET, THOMAS, and JOHN
        FLEETS POCKET ALMANACK FOR THE YEAR OF OUR LORD 1793. BEING THE FIRST
        AFTER LEAP-YEAR, AND SEVENTEENTH OF AMERICAN INDEPENDENCE CALCULATED
        CHIEFLY FOR THE USE OF THE COMMONWEALTH OF MASSACHUSETTS, BOSTON, THE
        METROPOLIS, BEING IN THE LATITUDE 42 DEG. 25 MIN. NORTH LONGITUDE 71 DEG.
        4 MIN. WEST FROM THE ROYAL OBSERVATORY AT GREENWICH. TO WHICH IS
        ANNEXED, THE MASSACHUSETTS REGISTER, &C.
            Boston: Printed and sold by T. & J. Fleet, at the Bible and Heart in Corn-
        hill. [1792.] pp. [20]; [143], (1). 24mo.   AAS. BA. HC. LOC. MHS. NYPL.
        35th Massachusetts District Copyright, issued to Thomas & John Fleet,
        as Proprietors, 11 October, 1792.

24321   FLEMING, FRANCIS A.   – 1793
        THE CALUMNIES OF VERUS: OR, CATHOLICS VINDICATED FROM CERTAIN OLD SLAND-
        ERS REVIVED; IN A SERIES OF LETTERS PUBLISHED IN DIFFERENT GAZETTES AT
        PHILADELPHIA. COLLECTED AND REVISED BY "VERAX," WITH THE ADDITION OF
        A PREFACE AND A FEW NOTES.
            Philadelphia: Printed by Johnston & Justice, 1792.

24322   FLETCHER, OF DE LA FLECHIERE, JOHN WILLIAM   1729 – 1785
        THE WORKS OF THE REV. JOHN FLETCHER. VOLUME III. THE FIRST AMERICAN
        EDITION.
            Philadelphia: Printed by Joseph Cruikshank: Sold by John Dickins, No.
        182, *in Race-Street, near Sixth-Street.* 1792. pp. 340. 12mo.   AAS. JCB.

24323 | FOLIE, A. P.
PLAN OF THE TOWN OF BALTIMORE AND ITS ENVIRONS. BY A. P. FOLIE.
Philadelphia: 1792.   HC.

24324 | FORD, TIMOTHY   1762 – 1830
AN ENQUIRY INTO THE CONSTITUTIONAL AUTHORITY OF THE SUPREME FEDERAL
COURT, OVER THE SEVERAL STATES, IN THEIR POLITICAL CAPACITY. BEING AN
ANSWER TO OBSERVATIONS UPON THE GOVERNMENT OF THE UNITED STATES OF
AMERICA. BY JAMES SULLIVAN, ESQ. ATTORNEY GENERAL OF THE STATE OF
MASSACHUSETTS. BY A CITIZEN OF SOUTH-CAROLINA. [Signed, Hortensius.
Charleston, April 12, 1792.]
Charleston: Printed by W. P. Young, Broad-Street. M.DCC.XCII. pp.
(49). 8vo.   BA. HC. JCB. LOC. NYHS. NYPL.
Attributed wrongly, also, to David Ramsay.

24325 | FOSTER, EDMUND   1752 – 1826
THE MINISTRY OF RECONCILIATION ILLUSTRATED. A SERMON, PREACHED AT THE
ORDINATION OF THE REV. JONATHAN OSGOOD, TO THE PASTORAL CARE OF THE
CHURCH AND CONGREGATION IN GARDNER, OCTOBER 19, MDCCXCI. BY EDMUND
FOSTER, A. M. PASTOR OF THE CHURCH OF CHRIST IN LITTLETON.
*Printed at Worcester, Massachusetts, by Isaiah Thomas & Leonard Wor-
cester.* MDCCXCII. pp. 40. 8vo   AAS. BA. HC. JCB. NYPL. UTS. YC.

24326 | FOSTER, JOEL
Half-title: MR. FOSTER'S SERMON AT THE INTERMENT OF THE REV. SAMUEL
KENDALL. NEW-SALEM, FEBRUARY 3, 1792.
Title: A DISCOURSE, OCCASIONED BY THE DEATH, AND DELIVERED AT THE INTER-
MENT, OF REV. SAMUEL KENDALL, A. M. FORMER MINISTER OF NEW-SALEM; WHO
DIED THE 31ST OF JANUARY, AND WAS INTERRED THE 3D OF FEBRUARY, 1792, IN
THE 85TH YEAR OF HIS AGE. BY JOEL FOSTER, A. M. PASTOR OF THE CHURCH IN
NEW-SALEM. [Two lines from] ST. PAUL.
Springfield: Printed by Ezra Waldo Weld. MDCCXCII. pp. 18. 8vo. AAS.

24327 | FOTHERGILL, SAMUEL   1715 – 1772
THE NECESSITY AND DIVINE EXCELLENCY OF A LIFE OF PURITY AND HOLINESS, SET
FORTH WITH PATHETIC ENERGY, BY AN EMINENT MINISTER AMONG THE PEOPLE
CALLED QUAKERS. IN SEVEN DISCOURSES AND THREE PRAYERS, AND AN EPISTLE
TO HIS BRETHREN IN RELIGIOUS PROFESSION IN THE ISLAND OF TORTOLA. NOW
COLLECTED AND REPUBLISHED, THAT THE INSTRUCTIVE AND IMPORTANT TRUTHS
THEREIN CONTAINED, MAY BE SPREAD, AND BECOME GENERALLY USEFUL. GATHER
UP THE FRAGMENTS, THAT NOTHING BE LOST. JOHN VI. 12. THE FIRST SALEM
EDITION. FROM MR. CRUKSHANK'S PHILADELPHIA EDITION OF 1783.
*Salem: (Massachusetts): Printed and sold by Thomas C. Cushing.—Sold
also by William Carlton, at his Shop opposite the Rev. Mr. Prince's meeting-house.*
M.DCC.XCII. pp. 112. 8vo.   AAS. BA.
Second title: TWO DISCOURSES, AND A PRAYER. PUBLICLY DELIVERED, ON SUNDAY
THE SEVENTH AND TUESDAY THE NINETEENTH DAYS OF MAY, 1767, AT THE
QUAKERS' YEARLY MEETING, AT THE FRYERS, IN BRISTOL. THE WHOLE TAKEN
DOWN IN CHARACTERS, BY A MEMBER OF THE CHURCH OF ENGLAND. TO WHICH
IS ADDED, A PREFACE.
Salem: Printed by T. C. Cushing; and sold by W. Carlton, Main-Street.
M.DCC.XCII. pp. (2), 15—37.

FOTHERGILL, Samuel, continued.

Third title: The Prayer of Agur illustrated in a funeral discourse; and the advantages resulting from an early steadfast piety. Preached extempore. By the Author of Two discourses and a prayer, publicly delivered at the Quakers' yearly meeting in Bristol. The whole taken down in characters, by a Member of the Church of England.

    Salem: Printed by T. C. Cushing; and sold by W. Carlton, Main-Street. M.DCC.XCII. pp. (2), 43—68.

Fourth title: The Grace of our Lord Jesus Christ, the love of God, and a divine communion, recommended and inforced in a sermon, publicly delivered at a meeting of the people called Quakers, held in Leeds, the 26th of the sixth month, commonly called June, 1769. Carefully taken down in characters, at the same time, by James Blakes, jun.

    Salem: Printed by T. C. Cushing; and sold by W. Carlton, Main-Street. M.DCC.XCII. pp. (1), 70—87.

Fifth title: Repent and be converted: a sermon, preached at a meeting of the people called Quakers, 1768. Also, the Heads of a sermon, preached at Horsleydown meeting, upon the close of a visit to Friends families in that quarter, the 19th of the eleventh month, 1769.

    Salem: Printed by T. C. Cushing; and sold by W. Carlton, Main-Street. M.DCC.XCII. pp. (2), 91—112.

24328   FOWLER, Andrew   1760 – 1850
    A Short introduction to christian knowledge, designed particularly for the use of the Protestant Episcopal Church at East-Woods, Oysterbay.

    New-York: 1792. pp. 31. 16mo.   HC. LOC.

24329   FOX, Thomas
    The Wilmington Almanack, or ephemeris, for the year of our Lord 1793.

    Wilmington: [1792.]

24330   FRANCE. Kingdom.
    The French Constitution, decreed by the National Assembly, at the session of the years 1789, 1790, and 1791, and accepted by the King on the 13th and 14th of September, 1791; with the Declaration of rights of man and citizen, and the Message of the King to the National Assembly, on the 13th of September, 1791; his Speech on accepting and ratifying it, in the Assembly; and the Answer of M. Thouvet, then president of the National Assembly, with this motto—"Vivre, libre ou mourir!" "To live free, or to die!" Translated from the French, with the greatest care and accuracy, and preceded by an introduction of the translator, dedicated to the republicans of the new world. By a Friend of Liberty.—D. F. Dounant.

    Alexandria: Printed by Hanson and Bond, 1792. pp. 50? 8vo.

24331   THE FREEMAN'S [cut] Journal; or, the North-American intelligencer. Open to all parties, but influenced by none. Numb. dlix. Wednesday, January 4, [—Numb. dlxxviii. Wednesday, May 16, 1792.]

    Philadelphia, Printed by Francis Bailey, at Yorick's Head, in High-Street. 1792. fol.

    With the issue for May 16th, publication of the Freeman's Journal ceased.

24332   FRIENDS. SOCIETY OF
THE EPISTLE FROM THE YEARLY-MEETING, HELD IN LONDON, BY ADJOURNMENTS,
FROM THE 21ST TO THE 29TH OF THE FIFTH MONTH, 1792, INCLUSIVE, TO THE
QUARTERLY AND MONTHLY MEETINGS OF FRIENDS IN GREAT-BRITAIN, IRELAND,
AND ELSEWHERE.
        [Philadelphia? 1792.] pp. (4). fol.   AAS.

24333   —— SOME TRANSACTIONS BETWEEN THE INDIANS AND FRIENDS IN PENNSYLVANIA,
IN 1791 AND 1792.
        Philadelphia? 1792. pp. 16. 8vo.

24334   FROTHINGHAM'S LONG-ISLAND HERALD. [Motto.] VOL. I. No. 35. TUESDAY,
JANUARY 3, [—VOL. II. No. 84. THURSDAY, DECEMBER 27, 1792.]
        Sagg-Harbour, Printed by David Frothingham, near the Landing. 1792. fol.

24335   GAIFER, pseudonym.
THE CONVERSION OF A MEHOMETAN, TO THE CHRISTIAN RELIGION, DESCRIBED IN A
LETTER FROM GAIFER, IN ENGLAND, TO HIS FRIEND IN TURKEY.
        Catskill Landing: Printed by M. Croswell & Co. 1792.

24336   GAINE, HUGH   1726 – 1807
HUGH GAINE'S CATALOGUE OF BOOKS, LATELY IMPORTED FROM ENGLAND, IRELAND,
AND SCOTLAND, AND TO BE SOLD AT HIS BOOK-STORE AND PRINTING-OFFICE, AT
THE BIBLE IN HANOVER-SQUARE. [Ornament.]
        New-York: Printed by Hugh Gaine.—1792.—pp. 24. 8vo.   NYPL.

24337   —— GAINE'S UNIVERSAL REGISTER; OR, COLUMBIAN KALENDAR, FOR THE YEAR OF
OUR LORD 1793: BEING THE FIRST AFTER BISSEXTILE, AND OF THE AMERICAN
EMPIRE THE SEVENTEENTH. [New York arms.]
        New-York: Printed by Hugh Gaine, at the Bible, in Hanover-Square.
M,DCC,XCIII. [1792.] pp. (214), (2). 24mo.   HC. LOC.

24338   GARDINER, JOHN   1731 – 1793
THE SPEECH OF JOHN GARDINER, ESQ. DELIVERED IN THE HOUSE OF REPRESENT-
ATIVES. ON THURSDAY, THE 26TH OF JANUARY, 1792; ON THE SUBJECT OF THE
REPORT OF THE COMMITTEE, APPOINTED TO CONSIDER THE EXPEDIENCY OF RE-
PEALING THE LAW AGAINST THEATRICAL EXHIBITIONS WITHIN THIS COMMON-
WEALTH. [Nineteen lines of quotations.]
        Printed at Boston, by Joseph Bumstead, for the Author. MDCCXCII. pp.
vii, (65). 8vo.   AAS.
        Printed on thick paper. Contains the Speech only.

24339   —— — GARDINER ON THE THEATRE, OR, THE SPEECH OF JOHN GARDINER, ESQ.
DELIVERED IN THE HOUSE OF REPRESENTATIVES, ON THURSDAY, THE 26TH OF
JANUARY LAST, ON THE SUBJECT OF THE REPORT OF THE COMMITTEE, APPOINTED
TO CONSIDER THE EXPEDIENCY OF REPEALING THE LAW AGAINST THEATRICAL
EXHIBITIONS WITHIN THIS COMMONWEALTH; WITH AN ADDRESS TO THE PUBLICK,
MANY CRITICAL AND HISTORICAL NOTES, AND A BEAUTIFUL FRONTISPIECE, ENGRAV-
ED BY CALLENDER, REPRESENTING THE GROUND PART OF THE ANCIENT GREEK
THEATRE, PRICE THREE SHILLINGS, STITCHED ON BLUE PAPER. [Eight lines from]
POPE. TO WHICH ARE ADDED, A LETTER TO THE AUTHOR, ON THE THEATRE, BY A
FRIEND; AND A DISSERTATION ON THE ANCIENT POETRY OF THE ROMANS; WITH
INCIDENTAL OBSERVATIONS ON CERTAIN SUPERSTITIONS, &C.
        *Boston: Printed by Benjamin Russell, and to be had at Mr. John Ewing's
Grocery-Store, No. 42, Marlborough-Street; of the Author, and of no other persons
in town.* 1792.

GARDINER, JOHN, continued.

24340 —— — THE SPEECH OF JOHN GARDINER, ESQ. DELIVERED IN THE HOUSE OF REP-
RESENTATIVES, OF THURSDAY THE 26TH OF JANUARY LAST, ON THE SUBJECT OF
THE REPORT OF THE COMMITTEE, APPOINTED TO CONSIDER THE EXPEDIENCY OF
REPEALING THE LAW AGAINST THEATRICAL EXHIBITIONS WITHIN THIS COMMON-
WEALTH; WITH AN ADDRESS TO THE PUBLIC, MANY CRITICAL AND HISTORICAL
NOTES, AND A BEAUTIFUL FRONTISPIECE, ENGRAVED BY CALLENDER, REPRESENT-
ING THE GROUND PART OF THE ANCIENT GREEK THEATRE. [Eight lines from]
POPE. TO WHICH ARE ADDED, A LETTER TO THE AUTHOR, ON THE THEATRE;
BY A FRIEND; AND A DISSERTATION, ON THE ANCIENT POETRY OF THE ROMANS;
WITH INCIDENTAL OBSERVATIONS ON CERTAIN SUPERSTITIONS, &C.

Newburyport: Printed (?) Sold by John Mycall. 1792.

24341 —— — THE SPEECH OF JOHN GARDINER, ESQUIRE. DELIVERED IN THE HOUSE
OF REPRESENTATIVES. ON THURSDAY, THE 26TH OF JANUARY, 1792; ON THE
SUBJECT OF THE REPORT OF THE COMMITTEE, APPOINTED TO CONSIDER THE EX-
PEDIENCY OF REPEALING THE LAW AGAINST THEATRICAL EXHIBITIONS WITHIN
THIS COMMONWEALTH. [Twenty-six lines of quotations.]

Printed at the Apollo Press, in Boston, for the Author. MDCCXCII. pp.
159, (1), plate. 8vo.   AAS. BA. BM. BPL. HC. JCB. LCP. LOC. MHS. NYHS. NYPL.

Contains, a Plan of the ancient Greek theatre. The Letter to the
Author, on the Theatre [As referred to in page 99.] pp. 103–108.
And, A Dissertation on the ancient poetry of the Romans: with inci-
dental observations on certain superstitions, &c. pp. 110–159.
The copy in the Massachusetts Historical Society, contains manuscript
notes by the author.
27th Massachusetts District Copyright, issued to John Gardiner, as
Author, 20 March, 1792. 3d Maine District Copyright, issued to
John Gardiner, esq. as Author, 9 April, 1792.

24342 GAY, BUNKER   – 1815
A DISCOURSE IN TWO PARTS, DELIVERED AT HINSDALE, JULY 29, 1792; AND THE
SABBATH AFTER AT CHESTERFIELD: OCCASIONED BY THE DEATH OF MRS. ABIGAIL
GAY. WHO DEPARTED THIS LIFE JULY 15TH, 1792. . . . [Two lines of quo-
tations.]

Printed at Greenfield, Massachusetts, by Thomas Dickman. MDCCXCII.
pp. 24. 8vo.   HC. LOC.

24343 —— A GENUINE AND CORRECT ACCOUNT OF THE CAPTIVITY, SUFFERINGS & DE-
LIVERANCE OF MRS. JEMIMA HOWE, OF HINSDALE, IN NEW-HAMPSHIRE. TAKEN
FROM HER OWN MOUTH, AND WRITTEN, BY THE REV. BUNKER GRAY [*sic* GAY],
A. M. MINISTER OF HINSDALE, IN A LETTER TO THE AUTHOR OF THE HISTORY OF
NEW-HAMPSHIRE [JEREMY BELKNAP], EXTRACTED FROM THE THIRD VOLUME OF
SAID HISTORY, BY CONSENT OF SAID AUTHOR. IN THIS ACCOUNT THE MISTAKES
OF COL. HUMPHREYS, RELATING TO MRS. HOWE, IN HIS "LIFE OF GENERAL
PUTNAM," ARE RECTIFIED.

*Printed at the Apollo Press, in Boston, by Belknap and Young, north side
of the State-House, State-Street.* MDCCXCII. pp. 20. 8vo.   AAS. LOC. MHS.

$13

24344 GAZETTE OF MAINE. VOL. II. NO. 14. THURSDAY, JANUARY 5, [——NO. 117. SAT-
URDAY, DECEMBER 29, 1792.]

Portland, (District of Maine) Published by Benjamin Titcomb, jun. 1792.
fol.   AAS.

24345   *General title:* THE GAZETTE OF THE UNITED STATES. PUBLISHED AT THE SEAT OF GOVERNMENT. BEGINNING APRIL 27, 1791,—AND ENDING MAY 29, 1792; CONTAINING THE LAWS AND RESOLUTIONS OF THE LEGISLATURE OF THE UNION, PASSED AT THE FIRST SESSION OF THE SECOND CONGRESS, AND SKETCHES OF DEBATES IN THE HOUSE OF REPRESENTATIVES; ALSO A SERIES OF ORIGINAL ESSAYS, UPON THE MOST INTERESTING SUBJECTS OF LIFE, MANNERS, &C. VOL. THIRD. U S A.

       Philadelphia: Printed by the Editor (John Fenno) at his office in High-Street. 1792. pp. 456. fol.   LOC.

    Heading: GAZETTE OF THE UNITED STATES. NO. 72. OF VOL. III. WHOLE NO. 280. WEDNESDAY, JANUARY 4, [—NO. 61. OF VOL. IV. WHOLE NO. 383. SATURDAY, DECEMBER 29, 1792.]

       [A National paper.] Published Wednesdays and Saturdays by *John Fenno, No. 69, High-Street, between Second and Third-Streets, Philadelphia.* 1792. pp. 285–456; 1–244. fol.   LOC.

24346   GENERAL ADVERTISER. NUM. 393. MONDAY, JANUARY 2, [—NUM. 705. MONDAY, DECEMBER 31, 1792.]

       Published (daily) by Benj. Franklin Bache, up Franklin-Court, in Market, between Third and Fourth-Streets, Philadelphia. 1792. fol.   AAS. HC. LCP.

    From November 20th, the Printing-Office was "at No. 112, Market-street."

24347   A GEOGRAPHICAL CLOCK: CALCULATED FOR THE MERIDIAN OF THIS CITY; EXHIBITING AT ONE VIEW, THE TIME OF DAY OR NIGHT IN EVERY PART OF THE GLOBE; WITH A FULL DESCRIPTION, IN LETTER PRESS, OF THE CLOCK AND THEIR PLANISPHERE OF THE EARTH, AND A COPIOUS INDEX OF ALL THE PRINCIPAL KINGDOMS, ISLANDS AND CITIES IN THE WORLD, WITH THE LONGITUDE AND LATITUDE RECKONED FROM THE MERIDIAN OF PHILADELPHIA.

       Philadelphia: Printed and sold by Francis Bailey, No. 116, Market street, and by the principal Booksellers in this city. 1792.

24348   THE GEORGE-TOWN WEEKLY LEDGER. VOL. II. NO. 39. WHOLE NO. 91. SATURDAY, JANUARY 7, [—VOL. III. NO. 38. WHOLE NO. 142. SATURDAY, DECEMBER 28, 1792.]

       George-Town: Printed by Alexander Doyle. 1792. fol.

    In April, James Doyle, succeeded Alexander Doyle as Publisher.

24349   GEORGIA. STATE.
    AN ACT FOR ESTABLISHING AND REGULATING PATROLS, AND FOR PREVENTING ANY PERSON FROM PURCHASING PROVISIONS OR ANY OTHER COMMODITIES FROM, OR SELLING SUCH TO ANY SLAVE, UNLESS SUCH SLAVE SHALL PRODUCE A TICKET FROM HIS OR HER OWNER, MANAGER OR EMPLOYER. PASSED IN NOVEMBER 1765.

       Augusta: Printed by John E. Smith. 1792.

24350   —— AN ACT FOR GOVERNING SLAVES WITHIN THIS STATE, AND FOR ESTABLISHING A JURISDICTION FOR THE TRIAL OF OFFENCES COMMITTED BY SUCH SLAVES AND OTHER PERSONS THEREIN MENTIONED; AND TO PREVENT THE INVEIGLING AND CARRYING AWAY SLAVES FROM THEIR MASTERS, OWNERS AND EMPLOYERS. PASSED IN MAY 1770.

       Augusta: Printed by John E. Smith, 1792.

24351   —— JOURNALS OF THE LAST SESSION OF BOTH BRANCHES OF THE LEGISLATURE.

       Augusta: Printed by John E. Smith, 1792.

24352   —— LAWS PASSED AT THE LAST GENERAL ASSEMBLY.

       Augusta: Printed by John E. Smith, 1792.

24353   GEORGIA. CIRCUIT COURT.
THE OPINIONS OF THE JUDGES DELIVERED IN THE CIRCUIT COURT FOR THE DISTRICT OF GEORGIA, ON THE 2D OF MAY LAST, IN THE CASE OF MESSRS BRAILSFORD AND OTHERS VERSUS JAMES SPALDING; ALSO DOUGLAS VERSUS THE EXECUTORS OF STIRK.
Savannah: Printed by James & Nicholas Johnston, 1792. pp. 36. 8vo. NYHS.

24354   THE GEORGIA GAZETTE. NO. 467. THURSDAY, JANUARY 5, [—NO. 515. THURSDAY, DECEMBER 27, 1792.]
Savannah: Printed by James and Nicholas Johnston, Broughton-Street, 1792. fol.   GHS.

24355   GEORGIA. THE AUGUSTA CHRONICLE AND GAZETTE OF THE STATE. [Motto.] VOL. VI. NO. CCLXXIV. SATURDAY, JANUARY 7, [—NO. 325. SATURDAY, DECEMBER 29, 1792.]
Augusta; Printed by John E. Smith, Printer to the State. 1792. fol. GHS.

24356   DIE GERMANTAUNER ZEITUNG. NUM. 77. DIENSTAG, DEN 3TEN JANUAR, [— NUM. 128. DIENSTAG, DEN 25TEN DECEMBER, 1792.]
Diese Zeitung wird wochentlich Dienstag Nachmittags herausgegeben von Michael Billmeyer, Buchdrucker, zu Germantaun; fur einen halben Thaler des Jahrs. Ein Viertel Thaler wird beym Einschreiben bezahlt. 1792. 4to.   HSP.

24357   GIBSON, ROBERT
A TREATISE OF PRACTICAL SURVEYING; WHICH IS DEMONSTRATED FROM ITS FIRST PRINCIPLES. WHEREIN EVERY THING THAT IS USEFUL AND CURIOUS IN THAT ART, IS FULLY CONSIDERED AND EXPLAINED. PARTICULARLY THREE NEW AND VERY CONCISE METHODS FOR DETERMINING THE AREAS OF RIGHT-LINED FIGURES ARITH-METICALLY, OR BY CALCULATION, AS WELL AS THE GEOMETRICAL ONES HERETO-FORE TREATED OF. THE WHOLE ILLUSTRATED WITH COPPER-PLATES. THE SIXTH EDITION. BY ROBERT GIBSON, TEACHER OF THE MATHEMATICS. WITH ALTERATIONS AND AMENDMENTS, ADAPTED TO THE USE OF AMERICAN SURVEYORS.
Philadelphia: Printed by Joseph Crukshank, No. 87, High-Street, 1792. pp. viii, 288; (2), (2), 90, (2), 60, 12 plates. 8vo.   AAS.

Second title: MATHEMATICAL TABLES: DIFFERENCE OF LATITUDE AND DEPART-URE: LOGARITHMS, FROM 1 TO 10,000. ARTIFICIAL SINES, TANGENTS, AND SECANTS.
Philadelphia: Printed and sold by Joseph Crukshank, No. 87, Market-Street. 1794. pp. (2), (2), 90, (2), 60.

Third title: TABLES OF LATITUDE AND DEPARTURE: CONSTRUCTED TO EVERY QUARTER OF A DEGREE OF THE QUADRANT, AND CONTINUED FROM ONE, TO THE DISTANCE OF ONE HUNDRED MILES OR CHAINS. [By John Robertson.] [Ornament.]
Philadelphia: Printed and sold by Joseph Crukshank, in Market-street, between Second and Third-streets. MDCCXC. pp. (2), 90.

24358   GLEASON, EZRA
THOMAS'S MASSACHUSETTS, CONNECTICUT, RHODEISLAND, NEWHAMPSHIRE & VER-MONT ALMANACK, WITH AN EPHEMERIS, FOR THE YEAR OF OUR LORD 1793: BEING THE FIRST YEAR AFTER BISSEXTILE, OR LEAP YEAR, AND SEVENTEENTH OF THE INDEPENDENCE OF UNITED AMERICA. FROM CREATION, ACCORDING TO THE SCRIPTURES, 5755. [Six lines. Cut. Four lines of verse.]
Printed at Worcester, by I. Thomas and L. Worcester, for Isaiah Thomas. . . . [1792.] pp. [48.] 12mo.   AAS. LOC. NYPL. YC.

Contains, An Act more effectually to provide for the national defence, by establishing an uniform militia throughout the United States.

24359   A GOLDEN TREASURE FOR THE CHILDREN OF GOD, WHOSE TREASURE IS IN HEAVEN; CONSISTING OF SELECTED TEXTS OF THE BIBLE, WITH PRACTICAL OBSERVATIONS IN PROSE AND VERSE, FOR EVERY DAY IN THE YEAR. "WHERE YOUR TREASURE IS, THERE WILL YOUR HEART BE ALSO."
         Sold by William Carleton, at the Bible and Heart, Salem. 1792.

24360   GOLDSMITH, OLIVER   1728 – 1774
      THE VICAR OF WAKEFIELD: A NOVEL. BY DR. GOLDSMITH.
         Norwich: Re-printed and sold by Ebenezer Bushnell, 1792.

24361   —— —— THE VICAR OF WAKEFIELD: A TALE. SUPPOSED TO BE WRITTEN BY HIMSELF.
         Providence: Printed by Bennett Wheeler, 1792. 2 vols. in one. 12mo.

24362   GOOKIN, DANIEL   1612 – 1687
      HISTORICAL COLLECTIONS OF THE INDIANS IN NEW ENGLAND. OF THEIR SEVERAL NATIONS, NUMBERS, CUSTOMS, MANNERS, RELIGION, AND GOVERNMENT, BEFORE THE ENGLISH PLANTED THERE. ALSO A TRUE AND FAITHFUL ACCOUNT OF THE PRESENT STATE AND CONDITION OF THE PRAYING INDIANS, (OR THOSE WHO HAVE VISIBLY RECEIVED THE GOSPEL IN NEW ENGLAND:) DECLARING THE NUMBER OF THAT PEOPLE, THE SITUATION AND PLACE OF THEIR TOWNS AND CHURCHES, AND THEIR MANNER OF WORSHIPPING GOD, . . . BRIEFLY DECLARING THE PRUDENT AND FAITHFUL ENDEAVORS OF THE RIGHT HONORABLE THE CORPORATION OF LONDON, FOR PROMOTING THAT AFFAIR; ALSO SUGGESTING SOME EXPEDIENTS FOR THEIR FURTHER CIVILIZING AND PROPAGATING THE CHRISTIAN FAITH AMONG THEM. BY DANIEL GOOKIN.
         Printed at the Apollo Press, in Boston, by Belknap and Hall. MDCCXCII.
      pp. 89. 8vo.   BA. BM. BPL. NYHS. $11
      Also included in the first volume of the Collections of the Massachusetts Historical Society printed this year.

24363   THE GOSHEN REPOSITORY, AND WEEKLY INTELLIGENCER. [Motto.] VOL. III. No. 155. TUESDAY, JANUARY 3, [—VOL. IV. No. 206. TUESDAY, DECEMBER 25, 1792.]
         Goshen: Printed and published by David Mandeville and David M. Westcott, 1792. fol.
      Sometime this year David Mandeville withdrew, Wescott continuing publication alone.

24364   GRAFTON, JOSEPH   1757 – 1836
      A SERMON OCCASIONED BY THE DEATH OF JONATHAN SHEPARD, JAMES WARD, AND MICHAEL BRIGHT, WHO DIED OF SMALLPOX, 1792.
         Boston: 1792.

24365   GREEN, ASHBEL   1762 – 1848
      LETTER TO THE PREACHER OF LIBERAL SENTIMENTS.
         [Philadelphia:] 1792. 12mo.   HC.

24366   GREEN, TIMOTHY
      GREEN'S REGISTER, FOR THE STATE OF CONNECTICUT: [Ornamental line.] WITH AN ALMANACK, FOR THE YEAR OF OUR LORD, 1793, CALCULATED BY NATHAN DABOLL, FOR THE MERIDIAN OF NEW-LONDON, LAT. 41. 25. NORTH.
         New-London: Printed by T. Green & Son. [1792.] pp. 92; (15). 12mo.
                                          CHS. NL. RIHS. YC.

24367   GREENFIELD GAZETTE. VOL I. No. 27, THURSDAY, AUGUST 2, [—No. 48. THURSDAY, DECEMBER 27, 1792.]
         Greenfield: Printed by Thomas Dickman. 1792. fol.
      In continuation of the *Impartial intelligencer.*

24368 GROSS. —
AN HISTORICK RECITAL, OF THE DIFFERENT OCCURRENCES IN THE CAMPS OF GRAND-RIVIERE, DONDON, SAINTE-SUZANNE, AND OTHERS, FROM THE 26TH OF OCTOBER, 1791, TO THE 24TH OF DECEMBER, OF THE SAME YEAR. BY MR. GROSS, ATTORNEY SYNDIC OF VALIERE, TAKEN PRISONER BY JOHNNY.
Baltimore: 1792. 12mo.

24369 THE GUARDIAN; OR. NEW-BRUNSWICK ADVERTISER. VOL. I. NO. 1. WEDNESDAY, NOVEMBER 7, [—No. 8. WEDNESDAY, DECEMBER 26, 1792.]
New-Brunswick, New-Jersey: Printed by Arnett & Blauvelt. 1792. fol.
Established by Shelly Arnett and Abraham Blauvelt, in succession to *The Brunswick Gazette, and weekly monitor.* In the fall of 1793, the partnership was dissolved, Abraham Blauvelt assuming the entire control and continuing its publication for twenty years or more.

24370 GURNEY, THOMAS 1705 – 1770
Half-title: GURNEY'S BRACHYGRAPHY IMPROVED.
Title: AN EASY AND COMPENDIOUS SYSTEM OF SHORT-HAND; ADAPTED TO THE ARTS AND SCIENCES, AND TO THE LEARNED PROFESSIONS. FOR THE USE OF SCHOOLS. ABSTRACTED FROM THE LARGER EDITION. BY THOMAS SARJEANT. [Four lines of verse.] ILLUSTRATED WITH TEN COPPER-PLATES. [Second American edition.]
Philadelphia: Printed by T. Lang; sold by T. Dobson. 1792. pp. 21, (1), portrait, 9 plates. 12mo.
          AAS. LOC.
"Revised, corrected, abridged, and rendered so familiar and easy, that a complete knowledge of the art may be obtained without the assistance of a tutor, from a few hours application only, and reduced to a convenient size for a pocket book."

24371 HALIBURTON, WILLIAM
EFFECTS OF THE STAGE ON THE MANNERS OF A PEOPLE: AND THE PROPRIETY OF ENCOURAGING A VIRTUOUS THEATRE. BY A BOSTONIAN. [Vignette.]
Boston: Printed by Young and Etheridge, Market-Square. Sold by them and the several Booksellers. MDCCXCII. pp. 75, (1). plate. 8vo.
        AAS. BA. BM. LOC. MHS. **$16**
Contains, A ground plan of the proposed theatre. Also, A Letter from a friend to the Author, giving a summary of the advantages included in his system. 38th Massachusetts District Copyright, issued to William Haliburton, as Author, 18 October, 1792.

24372 HALL, JAMES 1744 – 1826
A SERMON, BASED ON PROVERBS XIV. 34, PREACHED AT THE OPENING OF A COURT IN SOUTH CAROLINA.
Charleston: 1792.

24373 —— A SERMON PREACHED AT THE ORDINATION OF SAMUEL C. CALDWELL, AS PASTOR OF SUGAR-CREEK CHURCH.
Charleston: 1792.

24374 HALL, PRINCE
A CHARGE DELIVERED TO THE BRETHREN OF THE AFRICAN LODGE ON THE 25TH OF JUNE, 1792. AT THE HALL OF BROTHER WILLIAM SMITH, IN CHARLESTOWN. BY THE RIGHT WORSHIPFUL MASTER PRINCE HALL. PRINTED AT THE REQUEST OF THE LODGE.
Printed and sold [by Thomas and John Fleet] at the Bible and Heart, Cornhill, Boston. [1792.] pp. (13). 8vo. AAS. HC. MHS. NYPL.

24375 HALL, SAMUEL   1740 – 1807
CATALOGUE OF BOOKS SOLD BY SAMUEL HALL AT NO, 53 CORNHILL, BOSTON.
APRIL, 1792.
[*Boston: Printed by Samuel Hall,* 1792.] Broadside. fol.

24376 HAMILTON, ALEXANDER   1739 – 1802
A TREATISE ON THE MANAGEMENT OF FEMALE COMPLAINTS, AND OF CHILDREN IN
EARLY INFANCY. A NEW EDITION.
New-York: Printed for Samuel Campbell, 1792. pp. 379. 12mo. BA. SGO.

24377 HAMMET, WILLIAM
AN APPEAL TO THE TRUTH AND CIRCUMSTANCES. BY WILLIAM HAMMET, E. M. C.
Charleston: Printed for the Author. 1792. 8vo.

24378 —— A REJOINDER: BEING A DEFENCE OF THE TRUTHS, CONTAINED IN AN APPEAL
TO TRUTH AND CIRCUMSTANCES; IN SEVEN LETTERS, ADDRESSED TO THE REVER-
END MR. MORRELL. BY THE AUTHOR OF THE APPEAL.
Charleston: Printed for the Author. 1792. 8vo.

24379 HAMPSHIRE AND BERKSHIRE CHRONICLE. POLITICAL AND HISTORICAL, MORAL AND
ENTERTAINING. OPEN, FREE, AND IMPARTIAL—BUT NOT LICENTIOUS. [Motto.]
VOL. V. NUMB. 253. WEDNESDAY, JANUARY 4, [—VOL. VI. NO. 304. WEDNESDAY,
DECEMBER 26, 1792.
*Printed and published by Ezra Waldo Weld, opposite the Court-House, in
Springfield, (Massachusetts)* 1792. fol.   AAS.
With the issue for December 26th, Ezra Waldo Weld withdrew from its
publication, and was succeeded by Edward Gray.

24380 THE HAMPSHIRE GAZETTE. VOL. VI. NUMB. 279. WEDNESDAY, JANUARY 4, [—
NUMB. 329. WEDNESDAY, DECEMBER 26TH, 1792.]
Northampton, (Massachusetts) Published by William Butler. 1792. fol.
AAS. MHS.

24381 HART, LEVI   1738 – 1808
Half-title: MR. HART'S ANNIVERSARY SERMON FOR FEBRUARY 28TH, 1792.
Title: THE IMPORTANCE OF PARENTAL FIDELITY IN THE EDUCATION OF CHILDREN
ILLUSTRATED, IN A DISCOURSE, ADDRESSED TO THE CONGREGATION IN THE NORTH
SOCIETY OF PRESTON, THE LORD'S-DAY FOLLOWING THE 28TH OF FEB. 1792. BY
LEVI HART, A. M. PASTOR OF A CHURCH IN PRESTON. BEING THE THIRTIETH
ANNIVERSARY OF HIS FIRST SERMON TO THAT PEOPLE. [Four lines of Scripture
texts.]
Norwich, Printed by Bushnell & Hubbard. M,DCC,XCII. pp. 38. 8vo.
AAS. BM. JCB.

24382 —— *Half-title:* MR. HART'S SERMON OCCASIONED BY THE DEATH OF MRS. KING.
Title: GOD THE UNFAILING SOURCE OF COMFORT TO AFFLICTED SAINTS; OR, THE
DIVINE ALL-SUFFICIENCY IN THE DAY OF TROUBLE, ILLUSTRATED IN A DISCOURSE:
DELIVERED AT CHELSEA IN NORWICH, MAY 22, 1791: THE LORD'S-DAY FOLLOW-
ING THE DEATH AND FUNERAL OF MRS. SARAH KING THE AMIABLE AND PIOUS CON-
SORT OF THE REV. WALTER KING. BY LEVI HART, A. M. PASTOR OF A CHURCH
IN PRESTON. [Four lines of Scripture texts.]
Norwich: Printed by Ebenezer Bushnell. M,DCC,XCII. pp. (34). 8vo. AAS.

24383 HARVARD UNIVERSITY.
HARVARD UNIVERSITY, IN CAMBRIDGE. THE ORDER OF THE EXERCISES OF COM-
MENCEMENT. JULY 18, 1792. [Colophon:]
[*Boston:*] (*Typis T. & J. Fleet.*) [1792.] Broadside. fol.   AAS. HC.

HARVARD UNIVERSITY, continued.

24384 —— ILLUSTRISSIMO JOHANNI HANCOCK, ARMIGERO, LL. D. HONORATISSIMO SAMUELI ADAMS, ARMIGERO, LL. D. VICE-GUBERNATORI; CONSILARIIS ET SENATORIBUS REIPUBLICÆ MASSACHUSETTENSIS; REVERENDISQUE ECCLESIARUM IN OPPIDIS SEX VICINIS, PRESBYTERIS, UNIVERSITATIS HARVARDIANÆ CURATORIBUS; REVERENDO JOSEPHO WILLARD, S. T. D. LL. D. PRÆSIDI; [Four lines.] THESES HASCE, JUVENES IN ARTIBUS INITIATI, [Thirty-seven names.] HUMILLIMÈ DEDICANT. . . . HABITA IN COMITIIS UNIVERSITATIS CANTABRIGIÆ MASSACHUSETTENSIS DIE JULII XVIII. ANNO SALUTIS MDCCXCII. RERUMQUE PUBLICARUM FŒDERATARUM AMERICÆ SUMMÆ POTESTATIS XVII. [Colophon:]
Bostoniæ: Typis Belknap et Hall. [1792.] Broadside. fol. AAS. BM. HC.

24385 HAVEN, SAMUEL   1727 – 1806
A FUNERAL DISCOURSE, DELIVERED AT THE INTERMENT OF THE REV. BENJAMIN STEVENS, D. D. WHO DEPARTED THIS LIFE, MAY 18, 1791, IN THE 71ST YEAR OF HIS AGE. BY SAMUEL HAVEN, D. D. PASTOR OF THE SOUTH CHURCH IN PORTSMOUTH. [Two lines from] PARABLE OF THE TALENTS.
Newburyport: Printed by John Mycall, M,DCC,XCII. pp. (32). 8vo.
AAS. BM.

24386 HAWEIS, THOMAS   1734 – 1820
HAWEIS' COMMUNICANT'S COMPANION: OR AN EVANGELICAL PREPARATION FOR THE LORD'S SUPPER. IN WHICH THE NATURE OF THE ORDINANCE IS SHEWN—THE DISPOSITIONS REQUISITE FOR A PROFITABLE PARTICIPATION THEREOF—WHEREIN THE CARELESS SINNER IS ADMONISHED—THE FORMALIST DETECTED AND REPROVED—THE FEEBLE-MINDED COMFORTED—THE DOUBTING RELIEVED—THE SINCERE ASSISTED—AND THE FAITHFUL CONFIRMED.
New-York: Printed by Samuel Loudon, 1792.

24387 HAYLEY, WILLIAM   1745 – 1820
THE TRIUMPHS OF TEMPER. A POEM, IN SIX CANTOS. BY WILLIAM HAYLEY, ESQ.
Winchester: Printed and sold by Richard Bowen, 1792.

24388 HAZARD, EBENEZER   1744 – 1817
HISTORICAL COLLECTIONS; CONSISTING OF STATE PAPERS, AND OTHER AUTHENTIC DOCUMENTS; INTENDED AS MATERIALS FOR AN HISTORY OF THE UNITED STATES OF AMERICA. BY EBENEZER HAZARD, A. M. MEMBER OF THE AMERICAN PHILOSOPHICAL SOCIETY, HELD AT PHILADELPHIA, FOR PROMOTING USEFUL KNOWLEDGE; AND FELLOW OF THE AMERICAN ACADEMY OF ARTS AND SCIENCES. VOLUME I. [Three lines of Latin quotation.]
. Philadelphia: Printed by T. Dobson, for the Author. MDCCXCII. pp. iv, [639], [x]. 4to.   AAS. BA. BM. HC. JCB. NL. NYHS. NYPL.
The second volume was printed at Philadelphia, in 1794. 31st Pennsylvania District Copyright, issued to Ebenezer Hazard, as Author, 8 March, 1792.

24389 HEMMENWAY, MOSES   1735 – 1811
A DISCOURSE CONCERNING THE CHURCH; IN WHICH THE SEVERAL ACCEPTATIONS OF THE WORD ARE EXPLAINED AND DISTINGUISHED; THE GOSPEL COVENANT DELINEATED: A RIGHT OF ADMISSION AND ACCESS TO SPECIAL ORDINANCES, IN THEIR OUTWARD ADMINISTRATION, AND INWARD EFFICACY, STATED AND DISCUSSED. DESIGNED TO REMOVE THE SCRUPLES AND RECONCILE THE DIFFERENCES OF CHRISTIANS. BY MOSES HEMMENWAY, D. D. PASTOR OF THE CONGREGATIONAL CHURCH IN WELLS. [One line from] ISAIAH LVII, 14.
Printed at Boston by I. Thomas and E. T. Andrews, Faust's Statue, No. 45, Newbury street. MDCCXCII. pp. 123. 8vo.
AAS. BA. BM. HC. JCB. LOC. MHS. NYHS. NYPL.
"Such is the reputation of this work that nearly two thousand subscribers for it have been obtained, besides what are on more than a hundred subscription papers that are not yet returned."

HEMMENWAY, Moses, continued.

24390 —— A DISCOURSE TO CHILDREN. BY THE REV. MOSES HEMMENWAY, D. D. ALSO, THE CONVERSION AND DEATH OF JOSEPH: AN AFFECTING STORY, FOUNDED ON FACT. EMBELLISHED WITH TWO ELEGANT ENGRAVINGS. PUBLISHED ACCORDING TO ACT OF CONGRESS.

> *Printed at Portland, by Thomas B. Wait.* 1792. pp. 23, 2 plates. 12mo.
> Second District of Maine Copyright, issued to Elijah Kellogg, as Proprietor, 6 December, 1791.

24391 —— A SERMON DELIVERED AT SOMERSWORTH, MARCH 11TH, AT THE INTERMENT OF THE REVEREND JAMES PIKE, A. M. WHO DIED MARCH 8, 1792, IN THE NINETIETH YEAR OF HIS AGE, AND SIXTY-FIFTH OF HIS MINISTRY. BY MOSES HEMMENWAY, D. D.

> *Dover: Printed by Eliphalet Ladd, for the Subscribers, at his Printing-Office near the Court-House.* M,DCC,XCII. pp. 28. 8vo. AAS. BA. BPL. JCB. LOC.

24392 HERALD OF THE UNITED STATES. NO. 1. OF VOL. I. WHOLE NO. 1. SATURDAY, JANUARY 14, [— NO. 51. OF VOL. I. WHOLE NO. 51. SATURDAY, DECEMBER 29, 1792.]

> *Printed and published on Saturdays, by Nathaniel Phillips, [at the Post Office] in Warren, State of Rhode-Island, &c.* 1792. pp. 204. fol.
> Established by Nathaniel Phillips, and continued by him until after the year 1807. In 1810 and 1811, publication was made in the name of John F. Phillips. In 1794, "Printer to the honorable the General Assembly of the State of Rhode-Island and Providence Plantations" was added to the imprint. A peculiarity of publication is that the numbers are consecutively paged from the first number up to, certainly, the issue for 8 April, 1805, and perhaps later.

24393 THE HERALD OF VERMONT; OR RUTLAND COURIER. [Motto.] VOL. I. No. 1. MONDAY, JUNE 25, [—No. 12. MONDAY, SEPTEMBER 10, 1792.]

> *Printed in Rutland, at the south west angle of the Court House Square, [every Monday morning] by Anthony Haswell.* 1792. fol.
> Established by Anthony Haswell, and publication suspended, and never resumed, after twelve numbers had been issued, owing to a fire which destroyed the Printing-Office. The Legislature, then sitting in Rutland, in October, passed an Act granting him the privileges of a Lottery to raise two hundred pounds to replace his loss, but this failed to accomplish the purpose. The motto reads: "Let sentiment blow free, and candour guide—We own no party and espouse no side."

24394 HERVEY, JAMES   1713 – 1758
MEDITATIONS AND CONTEMPLATIONS. BY JAMES HERVEY, A. M. LATE RECTOR OF WESTON-FAVELL, NORTHAMPTONSHIRE.

> *New-York: Printed by Hugh Gaine, at the Bible in Hanover-Square.* 1792. 2 vols. in one.

24395 HINDMARSH, ROBERT   1759 – 1835
A SHORT ACCOUNT OF THE HONOURABLE EMANUEL SWEDENBORG, AND HIS THEOLOGICAL WRITINGS.

> *London, printed. Baltimore—Re-printed and sold by Samuel and John Adams.* M,DCC,XCII. pp. (4), 23, (1). 16mo.   BA.
> Appended is a List of books by R. Hindmarsh.

24396   HIRTE, Tobias
EIN NEUES, AUSERLESENES GEMEINNÜTZIGES HAND–BÜCHLEINS FÜR DIE DEUTSCHEN
IN AMERIKA. VON TOBIAS HIRTE, PHILADELPHIA.
Chesnuthill: Gedruckt bey Samuel Saur. 1792. pp. 96. 12mo.   HSP.
37th Pennsylvania District Copyright, issued to Tobias Hirte, as
Author, 19 November, 1792.

24397   HISTORY OF MASTER FRIENDLY: TOGETHER WITH A NUMBER OF FABLES: SELECTED
FROM ÆSOP.
Boston: Printed and sold by N. Coverly, 1792. pp. 16. 32mo.   AAS.

24398   THE HISTORY OF THE HOLY JESUS. CONTAINING A BRIEF AND PLAIN ACCOUNT OF
HIS BIRTH, LIFE, AND DEATH, RESURRECTION AND ASCENSION INTO HEAVEN; AND
HIS COMING AGAIN AT THE GREAT AND LAST DAY OF JUDGMENT. BEING A PLEAS-
ANT AND PROFITABLE COMPANION FOR CHILDREN COMPOSED ON PURPOSE FOR
THEIR USE. BY A LOVER OF THEIR PRECIOUS SOULS.
Boston: Printed and sold by Samuel Hall, No. 53 *Cornhill.* 1792. pp.
58, (4), frontispiece. 32mo.
   JCB.

24399   —— THE HISTORY OF THE HOLY JESUS. CONTAINING A BRIEF AND PLAIN ACCOUNT
OF HIS BIRTH, LIFE, DEATH, RESURRECTION AND ASCENSION INTO HEAVEN; AND
HIS COMING AGAIN AT THE GREAT AND LAST DAY OF JUDGMENT. BEING A PLEAS-
ANT AND PROFITABLE COMPANION FOR CHILDREN; COMPOSED ON PURPOSE FOR
THEIR USE. BY A LOVER OF THEIR PRECIOUS SOULS.
Portsmouth: Printed and sold by John Melcher, 1792.

24400   HOARE, PRINCE   1754 – 1834
NO SONG, NO SUPPER. AN OPERA IN TWO ACTS. WITH ADDITIONAL SONGS. AS PER-
FORMED WITH GREAT APPLAUSE BY THE OLD AMERICAN COMPANY OF COMEDIANS.
Philadelphia: From the Press of Mathew Carey, No. 118 *Market Street.*
1792.

24401   DER HOCH-DEUTSCHE AMERICANISCHE CALENDER, AUF DAS JAHR 1793. NACH
DER GNADEN REICHEN, GEBURT UNSERS HERRN UND HEYLANDES JESU CHRISTI,
(WELCHES EIN GEMEINES JAHR VON 365 TAGEN IST.) [Eight lines.] ZUM NEUN-
TENMAL HERAUS GEGEBEN.
Germantuun, gedruckt und zu finden bey Michael Billmeyer. [Six lines.]
[1792.] pp. (40). 4to.
   AAS. LOC.

24402   HOLCROFT, THOMAS   1744 – 1809
THE ROAD TO RUIN: A COMEDY. AS IT IS ACTED AT THE THEATRE ROYAL, COVENT-
GARDEN. . . .
London: Printed: New-York: Reprinted for Berry and Rogers, No. 35,
Hanover-Square. M.DCC.XCII. pp. 78, (2). 16mo.   LOC.

24403   HOLDEN, OLIVER   1765 – 1831
AMERICAN HARMONY: CONTAINING, A VARIETY OF AIRS, SUITABLE FOR DIVINE WOR-
SHIP, ON THANKSGIVINGS, ORDINATIONS, CHRISTMAS, FASTS, FUNERALS, AND OTHER
OCCASIONS. TOGETHER WITH A NUMBER OF PSALM TUNES, IN THREE AND FOUR
PARTS. THE WHOLE INTIRELY NEW. BY OLIVER HOLDEN, TEACHER OF MUSIC
IN CHARLESTOWN. [One line from] PSALM LXVIII. 25. PUBLISHED ACCORDING
TO ACT OF CONGRESS.
*Printed, typographically, at Boston, by Isaiah Thomas, and Ebenezer T.
Andrews, Faust's Statue, No.* 45. *Newbury Street.*—MDCCXCII. pp. 32. obl.
16mo.
   AAS. HC. MHS.
34th Massachusetts District Copyright, issued to Oliver Holden, as
Author, 25 September, 1792.

24404 HOLMES, JOHN
THE ART OF RHETORICK MADE EASY: OR, THE ELEMENTS OF ORATORY . . .
New-York: Printed by Hugh Gaine, at the Bible, in Hanover-Square. 1792.

24405 HOLT, THOMAS   1762 – 1836
A SERMON, DELIVERED AT THE ORDINATION OF THE REV. REED PAIGE, M. A. TO
THE PASTORAL CARE OF THE CHURCH IN HANCOCK, STATE OF NEWHAMPSHIRE,
SEPTEMBER 21ST, MDCCXCI. BY THOMAS HOLT, M. A. PASTOR OF THE CHURCH
IN HARDWICK. [Five lines of Scripture texts.]
*Printed at Worcester, Massachusetts: by Isaiah Thomas & Leonard Wor-
cester.* MDCCXCII. pp. 44. 8vo.   AAS. BM. LOC. YC.

24406 HOMER, JONATHAN   1759 – 1843
THE SUCCESSION OF GENERATIONS AMONG MANKIND, ILLUSTRATED AND IMPROVED IN
A CENTURY SERMON, PREACHED AT NEWTON, ON LORD'S DAY, DEC. 25, 1791;
BEING THE COMMENCEMENT OF A NEW CENTURY, FROM THE INCORPORATION OF
SAID TOWN. BY JONATHAN HOMER, A. M. PASTOR OF THE FIRST CHURCH IN
NEWTON.
Printed at the Apollo Press in Boston, by Belknap and Young, State Street.
MDCCXCII. pp. 27. 8vo.   AAS. BA. BM. HC. JCB. LOC. MHS.

24407 HOPKINSON, FRANCIS   1737 – 1791
THE MISCELLANEOUS ESSAYS AND OCCASIONAL WRITINGS OF FRANGIS [*sic*] HOPKIN-
SON, ESQ. VOLUME I. [—III.]
*Philadelphia: Printed by T. Dobson, at the Stone House, No. 41, Second
Street,* M,DCC,XCII. 3vols. pp. vi, [384], 2 plates; iv, [422]; vi, [215], [204.]
8vo.   BA. BM. BPL. LCP. LOC. NYHS. NYPL.
On the title-pages of volumes one, and three, the Author's name is mis-
spelled Frangis. His Poems on several subjects, occupies 204 pages, in
the third volume. The volumes were prepared for the press by the
Author, and published from his manuscripts after his death.   36th
Pennsylvania District Copyright, issued to Joseph Hopkinson, as
Proprietor, 2 October, 1792.

24408 HORNE, GEORGE   1730 – 1792
A COMMENTARY ON THE BOOK OF PSALMS. IN WHICH THEIR LITERAL OR HISTOR-
ICAL SENSE, AS THEY RELATE TO KING DAVID, AND THE PEOPLE OF ISRAEL, IS
ILLUSTRATED: AND THEIR APPLICATION TO MESSIAH, TO THE CHURCH, AND TO IN-
DIVIDUALS, AS MEMBERS THEREOF, IS POINTED OUT: WITH A VIEW TO RENDER THE
USE OF THE PSALTER PLEASING AND PROFITABLE TO ALL ORDERS AND DEGREES OF
CHRISTIANS. THE FIRST AMERICAN EDITION, FROM THE FOURTH BRITISH. BY
GEORGE, LORD BISHOP OF NORWICH, AND PRESIDENT OF MAGDALEN COLLEGE,
OXFORD. [Three lines of Scripture texts.] VOL. I. [—II.]
*Philadelphia: Printed by William Young, Bookseller, No. 52, Second-
street, the corner of Chesnut-street.* M,DCC,XCII. 2 vols. pp. (2), xxxiv, (1),
260; (2), 261—554. 8vo.   AAS. BA.
Printed on thick, and on thin paper; and in one volume with this general
title-page, also. The American Antiquarian Society has copies of the
three variants.

24409 HOSACK, DAVID   1769 – 1835
AN INQUIRY INTO THE CAUSES OF SUSPENDED ANIMATION FROM DROWNING, WITH THE
MEANS OF RESTORING LIFE. BY DAVID HOSACK, M. D.
New-York: Printed by T. & J. Swords, 1792. pp. v, 7–37. 8vo.
                                                        BA. NYHS. SGO.

24410   HOUGH, SIMON
AN ALARM TO THE WORLD: DEDICATED TO ALL RANKS OF MEN; BY A PROFESSED
FRIEND TO ALL MANKIND—BEGGING THEY WOULD PREPARE FOR CHRIST'S SECOND
COMING, WHICH IS NEAR, EVEN AT THE DOORS. AND THE ANGEL WHICH I SAW
STAND UPON THE SEA, AND UPON THE EARTH, LIFTED UP HIS HAND TO HEAVEN,
AND SWARE BY HIM THAT LIVETH FOREVER AND EVER, THAT THERE SHOULD BE
TIME NO LONGER. BUT IN THE DAYS OF THE VOICE OF THE SEVENTH ANGEL,
WHEN HE SHALL BEGIN TO SOUND THE MYSTERY OF GOD SHALL BE FINISHED*
REV. 10. 7. *THIS ANGEL COMES BETWIXT THE 6TH AND 7TH TRUMPET, AND IS
THE UNITED STATES OF AMERICA.
Printed at Stockbridge, by Loring Andrews. MDCCXCII. pp. 41. 8vo.
LOC.

"The above pamphlet & dialogue was fitted for the press in June, 1791,
since which the writer has, Sept. 1792, been excommunicated by the
minister and a small majority of the church, as I am informed." Simon
Hough, Richmond, Sept. 22, 1792. To David Perry.

24411   HOWELL, READING
A MAP OF THE STATE OF PENNSYLVANIA, WITH PART OF LAKE ERIE AND PRESQUE
ISLE, ALSO, THE RIVERS SUSQUEHANNA. OHIO, ALLEGHANY, MONONGAHELA,
AND LESSER STREAMS, THE MOUNTAINS, ROADS, PORTAGES, ETC.
[Philadelphia: Printed for the Author, 1792.] 63 x 36.
Dedicated to Governor Thomas Mifflin. Advertised, November 12,
1792, as follows: "Howell's large Map of Pennsylvania, may be had of
the Author in North Fifth Street, No. 88, completed in the following
manner, viz. Counties coloured, pasted on linen, varnished, and
mounted on rollers, all performed by himself, and in every part supe-
rior to those done in London. Specimens of both may be seen at his
house." The London edition, is 64 x 75 inches, mounted on canvas, and
folded into quarto, in slip case. The American Copyright notice is
dated August, 1792. Published for the Author and sold, London:
J. Phillips, 1792.

24412   —— A MAP OF PENNSYLVANIA, & THE PARTS CONNECTED THEREWITH, RELATING TO
THE ROADS AND INLAND NAVIGATION, ESPECIALLY AS PROPOSED TO BE IMPROVED
BY THE LATE PROCEEDINGS OF ASSEMBLY. 1792. [COPIED FROM HIS LARGER MAP.]
BY READING HOWELL. J. TRENCHARD, SCULP.
[Philadelphia: Printed for the Author, 1792.] 18 x 26.   LOC.

24413   HUDSON GAZETTE. VOL. VII. NUMB. 353. TUESDAY, JANUARY 3, [—VOL. VIII.
NUMB. 404. THURSDAY, DECEMBER 27, 1792.]
[Hudson:] Printed by Ashbel Stoddard. 1792. fol.
In continuation of *The Hudson Weekly Gazette.*

24414   HULL, WILLIAM   1753 – 1825
(CIRCULAR.) PHILADELPHIA, APRIL 1792. SIR, IN CONFORMITY TO AN APPOINTMENT
AND INSTRUCTIONS FROM THE OFFICERS OF THE MASSACHUSETTS LINE OF THE LATE
AMERICAN ARMY, I HAVE ATTENDED AT THE SEAT OF GOVERNMENT FROM THE
20TH OF MARCH TO THE PRESENT PERIOD. THE OBJECT OF MY COMMISSION WAS
TO OBTAIN A DECISION ON A MEMORIAL WHICH THEY HAVE HERETOFORE PRESENTED
TO CONGRESS, ON THE SUBJECT OF FURTHER COMPENSATION FOR THEMSELVES AND
THE SOLDIERS WHO SERVED DURING THE WAR. . . . [Signed, in autograph,
William Hull.]
[Philadelphia: 1792.] pp. (2). fol.   LOC.

24415   HUMPHREYS, DANIEL
THE COMPENDIOUS AMERICAN GRAMMAR, OR GRAMMATICAL INSTITUTES IN VERSE;
DESIGNED FOR THE USE OF SCHOOLS IN THE UNITED STATES. WITH AN APPENDIX,
CONTAINING RULES FOR THE FORMATION OF VERBS, AND THE RIGHT USE OF THE
POINTS AND STOPS. INSCRIBED TO THE AMERICAN INSTRUCTORS OF YOUTH. BY
DANIEL HUMPHREYS, ESQ. PUBLISHED ACCORDING TO ACT OF CONGRESS. [TWO
lines of Latin from] OVID.

Portsmouth. (N. H.) Printed by John Osborne, at the Spy Printing-office,
(for the Author). M,DCC.XCII. pp. (71). 12mo.   LOC. MHS.

5th New Hampshire District Copyright, issued to Daniel Humphreys,
as Author, 15 September, 1792.

24416   HUTCHINS, FATHER ABRAHAM, pseudonym.
FATHER HUTCHINS REVIVED; BEING AN ALMANAC AND EPHEMERIS; OF THE MOTIONS
OF THE SUN AND MOON; THE TRUE PLACES AND ASPECTS OF THE PLANETS; THE RIS-
ING AND SETTING OF THE SUN; AND THE RISING, SETTING, AND SOUTHING OF THE
MOON; FOR THE YEAR OF OUR LORD 1793: BEING THE FIRST AFTER BISSEXTILE,
OR LEAP-YEAR, AND THE 17TH OF AMERICAN INDEPENDENCE, UNTIL THE 4TH OF
JULY. CALCULATED FOR THE MERIDIAN OF NEW-YORK; BUT WITHOUT ANY MA-
TERIAL ALTERATION WILL ANSWER FOR THE STATES OF NEW-JERSEY AND CON-
NECTICUT, AS WELL AS THE ADJACENT STATES. CONTAINING ALSO, THE LUNATIONS,
CONJUNCTIONS, ECLIPSES, JUDGMENT OF THE WEATHER, RISING AND SETTING OF
THE PLANETS, LENGTH OF DAYS AND NIGHTS, COURTS, ROADS. &C. TOGETHER WITH
USEFUL TABLES, CHRONOLOGICAL OBSERVATIONS, AND ENTERTAINING REMARKS.
BY FATHER ABRAHAM HUTCHINS, MATHEMATICIAN.

New-York: Printed and sold by Samuel Campbell, No. 37, Hanover-Square.
[1792.] pp. (36), 12mo.   AAS.

24417   —— FATHER HUTCHIN'S REVIVED BEING AN ALMANAC AND EPHEMERIS; OF
THE MOTIONS OF THE SUN AND MOON; THE TRUE PLACES AND ASPECTS OF THE
PLANETS: THE RISING AND SETTING OF THE SUN; AND THE RISING, SETTING, AND
SOUTHING OF THE MOON; FOR THE YEAR OF OUR LORD 1793: BEING THE FIRST
AFTER BISSEXTILE. OR LEAP-YEAR, AND THE 17TH OF AMERICAN INDEPENDENCE,
UNTIL THE 4TH OF JULY. CALCULATED FOR THE MERIDIAN OF NEW-YORK; BUT
WITHOUT ANY MATERIAL ALTERATION WILL ANSWER FOR THE STATE OF NEW-
JERSEY AND CONNECTICUT, AS WELL AS THE ADJACENT STATES. CONTAIN-
ING ALSO, THE LUNATIONS, CONJUNCTIONS, ECLIPSES, JUDGMENT OF THE WEATHER;
RISING AND SETTING OF THE PLANETS, LENGTH OF DAYS AND NIGHTS, COURTS,
ROADS, &C. TOGETHER WITH USEFUL TABLES, CHRONOLOGICAL OBSERVATIONS,
AND ENTERTAINING REMARKS. BY FATHER ABRAHAM HUTCHINS, MATHEMATICIAN.

New-York: Printed for Robert Hodge, No. 11, Water-Street. [1792.] pp.
(48). 12mo.   NYHS.

24418   —— THE FEDERAL ALMANAC, FOR THE YEAR OF OUR LORD 1793: BEING THE FIRST
AFTER BISSEXTILE OR LEAP-YEAR, AND THE XVIITH OF AMERICAN INDEPENDENCE,
'TILL THE 4TH OF JULY. CALCULATED FOR THE MERIDIAN OF NEW-JERSEY; BUT
WITHOUT ANY MATERIAL ALTERATION WILL ANSWER FOR THE STATES OF NEW
YORK AND PENNSYLVANIA. CONTAINING ALSO, THE LUNATIONS, CONJUNCTIONS,
ECLIPSES, JUDGMENT OF THE WEATHER, RISING AND SETTING OF THE PLANETS.
LENGTH OF DAYS AND NIGHTS, COURTS, ROADS, &C. TOGETHER WITH USEFUL
TABLES, CHRONOLOGICAL OBSERVATIONS, AND A VARIETY OF USEFUL AND ENTER-
TAINING MATTER, IN PROSE AND VERSE. BY FATHER ABRAHAM HUTCHINS, MATH-
EMATICIAN.

New-Brunswick: Printed by Arnett and Blauvelt. [1792.] pp. (36). 12mo.
     AAS.

24419 HUTCHINS, John Nathan
HUTCHINS IMPROVED: BEING AN ALMANACK AND EPHEMERIS OF THE MOTIONS OF THE SUN AND MOON; THE TRUE PLACES AND ASPECTS OF THE PLANETS; THE RISING AND SETTING OF THE SUN; AND THE RISING, SETTING AND SOUTHING OF THE MOON; FOR THE YEAR OF OUR LORD 1793: BEING THE FIRST AFTER BISSEXTILE, OR LEAP-YEAR, AND 17TH YEAR OF AMERICAN INDEPENDENCE,'TILL 4TH JULY. [Five lines.] BY JOHN NATHAN HUTCHINS, PHILOM.
New-York: Printed and sold by H. Gaine, at his Printing office, at the Bible, in Hanover-Square. Where may be had, the New-York Pocket Almanack. [1792.] pp. (36). 12mo.
AAS. LOC.

24420 IMPARTIAL INTELLIGENCER. VOL. I. No. 1. WEDNESDAY, FEBRUARY 1, [—No. 26. THURSDAY, JULY 26, 1792.]
Greenfield: Printed by Thomas Dickman. 1792. fol.
Established by Thomas Dickman, Postmaster at Greenfield. With the issue for 2 August, 1792, he altered the title to *Greenfield Gazette*, to which was added, in 1795, the sub-title: "Or, Massachusetts and Vermont Telegraphe;" for which was substituted, in 1798: "An impartial register of the times." In August, 1798, he sold all his interests to Francis Barker, an apprentice of Thomas and Andrews at Boston, who had obtained appointment as Postmaster at Greenfield. Barker enlarged the paper and substituted for its sub-title: "A register of genuine Federalism." Within a year Barker, apparently sick of his bargain, in June, 1799, arranged with Dickman to take back the Gazette, Printing-office, Bookstore, Post-office, and all, and obtained for himself a commission in the army. Dickman continued publication to the year 1805, when he relinquished it to John Denio, who had served his apprenticeship under him, and removed permanently to Springfield, Massachusetts. Denio continued publication to after 1810. The Gazette afterwards passed through several hands, and was called, after it was consolidated with the Greenfield Courier, in the middle of the next century, Gazette and Courier.

24421 AN IMPARTIAL STATEMENT OF THE CONTROVERSY, RESPECTING THE DECISION OF THE LATE COMMITTEE OF CANVASSERS. CONTAINING. THE OPINIONS OF EDMUND RANDOLPH, ESQ. ATTORNEY GENERAL OF THE UNITED STATES; OF JONATHAN D. SERGEANT, ESQ. PHILADELPHIA; OF PIERPONT EDWARDS, ESQ. CONNECTICUT, AND SEVERAL OTHER EMINENT LAW CHARACTERS.
New-York—Printed by Thomas Greenleaf. M.DCC.XCII. pp. [46.] 8vo.
AAS. BM. JCB. LOC. MHS. NYHS.

24422 INCHBALD, Elizabeth Simpson   1753 – 1821
A SIMPLE STORY. BY MRS. INCHBALD.
Philadelphia: Printed for Robert Campbell, No. 54, South Second-Street. 1792.

24423 THE INDEPENDENT [Mass. arms] CHRONICLE: AND THE UNIVERSAL ADVERTISER. VOL. XXIV. No. 1210. THURSDAY, JANUARY 5, [—No. 1261. THURSDAY. DECEMBER 27. 1792.]
Boston: Printed and published by Thomas Adams, Printer to the honorable the General Court of the Commonwealth of Massachusetts, at his Printing-office, opposite the Court-House, Court-Street. 1792. fol.
MHS.

24424 THE INDEPENDENT GAZETTEER, AND AGRICULTURAL REPOSITORY. [Mottoes.] No. 1374. SATURDAY, JANUARY 7, [—No. 1425. SATURDAY, DECEMBER 29, 1792.]
Philadelphia: Printed by Eleazer Oswald, in Market-Street, between Fourth and Fifth-Streets. 1792. fol.

24425 AN INDEX OF THE VARIOUS SUBJECTS CONTAINED IN THE SACRED SCRIPTURES. TO WHICH IS PREFIXED AN ANALYSIS OF THE SCRIPTURES OF THE OLD AND NEW TESTAMENTS, AND OF THE APOCRYPHA. [Sixteen lines from] BISHOP ATTERBURY.
Salem: Printed by Thomas C. Cushing; and sold by W. Carlton, at the Bible and Heart. M.DCC.XCII. pp. 96. 8vo.
AAS. JCB. MHS.

24426   AN INQUIRY INTO THE CAUSES OF THE INSURRECTION OF THE NEGROES IN THE ISLAND OF ST. DOMINGO. TO WHICH ARE ADDED, OBSERVATIONS OF M. GARRAN-COULON ON THE SAME SUBJECT, READ IN HIS ABSENCE BY M. GAUDET, BEFORE THE NATIONAL ASSEMBLY, 29TH FEB. 1792.

London: Printed: Philadelphia: Re-printed and sold by Joseph Crukshank, No. 87, High-Street, 1792. pp. (2), (2), (39). 8vo.

AAS. BA. JCB. LOC. NYHS. NYPL.

Page 36 is mispaged 35.

24427   JANEWAY, JAMES   1636 – 1674
INVISIBLE REALITIES DEMONSTRATED IN THE LIFE AND DEATH OF JOHN JANEWAY. SECOND AMERICAN EDITION.

Lancaster: Printed by William Dickson, in King-Street. 1792. 12mo. BA.

24428   —— A TOKEN FOR CHILDREN; OR, AN ACCOUNT OF SEVERAL PIOUS CHILDRENS LIVES AND DEATHS.

Philadelphia: Printed by Johnson & Justice, Franklin's Head, No. 41, Chesnut street. 1792.

24429   JARRATT, DEVEREUX   1733 – 1801
THE NATURE OF LOVE TO CHRIST, AND THE DANGER OF NOT LOVING HIM, OPENED AND EXPLAINED. BY THE REV. MR. DEVEREUX JARRATT, RECTOR OF BATH, IN THE STATE OF VIRGINIA.

Philadelphia: Printed by Johnson & Justice, at Franklin's Head, No. 41, Chesnut-Street. MDCCXCII. *For William Glendinning, preacher of the Gospel.* pp. [24.] 12mo.

AAS.

24430   —— A SERMON, PREACHED BEFORE THE CONVENTION OF THE PROTESTANT EPISCOPAL CHURCH, IN VIRGINIA, AT RICHMOND, MAY 3, 1792. BY DEVEREUX JARRATT, RECTOR OF BATH PARISH, DINWIDDIE COUNTY.

Richmond: 1792. pp. 31. 8vo.   BA.

24431   —— — A SERMON, PREACHED BEFORE THE CONVENTION OF THE PROTESTANT EPISCOPAL CHURCH, IN VIRGINIA, AT RICHMOND, MAY 3, 1792. BY DEVEREUX JARRATT, RECTOR OF BATH PARISH, DINWIDDIE COUNTY.

Richmond: (Virginia) Printed. New-London: Re-printed by T. Green and Son. M,DCC,XCII. pp. [31.] 8vo.   JCB. MHS. NL. NYPL.

"This sermon has been judged worthy of a second publication." Re-printed in Bristol, Rhode Island, in 1808; and, in a third edition, at New-Haven, in 1809.

24432   —— A SOLEMN CALL TO SLEEPING SINNERS: A SERMON. BY THE REV. MR. DEVEREUX JARRATT, RECTOR OF BATH, IN THE STATE OF VIRGINIA.

Philadelphia: Printed by Johnson & Justice, at Franklin's Head, No. 41, Chesnut-Street. 1792.

24433   JOCELYN, SIMEON
THE CHORISTER'S COMPANION: TO WHICH IS NOW ADDED, A SUPPLEMENT OF PSALM AND HYMN TUNES, NEWLY COMPOSED OR NEVER BEFORE PRINTED IN AMERICA.

New-Haven: Printed by T. and S. Green. Sold by Simeon Jocelyn. 1792. pp. 164.

24434   —— — SUPPLEMENT TO THE CHORISTER'S COMPANION, CONTAINING SIXTEEN PAGES OF PSALM AHD HYMN TUNES NEWLY COMPOSED AND NOT BEFORE PRINTED IN AMERICA.

New-Haven: Printed by T. & S. Green, for Simeon Jocelyn, 1792. pp. 16. obl.8vo.   MHS.

Connecticut District Copyright, issued to Simeon Jocelin, as Author and Proprietor, 30 January, 1791.

24435   JOHNSON, GORDON
An INTRODUCTION TO ARITHMETIC, DESIGNED FOR THE USE OF SCHOOLS. BY GORDON JOHNSON.

Springfield: Printed by Ezra Waldo Weld. 1792.

24436   JOHNSON, JOHN
THE RAPE OF BETHESDA; OR, THE GEORGIA ORPHAN HOUSE DESTROYED. A POEM. BY JOHN JOHNSON. [Two lines from] SANDYS.

Charleston, Printed by Markland and M'Iver, No. 27, Bay. MDCCXCII.
pp. 16. 16mo.
           AAS. JCB.

24437   JOSEPHUS, FLAVIUS   37 – 95
THE WHOLE GENUINE AND COMPLETE WORKS OF FLAVIUS JOSEPHUS THE LEARNED AND AUTHENTIC JEWISH HISTORIAN, AND CELEBRATED WARRIOR. CONTAINING, I. THE ANTIQUITIES OF THE JEWS, IN TWENTY BOOKS; WITH THEIR WARS, MEMORABLE TRANSACTIONS, REMARKABLE OCCURRENCES, THEIR VARIOUS TURNS OF GLORY AND MISERY, PROSPERITY AND ADVERSITY, FROM THE CREATION OF THE WORLD. II. THE WARS OF THE JEWS WITH THE ROMANS, FROM THEIR COMMENCEMENT TO THE FINAL DESTRUCTION OF JERUSALEM BY TITUS IN THE REIGN OF VESPASIAN. IN SEVEN BOOKS. III. THE BOOK OF JOSEPHUS AGAINST APION IN DEFENCE OF THE JEWISH ANTIQUITIES. IN TWO PARTS. IV. THE MARTYRDOMS OF THE MACABEES. V. THE EMBASSY OF PHILO FROM THE JEWS OF ALEXANDRIA, TO THE EMPEROR CAIUS CALIGULA. VI. THE LIFE OF FLAVIUS JOSEPHUS, WRITTEN BY HIMSELF. VII. TESTIMONIES OF JOSEPHUS CONCERNING OUR BLESSED SAVIOUR, ST. JOHN THE BAPTIST, &c. CLEARLY VINDICATED. TRANSLATED FROM THE ORIGINAL IN THE GREEK LANGUAGE. AND DILIGENTLY REVISED AND COMPARED WITH THE WRITINGS OF CONTEMPORARY AUTHORS, OF DIFFERENT NATIONS, ON THE SUBJECT. ALL TENDING TO PROVE THE AUTHENTICITY OF THE WORK. TO WHICH IS ADDED VARIOUS USEFUL INDEXES, PARTICULARLY OF THE COUNTRIES, CITIES, TOWNS, VILLAGES, SEAS, RIVERS, MOUNTAINS, LAKES, &c. WHICH ARE RELATED IN THE HISTORY. ALSO A CONTINUATION OF THE HISTORY OF THE JEWS, FROM JOSEPHUS DOWN TO THE PRESENT TIME, INCLUDING A PERIOD OF MORE THAN ONE THOUSAND SEVEN HUNDRED YEARS. CONTAINING AN ACCOUNT OF THEIR DISPERSION INTO VARIOUS PARTS OF EUROPE, ASIA, AFRICA, AND AMERICA; THEIR DIFFERENT PERSECUTIONS, TRANSACTIONS, VARIOUS OCCURRENCES, AND PRESENT STATE THROUGHOUT THE KNOWN WORLD. WITH A GREAT VARIETY OF THEIR INTERESTING AND AUTHENTIC PARTICULARS COLLECTED FROM VARIOUS VALUABLE WORKS, RECORDING THE PRINCIPAL TRANSACTIONS OF THE JEWS SINCE THE TIME OF JOSEPHUS. BY GEORGE HENRY MAYNARD, LL. D. ILLUSTRATED WITH MARGINAL REFERENCES AND NOTES, HISTORICAL, BIOGRAPHICAL, CLASSICAL, CRITICAL, GEOGRAPHICAL, AND EXPLANATORY. BY THE REV. EDWARD KIMPTON, AUTHOR OF THE COMPLEAT UNIVERSAL HISTORY OF THE HOLY BIBLE. EMBELLISHED WITH UPWARDS OF SIXTY BEAUTIFUL ENGRAVINGS, TAKEN FROM ORIGINAL DRAWINGS OF MESSRS. METZ, STOTHARD, AND CORBOULD, MEMBERS OF THE ROYAL ACADEMY, AND ENGRAVED BY AMERICAN ARTISTS.

New-York: Printed and sold by William Durell, at his Book Store and Printing office, No. 19, Queen-Street, near the Fly-Market. M,DCC,XCII. Part I. —xxv? fol.
           AAS. BPL.

First issued in parts, to be completed in sixty numbers, each number to contain an engraving, and the names of subscribers to be printed. The first number, containing the title-page, dated 1792, and frontispiece, was issued in June, 1792, and publication was not finally concluded until 1794.

24438   JUDD, EBEN W
THE UNITED STATES ALMANAC FOR THE YEAR OF OUR LORD 1793: BEING THE FIRST
AFTER BISSEXTILE, OR LEAP YEAR. . . . BY EBEN W. JUDD.
Elizabeth-Town: Printed by Shepard Kollock. [1792.]

24439   ——— WEBSTER'S CALENDAR: OR, THE ALBANY ALMANACK, FOR THE YEAR OF OUR
LORD 1793; FROM THE CREATION OF THE WORLD 5742. AND OF AMERICAN IN-
DEPENDENCE (WHICH WAS DECLARED THE 4TH OF JULY, 1776) PART OF THE 17TH
AND 18TH YEARS. BEING THE FIRST AFTER BISSEXTILE OR LEAP YEAR. [Twenty-
seven lines.] CALCULATED FOR LATITUDE 42:40 NORTH. BY EBEN W. JUDD,
PHILO.
*Printed by Charles R. & George Webster, No. 46, State Street, Albany:
where printing is performed on reasonable terms.* [1792.] pp. (36). 12mo. AAS.
The Sketch of the life of Frederic, baron Trenck, is continued.

24440   JULIA, OR, THE ADVENTURES OF A CURATE'S DAUGHTER. A NOVEL. TO WHICH IS
ADDED, THE SHIPWRECK, A TALE; AND A PASTORAL BALLAD, IN FOUR PARTS. BY
W. SHENSTONE, ESQ.
Burlington: Printed by Isaac Neale, 1792. pp. 140. 12mo.

24441   KEATE, GEORGE   1729 – 1797
AN ACCOUNT OF THE PELEW ISLANDS, SITUATED IN THE WESTERN PART OF THE
PACIFIC OCEAN. COMPOSED FROM THE JOURNALS AND COMMUNICATIONS OF CAP-
TAIN HENRY WILSON, AND SOME OF HIS OFFICERS, WHO, IN AUGUST 1783, WERE
THERE SHIPWRECKED, IN THE ANTELOPE, A PACKET BELONGING TO THE HON.
EAST INDIA COMPANY. BY GEORGE KEETE [*sic*], ESQ. F. R. S. AND S. A. [THE
SECOND AMERICAN EDITION.]
*Philadelphia: Printed and sold by Joseph Crukshank, No. 87, High-
Street.* 1792. pp. xx, 256. 12mo.   AAS. JCB.

24442   KEIR, SUSANNA HARVEY   1747 – 1802
INTERESTING MEMOIRS. BY A LADY. IN TWO VOLUMES. VOL. I. [—II.] THE
FOURTH EDITION.
*New-York: Printed by T. Allen, Bookseller and Stationer, No. 12, Queen-
Street.*—1792.—pp. 127; 136. 16mo.   JCB.
Reprinted in Boston, in 1802.

24443   KENTUCKY. STATE.
A CONSTITUTION OR FORM OF GOVERNMEN [*sic*] FOR THE STATE OF KENTUCKY.
Lexington: Printed by John Bradford. M.DCC.XCII. pp. (32). 16mo.
LOC.
This Constitution was superseded by the Constitutions of 1799, and 1850.

24444   THE KENTUCKY GAZETTE. VOL. V. NUMB. XX. SATURDAY, JANUARY 7, [—VOL.
VI. NUMB. XIX. SATURDAY, DECEMBER 29, 1792.]
*Lexington: Printed by John Bradford, at his Printing-Office in Main
Street, . . .* 1792. fol.

24445   DIE KLEINE HARFE, GESTIMMET VON UNTERSCHIEDLICHEN LIEBLICHEN LIEDERN
ODER LOB-GESÄNGEN, WELCHE GEHÖRET WERDEN VON DEN ENDEN DER ERDEN,
ZU EHREN DEM GERECHTEN. DIESE KLEINE HARFE KLINGET ZWAR LIEBLICH,
ABER DOCH NOCH IM NIEDRIGEN SHON; BIS DAS GROSSE HARFEN-SPIELER HEER
DEN GESANG ERHÖHEN WIRD. GOTT UND DEM LAMM SEY DIE EHRE UND DAS LOB
IN ZEIT UND EWIGKEIT! AMEN. ZUM ERSTEN MAL ANS LICHT GEGEBEN.
Chesnuthill, gedruckt bey Samuel Saur, 1792. pp. 55, (1). 8vo. LOC. NYPL.

24446   KNIGHT, ELLIS CORNELIA   1757 – 1837
DINARBAS; A TALE: BEING A CONTINUATION OF RASSELAS, PRINCE OF ABISSINIA.
[Seven lines from] HORACE.
> *Philadelphia: Printed by F. Bailey, No. 116, Market-Street, and T. Lang,*
> *No. 21, Church-Alley.* MDCCXCII. pp. (2), 200. 16mo.   AAS. MHS.

Usually found bound with Samuel Johnson's Rasselas, printed, as above,
in 1791.

24447   KNOX, VICESIMUS   1752 – 1821
ESSAYS MORAL AND LITERARY. BY VICESIMUS KNOX, M. A. LATE FELLOW OF ST.
JOHN'S COLLEGE, OXFORD.
> *Philadelphia: Printed for and sold by Benjamin Johnson, No. 147, and*
> *H. & P. Rice, No. 50, Market-Street.* 1792. 2 vols.

24448   KNOXVILLE GAZETTE. VOL. I. NO. 6. SATURDAY, JANUARY 14, [—VOL. II. NO. 5.
(NO. 31). SATURDAY, DECEMBER 29, 1792.]
> *Rogersville, Hawkins County, Tennessee: Printed by George Roulstone.*
> 1792. fol.

In November, Roulstone permanently removed his press to Knoxville,
and continued the publication of the Gazette there until publication
was suspended in 1797.

24449   KURGEFASSTES ARZNEY-BÜCHLEIN FÜR MENSCHEN UND VIEH. [VIERTE AUF-
LAGE.]
> *Ephrata: Klosterpresse.* 1792. pp. 24. 12mo.

24450   LADIES' LITERARY COMPANION.
> *Burlington: Printed by Isaac Neale,* 1792.

24451   THE LADY'S MAGAZINE; AND REPOSITORY OF ENTERTAINING KNOWLEDGE. VOL. I.
FOR [JUNE—NOVEMBER] 1792. BY A LITERARY SOCIETY THE MIND T'IMPROVE
& YET AMUSE.
> *Philadelphia: Printed for the Proprietors, by W: Gibbons North Third*
> *Street No. 144.* [1792.] pp. (2), 303, (1), frontispiece, and engraved title. 8vo.
>   AAS. BPL. LCP. LOC.

38th Pennsylvania District Copyright, issued to Joseph C. Sykes, as
Proprietor, 1 December, 1792.

24452   THE LADY'S POCKET LIBRARY. CONTAINING: 1. MISS MORE'S ESSAYS. 2. DR.
GREGORY'S LEGACY TO HIS DAUGHTERS. 3. LADY PENNINGTON'S UNFORTUNATE
MOTHER'S ADVICE TO HER DAUGHTERS. 4. MARCHIONESS OF LAMBERT'S ADVICE
OF A MOTHER TO HER DAUGHTER. 5. MRS. CHAPONE'S LETTER ON THE GOVERN-
MENT OF THE TEMPER. 6. SWIFT'S LETTER TO A YOUNG LADY NEWLY MARRIED.
7. MOORE'S FABLES FOR THE FEMALE SEX. [Ornament.]
> *Philadelphia: From the Press of Mathew Carey, No. 118, Market-Street.*
> *March* 20, M.DCC.XCII. pp. 297, (2). 12mo.   AAS.

24453   LAMBERT, ANNE THÉRÈSE; marquise DE   1647 – 1733
THE POLITE LADY; OR, A COURSE OF FEMALE EDUCATION. IN A SERIES OF LETTERS
FROM A MOTHER TO HER DAUGHTER. [Two lines from] POPE.
> *Salem: Printed by Thomas C. Cushing?* 1792.

"A few copies" for sale by William Carleton, Salem. 1792.

24454   LANGDON, Samuel   1723 – 1797
A Correction of some great mistakes committed by the rev. John Cosens
Ogden, a presbyter in the Protestant Episcopal Church, in the United
States of America, in his late letters published at Boston. By Samuel
Langdon, d. d. minister of Hampton-Falls, in the State of New-Hamp-
shire.
Portsmouth: Printed by John Melcher. M,DCC,XCII. pp. 5–22. 8vo.
AAS. BA. LOC. NYHS.

24455   —— A Discourse on the unity of the church as a monumental pillar of the
truth; designed to reconcile christians of all parties and denominations in charity and fellowship, as one body in Christ; delivered before
the association of ministers convened at Portsmouth, October 12, 1791,
and in substance repeated at a lecture in Hamptonfalls, January 26,
1792. By Samuel Langdon, d. d. minister of the church in Hamptonfalls,
in the State of Newhampshire.
Printed at Exeter, by Henry Ranlet, 1792. pp. 30. 8vo.
AAS. BA. BM. JCB. MHS. NYHS.

24456   LANGWORTHY, Edward
Memoirs of the life of the late Charles Lee, esq. lieutenant-colonel of
the forty-fourth regiment; colonel in the Portuguese service; major-
general and aid de camp to the King of Poland, and second in command
in the service of the United States of America during the Revolution.
To which are added, his political and military essays; also, letters to
and from many distinguished characters, both in Europe and America.
New-York: Printed by T. Allen, Bookseller and Stationer, No. 12, *Queen-
Street.* 1792. pp. (viii), 284. 12mo.   AAS. HC. JCB. LOC. MHS. NL. NYPL.

In two states: on thick paper, and ordinary book paper. The Memoirs,
ending on page 47, are signed, Edward Langworthy, Baltimore, March
10th, 1787. The preface is dated, London, Feb. 1792,—in which year
it was reprinted there, and in Dublin.

24457   LATHROP, John   1740 – 1816
A Catechism, compiled for the use of children. By John Lathrop, d. d.
Boston, Printed by John West Folsom, No. 30, *Union-Street.* MDCCXCII.
pp. 16. 32mo.   AAS.

Dedicated, To the Second Religious Society in Boston. Based on the
Shorter Catechism of the Westminster Assembly of Divines.

24458   —— — A Catechism, compiled for the use of children. By John Lathrop,
d. d. Second edition.
Boston: Printed by John West Folsom, No. 30, *Union-Street.* 1792. 12mo.
BA.

24459   LATHROP, Joseph   1731 – 1820
Christ's warning to the churches, to beware of false prophets, who come
as wolves in sheep's clothing: and the marks by which they are known:
illustrated in two discourses. By Joseph Lathrop, d. d. pastor of a
church in West-Springfield. [Three lines from] Apostle Peter. Third
edition, with an appendix and other enlargements.
Printed at Springfield: Exeter Re-printed by Henry Ranlet. M,DCC,XCII.
pp. 55. 8vo.   AAS. JCB.

24460   LATHROP, Joseph, continued.
—— A Church of God described, the qualifications for membership stated, and Christian fellowship illustrated. In two discourses. By Joseph Lathrop, D. D. minister of a Congregational church, in West-Springfield.
Hartford: Re-printed by Hudson and Goodwin. MDCCXCII. pp. 51. 8vo.
AAS. BA. JCB. LOC.
Reprinted in Charlestown, in 1804.

24461   LAUS DEO! The Worcester collection of sacred harmony. First and second parts. Containing, i. An introduction to the grounds of musick: or, rules for learners. ii. A large number of celebrated psalm and hymn tunes, from the most approved authors. Suited to all metres usually sung in churches. To which is added, an appendix. Containing a number of excellent psalm tunes, (several of which are entirely new) and other pieces of sacred vocal musick, many of which were composed by eminent European authors, and never before published in this country. The whole compiled for the use of schools and singing societies. Praise ye the Lord: for it is good to sing praises unto our God.—Psalm cxlvii. The fourth edition, with additions.
Printed, typographically, at Boston, by Isaiah Thomas and Ebenezer T. Andrews. Sold by them at Faust's Statue, No. 45, Newbury Street; and by said Thomas in Worcester. Sold also by the Booksellers in town and country. MDCC-XCII. pp. (2), (2), 151, (1). obl.16mo.
AAS.

24462   LA VALINIERE, Pierre Huet de
Vraie histoire: ou, simple précis des infortunes, pour ne pas dire des persécutions qu'a souffert et souffre encore le rev. P. H. de La V., mis en vers par lui-même en Juillet, 1792.
A Albany, Imprimé aux dépens de Auteur. [1792.]

24463   LAW, Andrew   1748 – 1821
A Collection of hymn tunes, from the most modern and approved authors. By Andrew Law, a. m.
Cheshire: Connecticut. Printed and sold by William Law. 1792.
Connecticut District Copyright, issued to Andrew Law, as Author, 28 August, 1792.

24464   —— The Musical magazine; containing a variety of favorite pieces. A periodical publication. By Andrew Law, a. m. Number first.
Cheshire: Connecticut. Printed and sold by William Law, A. D. 1792. pp. (2), 16. obl.16mo.
NL.
Connecticut District Copyright, issued to Andrew Law, as Author, 8 October, 1792.

24465   —— The Rudiments of music, or a short and easy treatise on the rules of psalmody. To which are annexed, a number of plain tunes and chants. By Andrew Law, a. m. author of Select harmony, A Collection of plain tunes for the Psalm-book, and A Collection of hymn tunes, with their hymns, lately published.
Cheshire: Connecticut. Printed and sold by William Law. 1792.
Connecticut District Copyright, issued to Andrew Law, as Author, 28 August, 1792.

LAW, ANDREW, continued.

24466 —— — THE RUDIMENTS OF MUSIC: OR A SHORT AND EASY TREATISE ON THE RULES OF PSALMODY. TO WHICH ARE ANNEXED, A NUMBER OF PSALM AND HYMN TUNES. BY ANDREW LAW, A. M. FOURTH EDITION, WITH THE ADDITION OF A NUMBER OF PIECES, NEVER BEFORE PUBLISHED.
Cheshire: Printed and sold by William Law. 1792. pp. (6), 76.
Connecticut District Copyright, issued to Andrew Law, as Author, 18 September, 1792.

24467 —— SELECT HARMONY. CONTAINING IN A PLAIN AND CONCISE MANNER, THE RULES OF SINGING: TOGETHER WITH A COLLECTION OF PSALM TUNES, HYMNS, AND ANTHEMS. BY ANDREW LAW, A. B.
Cheshire: Connecticut. Printed and sold by William Law. 1792.
Connecticut District Copyright, issued to Andrew Law, as Author, 28 August, 1792.

24468 LEE, RICHARD
LINES ON THE LAST AND DYING WORDS OF REV. OLIVER WILLIAMS (OF GRAFTON BAPTIST CHURCH), WHO DIED AUGUST 29, 1790. [Fifteen four-line verses, followed by an acrostic on Richard Lee.]
Warren [R. I.] Printed [by Nathaniel Phillips] for Richard Lee. [1792.]
Broadside. 4to.   AAS.

24469 LELAND, JOHN   1754 – 1841
THE HISTORY OF JACK NIPS. [Ornament.]
Albany: Printed for John Asplund, of Virginia; by Charles R. and George Webster, No. 46, on the north side of State street, corner of Middle-lane. MDCC-XCII. pp. (8). 8vo.   AAS.

24470 LELAND, JOSEPH
THE FARMER'S DIARY: OR THE UNITED STATES ALMANACK, FOR THE YEAR OF OUR LORD CHRIST, 1793. . . . BY JOSEPH LELAND, PHILOM.
Danbury: Printed by Nathan Douglas and Edwards Ely. [1792.]

24471 L'ENFANT, PETER CHARLES   1755 – 1825
PLAN OF THE CITY INTENDED FOR THE PERMANENT SEAT OF THE GOVERNMENT OF THE UNITED STATES, PROJECTED AGREEABLY TO THE DIRECTION OF THE PRESIDENT OF THE UNITED STATES, IN PURSUANCE OF AN ACT OF CONGRESS, PASSED ON THE 16TH OF JULY, 1790 "ESTABLISHING THE PERMANENT SEAT ON THE BANKS OF THE POTOWMACK." BY PETER CHARLES L'ENFANT.
Philadelphia: Printed by John Dunlap, 1792.

24472 LE PRINCE DE BEAUMONT, JEANNE MARIE   1711 – 1780
THE YOUNG MISSES' MAGAZINE: CONTAINING DIALOGUES BETWEEN A GOVERNESS AND SEVERAL YOUNG LADIES OF QUALITY, HER SCHOLARS. IN WHICH EACH LADY IS MADE TO SPEAK ACCORDING TO HER PARTICULAR GENIUS, TEMPER, AND INCLINATION: THEIR SEVERAL FAULTS ARE POINTED OUT, AND THE EASY WAY TO MEND THEM, AS WELL AS TO THINK, AND SPEAK, AND ACT PROPERLY; NO LESS CARE BEING TAKEN TO FORM THEIR HEARTS TO GOODNESS, THAN TO ENLIGHTEN THEIR UNDERSTANDINGS WITH USEFUL KNOWLEDGE. A SHORT AND CLEAR ABRIDGMENT IS ALSO GIVEN OF SACRED AND PROFANE HISTORY, AND SOME LESSONS IN GEOGRAPHY. THE USEFUL IS BLENDED THROUGHOUT WITH THE AGREEABLE, THE WHOLE BEING INTERSPERSED WITH PROPER REFLEXIONS AND MORAL TALES. TRANSLATED FROM THE FRENCH OF MADEM. LE PRINCE DE BEAUMONT. IN FOUR VOLUMES. VOL. I. [—IV.]
Philadelphia: Printed by Mathew Carey. M.DCC.XCII. 4 vols. pp. 175; (2) 179;— — 328; — —. 24mo.   AAS.
First published in 1757. To be had in four volumes, or in two volumes, with continuous paging and signatures.

24473 LEWIS, AMZI 1746 – 1819
A SERMON DELIVERED AT GILEAD IN FREDERICKTOWN, 1792.
Danbury: Printed by Nathan Douglas and Edwards Ely? 1792.

24474 LEWIS, ELI
ST. CLAIR'S DEFEAT. A POEM. "A TALE WHICH STRONGLY CLAIMS THE PITYING TEAR, AND EVERY FEELING HEART MUST BLEED TO HEAR."
Harrisburgh: Printed by John W. Allen and John Wyeth. MDCCXCII. pp. 14. 16mo.

24475 LIBERALISSIMUS, ELIPHAZ, pseudonym.
A LETTER TO THE PREACHER OF LIBERAL SENTIMENTS, CONTAINING A LIBERAL MAN'S CONFESSION OF FAITH. BY ELIPHAZ LIBERALISSIMUS.
Printed in the year 1792. pp. [23.] 8vo.   BA. JCB. LOC.

24476 LINES ADDRESSED TO THE PATIENTS UNDER INOCULATION FOR THE SMALL POX. [Five four-line verses.] EXTRACT FROM THE CELEBRATED PINDAR. THE APPLE-DUMPLINGS AND A KING. [Thirty-four lines.]
[Boston: 1792.] Broadside. nar.fol.   NYHS.

24477 LIPPINCOTT, JOSEPH
A COLLECTION OF TABLES. 1. A TABLE SHEWING THE VALUE OF ANY NUMBER OF POUNDS, SHILLINGS AND PENCE IN DOLLARS AND CENTS FROM ONE CENT TO TEN THOUSAND DOLLARS. 2. A TABLE OF THE WEIGHT AND VALUE OF COINS AS THEY NOW PASS IN THE RESPECTIVE STATES OF THE UNION WITH THEIR STERLING AND FEDERAL VALUE. 3. A TABLE OF THE MONEY OF THE UNITED STATES. 4. TABLES OF INTEREST AT SIX AND SEVEN PER CENT, PER ANNUM. WITH SEVERAL OTHER USEFUL TABLES. CALCULATED BY JOSEPH LIPPINCOTT.
Philadelphia: 1792.
33d Pennsylvania District Copyright, issued to Joseph Lippincott, as Author, 30 March, 1792.

24478 LITCHFIELD [cut] MONITOR. VOL. VI. No. 4. TOTAL NO. 286. MONDAY, JANUARY 3, [—VOL. VII. No. 338. WEDNESDAY, DECEMBER 28, 1791.]
Litchfield: Printed by Thomas Collier. 1791. fol.   AAS. YC.
In December, David Buel, was admitted to partnership under the firm name of Collier and Buel. After 11 January, 1792, called *The Monitor,* only.

24479 LIVERMORE, EDWARD ST. LOE 1762 – 1832
AN ORATION DELIVERED BEFORE THE . . . MASONS, OF . . . NEW-HAMPSHIRE . . . THE TWENTY-FIFTH . . . OF JUNE . . . 5792. . . .
Portsmouth: Printed by John Melcher. M,DCC,XCII. pp. 23. 8vo.

24480 LOGAN, GEORGE 1753 – 1821
FIVE LETTERS, ADDRESSED TO THE YEOMANRY OF THE UNITED STATES: CONTAINING SOME OBSERVATIONS ON THE DANGEROUS SCHEME OF GOVERNOR DUER AMD MR. SECRETARY HAMILTON, TO ESTABLISH NATIONAL MANUFACTORIES. [Ornament.] BY A FARMER.
Philadelphia: Printed by Eleazer Oswald, No. 156, *Market-street, between Fourth and Fifth-streets.* M,DCC,XCII. pp. [28.] 8vo.   AAS. BA. JCB. LOC.

24481 LONDON. ENGLAND. CHURCH OF CHRIST.
A DECLARATION OF THE FAITH AND PRACTICE OF THE CHURCH OF CHRIST IN CARTER LANE, SOUTHWARK, LONDON, UNDER THE PASTORAL CARE OF DR. JOHN GILL; READ AND ASSENTED TO AT THE ADMISSION OF MEMBERS.
Wilmington: Printed and sold by James Adams, 1792.

24482   LOVE, CHRISTOPHER   1618 – 1651
SIXTEEN SERMONS; WHEREIN IS PLAINLY SHEWN TRUE GRACE, WITH ITS DIFFERENT
DEGREES;—AND SEVERAL IMPORTANT CASES OF CONSCIENCE ANSWERED IN THE
COURSE OF THE WORK. BY THE WORTHY AND EMINENTLY PIOUS CHRISTOPHER
LOVE, MINISTER OF THE GOSPEL, IN LAURENCE-JURY, LONDON; WHO WAS BE-
HEADED ON TOWER-HILL, IN THE TIME OF CROMWELL'S USURPATION, BEING THE
LAST HE PREACHED. [Sixteen lines of verse from] DR. WILD.
> *Wilmington, Printed and sold by James Adams, 1792.* pp. (244). 12mo.
> AAS.

24483   LOW, NATHANAEL   1740 – 1808
AN ASTRONOMICAL DIARY: OR ALMANACK, FOR THE YEAR OF CHRISTIAN ÆRA 1793.
BEING THE FIRST YEAR AFTER BISSEXTILE, OR LEAP-YEAR. AND THE SEVEN-
TEENTH OF THE INDEPENDENCE OF AMERICA, WHICH BEGAN JULY 4TH, 1776. [Seven
lines.] BY NATHANAEL LOW. [Twelve lines of verse.]
> *Printed and sold by T. & J. Fleet, in Boston. [The only proprietors of Dr.
> Low's copy right.] Where may be had their Pocket Almanack and Register, for
> 1793.* [1792.] pp. [24.] 12mo.   AAS. LOC. NYPL. YC.
> 36th Massachusetts District Copyright, issued to T. & J. Fleet, as Pro-
> prietors, 11 October, 1792.

24484   —— THE YORK, CUMBERLAND & LINCOLN ALMANACK, FOR THE YEAR OF CHRISTIAN
ERA 1793: . . .
> *Portland: Printed and sold by Thomas B. Wait, . . .* [1792.] 12mo.

24485   LUKINS, GEORGE
A NARRATIVE OF THE EXTRAORDINARY CASE OF GEORGE LUKINS, OF YATTON,
SOMERSETSHIRE, WHO WAS POSSESSED OF EVIL SPIRITS, FOR NEAR EIGHTEEN YEARS.
ALSO AN ACCOUNT OF HIS REMARKABLE DELIVERANCE, IN THE VESTRY-ROOM OF
TEMPLE CHURCH, IN THE CITY OF BRISTOL. EXTRACTED FROM THE MANUSCRIPTS
OF SEVERAL PERSONS WHO ATTENDED. TO WHICH IS PREFIXED, A LETTER FROM
THE REV. W. R. W[ILD.] [Dated, Wrington, June 5, 1788.]
> *—Bristol, Printed—Philadelphia: Reprinted and sold by Parry Hall, No.
> 149, Chesnut Street, near Fourth Street.* M.DCC.XCII. pp. [19.] 8vo.   NYPL.

24486   McCLURE, DAVID   1748 – 1820
Half-title: HOPE IN DEATH. [Cut.] REV. MR. M'CLURE'S SERMON, ON THE DEATH
OF THE REV. DOCTOR POMEROY.
Title: A SERMON, DELIVERED AT HEBRON, IN CONNECTICUT, ON THE DEATH OF
THE LATE PIOUS AND REVEREND BENJAMIN POMEROY, D. D. MINISTER OF THE
FIRST CHURCH THERE. WHO DEPARTED THIS LIFE DEC. 22, 1784; IN THE 81ST
YEAR OF HIS AGE, AND 49TH OF HIS MINISTRY. BY DAVID M'CLURE, A. M. MINIS-
TER OF THE FIRST CHURCH IN EAST-WINDSOR. [Six lines of quotations.]
> *Hartford: Printed by Elisha Babcock.* MDCCXCII. pp. 24. 8vo.
> AAS. BM. CHS. HC. JCB. LOC. MHS. NYHS. NYPL. YC.

24487   —— A SERMON, DELIVERED AT ELLINGTON IN CONNECTICUT, AT THE INTERMENT OF
THE REVEREND JOHN ELSWORTH, A. M. LATE MINISTER OF THE PRESBYTERIAN
CHURCH IN THE ISLAND OF SABA, IN THE WEST-INDIES, WHO DEPARTED THIS
LIFE NOV. 22, 1791, AGED 29 YEARS. PUBLISHED AT THE REQUEST OF THE
MOURNING PARENTS. BY DAVID M'CLURE, A. M. MINISTER OF THE FIRST CHURCH
IN EAST-WINDSOR. [Three lines from] PORTEUS.
> *Printed at Hartford, by Hudson and Goodwin.* MDCCXCII. pp. 32. 8vo.
> AAS. BA. BM. CHS. JCB. LOC. MHS. NYPL. YC.

24488   Mc CORKLE, SAMUEL EUSEBIUS   1746 – 1811
A SERMON ON SACRIFICES.
Halifax: Printed by Abraham Hodge? 1792.

24489   M' CORMICK, JAMES
THE WESTERN ALMANAC, FOR THE YEAR OF OUR LORD 1793. ADAPTED TO THE LATITUDE AND MERIDIAN OF CARLISLE. THE ASTRONOMICAL CALCULATIONS BY JAMES M'CORMICK, PROFESSOR OF MATHEMATICKS IN DICKINSON COLLEGE, CARLISLE.
Carlisle: Printed by George Kline. [1792.]

24490   M' CULLOCH, JOHN
M'CULLOCH'S POCKET ALMANAC, FOR THE YEAR 1793: BEING THE FIRST AFTER LEAP-YEAR; AND THE SEVENTEENTH OF AMERICAN INDEPENDENCE. CONTAINING, BESIDES THE ASTRONOMICAL CALCULATIONS, A VARIETY OF LISTS AND TABLES. THE CALCULATIONS OF THIS ALMANAC ARE MADE TO APPARENT TIME BY THE MERIDIAN OF PHILADELPHIA: AND THE SUN'S, PLANETS', AND MOON'S PLACES, ARE COMPUTED TO THE TIME OF THE SUN'S PASSING THE MERIDIAN.
Philadelphia: Printed and sold by John M'Culloch, at No. 1, North Third-Street. [1792.] pp. (32). 32mo.   HC. NYHS.
The interleaved copy in the New York Historical Society, contains, in manuscript, a nearly daily record by Judge William Cushing.

24491   Mc EWEN, WILLIAM   1735 – 1762
GRACE AND TRUTH: OR, THE GLORY AND FULNESS OF THE REDEEMER DISPLAYED. IN AN ATTEMPT TO EXPLAIN, ILLUSTRATE, AND ENFORCE THE MOST REMARKABLE TYPES, FIGURES, AND ALLEGORIES OF THE OLD TESTAMENT. BY THE REV. WILLIAM M'EWEN, LATE MINISTER OF THE GOSPEL IN DUNDEE. THE FIRST AMERICAN EDITION FROM THE NINTH BRITISH.
Philadelphia: Printed by Johnson and Justice, at Franklin's Head, No. 41, Chesnut-Street. M.DCC.XCII. pp. viii, (2), 239. 12mo.   AAS. HC. JCB.

24492   MACGOWAN, JOHN   1726 – 1780
PRIESTCRAFT DEFENDED. A SERMON, OCCASIONED BY AN EXTRAORDINARY OCCURRENCE THAT HAPPENED TO SIX YOUNG GENTLEMEN, TRULY ORIGINAL IN ITS KIND; REPLETE WITH WIT, HUMOR, AND GOOD SENSE; CALCULATED TO PLEASE AND INSTRUCT, AND WHICH SETS IN A CLEAR POINT OF VIEW, SOME IMPORTANT MATTERS, IN WHICH PERSONS OF ALL DENOMINATIONS ARE DEEPLY INTERESTED. SO GENERALLY APPROVED OF, AS TO HAVE ALREADY GONE THROUGH TEN EDITIONS, IN LONDON. HUMBLY DEDICATED TO MR. V— C—, AND THE H— OF —, NOT BY PRELATE, PRIEST, NOR DEACON, BUT BY THEIR HUMBLE SERVANT, THE SHAVER.
Baltimore: Printed and sold by Philip Edwards, at the new Printing-Office, in Market-Street, a few doors below Tripolet's Alley, and nearly opposite the Card Manufactory. 1792.

24493   MACK, VALENTINE
EIN GESPRÄCH ZWISCHEN EINEM PILGER UND BÜRGER AUF IHRER REISE NACH UND IN DER EWIGKEIT.
Chesnuthill: Gedruckt bey Samuel Saur. 1792. pp. 72. 12mo.

24494   MACKENZIE, HENRY, and others:
THE MIRROR. A PERIODICAL PAPER, PUBLISHED AT EDINBURGH IN THE YEARS [NO. 1. SATURDAY, JANUARY 23,] 1779 AND [NO. 110. SATURDAY, MAY 27,] 1780. VELUTI IN SPECULO. IN TWO VOLUMES. VOL. I. [—II.] FIRST AMERICAN EDITION.
Printed at the Apollo Press, in Boston, by Belknap and Hall, for the Proprietor of the Boston Book Store, No. 59, Cornhill. MDCCXCII. pp. 316; 316. 12mo.   AAS. BA. HC. JCB.

24495 MACKINTOSH, Sir James   1765 – 1832
Vindiciæ Gallicæ. Defence of the French Revolution and its English ad-
mirers against the accusations of the right hon. Edmund Burke; including some strictures on the late production of mons. de Calonne. By James
Mackintosh.
> *Philadelphia: Printed by William Young, Bookseller, No. 52, Second-*
> *Street, the corner of Chesnut-Street.* M,DCC,XCII. pp. 175, (1). 8vo.
>   AAS. LOC. RIHS.
> Some copies have appended, the French Constitution, as accepted by
> the King, 13th September, 1791. The first English edition, printed in
> London, in 1791, contains many passages suppressed in later editions.
> This is esteemed the most able of the answers to Burke.

24496 MACPHERSON, John
McPherson's Vorlesungen über philosophische Sittenlehre. Uebersetzt
von G. F. Götz.
> *Philadelphia: Printed for William Woodhouse, No. 6 South Front-Street.*
> *And the Author No. 417 South Front-Street.* 1792. 8vo.   HC.
> Advertisement: John Macpherson's Lectures on the divinity of Christ
> and morality. In English (see 1791) or in German, are sold by George
> Reinholdt, No. 201 Market-Street; H. & P. Rice, Market-Street, No.
> 59; Godfrey Baker & Co. Race-Street, No, 59; William Young, South
> Second Street, No. 52; William Woodhouse, South Front Street, No. 2;
> and Mrs. Griffith, South Front Street, No. 417. Philadelphia, 1792.

24497 MADISON, James   1749 – 1812
An Address to the Convention of the Protestant Episcopal Church, in Virginia, By the right reverend J. Madison, d. d. Bishop of said church.
> *Baltimore: Printed by W. Goddard and J. Angell, in Market-Street.* 1792.

24498 MAGAW, Samuel   1740 – 1812
The Substance of an address, delivered in the Young Ladies' Academy of
Philadelphia, June 20th, 1792. By the rev. doctor Magaw.
> *Philadelphia: Printed by Stewart & Cochran, No. 34, South Second-street.*
> [1792.] pp. (6). 8vo.   AAS.

24499 THE MAIL; or, Claypoole's daily advertiser. Number 185. Tuesday, January
2, [--Number 497. Monday, December 31, 1792.]
> *Philadelphia: Printed and sold by D. C. Claypoole, at his Office, No. 2,*
> *South Third-street, . . .* 1792. fol.   AAS.

24500 MARMONTEL, Jean François   1723 – 1799
Selima & Azore. A new comic opera. Translated into English from the
Italian, by mrs. Rigaud, the music by the most celebrated composer, sig-
nor Gretry. Performed by the American Company, Philadelphia. [Mon-
ogram.]
> *Philadelphia: Printed and sold by Enoch Story.* [1792.] pp. 36. 12mo.
>   LCP.

24501 MARTIN, Georg Adam
Christliche Bibliothek, enthält dasjenige was allen Pilgern auf der
Reise nach der verlorenen Herrlichkeit zu wissen nöthig isт. Heraus-
gegeben durch deinen Getreuen Aufrichtigen Mitbruder.
> *Ephrata: Der Klosterpresse.* 1792. pp. 148. 8vo.   AAS. BM.
> The initial letters of the last three words are those of the author's
> name. An autobiographical account of his conversion, spiritual life
> and connection with the Ephrata Brotherhood is in the thirty-first
> chapter of the Chronicon Ephratense.

24502   MARTINET, JOANNES FLORENTIUS   1729 – 1795
THE CATECHISM OF NATURE; OR, FAMILIAR DIALOGUES BETWEEN A PUPIL AND HIS
TUTOR UPON THE WORKS OF CREATION. COMPOSED FOR THE USE OF CHILDREN.
BY DOCTOR MARTINET, PROFESSOR OF PHILOSOPHY AT ZUTPHEN. TRANSLATED
FROM THE DUTCH. [By John Hall.] READ NATURE—NATURE IS A FRIEND TO
TRUTH. THE SECOND PHILADELPHIA EDITION, WITH ADDITIONS AND AMENDMENTS.
    Philadelphia: Printed and sold by Thomas Lang, No. 21, Church-Alley.
MDCCXCII. pp. 144. 18mo.
                AAS.

24503   MARYLAND. STATE.
LAWS OF MARYLAND, MADE AND PASSED AT A SESSION OF ASSEMBLY, BEGUN AND
HELD AT THE CITY OF ANNAPOLIS ON MONDAY, THE SEVENTH OF NOVEMBER, IN
THE YEAR OF OUR LORD ONE THOUSAND SEVEN HUNDRED AND NINETY-ONE [—30
December, 1791.] [Arms.]
    Annapolis: Printed by Frederick Green, Printer to the State. [1792.] pp.
(2), (100). fol.
              AAS. HC. LOC. NYPL.

24504   —— LAWS OF MARYLAND, MADE AND PASSED AT A SESSION OF ASSEMBLY, BEGUN AND
HELD AT THE CITY OF ANNAPOLIS ON MONDAY THE SECOND OF APRIL, IN THE
YEAR OF OUR LORD ONE THOUSAND SEVEN HUNDRED AND NINETY-TWO [—6 April,
1792.] [Arms.]
    Annapolis: Printed by Frederick Green, Printer to the State. [1792.] pp.
(7). fol.
              AAS. HC. LOC. NYPL.

24505   —— VOTES AND PROCEEDINGS OF THE HOUSE OF DELEGATES OF THE STATE OF
MARYLAND. NOVEMBER SESSION, 1791. BEING THE FIRST SESSION OF THIS
ASSEMBLY [8 November,—30 December, 1791.]
    [Annapolis: Printed by Frederick Green, 1792.] pp. 146. fol.   NYPL.

24506   —— — VOTES AND PROCEEDINGS OF THE HOUSE OF DELEGATES OF THE STATE OF
MARYLAND. NOVEMBER SESSION, 1791. BEING THE FIRST SESSION OF THIS
ASSEMBLY [—6 April, 1792.]
    [Annapolis: Printed by Frederick Green, 1792.] pp. 146. fol.   LOC.

24507   —— VOTES AND PROCEEDINGS OF THE SENATE OF THE STATE OF MARYLAND. NOV-
EMBER SESSION, 1791. BEING THE FIRST SESSION OF THE FOURTH SENATE [7
NOVEMBER,—30 DECEMBER, 1791.]
    [Annapolis: Printed by Frederick Green, 1792.] pp. 57, fol. LOC. NYPL.

24508   —— — VOTES AND PROCEEDINGS OF THE SENATE OF THE STATE OF MARYLAND.
APRIL SESSION, 1792. BEING THE SECOND SESSION OF THE FOURTH SENATE
[—6 APRIL, 1792.]
    [Annapolis: Printed by Frederick Green, 1792.] pp. (59)—66. fol. LOC.

24509   MARYLAND SOCIETY FOR PROMOTING THE ABOLITION OF SLAVERY.
AT A MEETING OF "THE MARYLAND SOCIETY FOR PROMOTING THE ABOLITION OF
SLAVERY, AND THE RELIEF OF FREE NEGROES, AND OTHERS, UNLAWFULLY HELD
IN BONDAGE," HELD AT BALTIMORE, THE 4TH OF FEBRUARY, 1792, RESOLVED,
THAT THE REPORT OF THE COMMITTEE OF GRIEVANCES, IN CONSEQUENCE OF THE
COMPLAINT OF MESSRS. EZEKIEL JOHN, AND EDWARD DORSEY, TOGETHER WITH
THE MEMORIAL PRESENTED TO THE GENERAL ASSEMBLY BY THIS SOCIETY, AND
THE RESOLVES OF THE HOUSE OF DELEGATES, UPON THE SAID REPORT AND MEM-
ORIAL, BE PUBLISHED, FOR THE INFORMATION OF THEIR FELLOW-CITIZENS, IN
THE MARYLAND JOURNAL, &c. RESOLVED, THAT THE SAME BE ACCOMPANIED
WITH AN ADDRESS TO THE PUBLIC, IN VINDICATION OF THE CONDUCT OF THIS
SOCIETY FROM THE CHARGES CONTAINED IN THOSE RESOLVES OF THE HOUSE OF
DELEGATES. EXTRACTS FROM THE MINUTES, JOSEPH TOWNSEND, SECRETARY.
[Colophon:]
    Baltimore: Printed by William Goddard and James Angell. [1792.] pp.
[8.] 4to.
              LOC. MHS.

24510 THE MARYLAND GAZETTE. XLVII TH YEAR. NO. 2347. THURSDAY, JANUARY 5, [—XLVIII TH YEAR. NO. 2398. THURSDAY, DECEMBER 27, 1792.]
Annapolis: Printed by Frederick and Samuel Green. 1792. fol. MdHS.

24511 THE MARYLAND GAZETTE, AND FREDERICK WEEKLY ADVERTISER. VOL. II. NO. 99. SATURDAY, JANUARY 7, [—VOL. III. NO. 150. SATURDAY, DECEMBER 29, 1792.]
Frederick-Town: Printed by John Winter, at the Printing-Office in Patrick-Street, . . . 1792. fol.
Apparently publication was made throughout the year.

24512 THE MARYLAND GAZETTE: OR, THE BALTIMORE ADVERTISER. PUBLISHED EVERY TUESDAY AND FRIDAY. VOL. IX. NO. 756. TUESDAY, JANUARY 3, [— ——]
Baltimore: Printed and published by John Hayes, the corner of Market and Calvert Streets, . . . 1792. fol.
At what date this year the Gazette was discontinued is not known.

24513 THE MARYLAND HERALD, AND EASTERN SHORE INTELLIGENCER. VOL. II. NO. 84. TUESDAY, JANUARY 3, [—VOL. III. NO. 135. TUESDAY, DECEMBER 25, 1792.]
Easton: Printed by James Cowan. 1792. fol. MdHS.

24514 THE MARYLAND JOURNAL AND BALTIMORE ADVERTISER. NO. 1. OF VOL. XIX. NO. 1416. TUESDAY, JANUARY 3, [—NO. 104. OF VOL. XIX. NO. 1519. FRIDAY, DECEMBER 28, 1792.]
Baltimore: Printed by W. Goddard and J. Angell, Market-Street. 1792. fol. MdHS.
The partnership of William Goddard, and James Angell, his brother-in-law, expired on the 23 October, 1792; but the name of William Goddard was carried in the imprint until 19 February, 1793, when it was permanently dropped from the Journal, which he founded in 1773.

24515 MASSACHUSETTENSIS, pseudonym.
STRICTURES AND OBSERVATIONS UPON THE THREE EXECUTIVE DEPARTMENTS OF THE GOVERNMENT OF THE UNITED STATES; CALCULATED TO SHEW THE NECESSITY OF SOME CHANGE THEREIN, THAT THE PUBLIC MAY DERIVE THAT ABLE AND IMPARTIAL EXECUTION OF THE POWERS DELEGATED, UPON WHICH ALONE THEIR HAPPINESS AT HOME AND THEIR RESPECTABILITY ABROAD MUST MATERIALLY DEPEND. BY MASSACHUSETTENSIS.
Printed in the United States of America. M,DCC,XCII. pp. 32. 8vo.
AAS. JCB. LOC. NYHS.

24516 MASSACHUSETTS. STATE.
[Arms.] ACTS AND LAWS, PASSED BY THE GENERAL COURT OF MASSACHUSETTS. BEGUN AND HELD AT BOSTON, IN THE COUNTY OF SUFFOLK, ON WEDNESDAY THE ELEVENTH DAY OF JANUARY, ANNO DOMINI, 1792. [Colophon:]
Printed in Boston, at the State Press, by Thomas Adams, Printer to the honorable the General Court. M,DCC,XCII. pp. 121–189. fol. AAS. LOC. NYPL.

24517 —— — [Arms.] ACTS AND LAWS, PASSED BY THE GENERAL COURT OF MASSACHUSETTS. BEGUN AND HELD AT BOSTON, IN THE COUNTY OF SUFFOLK, ON WEDNESDAY THE THIRTIETH DAY OF MAY, ANNO DOMINI, 1792. [Colophon:]
Printed in Boston, Massachusetts: at the State Press, by Thomas Adams, Printer to the honourable, the General Court. 1792. pp. 191–222. fol.
AAS. LOC. NYPL.

MASSACHUSETTS, continued,

24518 —— — [Arms.] ACTS AND LAWS, PASSED BY THE GENERAL COURT OF MASSACHU-
SETTS. BEGUN AND HELD AT BOSTON, IN THE COUNTY OF SUFFOLK, ON WEDNES-
DAY THE THIRTIETH DAY OF MAY, ANNO DOMINI, 1792; AND FROM THENCE CON-
TINUED BY PROROGATION AND PROCLAMATION TO WEDNESDAY, THE SEVENTH DAY
OF NOVEMBER, AT CONCORD, IN THE COUNTY OF MIDDLESEX. [Colophon:]
Boston: Printed by Thomas Adams. [1792.] pp. 223–230. fol.
AAS. LOC. NYPL.

24519 —— COMMONWEALTH [Arms] OF MASSACHUSETTS. BY HIS EXCELLENCY JOHN HAN-
COCK, ESQUIRE, GOVERNOR OF THE COMMONWEALTH OF MASSACHUSETTS. A
PROCLAMATION FOR A DAY OF FASTING, HUMILIATION AND PRAYER [on Thurs-
day, the twenty-ninth day of March.] GIVEN AT THE COUNCIL-CHAMBER IN
BOSTON, THE TWENTY-FOURTH DAY OF FEBRUARY, IN THE YEAR OF OUR LORD,
ONE THOUSAND SEVEN HUNDRED AND NINETY-TWO, AND IN THE SIXTEENTH YEAR
OF THE INDEPENDENCE OF THE UNITED STATES OF AMERICA. JOHN HANCOCK.
BY HIS EXCELLENCY'S COMMAND, WITH THE ADVICE AND CONSENT OF COUNCIL,
JOHN AVERY, JUN. SECRETARY. GOD SAVE THE COMMONWEALTH OF MASSA-
CHUSETTS! [Colophon:]
*Boston, Massachusetts: Printed by Thomas Adams, Printer to the honour-
able the General Court.* [1792.] Broadside. fol.   AAS.

24520 —— COMMONWEALTH [Arms] OF MASSACHUSETTS. BY HIS EXCELLENCY JOHN HAN-
COCK, ESQUIRE, GOVERNOR OF THE COMMONWEALTH OF MASSACHUSETTS. A
PROCLAMATION FOR A DAY OF PUBLIC THANKSGIVING [on Thursday, the twen-
ty-ninth day of November next.] GIVEN AT THE COUNCIL-CHAMBER IN
BOSTON, THE TWENTY-FIFTH DAY OF OCTOBER, IN THE YEAR OF OUR LORD, ONE
THOUSAND SEVEN HUNDRED AND NINETY-TWO, AND IN THE SEVENTEENTH YEAR
OF THE INDEPENDENCE OF THE UNITED STATES OF AMERICA. JOHN HANCOCK.
BY HIS EXCELLENCY'S COMMAND, WITH THE ADVICE AND CONSENT OF COUNCIL.
JOHN AVERY, JUN. SECRETARY. GOD SAVE THE COMMONWEALTH OF MASSA-
CHUSETTS! [Colophon:]
*Printed at Boston, Massachusetts, at the State Press: by Thomas Adams,
Printer to the honourable the General Court.* [1792.] Broadside. fol.
AAS. BPL. NYHS.

24521 —— COMMONWEALTH OF MASSACHUSETTS. IN THE YEAR OF OUR LORD, ONE THOU-
SAND SEVEN HUNDRED AND NINETY-TWO. AN ACT FOR ENQUIRING INTO THE
RATEABLE ESTATES WITHIN THIS COMMONWEALTH. [Colophon:]
*Printed at Boston, by Thomas Adams, Printer to the honourable, the General
Court.* M,DCC,XCII. pp. 8. 4to.   HSP.

24522 —— COMMONWEALTH OF MASSACHUSETTS. IN THE YEAR OF OUR LORD, ONE THOU-
SAND SEVEN HUNDRED AND NINETY-TWO. AN ACT TO INCORPORATE SUNDRY PER-
SONS BY THE NAME OF "THE PRESIDENT AND DIRECTORS OF THE MASSACHUSETTS
STATE BANK. [Colophon:]
*[Published by order of the House of Representatives] by Thomas Adams, at
the State Press in Boston, [Massachusetts] 1792.* pp. 8. 8vo.   AAS. LOC.

24523 —— COMMONWEALTH OF MASSACHUSETTS. IN THE YEAR OF OUR LORD ONE THOU-
SAND SEVEN HUNDRED AND NINETY-TWO. AN ACT TO INCORPORATE SUNDRY PER-
SONS BY THE NAME OF "THE PRESIDENT AND TRUSTEES OF THE BOSTON TONTINE
ASSOCIATION."
[Boston: Printed by Thomas Adams, 1792.] Broadside. fol.   AAS.

24524 —— RESOLVE FOR DISTRICTING THE COMMONWEALTH FOR THE PURPOSE OF CHOOS-
ING ELECTORS OF PRESIDENT, 1792.
Boston: Printed by Thomas Adams. 1792. pp. 4. 4to.   MHS.

MASSACHUSETTS, continued.

24525 —— — RESOLVE FOR DISTRICTING THE COMMONWEALTH, FOR THE PURPOSE OF CHOOSING FEDERAL REPRESENTATIVES. IN SENATE, JUNE 30, 1792.
[*Boston: Printed by Thomas Adams, 1792.*] pp. 7. 4to.
AAS. JCB. MHS. NYPL.

24526 —— — RESOLVE FOR DISTRICTING THE COMMONWEALTH FOR THE PURPOSE OF CHOOSING FEDERAL REPRESENTATIVES. COMMONWEALTH OF MASSACHUSETTS. IN SENATE, JUNE 30, 1792.

Second heading: RESOLVE FOR DISTRICTING THE COMMONWEALTH FOR THE PURPOSE OF CHOOSING ELECTORS OF PRESIDENT AND VICE-PRESIDENT. COMMONWEALTH OF MASSACHUSETTS. IN THE HOUSE OF REPRESENTATIVES, JUNE 29, 1792. [Colophon:]
Printed in Boston, Massachusetts: At the State Press, by Thomas Adams, Printer to the honourable, the General Court. M,DCC,XCII. pp. 12. 4to. NYPL.

24527 —— RESOLVES OF THE GENERAL COURT OF THE COMMONWEALTH OF MASSACHU-SETTS: BEGUN AND HELD AT BOSTON, IN THE COUNTY OF SUFFOLK, ON WEDNES-DAY THE TWENTY-FIFTH DAY OF MAY, ANNO DOMINI, 1791; AND FROM THENCE CONTINUED BY ADJOURNMENT, TO WEDNESDAY THE ELEVENTH DAY OF JANUARY FOLLOWING [— 9 March, 1792.]
[*Boston: Printed by Thomas Adams, 1792.*] pp. [33] – 78. Index, [8.] fol. AAS. LOC. NYPL.

24528 —— — RESOLVES OF THE GENERAL COURT OF THE COMMONWEALTH OF MASSA-CHUSETTS. BEGUN AND HELD AT BOSTON, IN THE COUNTY OF SUFFOLK, ON WEDNESDAY THE THIRTIETH DAY OF MAY, ANNO DOMINI, 1792 [— 30 June, 1792.]
Boston: Printed by Thomas Adams, Printer to the honourable General Court. M,DCC,XCII. pp. 28. fol. AAS. NYPL.

24529 —— — RESOLVES OF THE GENERAL COURT OF THE COMMONWEALTH OF MASSA-CHUSETTS: BEGUN AND HELD AT BOSTON, IN THE COUNTY OF SUFFOLK, ON WED-NESDAY THE THIRTIETH DAY OF MAY, ANNO DOMINI, 1792; AND FROM THENCE CON-TINUED BY PROROGATION AND PROCLAMATION TO WEDNESDAY, THE SEVENTH DAY OF NOVEMBER, AT CONCORD, IN THE COUNTY OF MIDDLESEX [— 16 November, 1792.]
[*Boston: Printed by Thomas Adams, 1792.*] pp. [79 *sic* 29] — 37. fol. AAS. NYPL.
Pages 29 to 32, are mispaged, 79, 80, 81, 82.

24530 MASSACHUSETTS HISTORICAL SOCIETY.
COLLECTIONS OF THE MASSACHUSETTS HISTORICAL SOCIETY, FOR THE YEAR 1792. VOLUME I.
Printed at the Apollo Press in Boston, by Belknap and Hall. MDCCXCII. pp. (2), (2), 288. 8vo. AAS. HC. JCB. LOC. NL. NYHS.
Reprinted in Boston, in 1806.

24531 THE MASSACHUSETTS MAGAZINE, OR MONTHLY MUSEUM. CONTAINING THE LITER-ATURE, HISTORY, POLITICS, ARTS, MANNERS & AMUSEMENTS OF THE AGE. [One line of Latin.] VOL. IV FOR [January—December] 1792. [Cut.]
Printed at Boston, by I. Thomas and E. T. Andrews; at Faust's Statue, No. 45, Newbury Street. MDCCXCII. pp. (2), iv, 770. 9 plates, engraved title-page. 8vo. AAS. BA. HC. JCB. LOC. MHS.

24532 MATHER, Ralph
FAMILIAR LETTERS. BY THE REV. MR. RALPH MATHER, MEMBER OF THE NEW-JERUSALEM CHURCH, IN LIVERPOOL; ADDRESSED TO THE JUDGMENT OF THE LOVERS OF TRUTH.
Baltimore: Printed by Samuel and John Adams, in Market-street. 1792. pp. 200. 8vo.

24533 MATTHEWS, William
AN ADDRESS TO THE PUBLIC.
[Baltimore: 1792.] pp. 94. 16mo.   BA.

24534 MEASE, James   1771 – 1846
AN INAUGURAL DISSERTATION ON THE DISEASE PRODUCED BY THE BITE OF A MAD DOG, OR OTHER RABID ANIMAL.: SUBMITTED TO THE EXAMINATION OF THE REV. JOHN EWING, S. T. P. PROVOST; THE TRUSTEES AND MEDICAL FACULTY OF THE UNIVERSITY OF PENNSYLVANIA, ON THE ELEVENTH DAY OF MAY, 1792, FOR THE DEGREE OF DOCTOR OF MEDICINE. BY JAMES MEASE, A. M. OF PHILADELPHIA. [Two lines from] LUCAN. PHARSAL.
Philadelphia: Printed by Thomas Dobson, at the Stone-House, Second-Street. M,DCC,XCII. pp. (2), (3), v, [130], (1). 8vo.
     AAS. BA. BM. HC. JCB. SGO.

24535 THE MEDLEY OR NEWBEDFORD MARINE JOURNAL. VOL. I. No. 1. SATURDAY, NOVEMBER 24, [—No. 6. SATURDAY, DECEMBER 29, 1792.]
Newbedford, (Massachusetts). Printed and published by John Spooner at his office, corner of Water & Prospect Streets. 1792. fol.
Established by John Spooner, and continued by him into the year 1799, when publication was suspended.

24536 MEMORIALS PRESENTED TO THE CONGRESS OF THE UNITED STATES OF AMERICA, BY THE DIFFERENT SOCIETIES INSTITUTED FOR PROMOTING THE ABOLITION OF SLAVERY, &C. &C. IN THE STATES OF RHODE-ISLAND, CONNECTICUT, NEW-YORK, PENNSYLVANIA, MARYLAND, AND VIRGINIA. PUBLISHED BY ORDER OF "THE PENNSYLVANIA SOCIETY FOR PROMOTING THE ABOLITION OF SLAVERY, AND THE RELIEF OF FREE NEGROES UNLAWFULLY HELD IN BONDAGE, AND FOR IMPROVING THE CONDITION OF THE AFRICAN RACE. [Monogram.]
Philadelphia: Printed by Francis Bailey, No. 116. High-street. MDCC-XCII. pp. (4), [31.] 8vo.   BA. JCB. LCP. LOC. MHS.

24537 MERCER, John
AN ORATION DELIVERED ON THE 4TH OF JULY 1792. BEFORE THE PRESIDENT, PROFESSORS AND MASTERS OF WILLIAM & MARY COLLEGE. BY JOHN MERCER, STUDENT. [Ornament.]
Richmond: Printed by T. Nicolson. [1792.] pp. [19.] 8vo.
     JCB. LOC. MHS.

24538 MERCER, John Francis   1759 – 1821
MR. MERCER CONSIDERS MR. [DAVID] ROSS'S PUBLICATION AGAINST HIM IN NO OTHER RESPECT WORTHY OF REPLY, THAN AS IT CONTAINS ONE CONTINUED TISSUE OF MISREPRESENTATION OF SENTIMENT AND MISSTATEMENT OF FACT, [Twenty-two lines.]
Annapolis, [Printed by F. & S. Green] September 15, 1792. Broadside. 4to.
This is in answer to "Strictures on Mercer's Introductory discourse relative to the payments made of the British debts into the Treasury of Maryland during the late war," (published in 1789), and issued anonymously in London, in 1790.

24539   MEREDITH. New-Hampshire. Baptist Association.
Minutes of the Meredith Association, held at Sandbornton, September 13-14, 1792.
     Concord: Printed by George Hough. 1792. 12mo.   BM.

24540   MERRIAM, Matthew   1739 – 1797
Sermons preached to Joshua Abbott; at York, September 3, 1792: preparatory to the sixth: the day appointed for his execution; when his pardon was publicly read by the minister, at the desire of the sheriff, in the meeting-house to a numerous assembly of people. By Mathew Merriam, of Berwick, and Joseph Buckminster of Portsmouth, N. H. With an address to John Hancock, by Mathew Merriam, of Berwick, and Joseph Buckminster of Portsmouth, N. H.
     [Newburyport:] Printed and sold by John Mycall. [1792.] pp. 83.
8vo.   BA. BPL. JCB. LOC. NYHS.

     Second title: A Discourse; the substance of which was delivered at York, on Monday, September 3, 1792: the day on which Joshua Abbott, jun. received a pardon, from the Governor and Council of the Commonwealth of Massachusetts. By Joseph Buckminster.
     [Newburyport: Printed by John Mycall, 1792.] pp. 53–83.

24541   MERRIMACK HUMANE SOCIETY.
By-laws of the Merrimack Humane Society.
     Newburyport: Printed by John Mycall. 1792. 8vo.

24542   —— Laws of the Merrimack Humane Society.
     Newburyport: Printed by John Mycall. [1792.] 8vo.

24543   METHODIST EPISCOPAL CHURCH in America.
The Doctrines and discipline of the Methodist Episcopal Church in America, revised and approved at the General Conference held at Baltimore, in the State of Maryland, in November, 1792: in which Thomas Coke, and Francis Asbury, presided: arranged under proper heads, and methodised in a more acceptable and easy manner. The eighth edition.
     Philadelphia: Printed by Parry Hall, No. 148. Chesnut street, and sold by John Dickins, No. 182. Race street, between Fifth and Sixth street. M.DCC.-XCII. pp. (264), (4). 12mo.   AAS. PHS. PTS.

24544   —— Minutes, taken at the several conferences of the Methodist Episcopal Church, in America. For the year 1792.
     Philadelphia: Printed by Parry Hall, No. 149, Chesnut Street, near Fourth Street. 1792.

24545   —— A Pocket hymn-book, designed as a constant companion for the pious. Collected from various authors. The thirteenth edition. Psalm civ. 33. [Three lines.]
     Philadelphia: Printed by Parry Hall, No. 149, Chesnut Street, near Fourth Street. 1792.
     A fourteenth edition may have been printed this year, also.

24546   THE MIDDLESEX Gazette, or, Fœderal adviser. Vol. VII. Numb. 323. Saturday, January 7, [—Vol. VIII. Numb. 371. Saturday, December 29, 1792.]
     Printed by Moses H. Woodward, in the Town-House Chamber, Middletown.
1792. fol.   AAS. CHS.
     Beginning March 3d, the title was shortened to, *The Middlesex Gazette.*

24547   MISCELLANEOUS reflections in verse when under long confinement by a
        complication of nervous disorders. By a Valetudinary.
                Greenfield, Massachusetts: Printed by Thomas Dickman. 1792. pp. 40. 16mo.

24548   MISCELLANIES, moral and instructive, in prose and verse; collected from
        various authors, for the use of schools, and improvement of young per-
        sons of both sexes. Second edition.
                Burlington: Printed by Isaac Neale. 1792.   pp. 180. 12mo.

24549   MITCHILL, Samuel Latham   1764 – 1831
        Outline of the doctrines in natural history, chemistry, and economics
        . . . now delivering in the College of New-York.
                New-York: 1792. 8vo.   BM.

24550   THE [cut] MONITOR. Vol. vii. No. 339. Wednesday, January 4, [—Vol. viii.
        No. 386. Wednesday, December 26, 1792.]
                Litchfield, (Connecticut) Printed by Collier and Buel. 1792. fol.   YC.

        Beginning January 11th, the title of the *Litchfield Monitor* was short-
        ened as above.

24551   MONSTROUS good songs for 1792.
                Boston: 1792. 12mo.

24552   MOORE, Benjamin   1748 – 1816
        The Doctrine of regeneration asserted and explained: a sermon, preached
        in St. George's chapel, New-York, July 7, 1791. The second edition. By
        Benjamin Moore, d. d.
                New-York: Printed by Hugh Gaine, in Hanover-Square. — 1792. — pp.
        24. 4to.   JCB.

        Ends with the catchword "We" on page 24.

24553   MOORE, John   1730 – 1802
        A View of society and manners in France, Switzerland. and Germany: with
        anecdotes relating to some eminent characters. By John Moore, m. d.
        [Two lines of Latin from] Horace. [Vignette.]
                *Printed at the Apollo Press, in Boston, by Belknap and Young, for David
        West, No. 36, Marlborough Street, and Ebenezer Larkin, jun. No. 50, Cornhill.*
        MDCCXCII. pp. xx, 430. 8vo.   AAS.

24554   —— A View of society and manners in Italy: with anecdotes relating to
        some eminent characters. By John Moore, m. d. [Two lines of Latin from]
        Horace. [Vignette.]
                *Printed at the Apollo Press, in Boston, by Belknap and Young, for David
        West, No. 36, Marlborough Street, and Ebenezer Larkin, jun. No. 50, Cornhill.*
        MDCCXCII. pp. xvi, 512. 8vo.   AAS. BPL. JCB.

24555   —— Zeluco. Various views of human nature, taken from life and manners,
        foreign and domestic. [Seven lines of Latin from] Juv. [Vignette.]
                *Boston: Printed by Alexander Young, in State Street, for David West, No.
        36, Marlborough Street, and Ebenezer Larkin, jun. No. 50, Cornhill.* MDCCXCII.
        pp. 560. 8vo.   AAS. BA.

24556 MOORE, John Hamilton – 1807
THE YOUNG GENTLEMAN AND LADY'S MONITOR, AND ENGLISH TEACHER'S ASSISTANT:
BEING A COLLECTION OF SELECT PIECES FROM OUR BEST MODERN WRITERS: CAL-
CULATED TO ERADICATE VULGAR PREJUDICES AND RUSTICITY OF MANNERS; IM-
PROVE THE UNDERSTANDING: RECTIFY THE WILL; PURIFY THE PASSIONS; DIRECT
THE MINDS OF YOUTH TO THE PURSUIT OF PROPER OBJECTS; AND TO FACILITATE
THEIR READING, WRITING, AND SPEAKING THE ENGLISH LANGUAGE, WITH ELE-
GANCE AND PROPRIETY. PARTICULARLY ADAPTED FOR THE USE OF OUR EMINENT
SCHOOLS AND ACADEMIES, AS WELL AS PRIVATE PERSONS, WHO HAVE NOT HAD AN OP-
PORTUNITY OF PERUSING THE WORKS OF THOSE CELEBRATED AUTHORS, FROM
WHENCE THIS COLLECTION IS MADE. DIVIDED INTO SMALL PORTIONS FOR THE EASE
OF READING IN CLASSES. THE SEVENTH EDITION. BY J. HAMILTON MOORE,
AUTHOR OF THE PRACTICAL NAVIGATOR AND SEAMAN'S NEW DAILY ASSISTANT.
*London: Printed: New-York: Re-printed by Hugh Gaine, at the Bible,
in Hanover-Square.* M.DCC.XCII. pp. (2), (2), 368; (28), (6), (6), 4 plates.
12mo. AAS. NYPL.
"This last edition of the Monitor is greatly enrich'd by a number of choice
pieces, viz. The History of the Old and New Testament.—A Compar-
ative view of the blessed and cursed at the last day, and the inference
to be drawn from it.—Life of Columbus, and the discovery of America.
To which is also added a poem, entitled, Philosophic solitude; or, the
choice of a rural life. Written by the late William Livingston, esq; formerly Governor of New-Jersey. Together with the Elements of gesture."

24557 MOORE, Thomas, pseudonym
GAINE'S NEW-YORK POCKET ALMANACK, FOR THE YEAR 1793: BEING THE FIRST
AFTER LEAP YEAR, AND 17TH OF AMERICAN INDEPENDENCE, TILL 4TH JULY.
CALCULATED FOR THIS AND THE NEIGHBOURING STATES. SIGNS, PLANETS, AND
ASPECTS. . . . BY THOMAS MOORE, PHILO.
New-York: Printed by H. Gaine, at the Bible, in Hanover-Square. [1792.]
pp. [72.] 48mo. AAS. NYPL.

24558 MOORE, Thomas Lambert
A SERMON DELIVERED IN TRINITY-CHURCH AND ST. PAUL'S, IN THE CITY OF NEW-
YORK, ON SUNDAY THE 14TH OF OCTOBER, 1792; AND ON SUNDAY THE 21ST OF
THE SAME MONTH, IN THE CHURCH UNDER THE CHARGE OF THE AUTHOR. BY
THOMAS LAMBERT MOORE, A. M. RECTOR OF ST. GEORGE-CHURCH, SOUTH-HEMP-
STEAD. [Five lines of Scripture texts.]
New-York: Printed by Hugh Gaine, at the Bible, in Hanover-Square, 1792.
pp. (16). 8vo. NYHS. NYPL.

24559 THE MORALIST: OR YOUNG GENTLEMAN AND LADY'S ENTERTAINING COMPANION:
BEING A COLLECTION OF MORAL TALES AND STORIES.
Providence: Sold by Bennett Wheeler. 1792.

24560 MORGAN, James
THE LIFE AND DEATH OF THOMAS WALSH. TO WHICH IS ADDED AN EXTRACT FROM
JOHN NELSON'S JOURNAL. [Ornament.]
*Philadelphia: Printed by Parry Hall, No. 149, Chesnut Street and sold
by John Dickins, No. 182, Race Street near Sixth Street.* M.DCC.XCII. pp.
356, (2). 12mo. JCB.
Second title: THE LIFE AND DEATH OF THOMAS WALSH, COMPOSED IN GREAT PART
FROM HIS OWN ACCOUNTS. BY JAMES MORGAN. [Two lines of Scripture texts.]
pp. [3] — 190.
Third title: AN EXTRACT FROM JOHN NELSON'S JOURNAL; BEING AN ACCOUNT OF
GOD'S DEALING WITH HIM FROM HIS YOUTH TO THE FORTY-SECOND YEAR OF HIS
AGE. WRITTEN BY HIMSELF. [Six lines.] pp. 191 — 338.

MORGAN, JAMES, continued,
Fourth title: A RACE FOR ETERNAL LIFE: BEING AN EXTRACT FROM THE
HEAVENLY FOOTMAN. A SERMON ON I CORINTHIANS, IX. 24. WRITTEN BY THE
AUTHOR OF THE PILGRIM'S PROGRESS. BY THE REV. MR. FLETCHER.
*Philadelphia: Printed by Parry Hall, No. 149, Chesnut Street and sold by
John Dickins, No. 182, Race Street, near Sixth Street.* M.DCC.XCII. pp. 339 — 356.

24561   THE MORNING POST, AND DAILY ADVERTISER. No. 2161. MONDAY JANUARY 2,
[—No. 2300. TUESDAY, JUNE 12, 1792.]
*New-York: Printed and published by William Morton, at his Printing-
office, No. 55, King-Street.* 1792. fol.
How long the Post was continued after the above date is not known.

24562   THE MORNING RAY: OR, IMPARTIAL ORACLE. [Motto.] VOL. I. NO. 11. TUES-
DAY, JANUARY 3, [—No. 51. TUESDAY, OCTOBER 9, 1792.]
*Windsor (Vermont)—Published by Hutchins & Spooner, on the Mainstreet,
every Tuesday morning.* 1792. fol.

"The Printers in the several towns are hereby notified *The Morning Ray*
lately published in Windsor, Vermont, by Mr. James Reed Hutchins,
is now discontinued."—Spooner's Vermont Journal. October 15, 1792.

24563   MORRISON, WILLIAM   1748 – 1818
A SERMON, DELIVERED AT DOVER, STATE OF NEW-HAMPSHIRE; BEFORE THE HON-
ORABLE GENERAL COURT, AT THE ANNUAL ELECTION, JUNE 7TH, 1792. BY WIL-
LIAM MORISON [*sic*] MINISTER OF A PRESBYTERIAN CHURCH, LONDONDERRY.
[New Hampshire Arms.]
*New-Hampshire: Exeter, Printed by Henry Ranlet, for the General Court
of said State—and sold at his office*—1792. pp. 43. 4to.   BM. JCB. NYHS.

24564   MOZART, JOHANN CHRYSOSTOMUS SIGISMUND WOLFGANG AMADEUS   1756 – 1791
DON JUAN; OR THE LIBERTINE DESTROYED. A GRAND PANTOMIMICAL BALLET, IN
TWO PARTS. AS PERFORMED WITH GREAT APPLAUSE BY THE OLD AMERICAN
COMPANY AT THE THEATRE IN SOUTHWARK. FIRST AMERICAN EDITION.
Philadelphia: From the Press of Mathew Carey, Dec. 22, 1792. pp. 12.
12mo.   BPL.

24565   MUCKARSIE, JOHN
THE CHILDREN'S CATECHISM: OR, AN HELP TO THE MORE EASY UNDERSTANDING OF
THE DOCTRINE TAUGHT IN OUR CONFESSION OF FAITH; AND CATECHISMS, LARGER
AND SHORTER; HUMBLY OFFERED FOR INSTRUCTING THE YOUNG AND IGNORANT.
BY JOHN MUCKARSIE, MINISTER OF THE GOSPEL AT KINKELL. [Five lines of
Scripture texts.] A NEW EDITION, CORRECTED AND IMPROVED.
*Philadelphia: Printed by William Young, Bookseller, No. 52, Second
Street, the corner of Chesnut-Street.* MDCCXCII. pp. 35, (1). 12mo.   BA.

24566   NANCREDE, PAUL JOSEPH GUÉRARD DE   1760 – 1841
L'ABEILLE FRANÇOISE, OU NOUVEAUX RECUEIL, DE MORCEAUX BRILLANS, DES AU-
TEURS FRANÇOIS LES PLUS CELEBRES. OUVRAGE UTILE À CEUX QUI STUDIENT LA
LANGUE FRANÇOISE, ET AMUSANT POUR CEUX QUI LA CONNOISSENT. A L'USAGE
DE L'UNIVERSITÉ DE CAMBRIDGE. PAR P. J. G. DE NANCREDE, MAÎTRE DE
LANGUE FRANÇOISE EN CETTE UNIVERSITÉ. [Eight lines of quotations.]
*A Boston, De l'Imprimerie de Belknap et Young, Rue de l'Etat, vis-à-vis la
Banque Nationale.* MDCCXCII. [*Published according to Act of Congress.*] pp.
352, v, (3). 12mo.   AAS. BU.
Contains, a three-page Liste des souscripteurs. 30th Massachusetts
District Copyright, issued to P. J. G. de Nancrede, 27 April, 1792.

24567 NASH, JUDAH   1728 – 1805
Half-title: MR. NASH'S SERMON AT THE FUNERAL OF MADAM KENDALL. NEW-
SALEM, APRIL 22, 1790.
Title: A DISCOURSE, DELIVERED AT THE FUNERAL OF MRS. ANNA KENDALL,
CONSORT OF THE REV. SAMUEL KENDALL, OF NEW-SALEM, ON THE 22D DAY OF
APRIL, 1790, IN THE EIGHTIETH YEAR OF HER AGE. BY JUDAH NASH, A. M.
PASTOR OF THE CHURCH IN MONTAGUE. [Ornament.]
Springfield : Printed by Ezra Waldo Weld. MDCCXCII. pp. 13. 8vo. AAS.

24568 NATIONAL GAZETTE. BY PHILIP FRENEAU. NUMB. 19 OF VOL. I. MONDAY, JAN-
UARY 2, [—NUMB.·18 OF VOL. II. TOTAL NO. 122. SATURDAY, DECEMBER 29,
1792.]
*Printed by Childs and Swaine, at their office, No. 239, High-Street. near
Sixth-Street, Philadelphia.* 1792. pp. 73—416; 1—72. fol. HC. LCP. LOC.
In July, the days of publication were changed from Mondays and
Thursdays, to Wednesdays and Saturdays.

24569 DER NEUE, GEMEINNÜTZIGE LANDWIRTHSCHAFT CALENDER, AUF DAS JAHR, NACH
DER HEILBRINGENDEN GEBURT UNSERS HERRN JESU CHRISTI, 1793. WELCHES
EIN GEMEIN JAHR VON 365 TAGEN IST. [Nine lines.] ZUM SECHSTENMAL HER-
AUSGEGEBEN.
*Lancäster, Gedruckt und zu haben bey Johann Albrecht und Comp. in der
Neuen Buchdruckerey, in der Prinz-strasse, das Zweyte Haus, nordwärts vom Ges-
ängniss.* [1792.] pp. (42). 4to. AAS. LOC.

24570 DER NEUE HOCH DEUTSCHE AMERICANISCHE CALENDER. AUF DAS JAHR 1793.
Chesnuthill: Gedruckt bey Samuel Saur. [1792.]

24571 NEUE PHILADELPHISCHE CORRESPONDENZ. NUM. 131. DIENSTAG DEN 3 JANU-
ARY, [—NUM. 189. DIENSTAG DEN 25TEN DECEMBER, 1792.]
*Diese Zeitung wird alle Dienstag und Freytag heraus gegeben von Melchior
Steiner, Buchdrucker, in der Rees-Strasse, zwischen der Zweyten und Dritten-
Strasse, No. 71; . . . .* 1792. fol. HSP.
Before May, publication was changed to a weekly issue on Tuesdays.
Beginning with the issue for November 6th, Heinrich Kämmerer was
admitted to partnership, under the firm name of Steiner und Käm-
merer. After November 20th, the word "Neue" was dropped, and
publication continued as: *Philadelphische Correspondenz.*

24572 NEUE, UNPARTHEYISCHE LANCÄSTER ZEITUNG UND ANZEIGS-NACHRICHTEN. JANUAR-
DECEMB, 1792.
Lancaster: Gedruckt bey Albrecht & Comp. 1792. fol.

24573 THE NEW-ENGLAND PRIMER IMPROVED, FOR THE MORE EASY ATTAINING THE
TRUE READING OF ENGLISH. TO WHICH IS ADDED THE ASSEMBLY OF DIVINES
CATECHISM.
Hudson: Printed by Ashbel Stoddard. 1792.

24574 —— — THE AMERICAN PRIMER, IMPROVED, OR AN EASY AND PLEASANT GUIDE TO
THE ART OF READING. ADORNED WITH CUTS. TO WHICH IS ADDED, THE ASSEM-
BLY OF DIVINES' CATECHISM.
Boston: Printed by Nathaniel Coverly, for James Gardner, of Providence.
[1792.] pp. (64). 32mo.

AUCTION
VALUES

THE NEW-ENGLAND PRIMER, continued.

24575   —— —— THE AMERICAN PRIMER, IMPROVED, OR AN EASY AND PLEASANT GUIDE TO THE ART OF READING. ADORNED WITH CUTS. TO WHICH IS ADDED, THE ASSEMBLY OF DIVINES' CATECHISM.

Catskill-Landing: Printed by M. Croswell & Co. 1792.

24576   THE NEW GAME OF CARDS, OR, A PACK OF CARDS CHANGED INTO A COMPLEAT AND PERPETUAL ALMANACK, IN A DIALOGUE BETWEEN A NOBLEMAN AND HIS SERVANT. FIRST, SHEWING THE USE OF HIS ALMANACK, BY THE QUARTERS, MONTHS, WEEKS, AND DAYS OF THE YEAR. SECONDLY, SHEWING HOW HE CONVERTS HIS CARDS INTO A COMPLEAT MONITOR, OR PRAYER BOOK; WITH HIS CURIOUS REMARKS ON THE KNAVE. THE WHOLE ADAPTED TO THE ENTERTAINMENT OF THE HUMOROUS, AS WELL AS TO THE SATISFACTION OF THE GRAVE, LEARNED AND INGENIOUS.

[Printed by John Byrne, and] Sold at the Printing-office, Windham. [1792.] pp. 11. 12mo.   AAS.

24577   NEW HAMPSHIRE. STATE.
ARTICLES IN ADDITION TO AND AMENDMENT OF THE CONSTITUTION OF THE STATE OF NEWHAMPSHIRE, AGREED TO BY THE CONVENTION OF SAID STATE, AND SUBMITTED TO THE PEOPLE THEREOF FOR THEIR APPROBATION.

Dover: Printed by E. Ladd, for the State, 1792. pp. 31. 4to.
      JCB. LOC. NYPL.

24578   —— —— ARTICLES IN ADDITION TO AND AMENDMENT OF THE CONSTITUTION OF THE STATE OF NEW HAMPSHIRE. AGREED TO BY THE CONVENTION OF SAID STATE, AND SUBMITTED TO THE PEOPLE THEREOF FOR THEIR APPROBATION. [Ornament.]

Printed at Exeter, New-Hampshire, by Henry Ranlet, and sold at his Office in Mainstreet.—1792.—pp. 33, (1). 4to.   AAS. JCB. LOC. NYPL.

> The copy in the New York Public Library bears the attestation of 124 voters of Gilmantown to all the amendments. The copy in the Library of Congress, the attestation of the voters of Plastow.

24579   —— BY HIS EXCELLENCY JOSIAH BARTLETT, ESQUIRE, PRESIDENT AND COMMANDER IN CHIEF OF THE STATE OF NEW-HAMPSHIRE. A PROCLAMATION FOR A PUBLIC THANKSGIVING. . . . THURSDAY THE FIFTEENTH DAY OF NOVEMBER NEXT, . . . GIVEN AT THE COUNCIL-CHAMBER IN EXETER, THE FIRST DAY OF SEPTEMBER, IN THE YEAR OF OUR LORD ONE THOUSAND SEVEN HUNDRED AND NINETY-TWO, AND OF THE SOVEREIGNTY AND INDEPENDENCE OF THE UNITED STATES OF AMERICA, THE SEVENTEENTH. JOSIAH BARTLETT. [Colophon:]

Exeter: Printed by Henry Ranlet. [1792.] Broadside. fol.

24580   —— THE CONSTITUTION OF NEW HAMPSHIRE, AS ALTERED AND AMENDED BY A CONVENTION OF DELEGATES, HELD AT CONCORD, IN SAID STATE, APPROVED BY THE PEOPLE, AND ESTABLISHED BY THE CONVENTION, ON THE FIRST WEDNESDAY OF SEPTEMBER, 1792. [Arms.]

Concord: Printed by George Hough, by the authority of the Convention. M.DCC.XCII. pp. 70, (1). 8vo.   AAS. HC. JCB. LOC. NYPL.

24581   —— A JOURNAL OF THE PROCEEDINGS OF THE HONORABLE HOUSE OF REPRESENTATIVES OF THE STATE OF NEW-HAMPSHIRE, BEGUN AND HOLDEN AT PORTSMOUTH, NOVEMBER, 1791.

Portsmouth: Printed by J. Melcher. 1792. pp. 151. 8vo.   NHSL.

NEW HAMPSHIRE, continued.

24582 —— — A JOURNAL OF THE PROCEEDINGS OF THE HONORABLE HOUSE OF REPRE-
SENTATIVES OF THE STATE OF NEW-HAMPSHIRE, BEGUN AND HOLDEN AT DOVER,
JUNE, 1792.
Portsmouth: Printed by J. Melcher, 1792. pp. 88. 8vo. NHSL.

24583 —— A JOURNAL OF THE PROCEEDINGS OF THE HONORABLE SENATE OF THE STATE
OF NEW-HAMPSHIRE, AT A SESSION OF THE GENERAL COURT, BEGUN AND HOLDEN
AT PORTSMOUTH, ON NOVEMBER, 1791.
Portsmouth: Printed by J. Melcher, 1792. pp. 71. 8vo. NHSL.

24584 —— — A JOURNAL OF THE PROCEEDINGS OF THE HONORABLE SENATE OF THE
STATE OF NEW-HAMPSHIRE, AT A SESSION OF THE GENERAL COURT, BEGUN AND
HOLDEN AT DOVER, JUNE, 1792.
Portsmouth: Printed by J. Melcher, 1792. pp. 47. 8vo. NHSL.

24585 —— THE LAWS OF THE STATE OF NEW-HAMPSHIRE, TOGETHER WITH THE DECLAR-
ATION OF INDEPENDENCE : THE DEFINITIVE TREATY OF PEACE BETWEEN THE
UNITED STATES OF AMERICA AND HIS BRITANNIC MAJESTY: THE CONSTITUTION
OF NEW-HAMPSHIRE, AND THE CONSTITUTION OF THE UNITED STATES, WITH ITS
PROPOSED AMENDMENTS. [Ornament.] PRINTED BY ORDER OF THE HONORABLE
THE GENERAL-COURT OF THE STATE OF NEW-HAMPSHIRE, FROM ATTESTED COPIES,
AND HAVE SINCE BEEN CAREFULLY COMPARED WITH THE ORIGINALS IN THE SEC-
RETARY'S OFFICE.
Portsmouth: Printed by John Melcher, 1792. pp. 396. 8vo. AAS. BA. HC.

24586 —— — THE LAWS OF THE STATE OF NEW-HAMPSHIRE, PASSED AT A SESSION OF
THE HONORABLE GENERAL COURT, BEGUN AND HOLDEN AT DOVER, JUNE, 1792.
PRINTED FROM ATTESTED COPIES, AND SINCE COLLATED WITH THE ORIGINALS IN
THE SECRETARY'S OFFICE.
Portsmouth: Printed and sold by John Melcher, 1792. pp. (2), 397-422.
8vo. AAS. LOC.

24587 —— STATE OF NEW-HAMPSHIRE. IN THE YEAR OF OUR LORD, ONE THOUSAND
SEVEN HUNDRED AND NINETY-ONE. [L S.] AN ACT TO ESTABLISH A BANK IN THIS
STATE, AND TO INCORPORATE THE SUBSCRIBERS THERETO. [Fifty-four lines.]
STATE OF NEW-HAMPSHIRE. IN THE HOUSE OF REPRESENTATIVES, DECEMBER
31, 1791. THE FOREGOING BILL HAVING BEEN READ A THIRD TIME, PASSED TO
BE ENACTED. WILLIAM PLUMER, SPEAKER. IN SENATE, JANUARY 3, 1792.
THIS BILL HAVING BEEN READ A THIRD TIME, VOTED THAT THE SAME BE ENACTED.
JOSIAH BARTLETT, PRESIDENT. A TRUE COPY. ATTEST, JOSEPH PEARSON,
SECRETARY.
[Portsmouth: Printed by John Melcher. 1792.] pp. (2). fol. JCB.

24588 NEW HAMPSHIRE MEDICAL SOCIETY.
THE CHARTER OF THE NEW-HAMPSHIRE MEDICAL SOCIETY: TOGETHER WITH THEIR
LAWS AND REGULATIONS. TO WHICH ARE PREFIXED A LIST OF THE PRESENT
FELLOWS AND OF THEIR OFFICERS FOR THE CURRENT YEAR. PUBLISHED BY THEIR
ORDER. [Ornament.]
Printed at Exeter, by Henry Ranlet. M,DCC,XCII. pp. 35. 12mo. JCB.

24589 THE NEW-HAMPSHIRE GAZETTE, AND THE GENERAL ADVERTISER. VOL. XXXV.
Nȯ. 1826. WEDNESDAY, JANUARY 4, [—VOL. XXXVI. NUMB. 1876. WEDNESDAY,
DECEMBER 26, 1792.]
Portsmouth: Printed by John Melcher, at his office in Market-Street. 1792.
fol.

24590   THE NEWHAMPSHIRE [U. S. Arms] GAZETTEER. VOL. VI. No. 26. SATURDAY, JANUARY 7, [—VOL. VII. No. 25. WEDNESDAY, DECEMBER 26, 1792.]

Exeter (New-Hampshire) Printed and published by Henry Ranlet, in Main-Street. 1792. fol.

24591   NEW JERSEY. STATE.
ACTS OF THE SIXTEENTH GENERAL ASSEMBLY OF THE STATE OF NEW-JERSEY. AT A SESSION BEGUN AT TRENTON THE 25TH DAY OF OCTOBER, 1791, AND CONTINUED BY ADJOURNMENTS. BEING THE SECOND SITTING [18 MAY, — 2 JUNE, 1792.]

Burlington: Printed by Isaac Neale. M,DCC,XCII. pp. (2), (766)–814, (1). fol.   NYPL.

Second heading: APPENDIX TO THE ACTS OF THE SIXTEENTH GENERAL ASSEMBLY OF THE STATE OF NEW-JERSEY: CONTAINING SUNDRY ACTS OF THE CONGRESS OF THE UNITED STATES, DIRECTED TO BE RE-PUBLISHED FOR THE INFORMATION OF THE CITIZENS OF THIS STATE, BY A RESOLUTION OF THE LEGISLATURE, PASSED THE SECOND DAY OF JUNE, ONE THOUSAND SEVEN HUNDRED AND NINETY-TWO [23 JANUARY, — 8 MAY, 1792.] pp. (782)–814.

24592   —— — ACTS OF THE SEVENTEENTH GENERAL ASSEMBLY OF THE STATE OF NEW-JERSEY. AT A SESSION BEGUN AT TRENTON THE 23D DAY OF OCTOBER 1792, AND CONTINUED BY ADJOURNMENTS. BEING THE FIRST SITTING. [31 OCTOBER, — 30 NOVEMBER, 1792.]

Trenton: Printed by Isaac Collins. M.DCC.XCII. pp. (2), (783) — 829, (1). fol.   NYPL.

24593   —— JOURNAL OF PROCEEDINGS OF LEGISLATIVE COUNCIL OF THE STATE OF NEW-JERSEY. [25 OCTOBER, 1791—2 JUNE, 1792.]

Burlington: Printed by Isaac Neale. 1792.

24594   —— VOTES AND PROCEEDINGS OF THE GENERAL ASSEMBLY OF THE STATE OF NEW-JERSEY. [18 MAY, —2 JUNE, 1792.]

Burlington: Printed by Isaac Neale. 1792.

24595   NEW JERSEY. COLLEGE OF, now popularly known as PRINCETON UNIVERSITY. CATALOGUS COLLEGII NÆO-CÆSARIENSIS.

Trenton: E typis Isaaci Collins. M.DCC.XCII. pp. 16. 8vo.   MHS.

24596   THE NEW-JERSEY, PENNSYLVANIA, DELAWARE, MARYLAND AND VIRGINIA ALMANAC AND EPHEMERIS. FOR THE YEAR OF OUR LORD 1793.

Baltimore: Printed and sold by Samuel and John Adams. [1792.] pp. (36). 12mo.   MHS.

24597   THE NEW-JERSEY JOURNAL, AND POLITICAL INTELLIGENCER. No. 429. WEDNESDAY, JANUARY 4, [—No. 480. WEDNESDAY, DECEMBER 26, 1792.]

Elizabeth-Town: Printed and published by Shepard Kollock, every Wednesday. . . . 1792. fol.   LOC.

In June the sub-title was dropped. The issues from October 3 to November 21, are attractively printed on blue paper.

24598   NEW-JERSEY State Gazette. Vol. i. No. 1. Wednesday, September 12, [—
No. 16. Wednesday, December 26, 1792.]

Trenton: Printed by George Sherman and John Mershon. 1792. fol.

Established by George Sherman, and John Mershon, and continued by
them, as a weekly publication, into the year 1794. At about the end
of the second volume, in September, 1794, they sold their interests to
Matthias Day, who continued publication, under the same title to July,
1796, when he changed the name to *The State Gazette and New-Jersey
Advertiser,* which he continued to February, 1799, when he relinquished
its publication to its former proprietors, and removed to Newark. Sherman and Mershon revived the original title, and began, with a new
numbering, in March, 1799, the publication of the *New-Jersey State
Gazette,* admitting, in a short time, Isaiah Thomas as a member of the
firm. In June, 1800, Sherman, Mershon and Thomas entered into an
agreement with Gershom Craft, proprietor of The Federalist, a rival
newspaper published across the street, to consolidate the two publications, under their joint management, and the united papers were issued
from the Gazette office, with the consecutive volume and number of
that paper, as, *The Federalist & New-Jersey State Gazette.* Craft withdrew from the firm in September. In 1802, the title was again changed
to the *Trenton Federalist.* And, in June, 1828, after consolidation with
the True American, to *State Gazette,* which was again changed to *New
Jersey State Gazette,* in July, 1829. In January, 1840. publication was
made tri-weekly, under the title of *State Gazette,* until January, 1847,
when it became a daily newspaper. In 1857, the title was changed to,
Daily State Gazette and Republican; and this was shortened to *Daily
State Gazette* from May 1863 to 1901. Being continued at the present
time as the *Trenton Daily Gazette.*

24599   NEW JERUSALEM. Church of
The Liturgy of the New Church, signified by the New Jerusalem in the
Revelation. Together with the forms for the administration of baptism and the Holy Supper: and a Catechism for the use of the New
Church. Also, Hymns and spiritual songs, by the Rev. mr. Joseph Proud,
minister of the New Church. The fourth edition. [Two lines from] Rev.
xxi. 5.

Baltimore: Printed and sold by Samuel and John Adams, in Market-Street.
1792. pp. (342), (2). 12mo.   AAS. BA. LCP.

Second title: Hymns and spiritual songs, for the use of the Lord's New
Church, signified by the New Jerusalem in the Revelation. pp. (2), 85–342.

24600   NEW YORK. State.
Journal of the Assembly of the State of New-York. Fifteenth session.
[4 January,—12 April, 1792.] [Arms.]

*New-York: Printed by Francis Childs and John Swaine, Printers to the
State.* M,DCC,XCII. pp. [207.] fol.   AAS. NYHS. NYPL,

24601   —— Journal of the Senate of the State of New-York. Fifteenth session.
[5 January,—12 April, 1792.] [Arms.]

*New-York: Printed by Francis Childs and John Swaine, Printers to the
State.* M,DCC,XCII. pp. [89.] fol.   NYHS. NYPL.

24602   —— Laws of the State of New-York. Comprising the Constitution, and
the Acts of the Legislature, since the Revolution, from the first to
the fifteenth session, inclusive. [Arms.] In two volumes. Volume i.
[—ii.] [Three lines of Latin quotations.]

*New-York—Printed by Thomas Greenleaf—*M,DCC,XCII. 2vols. pp. (2),
(2), 511; (2), (2), 521, (1), (14). 8vo.   BA. HC. JCB. NYHS.

A third volume was printed in 1797.

NEW YORK, continued.

24603   ——— — LAWS OF THE STATE OF NEW-YORK. FIFTEENTH SESSION. [12 January, —12 April, 1792.] [Arms.]
New-York: Printed by Francis Childs and John Swaine, Printers to the State. M,DCC,XCII. pp. 74, (2). fol.   LOC. NYHS. NYPL.

24604   ——— THE REPORT OF A COMMITTEE, APPOINTED TO EXPLORE THE WESTERN WATERS IN THE STATE OF NEW-YORK: FOR THE PURPOSE OF PROSECUTING THE INLAND LOCK NAVIGATION.
Albany: Printed by Barber and Southwick. M,DCC,XCII. pp. [24.] 12mo.   NYHS. NYPL.
Reprinted in Volume 3, of O'Callaghan's Documentary History of New York. Albany, 1850.

24605   NEW YORK. SOCIETY FOR AGRICULTURE, ARTS, AND MANUFACTURES. TRANSACTIONS OF THE SOCIETY, INSTITUTED IN THE STATE OF NEW-YORK, FOR THE PROMOTION OF AGRICULTURE, ARTS, AND MANUFACTURES. PART I. PUBLISHED BY ORDER OF THE SOCIETY.
New-York: Printed by Childs and Swaine. M,DCC,XCII. pp. xiii, (3), 122, 2 plates. 4to.   AAS. BA. BM. MHS. NYHS.

24606   NEW YORK. CITY. ASSOCIATED BODY OF HOUSE CARPENTERS. THE CONSTITUTION OF THE ASSOCIATED BODY OF HOUSE CARPENTERS OF THE CITY OF NEW-YORK.
New-York: 1792. 12mo.

24607   NEW YORK. CITY. FRIAR'S TONTINE. CONSTITUTION OF THE NEW-YORK FRIAR'S TONTINE, INSTITUTED IN THE CITY OF NEW-YORK, 3 MARCH, 1792.
New-York: Printed by Archibald M'Lean. 1792. pp. 15. 8vo.

24608   NEW YORK. CITY. GENERAL SOCIETY OF MECHANICS AND TRADESMEN. AN ACT TO INCORPORATE THE SOCIETY OF MECHANICS AND TRADESMEN OF THE CITY OF NEW-YORK, FOR CHARITABLE PURPOSES. PASSED THE 14TH OF MARCH, 1792.
New-York: Printed by Samuel Loudon, jun. [1792.] pp. 11. 12mo.
This also forms the first eleven pages of the following:

24609   ——— THE CHARTER AND BYE-LAWS OF THE GENERAL SOCIETY OF MECHANICS & TRADESMEN OF THE CITY OF NEW-YORK. ALSO, THE RULES AND ORDERS WITH A CATALOGUE OF NAMES OF THE MEMBERS. PUBLISHED BY ORDER OF THE SOCIETY.
New-York: Printed by John Harrisson, at Yorick's Head, No. 3, Peck-Slip.—1792.—pp. 30. 8vo.   AAS.

24610   NEW YORK. CITY. SOCIETY LIBRARY. A FARTHER CONTINUATION OF THE [1789] CATALOGUE OF THE NEW-YORK SOCIETY LIBRARY.
[New-York: Printed by Thomas and James Swords, 1792.] pp. 109— 131. 8vo.

24611   ——— — A FARTHER CONTINUATION OF THE CATALOGUE OF BOOKS BELONGING TO THE NEW-YORK SOCIETY LIBRARY, WITH THE NAMES OF THE ADDITIONAL MEMBERS OF THE SAID SOCIETY. [Monogram.]
New-York: Printed by Thomas & James Swords, at their Printing-Office, No. 27, William-Street; where printing in general is executed with neatness, accuracy and dispatch, and on reasonable terms.—1792.—pp. 100. 8vo.
A "Circular" was also issued by the Society Library this year.

24612 NEW YORK. CITY. TAMMANIAL TONTINE ASSOCIATION.
PLAN OF THE NEW-YORK TAMMANIAL TONTINE ASSOCIATION.
New-York: Printed by Thomas & James Swords? 1792. pp. 12. 8vo.
NYHS.

24613 NEW-YORK DAILY GAZETTE. NUMB. 942. MONDAY, JANUARY 2, [—NUMB. 1254.
MONDAY, DECEMBER 31, 1792.]
*New-York: Published by Archibald M'Lean, at Franklin's Head, No. 41,
Hanover-Square.* 1792. fol.

24614 THE NEW-YORK JOURNAL & PATRIOTIC REGISTER. [Motto.] VOL. XLVI. NUMB.
1. TOTAL NUMBER 2625. WEDNESDAY, JANUARY 4, [—NUMB. 104 OF VOL. XLVI.
TOTAL NUMBER 2728. SATURDAY, DECEMBER 29, 1792.]
*New-York: Printed and published (on Wednesdays and Saturdays) by
Thomas Greenleaf, at his Printing-Office, No. 196, Water-Street.* 1792. fol.
An Extraordinary number was issued March 24th.

24615 THE NEW-YORK MAGAZINE; OR, LITERARY REPOSITORY. VOL. III. [JANUARY—
DECEMBER] 1792. [Two lines of verse.]
*New-York: Printed and sold by Thomas and James Swords, at their office,
No. 27, William-Street.* 1792. pp. vii, (1), 768, 12 plates, 1 plan. 8vo.
AAS. BA. HC. LOC. NYHS.

24616 THE NEW-YORK PACKET. [Motto.] No. 1219. TUESDAY, JANUARY 3, [—No. 1226.
THURSDAY, JANUARY 19, 1792.]
*New-York: Published every Tuesday, Thursday and Saturday, by Samuel
Loudon, No. 5, Water-Street, between the Coffee-House and Old-Slip.* 1792. fol.
Discontinued shortly after the above date, and succeeded in February,
by *The Diary; or, Loudon's Register*, with a daily issue.

24617 NEWARK. NEW JERSEY. STOCKING MANUFACTORY.
NEWARK STOCKING MANUFACTORY. A NUMBER OF JOURNEYMEN STOCKING MAKERS
ARE WANTED, WHO WILL FIND CONSTANT EMPLOYMENT AND GENEROUS WAGES, AT
THE STOCKING MANUFACTORY, LATELY ESTABLISHED IN THE FLOURISHING, PLEAS-
ANT AND HEALTHY, TOWN OF NEWARK, IN NEW-JERSEY. [Twenty-three lines.]
MICHAEL TRAPPEL, SUPERINTENDANT. NEWARK, JUNE 5, 1792.
[*Newark: Printed by John Woods,* 1792.] Broadside. 4to. NYHS.

24618 NEWPORT. RHODE ISLAND. ASSOCIATION OF MECHANICS AND MANUFACTURERS.
THE CHARTER, CONSTITUTION AND BY-LAWS OF THE NEWPORT ASSOCIATION OF
MECHANICS AND MANUFACTURERS, WITH A LIST OF OFFICERS AND COMMITTEE OF
CORRESPONDENCE.
Newport: Printed by Henry Barber. 1792. pp. vi, 24. 16mo. BU.

24619 THE NEWPORT MERCURY. No. 1551. SATURDAY, JANUARY 7, [—No. 1602. SAT-
URDAY, DECEMBER 29, 1792.]
*Newport, (Rhode-Island) Printed by Henry Barber, at the foot of the Pa-
rade.* 1792. fol.
The imprint was changed in this year to: Published by Henry Barber,
near the State-House.

24620 NEWTON, JOHN 1725 – 1807
CARDIPHONIA: OR, THE UTTERANCE OF THE HEART; IN THE COURSE OF A REAL COR-
RESPONDENCE. BY THE AUTHOR OF OMICRON'S LETTERS. [Two lines of quotations.] THE FIFTH EDITION. IN TWO VOLUMES. VOL. I. [—II.]
*Philadelphia: Printed by William Young, Bookseller, No. 52, Second-
street, the corner of Chesnut-street.* M,DCC,XCII. 2 vols. pp. 307; [4], 312.
12mo. AAS.

NEWTON, JOHN, continued.

24621　—— LETTERS, ORIGINALLY PUBLISHED UNDER THE SIGNATURES OF OMICRON AND VIGIL. BY THE REV. MR. JOHN NEWTON, MINISTER OF THE GOSPEL IN LONDON. TO WHICH IS PREFIXED, AN AUTHENTIC NARRATIVE OF SOME REMARKABLE AND INTERESTING PARTICULARS IN THE LIFE OF MR. NEWTON. COMMUNICATED, IN A SERIES OF LETTERS TO THE REV. MR. HAWEIS, RECTOR OF ALDWINCKLE, NORTHAMPTONSHIRE.

Philadelphia: Printed by William Young, Bookseller. No. 52, Second-street, the corner of Chesnut-street. M,DCC,XCII, pp. (2), (2), 372. 12mo. AAS. JCB.

24622　—— LETTERS AND SERMONS, WITH A REVIEW OF ECCLESIASTICAL HISTORY, AND HYMNS. BY JOHN NEWTON, RECTOR OF ST. MARY, WOOLNOTH, LONDON. IN SIX VOLUMES. VOL. VI.

Philadelphia: Printed by William Young, Bookseller, No. 52, Second-Street the corner of Chesnut-Street. M,DCC,XCII. pp. 348. 12mo.　　　JCB.

24623　NISBET, RICHARD
THE CAPACITY OF NEGROES, FOR RELIGIOUS AND MORAL IMPROVEMENT, CONSIDERED: WITH CURSORY HINTS, TO PROPRIETORS AND TO GOVERNMENT, FOR THE IMMEDIATE MELIORATION OF THE CONDITION OF SLAVES IN THE SUGAR COLONIES: TO WHICH IS SUBJOINED, SHORT AND PRACTICAL DISCOURSES TO NEGROES, ON THE PLAIN AND OBVIOUS PRINCIPLES OF RELIGION AND MORALITY.

Baltimore: Sold by Rice and Co. 1792.

24624　—— THE SOURCE OF VIRTUE: A POEM. BY RICHARD NISBET.
Baltimore: Sold by Rice and Co. 1792.

24625　NIXON, WILLIAM
ANALOGICAL VOCABULARY, CONTAINING ABOVE TWO THOUSAND LATIN WORDS, WHICH AN UTTER STRANGER TO THE LANGUAGE MAY LEARN TO CONSTRUE IN THE SHORT SPACE OF A SINGLE DAY. [Nineteen lines.] BY THE REV. WILLIAM NIXON, AUTHOR OF PROSODY MADE EASY, FORMERLY PRINCIPAL OF THE DUBLIN ACADEMY, IN THE CITY OF DUBLIN, NOW MASTER OF A PRIVATE SCHOOL IN CHARLESTON, SOUTH-CAROLINA. [Two lines of Latin from] CICERO.

Philadelphia: From the Press of M. Carey, No. 118, High-Street, Nov. 10, M.DCC.XCII. pp. [28.] 8vo.　　　SCHS.

24626　THE NORFOLK AND PORTSMOUTH CHRONICLE. VOL. III. NUMB. 124. SATURDAY, JANUARY 7, [—NUMB. 145. SATURDAY, JUNE 2, 1792.]
Norfolk: Printed by Prentis & Baxter. 1792. fol.

In June, Prentis retired, and was succeeded by Thomas Wilson, under the firm name of Baxter and Wilson. Later in the year the title was altered to, *Virginia Chronicle and Norfolk and Portsmouth General Advertiser.*

24627　NORTH CAROLINA. STATE.
A COLLECTION OF THE STATUTES OF THE PARLIAMENT OF ENGLAND IN FORCE IN THE STATE OF NORTH-CAROLINA. PUBLISHED ACCORDING TO A RESOLVE OF THE GENERAL ASSEMBLY. BY FRANCOIS-XAVIER MARTIN, ESQ. COUNSELLOR AT LAW.

Newbern: From the Editor's Press. 1792. pp. (iv), (424), (v)—(xxvi), (3). 4to.　　　AAS. HC. JCB. LOC. NCSL. NCU. NYHS. NYPL.

Contains, a list of subscribers, headed by The State of North-Carolina, (Seventy copies.)

NORTH CAROLINA, continued.

24628 —— JOURNAL OF THE HOUSE OF COMMONS OF THE GENERAL ASSEMBLY OF NORTH-CAROLINA, DECEMBER SESSION, 1791. [Colophon:]
Edenton: Printed by Hodge & Wills, Printers to the State. 1792. pp. 66. fol.
NCSL.

24629 —— JOURNAL OF THE SENATE OF THE GENERAL ASSEMBLY OF NORTH-CAROLINA. DECEMBER SESSION, 1791.
[Edenton: Printed by Hodge and Wills. 1792.] pp. 41. fol.
NCSL.

24630 —— LAWS OF NORTH-CAROLINA. AT A GENERAL ASSEMBLY, BEGUN AND HELD AT NEWBERN, ON THE FIFTH DAY OF DECEMBER, IN THE YEAR OF OUR LORD ONE THOUSAND SEVEN HUNDRED AND NINETY-ONE, AND IN THE SIXTEENTH YEAR OF THE INDEPENDENCE OF THE SAID STATE: BEING THE FIRST SESSION OF THE SAID ASSEMBLY [—19 JANUARY, 1792.]
[Edenton: Printed by Hodge and Wills, 1792.] pp. 713–732. fol.
HC. LOC. NCSL. NCU. NYPL.

24631 THE NORTH-CAROLINA GAZETTE. VOL. VII. NUMB. 313. THURSDAY, JANUARY 5, [—NUMB. 364. SATURDAY, DECEMBER 29, 1792.]
Newbern: Printed by F. X. Martin. 1792. fol.

24632 THE NORTH-CAROLINA JOURNAL. VOL. I. NO. 1. WEDNESDAY, JULY 18, [—NO. 24. WEDNESDAY, DECEMBER 26, 1793.]
Halifax: Printed by Abraham Hodge, joint printer to the State with H. Wills. 1792. fol.

Established by Abraham Hodge, after his withdrawal from the firm of Hodge and Wills, publishers of the "State Gazette of North-Carolina," at Edenton, and continued by him certainly into the year 1807.

24633 NORTHWEST TERRITORY.
LAWS PASSED IN THE TERRITORY OF THE UNITED STATES NORTHWEST OF THE RIVER OHIO, FROM THE COMMENCEMENT OF THE GOVERNMENT TO THE 31ST OF DECEMBER. 1791. PUBLISHED BY AUTHORITY.
Philadelphia: Printed by Francis Childs and John Swaine. M,DCC,XCII. pp. 68, (2). 4to.
LOC.

24634 NORTHERN INLAND-LOCK NAVIGATION COMPANY.
THE NORTHERN INLAND LOCK NAVIGATION COMPANY, WILL PURCHASE THE FOLLOWING ARTICLES, BY CONTRACT. . . . PH. SCHUYLER, PRESIDENT. OCTOBER 10TH, 1792. [Colophon:]
Printed by Charles R. and George Webster, No. 46, north side of State-Street, corner of Middle-lane, Albany. [1792.] Broadside. fol.
NYPL.

24635 —— A REPORT OF THE COMMITTEE APPOINTED BY THE DIRECTORS OF THE NORTHERN INLAND LOCK NAVIGATION COMPANY, IN THE STATE OF NEW-YORK, TO EXAMINE HUDSONS RIVER. [Ornament.]
[New-York:] From the Press of W. Durell. [1792.] pp. (20). 8vo.
AAS. NYPL.

24636 NORWICH PACKET. VOX POPULI—THE VOICE OF THE PEOPLE. VOL. XIX. NO. 928. THURSDAY, JANUARY 5, [—VOL. XX. NO. 979. THURSDAY, DECEMBER 27, 1792.]
[Norwich:] Printed and published by John Trumbull, near the Meeting-House. 1792. fol.
AAS.

24637 NOYES, NATHANIEL   1735 – 1810
A DIALOGUE BETWEEN POIMEN AND AGAMOS, WHEREIN THE DIVINE RIGHT OF INFANT BAPTISM IS EXHIBITED AND DEFENDED. BY NATHANIEL NOYES, A. M. [Five lines of Scripture texts.]
Newburyport: Printed by John Mycall. MDCCXCII. pp. (16). 8vo. NYPL.

24638   OBSERVATIONS OCCASIONED BY WRITINGS AGAINST ALTERATIONS, PROPOSED IN THE
CONVENTION, TO BE MADE IN THE JUDICIARY SYSTEM. BY A MEMBER OF THE
CONVENTION. [Ornament.]
*Portsmouth, (N. H.) Printed by George and John Osborne, at the Spy
Printing-Office.* M;DCC,XCII. pp. [23.] 12mo.   AAS. BPL. LOC.

24639   OBSERVATIONS ON NOVEL-READING: IN AN ESSAY, WRITTEN BY A MEMBER OF THE
BELLES-LETTRES SOCIETY OF DICKINSON COLLEGE, AT CARLISLE, IN THE YEAR 1789.
*Philadelphia: Printed by Thomas Dobson, at the Stone House, No. 41, South
Second-Street.* 1792.

24640   OBSERVATIONS ON THE PRESENT SITUATION OF LANDED PROPERTY IN AMERICA.
New-York: [London?] January, 1792. pp. 4. fol.

24641   OCCOM, SAMSON   1723 – 1792
A CHOICE COLLECTION OF HYMNS AND SPIRITUAL SONGS; INTENDED FOR THE EDIFI-
CATION OF SINCERE CHRISTIANS OF ALL DENOMINATIONS. BY SAMSON OCCOM,
MINISTER OF THE GOSPEL. THE THIRD EDITION, WITH ADDITIONS.
New-London: Printed by Timothy Green & Son. 1792. pp. 112. 16mo.

24642   ODE FOR THE 23D OF OCTOBER, 1792. [Twelve verses, with chorus beginning
"Hail! Great Columbia! favour'd soil."]
[Without Place or Printer. 1792.] Broadside. fol.   AAS.

24643   ODIORNE, THOMAS   1769 – 1851
THE PROGRESS OF REFINEMENT, A POEM, IN THREE BOOKS. TO WHICH ARE
ADDED, A POEM ON FAME, AND MISCELLANIES. BY THOMAS ODIORNE. [Ornament.]
*Boston: Printed by Young and Etheridge, opposite the entrance of the
Branch-Bank, State-Street.* MDCCXCII. pp. 176, frontispiece. 16mo.
     AAS. BA. BM. BPL. BU. HC. NYPL.
3d New Hampshire District Copyright, issued to Thomas Odiorne, as
Author, 6 November, 1792.

24644   O'KEEFFE, JOHN   1747 – 1833
THE FARMER: A COMIC OPERA. IN TWO ACTS. AS PERFORMED WITH GREAT AP-
PLAUSE, BY THE OLD AMERICAN COMPANY AT THE THEATRE IN SOUTHWARK. BY
JOHN O'KEEFFE, ESQ. FIRST AMERICAN EDITION.
*Philadelphia: From the Press of Mathew Carey, Dec. 14,—*M.DCC.XCII.
pp. [40.] 8vo.   BPL. NYPL.

24645   THE ORACLE OF DAUPHIN. AND HARRISBURGH ADVERTISER. VOL. I. NO. 1. SAT-
URDAY, OCTOBER 20, [—NO. IX. SATURDAY, DECEMBER 29, 1792.]
Printed by Allen and Wyeth, adjoining the Register's Office, Harrisburgh.
1792. fol.
Established by John W. Allen, and John Wyeth: the Printing-office
being removed in a short time to "Mulberry-Street, opposite the residence of Adam Boyd, esq. near the Bank." There appears to be some
evidence that Eli Lewis, author of "St. Clair's Defeat. A poem,"
(Harrisburgh, 1792,) was editorially connected with its early publication. At the end of the first volume, in October, 1793, Allen
withdrew, and from that time the Oracle was published in succession,
by John Wyeth; John Wyeth, junior; and by Francis Wyeth, for
about forty years. After January, 1808, the sub-title was dropped.
Latterly the Printing-office was at "the north-east corner of the Market-Square and Market-Street" until the end.

24646 OSBORNE'S NEW-HAMPSHIRE SPY. A FREE AND IMPARTIAL PAPER. VOL. XI. NO.
XXI. WEDNESDAY, JANUARY 4, [—VOL. XIII. NO. 9. SATURDAY, DECEMBER 29,
1792.]
Published on Wednesdays and Saturdays—By George and John Osborne—
near the State-House, Guttemberg's [sic] Head, Congress-Street, Portsmouth.—
Twelve shillings per annum. 1792. fol.
On May 26th the partnership was dissolved by mutual consent. George
Jerry Osborne, junior retiring, and John Osborne continuing the
paper as sole publisher. The change being signalized, in the heading
of the Spy. by a cut of the New-Hampshire Arms dividing the title.
In November, this cut was replaced by one of an eye surrounded by
thirteen stars.

24647 OTTAWA INDIANS.
DEBATES IN COUNCIL, ON THE BANKS OF THE OTTAWA RIVER, NOVEMBER, 1791.
Philadelphia: 1792. 8vo.   LCP.

24648 OWEN, JOHN   1616 – 1683
THE DEATH OF DEATH IN THE DEATH OF CHRIST. BEING A TREATISE OF THE RE-
DEMPTION AND RECONCILIATION THAT IS IN THE BLOOD OF CHRIST; WHEREIN THE
WHOLE CONTROVERSY ABOUT UNIVERSAL REDEMPTION, IS FULLY DISCUSSED: IN
FOUR PARTS. BY JOHN OWEN, D. D. FIRST AMERICAN EDITION, CAREFULLY RE-
VISED AND CORRECTED.
Carlisle, (Pennsylvania) Printed by George Kline. M,DCC,XCII. pp.
320. 8vo.   AAS.

24649 PAINE, THOMAS   1737 – 1809
A LETTER FROM MR. PAINE TO MR. SECRETARY DUNDAS, ON HIS OPENING THE DE-
BATE IN THE HOUSE OF COMMONS, ON THE PROCLAMATION OF THE 25TH OF MAY,
FOR SUPPRESSING PUBLICATIONS, &C. WHEREIN IS ANSWERED THE CAVILS OF
OTHER COURT-PARASITES' AGAINST HIS RIGHTS OF MAN. INTERESTING TO EVERY
AMERICAN.
New-York—Printed by Samuel Loudon, No. 5, Water-Street. [1792.] pp.
14. 8vo.   NYPL.

24650 ——— RIGHTS OF MAN: PART THE FIRST. BEING AN ANSWER TO MR. BURKE'S ATTACK
ON THE FRENCH REVOLUTION. BY THOMAS PAINE, SECRETARY FOR FOREIGN AF-
FAIRS TO CONGRESS IN THE AMERICAN WAR, AND AUTHOR OF THE WORK INTITLED
COMMON SENSE.
London: Printed: New-York: Reprinted for Berry, Rogers and Berry, No.
35, Hanover-Square. M.DCC.XLII [sic 1792.] pp. 76. 8vo.   BU. IOC. MHS.

24651 ——— — RIGHTS OF MAN. PART THE SECOND. COMBINING PRINCIPAL [sic] AND PRAC-
TICE. BY THOMAS PAINE, SECRETARY FOR FOREIGN AFFAIRS TO CONGRESS IN THE
AMERICAN WAR, AND AUTHOR OF THE WORK, ENTITLED, COMMON SENCE [sic];
AND THE FIRST PART OF THE RIGHTS OF MAN.
London, Printed: New-York: Re.printed, by Hugh Gaine,—1792.—pp.
88. 8vo.   NYPL.

24652 ——— — RIGHTS OF MAN. PART THE SECOND. COMBINING PRINCIPLE AND PRAC-
TICE. BY THOMAS PAINE, SECRETARY FOR FOREIGN AFFAIRS TO CONGRESS IN
THE AMERICAN WAR, AND AUTHOR OF THE WORK, ENTITLED COMMON SENSE, AND
THE FIRST PART OF THE RIGHTS OF MAN. [Ornament.]
London, Printed 1792. *United States of America. Printed by Thomas*
and John Fleet, at the Bible and Heart in Boston, 1792. pp. ix, 108. 8vo.
AAS. BA. JCB. LOC. NYPL.

PAINE, THOMAS, continued.

24653 —— — RIGHTS OF MAN. PART THE SECOND. COMBINING PRINCIPLE AND PRAC-
TICE. BY THOMAS PAINE, SECRETARY FOR FOREIGN AFFAIRS TO CONGRESS IN
THE AMERICAN WAR, AND AUTHOR OF THE WORK, ENTITLED, COMMON SENSE;
AND THE FIRST PART OF THE RIGHTS OF MAN.
*Philadelphia: Printed by and for Messrs. Rice and Company, Market-Street,
and S. H. Smith.* M,DCC,XCII. pp. 120. 8vo.   NYPL.

24654 —— — RIGHTS OF MAN. PART THE SECOND. COMBINING PRINCIPLE AND PRAC-
TICE. BY THOMAS PAINE, SECRETARY FOR FOREIGN AFFAIRS TO CONGRESS IN
THE AMERICAN WAR, AND AUTHOR OF THE WORK ENTITLED COMMON SENSE; AND
THE FIRST PART OF THE RIGHTS OF MAN. SECOND PHILADELPHIA EDITION.
*Philadelphia: Printed by and for Messrs. H. and P. Rice, No. 50, Market-
Street, and S. H. Smith.* M,DCC.XCII. pp. 96. 8vo.   AAS.

24655 —— — RIGHTS OF MAN. PART THE SECOND. COMBINING PRINCIPLE AND PRAC-
TICE. BY THOMAS PAINE.
Baltimore: Printed by David Graham, 1792.

24656 —— — RIGHTS OF MAN. PART THE SECOND. COMBINING PRINCIPLE AND PRAC-
TICE. BY THOMAS PAINE. DEDICATED TO M. DE LAFAYETTE.
Carlisle: Printed by George Kline. 1792.

24657 —— — RIGHTS OF MAN. PART THE SECOND. COMBINING PRINCIPLE AND PRAC-
TICE. BY THOMAS PAINE, SECRETARY FOR FOREIGN AFFAIRS TO CONGRESS IN
THE AMERICAN WAR, AND AUTHOR OF THE WORK ENTITLED COMMON SENSE; AND
THE FIRST PART OF THE RIGHTS OF MAN.
New-London: Printed by Timothy Green and Son. 1792.
First printed in The Connecticut Gazette, in successive numbers from
June 21, 1792.

24658 —— THE WRITINGS OF THOMAS PAINE, SECRETARY FOR FOREIGN AFFAIRS TO THE
CONGRESS OF THE UNITED STATES OF AMERICA, IN THE LATE WAR. CONTAIN-
ING 1. RIGHTS OF MAN. 2. COMMON SENSE. 3. THE CRISIS. 4. PUBLIC GOOD.
5. LETTER TO ABBE RAYNAL. 6. LETTER TO THE EARL OF SHELBURNE. 7.
LETTER TO SIR GUY CARLTON. 8. LETTERS TO THE AUTHORS OF THE REPUBLI-
CAN. 9. LETTER TO ABBE SYEYES.
Albany—State of New-York: Printed by Charles R. & George Webster.
[1792.] pp. [xii], [124]; [60]; [186]; [41]; [70]; [24.] 8vo.
     AAS. HC. JCB. NL. NYHS. NYPL.
A second edition was published in 1794. Separately paged, but with
continuous signatures. Contains an eight-page list of subscriber's
names. A printed slip of paper pasted on the inside of the cover gives
an alphabetical summary of the contents, within an ornamental border.
Total number of pages, 517.

Second title: RIGHTS OF MAN: BEING AN ANSWER TO MR. BURKE'S ATTACK ON
THE FRENCH REVOLUTION. BY THOMAS PAINE, SECRETARY FOR FOREIGN AF-
FAIRS TO CONGRESS IN THE AMERICAN WAR, AND AUTHOR OF THE WORK ENTITLED
COMMON SENSE. THE FOURTH AMERICAN EDITION.
*Albany, Re-printed by Charles R. & George Webster, No. 46, on the north
side of State-Street, corner of Middle-lane, between the Dutch and English Churches
—Where printing is performed with dispatch and on reasonable terms.* [1792.]
pp. [124.]

PAINE, THOMAS, continued.

Third title: COMMON SENSE; ADDRESSED TO THE INHABITANTS OF AMERICA, ON THE FOLLOWING INTERESTING SUBJECTS, VIZ. I. OF THE ORIGIN AND DESIGN OF GOVERNMENT IN GENERAL, WITH CONCISE REMARKS ON THE ENGLISH CONSTITUTION. II. OF MONARCHY AND HEREDITARY SUCCESSION. III. THOUGHTS ON THE PRESENT STATE OF AMERICAN AFFAIRS. IV. OF THE PRESENT ABILITY OF AMERICA, WITH SOME MISCELLANEOUS REFLECTIONS. TO WHICH IS ADDED, AN APPENDIX. [Two lines from] THOMSON.

    Albany: Re-printed by Charles R. and George Webster. M.DCC.XCI. pp. [60.]

Fourth title: THE CRISIS: IN THIRTEEN NUMBERS. WRITTEN DURING THE LATE WAR. BY THE AUTHOR OF COMMON SENSE.

    Albany: Printed & sold by Charles R. & George Webster, No. 46, *State-street, corner of Middle-lane.* M.DCC.XCII. pp. [186.]

Numbers X, and XII, were not printed in regular order as above.

Fifth title: PUBLIC GOOD: BEING AN EXAMINATION INTO THE CLAIM OF VIRGINIA TO THE VACANT WESTERN TERRITORY, AND OF THE RIGHT OF THE UNITED STATES TO THE SAME. TO WHICH IS ADDED, PROPOSALS FOR LAYING OFF A NEW STATE, TO BE APPLIED AS A FUND FOR CARRYING ON THE WAR, OR REDEEMING THE NATIONAL DEBT. BY THE AUTHOR OF COMMON SENSE. WRITTEN IN THE YEAR 1780.

    Albany: Printed by Charles R. & George Webster, No. 46, *State-street, corner of Middle-lane.* [1792.] pp. [41.]

Sixth title: LETTER ADDRESSED TO THE ABBE RAYNAL, ON THE AFFAIRS OF NORTH-AMERICA. IN WHICH THE MISTAKES IN THE ABBE'S ACCOUNT OF THE REVOLUTION OF AMERICA ARE CORRECTED AND CLEARED UP. BY THOMAS PAINE, M. A. OF THE UNIVERSITY OF PENNSYLVANIA, AND AUTHOR OF THE PAMPHLET AND OTHER PUBLICATIONS ENTITLED, OR SIGNED, "COMMON SENSE." [Dated, Philadelphia, August 21, 1782.]

    Albany: Printed by Charles R. & George Webster, No. 46, *State-street, corner of Middle-lane.* [1792.] pp. [170.]

Seventh title: LETTERS, BY THE AUTHOR OF COMMON SENSE. *First,* TO THE EARL OF SHELBURNE, NOW MARQUIS OF LANSDOWNE, ON THE SUBJECT OF AMERICAN INDEPENDENCE. *Second,* TO SIR GUY CARLTON, NOW LORD DORCHESTER, ON THE MURDER OF CAPTAIN HUDDY. *Third,* TO THE AUTHORS OF "THE REPUBLICAN," A FRENCH PAPER; TENDERING HIS SERVICES IN SUPPORT OF THE REPUBLICAN SYSTEM. *Fourth,* TO THE ABBE SYEYES, A MEMBER OF THE FRENCH NATIONAL ASSEMBLY; ACCEPTING THE ABBE'S CHALLENGE ON THE SUBJECT OF GOVERNMENT, BY OFFERING TO DEFEND THE REPUBLICAN AGAINST THE MONARCHIAL SYSTEM.

    Albany: Printed by Charles R. & George Webster, No. 46, *State-street, corner of Middle-lane.* M.DCC.XCII. pp. [24.]

The Letter to the Earl of Shelburne, is Number xii of The Crisis. And that to Sir Guy Carleton is considered Number xiv, in the series, although Paine, himself, always referred to The Crisis as having the same number as the thirteen original States of the Union.

24659   A PARENT'S ADVICE FOR HIS FAMILY.

    New-London: Printed by Timothy Green and Son. M,DCC.XCII. pp. (24). 12mo.   AAS.

24660   PARISH, Elijah   1762 – 1825
A Sermon, preached at the ordination of the rev. Ariel Parish, a. m. pastor of the church in Manchester, April 4, 1792. By Elijah Parish, a. m. [Six lines of verse.]
     Salem: Printed by Thomas C. Cushing, 1792.   pp. (40). 8vo.
                                        AAS. BA. HC. JCB. LOC.

24661   PARKER, James   1714 – 1770
The Conductor generalis: or, the office, duty and authority of justices of the peace, high-sheriffs, under-sheriffs, coroners, constables, gaolers, jury-men, and overseers of the poor. As also, the office of clerks of assize, and of the peace, &c. Compiled chiefly from Burn's Justice, and the several other books, on those subjects, by James Parker, late one of the justices of the peace for Middlesex County, in New-Jersey; and now revised and adapted to the United States of America. By a Gentleman of the law. The whole alphabetically digested under the several titles; with a table, directing to the ready finding out the proper matter under those titles. To which are added, the Excise and Militia laws of the United States; and the Acts called the Ten pound Act of the States of Pennsylvania and New-York.
     Philadelphia: Printed for Robert Campbell. 1792. pp. xv. 464. 8vo. AAS. JCB.

24662   PENN, William   1644 – 1718
Fruits of a father's love: being the advice of William Penn to his children, relating to their civil and religious conduct.
     Philadelphia: Printed by Benjamin Johnson. M,DCC,XCII. pp. 86
12mo.   BM. JCB. LOC.

24663   —— Fruits of solitude, in reflections and maxims relating to the conduct of human life. By William Penn. The tenth edition.
     Philadelphia: Printed by Benjamin Johnson. M.DCC.XCII. pp. xi, 166, (8). 12mo.   AAS. BM. JCB. LOC.

24664   PENNSYLVANIA. State.
An Act for incorporating the Society formed for the relief of poor, aged and infirm masters of ships, their widows and children.
     Philadelphia: Printed by Hall and Sellers. 1792. pp. 35. 12mo. NYHS.

24665   —— An Act for making an artificial road from the city of Philadelphia to the borough of Lancaster.
     [Philadelphia:] Printed by Hall and Sellers. 1792. 4to.   LCP.

24666   —— Acts of the General Assembly of the Commonwealth of Pennsylvania, passed at a session, which was begun and held at the city of Philadelphia on Tuesday, the sixth day of December, in the year one thousand seven hundred and ninety-two [sic one], and of the independence of the United States of America, the sixteenth [—10 April, 1792.] Published by authority.
     Philadelphia: Printed by Hall and Sellers, No. 51, Market-street. M.DCC.-XCII. pp. (2), (177)—[289.] fol.   LOC.

24667   —— Journal of the first session of the second House of Representatives of the Commonwealth of Pennsylvania, which commenced at Philadelphia, on Tuesday, the sixth day of December, in the year of our Lord one thousand seven hundred and ninety-one [—10 April, 1792.] [Arms.]
     Philadelphia: Printed by Francis Bailey and Thomas Lang. MDCCXCI. [1792.] pp. [327], (34). fol.   LOC. PSL.
The Appendix contains: Report of Comptroller general. pp. 10. Report of Register general. pp. 7. Report of Treasurer of the Commonwealth. pp. 20.

PENNSYLVANIA, continued.

24668 —— TAGEBUCH DER ERSTEN SITZUNG DES ZWEYTEN HAUSES DER REPRESENTANTEN DER REPUBLIK PENNSYLVANIEN, WELCHE IN PHILADELPHIA, AM DIENSTAG, DEN SECHSTEN TAG DECEMBERS IM JAHR 1790 IHREN ANFANG NAHM. AUS DEM ENGLISCHEN ÜBERSETZT. [Und Anhang.]
Germantaun: Gedruckt bey Michael Billmeyer. [1792.] pp. 327; 33. fol.

24669 —— TAGEBUCH DES DRITTEN HAUSES DER REPRÄSENTANTEN DER REPUBLIK PENNSYLVANIEN. 1791-1792.
Germantaun: Gedruckt bey Michael Billmeyer. 1792.

24670 —— JOURNAL OF THE SENATE OF THE COMMONWEALTH OF PENNSYLVANIA. COMMENCING ON TUESDAY, THE SIXTH DAY OF DECEMBER, IN THE YEAR OF OUR LORD ONE THOUSAND SEVEN HUNDRED AND NINETY-ONE, AND OF THE INDEPENDENCE OF THE UNITED STATES OF AMERICA THE SIXTEENTH [—10 April, 1792.]
Philadelphia: Printed by Zachariah Poulson, junior, in Fourth-street, near the University. [1792.] pp. (266). fol. LOC.

24671 —— TAGEBUCH DES SENATS DER REPUBLIK PENNSYLVANIEN. 1791-1792.
Germantaun: Gedruckt bey Michael Billmeyer. 1792.

24672 —— [Arms.] PENNSYLVANIA; SS. BY THOMAS MIFFLIN, ESQ; GOVERNOR OF THE COMMONWEALTH OF PENNSYLVANIA. A PROCLAMATION. [Offering a reward of three hundred dollars for the murderers of Elizabeth Reeves, spinster. Dated, 22 August, 1792.] THOMAS MIFFLIN.
[Philadelphia: Printed by John Dunlap, 1792.] Broadside. 4to.

24673 THE PENNSYLVANIA GAZETTE. NUMBER 3214. WEDNESDAY, JANUARY 4, [—NUMBER 3267. WEDNESDAY, DECEMBER 26, 1792.]
Philadelphia: Printed by Hall and Sellers, at the New Printing-Office, near the Market. 1792. fol. NYPL.

24674 THE PENNSYLVANIA HERALD AND YORK GENERAL ADVERTISER.. VOL. III. NO. 51. TOTAL NO. 155. WEDNESDAY, JANUARY 4, [—VOL. IV. NO. 50. TOTAL NO. 206. WEDNESDAY, DECEMBER 26, 1792.]
York: Printed every Wednesday, by John Edie. 1792. fol.

24675 THE PENNSYLVANIA [cut] JOURNAL, AND THE WEEKLY ADVERTISER. PUBLISHED EVERY WEDNESDAY.--PRICE FOUR-PENCE. NO. 2537. WEDNESDAY, JANUARY 4, [—NO. 2588. WEDNESDAY, DECEMBER 26, 1792.]
Philadelphia: Printed by Thomas Bradford, . . . at his Printing-Office, Lætitia-Court. 1792. fol.

24676 THE PENNSYLVANIA, MARYLAND, AND VIRGINIA ALMANACK, FOR THE YEAR 1793. BEING THE FIRST AFTER LEAP YEAR, THE SEVENTEENTH OF AMERICAN INDEPENDENCE, AND THE FIFTH YEAR OF OUR FEDERAL GOVERNMENT. CONTAINING BESIDES THE USUAL ASTRONOMICAL CALCULATIONS A VARIETY OF INTERESTING ESSAYS, IN PROSE AND VERSE.
Frederick-Town: Printed by Matthias Bartgis, at his English and German Printing-office. [1792.]

24677 THE PENNSYLVANIA MERCURY, AND PHILADELPHIA PRICE-CURRENT. NO. 801. TUESDAY, JANUARY 3, [—NO. 826. THURSDAY, MARCH 1, 1792.]
Philadelphia: Printed (on Tuesdays, Thursdays and Saturdays) by Daniel Humphreys. 1792. 4to.
How much longer publication was continued is not known.

24678   PERKINS, NATHAN   1748 – 1838
A DISCOURSE, DELIVERED AT THE ORDINATION OF THE REV. WILLIAM F. MILLER, TO THE MINISTERIAL OFFICE IN THE CHRISTIAN CHURCH AT WINTONBURY, NOVEMBER 30TH, 1791. BY NATHAN PERKINS, A. M. PASTOR OF A CHURCH OF CHRIST IN HARTFORD. THIS DISCOURSE IS PUBLISHED BY PARTICULAR REQUEST OF THE SOCIETY; TO WHOM IT IS RESPECTFULLY INSCRIBED BY THE AUTHOR.
Hartford: Printed by Elisha Babcock. MDCCXCII. pp. 22. 8vo. AAS. JCB.

24679   PERRY, WILLIAM
THE ONLY SURE GUIDE TO THE ENGLISH TONGUE: OR, NEW PRONOUNCING SPELLING BOOK. UPON THE SAME PLAN AS PERRY'S ROYAL STANDARD ENGLISH DICTIONARY; NOW MADE USE OF IN ALL THE CELEBRATED SCHOOLS IN GREATBRITAIN, IRELAND AND AMERICA. TO WHICH IS ADDED, A COMPREHENSIVE GRAMMAR OF THE ENGLISH LANGUAGE; AND, A SELECT NUMBER OF MORAL TALES AND FABLES, FOR THE INSTRUCTION OF YOUTH. WITH AN APPENDIX. CONTAINING, DIRECTIONS FOR THE DIFFERENT SOUNDS OF THE CONSONANTS BEFORE ALL THE VOWELS, WITH EVERY EXCEPTION THAT IS TO BE MET WITH IN OUR LANGUAGE, FROM SUCH GENERAL RULES: ALSO, A COMPLETE LIST OF ALL THE WORDS IN WHICH E FINAL DOES NOT LENGTHEN THE SYLLABLE: LIKEWISE, SEVERAL VALUABLE APHORISMS RESPECTING THE SOUNDS OF THE VOWELS IN THE LAST SYLIABLE OF WORDS ENDING WITH E. AND, A COMPLETE LIST OF ALL THE WORDS IN THE ENGLISH LANGUAGE, WHICH, THOUGH WRITTEN DIFFERENTLY HAVE A SIMILARITY OF SOUND.—OF THOSE SUBSTANTIVES AND VERBS OF THE SAME ORTHOGRAPHY, BUT OF A DIFFERENT ACCENT.—OF THOSE SUBSTANTIVES AND VERBS, WHICH VARY IN THEIR SOUND, EITHER BY A DIFFERENT CONSONANT, OR BY CHANGING THE HARD SOUND OF THAT CONSONANT INTO THE SOFT SOUND.—OF THOSE ADJECTIVES AND VERBS ALIKE IN ORTHOGRAPHY, BUT DIFFERENTLY ACCENTED.—OF THE SUBSTANTIVES AND ADJECTIVES CHANGING THE SEAT OF THE ACCENT. BY W. PERRY. LECTURER ON THE ENGLISH LANGUAGE, IN THE ACADEMY, EDINBURGH. SIXTH WORCESTER EDITION. ILLUSTRATED WITH CUTS. CAREFULLY REVISED BY PERRY'S ROYAL STANDARD ENGLISH DICTIONARY. BY ISAIAH THOMAS, AND CORRECTED OF THE NUMEROUS ERRORS, WHICH ARE IN ALL OTHER EDITIONS BOTH BRITISH AND AMERICAN.
Printed at Worcester, Massachusetts, by Isaiah Thomas and Leonard Worcester, for Isaiah Thomas. Sold wholesale and retail, at his Bookstore in Worcester, and by him and Company in Boston, MDCCXCII. pp. 180. frontispiece. 12mo.   AAS.

24680   PEYTON, V. J.
THE ELEMENTS OF THE ENGLISH LANGUAGE, EXPLAINED IN A NEW, EASY, AND CONCISE MANNER, BY WAY OF DIALOGUES; IN WHICH THE PRONUNCIATION IS TAUGHT BY AN UNION OF LETTERS THAT PRODUCE SIMILAR SOUNDS IN FRENCH, AND THE TRUE QUANTITY OF EACH SYLLABLE IS DETERMINED; WITH FAMILIAR PHRASES AND DIALOGUES, VERY USEFUL FOR THOSE WHO DESIRE TO SPEAK ENGLISH CORRECTLY IN A SHORT TIME. BY V. J. PEYTON.
Philadelphia: From the Press of Mathew Carey, 1792.

24681   THE [cut] PHENIX. VOL. II. NUMB. 77. WEDNESDAY, JANUARY 25, [—VOL. III. NUMB. 125. WEDNESDAY, DECEMBER 26, 1792.]
Dover (N. H.) Published by Eliphalet Ladd, near the Court-House—18s per ann. 1792. fol.
In continuation of, *The Political Repository and Strafford Recorder.*

24682   THE [cut] PHENIX; OR WINDHAM HERALD. VOL. I. No. 44. SATURDAY, JANUARY 7, [—VOL. II. NUMB. 95. SATURDAY, DECEMBER 29, 1792.]
Windham: Printed by John Byrne, north of the Court-House. 1792. fol.
AAS. CHS.

24683 PHILADELPHIA. PENNSYLVANIA.
DIRECTIONS FOR THE INSPECTORS, &C. OF THE GAOL OF THE CITY AND COUNTY OF
PHILADELPHIA. [Two columns.] GEORGE MEADE, CHAIRMAN. 26TH FEBRU-
ARY, 1792.
[Philadelphia: Printed by D. Humphreys. 1792.] Broadside. 4to. NYHS.

24684 —— RULES, ORDERS, AND REGULATIONS FOR THE GAOL OF THE CITY AND COUNTY
OF PHILADELPHIA. [Two columns.] GEORGE MEADE, CHAIRMAN. 26TH FEB-
RUARY, 1792. [Colophon:]
Philadelphia: Printed by D. Humphreys, No. 132, S. Front-Street. [1792.]
Broadside. fol. NYHS.

24685 PHILADELPHIA. PENNSYLVANIA. BAPTIST ASSOCIATION.
MINUTES OF THE PHILADELPHIA BAPTIST ASSOCIATION, HELD AT PHILADELPHIA,
OCTOBER 2, 3, 4, & 5, 1792.
[Philadelphia: 1792.] pp. 8. 4to. BU.

24686 PHILADELPHIA. PENNSYLVANIA. CHRIST CHURCH.
AN ACCOUNT OF THE BIRTHS AND BURIALS IN THE UNITED CHURCHES OF CHRIST-
CHURCH AND ST. PETER'S, FROM DECEMBER 24, 1791, TO DECEMBER 24, 1792.
[Philadelphia: 1792.] Broadside. fol. LCP.

24687 PHILADELPHIA. PENNSYLVANIA. FRANKLIN SOCIETY.
CONSTITUTION OF THE FRANKLIN SOCIETY, (PRINTERS) OF THE CITY OF PHILADEL-
PHIA; INSTITUTED MARCH 8, 1788. ARS ARTIUM OMNIUM CONSERVATRIX.
Printed by Stewart & Cochran, No. 34, South Second-Street. December,
1792. pp. (15). 8vo. NYPL.

24688 PHILADELPHISCHE CORRESPONDENZ. NUM. 190. DIENSTAG, DEN 27 NOVEMBER,
[—NUM. 194. DIENSTAG, DEN 25 DECEMBER, 1792.]
Diese Zeitung wird alle Dienstag heraus gegeben bey Melchior Steiner und
Heinrich Kammerer, in der Rees-Strasse, zwischen der Zweyten-und Dritten-
Strasse, No. 71; für Zehn Schillinge des Jahrs, Fünf Schillinge werden beym
Einschreiben bezahlt. 1792. fol.
In continuation of *Neue Philadelphische Correspondenz.*

24689 PHILLIPS, NATHANIEL
PHILLIPS'S UNITED STATES DIARY, OR AN ALMANACK, FOR THE YEAR OF OUR LORD
1793: BEING THE FIRST AFTER BISSEXTILE, OR LEAP-YEAR, AND SEVENTEENTH OF
THE INDEPENDENCE OF UNITED AMERICA. [Five lines. U. S. Arms. Four lines
of verse.]
Printed at Warren (R. I.) by Nathaniel Phillips. Great encouragement
will be given to the whole-sale purchasers. [1792.] pp. (24). 12mo. RIHS.

24690 —— SECOND EDITION. PHILLIPS'S UNITED STATES DIARY, OR AN ALMANACK, FOR
THE YEAR OF OUR LORD 1793: BEING THE FIRST AFTER BISSEXTILE, OR LEAP-
YEAR, AND SEVENTEENTH OF THE INDEPENDENCE OF UNITED AMERICA. [Five
lines. U. S. Arms. Four lines of verse.]
Printed at Warren (R. I.) by Nathaniel Phillips. Great encouragement
will be given to the whole-sale purchasers. [1792.] pp. (24). 12mo. LOC.

24691 PHILO DRAMATIS, pseudonym.
THE RIGHTS OF THE DRAMA: OR, AN INQUIRY INTO THE ORIGIN, PRINCIPLES, AND
CONSEQUENCES OF THEATRICAL ENTERTAINMENTS. BY PHILO DRAMATIS. [Ten
lines from] L'ALLEGRO.
Boston: Printed [by Thomas and Andrews] for the Author. MDCCXCII.
pp. [48.] 8vo. AAS. BU. LOC. MHS.

24692　PILMORE, JOSEPH　　　　　　　　　　　　　　　1734 – 1825
THE RENOVATION OF MAN: BEING THE SUBSTANCE OF A SERMON, DELIVERED IN ST.
PAUL'S CHURCH, PHILADELPHIA. BY THE REV. JOSEPH PILMORE.
Philadelphia: Printed by Johnson and Justice, Franklin's Head, No. 41,
Chesnut-Street. M.DCC.XCII. pp. [23.] 8vo.　　　　　AAS. JCB.

24693　PINCHARD, Mrs. —
THE BLIND CHILD, OR ANECDOTES OF THE WINDHAM FAMILY; WRITTEN FOR THE
USE OF YOUNG PEOPLE. BY A LADY.
New-York: Printed for Berry,Rogers & Berry,No.35, Hanover-Square. 1792.

24694　——— — THE BLIND CHILD, OR ANECDOTES OF THE WINDHAM FAMILY. WRITTEN
FOR THE USE OF YOUNG PEOPLE. BY A LADY. EMBELLISHED WITH A HANDSOME
ENGRAVED FRONTISPIECE.
Philadelphia: Printed for William Spotswood, No. 69. Market-Street, near
Second-Street. 1792.

24695　THE PIOUS GUIDE TO PRAYER AND DEVOTION. CONTAINING VARIOUS PRACTICES OF
PIETY AND DEVOTION CALCULATED TO ANSWER THE VARIOUS DEMANDS OF THE
DIFFERENT DEVOUT MEMBERS OF THE ROMAN CATHOLIC CHURCH. PERMISSU
SUPERIORUM.
George-Town, (Potowmack): Printed by James Doyle. MDCCXCII. pp.
282. 12mo.
Prepared by the Jesuit fathers of Georgetown College.

24696　THE PITTSBURGH GAZETTE. NUMBER 279. SATURDAY, JANUARY 7, [—NUMBER
330. SATURDAY, DECEMBER 29, 1792.]
Pittsburgh: Printed by John Scull. 1792. fol.

24697　PLATTES, GABRIEL
A DISCOVERY OF SUBTERRANEAN TREASURE, VIZ. ALL MANNER OF MINES & MINERALS,
FROM THE GOLD TO THE COAL, WITH PLAIN DIRECTIONS AND RULES FOR FINDING
THEM IN ALL KINGDOMS AND COUNTRIES. ALSO THE ART OF MELTING, REFINING
AND ASSAYING THEM MADE PLAIN AND EASY TO EVERY ORDINARY CAPACITY, SO
THAT THEY MAY WITH SMALL CHARGE TRY THE VALUE OF SUCH ORES AS SHALL BE
FOUND EITHER BY RULE OR ACCIDENT. TO WHICH IS ADDED, A REAL EXPERIMENT,
TO TRY WHETHER A PIECE OF GOLD BE TRUE OR COUNTERFEIT, WITHOUT DEFACING
OR ALTERING THE FORM THEREOF, WITH MORE CERTAINTY THAN ANY GOLDSMITH
OR REFINER COULD FORMERLY DO. ALSO A SURE WAY TO TRY WHAT COLOUR ANY
BERRY, LEAF, FLOWER, STALK, ROOT, FRUIT, SEED, BARK OR WOOD WILL GIVE:
TOGETHER WITH DIRECTIONS FOR MAKING COLOURS THAT SHALL NOT STAIN NOR
FADE. VERY NECESSARY FOR EVERY ONE TO KNOW, WHETHER HE BE A TRAVEL-
LER BY LAND OR SEA, OR IN WHAT COUNTRY, DOMINION, OR PLANTATION SOEVER
HE MAY INHABIT. . . .
Philadelphia: Printed M,DCC,XCII. pp. (24). 8vo. AAS. HC. LCP. LOC. MHS.

24698　PLUMMER, JONATHAN, JUNIOR
AN ADDRESS TO MISS KATHERINE WIGGLESWORTH OF NEWBURY PORT ON HER RE-
TURN FROM BOSTON WHERE SHE HAD THE SMALL POX BY INOCULATION. NEW-
BURY, OCTOBER 16, 1792. LOVELY NYMPH; HAVING BEEN LATELY SHOCK'D
WITH NEWS THAT YOU WERE DEAD IN BOSTON OF THE SMALL POX AND SOON AFTER
TRANSPORTED WITH THE AGREEABLE INTELLIGENCE THAT THE MELANCHOLY RE-
PORT WAS FALSE, AND THAT YOU WERE OUT OF DANGER FROM THAT ALARMING IN-
DISPOSITION, I CANNOT (THOUGH AN UNFORTUNATE SWAIN AND PERHAPS UNKNOWN
TO YOU) SUPPRESS THE PLEASURE I FEEL ON THIS JOYFUL OCCASION, AND THERE-
FORE BEG YOUR ACCEPTANCE OF THE FOLLOWING POEM. [Fifty-six lines.] I AM
DEAR NYMPH WITH ZEAL MOST FERVENT, YOUR MOST OBEDIENT HUMBLE SER-
VANT – – – – JONATHAN PLUMER, JUNR.
[Newburyport: Printed by John Mycall, 1792.] Broadside. fol. NYHS.

24699   THE POLITICAL REPOSITORY AND STRAFFORD RECORDER. VOL. II. No. 77. WED-
NESDAY, JANUARY 4, [—No. 78. WEDNESDAY, JANUARY 11, 1792.]
Dover: Printed by Eliphalet Ladd. 1792. fol.
On January 14th, the Printing-office was destroyed by fire, and begin-
ning with January 25th, Ladd established, with a continuous number-
ing, *The Phenix.*

24700   POMFRET, JOHN   1667 – 1703
POEMS UPON SEVERAL OCCASIONS. BY THE REVEREND MR. JOHN POMFRET.
New-York: Printed by Hugh Gaine, at the Bible, in Hanover-Square.
1792.
"Printed on fine paper."

24701   PÓOR ROBIN, pseudonym.
POOR ROBIN'S ALMANACK FOR THE YEAR 1793.
Philadelphia: [1792.]

24702   POPE, ALEXANDER   1688 – 1744
AN ESSAY ON MAN: IN FOUR EPISTLES, TO HENRY ST. JOHN, L. BOLINGBROKE, BY
ALEXANDER POPE, ESQUIRE.
Philadelphia: Printed for Thomas Dobson, at the Stone House, No. 41,
South, Second-Street. M,DCC,XCII. pp. 48. 12mo.   NYPL.
The Universal prayer, is added at the end.

24703   —— — AN ESSAY ON MAN; IN FOUR EPISTLES TO H. ST. JOHN, LORD BOLING-
BROKE. TO WHICH IS ADDED, THE UNIVERSAL PRAYER.. BY ALEXANDER POPE,
ESQ. [Ornament.]
Boston: Printed and sold by John W. Folsom, No. 30, *Union-Street.*
M,DCC,XCII. pp. 65. (3). 18mo.   AAS.
Contains, "The following Books may be had of Daniel Brewer, upon
Taunton-Green." pp. (3).

24704   POPE, AMOS   1771 – 1837
AN ASTRONOMICAL DIARY: OR ALMANACK, FOR THE YEAR OF OUR LORD 1793. BE-
ING THE FIRST AFTER LEAP-YEAR, AND THE SEVENTEENTH OF AMERICAN INDE-
PENDENCE. [Nine lines.] BY AMOS POPE, PHILOM. [Six lines of verse.]
Boston: Printed and sold by John W. Folsom, No. 30, *Union-Street. Sold
also by the Booksellers in town and country.* [1792.] pp. [24.] 12mo.
                                        BPL. LOC. NYPL.
To the reader is dated, Amos Pope, Danvers, May 24th, 1792.

24705   POPE, JOHN   1770 – 1845
A TOUR THROUGH THE SOUTHERN AND WESTERN TERRITORIES OF THE UNITED
STATES OF NORTH-AMERICA; THE SPANISH DOMINIONS ON THE RIVER MISSISSIPPI,
AND THE FLORIDAS; THE COUNTRIES OF THE CREEK NATIONS; AND MANY UNIN-
HABITED PARTS. BY JOHN POPE. MALFORUM, PAUCORUM, PLURIUM, OMNIUM, IN-
TEREST.
*Richmond: Printed by John Dixon. For the Author and his three child-
ren, Alexander D. Pope, Lucinda C. Pope, and Anne Pope.* M,DCC,XCII. pp.
(104). 8vo.   JCB.
5th Virginia District Copyright, March, 1792. Literally reprinted,
with index, in New York, in 1888.

24706   THE POTOMAK ALMANAC, OR, THE WASHINGTON EPHEMERIS, FOR THE YEAR OF OUR
LORD 1793, BEING THE FIRST AFTER LEAP-YEAR. [Seventeen lines.]
George-Town, (Potomak) Printed and sold by James Doyle. [1792.] pp.
(40). 16mo.   LOC.
The Editor's Preface states that this is the first issue.

24707 | THE POTOWMAC GUARDIAN, AND BERKELEY ADVERTISER. VOL. 2. NUMBER 59. MONDAY, JANUARY 2, [—VOL. 3. NUMBER 111. MONDAY, DECEMBER 31, 1792.]
Martinsburg, Virginia: Printed and published every Monday, by N. Willis, Burke-Street, near the Court-House. 1792. fol.

24708 | THE POUGHKEEPSIE JOURNAL. NUMB. 336. THURSDAY, JANUARY 5, [—NUMB. 388. WEDNESDAY, DECEMBER 26, 1792.]
Poughkeepsie, Dutchess County: Printed by Nicholas Power, near the Court-House. 1792. fol.

24709 | PRESBYTERIAN CHURCH IN PENNSYLVANIA.
AN ACT OF THE ASSOCIATE PRESBYTERY OF PENNSYLVANIA CONCERNING PUBLIC COVENANTING. . . . PHILADELPHIA, APRIL 29, 1791. . . . ADDED AN ACT CONCERNING THE ADMISSION OF CHURCH MEMBERS TO COMMUNION.
Philadelphia: Printed by W. Young. MD,CC,XCII. pp. (2), 5–53. 18mo. HC.

24710 | PRESBYTERIAN CHURCH IN THE UNITED STATES.
ACTS AND PROCEEDINGS OF THE GENERAL ASSEMBLY OF THE PRESBYTERIAN CHURCH IN THE UNITED STATES OF AMERICA, A. D. 1792.
Philadelphia: Printed by R. Aitken & Son. No. 22, Market Street. M.DCC.XCII. pp. (14). 8vo. AAS. PHS. PTS.

24711 | —— THE CONSTITUTION OF THE PRESBYTERIAN CHURCH IN THE UNITED STATES OF AMERICA; CONTAINING THE CONFESSION OF FAITH, THE CATECHISMS, THE GOVERNMENT AND DISCIPLINE AND THE DIRECTORY FOR THE WORSHIP OF GOD. RATIFIED AND ADOPTED BY THE SYNOD OF NEW-YORK AND PHILADELPHIA, HELD AT PHILADELPHIA MAY THE 16TH 1788, AND CONTINUED BY ADJOURNMENTS UNTIL THE 28TH OF THE SAME MONTH.
Philadelphia: Printed and sold by Thomas Bradford, No. 8, South Front Street. MDCCXCII. pp. vii, 215. 12mo. AAS. PHS.
An exact reprint of the edition printed in Philadelphia in 1789.

24712 | PRICHARD, WILLIAM
LITERATURE, WILLIAM PRICHARD'S SALE OF BOOKS BY AUCTION WILL COMMENCE ON MONDAY EVENING, FEBRUARY 13, 1792, AT MR. A. HUBLEY'S VENDUE-STORE, IN FRONT-STREET, A FEW DOORS BELOW CHESNUT-STREET. WHEN WILL BE SOLD A VALUABLE COLLECTION OF ANCIENT AND MODERN AUTHORS.
Philadelphia: Printed for William Prichard, 1792.

24713 | PRIESTLEY, JOSEPH   1733 – 1804
A DESCRIPTION OF A NEW CHART OF HISTORY. CONTAINING A VIEW OF THE PRINCIPAL REVOLUTIONS OF EMPIRE, THAT HAVE TAKEN PLACE IN THE WORLD. . . . [One line of Latin from] HORACE. FROM THE SEVENTH LONDON EDITION.
London: Printed. New-Haven: Re-printed [by T. and S. Green] for Amos Doolittle [Engraver.] MDCCXCII. pp. 91, (4), folded chart. 8vo.
AAS. BA. BPL. JCB. LOC. MHS.
Title of Chart: A NEW CHART OF HISTORY; EXHIBITING A CLEAR VIEW OF THE RISE, PROGRESS, EXTENT AND DURATION OF EVERY CONSIDERABLE STATE AND EMPIRE, . . .
New-Haven: Engraved by Amos Doolittle. 1792. 2 sheets.

24714 | PROPRIETORS OF THE LOCKS AND CANALS ON MERRIMAC RIVER.
ACT INCORPORATING THE PROPRIETORS OF THE LOCKS AND CANALS ON THE MERRIMAC RIVER.
Boston: Printed by Thomas Adams, 1792. pp. 12. 8vo. MHS.

24715 | —— BY-LAWS, PASSED AUGUST 8, 1792
Newburyport: Printed by John Mycall. 1792. pp. 14. 8vo. BA. MHS.

24716 PROTESTANT EPISCOPAL CHURCH. Diocese of Delaware.
JOURNAL OF THE PROCEEDINGS OF A CONVENTION OF THE PROTESTANT EPISCOPAL
CHURCH, IN THE STATE OF DELAWARE, 1792.
New-York: Printed by Hugh Gaine? 1792.

24717 PROTESTANT EPISCOPAL CHURCH. Diocese of Maryland.
JOURNAL OF THE PROCEEDINGS OF A CONVENTION OF THE PROTESTANT EPISCOPAL
CHURCH IN THE STATE OF MARYLAND, 1792.
Baltimore: 1792.

24718 PROTESTANT EPISCOPAL CHURCH. Diocese of Massachusetts.
JOURNAL OF THE PROCEEDINGS OF A CONVENTION OF THE PROTESTANT EPISCOPAL
CHURCH IN THE STATE OF MASSACHUSETTS, 1792.
Boston: 1792.

24719 PROTESTANT EPISCOPAL CHURCH. Diocese of New Jersey.
PROCEEDINGS OF A CONVENTION OF THE PROTESTANT EPISCOPAL CHURCH, IN THE
STATE OF NEW-JERSEY, 1792.
Newark: Printed by John Woods. 1792.

24720 PROTESTANT EPISCOPAL CHURCH. Diocese of New York.
JOURNAL OF THE CONVENTION OF THE PROTESTANT EPISCOPAL CHURCH OF THE
STATE OF NEW-YORK, HELD IN THE CITY OF NEW-YORK,—FROM TUESDAY, NOV-
EMBER 6TH, 1787,—TO TUESDAY, OCTOBER 13TH, 1791.
New-York: Printed by Hugh Gaine, at the Bible, Hanover-Square,
M,DCC,XCII. pp. 32. 8vo.   AAS. HC. NYHS.

24721 PROTESTANT EPISCOPAL CHURCH IN THE UNITED STATES OF AMERICA.
A CATECHISM FROM THE BOOK OF COMMON PRAYER OF THE PROTESTANT EPISCOPAL
CHURCH.
Philadelphia: Printed by Zachariah Poulson, jun. 1792. 8vo.

24722 —— JOURNAL OF THE PROCEEDINGS OF THE BISHOPS, CLERGY AND LAITY OF THE
PROTESTANT EPISCOPAL CHURCH IN THE UNITED STATES OF AMERICA, IN A CON-
VENTION HELD IN THE CITY OF NEW-YORK, SEPTEMBER, 1792.
New-York: Printed by Hugh Gaine, at the Bible, Hanover-Square. 1792.
pp. 35. 8vo.   MHS.

24723 PROVIDENCE. Rhode Island. Assembly.
RULES FOR THE PROVIDENCE [Dancing] ASSEMBLY. [Forty-eight lines.]
Providence: [Printed by Bennett Wheeler] 1792. Broadside. fol. RIHS.

24724 PROVIDENCE. Rhode Island. St. John's Lodge.
THE BRETHREN OF ST. JOHN'S LODGE ARE REQUESTED TO ATTEND THE FUNERAL OF
OUR BROTHER REV. MOSES BADGER, TO-MORROW AFTERNOON,—TO MEET AT THE
COUNCIL-CHAMBER PRECISELY AT TWO O'CLOCK. BY ORDER, B. WHEELER, SEC'RY.
PROVIDENCE, SEPTEMBER 21, 5792. ☞ EACH BROTHER WILL FURNISH HIM-
SELF WITH WHITE GLOVES, PLAIN WHITE APRON, AND WHITE STOCKINGS.
[Providence: Printed by Bennett Wheeler, 1792.] Broadside. 16mo. BU.

24725 THE PROVIDENCE GAZETTE AND COUNTRY JOURNAL. NO. 1. OF VOL. XXIX. NO.
1462. SATURDAY, JANUARY 7, [—NO. 52. OF VOL. XXIX. NO. 1513. SATURDAY,
DECEMBER 29, 1792.]
*[Providence:] Published by John Carter, at the Post-office, near the State-
House.* 1792. fol.   JCB. NYPL.
After the resignation of John Carter as postmaster, "at the Post-office"
was dropped from the imprint.

24726   RANLET, HENRY
THE YOUTH'S INSTRUCTOR OR SPELLING BOOK COMPRISING THE FIRST PRINCIPLES OF THE ENGLISH LANGUAGE. THE WORDS SELECTED FOR SPELLING ARE SUCH AS ARE MOST FREQUENTLY USED IN WRITING AND CONVERSATION, AND THESE ARE SUITABLY ARRANGED, ACCENTED AND DIVIDED. THE LESSONS FOR READING ARE EASY AND VERY PROPER FOR YOUNG BEGINNERS. THE WHOLE ADAPTED FOR THE IMPROVEMENT OF SCHOOLS. BY HENRY RANLET.
Printed at Exeter, by Henry Ranlet, 1792.
6th New Hampshire District Copyright, issued to Henry Ranlet, as Author and Proprietor, 5 October, 1792.

24727   RASPE, RUDOLF ERICH   1737 – 1794.
GULLIVER REVIVED, CONTAINING SINGULAR TRAVELS, CAMPAIGNS, VOYAGES, AND ADVENTURES, IN RUSSIA, ICELAND, TURKEY, EGYPT, GIBRALTAR, UP THE MEDITERRANEAN, AND ON THE ATLANTIC OCEAN: ALSO AN ACCOUNT OF A VOYAGE INTO THE MOON, WITH MANY EXTRAORDINARY PARTICULARS RELATIVE TO THE COOKING ANIMAL IN THAT PLANET, WHICH ARE HERE CALLED HUMAN SPECIES. BY BARON MUNCHAUSEN.
New-York: Printed for Samuel Campbell, 1792.

24728   RAYNAL, GUILLAUME THOMAS FRANÇOIS, l'abbé   1713 – 1796
THE REVOLUTION OF AMERICA. BY THE ABBE RAYNAL, AUTHOR OF THE PHILOSOPHICAL AND POLITICAL HISTORY OF THE ESTABLISHMENTS AND COMMERCE OF THE EUROPEANS IN BOTH THE INDIES. A NEW TRANSLATION, WITH NOTES.
Hudson: Printed and sold by Ashbel Stoddard. M,DCC,XCII. pp. [124.]
12mo.   JCB. LOC.

24729   READ, DANIEL   1757 – 1841
THE AMERICAN SINGING BOOK; OR A NEW AND EASY GUIDE TO THE ART OF PSALMODY. DESIGNED FOR THE USE OF SINGING SCHOOLS IN AMERICA. CONTAINING IN A PLAIN AND FAMILIAR MANNER, THE RULES OF PSALMODY, TOGETHER WITH A NUMBER OF PSALM TUNES, &C. THE THIRD EDITION. WITH SUPPLEMENT.
Printed [by T. and S. Green] for and sold by the Author, in New-Haven. 1792.
Connecticut District Copyright, issued to Daniel Read, as Author, 3 September, 1791.

24730   REASONS IN SUPPORT OF AN OPINION OFFERED TO THE PUBLIC, RESPECTING THE VOTES OF OTSEGO COUNTY, ON THE 7TH OF JUNE, 1792. [By Richard Harrison, and others.]
New-York: Printed by T. and J. Swords, No. 27, William-Street—1792— pp. (30). 8vo.   JCB. MHS. NYHS. NYPL.

24731   REID, THOMAS   1710 – 1796
ESSAYS ON THE INTELLECTUAL AND ACTIVE POWERS OF MAN. BY THOMAS REID, D. D. F. R. S. EDINBURGH. PROFESSOR OF MORAL PHILOSOPHY IN THE UNIVERSITY OF GLASGOW.
Philadelphia: Printed by William Young, Bookseller, No. 52. Second-Street, the corner of Chesnut-Street. 1792. 2vols. 8vo.

24732   RHODE ISLAND. STATE.
FEBRUARY, 1792. AT THE GENERAL ASSEMBLY OF THE GOVERNOR AND COMPANY OF THE STATE OF RHODE-ISLAND, AND PROVIDENCE-PLANTATIONS, BEGUN AND HOLDEN (BY ADJOURNMENT) AT PROVIDENCE, WITHIN AND FOR THE STATE AFORESAID, ON THE LAST MONDAY IN FEBRUARY, IN THE YEAR OF OUR LORD ONE THOUSAND SEVEN HUNDRED AND NINETY-TWO, AND IN THE SIXTEENTH YEAR OF INDEPENDENCE. [Colophon:]
Providence: Printed by Bennett Wheeler. [1792.] pp. 40. fol. HSP. JCB. LOC.

RHODE ISLAND, continued.

24733 —— May, 1792. At the General Assembly of the governor and company of the State of Rhode-Island, and Providence-Plantations, begun and holden at Newport, within and for the State aforesaid, on the first Wednesday in May, in the year of our Lord one thousand seven hundred and ninety-two, and in the sixteenth year of independence. [Colophon:]
Providence: Printed by Bennett Wheeler. [1792.] pp. 30. fol.
HSP. JCB. LOC.

24734 —— June, 1792. At the General Assembly of the governor and company of the State of Rhode-Island and Providence-Plantations, begun and holden by adjournment at Newport, within and for the State aforesaid, on the third Monday of June, in the year of our Lord one thousand seven hundred and ninety-two, and in the sixteenth year of independence. [Colophon:]
Providence: Printed by J. Carter. [1792.] pp. 30. fol. HSP. JCB. LOC.

24735 —— August, 1792. At the General Assembly of the governor and company of the State of Rhode-Island, and Providence-Plantations, begun and holden, in consequence of warrants issued by his Excellency the governor, at Newport, within and for the State aforesaid, on the second Wednesday in August, in the year of our Lord one thousand seven hundred and ninety-two, and in the seventeenth year of independence. [Colophon:]
Providence: Printed by Bennett Wheeler. [1792.] pp. 18. fol.
HSP. JCB. LOC.

24736 —— October, 1792. At the General Assembly of the governor and company of the State of Rhode-Island, and Providence-Plantations, begun and holden, at Providence, within and for the State aforesaid, on the last Monday in October, in the year of our Lord one thousand seven hundred and ninety-two, and in the seventeenth year of independence. [Colophon:]
Providence: Printed by Bennett Wheeler. [1792.] pp. 42. fol.
HSP. JCB. LOC.

24737 —— State of Rhode-Island, &c. In General Assembly, June session, A. D. 1792. It is voted and resolved, That two Representatives, qualified agreeably to law, to represent this State in the third Congress of the United States, be elected, by the freemen of this State, in town-meeting legally assembled, on the last Tuesday in August next: [Twelve lines.] A true copy, witness, Henry Ward, sec'ry. [Colophon:]
Providence: Printed by Bennett Wheeler. [1792.] Broadside. 4to. AAS. RIHS.

24738 —— State of Rhode-Island, &c. In General Assembly. August session, 1792. It is voted and resolved, That the freemen of this State, in the election of two Representatives to represent this State in the Congress of the United States, [shall designate their ballots, first and second Representative, or they will be rejected.] A true copy: witness, Henry Ward, sec'ry. [Colophon:]
[Providence:] Printed by J. Carter. [1792.] Broadside. 4to. RIHS.

24739 RHODE ISLAND. College of, now Brown University.
Catalogus eorum qui in Collegio Rhod. Ins. et Prov. Plant. ab anno 1769, ad annum 1792, alicujus gradus laureâ donati sunt.
Providentiæ: Typis Bennett Wheeler? 1792. Broadside. fol.

24740   RHODE ISLAND, COLLEGE OF, now BROWN UNIVERSITY, continued.
—— HONORATISSIMO JABEZ BOWEN, ARMIGERO, COLLEGII RHOD. INSULÆ QUOD PROVIDENTIÆ EST CANCELLARIO; [Nine lines.] HÆC PHILOSOPHEMATA, JUVENES IN ARTIBUS INITIATI, [Seventeen names] HUMILLIMÈ DEDICANT. THESES [Three columns.] [Colophon:]
Habita in solennibus Academicis Providentiæ, in Rep. Ins. Rhod. et Prov. Plant. nonis Septembris, A. D. M,DCC,XCII. *Rerumpublicarum Foederatarum Americæ summæ potestatis* XVII. *Providentiæ: Typis Bennett Wheeler.* Broadside. fol.
        AAS. BU.

24741   RICE, DAVID   1733 – 1816
SLAVERY INCONSISTENT WITH JUSTICE AND GOOD POLICY. BY PHILANTHROPOS.
Lexington; Printed by J. Bradford. M.DCC.XCII. pp. [34.] 12mo. LOC.

24742   —— SLAVERY INCONSISTENT WITH JUSTICE AND GOOD POLICY; PROVED BY A SPEECH DELIVERED IN THE CONVENTION, HELD AT DANVILLE, KENTUCKY. BY THE REV. DAVID RICE. LET THE OPPRESSED GO FREE.—ISAIAH LVIII. 6.
Philadelphia: Printed by Parry Hall, 1792. 12mo.
Reprinted in London, in 1793; and in New York in 1804, and in 1862.

24743   RICHARD, ASTROLOGER, pseudonym.
THE NEW-ENGLAND CALENDAR: OR ALMANACK, FOR THE YEAR OF OUR LORD, 1793. [Cut. Four lines.] BY RICHARD ASTROLOGER.
Boston: Printed and sold by Nathaniel Coverly, by the gross, or single dozen. [1792.] pp. (24). 12mo.
        AAS. LOC.

24744   RICHARDSON, SAMUEL   1689 – 1761
THE HISTORY OF PAMELA: OR VIRTUE REWARDED. ABRIDGED FROM THE WORKS OF SAMUEL RICHARDSON, ESQ.
Philadelphia: Printed and sold by W. Woodhouse, at the Bible No. 6, South Front-street. M.DCC.XCII.

24745   RILEY, GEORGE
THE BEAUTIES OF THE CREATION; OR, A NEW MORAL SYSTEM OF NATURAL HISTORY; DISPLAYED IN THE MOST SINGULAR, CURIOUS, AND BEAUTIFUL, QUADRUPEDS, BIRDS, INSECTS, TREES, AND FLOWERS: DESIGNED TO INSPIRE YOUTH WITH HUMANITY TOWARDS THE BRUTE CREATION, AND BRING THEM EARLY ACQUAINTED WITH THE WONDERFUL WORKS OF THE DIVINE CREATOR. [Three lines from] BLACKMORE ON THE CREATION.
Philadelphia: Printed by William Young, Bookseller, No. 52, Second-street, the corner of Chesnut-Street. M,DCC,XCII. pp. 348. 12mo.   AAS. JCB.

24746   RIPLEY, EZRA   1751 – 1841
THE DESIGN AND BLESSEDNESS OF THE GOSPEL. A SERMON, DELIVERED, MAY 23, 1792, AT THE ORDINATION OF THE REV. WILLIAM EMERSON, TO THE CARE OF THE CONGREGATIONAL CHURCH AND SOCIETY IN HARVARD. BY EZRA RIPLEY, A. M. PASTOR OF THE CHURCH IN CONCORD. [Publishers monogram.]
Printed at Boston, by Isaiah Thomas and Ebenezer T. Andrews, Faust's Statue, No. 45, Newbury Street. MDCCXII [sic 1792.] pp. 43. 8vo.
        AAS. BA. JCB. LOC. MHS. NYPL.

24747   —— *Half-title:* MR. RIPLEY'S SERMON AT THE DEDICATION OF HIS MEETING-HOUSE. *Title:* [THE CHURCH GOD'S PECULIAR CARE.] A SERMON PREACHED ON THE COMPLETION OF A GENERAL REPAIR OF THE MEETING HOUSE IN CONCORD, JANUARY 24TH, 1792. BY EZRA RIPLEY, A. M. PASTOR OF THE CHURCH IN THAT TOWN.
Boston: Printed by B. Edes and Son, in Kilby-Street, M,DCC,XCII. pp. [52.] 4to.
        AAS. BA. JCB. MHS. NYHS.

24748   RIPPON, JOHN   1751 – 1836
RIPPON'S HYMNS, BEING A SELECTION OF HYMNS, FROM THE BEST AUTHORS, INTEND-
ED TO BE AN APPENDIX TO DOCTOR WATTS'S PSALMS AND HYMNS, AND SUITABLE
FOR CHRISTIANS OF EVERY DENOMINATION.
Elizabeth-Town: Printed by Shepard Kollock. MDCCXCII. pp. ix, 416.
16mo.   AAS. BM.

24749   —— — A SELECTION OF HYMNS FROM THE BEST AUTHORS, INTENDED TO BE AN
APPENDIX TO DR. WATT'S PSALMS AND HYMNS. BY JOHN RIPPON, A. M. FIRST
AMERICAN EDITION.
*New-York: Printed and sold by William Durell, at his Book-store and
Printing-office, No.* 19, *Queen-Street.* M,DCC,XCII. pp xiii, (19), (1), (489),
(6), (20). 12mo. unpaged.   AAS. NYPL.

24750   ROBBINS, ROBERT   1741 – 1804
DIVINE SOVEREIGNTY IN THE SALVATION, AND DAMNATION OF SINNERS VINDICATED;
IN A DISCOURSE, DELIVERED AT WEST CHESTER, IN COLCHESTER. BY ROBERT
ROBBINS A. M. PASTOR OF A CHURCH IN COLCHESTER. SUBMITTED TO PUBLIC IN-
SPECTION IN COMPLIANCE WITH THE REQUEST OF SEVERAL RESPECTABLE GENTLE-
MEN. [One line from] PROPHET ISAIAH.
Norwich: Printed by Ebenezer Bushnell. M,DCC,XCII. pp. (67). 8vo.
                                   BM. CHS. JCB. LOC. YC.

24751   ROBERTSON, JOSEPH   1726 – 1802
A CLEAR AND PRACTICAL SYSTEM OF PUNCTUATION: ABRIDGED FROM ROBERTSON'S
ESSAY ON PUNCTUATION. [By Thaddeus Mason Harris.] FOR THE USE OF SCHOOLS.
[Publisher's monogram.]
*Printed at Boston, [according to Act of Congress.] By I. Thomas and E.
T. Andrews, Faust's Statue, No.* 45, *Newbury Street.* MDCCXCII. pp. (2), (2),
(2), (11)—48. 12mo.   LOC.

32d Massachusetts District Copyright, issued to Thomas & Andrews,
as Proprietors, 16 July, 1792.

24752   ROBERTSON, WILLIAM   1721 – 1793
AN HISTORICAL DISQUISITION CONCERNING THE KNOWLEDGE WHICH THE ANCIENTS
HAD OF INDIA; AND THE PROGRESS OF TRADE WITH THAT COUNTRY PRIOR TO THE
DISCOVERY OF THE PASSAGE TO IT BY THE CAPE OF GOOD HOPE. WITH AN AP-
PENDIX, CONTAINING OBSERVATIONS ON THE CIVIL POLICY—THE LAWS AND JU-
DICIAL PROCEEDINGS—THE ARTS—THE SCIENCES—AND RELIGIOUS INSTITUTIONS
OF THE INDIANS. BY WILLIAM ROBERTSON, D. D. F. R. S. EDINBURGH, PRINCIPAL
OF THE UNIVERSITY, AND HISTORIOGRAPH TO HIS MAJESTY FOR SCOTLAND.
Philadelphia: Printed by William Young, Bookseller, No. 52, *Second-Street,
the corner of Chesnut-Street.* M,DCC,XCII. pp. viii, 13—420. 8vo.
                                   AAS. HC. LCP. MHS.

24753   ROGERS, MEDAD   1750 – 1824
AN ADDRESS TO THE LIVING; OR THE LANGUAGE OF DIVINE PROVIDENCE IN DEATH:
AT THE FUNERAL OF THE WIFE OF BENJAMIN BEARSS, JUN. AND THE DAUGHTER
OF MARTIN KELLOGG, OF NEW-FAIRFIELD, WHO DIED SUDDENLY, MARCH XXV,
M,DCC,XC,II. IN THE XXTH YEAR OF HER AGE. . . .
Danbury: Printed by Douglas and Ely. 1792. pp. 12. 12mo.   BA.

24754   ROGERS, RANSFORD

AN ACCOUNT OF THE BEGINNING, TRANSACTIONS AND DISCOVERY, OF RANSFORD ROGERS, WHO SEDUCED MANY BY PRETENDED HOBGOBLINS AND APPARITIONS, AND THEREBY EXTORTED MONEY FROM THEIR POCKETS. IN THE COUNTY OF MORRIS AND STATE OF NEW-JERSEY, IN THE YEAR 1788.

     [Newark:] Printed [by John Woods] for every purchaser—1792. pp. 28. 16mo.

The account of this impostor's pranks, locally known as the "Morristown Ghost," has been reprinted in Newark in 1814; in 1826; in 1850; in 1876; and in 1896.

24755   RÖMELING, CHRISTIAN ANTON

C. A. ROEMELINGS, GEWESEN PREDIGERS ZU HAARBURG, NACHRICHT SEINER VON GOTT GESCHEHENEN VÖLLIGEN HERAUSFÜHRUNG AUS BABEL. WIE AUCH TREUHERZIGE ERWECKUNGS-STIMME ZUM AUSGANG AUS BABEL, DEME ANGEHÄNGT EIN THEOSOPHISCHER ENTWURF VON DENEN ZWEI ERZ-KAETZERN, VERNUNFT UND EIGENLIEBE, UND G. ARNOLD'S HEILSAME WAHRNEHMUNG JETZIGER ZEITEN, WIE AUCH EIN STÜCK AUS G. T. STEEGENS VON DER MYSTIK UND EIN TRACTAT VOM INNERN LEBEN UND DER REINEN LIEBE GOTTES.

     Ephrata gedruckt im Jahr 1792. pp. (2), (10), (466); (2). 23—96. 8vo.

Second title: THEOSOPHISCHER ENTWURF, AUS WAS URSACHEN DAS VERWORRENE RELIGIONS-GEZANK IN DER CHRISTENHEIT ENTSPRUNGEN, DURCH WAS MITTEL ES FORTGEFÜHRET, UND AUF WAS ART ES ENDLICH ZERNICHTET MÖGE WERDEN. IN CHRISTLICHER FREYHEIT UND AUFRICHTIGER LIEB, AUS DEM LICHT VON OBEN VERFASSET. [Seven lines of Scripture texts.] pp. (349) — (407.)

Third title: HEILSAME WAHRNEHMUNG JETZIGER ZEITEN. BEREITS 1699, HERAUSGEGEBEN ABER BEY ABGANG DER EXEMPLARIEN, UM SEINES ERBAULICHEN UND AUF GEGENWÄRTIGE ZEIT SICH SONDERLICH SCHICKENDEN INHALTS WILLEN, ZU ALLGEMEINER ERBAUUNG UND ERWECKUNG AUFS NEUE ZUM DRUCK BEFÖRDERT. [Five lines of Scripture texts.] pp. (407)—(459).

Fourth title: KURZER BERICHT VON DER MYSTIC.

Fifth title: KURZE ANLEITUNG ZUM INNERN LEBEN, NACH DESSIN RECHTEN, BESTÄNDIGEN UND SICHERN GRUNDE, MORAN UNSERE ZEITLICHE UND EWIGE GLÜCKSELIGKEIT GELEGEN IST. B 3 pp. (2), (23)—(96).   AAS. JCB. NYPL.

First printed in Frankfurt and Leipzig in 1710. The year the author was excommunicated and banished from the Lutheran Church at Harburg, for his leaning towards pietistic and mystical religion. In Holland, where he found refuge, he joined the Mennonites. The appended tracts of Arnold, and Tersteegen, were also printed separately at Ephrata.

24756   ROSS, DAVID   1750 –

ADDRESS TO THE CITIZENS OF ANN ARUNDEL AND PRINCE GEORGE'S COUNTIES. [Against electing Colonel John Francis Mercer to Congress.]

     Annapolis: Printed by F. and S. Green. 1792. 12mo.

24757   ROUELLE, JOHN

A COMPLETE TREATISE ON THE MINERAL WATERS OF VIRGINIA; CONTAINING A DESCRIPTION OF THEIR SITUATION, THEIR NATURAL HISTORY, THEIR ANALYSIS, CONTENTS, AND THEIR USE IN MEDICINE. BY JOHN ROUELLE, M. D. [Two lines of verse.]

     Philadelphia: Printed for the Author, by Charles Cist, and to be sold by Thomas Dobson. M,DCC,XCII. pp. (2), (2), (4), xix, 68. 8vo.

                   AAS. BA. BM. CLS. HC. LOC. NYHS. NYPL. SGO.

29th Pennsylvania District Copyright, issued to John Rouelle, as Author, 18 January, 1792.

24758   ROWE, Elizabeth Singer   1674 – 1737
DEVOUT EXERCISES OF THE HEART, IN MEDITATION AND SOLILOQUY, PRAYER AND
PRAISE. *Windsor: Printed by Alden Spooner.* 1792. 12mo.   BM.

24759   —— —— AN ABRIDGEMENT OF MRS. ROWE'S DEVOUT EXERCISES OF THE HEART.
*Philadelphia: Printed by Parry Hall, No. 149, in Chesnut-Street; and
sold by John Dickins No. 43, Fourth-Street, near Race-Street.* 1792.

24760   —— FRIENDSHIP IN DEATH: IN TWENTY LETTERS FROM THE DEAD TO THE LIVING.
TO WHICH ARE ADDED, LETTERS MORAL AND ENTERTAINING, IN PROSE AND
VERSE. IN THREE PARTS. BY MRS. ELIZABETH ROWE. TO WHICH IS PREFIXED,
AN ACCOUNT OF THE LIFE OF THE AUTHOR.
*Printed at Boston, for David West, No. 36, Marlboro-street, and E. Larkin, jun.
No. 50, Cornhill. By Joseph Bumstead.* M.DCC.XCII. pp. xxix, 310. 12mo.   AAS.

24761   RUSH, Benjamin   1745 – 1813
AN ACCOUNT OF THE SUGAR MAPLE TREE, OF THE UNITED STATES: AND OF THE
METHODS OF OBTAINING SUGAR FROM IT; TOGETHER WITH OBSERVATIONS UPON
THE ADVANTAGES, BOTH PUBLIC AND PRIVATE, OF THIS SUGAR; IN A LETTER TO
THOMAS JEFFERSON, ESQ. SECRETARY OF STATE OF THE UNITED STATES, AND
ONE OF THE VICE-PRESIDENTS OF THE AMERICAN PHILOSOPHICAL SOCIETY. READ
IN THE AMERICAN PHILOSOPHICAL SOCIETY, ON THE 19 OF AUGUST, 1791, AND
EXTRACTED FROM THE THIRD VOLUME OF THEIR TRANSACTIONS, NOW IN THE
PRESS. BY BENJAMIN RUSH, M. D. PROFESSOR OF THE INSTITUTES AND OF CHEM-
ICAL MEDICINE IN THE UNIVERSITY OF PENNSYLVANIA.
Philadelphia: Printed by R. Aitken & Son. M.DCC.XCII. pp. 16. 8vo.
Reprinted in London in 1792.   BM. JCB.

24762   —— CONSIDERATIONS ON THE INJUSTICE AND IMPOLICY OF PUNISHING MURDER BY
DEATH. EXTRACTED FROM THE AMERICAN MUSEUM. WITH ADDITIONS. BY
BENJAMIN RUSH, M. D. PROFESSOR OF THE INSTITUTES, AND OF CLINICAL MEDI-
CINE, IN THE UNIVERSITY OF PENNSYLVANIA. [Ornament.]
Philadelphia: From the Press of Mathew Carey, May 4—M.DCC.XCII.
pp. (19). 8vo.   BM. LOC. NYHS.
Reprinted in London in 1793.

24763   RUSSEL, Robert
SEVEN SERMONS, VIZ. I. OF THE UNPARDONABLE SIN AGAINST THE HOLY GHOST;
OR, THE SIN UNTO DEATH. II. THE SAINT'S DUTY AND EXERCISE: IN TWO PARTS:
BEING AN EXHORTATION TO, AND DIRECTION FOR PRAYER. III. THE ACCEPTED
TIME AND DAY OF SALVATION. IV. THE END OF TIME, AND BEGINNING OF ETER-
NITY. V. JOSHUA'S RESOLUTION TO SERVE THE LORD. VI. THE WAY TO HEAVEN
MADE PLAIN. VII. THE FUTURE STATE OF MAN: OR, A TREATISE OF THE RESUR-
RECTION. BY ROBERT RUSSEL.
Baltimore: Printed and sold by David Graham, 1792.

24764   RUSSELL, Elijah
RUSSELL'S NEWHAMPSHIRE & VERMONT ALMANACK, FOR THE YEAR OF CREATION,
ACCORDING TO MOSAIC HISTORY, 5755: AND OF THE CHRISTIAN ÆRA, 1793. BEING
THE FIRST AFTER BISSEXTILE OR LEAPYEAR, AND OF THE INDEPENDENCE OF THE
UNITED STATES OF AMERICA THE SEVENTEENTH. CALCULATED FOR THE LATI-
TUDE AND LONGITUDE OF THE STATE OF NEWHAMPSHIRE; BUT WILL ANSWER,
WITHOUT ESSENTIAL VARIATION, FOR THE STATE OF VERMONT. CONTAINING,
THE USUAL ASTRONOMICAL CALCULATIONS, WITH A VARIETY OF OTHER MATTER,
USEFUL, INSTRUCTIVE, AND ENTERTAINING.
*Printed at Concord, [Newhampshire] by Elijah Russell. Sold by the thou-
sand, gross, hundred, dozen, or single.* [1792.] pp. (24). 12mo. AAS. LOC. NYHS.
Contains an Essay on political corruption.

24765 SAINT DOMINGO. COLONY. ASSEMBLÉE GÉNÉRALE DE LA PARTIE FRANÇAISE.
A PARTICULAR ACCOUNT OF THE INSURRECTION OF THE NEGROES OF ST. DOMINGO,
BEGUN IN AUGUST, 1791: TRANSLATED FROM THE FRENCH. THE THIRD EDITION:
WITH NOTES AND AN APPENDIX EXTRACTED FROM AUTHENTIC ORIGINAL PAPERS.
[Without Place or Printer, 1792.] pp. (32). 8vo. NYPL.

24766 —— — A PARTICULAR ACCOUNT OF THE INSURRECTION OF THE NEGROES OF ST.
DOMINGO, BEGUN IN AUGUST, 1791: TRANSLATED FROM THE FRENCH. THE
FOURTH EDITION : WITH NOTES AND AN APPENDIX EXTRACTED FROM AUTHENTIC
ORIGINAL PAPERS.
[Without Place or Printer, 1792.] pp. (32). 8vo. NYPL.

24767 THE SALEM GAZETTE. VOLUME VI. NUMBER 273. TUESDAY, JANUARY 3, [—NUM-
BER 324. TUESDAY, DECEMBER 25, 1792.]
*Published by Thomas C. Cushing, No. 8, Main-Street, near [corner] Court
and Washington Streets, Salem, Massachusetts.* 1792. fol. HC. LOC.

24768 SANDERS, DANIEL CLARKE 1768 – 1850
THE PLEASURES AND ADVANTAGES OF FRIENDLY SOCIETY. A SERMON PREACHED AT
VERGENNES, STATE OF VERMONT, ON ST. JOHN'S FESTIVAL. JUNE 26TH, A. D.
1792, BEFORE THE FREE AND ACCEPTED MASONS OF DORCHESTER LODGE. NO.
XII. AND PUBLISHED AT THEIR REQUEST. BY DANIEL CLARKE SANDERS, A. M.
A CANDIDATE FOR THE GOSPEL MINISTRY.
*Printed at Windsor, State of Vermont. By James Reed Hutchins, for the
Masonic Fraternity of Vergennes.* 1792. pp. 16. 4to. AAS.

24769 SANDS, JOSHUA?
THE RIGHTS OF SUFFRAGE. [Six lines from] ADDISON's CATO.
Hudson: Printed by Ashbel Stoddard. M,DCC,XCII. pp. [45], (1).
12mo. AAS. LOC. MHS.
Signed, Plain sense. September 10, 1791. Refers to the votes of
Otsego County being thrown out to elect George Clinton, governor.

24770 SAUNDERS, RICHARD, pseudonym.
POOR RICHARD IMPROVED: BEING AN ALMANACK AND EPHEMERIS OF THE MOTIONS
OF THE SUN AND MOON, THE TRUE PLACES AND ASPECTS OF THE PLANETS; THE
RISING AND SETTING OF THE SUN; AND THE RISING, SETTING AND SOUTHING OF THE
MOON, FOR THE YEAR OF OUR LORD 1793: BEING THE FIRST AFTER LEAP-YEAR.
[Eight lines.] BY RICHARD SAUNDERS, PHILOM.
Philadelphia: Printed and sold by Hall & Sellers—No. 51—Market-street.
[1792.] pp. (44). 12mo. AAS. LOC.

24771 SAUR, CHRISTOPH 1721 – 1784
EINE NUETZLICHE ANWEISUNG ODER BEYHÜLFE VOR DIE TEUTSCHEN UM ENGLISCH
ZU LERNEN: WIE ES VOR NEU-ANKOMMENDE UND ANDERE IM LAND GEBOHRNE
LAND UND HANDWERKSLEUTE WELCHEN IN DER ENGLISCHEN SPRACHE ERFAHR-
ENE UND GEÜBTE SCHULMEISTER UND PRECEPTORES ERMANGELEN, VOR DAS BE-
QUEMSTE ERACHTET WORDEN; MIT IHRER, GEWÖHNLICHEN ARBEIT UND WERCK-
ZEUG ERLÄUTERT. NEBST EINER GRAMMATIC, VOR DIEJENIGEN, WELCHE IN AN-
DERN SPRACHEN UND DEREN FUNDAMENTEN ERFAHREN SIND. VIERTE AUFLAGE.
Germantaun: Gedruckt bey Peter Leibert. 1792. pp. 282+ 12mo. HSP.

24772 SCHNEIDER, PETER
MERKWÜRDIGE PROPHEZEYUNG EINES EINSIEDLERS, WELCHER 15 JAHRE ALLEIN
IN DER WÜSTEN GEWOHNET. ENTDECKT VON DR. PETER SCHNEIDER.
[Ephrata?] Gedruckt für den Verfasser. 1792.

24773   SCOTT, Thomas
A Sermon, preached at St. Peter's church, Philadelphia, on Sunday the
26th of August, 1792. Luke 15, 18. [Two lines.] By the rev. Thomas
Scot, of St. John's College, Annapolis.
> *Philadelphia: Printed by Stewart & Cochran, No. 34, South Second-street.*
M,DCC,XCII. pp. (19). 8vo.   JCB. LOC.

24774   SEABURY, Samuel   1729 – 1796
A Discourse delivered before the triennial Convention of the Protestant
Episcopal Church in the United States of America, in Trinity-church,
New-York, on the twelfth day of September, one thousand seven hundred and ninety-two. By Samuel Seabury, d. d. bishop of Connecticut
and Rhode-Island.
> *New-York: Printed by Hugh Gaine, at the Bible, in Hanover-Square.*
—1792.— pp. (27). 8vo.   JCB. NYHS. NYPL.

24775   SEAMAN, Valentine   1765 –
An Inaugural dissertation on opium.
> *Philadelphia: Printed by Johnson & Justice,* 1792. pp. 32. 8vo.   SGO.

24776   THE SECURITY of the rights of citizens in the State of Connecticut
considered.
> *Printed at Hartford, by Hudson & Goodwin.* MDCCXCII. pp. 102. 8vo.
BA. NYHS.

24777   A SELECTION of miscellaneous pieces, in verse and prose. Respectfully
dedicated to the youth of both sexes. Part I. [—II.]
> *Philadelphia: Printed and sold by Daniel Lawrence, No. 78, North 4th*
Street, near Race. M.DCC.XCII. pp. (2), (80), (2). 12mo.   LOC.

24778   SENECA, Lucius Annæus   5 B C—65 A D
Seneca's Morals, by way of abstract. To which is added, a discourse, under
the title of An After-thought. Adorned with cuts. - By sir Roger
L'Estrange, knt.
> *Printed at Boston, by I. Thomas and E. T. Andrews, at Faust's Statue,*
No. 45, Newbury-Street. MDCCXCII. pp. xxiv, 383, 4 plates. 12mo. AAS. JCB.

24779   A SERIOUS address to the candid and impartial members of the Methodist
communion, as well preachers as people. By a Member.
> *New-York: Printed by Samuel Loudon, jun.?* 1792. 12mo.

24780   SERJENT, Abel
An Humble address to the Independent Universal Church in Philadelphia;
and others of the same faith. By Abel Serjent.
> *New-York: Printed by Samuel Loudon, jun.? Sold by L. Jones, No. 54,*
King Street. 1792.

24781   SEWALL, Daniel   1755 – 1842
An Astronomical diary, or Almanac, for the year of christian æra 1793: being 1st after bissextile or leap year. Calculated for the meridian of
Portsmouth, New-Hampshire, lat. 43 deg. 5 min. north. But will serve
for any of the New-England States; containing every thing necessary
for such a work, with a variety of other useful matters. By Daniel Sewall. [Nine lines of verse.]
> *Portsmouth: New-Hampshire, Printed and sold (wholesale and retail, cheap,)*
by John Melcher, at his office, corner of Market-Street: Sold also by most of the
shop keepers in town and country. [1792.] pp. (24). 12mo.   LOC.

24782　SEWARD, ANNA　　　　　　　　　　　　　　　1747 – 1809
MONODY ON THE UNFORTUNATE MAJOR ANDRE; WHO WAS EXECUTED AT TAPPAN,
NOVEMBER — 1780. BY MISS SEWARD. TO WHICH ARE ADDED, MAJOR ANDRE'S
LETTERS. ADDRESSED TO MISS SEWARD, WHEN AT HIS 18TH YEAR. THE SEC-
OND NEW-YORK EDITION.
　　　New-York: Printed for T. Allen, Bookseller and Stationer, No. 12, *Queen-
Street.* 1792. pp. 48. 12mo.　　　　　　　　　　　　AAS. BA. HC.

24783　SÈZE, RAYMOND, called ROMAIN, comte DE　　　　　1748 – 1828
THE DEFENCE OF LOUIS XVI, PRONOUNCED AT THE BAR OF THE NATIONAL CONVEN-
TION, 26TH DECEMBER, 1792. TRANSLATED FROM THE FRENCH BY C. DUBUC.
　　　Boston, Re-printed, 1792. pp. 76. 16mo.　　　　　　　MHS.

24784　SHAFTSBURY. VERMONT. BAPTIST ASSOCIATION.
MINUTES OF THE SHAFTSBURY ASSOCIATION, AT THEIR ANNUAL CONVENTION, HELD
IN STILLWATER, 1792.
　　　Bennington: Printed by Anthony Haswell? 1792.

24785　SHERIDAN, RICHARD BRINSLEY BUTLER　　　　　　1751 – 1816
THE SCHOOL FOR SCANDAL. A COMEDY, IN FIVE ACTS. AS PERFORMED AT THE
THEATRE ROYAL, DRURY LANE, LONDON. BY R. B. SHERIDAN, ESQ.
　　　*Printed at Boston, by J. Belknap and T. Hall, sold at their office, State
Street.* MDCCXCII. pp. 96. 12mo.　　　　　　　　　AAS.

24786　SHERWIN, THOMAS
DIVINE BREATHINGS: OR, A PIOUS SOUL THIRSTING AFTER CHRIST. IN A HUNDRED
PATHETICAL MEDITATIONS. THE FIRST AMERICAN EDITION [FROM THE SIXTEENTH
ENGLISH.] PSALM LXXIII. 25. [Two lines.]
　　　Philadelphia: Printed by William Gibbons, No. 144, *Third Street, near
Vine Street.* M.DCC.XCII. pp. 104, (4). 18mo.　　　　　AAS.
A second American edition was printed in Boston, in 1805.

24787　A SHORT INTRODUCTION TO LATIN GRAMMAR, FOR THE USE OF THE UNIVERSITY AND
ACADEMY OF PENNSYLVANIA, IN PHILADELPHIA. [Two lines of Latin from] HOR.
FIFTH EDITION, CAREFULLY REVISED.
　　　Boston: Printed and sold by John W. Folsom, No. 30, *Union-Street.*
M,DCC,XCII. pp. (126), (1). 12mo.　　　　　　　　　AAS.
Folsom's second edition—a reprint of the fifth Philadelphia edition.

24788　SHUTTLESWORTH, SAMUEL　　　　　　　　　　　1750 – 1834
A DISCOURSE DELIVERED IN PRESENCE OF HIS EXCELLENCY, THOMAS CHITTENDEN,
ESQ. GOVERNOR; HIS HONOR PETER OLCOTT, ESQ. LIEUTENANT-GOVERNOR: THE HON-
ORABLE COUNCIL, AND HOUSE OF REPRESENTATIVES OF THE STATE OF VERMONT;
AT WINDSOR OCTOBER 13, 1791. BEING THE DAY OF GENERAL ELECTION. BY
SAMUEL SHUTTLESWORTH, A. M. PASTOR OF A CHURCH IN WINDSOR.
　　　*Printed at Windsor, State of Vermont, by James Reed Hutchins, for, and
by order of the General Assembly.* MDCCXCII. pp. 16. 8vo.　BA. CLS. HC. MHS.

24789　SIRET, PIERRE LOUIS　　　　　　　　　　　　　1745 – 1798
ELÉMENS DE LA LANGUE ANGLAISE. NOUVELLE ÉDITION . . . CORRIGÉE ET AUG-
MENTÉE PAR UN ÉDITEUR ANGLOIS.
　　　Philadelphia: 1792. 12mo.　　　　　　　　　　BA.

24790 SLACK, Mrs. —
THE AMERICAN INSTRUCTOR: OR, YOUNG MAN'S BEST COMPANION. CONTAINING, SPELLING, READING, WRITING, AND ARITHMETICK, IN AN EASIER WAY THAN ANY YET PUBLISHED; AND HOW TO QUALIFY ANY PERSON FOR BUSINESS, WITHOUT THE HELP OF A MASTER. INSTRUCTIONS TO WRITE VARIETY OF HANDS, WITH COPIES BOTH IN PROSE AND VERSE. HOW TO WRITE LETTERS ON BUSINESS OR FRIEND-SHIP. FORMS OF INDENTURES, BONDS, BILLS OF SALE, RECEIPTS, WILLS, LEASES, RELEASES, &C. ALSO MERCHANTS ACCOUNTS, AND A SHORT AND EASY METHOD OF SHOP AND BOOK-KEEPING. TOGETHER WITH THE METHOD OF MEASURING CAR-PENTERS, JOINERS, SAWYERS, BRICKLAYERS, PLASTERERS, PLUMBERS, MASONS, GLAZIERS AND PAINTERS WORK. WITH THE DESCRIPTION OF GUNTER'S LINE, AND COGGESHALL'S SLIDING RULE. LIKEWISE THE PRACTICAL GAUGER MADE EASY; THE ART OF DIALLING, AND HOW TO ERECT AND FIX DIALS; WITH INSTRUCTIONS FOR DYING, COLOURING, AND MAKING COLOURS; AND SOME GENERAL OBSERVATIONS FOR GARDENING EVERY MONTH IN THE YEAR. WITH INSTRUCTIONS HOW TO PICKLE AND PRESERVE; TO MAKE DIVERS SORTS OF WINE; AND MANY EXCELLENT PLASTERS AND MEDICINES, NECESSARY IN ALL FAMILIES. A COMPENDIUM OF THE SCIENCES OF GEOGRAPHY AND ASTRONOMY. ALSO SOME USEFUL INTEREST TABLES. BY GEORGE FISHER, ACCOUNTANT.
New-York: Printed by Hugh Gaine, at the Bible, in Hanover-Square. 1792.

24791 SMITH, EUNICE
PRACTICAL LANGUAGE INTERPRETED: IN A DIALOGUE BETWEEN A BELIEVER AND AN UNBELIEVER. IN TWO PARTS. REPRESENTING A BELIEVER UNDER THE INFLU-ENCE OF GRACE, SPEAKING CANAAN'S LANGUAGE. PART I. REPRESENTS AN UNBE-LIEVER UNDER THE INFLUENCE OF A CARNAL MIND, REFUSING TO ACCEPT OF THE INVITATIONS OF THE GOSPEL; WHOSE PRACTICE OFTEN SPEAKS PLAINER AND LOUDER THAN WORDS, SAYING OF CHRIST THE KING, WE WILL NOT HAVE THIS MAN TO REIGN OVER US. PART II. SHEWS SOME OF THE LANGUAGE OF A SOUL UN-DER CONVICTION: AND HOW THE UNBELIEVER BECOMES A BELIEVER. [Ornament.]
America: Boston; Printed by E. Russell, next the stump of Liberty-Tree, 1792; *for Zadok King, and sold by him at his house in Conway.* [*Price nine pence.*] pp. 24. 8vo. JCB. LOC.

24792 —— — PRACTICAL LANGUAGE INTERPRETED: IN A DIALOGUE BETWEEN A BELIEVER AND AN UNBELIEVER. IN TWO PARTS. REPRESENTING A BELIEVER UNDER THE INFLUENCE OF GRACE, SPEAKING CANAAN'S LANGUAGE.—PART I.—REPRESENTS AN UNBELIEVER UNDER THE INFLUENCE OF A CARNAL MIND, REFUSING TO ACCEPT OF THE INVITATIONS OF THE GOSPEL; WHOSE PRACTICE OFTEN SPEAKS PLAINER AND LOUDER THAN WORDS, SAYING OF CHRIST THE KING, WE WILL NOT HAVE THIS MAN TO REIGN OVER US.—PART II.—SHEWS SOME OF THE LANGUAGE OF A SOUL UNDER CONVICTION: AND HOW THE UNBELIEVER BECOMES A BELIEVER.
Warren, [*R. I.*] *Printed* [*by Nathaniel Phillips*] *for Richard Lee.* [1792.] pp. 24. 12mo. JCB. RIHS.
The Preface is signed, Eunice Smith. Ashfield, January, 1792.

24793 —— SOME ARGUMENTS AGAINST WORLDLY-MINDEDNESS, AND NEEDLESS CARE AND TROUBLE. WITH SOME OTHER USEFUL INSTRUCTIONS. REPRESENTED BY WAY OF A DIALOGUE OR DISCOURSE, BETWEEN TWO, BY THE NAMES OF MARY AND MARTHA.
Springfield: Printed by Edward Gray. [1792.] pp. 23. 24mo. AAS.

24794 —— — SOME ARGUMENTS AGAINST WORDLY-MINDEDNESS AND NEEDLESS CARE AND TROUBLE. WITH SOME OTHER USEFUL INSTRUCTIONS. REPRESENTED BY WAY OF A DIALOGUE OR DISCOURSE BETWEEN MARY AND MARTHA.
Warren [*R. I.*] *Printed* [*by Nathaniel Phillips*] *for Richard Lee.* [1792.] pp. 23. 12mo. RIHS.
Dated, Ashfield, March 17, 1791.

24795 SMITH, EUNICE, continued.

—— —— SOME ARGUMENTS AGAINST WORLDLY-MINDEDNESS, AND NEEDLESS CARE AND TROUBLE. WITH SOME OTHER USEFUL INSTRUCTIONS. REPRESENTED BY WAY OF A DIALOGUE OR DISCOURSE BETWEEN TWO CALLED BY THE NAMES OF MARY AND MARTHA. THE SECOND EDITION.

Boston: Printed and sold by E. Russell, in Essex-Street, next the Stump of Liberty-Tree. 1792.

24796 SMITH, HUGH 1736 – 1789

LETTERS TO MARRIED WOMEN, ON NURSING AND THE MANAGEMENT OF CHILDREN. THE FIRST AMERICAN EDITION. PRINTED FROM THE SIXTH LONDON ONE. BY THE LATE HUGH SMITH, M. D.

*Philadelphia: From the Press of Mathew Carey, August 14,—*M.DCC.- XCII. pp. 167. 12mo. AAS. LOC. RIMS.

24797 SMITH, ROBERT 1723 – 1793

THREE SERMONS, ON THE NATURE AND EXCELLENCY OF SAVING FAITH; DELIVERED AT PEQUEA, THE 21ST OF AUGUST, AND THE 10TH OF SEPTEMBER, 1791. BY THE REVEREND ROBERT SMITH, D. D. PASTOR OF THE PRESBYTERIAN CHURCH OF PE- QUA. PUBLISHED BY REQUEST.

Lancaster, Printed—Carlisle, Re-printed and to be sold by George Kline, 1792. pp. (68). 8vo. AAS. PHS.

Reprinted also in Austin's American preacher, Vol. IV. New Haven, 1793.

24798 SMITH, SAMUEL STANHOPE 1750 – 1819

THREE DISCOURSES, I. ON THE GUILT AND FOLLY OF BEING ASHAMED OF RELIGION, II. ON THE GREAT EVIL OF SLANDER, III. ON THE NATURE AND DANGER OF SMALL FAULTS, DELIVERED AT BOSTON, IN OCTOBER, 1790. BY THE REVEREND SAMUEL STANHOPE SMITH, D. D. VICEPRESIDENT, AND PROFESSOR OF MORAL PHILOSOPHY, IN THE UNIVERSITY AT PRINCETON, NEWJERSEY. FIRST PUBLISHED AT REQUEST OF THE HEARERS.

Lancaster, Reprinted by William Dickson, in Kingstreet, M,DCC,XCII. pp. [54.] 12mo. AAS.

24799 SMITH, WILLIAM 1727 – 1803

EULOGIUM ON BENJAMIN FRANKLIN, L. L. D. PRESIDENT OF THE AMERICAN PHILO- SOPHICAL SOCIETY, HELD AT PHILADELPHIA, FOR PROMOTING USEFUL KNOWLEDGE, FELLOW OF THE ROYAL SOCIETY OF LONDON, MEMBER OF THE ROYAL ACADEMY OF SCIENCES AT PARIS, OF THE ROYAL SOCIETY AT GOTTINGEN, THE BATAVIAN SOCIETY IN HOLLAND, AND OF MANY OTHER LITERARY SOCIETIES IN EUROPE AND AMERICA: LATE MINISTER PLENIPOTENTIARY FOR THE UNITED STATES OF AMERICA AT THE COURT OF PARIS, SOMETIME PRESIDENT, AND FOR MORE THAN HALF A CENTURY A REVERED CITIZEN, OF THE COMMONWEALTH OF PENNSYLVANIA. DELIVERED MARCH 1, 1791, IN THE GERMAN LUTHERAN CHURCH OF THE CITY OF PHILADELPHIA, BEFORE THE AMERICAN PHILOSOPHICAL SOCIETY, AND AGREE- ABLY TO THEIR APPOINTMENT, BY WILLIAM SMITH, D. D. ONE OF THE VICE-PRESI- DENTS OF THE SAID SOCIETY, AND PROVOST OF THE COLLEGE AND ACADEMY OF PHILADELPHIA. THE MEMORY OF THE DECEASED WAS HONORED ALSO, AT THE DELIVERY OF THIS EULOGIUM, WITH THE PRESENCE OF THE PRESIDENT, SEN- ATE AND HOUSE OF REPRESENTATIVES OF THE UNITED STATES OF AMERICA, THE SENATE AND HOUSE OF REPRESENTATIVES OF THE COMMONWEALTH OF PENNSYL- VANIA, THE CORPORATION AND MOST OF THE PUBLIC BODIES, AS WELL AS RESPECT- ABLE PRIVATE CITIZENS, OF PHILADELPHIA.

Printed by Benjamin Franklin Bache, Philadelphia, 1792. pp. (2), (2), (40), (v,) (1). 8vo. AAS. BA. JCB. LOC. MHS. NYHS.

32d Pennsylvania District Copyright, issued to Benjamin Franklin Bache, as Proprietor, 13 March, 1792. Reprinted in London in 1792.

24800   SMITH, WILLIAM   1728 – 1793
THE HISTORY OF THE PROVINCE OF NEW-YORK, FROM THE FIRST DISCOVERY TO
THE YEAR 1732. TO WHICH IS ANNEXED, A DESCRIPTION OF THE COUNTRY, WITH
A SHORT ACCOUNT OF THE INHABITANTS, THEIR RELIGIOUS AND POLITICAL STATE,
AND THE CONSTITUTION OF THE COURTS OF JUSTICE IN THAT COLONY. [Four lines
of quotations.] THE SECOND EDITION. BY WILLIAM SMITH, A. M.
> *Philadelphia: From the Press of Mathew Carey, April 9—* M.DCC.XCII.
pp. 276. 8vo.   AAS. JCB. MHS, NL. NYHS. NYPL.
Reprinted, with a continuation to 1814, by J. V. N. Yates, in Albany
in 1814.

24801   SMITH, WILLIAM LOUGHTON   1757 – 1812
THE POLITICKS AND VIEWS OF A CERTAIN PARTY, DISPLAYED.
> *Printed in the year* M,DCC,XCII. pp. (36). 12mo.
                     BA. CLS. JCB. LCP. MHS. NYHS. NYPL.
This has been sometimes attributed to Alexander Hamilton; but there
seems to be good reasons for ascribing the authorship to William
Loughton Smith, who shared his political views.

24802   SOME MODERN DIRECTIONS FOR THE CULTURE OF SILK. . . . FROM THE ITALIAN.
> *Windham: Printed by John Byrne.* 1792.

24803   SOME THOUGHTS ON THE GLOOMY CLOUD THAT HANGS OVER NEW-ENGLAND, BY THE
NUMEROUS ERRORS IN DOCTRINE, AS WELL AS SCHOOLS OF INSTRUCTION, SUCH AS
UNIVERSALISTS, HOPKINTONIANS, ARMENIANS, AND SHAKERS.
> *Boston: Printed for the Author,* 1792. pp. (8). 8vo.   LOC.

24804   SOUTH CAROLINA. STATE.
ACTS AND RESOLUTIONS OF THE GENERAL ASSEMBLY OF THE STATE OF SOUTH-CAR-
OLINA, PASSED IN DECEMBER, 1791.
> *Charleston: Printed by T. B. Bowen, No.* 38, *Bay.* M.DCC.XCII. pp.
(60), (3), fol.   BM. LOC.

24805   THE SOUTH CAROLINA GAZETTE. NO. 1. TUESDAY, APRIL 3, [—NO. 39. TUES-
DAY, DECEMBER 25, 1792.]
> *Columbia: Printed by D. Constable.* 1792. fol.
Established by D. Constable, and how long continued by him after
September, 1793, is not known.

24806   THE SOUTH CAROLINA GAZETTE AND GENERAL ADVERTISER. JANUARY—DECEM-
BER?; 1792.
> *Charleston: Printed by John Miller.* 1792. fol.
It appears that about this year, John Miller sold his Gazette to Benjamin
Franklin Timothy, and William Mason, junior, and removed to Pen-
dleton, South Carolina.

24807   SPIRITUAL FOOD: OR, TRUTH DISPLAYED, IN A LETTER ADDRESSED TO YOUNG PER-
SONS, WHEREIN MANY OF THE PRINCIPLES OF THE CHRISTIAN RELIGION ARE
BRIEFLY EXPLAINED. BY A LAYMAN. [Four lines of quotations.]
> *Philadelphia: Printed by Zachariah Poulson, junior, No.* 30, *North
Fourth-street.* MDCCXCII. pp. (72). 12mo.   AAS. JCB.
N. B. If encouragement be given, the Author will be induced to pub-
lish twelve letters, which were written at different times to sundry
persons, and which (he hopes) might be profitable for the instruction
of youth.

24808   SPOONER'S VERMONT JOURNAL. VOL. X. NUMBER 453. TUESDAY, APRIL 3, [—VOL.
X. NUMBER 492. MONDAY, DECEMBER 31, 1792.]
*Windsor: Printed by Alden Spooner, Printer to the State of Vermont for
the Eastern district.* 1792. fol.
In continuation of *The Vermont Journal, and the universal advertiser.*

24809   THE SPORTSMAN'S COMPANION OR AN ESSAY ON SHOOTING: ILLUSTRIOUSLY SHEWING
IN WHAT MANNER TO FIRE AT BIRDS OF GAME, IN VARIOUS DIRECTIONS AND SIT-
UATIONS. AND, DIRECTIONS TO GENTLEMEN FOR THE TREATMENT AND BREAKING
THEIR OWN POINTERS AND SPANIELS, AND THE NECESSARY PRECAUTIONS, TO GUARD
AGAINST MANY ACCIDENTS THAT ATTEND THIS PLEASANT DIVERSION : WITH SEVERAL
OTHER USEFUL AND INTERESTING PARTICULARS RELATIVE THERETO. BY A GENT-
LEMAN, WHO HAS MADE SHOOTING HIS FAVORITE AMUSEMENT UPWARDS OF TWENTY-
SIX YEARS, IN GREAT-BRITAIN, IRELAND, AND NORTH-AMERICA. THIRD EDITION.
Philadelphia: Printed for the purchasers. [1792.]   LOC.

24810   SPRING, SAMUEL   1746 – 1819
A SERMON, PREACHED AT THE ORDINATION OF THE REVEREND PEARSON THURSTON,
PASTOR OF THE CHURCH IN SOMERSWORTH. FEBRUARY 1ST. 1792. BY SAMUEL
SPRING, PASTOR OF THE NORTH CHURCH IN NEWBURY-PORT.
*Dover: Printed by Eliphalet Ladd, at his Printing-office, near the Court-
House.* M,DCC,XCII. pp. 25. 8vo.   AAS. BPL. JCB.

24811   STANFORD, JOHN   1754 – 1834
THE DEATH OF EUPHEMIA MITCHELL IMPROVED IN A LETTER TO A YOUNG FRIEND.
New-York: Printed by T. & J. Swords, 1792. 12mo.   BM.

24812   —— HYMNS FOR YOUTH.
New-York: Printed by T. & J. Swords, 1792.

24813   STANHOPE, PHILIP DORMER, 4th earl of CHESTERFIELD.   1694 – 1773
PRINCIPLES OF POLITENESS, AND OF KNOWING THE WORLD: BY THE LATE LORD
CHESTERFIELD. WITH ADDITIONS, BY THE REV. DR. JOHN TRUSLER. CONTAIN-
ING EVERY INSTRUCTION NECESSARY TO COMPLETE THE GENTLEMAN AND MAN OF
FASHION, TO TEACH HIM A KNOWLEDGE OF LIFE, AND MAKE HIM WELL RECEIVED
IN ALL COMPANIES. FOR THE IMPROVEMENT OF YOUTH : YET NOT BENEATH THE
ATTENTION OF ANY.
*Printed at Worcester, Massachusetts, by Isaiah Thomas & Leonard Worces-
ter, for Isaiah Thomas. Sold at his Bookstore in Worcester, and by said Thomas,
and Andrews, in Boston.* MDCCXCII. pp. 188. 24mo.   AAS.

24814   STATE GAZETTE OF NORTH-CAROLINA. VOL. VII. NUMB. 312. FRIDAY, JANUARY 6,
[-—VOL. VIII. NUMB. 363. SATURDAY, DECEMBER 29, 1792.]
Edenton: Printed by Hodge and Wills. 1792. fol.
With the issue for March 30th, Abraham Hodge withdrew, and in July,
established at Halifax, The North-Carolina Journal. Henry Wills con-
tinuing publication of the State Gazette at Edenton.

24815   THE STATE GAZETTE OF SOUTH-CAROLINA. JANUARY—DECEMBER, 1792.
Charleston, Printed for A. Timothy, 1792. fol.
Anne Timothy died in September of this year, and the Gazette was continued by her son, Benjamin Franklin Timothy, and William Mason,
junior, as the *South-Carolina State Gazette & Timothy & Mason's daily
advertiser*

24816   STEARNS, CHARLES   1753 – 1826
A SERMON: PREACHED AT AN EXHIBITION OF SACRED MUSICK, IN LINCOLN, ON THE
NINETEENTH OF APRIL, 1792. BY CHARLES STEARNS, A. M. PASTOR OF THE
CHURCH IN LINCOLN. [Ornament.]
*Printed at Boston, by Isaiah Thomas and Ebenezer T. Andrews, at Faust's
Statue, No. 45, Newbury Street.* MDCCXCII. pp. 15. 8vo.
AAS. BA. BM, HC. JCB. MHS. NYPL.

24817   STEARNS, SAMUEL   1747 – 1819
THE FREE MASON'S CALENDAR, AND CONTINENTAL ALMANAC; FOR THE YEAR OF
OUR LORD 1793: CONTAINING, ASTRONOMICAL CALCULATIONS, – – – AN ACCOUNT
OF THE ANCIENT AND HONORABLE SOCIETY OF FREE MASONS, WITH OTHER THINGS
NECESSARY FOR AN ALMANAC. BY THE HON. SAMUEL STEARNS, L. L. D.
*New-York: Printed and sold, wholesale and retail, by Samuel Campbell,
No. 37, Hanover-Square. The Copy right of this Calendar and Almanac is secured
according to law.* [1792.] pp, (68). 18mo.   AAS. HC.
10th New York District Copyright, issued to Samuel Stearns, as Author,
4 JUNE, 1792.

24818   STERNE, LAURENCE   1713 – 1768
A SENTIMENTAL JOURNEY THROUGH FRANCE AND ITALY. BY MR. YORICK. VOL. I.
[—II.]
Norwich: Printed by Bushnell and Hubbard. M,DCC,XCII. 2 vols. in
one. pp. 254. 16mo.   AAS.

24819   STEWART, WILLIAM M.
THE YOUNG MASON'S MONITOR. TO WHICH IS ANNEXED A COLLECTION OF MASONIC
SONGS, ODES, ETC.
Portsmouth: Printed by John Melcher. 5792. [1792.] pp. 62. 16mo.

24820   STONE, TIMOTHY   1742 – 1797
A SERMON, PREACHED BEFORE HIS EXCELLENCY SAMUEL HUNTINGTON, ESQ. L. L. D.
GOVERNOR, AND THE HONORABLE THE GENERAL ASSEMBLY OF THE STATE OF
CONNECTICUT, CONVENED AT HARTFORD, ON THE ANNIVERSARY ELECTION, MAY
10TH, 1792. BY TIMOTHY STONE, A. M. PASTOR OF A CHURCH IN LEBANON. [Pub-
lishers monogram.]
Printed at Hartford, by Hudson and Goodwin. MDCCXCII. pp. 35. 8vo.
AAS. BA. BM. CHS. JCB. MHS. NYHS. NYPL. YC.

24821   STONINGTON. CONNECTICUT. BAPTIST ASSOCIATION.
MINUTES OF THE STONINGTON BAPTIST ASSOCIATION, 1792.
New-London: Printed by T. Green and Son? 1792.

24822   STORY, ISAAC   1774 – 1803
AN EPISTLE FROM YARICO TO INKLE, TOGETHER WITH THEIR CHARACTERS, AS RE-
LATED IN THE SPECTATOR. [Three lines of Latin. Author's monogram.]
Marblehead [Salem]: Printed for the Sons and Daughters of Columbia.
M.DCC.XCII. pp. 31. 8vo.   AAS. BU. NYPL.

24823   STRICTURES UPON THE OBSERVATIONS OF A 'MEMBER OF CONVENTION'; IN ANSWER
TO THE "AUTHOR OF SOME REMARKS, &C." BY A FREEMAN.
New-Hampshire: Printed—Seventeen Hundred, Ninety-two. pp. 15. 8vo.

24824   STRONG, NEHEMIAH   1729 – 1807
AN ASTRONOMICAL DIARY, CALENDAR, OR ALMANACK, FOR THE YEAR OF OUR LORD,
1793. AND FROM THE CREATION OF THE WORLD 5742. AND, TILL JULY 4TH,
THE 17TH OF AMERICAN INDEPENDENCE. BEING THE FIRST AFTER BISSEXTILE
OR LEAP YEAR. [Seven lines.] BY N. STRONG, LATE PROFESSOR OF MATHE-
MATICKS, AND NATURAL PHYLOSOPHY [*sic*] IN YALE-COLLEGE. [Eight lines of
verse.]
     Hartford: Printed for Nathaniel Patten. [1792.] pp. (24). 12mo.
                                    CHS. LOC. YC.
   Apparently the same as West's Astronomical diary, etc. for 1793.
Printed for Nathaniel Patten, this year.

24825   —— — AN ASTRONOMICAL DIARY, KALENDER, OR ALMANACK, FOR THE YEAR OF
OUR LORD 1793. . . . BY NEHEMIAH STRONG.
     Hartford: Printed by Elisha Babcock. [1792.] pp. (24). 12mo.   CHS.

24826   —— — AN ASTRONOMICAL DIARY, KALENDAR, OR ALMANACK, FOR THE YEAR OF
OUR LORD, 1793. AND FROM THE CREATION OF THE WORLD 5742. AND, FROM
THE 4TH OF JULY, THE 17TH OF AMERICAN INDEPENDENCE. BEING THE FIRST
AFTER BISSEXTILE, OR LEAP-YEAR. ADAPTED TO THE HORIZON AND MERIDIAN OF
LITCHFIELD, 41 DEG. 45 MIN. NORTH. BUT WILL SERVE FOR ALL THE ADJACENT
STATES. BY NEHEMIAH STRONG, ESQ. LATE PROFESSOR OF MATHEMATICS AND
NATURAL PHILOSOPHY IN YALE COLLEGE.
     Litchfield: Printed by Collier and Buel. [1792.] pp. (24). 12mo.
                                    AAS. CHS. YC.

24827   —— — AN ASTRONOMICAL DIARY, KALENDAR, OR ALMANACK, FOR THE YEAR OF
OUR LORD, 1793: AND FROM THE CREATION OF THE WORLD, 5742. AND, AFTER
THE 4TH OF JULY, THE 17TH OF AMERICAN INDEPENDENCE. BEING THE FIRST
AFTER BISSEXTILE OR LEAP YEAR. [Five lines.] BY H. STAFFORD, PHILO MATH.
[Eight lines of verse.]
     New-Haven: Printed and sold by T. & S. Green. [1792.] pp. [20.] 12mo.
                                AAS. LOC. NYPL. YC.

24828   —— SHEET ALMANACK FOR THE YEAR 1793.
     Hartford: Printed by Elisha Babcock. 1792. Broadside. fol.

24829   SULLIVAN, JAMES   1744 – 1808
THE PATH TO RICHES. [Ornament.] AN INQUIRY INTO THE ORIGIN AND USE OF
MONEY; AND INTO THE PRINCIPLES OF STOCKS AND BANKS. TO WHICH ARE SUB-
JOINED SOME THOUGHTS RESPECTING A BANK FOR THE COMMONWEALTH. BY A
CITIZEN OF MASSACHUSETTS. [Four lines of verse.]
     *Printed at Boston, by P. Edes, for I. Thomas and E. T. Andrews, Faust's
statue, No. 45, Newbury-Street.* MDCCXCII. pp. 77. 8vo.
                       AAS. BA. JCB. LOC. MHS. NYPL.
   Reprinted in Boston, in 1809.

24830   THE SUNBURY AND NORTHUMBERLAND GAZETTE. VOL. I. NO. 1. SATURDAY, JULY 7,
[—NO. 26. SATURDAY, DECEMBER 29, 1792.]
     Northumberland—Printed by George Schuster. 1792. fol.

24831   SWAN, TIMOTHY   1758 – 1842
THE FEDERAL HARMONY: IN THREE PARTS. PART I. AN INTRODUCTION TO THE ART
OF SINGING. PART II. A LARGE COLLECTION OF PSALM TUNES. PART III. SELECT
ANTHEMS, &C. COMPILED FOR THE USE OF SCHOOLS AND SINGING SOCIETIES.
     Boston: Printed and sold by John Norman, 1792. pp. 130. obl. 8vo.

24832   SWEDENBORG or SWEDBERG, EMANUEL   1688 – 1772
APHORISMS OF WISDOM.
     Boston: 1792. 8vo.   MHS.

24833   —— THE DOCTRINE OF LIFE FOR THE NEW JERUSALEM, FROM THE COMMAND-
MENTS OF THE DECALOGUE. TRANSLATED FROM THE LATIN OF THE HONORABLE
AND LEARNED EMANUEL SWEDENBORG. THE THIRD EDITION.
     Philadelphia: Printed by F. Bailey, No. 116, *High-street, and T. Lang,
No.* 21, *Church-alley.*—M,DCC,XCII.—pp. 140. 24mo.   AAS. BA. JCB.

24834   —— QUERIES CONCERNING THE TRINITY, WITH EMANUEL SWEDENBORG'S ANSWERS.
     Baltimore: Printed and sold by Samuel and John Adams, in Market-street.
1792.

24835   —— TRUE CHRISTIAN RELIGION; CONTAINING THE UNIVERSAL THEOLOGY OF THE
NEW CHURCH: WHICH WAS FORETOLD BY THE LORD IN DANIEL, CHAP. VII. 5, 13,
14, AND IN THE APOCALYPSE, CHAP. XXI. 1, 2. BY EMANUEL SWEDENBORG, SER-
VANT OF THE LORD JESUS CHRIST. TRANSLATED FROM THE ORIGINAL LATIN. [BY
John Clowes.] IN TWO VOLUMES. VOL. II. THE THIRD EDITION.
     Philadelphia: Printed by Francis Bailey. 1792. pp. 478, (2). 8vo.
                                           AAS. BA. HC. JCB. MHS.
     The first volume was printed in 1789.

24836   SWEETING, WHITING   – 1791
THE NARRATIVE OF WHITING SWEETING, WHO WAS EXECUTED AT ALBANY THE 26TH
OF AUGUST, 1791: CONTAINING AN ACCOUNT OF HIS TRIAL BEFORE THE SUPREME
COURT OF JUDICATURE OF THE STATE OF NEW-YORK, AT THE JULY TERM, 1791,
FOR THE MURDER OF DARIUS QUIMBY, THE SUBSTANCE OF THE CHARGE OF HIS
HONOUR THE CHIEF JUSTICE TO THE JURY, WITH THE SENTENCE OF DEATH ON THE
PRISONER. AN ADDRESS TO THE PUBLIC, ON THE FATAL CONSEQUENCES OF A LIFE
SPENT IN SIN, INSTANCED IN HIS OWN CONDUCT, SETTING FORTH THE GREAT NECES-
SITY OF REMEMBERING OUR CREATOR IN THE DAYS OF OUR YOUTH, AND PRACTIS-
ING RELIGION AND VIRTUE IN OUR WHOLE LIVES; WITH AN ADDRESS TO HIS PAR-
ENTS, BROTHERS AND SISTERS, WIFE AND CHILDREN, AND MANY OTHERS; ALSO A
BRIEF ACCOUNT OF HIM BY WILLIAM CARTER, FROM HIS FIRST CONFINEMENT TILL
THE TIME OF EXECUTION.
     Philadelphia: Printed and sold by Daniel Lawrence. 1792. pp. 72. 12mo.

24837   —— — THE NARRATIVE OF WHITING SWEETING, WHO WAS EXECUTED AN ALBANY
THE 26TH OF AUGUST, 1791. CONTAINING, AN ACCOUNT OF HIS TRIAL BEFORE
THE SUPREME COURT OF JUDICATURE OF THE STATE OF NEW-YORK, AT THE JULY
TERM, 1791, FOR THE MURDER OF DARIUS QUIMBY, THE SUBSTANCE OF THE
CHARGE OF HIS HONOUR THE CHIEF-JUSTICE TO THE JURY, WITH THE SENTENCE
OF DEATH ON THE PRISONER. AN ADDRESS TO THE PUBLIC ON THE FATAL CONSE-
QUENCES OF A LIFE SPENT IN SIN, INSTANCED IN HIS OWN CONDUCT SETTING
FORTH THE GREAT NECESSITY OF REMEMBERING OUR CREATOR IN THE DAYS OF OUR
YOUTH, AND PRACTISING RELIGION AND VIRTUE IN OUR WHOLE LIVES. WITH AN
ADDRESS TO HIS PARENTS, BROTHERS AND SISTERS, WIFE AND CHILDREN, AND MANY
OTHERS; ALSO A BRIEF ACCOUNT OF HIM, BY WILLIAM CARTER, FROM HIS FIRST
CONFINEMENT TILL THE TIME OF EXECUTION.
     *Wilmington: Printed and sold by Peter Brynberg and Samuel Andrews in
Market-Street.* 1792.

24838   —— — THE VERY EXTRAORDINARY NARRATIVE OF WHITING SWEETING, WHO WAS
EXECUTED AT ALBANY, AUGUST 26, 1791, FOR THE MURDER OF DARIUS QUIMBY.
     Providence: Printed by Bennett Wheeler. 1792.

24839 THE SYREN; OR, MUSICAL BOUQUET. BEING A NEW SELECTION OF FAVOURITE
SONGS SUNG AT THE VARIOUS PLACES OF AMUSEMENT IN GREAT-BRITAIN, IRELAND
AND AMERICA.
New-York: Printed for Berry and Rogers, No. 35, Hanover-Square. 1792.

24840 TAPPAN, DAVID   1752 – 1803
THE CONNEXION BETWEEN FAITH IN GOD, OR IN THE PRINCIPLES OF NATURAL RE-
LIGION, AND A SUITABLE REGARD TO JESUS CHRIST AND HIS GOSPEL.—— ILLUS-
TRATED IN A DISCOURSE, DELIVERED AT PORTSMOUTH, N. HAMPSHIRE, BEFORE
THE REVEREND ASSOCIATION OF CONGREGATIONAL MINISTERS, OF THAT TOWN AND
VICINITY. . . . PUBLISHED BY DESIRE OF THE HEARERS.
Portsmouth: Printed and sold by John Melcher, M,DCC,XCII. pp. (29).
8vo.   AAS. BA. JCB. LOC. NYHS.

24841 —— A SERMON PREACHED BEFORE HIS EXCELLENCY JOHN HANCOCK, ESQ. GOVERN-
OUR; HIS HONOR SAMUEL ADAMS, ESQ. LIEUTENANT-GOVERNOUR; THE HONOUR-
ABLE THE COUNCIL, SENATE, AND HOUSE OF REPRESENTATIVES, OF THE COMMON-
WEALTH OF MASSACHUSETTS, MAY 30, 1792. BEING THE DAY OF GENERAL ELEC-
TION. BY DAVID TAPPAN, A. M. PASTOR OF A CHURCH IN NEWBURY.
*Printed in Boston, Massachusetts: at the State Press, by Thomas Adams,
Printer to the honourable the General Court.* M,DCC,XCII. pp. 39. 8vo.
AAS. BA. BPL. HC. JCB. LOC. MHS. NYHS. NYPL.

24842 TAYLER, THOMAS
THE OBSERVATION OF THE LORD'S-DAY RECOMMENDED, IN A SERMON UPON MARK
II. 27. BY T. TAYLER. TO WHICH ARE ADDED, TWO PRAYERS FOR THE LORD'S-
DAY, BY MATTHEW HENRY. [Ornament.]
Boston: Printed by Samuel Hall, in Cornhill. 1792. pp. [32.] 8vo. AAS. BA.
☞This Sermon is re-printed at the expense of the Society for propa-
gating the Gospel among the Indians and others in North-America, to
be distributed by their Missionaries.

24843 TERSTEEGEN, GERHARD   1697 – 1769
VOM CHRISTLICHEN GEBRAUCH DER LIEDER, UND DES SINGENS. COLOSS. 3, 16.
SINGET UND SPIELET DEM HERRN IN EURENT HERZEN, HERAUSGEGEBEN VON
G. T. STEEGEN, [Line of thirty-six stars.]
Ephrata, Gedruckt im Jahr 1792. pp. 88. 8vo.   AAS.

24844 THEATRE. [A POEM.]
[Boston: 1792.] pp. [7.] 8vo.   AAS.

24845 THOMAS, ISAIAH   1749 – 1831
CATALOGUE OF BOOKS TO BE SOLD BY ISAIAH THOMAS, AT HIS BOOKSTORE IN WOR-
CESTER, MASSACHUSETTS. CONSISTING OF HISTORY, VOYAGES, TRAVELS, GEOGRA-
PHY, ANTIQUITIES, PHILOSOPHY, NOVELS, MISCELLANIES, DIVINITY, PHYSICK, SUR-
GERY, ANATOMY, ARTS, SCIENCES, HUSBANDRY, ARCHITECTURE, NAVIGATION, MATH-
EMATICKS, LAW, PERIODICAL PUBLICATIONS, POETRY, PLAYS, MUSICK, &C. &C. NOV-
EMBER MDCCXCII.
*Printed at Worcester, Massachusetts, by Isaiah Thomas and Leonard Wor-
cester.* [1792.] pp. 42. 12mo.   AAS.

24846 THOMAS'S MASSACHUSETTS SPY: OR, THE WORCESTER GAZETTE. VOL. XX. NO.
979. THURSDAY, JANUARY 5, [—VOL. XXI. NO. 1030. THURSDAY, DECEMBER 27,
1792.]
*Printed at Worcester, Massachusetts, by Isaiah Thomas and Leonard Wor-
cester.* 1792. fol.
Beginning with the issue for January 5th, Leonard Worcester became
associated with Thomas in the publication of the Spy.

24847   THOMAS, ROBERT BAILEY   1766 – 1846
         [NO. 1.] THE FARMER'S ALMANAC, CALCULATED ON A NEW AND IMPROVED PLAN,
         FOR THE YEAR OF OUR LORD 1793: BEING THE FIRST AFTER LEAP YEAR, AND
         SEVENTEENTH OF THE INDEPENDENCE OF AMERICA. FITTED TO THE TOWN OF
         BOSTON, BUT WILL SERVE FOR ANY OF THE ADJOINING STATES. CONTAINING,
         BESIDES THE LARGE NUMBER OF ASTRONOMICAL CALCULATIONS AND FARMER'S CAL-
         ENDAR FOR EVERY MONTH IN THE YEAR, AS GREAT A VARIETY AS ARE TO BE
         FOUND IN ANY OTHER ALMANAC, OF NEW, USEFUL, AND ENTERTAINING MATTER.
         BY ROBERT B. THOMAS. [Four lines of verse.] PUBLISHED ACCORDING TO ACT
         OF CONGRESS.
              Printed at the Apollo Press, in Boston, by Belknap and Hall, sold at their
         office, State Street; also, by the Author and M. Smith, Sterling. [Six pence single,
         4s. per dozen, 40s. per groce.] [1792.] pp. (48). 12mo.   AAS. LOC.
              This is the first issue of the best known of all the New England Alman-
         acs, its publication having been continued, annually, down to number
         119, for the year 1911. Its popularity with all classes dated from the
         first issue, of which three thousand copies were sold; and this number
         was increased to nine thousand copies for the second issue, of the fol-
         lowing year. By the middle of the next century the sales approximated
         nearly a quarter of a million copies annually.

24848   THOMAS, TRISTRAM   1769 – 1847
         DISPUTATIO MEDICA INAUGURALIS DE PNEUMONIA STHENICA.
              Philadelphiæ: Apud Gulielmum Young. 1792. pp. 24. 8vo.   SGO.

24849   THOMSON, JAMES   1700 – 1748
         THE SEASONS. CONTAINING SPRING. SUMMER. AUTUMN. WINTER. BY JAMES
         THOMSON.
              Hartford: Printed by Elisha Babcock, 1792.

24850   THORNTON, ELISHA
         THE RHODE-ISLAND ALMANACK, FOR THE YEAR OF OUR LORD 1793; BEING THE
         FIRST AFTER LEAP-YEAR, AND SEVENTEENTH OF AMERICAN INDEPENDENCE.
         FROM CREATION, ACCORDING TO THE SCRIPTURES, 5755. CALCULATED FOR THE
         MERIDIAN OF NEWPORT, LATITUDE 41° 25′ N. AND LONGITUDE 71° 15′ W. BUT
         MAY SERVE FOR THE ADJACENT STATES. THE ASTRONOMICAL CALCULATIONS BY
         ELISHA THORNTON. [Eight lines of verse.]
              Printed at Warren (R. I.) by Nathaniel Phillips. Great encouragement will
         be given to whole-sale purchasers. [1792.] pp. (24). 12mo.   LOC. RIHS.

24851   THOUGHTS ON CHRISTIAN HOLINESS.
              Philadelphia: Printed by Johnson & Justice, Franklin's Head, No. 41,
         Chesnut Street. 1792.

24852   THURBER, LABAN
         A COMPOSITION UPON SEVERAL DIVINE SUBJECTS, AND WELL ADAPTED FOR RELIGIOUS
         WORSHIP. BY LABAN THURBER, MINISTER OF THE GOSPEL.
              Norwich: Printed by Ebenezer Bushnell. For sale by Laban Thurber. 1792.

24853   THURSTON, BENJAMIN   1756 – 1804
         TWO SERMONS ON THE DIVINE RIGHT OF INFANT BAPTISM, DELIVERED AT NORTH-
         HAMPTON, ON THE LORD'S DAY, JANUARY 5, 1792. BY BENJAMIN THURSTON,
         A. M. TO THE PEOPLE OF HIS CHARGE IN THAT PLACE, AND PUBLISHED BY DESIRE,
         WITH SOME ADDITION. [Ornament.]
              *Printed at Exeter, by Henry Ranlet, and sold at his Office—1792.—*pp.
         (2), 89. 4to.   JCB.

24854 TICKNOR, ELISHA   1757 – 1821
ENGLISH EXERCISES, IN WHICH SENTENCES, FALSELY CONSTRUCTED, ARE TO BE COR-
RECTED; COMPREHENDING ALL THE RULES NECESSARY FOR PARSING THE LANGUAGE;
AND ARRANGED IN SUCH A MANNER, AS WILL GREATLY FACILITATE THE ACQUISITION
OF GRAMMATICAL KNOWLEDGE. DESIGNED FOR SCHOOLS. BY ELISHA TICKNOR,
A. M.
  Boston: 1792. 18mo.
  29th Massachusetts District Copyright, issued to Elisha Ticknor, as
Author, 31 March, 1792.

24855 TIFFANY'S [cut] RECORDER. No. 16. TUESDAY, JANUARY 3, [—No. 67. TUESDAY,
DECEMBER 25, 1792.]
  *Lansingburgh: Printed by Silvester Tiffany, at his Office, over the Store of
Mr. W. Bell. 1792. fol.*

24856 CIRCULAR. TO THE FREE AND INDEPENDENT ELECTORS OF THE SEVERAL COUNTIES
IN THE STATE OF NEW-YORK. FRIENDS AND FELLOW COUNTRYMEN, COMBINED
IN A CAUSE WHICH INVOLVES THE RIGHTS AND HAPPINESS, NOT ONLY OF THIS GEN-
ERATION BUT OF THE MOST REMOTE POSTERITY, WE FEEL OURSELVES IMPELLED
BY EVERY PRINCIPLE OF DUTY AND AFFECTION, TO ADDRESS YOU IN THE LAN-
GUAGE OF SINCERITY AND FREEDOM. [Protesting against the rejection of the votes
of Otsego County which elected George Clinton governor, over John Jay.
Four columns.]
  / New-York: Printed by Francis Childs and John Swaine, 1792.] Broad-
side. fol.   NYHS.

24857 TO THE INDEPENDENT ELECTORS IN THE STATE OF NEW-YORK. THE TIME APPROACH-
ES WHEN YOU WILL BE CALLED AGAIN TO THE EXERCISE OF THE MOST IMPORTANT
PRIVILEGE OF FREE CITIZENS, . . . [Clinton-Jay election for governor.]
  [New-York: 1792.] Broadside. fol.   NYHS.

24858 TO THE INDEPENDENT ELECTORS OF THE STATE OF NEW-YORK. FELLOW CITIZENS, A
NUMEROUS MEETING OF RESPECTABLE INHABITANTS OF THIS CITY, IMPRESSED
WITH THE IMPORTANCE OF THE ENSUING ELECTION, HAVE APPOINTED AS A COM-
MITTEE TO ADDRESS YOU ON THE SUBJECT, . . . JOSEPH HALLETT, CHAIRMAN.
  [New-York: March 19, 1792.] Broadside. fol.   LOC.

24859 TO THE INDEPENDENT ELECTORS OF THE STATE OF NEW-YORK. FELLOW CITIZENS,
YOU WILL BE SHORTLY CALLED UPON TO EXERCISE ONE OF THE MOST IMPORTANT
DUTIES OF FREEMEN. [A refutation of the charge that Governor Clinton had
personally benefitted by the sale of State lands, circulated by the friends of Mr.
Jay.] PLAIN TRUTH. NEW-YORK, APRIL 11, 1792.
  [New-York: 1792.] Broadside. fol.   NYHS.

24860 TOWNSEND, SHIPPIE
THE GOSPEL CONSIDERED; AND THE MANNER IN WHICH IT SHOULD BE PREACHED;
WITH AN ENDEAVOR TO SHEW FROM THE SCRIPTURES, THAT ELECTION DOTH NOT
MILITATE WITH PREACHING THE GOSPEL TO EVERY CREATURE: SEVERAL OTHER
OBJECTIONS CONSIDERED. BY SHIPPIE TOWNSEND. [Four lines of quotations.]
  *Printed at Boston, for the Author, by Thomas Adams, and sold at his
Printing-Office, in Court-street.* M,DCC,XCII. pp. 21. 8vo. BA. JCB. LOC. NYPL.

24861   TRENCK, FRIEDRICH, freiherr VON DER   1726 – 1794
THE LIFE OF BARON FREDERIC TRENCK; CONTAINING HIS ADVENTURES; HIS CRUEL
AND EXCESSIVE SUFFERINGS, DURING TEN YEARS IMPRISONMENT, AT THE FORT-
RESS OF MAGDEBURG, BY COMMAND OF THE LATE KING OF PRUSSIA; ALSO, ANEC-
DOTES, HISTORICAL, POLITICAL, AND PERSONAL. TRANSLATED FROM THE GERMAN,
BY THOMAS HOLCROFT.
> *Printed at Boston: by J. Belknap and A. Young, for B. Guild, J. Boyle,*
> *B. Larkin, D. West, and E. Larkin, jun. sold at their respective Bookstores, and*
> *by the Printers, at their Office in State-Street.* MDCCXCII. pp. 417, plate.
> 12mo.   AAS. BM.

24862   —— —— THE LIFE OF BARON FREDERIC TRENCK; CONTAINING HIS ADVENTURES,
HIS CRUEL AND EXCESSIVE SUFFERINGS, DURING TEN YEARS IMPRISONMENT, AT
THE FORTRESS OF MAGDEBURG, BY COMMAND OF THE LATE KING OF PRUSSIA;
ALSO, ANECDOTES, HISTORICAL, POLITICAL AND PERSONAL.
> *Philadelphia: Printed and sold by W. Woodhouse, at the Bible No.* 6,
> *South Front-Street.* M.DCC.XCII. pp. 345, (1), plate. 12mo.   AAS.

Second title: THE HISTORY OF FRANCIS BARON TRENCK, A PARTISAN COLONEL,
AND COMMANDER IN CHIEF OF THE PANDOURS, IN THE SERVICE OF HER MAJESTY
THE EMPRESS-QUEEN; WRITTEN BY FREDERIC BARON TRENCK, AS A NECESSARY
SUPPLEMENT TO HIS OWN HISTORY.
> *Philadelphia: Printed and sold by W. Woodhouse, at the Bible, No.* 6,
> *South Front-street.* M.DCC.XII [*sic* 1792.] pp. (2), 271–309.

24863   A TRUE ACCOUNT OF THE LOSS OF THE SHIP COLUMBIA, OF EXETER, LATELY COM-
MANDED BY CAPTAIN ISAAC CHAUNCY: [cuts of fourteen coffins. Two columns.]
[Colophon:]
> *Printed [by George and John Osborne] and sold at the Spy Printing-office,*
> *Portsmouth, March* 28, 1792. Broadside. fol.   NYHS.

24864   [Cuts of twenty coffins, and of two vessels on beams end.] A TRUE AND PARTICULAR
NARRATIVE OF THE LATE TREMENDOUS TORNADO, OR HURRICANE, AT PHILADEL-
PHIA AND NEW-YORK, ON SABBATH-DAY, JULY 1, 1792: WHEN SEVERAL PLEAS-
URE-BOATS WERE LOST IN THE HARBOR OF THE LATTER, AND THIRTY MEN, WO-
MEN AND CHILDREN, (TAKING THEIR PLEASURE ON THAT SACRED DAY) WERE UN-
HAPPILY DROWNED IN NEPTUNE'S RAGING AND TEMPESTUOUS ELEMENT !!!!!!!—
TELL THIS NOT IN MASSACHUSETTS! PUBLISH IT NOT IN THE STREETS OF CON-
NECTICUT! LEST THEIR SOBER-MINDED YOUNG MEN AND MAIDENS, SHOULD BIT-
TERLY REPROACH THEE IN THE DAY OF THY CALAMITY, AND TRIUMPH OVER THEE
WHEN THY DESOLATION COMETH; AND ASK OF THEE, WHERE ART THY MAGIS-
TRATES? OR DO THEY BEAR THE SWORD OF THE LORD IN VAIN?—WHERE ART
THY WATCHMEN?—HAVE THEY DESERTED THEIR WATCH-TOWER? OR HAVE THEY
FALLEN ASLEEP? [Thirty-one lines.] THE NEW-YORK TRAGEDY. BEING A RE-
LATION OF THE DROWNING OF THIRTY MEN, WOMEN AND CHILDREN, IN THE LATE
SHOCKING AND TREMENDOUS TEMPEST, IN THAT CITY ON LORD'S-DAY, JULY 1,
1792, WHEN TAKING THEIR PLEASURE ON THE WATER! !—O TEMPORA!! O MORES!!
[THE SERIOUS READER MAY, PERHAPS, DO HIMSELF A FAVOR BY TURNING TO
EXOD. CHAP. XX. V. 1, 2, 8, 9, 10, 11, 18, 19. DEUT. V. 15.] [Forty-four four-
line verses.] [Colophon:]
> *Boston: Printed and sold by E. Russell, next the stump of Lib. Tree. [Pr.*
> *six pence.]* Where may be had, Mary and Martha, &c. [1792.] Broadside. fol.
>   NYHS.

24865   THE UNEQUAL CONFLICT. A POEM. DEDICATED TO THE HONOURABLE MEMORY
OF THE BRAVE OFFICERS AND PRIVATES WHO FELL, NOBLY, IN DEFENCE OF THEIR
COUNTRY, IN THE LATE ENGAGEMENT WITH THE INDIANS, UNDER THE COMMAND
OF HIS EXCELLENCY GENERAL ST. CLAIR, NOVEMBER 4TH, 1791.
> *Carlisle: Printed by George Kline.* 1792.

24866   UNITED STATES of America.
AN ACT FOR THE GOVERNMENT AND REGULATION OF SEAMEN IN THE MERCHANTS'
SERVICE: PASSED, AT NEW-YORK, BY THE HONORABLE THE FIRST CONGRESS OF
THE UNITED STATES, AT THEIR SECOND SESSION.
Warren (Rhode-Island): Printed and sold by N. Phillips, M,DCC,XCII.
pp. 16. 16mo.
RIIIS.

24867   —— AN ACT TO EXPLAIN AND AMEND AN ACT, ENTITLED "AN ACT TO ENABLE THE
OFFICERS AND SOLDIERS OF THE VIRGINIA LINE ON CONTINENTAL ESTABLISH-
MENT TO OBTAIN TITLES TO CERTAIN LANDS LYING NORTH WEST OF THE RIVER
OHIO, BETWEEN THE LITTLE MIAMIS AND SCIOTA.
Philadelphia: Printed by John Fenno. [1792.] pp. 2. fol.

24868   —— ACTS PASSED AT THE FIRST SESSION OF THE SECOND CONGRESS OF THE UNITED
STATES OF AMERICA, BEGUN AND HELD IN THE CITY OF PHILADELPHIA, ON MON-
DAY, THE TWENTY-FOURTH OF OCTOBER, ONE THOUSAND SEVEN HUNDRED AND
NINETY-ONE. PUBLISHED BY AUTHORITY.
Philadelphia: Printed by Francis Childs and John Swaine, [1792.] pp.
175, 3. 8vo.
BA.
To which are added the Ratifications of the Amendments to the Con-
stitution, by the several ratifying States; the armistice between the
United States and Great-Britain; and the Treaty of peace and friend-
ship with the Cherokees, which with those in the other octavo vol-
ume, completes all the existing Treaties.

24869   —— — ACTS PASSED AT THE FIRST SESSION OF THE SECOND CONGRESS OF THE
UNITED STATES OF AMERICA, BEGUN AND HELD IN THE CITY OF PHILADELPHIA,
ON MONDAY THE TWENTY-FOURTH OF OCTOBER, ONE THOUSAND SEVEN HUNDRED
AND NINETY-ONE: AND OF THE INDEPENDENCE OF THE UNITED STATES THE SIX-
TEENTH.
Philadelphia: Printed by Andrew Brown, M,DCC,XCII. pp. 114, xvi,
(3), 8vo.
JCB.
Collated with and corrected by the original rolls in the office of the
Secretary of State. Attested by Thomas Jefferson.

24870   —— — ACTS PASSED AT THE FIRST SESSION OF THE SECOND CONGRESS OF THE
UNITED STATES OF AMERICA. BEGUN AND HELD AT THE CITY OF PHILADELPHIA,
IN THE STATE OF PENNSYLVANIA, ON MONDAY THE TWENTY-FOURTH OF OCTOBER,
ONE THOUSAND SEVEN HUNDRED AND NINETY-ONE: AND OF THE INDEPENDENCE
OF THE UNITED STATES, THE SIXTEENTH. [Ornament.]
Richmond: Printed by Augustine Davis, Printer for the public. M,DCC,-
XCII. pp. [74], x. fol.
LOC.

24871   —— THE COMMITTEE TO WHOM THE SUBJECT OF WEIGHTS AND MEASURES WAS RE-
FERRED. IN SENATE, APRIL 4, 1792.
[Philadelphia:] Printed by John Fenno. [1792.] pp. 2. fol.   NYPL.

24872   —— THE COMMITTEE TO WHOM WAS REFERRED THE MEMORIAL OF THE DIRECTORS
OF THE OHIO COMPANY OF ASSOCIATES, SO CALLED, HAVING ATTENDED THE DUTY
ASSIGNED TO THEM, REPORT ——
[Philadelphia: Printed by John Fenno, 1792.] pp. (9). fol.   LOC. NYPL.

24873   —— SECOND CONGRESS OF THE UNITED STATES. AT THE FIRST SESSION, BEGUN
AND HELD AT THE CITY OF PHILADELPHIA; IN THE STATE OF PENNSYLVANIA, ON
MONDAY THE TWENTY FOURTH OF OCTOBER, 1791. AN ACT FOR CARRYING INTO
EFFECT A CONTRACT BETWEEN THE UNITED STATES AND THE STATE OF PENN-
SYLVANIA. APPROVED JAN. 3, 1792.
[Philadelphia: Printed by Francis Childs and John Swaine, 1792.] pp.
(2). fol.
NYPL.

UNITED STATES, continued.

24874 —— SECOND CONGRESS OF THE UNITED STATES. AT THE FIRST SESSION, BEGUN AND HELD AT THE CITY OF PHILADELPHIA; IN THE STATE OF PENNSYLVANIA, ON MONDAY, THE TWENTY FOURTH OF OCTOBER, 1791. AN ACT TO EXTEND THE TIME LIMITED FOR SETTLING THE ACCOUNTS OF THE UNITED STATES WITH THE INDIVIDUAL STATES. APPROVED, JAN. 23, 1792.
[Philadelphia: Printed by Francis Childs and John Swaine, 1792.] pp. (2). fol.
NYPL.

24875 —— SECOND CONGRESS OF THE UNITED STATES. AT THE FIRST SESSION, BEGUN AND HELD AT THE CITY OF PHILADELPHIA; IN THE STATE OF PENNSYLVANIA, ON MONDAY THE TWENTY FOURTH OF OCTOBER, 1791. AN ACT CONCERNING CERTAIN FISHERIES OF THE UNITED STATES AND FOR THE REGULATION AND GOVERNMENT OF THE FISHERMEN EMPLOYED THEREIN. APPROVED, FEB. 16, 1792.
[Philadelphia: Printed by Francis Childs and John Swaine, 1792.] pp. (4). fol.
NYPL. RIHS.

24876 —— SECOND CONGRESS OF THE UNITED STATES. AT THE FIRST SESSION BEGUN AND HELD AT THE CITY OF PHILADELPHIA; IN THE STATE OF PENNSYLVANIA, ON MONDAY, THE TWENTY FOURTH OF OCTOBER, 1791. AN ACT TO ESTABLISH THE POST-OFFICE AND POST-ROADS WITHIN THE UNITED STATES. APPROVED, FEB. 20, 1792.
[Philadelphia: Printed by Francis Childs and John Swaine, 1792.] pp. 8. fol.
NYPL. RIHS.

24877 —— —— ACT TO ESTABLISH THE POST-OFFICE AND POST-ROADS WITHIN THE UNITED STATES.
Philadelphia: Printed by John Fenno, January 10, 1792. pp. 10. fol.

24878 —— SECOND CONGRESS OF THE UNITED STATES. AT THE FIRST SESSION, BEGUN AND HELD AT THE CITY OF PHILADELPHIA; IN THE STATE OF PENNSYLVANIA, ON MONDAY THE TWENTY FOURTH OF OCTOBER, 1791. AN ACT RELATIVE TO THE ELECTION OF A PRESIDENT AND VICE-PRESIDENT OF THE UNITED STATES, AND DECLARING THE OFFICER WHO SHALL ACT AS PRESIDENT IN CASE OF VACANCIES IN THE OFFICES BOTH OF PRESIDENT AND VICE-PRESIDENT. APPROVED, MARCH 1, 1792.
[Philadelphia:] Printed by Francis Childs and John Swaine. [1792.] pp. (2). fol.
NYPL.

24879 —— —— AN ACT RELATIVE TO THE ELECTION OF A PRESIDENT AND VICE-PRESIDENT OF THE UNITED STATES.
[Philadelphia: Printed by John Fenno, March 1, 1792.] pp. (2). fol.

24880 —— SECOND CONGRESS OF THE UNITED STATES. AT THE FIRST SESSION, BEGUN AND HELD AT THE CITY OF PHILADELPHIA; IN THE STATE OF PENNSYLVANIA, ON MONDAY THE TWENTY FOURTH OF OCTOBER, 1791. AN ACT FOR MAKING FARTHER AND MORE EFFECTUAL PROVISION FOR THE PROTECTION OF THE FRONTIERS OF THE UNITED STATES. APPROVED, MARCH 5, 1792.
[Philadelphia: Printed by Francis Childs and John Swaine, [1792.] pp. (4). fol.
NYPL.

24881 —— SECOND CONGRESS OF THE UNITED STATES. AT THE FIRST SESSION, BEGUN AND HELD AT THE CITY OF PHILADELPHIA; IN THE STATE OF PENNSYLVANIA, ON MONDAY THE TWENTY FOURTH OF OCTOBER, 1791. AN ACT DECLARING THE CONSENT OF CONGRESS TO A CERTAIN ACT OF THE STATE OF MARYLAND, AND TO CONTINUE FOR A LONGER TIME, AN ACT DECLARING THE ASSENT OF CONGRESS TO CERTAIN ACTS OF THE STATES OF MARYLAND, GEORGIA, AND RHODE ISLAND AND PROVIDENCE PLANTATIONS, SO FAR AS THE SAME RESPECTS THE STATES OF GEORGIA, AND RHODE ISLAND AND PROVIDENCE PLANTATIONS. APPROVED, MARCH 19, 1792.
[Philadelphia: Printed by Francis Childs and John Swaine, 1792.] pp. (2). fol.
NYPL.

UNITED STATES, continued.

24882 —— SECOND CONGRESS OF THE UNITED STATES. AT THE FIRST SESSION, BEGUN AND HELD AT THE CITY OF PHILADELPHIA; IN THE STATE OF PENNSYLVANIA. ON MONDAY THE TWENTY FOURTH OF OCTOBER, 1791. AN ACT TO PROVIDE FOR THE SETTLEMENT OF THE CLAIMS OF WIDOWS AND ORPHANS BARRED BY THE LIMITATIONS HERETOFORE ESTABLISHED AND TO REGULATE THE CLAIMS TO INVALID PENSIONS. APPROVED, MARCH 23, 1792.

[Philadelphia: Printed by Francis Childs and John Swaine, 1792.] pp. (2). fol.   NYPL.

24883 —— SECOND CONGRESS OF THE UNITED STATES. AT THE FIRST SESSION, BEGUN AND HELD AT THE CITY OF PHILADELPHIA; IN THE STATE OF PENNSYLVANIA, ON MONDAY THE TWENTY FOURTH OF OCTOBER, 1791. AN ACT FOR THE RELIEF OF CERTAIN WIDOWS, ORPHANS, INVALIDS AND OTHER PERSONS. APPROVED, MARCH 24, 1792.

[Philadelphia: Printed by Francis Childs and John Swaine, 1792.] pp. (2). fol.   NYPL.

24884 —— SECOND CONGRESS OF THE UNITED STATES. AT THE FIRST SESSION, BEGUN AND HELD AT THE CITY OF PHILADELPHIA; IN THE STATE OF PENNSYLVANIA, ON MONDAY THE TWENTY FOURTH OF OCTOBER, 1791. AN ACT PROVIDING FOR THE SETTLEMENT OF THE CLAIMS OF PERSONS UNDER PARTICULAR CIRCUMSTANCES BARRED BY THE LIMITATIONS HERETOFORE ESTABLISHED. APPROVED, MARCH 27, 1792.

[Philadelphia: Printed by Francis Childs and John Swaine, 1792.] pp. (2). fol.   NYPL.

24885 —— SECOND CONGRESS OF THE UNITED STATES. AT THE FIRST SESSION BEGUN AND HELD AT THE CITY OF PHILADELPHIA; IN THE STATE OF PENNSYLVANIA. ON MONDAY THE TWENTY FOURTH OF OCTOBER, 1791. AN ACT SUPPLEMENTAL TO THE ACT FOR MAKING FARTHER AND MORE EFFECTUAL PROVISION FOR THE PROTECTION OF THE FRONTIERS OF THE UNITED STATES. APPROVED, MARCH 28, 1792.

[Philadelphia: Printed by Francis Childs and John Swaine, 1792.] pp. (2). fol.   NYPL.

24886 —— SECOND CONGRESS OF THE UNITED STATES. AT THE FIRST SESSION, BEGUN AND HELD AT THE CITY OF PHILADELPHIA; IN THE STATE OF PENNSYLVANIA, ON MONDAY THE TWENTY FOURTH OF OCTOBER, 1791. AN ACT ESTABLISHING A MINT, AND REGULATING THE COINS OF THE UNITED STATES. APPROVED, APRIL 2, 1792.

[Philadelphia: Printed by Francis Childs and John Swaine, 1792.] pp. 5. fol.   NYPL.

24887 —— —— AN ACT ESTABLISHING A MINT, AND REGULATING THE COINS OF THE UNITED STATES.

Philadelphia: Printed by John Fenno. [1792.] pp. 6. fol.

24888 —— SECOND CONGRESS OF THE UNITED STATES. AT THE FIRST SESSION, BEGUN AND HELD AT THE CITY OF PHILADELPHIA; IN THE STATE OF PENNSYLVANIA, ON MONDAY THE TWENTY FOURTH OF OCTOBER, 1791. AN ACT TO INDEMNIFY THE ESTATE OF THE LATE MAJOR GENERAL NATHANIEL GREEN, FOR A CERTAIN BOND ENTERED INTO BY HIM DURING THE LATE WAR. APPROVED, APRIL 27, 1792.

[Philadelphia: Printed by Francis Childs and John Swaine, 1792.] pp. (2). fol.   NYPL.

UNITED STATES, continued.

24889 —— SECOND CONGRESS OF THE UNITED STATES. AT THE FIRST SESSION, BEGUN AND HELD AT THE CITY OF PHILADELPHIA; IN THE STATE OF PENNSYLVANIA, ON MONDAY THE TWENTY FOURTH OF OCTOBER, 1791. AN ACT TO PROVIDE FOR CALLING FORTH THE MILITIA TO EXECUTE THE LAWS OF THE UNION, SUPPRESS INSURRECTIONS AND REPEL INVASIONS. APPROVED, MAY 2, 1792.

[Philadelphia: Printed by Francis Childs and John Swaine. 1792.] pp.
(4). fol. NYPL.

24890 —— SECOND CONGRESS OF THE UNITED STATES: AT THE FIRST SESSION, BEGUN AND HELD AT THE CITY OF PHILADELPHIA; IN THE STATE OF PENNSYLVANIA, ON MONDAY THE TWENTY FOURTH OF OCTOBER, 1791. AN ACT FOR RAISING A FARTHER SUM OF MONEY FOR THE PROTECTION OF THE FRONTIERS, AND FOR OTHER PURPOSES THEREIN MENTIONED. APPROVED, MAY 2, 1792.

[Philadelphia: Printed by Francis Childs and John Swaine, 1792.] pp.
(4). fol. NYPL.

24891 —— SECOND CONGRESS OF THE UNITED STATES: AT THE FIRST SESSION, BEGUN AND HELD AT THE CITY OF PHILADELPHIA; IN THE STATE OF PENNSYLVANIA, ON MONDAY THE TWENTY FOURTH OF OCTOBER, ONE THOUSAND SEVEN HUNDRED AND NINETY-ONE. AN ACT AUTHORIZING THE GRANT AND CONVEYANCE OF CERTAIN LANDS TO JOHN CLEVES SYMMES, AND HIS ASSOCIATES. APPROVED, MAY 5, 1792.

[Philadelphia: Printed by Francis Childs and John Swaine, 1792.] Broadside. fol. LOC. NYPL.

24892 —— SECOND CONGRESS OF THE UNITED STATES. AT THE FIRST SESSION, BEGUN AND HELD AT THE CITY OF PHILADELPHIA; IN THE STATE OF PENNSYLVANIA, ON MONDAY THE TWENTY FOURTH OF OCTOBER, 1791. AN ACT TO ALTER THE TIME FOR THE NEXT ANNUAL MEETING OF CONGRESS. APPROVED, MAY 5, 1792.

[Philadelphia: Printed by Francis Childs and John Swaine, 1792.] pp.
(2). fol. NYPL.

24893 —— SECOND CONGRESS OF THE UNITED STATES. AT THE FIRST SESSION, BEGUN AND HELD AT THE CITY OF PHILADELPHIA; IN THE STATE OF PENNSYLVANIA. ON MONDAY THE TWENTY FOURTH OF OCTOBER, 1791. AN ACT CONCERNING THE CLAIM OF JOHN BROWN CUTTING AGAINST THE UNITED STATES. APPROVED, MAY 8, 1792. [And] RESOLUTION [requiring the Secretary of the Treasury] TO PROVIDE . . . PRINTED CLEARANCES. . . . APPROVED, MAY 8, 1792.

[Philadelphia: Printed by Francis Childs and John Swaine, 1792.] pp.
(2). fol. NYPL.

24894 —— SECOND CONGRESS OF THE UNITED STATES. AT THE FIRST SESSION, BEGUN AND HELD AT THE CITY OF PHILADELPHIA; IN THE STATE OF PENNSYLVANIA, ON MONDAY THE TWENTY FOURTH OF OCTOBER, 1791. AN ACT CONCERNING THE DUTIES ON SPIRITS DISTILLED WITHIN THE UNITED STATES. APPROVED. MAY 8, 1792.

[Philadelphia: Printed by Francis Childs and John Swaine, 1792.] pp.
(4). fol. NYPL.

24895 —— SECOND CONGRESS OF THE UNITED STATES. AT THE FIRST SESSION, BEGUN AND HELD AT THE CITY OF PHILADELPHIA; IN THE STATE OF PENNSYLVANIA, ON MONDAY THE TWENTY FOURTH OF OCTOBER, 1791. AN ACT FOR MAKING COMPENSATIONS TO THE COMMISSIONERS OF LOANS FOR EXTRAORDINARY EXPENSES. APPROVED, MAY 8, 1792.

[Philadelphia: Printed by Francis Childs and John Swaine, 1792.] pp.
(2). fol. NYPL.

UNITED STATES, continued.

24896 —— SECOND CONGRESS OF THE UNITED STATES. AT THE FIRST SESSION, BEGUN AND HELD AT THE CITY OF PHILADELPHIA; IN THE STATE OF PENNSYLVANIA, ON MONDAY THE TWENTY FOURTH OF OCTOBER, 1791. AN ACT FOR REGULATING PROCESSES IN THE COURTS OF THE UNITED STATES, AND PROVIDING COMPENSATIONS FOR THE OFFICERS OF THE SAID COURTS, AND FOR JURORS AND WITNESSES. APPROVED, MAY 8, 1792.

[Philadelphia: Printed by Francis Childs and John Swaine, 1792.] pp. (4). fol.   NYPL.

24897 —— SECOND CONGRESS OF THE UNITED STATES. AT THE FIRST SESSION, BEGUN AND HELD AT THE CITY OF PHILADELPHIA; IN THE STATE OF PENNSYLVANIA, ON MONDAY THE TWENTY FOURTH OF OCTOBER, 1791. AN ACT MAKING ALTERATIONS IN THE TREASURY AND WAR DEPARTMENTS. APPROVED, MAY 8, 1792.

[Philadelphia: Printed by Francis Childs and John Swaine, 1792.] pp. (4). fol.   NYPL.

24898 —— SECOND CONGRESS OF THE UNITED STATES. AT THE FIRST SESSION, BEGUN AND HELD AT THE CITY OF PHILADELPHIA; IN THE STATE OF PENNSYLVANIA, ON MONDAY THE TWENTY FOURTH OF OCTOBER, 1791. AN ACT MAKING CERTAIN APPROPRIATIONS THEREIN SPECIFIED. APPROVED, MAY 8, 1792.

[Philadelphia: Printed by Francis Childs and John Swaine, 1792.] pp. (2). fol.   NYPL.

24899 —— SECOND CONGRESS OF THE UNITED STATES. AT THE FIRST SESSION, BEGUN AND HELD AT THE CITY OF PHILADELPHIA; IN THE STATE OF PENNSYLVANIA, ON MONDAY THE TWENTY FOURTH OF OCTOBER, 1791. AN ACT MORE EFFECTUALLY TO PROVIDE FOR THE NATIONAL DEFENCE BY ESTABLISHING AN UNIFORM MILITIA THROUGHOUT THE UNITED STATES. APPROVED, MAY 8, 1792.

[Philadelphia: Printed by Francis Childs and John Swaine, 1792.] pp. (4). fol.   NYPL. RIHS.

24900 —— SECOND CONGRESS OF THE UNITED STATES. AT THE FIRST SESSION, BEGUN AND HELD AT THE CITY OF PHILADELPHIA; IN THE STATE OF PENNSYLVANIA, ON MONDAY THE TWENTY FOURTH OF OCTOBER. 1791. AN ACT RELATIVE TO THE COMPENSATION OF CERTAIN OFFICERS EMPLOYED IN THE COLLECTION OF DUTIES OF IMPOST TONNAGE. APPROVED, MAY 8, 1792.

[Philadelphia: Printed by Francis Childs and John Swaine, 1792.] pp. (2). fol.   NYPL.

24901 —— SECOND CONGRESS OF THE UNITED STATES. AT THE FIRST SESSION, BEGUN AND HELD AT THE CITY OF PHILADELPHIA; IN THE STATE OF PENNSYLVANIA, ON MONDAY THE TWENTY FOURTH OF OCTOBER, 1791. AN ACT SUPPLEMENTARY TO THE ACT FOR MAKING PROVISION FOR THE DEBT OF THE UNITED STATES. APPROVED, MAY 8, 1792.

[Philadelphia: Printed by Francis Childs and John Swaine, 1792] pp. (4). fol.   NYPL.

24902 —— SECOND CONGRESS OF THE UNITED STATES. AT THE FIRST SESSION, BEGUN AND HELD AT THE CITY OF PHILADELPHIA; IN THE STATE OF PENNSYLVANIA, ON MONDAY THE TWENTY FOURTH OF OCTOBER, 1791. AN ACT RESPECTING THE GOVERNMENT OF THE TERRITORIES OF THE UNITED STATES NORTH WEST AND SOUTH OF THE RIVER OHIO. APPROVED, MAY 8, 1792. [Also,] AN ACT TO COMPENSATE THE SERVICES OF THE LATE COLONEL GEORGE GIBSON. APPROVED, MAY 8, 1792.

[Philadelphia: Printed by Francis Childs and John Swaine, 1792.] pp. (2). fol.   NYPL. RIHS.

UNITED STATES, continued.

24903 —— SECOND CONGRESS OF THE UNITED STATES. AT THE FIRST SESSION, BEGUN AND HELD AT THE CITY OF PHILADELPHIA; IN THE STATE OF PENNSYLVANIA, ON MONDAY THE TWENTY FOURTH OF OCTOBER, 1791. AN ACT TO CONTINUE IN FORCE THE ACT, INTITULED, AN ACT TO PROVIDE FOR MITIGATING OR REMITTING THE PENALTIES AND FORFEITURES ACCRUING UNDER THE REVENUE LAWS IN CERTAIN CASES," AND TO MAKE FURTHER PROVISION FOR THE PAYMENT OF PENSIONS TO INVALIDS. APPROVED, MAY 8, 1792.

[Philadelphia: Printed by Francis Childs and John Swaine, 1792.] pp. (2). fol. NYPL.

24904 —— SECOND CONGRESS OF THE UNITED STATES. AT THE FIRST SESSION, BEGUN AND HELD AT THE CITY OF PHILADELPHIA; IN THE STATE OF PENNSYLVANIA, ON MONDAY THE TWENTY FOURTH OF OCTOBER, 1791. AN ACT TO PROVIDE FOR A COPPER COINAGE. APPROVED, MAY 8, 1792.

[Philadelphia: Printed by Francis Childs and John Swaine, 1792.] pp. (2). fol. NYPL.

24905 —— DUTIES PAYABLE ON ALL GOODS, WARES AND MERCHANDIZE, IMPORTED INTO THE UNITED STATES OF AMERICA, AFTER THE LAST DAY OF JUNE 1792, PURSUANT TO THE RESPECTIVE ACTS, ENTITLED, "AN ACT MAKING FURTHER PROVISION FOR THE PAYMENT OF THE DEBTS OF THE UNITED STATES,"—AND "AN ACT FOR RAISING A FARTHER SUM OF MONEY FOR THE PROTECTION OF THE FRONTIERS, AND FOR OTHER PURPOSES THEREIN MENTIONED."—THE INWARD COLUMN EXHIBITING THE RATES PAYABLE ON THOSE IMPORTED IN SHIPS OR VESSELS OF THE UNITED STATES, —AND THE OUTWARD COLUMN THE RATES PAYABLE IN FOREIGN SHIPS OR VESSELS, INCLUDING THE ADDITIONAL DUTIES TO WHICH THE RESPECTIVE ARTICLES ARE LIABLE.

[Philadelphia: Printed by Francis Childs and John Swaine, 1792.] pp. (12). 8vo. LOC.

24906 —— — DUTIES PAYABLE ON GOODS, WARES AND MERCHANDISE, IMPORTED INTO THE UNITED STATES OF AMERICA, FROM JUNE 1792. THE DUTIES OF TONNAGE, AND THE RATES OF COINS, BY WHICH THE DUTIES ARE TO BE RECEIVED AND ESTIMATED. . . .

Philadelphia: Printed by Hall and Sellers. MDCCXCII. pp. 16. 8vo. JCB.

24907 —— — LIST OF DUTIES PAYABLE ON GOODS, WARES AND MERCHANDIZE, IMPORTED INTO THE UNITED STATES OF AMERICA.

[Without Place or Printer, 1792.] Broadside. fol.

24908 —— ESTIMATE OF THE EXPENDITURES FOR THE CIVIL LIST OF THE UNITED STATES, TOGETHER WITH THE INCIDENTAL AND CONTINGENT EXPENSES OF THE SEVERAL DEPARTMENTS AND OFFICES, FOR THE YEAR 1793. PUBLISHED BY ORDER OF THE HOUSE OF REPRESENTATIVES.

[Philadelphia:] Printed by Childs and Swaine. [1792.] pp. [23.] fol. BA. JCB. LOC.

24909 —— IN THE HOUSE OF REPRESENTATIVES OF THE UNITED STATES, TUESDAY THE 8TH OF MAY, 1792. MR. FITZSIMMONS, FROM THE COMMITTEE APPOINTED TO ENQUIRE INTO THE CAUSES OF THE FAILURE OF THE LATE EXPEDITION UNDER MAJOR GENERAL ST. CLAIR, REPORTED, THAT THE COMMITTEE HAD, ACCORDING TO ORDER, PROCEEDED TO EXAMINE ALL THE PAPERS FURNISHED BY THE EXECUTIVE DEPART-·MENT RELATIVE THERETO, SUNDRY PAPERS AND ACCOUNTS FURNISHED BY THE TREASURY AND WAR DEPARTMENTS, WITH EXPLANATION OF THE SAME BY THE HEADS OF THOSE DEPARTMENTS IN PERSON, TO HEAR THE TESTIMONY OF WITNESSES UPON OATH, AND WRITTEN REMARKS BY GENERAL ST. CLAIR, UPON THE FACTS ESTABLISHED BY THE WHOLE EVIDENCE, AND THAT, AS THE RESULT OF THEIR ENQUIRIES, THE COMMITTEE HAD AGREED TO THE FOLLOWING REPORT.

[Philadelphia: Printed by Francis Childs and John Swaine, 1792.] pp. 13. fol. LOC. NYPL.

UNITED STATES, continued.

24910   —— JOURNAL OF THE HOUSE OF REPRESENTATIVES OF THE UNITED STATES, AT THE FIRST SESSION OF THE SECOND CONGRESS. ANNO M,DCC,XCI, AND OF THE INDEPENDENCE OF THE UNITED STATES THE SIXTEENTH. [24 October, 1791—8 May, 1792.]
Philadelphia: Printed by Francis Childs and John Swaine. M,DCC,- XCII. pp. 245. fol.   AAS. BA. LOC. NYPL.

24911   —— JOURNAL OF THE SENATE OF THE UNITED STATES OF AMERICA, BEING THE FIRST SESSION OF THE SECOND CONGRESS, BEGUN AND HELD AT THE CITY OF PHILADELPHIA, OCTOBER 24TH, 1791 [—8 MAY, 1792]; AND IN THE SIXTEENTH YEAR OF THE SOVEREIGNTY OF THE SAID UNITED STATES.
Philadelphia: Printed by John Fenno, No. 69, *High-Street.* M.DCC.XCI. [1792.] pp. 224 [*sic* 228.] fol.   AAS. BA. BU. JCB. LOC. NL. NYPL. RIHS.
Page 228 is misnumbered 224. Reprinted in Washington, in 1820.

24912   —— LAWS FOR THE BETTER REGULATING SEAMEN IN THE MERCHANTS' SERVICE.
Norfolk: Printed by Nathaniel Baxter and Thomas Wilson, 1792.

24913   —— — SEAMAN'S ARTICLES, WITH THE ACT ENTITLED, "AN ACT FOR THE GOVERNMENT AND REGULATIONS OF SEAMEN IN THE MERCHANT'S SERVICE."
Savannah: Printed by James and Nicholas Johnston, 1792.

24914   —— LAWS OF THE UNITED STATES OF AMERICA; COMPRISING THE ACTS OF THE FIRST CONGRESS, AND THE TREATIES.
Exeter, N. H.: Printed by Henry Ranlet, for the General Court. 1792. pp. 700. 8vo.

24915   —— MANUAL EXERCISE; AND EVOLUTIONS OF THE CAVALRY, AS PRACTISED IN THE LATE AMERICAN ARMY.
Concord: Printed by George Hough? 1792.

24916   —— PROCEEDINGS IN THE HOUSE OF REPRESENTATIVES OF THE UNITED STATES OF AMERICA, RESPECTING THE CONTESTED ELECTION FOR THE EASTERN DISTRICT OF THE STATE OF GEORGIA. [Ornament.]
Philadelphia: Printed by Parry Hall, No. 149, *Chesnut Street, between Fourth and Fifth Streets.* M.DCC.XCII. pp. [71]. 8vo.
      AAS. BA. JCB. LCP. LOC. NYPL.

24917   —— — PROCEEDINGS IN THE HOUSE OF REPRESENTATIVES OF THE UNITED STATES OF AMERICA, RESPECTING THE CONTESTED ELECTION FOR THE EASTERN DISTRICT OF THE STATE OF GEORGIA. CONTAINING THE PETITION OF GENERAL JAMES JACKSON, AGAINST THE ELECTION OF GENERAL ANTHONY WAYNE, AND THE PROCEEDINGS RELATIVE TO THE RESOLUTIONS DIRECTING THE MODE OF CONDUCTING THE TRIAL; WITH A SKETCH OF THE DEBATES FROM THE COMMENCEMENT TO THE END OF THE BUSINESS; INCLUDING THE SPEECHES OF THE PARTIES, A SKETCH OF MR. LEWIS'S DEFENCE, COUNSEL FOR GENERAL WAYNE, AND THE CONCLUDING SPEECH OF GENERAL JACKSON, FOR WHICH HE RECEIVED THE APPLAUSE OF THE AUDITORS; ALSO THE SUBSEQUENT PROCEEDINGS OF THE HOUSE, RESPECTING HIS RIGHT TO A SEAT AFTER THE ELECTION OF THE SITTING MEMBER HAD BEEN DECLARED ILLEGAL. TOGETHER WITH A SUPPLEMENT, CONTAINING A SUMMARY OF THE PROCEEDINGS OF THE LEGISLATURE OF GEORGIA, RELATIVE TO THE IMPEACHMENT OF JUDGE OSBORNE; TAKEN FROM THE PAPERS SENT UNDER THE SEAL OF THE STATE, AND PRODUCED IN CONGRESS BY MR. BALDWIN, WHICH WERE REJECTED.
New-York: Printed by Samuel Loudon, jun. 1792.

UNITED STATES, continued.

24918 —— PURSUANT TO THE ORDER OF THE HOUSE OF REPRESENTATIVES OF THE 18TH OF JANUARY, 1791, DIRECTING THE SECRETARY OF THE TREASURY TO REPORT HIS OPINION WHETHER ANY AND WHAT FURTHER COMPENSATION OUGHT TO BE MADE TO THE RESPECTIVE OFFICERS EMPLOYED IN THE COLLECTION OF THE REVENUE, THE SAID SECRETARY RESPECTFULLY SUBMITS THE FOLLOWING REPORT . . . APRIL 5, 1792.

[Philadelphia: Printed by Francis Childs and John Swaine, 1792.] pp. 4. fol.
BA. NYPL. RIHS.

24919 —— REGULATIONS FOR THE ORDER AND DISCIPLINE OF THE TROOPS OF THE UNITED STATES. BY BARON DE STEUBEN.

Hartford: Printed and sold by Nathaniel Patten. MDCCXCII. pp. 95, (1), 8 plates. 8vo.

24920 —— —— REGULATIONS FOR THE ORDER AND DISCIPLINE OF THE TROOPS OF THE UNITED STATES. BY BARON DE STEUBEN, LATE MAJOR-GENERAL AND INSPECTOR-GENERAL IN THE ARMY OF THE UNITED STATES.

Windsor: Printed by Alden Spooner. M.DCC.XCII. pp. 91. 12mo.

24921 —— REPORT FROM THE COMMISSIONERS FOR PURCHASING THE PUBLIC DEBT. PUBLISHED BY ORDER OF THE HOUSE OF REPRESENTATIVES.

[Philadelphia:] Printed by Childs and Swaine. [1792.] pp. [19.] fol.
BA. JCB. LOC. RIHS.

24922 —— REPORT OF THE COMMISSIONERS ON THE ACCOUNTS OF THE STATES. DECEMBER 5, 1792.

[Philadelphia: Printed by Francis Childs and John Swaine, 1792.] pp. (4). fol.

Reprinted by order of the House of Representatives, November 4, 1803.

24923 —— REPORT OF THE COMMITTEE ON POST-OFFICE AND POST ROADS, ON WHAT ALTERATIONS AND AMENDMENTS WERE NECESSARY.

Philadelphia: Printed by John Fenno. 1792. pp. (2). fol.

24924 —— REPORT OF THE SECRETARY OF STATE ON THE SUBJECT OF THE COD AND WHALE FISHERIES, MADE CONFORMABLY TO AN ORDER OF THE HOUSE OF REPRESENTATIVES OF THE UNITED STATES, REFERRING TO HIM THE REPRESENTATION OF THE GENERAL COURT OF THE COMMONWEALTH OF MASSACHUSETTS ON THOSE SUBJECTS; FEB. 1, 1791.

Philadelphia: Printed by Francis Childs and John Swaine. M.DCC.XCII. pp. (45). 8vo.
LOC.

24925 —— REPORT OF THE SECRETARY OF THE TREASURY, ON THE ACT FOR LAYING DUTIES ON SPIRITS, &C. READ IN THE HOUSE OF REPRESENTATIVES, MARCH 6, 1792.

[Philadelphia:] Printed by Childs and Swaine. [1792.] pp. (20). fol.
AAS. BA. JCB. LOC. NYPL. RIHS.

24926 —— REPORT OF THE SECRETARY OF THE TREASURY, ON THE SUBJECT OF THE PUBLIC DEBT. PRESENTED TO THE HOUSE OF REPRESENTATIVES, FEBRUARY 7TH, 1792.

[Philadelphia:] Printed by Childs and Swaine. [1792.] pp. (15). fol.
AAS. JCB. LOC. NYPL. RIHS.

24927 —— REPORT OF THE SECRETARY OF THE TREASURY RESPECTING THE REDEMPTION OF THE PUBLIC DEBT; AND THE REIMBURSEMENT OF THE LOAN MADE OF THE BANK OF THE UNITED STATES. PUBLISHED BY ORDER OF THE HOUSE OF REPRESENTATIVES.

[Philadelphia:] Printed by Childs and Swaine. [1792.] pp. (2), (2), [10.] fol.
AAS. BA. JCB. LOC. RIHS.

UNITED STATES, continued.

24928 —— RETURN OF DUTIES ON IMPORTS AND TONNAGE, ALSO ON EXPORTS: TRANS-MITTED TO THE HOUSE OF REPRESENTATIVES BY THE SECRETARY OF THE TREAS-URY, MARCH 28, 1792.

[Philadelphia:] Printed by Childs and Swaine. [1792.] pp. (2), 9, fold-ed table. fol.   LOC. NYPL. RIHS.

24929 —— THE SECRETARY OF THE TREASURY, PURSUANT TO A RESOLUTION OF THE HOUSE OF REPRESENTATIVES OF THE 8TH INSTANT, DIRECTING THE SAID SECRE-TARY TO REPORT TO THE HOUSE HIS OPINION OF THE BEST MODE OF RAISING THE ADDITIONAL SUPPLIES REQUISITE FOR THE ENSUING YEAR. MARCH 16.

[Philadelphia:] Printed by Francis Childs and John Swaine. [1792.] pp. 8. fol.   BA. NYPL.

24930 —— THE SECRETARY OF THE TREASURY, TO WHOM THE HOUSE OF REPRESENTA-TIVES WERE PLEASED TO REFER THE SEVERAL PETITIONS ENUMERATED IN THE LISTS HEREWITH TRANSMITTED, MARKED A. B. & C, RESPECTFULLY SUBMITS THE FOLLOWING REPORT. [On claims in consequence of the late war. April 16, 1792.]

[Philadelphia: Printed by John Fenno, 1792.] pp. (3). fol.   BA. LOC. NYPL.

24931 —— THE SECRETARY OF THE TREASURY, TO WHOM WAS REFERRED THE SEVERAL PETITIONS IN THE LIST HEREUNTO ANNEXED SPECIFIED—RESPECTFULLY MAKES THE FOLLOWING REPORT THEREUPON, . . . ALEXANDER HAMILTON. NOVEMBER 19, 1792.

[Philadelphia: Printed by Childs and Swaine, 1792.] pp. (2). fol.   LOC.

24932 —— THE SECRETARY OF THE TREASURY, TO WHOM WERE REFERRED BY THE HOUSE OF REPRESENTATIVES, THE SEVERAL PETITIONS SPECIFIED, IN THE LIST HERE-WITH, PRAYING THE RENEWAL OF CERTAIN CERTIFICATES WHICH ARE ALLEDGED [*sic*] TO HAVE BEEN DESTROYED OR LOST, RESPECTFULLY MAKES THE FOLLOWING REPORT THEREUPON . . . APRIL 18, 1792.

[Philadelphia:] Printed by Francis Childs and John Swaine. [1792.] pp. 11. fol.   BA. JCB. NYPL. RIHS.

24933 —— THE SECRETARY OF THE TREASURY TO WHOM WERE REFERRED CERTAIN PAPERS CONCERNING A MARINE HOSPITAL, AT THE TOWN OF WASHINGTON IN THE STATE OF VIRGINIA, AND A MEMORIAL OF THE MARINE SOCIETY OF BOSTON, ON THE SUBJECT OF MARINE HOSPITALS RESPECTFULLY SUBMITS THE FOLLOWING REPORT . . . ALEXANDER HAMILTON. APRIL 17TH 1792.

[Philadelphia: Printed by Childs and Swaine, 1792.] Broadside. fol.   LOC. NYPL.

24934 —— SPEECH OF THE PRESIDENT OF THE UNITED STATES TO BOTH HOUSES OF CON-GRESS, NOVEMBER 6, 1792. [Three columns.] GO. WASHINGTON. UNITED STATES. NOVEMBER 6, 1792.

[Philadelphia: 1792.] Broadside. fol.   AAS.

24935 —— A TABLE OF POST-OFFICES IN THE UNITED STATES; WITH THEIR DISTANCE FROM PHILADELPHIA.

[Philadelphia: 1792.] 8vo.

AUCTION
VALUES

UNITED STATES, continued.

24936 —— TREASURY DEPARTMENT, DECEMBER 26, 1791. SIR, I HAVE THE HONOR TO SEND HEREWITH A REPORT, ON THE PETITION OF CATHARINE GREENE, PURSUANT TO A REFERENCE OF THE HOUSE OF THE 5TH OF MARCH, 1790, . . . ALEXANDER HAMILTON.
[*Philadelphia: Printed by John Fenno*, 1792.] pp. (2), (2), (5)—(35). fol.
LOC. NYPL. RIHS.

24937 —— TREASURY DEPARTMENT, JANUARY 23, 1792. SIR, I HAVE THE HONOR TO SEND HEREWITH A REPORT [on a surplus of revenue appropriated to the reduction of the public debt] PURSUANT TO THE ORDER OF THE HOUSE OF REPRESENTATIVES, OF THE 19TH INSTANT; . . . ALEXANDER HAMILTON.
[*Philadelphia: Printed by Childs and Swaine*, 1792.] pp. [4.] fol.
BA. LOC. RIHS.

24938 —— TREASURY OF THE UNITED STATES, FEBRUARY 28TH, 1792. SIR, MY SPECIE ACCOUNT, ENDING THE 31ST DECEMBER, 1791, HAVING PASSED THE TREASURY, PERMIT ME (THROUGH YOU) TO LAY IT BEFORE THE HONORABLE THE HOUSE OF REPRESENTATIVES, . . . SAMUEL MEREDITH, TREASURER OF THE UNITED STATES.
[*Philadelphia: Printed by Childs and Swaine*, 1792.] pp. 11. fol.
AAS. BA. LOC.

24939 —— .THE TREASURER OF THE UNITED STATES. ACCOUNTS OF PAYMENTS AND RECEIPTS OF PUBLIC MONIES. [January 1–September 20, 1792.] PRESENTED TO THE HOUSE OF REPRESENTATIVES, NOVEMBER 6, 1792.
[*Philadelphia: Printed by Childs and Swaine*. 1792.] pp. 67. fol.
AAS. BA.

24940 —— TREASURY DEPARTMENT, MARCH 16, 1792. THE SECRETARY OF THE TREASURY, PURSUANT TO A RESOLUTION OF THE HOUSE OF REPRESENTATIVES OF THE 8TH INSTANT, DIRECTING THE SAID SECRETARY TO REPORT TO THE HOUSE HIS OPINION OF THE BEST MODE OF RAISING THE ADDITIONAL SUPPLIES REQUISITE FOR THE ENSUING YEAR, RESPECTFULLY SUBMIT THE FOLLOWING REPORT. . . . [Colophon:]
[*Philadelphia:*] Printed by Childs and Swaine. [1792.] pp. (8). fol.
AAS. BA. LOC. RIHS.

24941 —— TREASURY DEPARTMENT, APRIL 16TH, 1792. SIR, I HAVE THE HONOR TO TRANSMIT HEREWITH A REPORT TO THE HOUSE OF REPRESENTATIVES, ACCOMPANYING AN ESTIMATE OF SUMS NECESSARY TO BE APPROPRIATED IN ADDITION TO THOSE PROVIDED FOR BY THE ACT PASSED THE 23D DECEMBER 1791. . . . ALEXANDER HAMILTON.
[*Philadelphia: Printed by Childs and Swaine*, 1792.] pp. (2). fol.
BA. LOC.

24942 —— TREASURY DEPARTMENT, DEC. 7, 1792. SIR, I HAVE THE HONOR HEREWITH TO TRANSMIT CERTAIN STATEMENTS, PURSUANT TO A RESOLUTION OF THE HOUSE OF REPRESENTATIVES OF THE 13TH ULTIMO, RELATIVE TO THE DISBURSEMENTS MADE BY THE DEPARTMENT OF WAR; ALSO, COPY OF A LETTER FROM THE COMPTROLLER OF THE TREASURY ON THE SUBJECT; . . . ALEXANDER HAMILTON.
[*Philadelphia: Printed by Childs and Swaine*, 1792.] pp. [8.] fol.
JCB. LOC. RIHS.

24943 —— UNITED STATES, IN SENATE, APRIL 4, 1792. THE COMMITTEE TO WHOM THE SUBJECTS OF WEIGHTS AND MEASURES WAS REFERRED,—REPORT . . . [Colophon:]
[*Philadelphia:*] Printed by John Fenno. [1792.] pp. (2). fol.   LOC.

UNITED STATES, continued.

24944　—— UNITED STATES, JANUARY THE 16TH, 1792. SIR, AS THE CIRCUMSTANCES WHICH HAVE ENGAGED THE UNITED STATES IN THE PRESENT INDIAN WAR MAY SOME OF THEM BE OUT OF THE PUBLIC RECOLLECTION, AND OTHERS PERHAPS BE UNKNOWN, IT MAY APPEAR ADVISABLE THAT YOU PREPARE AND PUBLISH, FROM AUTHENTIC DOCUMENTS, A STATEMENT OF THOSE CIRCUMSTANCES, AS WELL AS OF THE MEASURES WHICH HAVE BEEN TAKEN, FROM TIME TO TIME, FOR THE RE-ESTABLISHMENT OF PEACE AND FRIENDSHIP. WHEN THE COMMUNITY ARE CALLED UPON FOR CONSIDERABLE EXERTIONS TO RELIEVE A PART WHICH IS SUFFERING UNDER THE HAND OF AN ENEMY, IT IS DESIRABLE TO MANIFEST THAT DUE PAINS HAVE BEEN TAKEN BY THOSE ENTRUSTED WITH THE ADMINISTRATION OF THEIR AFFAIRS TO AVOID THE EVIL. G. WASHINGTON. THE SECRETARY FOR THE DEPARTMENT OF WAR.

THE CAUSES OF THE EXISTING HOSTILITIES BETWEEN THE UNITED STATES, AND CERTAIN TRIBES OF INDIANS NORTH-WEST OF THE OHIO, STATED AND EXPLAINED FROM OFFICIAL AND AUTHENTIC DOCUMENTS, AND PUBLISHED IN OBEDIENCE TO THE ORDERS OF THE PRESIDENT OF THE UNITED STATES. [Five columns.] H. KNOX, SECRETARY OF WAR. WAR DEPARTMENT, JAN. 26, 1792. [Colophon:]
　　Philadelphia, Printed by D. C. Claypoole. [1792.] Broadside. fol. NYHS.

24945　—— UNITED STATES, NOVEMBER THE 22D, 1792. GENTLEMEN OF THE SENATE, AND OF THE HOUSE OF REPRESENTATIVES. I SEND YOU HEREWITH THE ABSTRACT OF A SUPPLEMENTARY ARRANGEMENT WHICH HAS BEEN MADE BY ME, PURSUANT TO THE ACTS OF THE THIRD DAY OF MARCH, 1791, AND THE EIGHTH DAY OF MAY 1792, FOR RAISING A REVENUE UPON FOREIGN AND DOMESTIC DISTILLED SPIRITS, IN RESPECT TO THE SUBDIVISIONS AND OFFICERS WHICH HAVE APPEARED TO ME NECESSARY, AND TO THE ALLOWANCES FOR THEIR RESPECTIVE SERVICES TO THE SUPERVISORS, INSPECTORS, AND OTHER OFFICERS OF INSPECTION; TOGETHER WITH ESTIMATES OF THE AMOUNT OF COMPENSATIONS AND CHARGES. GO: WASHINGTON. [Colophon:]
　　[Philadelphia:] Printed by Childs and Swaine. [1792.] pp. [7.] fol.
　　　　　　　　　　　　　　　　　　　　　　　　　BA. LOC.

24946　—— WAR DEPARTMENT. AUGUST 6, 1792. INFORMATION IS HEREBY GIVEN TO ALL THE MILITARY INVALIDS OF THE UNITED STATES THAT THE SUMS TO WHICH THEY ARE ENTITLED FOR SIX MONTHS OF THEIR ANNUAL PENSION, . . . WILL BE PAID BY THE COMMISSIONERS OF THE LOANS WITHIN THE STATES RESPECTIVELY UNDER THE USUAL REGULATIONS, VIZ. . . . . [Form of application.] H. KNOX, SECRETARY OF WAR.
　　[Philadelphia: Printed by Childs and Swaine. 1792.] Broadside.

24947　[U. S. arms.] THE UNITED STATES CHRONICLE: POLITICAL, COMMERCIAL, AND HISTORICAL. [R. I. arms.] VOL. IX. No. 417. THURSDAY, JANUARY 5, [—No. 468, THURSDAY, DECEMBER 27, 1792.]
　　Published by Bennett Wheeler, in Westminster-Street, Providence. 1792. fol.　　　　　　　　　　　　　　　　　　　　　　AAS. NYPL.
In June, the Printing-Office was removed to the Market-House chambers.

24948　THE UNIVERSAL ASYLUM, AND COLUMBIAN MAGAZINE FOR [JANUARY—JUNE] 1792. VOL. [IV.] [Cut.]
　　Philadelphia: Printed for the Proprietors, by William Young, Bookseller, No. 52, Second-Street. [1792.] pp. (2), 383, (1), 50, (6), plan of Washington. 8vo.　　　　　　　　　　　　　　　　AAS. HC. JCB. LOC.

THE UNIVERSAL ASYLUM, continued.

24949 —— THE UNIVERSAL ASYLUM AND COLUMBIAN MAGAZINE FOR [JULY–DECEMBER]
1792. VOL. [V.] [Cut.]
*Philadelphia: Printed for the Proprietors by W. Young Bookseller No. 52
Second Street.* [1792.] pp. (2), 432, (4), (4). 8vo. AAS. HC. JCB. LOC.
Owing to an official ruling denying monthly publications the use
of the mails, the Proprietors relinquished their undertaking and publication ceased with the December number. A futile attempt was made,
by John Parker, to continue it as *The Columbian Magazine, or Universal
Asylum,* of which a single number was issued in January, 1793.

24950 THE UNIVERSAL TONTINE.
ARTICLES OF ASSOCIATION.
[Philadelphia: 1792.] pp. 21. 8vo. MHS.

24951 UNIVERSALIST CHURCH.
EVANGELICAL PSALMS, HYMNS AND SPIRITUAL SONGS; SELECTED FROM VARIOUS
AUTHORS, . . . AND PUBLISHED BY A COMMITTEE OF THE CONVENTION OF THE
CHURCHES BELIEVING IN THE RESTITUTION OF ALL MEN, MET IN PHILADELPHIA,
MAY 25, 1791.
Philadelphia: Printed by Thomas Dobson, 1792. 12mo. BM.

24952 —— PSALMS, HYMNS AND SPIRITUAL SONGS; SELECTED AND ORIGINAL. DESIGNED
FOR THE USE OF THE CHURCH UNIVERSAL IN PUBLIC AND PRIVATE DEVOTION.
[Four lines of quotations.]
*Printed at Boston, by I. Thomas and E. T. Andrews. Faust's Statue, No.
45, Newbury Street.* MDCCXCII. pp. (2), (2), (8), (12), 267, (9). 12mo.
AAS. NYPL.
Compiled by George Richards and Oliver W. Lane, for Rev. John Mur-
ray's Church, in Boston. 37th Massachusetts District Copyright, issued
to George Richards and Oliver W. Lane, as Authors, 15 October, 1792.

24953 VAN SOLINGEN, HENRY M.
AN INAUGURAL DISSERTATION ON WORMS OF THE HUMAN INTESTINES, . . . AT
QUEEN'S COLLEGE, NEW-JERSEY.
New-York: Printed by T. & J. Swords, 1792. pp. 32. 8vo. SGO.

24954 DER VERBESSERTE HOCH-DEUTSCHE AMERICANISCHE LAND UND STAATS CALEN-
DER. AUF DAS JAHR . . . 1793. ZUM NUENTENMAL HERAUSGEGEBEN.
Friedrich Stadt, Maryland: Gedruckt bey Matthias Bärtgis. [1792.]

24955 VERMONT. STATE.
ACTS AND LAWS, PASSED BY THE LEGISLATURE OF THE STATE OF VERMONT, AT
THEIR SESSION AT RUTLAND, IN OCTOBER. 1792. WESTERN DISTRICT.
*Rutland: Printed by order of the Legislature, at the Press of Anthony Has-
well.* [1792.] pp. 95. 8vo. AAS.

24956 —— THE CONSTITUTION OF VERMONT, AS REVISED AND AMENDED BY THE COUNCIL
OF CENSORS, AT THEIR SESSION HOLDEN IN RUTLAND, OCTOBER 1792.
*Printed by order of the Council. By Anthony Haswell, Printer for the
State in the Western District, at the Rutland Press.* [1792.]

24957   VERMONT, continued.

—— A Journal of the proceedings of the General Assembly of the State of Vermont, at their session at Windsor, October 13th, 1791. [—3 November, 1791.]

Printed at Windsor by Alden Spooner, Printer to the State. MDCCXCII. pp. 49. 4to.   AAS. LOC.

24958   —— Proceedings of the Council of Censors of the State of Vermont, at their sessions holden at Rutland, in the year 1792. Published by order of the Council, for the inspection of the people, in conformity to the xl.th section of the Constitution. And for the consideration of a Convention of the freemen of this State, to convene at Windsor, on the first Wednesday of July 1793.

Printed by Anthony Haswell in Rutland. MDCC,XCII. pp. 80. 8vo. JCB.

24959   [Vt. arms.] THE VERMONT Gazette. [U. S. arms.] [Motto.] Vol. IX. Numb. 32. Whole numb. 448. Monday, January 2, [—No. 31 of Vol. x. Whole no. 499. Friday, December 28, 1792.]

Printed and published (every Monday) by Anthony Haswell, at his Office, a few rods south of the Courthouse, Bennington. 1792. fol.

24960   THE VERMONT [cut] Journal, and the universal advertiser. Vol. IX. No. 440. Tuesday, January 3, [—No. 452. Tuesday, March 27, 1792.]

Windsor: Printed by Alden Spooner, Printer to the State of Vermont. 1792. fol.

Continued as, *Spooner's Vermont Journal.*

24961   VERSCHIEDENE alter und neuere Geschichten von Erscheinungen der Geister, Und etwas von dem Zustand der Seelen Nach dem Tode Nebst verschiedenen Geschichtern solcher die auch jetzo noch im Leben sind. Vierte Auflage.

Chesnuthill, Gedruckt bey Samuel Saur. 1792. pp. 168. 12mo.   PSL.

24962   VINALL, John

The Preceptor's assistant, or student's guide: being a systematical treatise of arithmetic, both vulgar and decimal; calculated for the use of schools, counting-houses, and private families. Wherein the most practical branches of that important art are laid down in so plain and concise a manner, that persons of common capacity may become acquainted, in a short time, with that beneficial science. By John Vinall, teacher of the mathematicks and writing, in Boston. "Mathematica est ars artium."

Printed at Boston, by P. Edes, for Thomas & Andrews, Faust's Statue, No. 45, Newbury-Street. MDCCXCII. pp. 288. 12mo.   AAS. BA. NYPL.

Dedicated to John Hancock, Governor of Massachusetts. Approved by the School Committee of Boston. Contains a four-page list of subscriber's names. 31st Massachusetts District Copyright, issued to John Vinall, as Author, 21 May, 1792.

24963   VIRGINIA. State.

Acts passed at a General Assembly of the Commonwealth of Virginia. Begun and held at the capitol, in the city of Richmond, on Monday, the seventeenth day of October, one thousand seven hundred and ninety one [—20 December, 1791.] [Ornament.]

Richmond: Printed by Augustine Davis, Printer for the Public. M,DCC,-XCI. [1792.] pp. [44.] fol.   HSP. LOC. NYPL. VSL.

VIRGINIA, continued.

24964 —— DRAUGHTS OF SUCH BILLS, AS HAVE BEEN PREPARED BY THE COMMITTEE AP-POINTED UNDER THE ACT INTITULED, "AN ACT, TO AMEND AN ACT, INTITULED, AN ACT, CONCERNING A NEW EDITION OF THE LAWS OF THIS COMMONWEALTH, REFORMING CERTAIN RULES OF LEGAL CONSTRUCTION, AND PROVIDING FOR THE DUE PUBLICATION OF THE LAWS AND RESOLUTIONS OF EACH SESSION," PASSED ON THE TWENTY-THIRD DAY OF DECEMBER, IN THE YEAR ONE THOUSAND SEVEN HUN-DRED AND NINETY, ON THE SUBJECTS OF THOSE LAWS WHICH FROM THEIR MULTI-PLICITY REQUIRE TO BE REDUCED INTO SINGLE ACTS. TRANSMITTED TO THE EX-ECUTIVE ON THE TWENTY-SIXTH OF MARCH, ONE THOUSAND SEVEN HUNDRED AND NINETY-TWO, IN ORDER TO BE PRINTED. VOL. I.
Richmond : Printed by Augustine Davis, Printer for the Public. M,DCC,-XCII. pp, (2), [194.] fol. LOC. VSL.
The interleaved copy in the Virginia State Library has corrections and additions in manuscript.

24965 —— DRAUGHTS OF SUCH BILLS, AS HAVE BEEN PREPARED BY THE COMMITTEE APPOINTED UNDER THE ACT, . . . TRANSMITTED TO THE EXECUTIVE ON THE EIGHTEENTH OF AUGUST, ONE THOUSAND SEVEN HUNDRED AND NINETY-TWO, IN ORDER TO BE PRINTED. VOL. II.
Richmond : Printed by Augustine Davis, Printer for the Public. M,DCC,-XCII. pp. [90.] fol. LOC. VSL.

24966 —— JOURNAL OF THE HOUSE OF DELEGATES OF THE COMMONWEALTH OF VIRGINIA, BEGUN AND HELD AT THE CAPITOL, IN THE CITY OF RICHMOND, ON MONDAY, THE SEVENTEENTH DAY OF OCTOBER, ONE THOUSAND SEVEN HUNDRED AND NINETY-ONE [—20 December, 1791.] [Ornament.]
Richmond : Printed by Augustine Davis, Printer for the Public. M,DCC,-XCI. [1792.] pp. [147.] fol. LOC. VSL.

24967 —— JOURNAL OF THE SENATE OF VIRGINIA. OCTOBER SESSION, ANNO DOM. 1791. [—20 December, 1791.] [Ornament.]
Richmond : Printed by Thomas Nicolson, two doors above the Eagle-Tavern. M,VCC,XCI [*sic* 1792.] pp. [72.] fol. LOC.

24968 THE VIRGINIA ALMANACK FOR THE YEAR 1793.
Norfolk : Printed and sold by Baxter and Wilson, at their Office near the Town-Point. [1792.]

24969 THE VIRGINIA ALMANACK, FOR THE YEAR OF OUR LORD 1793. BEING THE FIRST AFTER LEAP YEAR. AND THE SEVENTEENTH OF AMERICAN INDEPENDENCE. CAL-CULATED TO ANSWER EITHER VIRGINIA OR NORTH-CAROLINA. THE TWELVE SIGNS OF THE ZODIACK. [Six lines.]
Petersburg : Printed by William Prentis. [1792.] pp. [36.] 12mo. NYPL.

24970 THE VIRGINIA ALMANACK, FOR THE YEAR OF OUR LORD 1793; BEING THE FIRST AFTER LEAP-YEAR, AND THE SEVENTEENTH OF AMERICAN INDEPENDENCE. [Three lines from] YOUNG.
Richmond : Printed and sold, wholesale and retail, by James Carey, at his Printing-Office, near Shockœ Warehouse. [1792.] pp. (32). 16mo. LOC. VHS.

24971 THE VIRGINIA AND FARMER'S ALMANACK, FOR THE YEAR 1793.
Winchester : Printed and sold by Richard Bowen. [1792.]

24972 VIRGINIA CHRONICLE AND PORTSMOUTH GENERAL ADVERTISER. NO. 146? SAT-URDAY, JUNE 9? [—No. 175. SATURDAY, DECEMBER 29, 1792.]
Norfolk : Printed by Daniel Baxter and Thomas Wilson, at their Printing-Office, near the Town Point. . . . 1792. fol.
In continuation of *The Norfolk and Portsmouth Chronicle.*

AUCTION VALUES

24973   THE VIRGINIA GAZETTE AND ALEXANDRIA ADVERTISER. [Motto.] VOL. III. No. 128. THURSDAY, JANUARY 5, [—VOL. IV. No. 179. THURSDAY, DECEMBER 27, 1792.]
> *Alexandria: Printed by Hanson and Bond.* 1792. fol.

24974   THE VIRGINIA GAZETTE, AND GENERAL ADVERTISER. VOL. VI. NUMB. 313. WEDNESDAY, JANUARY 4, [—VOL. VII. NUMB. 335. WEDNESDAY, DECEMBER 26. 1792.]
> *[Richmond:] Printed by Aug. Davis, Printer for the Public.* 1792. fol.

24975   VIRGINIA GAZETTE AND PETERSBURG INTELLIGENCER. VOL. VI. No. 288. THURSDAY, JANUARY 5, [—VOL. VII. No. 339. THURSDAY, DECEMBER 29, 1792.]
> *Petersburg: Printed by William Prentis.* 1792. fol.

24976   THE VIRGINIA GAZETTE, AND WEEKLY ADVERTISER. No. 479. FRIDAY, JANUARY 6, [—NUMBER 517. FRIDAY, DECEMBER 28, 1792.]
> *Published by Thomas Nicolson, two doors above the Eagle-Tavern, Richmond.* 1792. fol.

24977   THE VIRGINIA HERALD & FREDERICKSBURG ADVERTISER. VOL. V. NUMB. 240. THURSDAY, JANUARY 5, [—NUMB. 291. THURSDAY, DECEMBER 27, 1792.]
> *Fredericksburg: Printed by Timothy Green.* 1792. fol.

24978   THE VOCAL MUSE; OR LADIES SONGSTER: CONTAINING A COLLECTION OF ELEGANT SONGS, SELECTED FROM BRITISH AND AMERICAN AUTHORS.
> *[Philadelphia:] Published and sold at Messrs. T. Dobson and W. Young's Book Stores, Second Street, also at Mr. H. Kammerer's Store, No. 24, North Third Street.* 1792.

24979   WALKER, JAMES L.
PAINTING IN GENERAL. BY JAMES L. WALKER, MARKET-STREET, NEAR THE COURT-HOUSE, BALTIMORE. SIGN OF THE PAINTING MUSE. . . . [Colophon:]
> *Baltimore: Printed by Philip Edwards, in Market-Street, nearly opposite the Card Manufactory.* [1792.] Broadside. fol.   LOC.

24980   WARING, WILLIAM
THE NEW-JERSEY ALMANACK FOR THE YEAR OF OUR LORD 1793; BEING THE FIRST AFTER BISSEXTILE OR LEAP-YEAR, AND THE EIGHTEENTH YEAR OF AMERICAN INDEPENDENCE AFTER THE 4TH OF JULY NEXT. [Fourteen lines.] CAREFULLY CALCULATED FOR THE LATITUDE AND MERIDIAN OF PHILADELPHIA, BY WILLIAM WARING.
> *Trenton: Printed and sold by Isaac Collins.* [1792.] pp. (44). 12mo. LOC.

24981   —— POOR WILL'S ALMANACK, FOR THE YEAR OF OUR LORD 1793; BEING THE FIRST AFTER BISSEXTILE OR LEAP-YEAR: [Nineteen lines.] THE ASTRONOMICAL CALCULATIONS BY WILLIAM WARING.
> *Philadelphia: Printed and sold by Joseph Crukshank, No. 87, High-Street.* [1792.] pp. (44), (4). 12mo.   AAS. LOC.

24982   —— POOR WILL'S POCKET ALMANACK, FOR THE YEAR 1793; BEING THE FIRST AFTER BISSEXTILE OR LEAP-YEAR. [Eighteen lines.]
> *Philadelphia: Printed and sold by Joseph Crukshank, No. 87, High Street.* [1792.] pp. (40). 48mo.   LOC.

24983   —— POULSON'S TOWN AND COUNTRY ALMANAC, FOR THE YEAR OF OUR LORD, 1793; BEING THE FIRST AFTER LEAP-YEAR. [Three lines. Constellation. Three lines.]
> *Philadelphia: Printed and sold by Zachariah Poulson, junior, No. 30, Fourth-Street, near the University.* [1792.] pp. (40). 12mo.   AAS. LOC.

The astronomical calculations of this Almanac, by William Waring.

WARING, WILLIAM, continued.

24984 —— THE SOUTH-CAROLINA AND GEORGIA ALMANAC, FOR THE YEAR OF OUR LORD, 1793: BEING THE FIRST AFTER LEAP YEAR, AND (TILL THE 4TH OF JULY) THE SEVENTEENTH OF AMERICAN INDEPENDENCE. [Four lines.] BY WILLIAM WARING. [Six lines. Ornament.]
Charleston: Printed by Markland & M'Iver, No. 47, Bay. [1792.] pp. (40). 12mo. LOC.

24985 WARREN. RHODE ISLAND. WARREN ASSOCIATION.
MINUTES OF THE WARREN ASSOCIATION HELD AT THE BAPTIST MEETING-HOUSE IN HARVARD. M,DCC,XCII.
Printed by S. Hall, in Boston. MDCCXCII. pp. 11, (1). 12mo.
AAS. BM. JCB.

24986 THE WASHINGTON SPY. VOL. II. NUM. 74. THURSDAY, JANUARY 5, [—VOL. III. NUM. 125. THURSDAY, DECEMBER 27, 1792.]
Elizabeth (Hager's) Town, Printed by Stewart Herbert, 1792. fol.

24987 WATERHOUSE, BENJAMIN   1754 – 1846
THE RISE, PROGRESS, AND PRESENT STATE OF MEDICINE. A DISCOURSE, DELIVERED AT CONCORD, JULY 6TH, 1791, BEFORE THE MIDDLESEX MEDICAL ASSOCIATION. BY B. WATERHOUSE, M. D. PROFESSOR OF THE THEORY AND PRACTICE OF PHYSIC IN THE UNIVERSITY OF CAMBRIDGE, AND VICE-PRESIDENT OF THE ASSOCIATION. [One line of Latin from] SALLUST.
Boston: Printed by Thomas and John Fleet. M,DCC,XCII. pp. xii, 31.
8vo.   AAS. BA. BM. HC. JCB. MHS. NYHS. NYPL. SGO.

24988 WATTS, ISAAC   1674 – 1748
HORÆ LYRICÆ. POEMS, CHIEFLY OF THE LYRIC KIND, IN THREE BOOKS. I. TO DEVOTION AND PIETY. II. VIRTUE, HONOUR AND FRIENDSHIP. III. TO THE MEMORY OF THE DEAD. BY I. WATTS, D. D. THE TENTH EDITION, CORRECTED. [Three lines of Latin from] HOR. OD. I. IMITAT.
New-York: Printed by Hugh Gaine, at the Bible, in Hanover-Square. 1792.

24989 —— —— HORÆ LYRICÆ. POEMS CHIEFLY OF THE LYRIC KIND. IN THREE BOOKS. SACRED I. TO DEVOTION AND PIETY. II. TO VIRTUE, HONOUR, AND FRIENDSHIP. III. TO THE MEMORY OF THE DEAD. BY I. WATTS, D. D. [Three lines of Latin from] HOR. OD. I. IMITAT.
Philadelphia: Printed by R. Aitken & Son, No. 22. Market Street. M.DCC.XCII. pp. 277. 24mo.   AAS.

24990 —— HYMNS AND SPIRITUAL SONGS, IN THREE BOOKS. I. COLLECTED FROM THE SCRIPTURES. II. COMPOSED ON DIVINE SUBJECTS. III. PREPARED FOR THE LORD'S SUPPER. BY I. WATTS, D. D. [Five lines of quotations.]
New-York: Printed for Berry and Rogers and John Reid. M.DCC.XCII. pp. 285. 12mo.   JCB. NYPL.

25991 —— —— HYMNS AND SPIRITUAL SONGS, IN THREE BOOKS. I. COLLECTED FROM THE SCRIPTURES. II. COMPOSED ON DIVINE SUBJECTS. III. PREPARED FOR THE LORD'S SUPPER. BY I. WATTS, D. D.
New-York: Printed and sold by William Durell. 1792.

25992 —— DR. WATTS' PLAIN AND EASY CATECHISMS FOR CHILDREN, AND PRESERVATIVE FROM THE SINS AND FOLLIES OF CHILDHOOD AND YOUTH; TO WHICH IS ADDED THE SHORTER CATECHISM OF THE ASSEMBLY OF DIVINES AT WESTMINSTER, WITH EXPLANATORY [*sic*] NOTES.
Exeter: Printed and sold by Henry Ranlet—1792. pp. 96. 24mo. LOC.

WATTS, Isaac, continued.

24993 —— The Young child's catechism, to begin at three or four years' old. *Hartford: Printed by Hudson & Goodwin.* 1792. pp. 14. 16mo.

24994 WEATHERWISE, Abraham, pseudonym
The Massachusetts and New-Hampshire Almanack, for the year of our Lord, 1793. [Portrait of Author. Four lines.] *Boston: Printed and sold by J. White and C. Cambridge, near Charles River Bridge.* [1792.] pp. (24). 12mo. AAS. LOC.
The Author's Greeting, says: Given under my hand, at my cottage a few miles from Boston, the 12th day of September, in the year of our Lord, 1792. A. Weatherwise.

24995 —— The New-England callendar: or Almanack, for the year of our Lord, 1793. . . . By Abraham Weatherwise.
Boston: Printed and sold by Nathaniel Coverly . . . [1792.] pp. (24). 12mo.

24996 THE FIRST edition of The Weavers' draft-book, and clothiers' assistant, printed on a beautiful copperplate, containing a choice collection of 52 drafts in the figured line of weaving, with proper directions how to draw in, tie up, and tread down each figure, and to size cotton warps; together with some valuable receipts in the dying-line, all performed with American materials. It is hoped the real friends to American manufactures will encourage this work, as it is calculated and designed to diffuse manufacturing knowledge through the States, and is the first book of the kind that has ever made its appearance in America (or perhaps in Europe). The dying-receipts are valuable, and the whole calculated for the domestic use of the farmer and manufacturer.
Baltimore: Sold, wholesale and retail, by John & George Hagerty, Stationers, in Water-Street. 1792.
"Compiled by an experienced weaver, of Harford County, in this State."

24997 WEBSTER, Noah, junior 1758 – 1843
An American selection of lessons in reading and speaking. Calculated to improve the minds and refine the taste of youth. And also, to instruct them in the geography, history, and politics of the United States. To which are prefixed, rules in elocution, and directions for expressing the principal passions of the mind. Being the third part of a Grammatical Institute of the English language. By Noah Webster, jun. esquire. Author of "Dissertations on the English language," "Collection of essays and fugitive writings," &c. Thomas and Andrews's second edition. With many corrections and improvements, by the author. [Two lines from] Mirabeau.
Printed at Boston, by Isaiah Thomas and Ebenezer T. Andrews at Faust's Statue, No. 45, Newbury Street. Sold, wholesale and retail, at their Bookstore; by said Thomas at his Bookstore in Worcester, and by the Booksellers in town and country. MDCCXCII. pp. 239, (1), portrait. 12mo. AAS. BM. NYPL.
The frontispiece portrait of Noah Webster, jun. esq. is headed: Part III.
Thomas & Andrews's second edition.

24998 —— —— An American selection of lessons in reading and speaking. Calculated to improve the minds and refine the taste of youth. And also to instruct them in the geography, history, and politicks of the United States. To which is prefixed, rules in elocution, and directions for expressing the principal passions of the mind. Being the third part of a Grammatical Institute of the English language. By Noah Webster, jun'r, esquire. The seventh Connecticut edition. [Two lines from] Mirabeau.
Hartford: Printed and sold by Hudson and Goodwin. [With the privilege of copy-right.] M,DCC,XCII. pp. [252.] 12mo. AAS. NYPL.

WEBSTER, Noah, junior, continued.

24999 —— The American spelling book: containing an easy standard of pronunciation. Being the first part of a Grammatical institute of the English language. By Noah Webster, jun. esquire. Author of "Dissertations on the English language." "Collection of essays and fugitive writings" &c. Thomas and Andrews's fourth edition.

Printed at Boston, by Isaiah Thomas and Ebenezer T. Andrews. At Faust's Statue, No. 45, Newbury Street. MDCCXCII. BM.

25000 —— —— The American spelling book: containing an easy standard of pronunciation. Being the first part of a Grammatical institute of the English language. By Noah Webster, jun'r, esquire. The fourteenth edition.

New-York: Printed for Samuel Campbell, Robert Hodge, . . . 1792.

Advertised by Samuel Campbell as "A neat and accurate edition (being the fourteenth of the American Spelling Book,) with plates, improvements, and frontispiece." Under date of September 15, 1792, the Author states, in the Connecticut Journal that the fourteenth edition of his Spelling book, printed in New York, for Samuel Campbell, Robert Hodge, &c. this year, is "the most incorrect edition he had ever seen. There are in it between two and three hundred errors in printing, great numbers of them very material ones, not to say anything of two or three sheets of the work which are printed on bad paper and old worn out letters: . . . that on account of the multitude of errors in this edition, I utterly disclaim it."

25001 —— A Grammatical institute of the English language; comprising an easy, concise and systematic method of education. Designed for the use of English schools in America. In three parts. Part second. Containing a plain and comprehensive grammar, grounded on the true principles and idioms of the language. By Noah Webster, jun. esquire. Author of "Dissertations on the English language," "Collection of essays and fugitive writings," &c. Thomas and Andrews's second edition. With many corrections and improvements, by the author.

Printed at Boston, by Isaiah Thomas and Ebenezer T. Andrews. At Faust's Statue, No. 45, Newbury Street. Sold, wholesale and retail, at their Bookstore; by said Thomas at his Bookstore in Worcester, and by the Booksellers in town and country. MDCCXCII. pp. 120, portrait, 12mo. AAS. BU. HC. LOC. NYPL. YC.

The frontispiece portrait of Noah Webster, jun. esq. is headed: Part II.
Thomas & Andrews's second edition.

25002 —— —— A Grammatical institute of the English language; comprising an easy, concise and systematic method of education. Designed for the use of English schools in America. In three parts. Part second. Containing a plain and comprehensive grammar, grounded on the true principles and idioms of the language. By Noah Webster, jun. esquire. Author of "Dissertations on the English language," "Collection of essays and fugitive writings," &c. The third Connecticut edition.

Printed at Hartford, by Hudson and Goodwin. MDCCXCII. pp. 131. 12mo. BM. LOC. YC.

In this edition the Appendix is enlarged and rewritten.

25003 —— The Prompter: or a commentary on common sayings and subjects, which are full of common sense, the best sense in the world. "To see all others faults and feel our own."

Albany: Printed by Charles R. & George Webster. 1792. pp. 92. 16mo.

WEBSTER, NOAH, JUNIOR, continued.

25004 —— — THE PROMPTER; OR A COMMENTARY ON COMMON SAYINGS AND SUBJECTS, WHICH ARE FULL OF COMMON SENSE, THE BEST SENSE IN THE WORLD. "TO SEE ALL OTHERS FAULTS AND FEEL OUR OWN."
Printed at Boston, by I. Thomas and E. T. Andrews, at Faust's Statue, No. 45, Newbury Street. MDCCXCII. pp. 96. 12mo.   AAS. BM. LOC. NYPL. YC.

25005 —— — THE PROMPTER; OR A COMMENTARY ON COMMON SAYINGS AND SUBJECTS, WHICH ARE FULL OF COMMON SENSE, THE BEST SENSE IN THE WORLD. "TO SEE ALL OTHERS FAULTS AND FEEL OUR OWN."
New-London: Printed by Timothy Green and Son. 1792.

25006 —— — THE PROMPTER; OR A COMMENTARY ON COMMON SAYINGS AND SUBJECTS, WHICH ARE FULL OF COMMON SENSE, THE BEST SENSE IN THE WORLD. "TO SEE ALL OTHERS FAULTS AND FEEL OUR OWN."
Philadelphia: Printed by Charles Cist, 1792.

25007 —— — THE PROMPTER: TO WHICH IS ADDED THE WHISTLE, A TRUE STORY; BY DR. FRANKLIN. I HAVE SEEN, AND I HAVE NOT SEEN; BY GOVERNOR LIVINGSTON. REMARKABLE SPEECHES OF GOOD OLD ROGER PINDAR, ESQ. A VULGAR ERROR. THE BEE. THE DRONE, IN ANSWER TO THE ABOVE, &C. &C. BEING AMERICAN PRODUCTIONS, AND CALCULATED TO INSTRUCT AND AMUSE THE READER.
Burlington: Printed by Isaac Neale. M.DCC.XCII. pp. [50.] 12mo. NYPL.

25008 THE WEEKLY MUSEUM. VOL. IV. NUMBER 191. SATURDAY, JANUARY 7, [—VOL. V. NUMBER 242. SATURDAY, DECEMBER 29, 1792.]
New-York: Printed and published by John Harrisson, at his Printing-Office, No. 3, Peck-Slip. 1792. 4to.

25009 THE WEEKLY REGISTER. VOL. I. No. 6. TUESDAY, JANUARY 3, [—VOL. II. No. 5. TUESDAY, DECEMBER 25, 1792.]
Norwich: Published by Ebenezer Bushnell, 24 rods west of the Meeting-House. 1792. fol.   LOC.
On June 7th, Ebenezer Bushnell and Thomas Hubbard, his brother-in-law "entered a partnership in the Printing and Stocking-Weaving business, under the firm of Bushnell & Hubbard." A full-page index for the first year forms a part of the issue for November 20th.

25010 DIE WEGE UND WERKE GOTTES IN DER SEELE.
Chesnuthill: Gedruckt bey Samuel Saur. 1792. pp. 59. 12mo.

25011 WESLEY, JOHN   1703 – 1791
EXPLANATORY NOTES UPON THE NEW TESTAMENT. BY JOHN WESLEY, M. A. LATE FELLOW OF LINCOLN-COLLEGE, OXFORD. VOLUME THE SECOND [—THIRD.] THE FIRST AMERICAN EDITION.
Philadelphia: Printed by Joseph Crukshank: Sold by John Dickins, No 43, Fourth-Street, near the corner of Race-Street. MDCCXCII. 2vols. 8vo.

25012 —— THE EXTRAORDINARY CASE OF ELIZABETH HOBSON; EXTRACTED FROM THE 15TH JOURNAL OF THE REV. MR. JOHN WESLEY.
Philadelphia: Printed by Johnson & Justice, Franklin's Head, No. 41, Chesnut street. 1792.

25013 —— THE NATURE AND DESIGN OF CHRISTIANITY. EXTRACTED FROM A LATE AUTHOR. [Moses Hemmenway.] THE NINTH EDITION. [Two lines of verse.]
Providence: Reprinted by John Carter. M,DCC,XCII. pp. (16). 8vo.
Reprinted in Boston, in 1804.   AAS. NYPL.

25014 —— THOUGHTS UPON SLAVERY.
Philadelphia: Printed by Parry Hall, No. 149, in Chesnut Street; and sold by John Dickins. 1792.

25015   WEST, BENJAMIN   1730 – 1813
AN ASTRONOMICAL DIARY, KALENDAR, OR, ALMANACK, FOR THE YEAR OF OUR LORD,
1793. AND FROM THE CREATION OF THE WORLD 5742. AND, TILL JULY 4TH,
THE 17TH OF AMERICAN INDEPENDENCE. BEING THE FIRST AFTER BISSEXTILE
OR LEAP YEAR. WHEREIN ARE CONTAINED. ALL THINGS NECESSARY TO SUCH A
COMPOSITION. ADAPTED TO THE HORIZON AND MERIDIAN OF HARTFORD, LAT. 41
DEG. 54 MIN. TO THE WESTWARD OF THE ROYAL OBSERVATORY AT GREENWICH
(ACCORDING TO THE LATEST OBSERVATIONS)—BUT MAY SERVE INDIFFERENTLY FOR
ALL THE TOWNS IN CONNECTICUT AND ADJACENT STATES. BY ISAAC BICKERSTAFF,
ESQ. [Four lines of verse.]
           Hartford: Printed for Nathaniel Patten. [1792.] pp. (24). 12mo.
                                                       AAS. CHS.
Apparently the same as Strong's Astronomical diary, etc. for 1793.
Printed for Nathaniel Patten this year.

25016   —— BICKERSTAFF'S GENUINE BOSTON ALMANACK OR FEDERAL CALENDAR, FOR
1793. FIRST AFTER LEAP-YEAR; SEVENTEENTH OF INDEPENDENCY. [Cut of
astronomer taking observation.]
           [Boston:] Printed by E. Russell, cheap to travelling-traders and others.
[1792.] pp. (24). 12mo.   AAS.

25017   —— — BICKERSTAFF'S GENUINE BOSTON ALMANACK OR FEDERAL CALENDAR, FOR
1793. FIRST AFTER LEAP-YEAR; SEVENTEENTH OF INDEPENDENCY. [Cut of
astronomer taking observation.] SECOND EDITION.
           [Boston:] Printed by E. Russell, cheap to travelling-traders and others.
[1792.] pp. (24). 12mo.   NYPL.

25018   —— BICKERSTAFF'S GENUINE MASSACHUSETTS, NEW-HAMPSHIRE, VERMONT, RHODE-
ISLAND, AND CONNECTICUT ALMANACK, FOR THE YEAR OF OUR LORD, 1793.
           Boston: Printed and sold by Nathaniel Coverly. [1792.]

25019   —— THE MASSACHUSETTS, CONNECTICUT, NEWHAMPSHIRE, RHODE-ISLAND, AND
VERMONT ALMANACK, FOR THE YEAR OF OUR LORD, 1793. [Cut.] . . . BY ISAAC
BICKERSTAFF, ESQ.
           *Boston: Printed and sold by Nathaniel Coverly, by the gross, or single
dozen.* [1792.] pp. (24). 12mo.   AAS. LOC.

25020   —— — THE MASSACHUSETTS, CONNECTICUT, NEWHAMPSHIRE, RHODE-ISLAND, AND
VERMONT ALMANACK, FOR THE YEAR OF OUR LORD, 1793. [Cut.] BEING FIRST
AFTER BISSEXTILE, OR LEAP YEAR, AND THE 17TH OF THE INDEPENDENCE OF
AMERICA. CALCULATED FOR THE LATITUDE OF BOSTON, BUT WILL SERVE FOR
EITHER OF THE ADJACENT STATES. BY ISAAC BICKERSTAFF, ESQ.
           *Boston: Printed by Nathaniel Coverly, and sold by James Gardner, nearly
opposite the Court-House Providence.* [1792.] pp. (24). 12mo.   AAS. NYPL.

25021   —— — THE MASSACHUSETTS, CONNECTICUT, NEWHAMPSHIRE, RHODE-ISLAND, AND
VERMONT ALMANACK, FOR THE YEAR OF OUR LORD, 1793. . . . BY ISAAC BICK-
ERSTAFF, ESQ.
           Boston: Printed and sold by Wm. T. Clapp. No. 90, Newbury Street.
[1792.] pp. (24). 12mo.   AAS.

25022   —— THE NEW-ENGLAND ALMANACK, OR LADY'S AND GENTLEMAN'S DIARY, FOR THE
YEAR OF OUR LORD CHRIST 1793: BEING THE FIRST AFTER BISSEXTILE, OR LEAP-
YEAR, AND THE SEVENTEENTH OF AMERICAN INDEPENDENCE, WHICH COM-
MENCED JULY 4, 1776. [Twenty-one lines.] BY ISAAC BICKERSTAFF, ESQ;
PHILOM. [Four lines of verse.]
           *Providence: Printed and sold, wholesale and retail, by John Carter, near
the State-House.* [1792.] pp. (24). 12mo.   AAS· LOC. RIHS.

25023   WEST, BENJAMIN, continued.

—— —— THE NEW-ENGLAND ALMANACK, OR LADY'S AND GENTLEMAN'S DIARY, FOR THE YEAR OF OUR LORD 1793. BY ISAAC BICKERSTAFF, ESQ; CONTAINING, BESIDES THE USUAL ASTRONOMICAL CALCULATIONS (WHICH ARE ALLOWED TO BE VERY AC- CURATE) A VARIETY OF MATTER, USEFUL AND ENTERTAINING.

Providence: Printed by John Carter. Sold by Jacob Richardson, esq; in Newport. [1792.]

25024   —— BICKERSTAFF'S NEW-ENGLAND ALMANACK, FOR THE YEAR OF OUR LORD 1793. . . .

Printed at Norwich, by John Trumbull. [1792.] pp. (24). 12mo.

25025   —— A SHEET ALMANACK FOR THE YEAR 1793.

Norwich: Printed by John Trumbull, 1792. Broadside. fol.

25026   —— THE NEW-ENGLAND CALLENDAR [*sic*]: OR ALMANACK, FOR THE YEAR OF OUR LORD, 1793. [Cut. Four lines.] BY ISAAC BICKERSTAFFE.

Boston: Printed and sold by Nathaniel Coverly, by the gross or single doz- en. [1792.] pp. (24). 12mo.   BPL. LOC

25027   —— WHEELER'S NORTH-AMERICAN CALENDAR, OR AN ALMANACK, FOR THE YEAR OF OUR LORD 1793: BEING THE FIRST AFTER BISSEXTILE OR LEAP YEAR, AND THE SEVENTEENTH OF AMERICAN INDEPENDENCE. [Cut of] ARMS OF THE UNITED STATES.

Printed at Providence, and sold by B. Wheeler by the groce, dozen or single, cheap for cash. [1792.] pp. (24). 12mo.   AAS. LOC. RIHS.

25028   WESTERN ADVERTISER AND CHAMBERSBURG WEEKLY NEWSPAPER. JANUARY– DECEMBER, 1792.

Chambersburg: Printed by William Davison. 1792. fol.

25029   THE WESTERN [cut] STAR. VOL. III. No. 6. WHOLE NO. 110. TUESDAY, JANUARY 3, [—No. 161. TUESDAY, DECEMBER 25, 1792.]

Printed and published by Loring Andrews, Stockbridge (Massachusetts). 1792. fol.   AAS.

25030   WESTMINSTER ASSEMBLY OF DIVINES.

THE SHORTER CATECHISM, WITH SCRIPTURE PROOFS AT LARGE. TO WHICH IS ADDED, A FORM OF PRAYER, AND SCRIPTURE EXPRESSIONS, DESIGNED AS A GUIDE TO YOUTH, IN THEIR FIRST ATTEMPTS IN THIS IMPORTANT DUTY.

Albany: Printed and sold by Charles R. & George Webster, 1792.

25031   WETHERILL, SAMUEL   1736 – 1816

THE DIVINITY OF JESUS CHRIST PROVED; BEING A REPLY TO DR. JOSEPH PRIEST- LEY'S "APPEAL TO THE SERIOUS AND CANDID "PROFESSORS OF CHRISTIANITY." AND TO A PAMPHLET PUBLISHED BY LEWIS NICHOLA, ENTITLED "THE DIVINITY OF JESUS CHRIST, CONSIDERED FROM SCRIPTURE EVIDENCES, &C." WITH SOME OBSERVATIONS UPON ARIANISM. BY SAMUEL WETHERILL. [Seven lines of Scripture texts.]

Philadelphia: Printed by Francis Bailey and Thomas Lang. M,DCC,- XCII. pp. (68), (1). 12mo.   AAS.

25032   WHELPLEY, Samuel, junior   1766 – 1817
Animadversions on mr. [Jeremiah] Day's sermon on infant baptism, with some remarks on the mode of baptism, and power of ordination; in several letters to a friend.
     Danbury: Printed by Douglas & Ely. 1792. pp. 62, (1). 8vo.

25033   WHITEFIELD, George   1714 – 1770
A Sermon, on Luke 8th, 18. Take heed therefore how you hear. Preached in one of the churches in London. By George Whitefield, before he embarked the first time for Georgia. [Three lines from] Mat. 16. 26. [Publisher's monogram.]
     Re-printed, 1792. pp. (16). 8vo.   JCB. NYPL.

25034   WHITMAN, Samuel   1752 – 1827
Half-title: Two sermons, on the importance of just and accurate distinctions in preaching.
     Title: Two sermons, the substance of which was preached at the ordination of the rev. Moses Hallock, to the pastoral care of the church in Plainfield, July 11, 1792. By Samuel Whitman, a. b. pastor of the church in Goshen. [Four lines from] Apostle Paul.
     Northampton: Printed by William Butler.—1792. pp. 43. 8vo.
                                          AAS. BA. BM. JCB. NYPL.

25035   WHITNEY, Eli   1765 – 1825
An Oration on the death of mr. Robert Grant, a member of the senior class, in Yale-College, Connecticut: who died on the fourth of April, 1792, ætat. xxiii. By Eli Whitney, a classmate of the deceased.
     New-Haven: Printed by Thomas and Samuel Green. [1792.] pp. (15). 8vo.   AAS.

25036   WILKINS, Henry
An Original essay on animal motion, . . .
     Philadelphia: 1792. 8vo.   BM.

25037   WILKINSON, Edward   1727 – 1809
Wisdom, a poem.
     Printed by M. Croswell, & Co. Catskill-Landing. 1792.

25038   WILLIAM and MARY. University of.
Statutes of the University of William & Mary. [Ornament.]
     Richmond: Printed by Augustine Davis, Printer for the Public. M,DCC,-XCII. pp. [16.] 16mo.   VSL.

25039   WILLIAMS, Helen Maria   1762 – 1827
Letters from France: containing many new ancedotes relative to the French Revolution, and the present state of French manners. By Helen Maria Williams. Vol. ii.
     Boston: Printed for Thomas and Andrews, David West, and E. Larkin, jun. M.DCC.XCII. pp. (2), (2), 138. 12mo.   AAS. NYPL.
     The first volume, printed in 1791, with the title: "Letters on the French Revolution."

25040   WILLIAMS, JONATHAN, JUNIOR   1750 – 1815
MEMOIR ON THE USE OF THE THERMOMETER IN NAVIGATION. PRESENTED TO THE
AMERICAN PHILOSOPHICAL SOCIETY, HELD AT PHILADELPHIA, FOR PROMOTING
USEFUL KNOWLEDGE. EXTRACTED FROM THE THIRD VOLUME OF THEIR TRANSAC-
TIONS.
> *Philadelphia:* 1792. pp. 82. 4to.   BM. NYHS.

25041   WILLIAMS, NATHAN   1735 – 1829
AN ENQUIRY CONCERNING THE DESIGN AND IMPORTANCE OF CHRISTIAN BAPTISM &
DISCIPLINE. IN WAY OF DIALOGUE BETWEEN A MINISTER AND HIS NEIGHBOUR. . . .
> *Printed at Boston, by Isaiah Thomas and Ebenezer T. Andrews, Faust's
> Statue, No. 45, Newbury Street.* M,DCC,XCII. pp. [70.] 8vo.
>> AAS. JCB. LOC. MHS.

25042   —— — AN ENQUIRY CONCERNING THE DESIGN AND IMPORTANCE OF CHRISTIAN
BAPTISM & DISCIPLINE. IN WAY OF DIALOGUE BETWEEN A MINISTER AND HIS
NEIGHBOUR. . . . [Five lines of quotations.] SECOND EDITION. [With an
appendix.]
> *Printed at Boston, by Isaiah Thomas and Ebenezer T. Andrews, Faust's
> Statue, No. 45, Newbury Street.* M,DCC,XCII. pp. [70.] 8vo.
>> AAS. BA. JCB. LOC. MHS.

25043   WILLIAMS, SAMUEL   1743 – 1817
THE EVIDENCE OF PERSONAL CHRISTIANITY, REPRESENTED IN A DISCOURSE DELIV-
ERED JUNE 17TH, 1792, AT RUTLAND, IN THE STATE OF VERMONT. BY SAMUEL
WILLIAMS, LL. D.
> *Printed in Rutland, [Vermont] by Anthony Haswell.* M,DCC,XCII. pp.
> 32. 8vo.   BM.

25044   —— THE LOVE OF OUR COUNTRY REPRESENTED AND URGED, IN A DISCOURSE, DE-
LIVERED OCTOBER 21ST, 1792, AT RUTLAND, IN THE STATE OF VERMONT; BY
SAMUEL WILLIAMS, LL. D. PRINTED AT THE REQUEST OF SEVERAL MEMBERS OF
THE LEGISLATURE.
> *From the Press of A. Haswell in Rutland.* M,DCC,XCII. pp. 28. 8vo.

25045   WILMER, JAMES JONES   1749 –
MEMOIRS BY JAMES WILMER.
> *Baltimore: Printed by Samuel & John Adams.* 1792. pp. 16. 16mo. BA.

25046   —— A SERMON, ON THE DOCTRINE OF THE NEW-JERUSALEM CHURCH: BEING THE
FIRST PROMULGATED WITHIN THE UNITED STATES OF AMERICA. DELIVERED ON
THE FIRST SUNDAY IN APRIL, 1792, IN THE COURT-HOUSE OF BALTIMORE-TOWN,
BY JAMES WILMER, EXAMINED AND APPROVED FOR THE MINISTERIAL OFFICE, BY
THE LATE DR. TERRICK, BISHOP OF LONDON.
> *Baltimore: Printed and sold by William Goddard and James Angell.*
> M.DCC.XCII. pp. (23). 8vo.   BA. LOC.

25047   WILSON, RACHEL
A DISCOURSE, DELIVERED ON SATURDAY, THE 10TH DAY OF AUGUST, 1769. AT THE
FRIENDS' MEETING-HOUSE, IN BEEKMAN'S PRECINCT, DUCHESS COUNTY, IN THE
PROVINCE OF NEW-YORK. BY THE CELEBRATED RACHEL WILSON, (ONE OF THE
PEOPLE CALLED QUAKERS). TO A NUMEROUS AUDIENCE OF DIFFERENT PER-
SUASION. TAKEN IN SHORT HAND, FROM THE MOUTH OF THE SPEAKER, BY ONE
OF THE AUDIENCE.
> *Dover: Printed by Eliphalet Ladd,* 1792.

25048   WINCHESTER, ELHANAN   1751 – 1797
AN ELEGY ON THE DEATH OF THE REV'D MR. JOHN WESLEY. BY ELHANAN WIN-
CHESTER.

> *Philadelphia: Printed and sold by Johnson & Justice, Franklin's Head,
> No. 41, Chesnut street.* 1792.

25049   —— TWO LECTURES ON THE PROPHECIES THAT REMAIN TO BE FULFILLED. DELIV-
ERED IN THE BOROUGH OF SOUTHWARK, AS ALSO AT THE CHAPEL IN GLASS-HOUSE
YARD, LONDON, IN THE YEAR MDCCLXXXIX. BY ELHANAN WINCHESTER. [TWO
lines of Scripture text.]

> *Norwich: Printed by John Trumbull,* MDCCXCII. pp. 77, (1) 8vo. JCB.

25050   —— THE UNIVERSAL RESTORATION, EXHIBITED IN FOUR DIALOGUES BETWEEN A MIN-
ISTER AND HIS FRIEND; COMPREHENDING THE SUBSTANCE OF SEVERAL REAL CON-
VERSATIONS WHICH THE AUTHOR HAD WITH VARIOUS PERSONS, BOTH IN AMERICA
AND EUROPE, ON THAT INTERESTING SUBJECT, CHIEFLY DESIGNED FULLY TO STATE,
AND FAIRLY TO ANSWER THE MOST COMMON OBJECTIONS THAT ARE BROUGHT
AGAINST IT FROM THE SCRIPTURES. A NEW EDITION. BY ELHANAN WINCHESTER.
TO THIS EDITION IS PREFIXED, A BRIEF ACCOUNT OF THE MEANS AND MANNER OF
THE AUTHOR'S EMBRACING THESE SENTIMENTS, INTERMIXED WITH SOME SKETCHES
OF HIS LIFE DURING FOUR YEARS.

> *Philadelphia: Printed by T. Dobson, at the Stone-House, No. 41, South
> Second-Street.* M,DCC,XCII. pp. lvi, 220. 12mo.   AAS. JCB. LCP.

25051   EIN WOHL EINGERICHTETES DEUTSCHES A. B. C. BUCHSTABIR-UND LESEBUCH ZUM
GEBRAUCH DEUTSCHER SCHULEN.

> *Germantaun: Gedruckt und zu haben bey Michael Billmeyer.* 1792.

34th Pennsylvania District Copyright, issued to Michael Billmeyer,
as Proprietor, 1 May, 1792.

25052   WOLCOT, JOHN   1738 – 1819
THE POETICAL WORKS OF PETER PINDAR, ESQ. A DISTANT RELATION TO THE POET
OF THEBES. TO WHICH ARE PREFIXED, MEMOIRS AND ANECDOTES OF THE
AUTHOR. A NEW EDITION, WITH ADDITIONS. VOL. I. [—II.]

> *Philadelphia: Printed for W. Spotswood, and Rice & Co.* M,DCC,XCII.
> 2vols. pp. [viii], (307), (1); iv, (324). 12mo.   AAS.

"To accommodate purchasers of the first and second American editions
in one or two volumes a few copies of the additional Poems have been
printed in one volume, by which sets may be completed."

"The pieces added in the new edition are the following—Peter's Pension; Peter's Prophecy; Sir Joseph Banks and the Emperor of Morocco; An Epistle to a falling minister; Subjects for painters; Expostu-
latory Odes, &c. &c."

25053   WOLLSTONECRAFT, afterwards GODWIN, MARY   1759 – 1797
A VINDICATION OF THE RIGHTS OF WOMAN. WITH STRICTURES ON MORAL AND PO-
LITICAL SUBJECTS. BY MARY WOLLSTONECRAFT. THE FIRST AMERICAN EDITION.

> *Philadelphia: Printed by William Gibbons, No. 144, North Third Street.*
> 1792.

25054   —— — A VINDICATION OF THE RIGHTS OF WOMAN: WITH STRICTURES ON POLITICAL
AND MORAL SUBJECTS. BY MARY WOLLSTONECRAFT. [Publisher's monogram.]

> *Printed at Boston, by Peter Edes for Thomas and Andrews, Faust's Statue,
> No. 45, Newbury-Street.* MDCCXCII. pp, (2), 340. 8vo.   AAS. BPL.

25055 WOODHOUSE, James   1770 – 1809
An Inaugural dissertation, on the chemical and medical properties of the
Persimmon tree, and the analysis of astringent vegetables; submitted
to the examination of the Revd. John Ewing, s. t. p. provost; the trustees and medical professors. of the University of Pennsylvania; for the
degree of doctor of medicine. By James Woodhouse, a. m. honorary member of the American and Philadelphia Medical Societies, [Two lines of
verse from] Gray.
            Philadelphia: Printed by William Woodhouse. [1792.] pp. 34. 8vo.
                                                     AAS. LCP. SGO.

25056 WOODMAN, Joseph   – 1807
A Sermon, on christian candour and condescension: preached at the baptism of mr. Levi Robinson, by immersion, November 22, 1791.
            Printed at Concord, by George Hough, for the Subscribers. M,DCC,XCII.
            pp. (30). 8vo.   BM. JCB. LOC.

25057 WOODS'S Newark Gazette and New-Jersey Advertiser. Vol. i. Numb. 34.
Thursday, January 5, [—Numb. 85. Thursday, December 27, 1792.]
            Newark, New-Jersey, Printed by John Woods. 1792. fol.

25058 WOODS'S Town and country Almanac, and ephemeris of the motion of the
sun and moon—the true places and aspects of the planets—the rising,.
setting and southing of the moon, for the year of our Lord 1793.
            Newark: Printed by John Woods. [1792.]

25059 WORKMAN, Benjamin
Father Tammany's Almanac for the year 1793; being the first after leap-
year. [Eighteen lines. Cut.]
            *Philadelphia, Printed and sold by John M'Culloch, No. 1. North Third-
            street.* [1792.] pp. (36). 12mo.   LOC.

25060 YALE COLLEGE.
Illustrissimo Samueli Huntington, arm. ll. d.   Reipublicæ Connecticut-
tensis Gubernatori: honoratissimo Olivero Wolcott, arm. vice-gubernatori: clarissimisque proceribus politiæ nostræ civilis: reverendo pariter
ac honorando Ezræ Stiles, s. t. d. ll. d. Collegii Yalensis præsidi. . . .
Hasce Theses quas in comitiis publicis Collegii Yalensis, . . . Habita in
comitiis Academicis Novo Portu Connecticutensium, m,dcc,xcii.
            *Novo-Portu: E. Typis Thomæ et Samuelis Green, Universitatis Typograph-
            orum.* [1792.] Broadside. fol.

25061 YOUNG, Arthur   1741 – 1820
Rural economy, or essays on the practical parts of husbandry: designed to
explain several of the most important methods of conducting farms
of various kinds; including many useful hints to gentlemen farmers,
relative to the economical management of their business. To which is
added, The Rural Socrates, being memoirs of a country philosopher. By
the Author of the Farmer's letters. [Two lines of Latin.] The third
edition.
            Burlington, Printed by Isaac Neale. M,DCC,XCII. pp. 299, (1). 8vo.
            Second title: The Rural Socrates: or a description of the economical
and moral conduct of a country philosopher. Written in German by mr.
Hirzel, president of the Physical Society of Zurich. [Three lines of
Latin from] Cato.   AAS. BA.

25062   YOUNG, WILLIAM
     BOOKS FOR SALE, AT WILLIAM YOUNG'S BOOK AND STATIONARY STORE, No. 52, SEC-
     OND-STREET, THE CORNER OF CHESNUT-STREET. 1792.
       [Philadelphia: Printed by William Young, 1792.] pp. 12. 12mo.   LOC.

25063   THE YOUNG CLERK'S MAGAZINE: OR, ENGLISH LAW-REPOSITORY: CONTAINING, A VA-
     RIETY OF THE MOST USEFUL PRECEDENTS OF ARTICLES OF AGREEMENT, BONDS,
     BILLS, RECOGNIZANCES, RELEASES, LETTERS AND WARRANTS OF ATTORNEY,
     AWARDS, BILLS OF SALE, GIFTS, GRANTS, LEASES, ASSIGNMENTS, MORTGAGES, SUR-
     RENDERS, JOINTURES, COVENANTS, COPARTNERSHIPS, CHARTERPARTIES, LETTERS
     OF LICENSE, COMPOSITIONS, CONVEYANCES, PARTITIONS, WILLS, AND ALL OTHER IN-
     STRUMENTS THAT RELATE TO PUBLIC BUSINESS. WITH NECESSARY DIRECTIONS
     FOR MAKING DISTRESSES FOR RENT, &c. AS THE LAW BETWEEN LANDLORD AND
     TENANT NOW STANDS. TO WHICH IS ADDED, THE DOCTRINE OF FINES, AND RE-
     COVERIES, AND THEIR FORMS. THE SEVENTH EDITION, REVISED AND CORRECTED.
       Philadelphia: Printed by Joseph Crukshank, No. 87, High-street. MDCC-
     XCII. pp. (2), (2), 299, (6). 12mo.   AAS. JCB.

25064   THE YOUNG GENTLEMAN'S PARENTAL MONITOR. CONTAINING I. LORD CHESTER-
     FIELD'S ADVICE TO HIS SON, ON MEN AND MANNERS, OR THE PRINCIPLES OF POLITE-
     NESS, AND ON THE ART OF ACQUIRING A KNOWLEDGE OF THE WORLD. II. MAR-
     CHIONESS DE LAMBERT'S ADVICE TO HER SON. III. LORD BURGHLEY'S TEN PRE-
     CEPTS TO HIS SON.
       Hartford: Printed by Nathaniel Patten, 1792. pp. 148, frontispiece. 16mo.

25065   —— THE YOUNG GENTLEMAN'S PARENTAL MONITOR. CONTAINING I. LORD CHES-
     TERFIELD'S ADVICE TO HIS SON, ON MEN AND MANNERS, OR THE PRINCIPLES OF
     POLITENESS, AND ON THE ART OF ACQUIRING A KNOWLEDGE OF THE WORLD. II.
     MARCHIONESS DE LAMBERT'S ADVICE TO HER SON. III. LORD BURGHLEY'S TEN
     PRECEPTS TO HIS SON.
       New-York: Printed by Samuel Loudon? 1792.

25066   THE YOUNG GENTLEMEN AND LADIES ACCIDENCE: OR A COMPENDIOUS AMERICAN
     GRAMMAR OF THE ENGLISH TONGUE, PLAIN AND EASY. DESIGNED FOR THE YOUTH
     OF BOTH SEXES.
       Printed at Boston, by I. Thomas and E. T. Andrews, 1792.
     24th Massachusetts District Copyright, issued to Isaiah Thomas, 21
     February, 1792.

25067   THE YOUNG LADY'S PARENTAL MONITOR: CONTAINING, I. DR. GREGORY'S "FATHER'S
     LEGACY TO HIS DAUGHTERS" II. LADY PENNINGTON'S "UNFORTUNATE" MOTHER'S
     ADVICE "TO HER ABSENT "DAUGHTERS." III. MARCHIONESS DE LAMBERT'S "AD-
     VICE OF A MO—"THER TO HER "DAUGHTER." [Ornament.]
       *London: Printed: Hartford, Re-printed, and sold by, Hathaniel [sic]
     Patten,* M.DCC.XCII. pp. 164, frontispiece. 16mo.   JCB. NL.

25068   —— THE YOUNG LADY'S PARENTAL MONITOR: CONTAINING I. DR. GREGORY'S FATH-
     ER'S LEGACY TO HIS DAUGHTERS. II. LADY PENNINGTON'S UNFORTUNATE MOTH-
     ER'S ADVICE TO HER ABSENT DAUGHTERS. III. MARCHIONESS DE LAMBERT'S AD-
     VICE OF A MOTHER TO HER DAUGHTER.
       New-London: Printed by Timothy Green & Son? 1792.

25069   —— THE YOUNG LADY'S PARENTAL MONITOR: CONTAINING I. DR. GREGORY'S FATH-
     ER'S LEGACY TO HIS DAUGHTERS. II. LADY PENNINGTON'S UNFORTUNATE MOTH-
     ER'S ADVICE TO HER ABSENT DAUGHTERS. III. MARCHIONESS DE LAMBERT'S
     ADVICE OF A MOTHER TO HER DAUGHTER.
       New-York: Printed by Samuel Loudon? 1792.

AUCTION
VALUES

25070 YOUTH'S WARNING-PIECE; OR, THE TRAGICAL HISTORY OF GEORGE BARNWELL, WHO WAS UNDONE BY A STRUMPET, WHO CAUSED HIM TO ROB HIS MASTER AND MURDER HIS UNCLE.
Printed and sold in the Printing Office, New-London, (Connecticut). [1792.] pp. 16. 16mo.

25071 —— YOUTH'S WARNING PIECE; OR, THE TRAGICAL HISTORY OF GEORGE BARNWELL, WHO WAS UNDONE BY A STRUMPET, WHO CAUSED HIM TO ROB HIS MASTER AND MURDER HIS UNCLE.
Norwich: Printed by John Trumbull. 1792.

25072 ZIMMERMANN, JOHANN GEORG, ritter VON   1728 – 1795
SOLITUDE CONSIDERED, WITH RESPECT TO ITS INFLUENCE UPON THE MIND AND HEART. BY M. ZIMMERMAN.
Philadelphia: Printed by William Young, 1792.

25073 ZSCHOKKE, JOHANN HEINRICH DANIEL   1771 – 1848
ABAELLINO, THE GREAT BANDIT. A DRAMATIC ROMANCE. TRANSLATED FROM THE GERMAN AND ADAPTED TO THE NEW-YORK STAGE. BY WILLIAM DUNLAP.
New-York: 1792. pp. 82. 12mo.

25074 ZUBLY, JOHANN JOACHIM   1724 –1781
EVANGELISCHES ZEUGNISS VOM ELEND UND ERLÖSUNG DER MENSCHEN, IN ZWEY PREDIGTEN ABGELEGT. . . . . VIERTE AUFLAGE.
Germantaun: Gedruckt bey Peter Leibert. 1792.

PRINTING INSTITUTED IN
CONNECTICUT, 1709, A. D.

CHESHIRE, 1782.
WILLIAM LAW, Printer and Bookseller, 1790–92.
DANBURY, 1789.
NATHAN DOUGLAS, Printer and Publisher. Nathan Douglas and Edwards Ely, near the Court-House, 1790–1792.
EDWARDS ELY, Printer. Douglas and Ely, 1790–1792.
FAIRFIELD, 1786.
FARMINGTON.
JOEL ALLEN, Engraver, 1790–1792.
HARTFORD, 1764.
ELISHA BABCOCK, Printer and Publisher, 1790–92.
GEORGE GOODWIN, Printer. Hudson and Goodwin, 1790–1792.
BARZILLAI HUDSON, Printer and Publisher. Hudson and Goodwin, near the Bridge, 1790–92.
NATHANIEL PATTEN, Printer and Bookseller, 1790–1792.
LITCHFIELD, 1784.
DAVID BUEL, Printer. Collier and Buel, 1792.
THOMAS COLLIER, Printer and Publisher. 1. Thomas Collier, in the lower room [south end] of the Court-House, 1790–1791. 2. Collier and Buel, 1791–1792.
MIDDLETOWN, 1785.
MOSES HAWKINS WOODWARD, Printer and Publisher. 1. Moses H. Woodward, 1790–1792. 2. In the Town-House Chamber, 1792.
NEW HAVEN, 1754.
ISAAC BEERS, Printer and Bookseller, 1790–92.
AMOS DOOLITTLE, Engraver, 1790–1792.
SAMUEL GREEN, Printer. T. and S. Green, 1790–1792.
THOMAS GREEN, Printer and Publisher. 1. T. and S. Green, opposite the Post-Office, 1790–1792. 2. Universitatis Typographi, 1790–1792.
SIMEON JOCELIN, Author-Bookseller, 1790–1792.
ABEL MORSE, Printer, Publisher and Bookseller, 1790–1792.
DANIEL READ, Author-Bookseller, 1790–1792.
ABRAHAM THOMPSON, Author-Bookseller. At his house in Broad-way, 1790.
NEW LONDON, 1709.
SAMUEL GREEN, Printer. Timothy Green and Son, 1790–1792.
TIMOTHY GREEN, Printer and Publisher. Timothy Green and Son, at the north-west corner of the Parade, 1790–1792.
NORWICH, 1773.
EBENEZER BUSHNELL, Printer and Publisher. 1. 24 Rods west of the Meeting-House, 1791–1792. 2. Bushnell and Hubbard, 1792.
THOMAS HUBBARD, Printer. Bushnell and Hubbard, 1792.

LABAN THURBER, Author-Bookseller, 1792.
JOHN TRUMBULL, Printer and Publisher. Near the Meeting-House, 1790–1792.
WALLINGFORD.
ELISHA WHITTELSEY, JUNIOR, Bookseller, 1790.
WINDHAM, 1791.
JOHN BYRNE, Printer and Publisher. North of the Court-House, 1791–1792.

PRINTING INSTITUTED IN
DELAWARE, 1761, A. D.

WILMINGTON, 1761.
JAMES ADAMS, Printer and Bookseller. In High-Street, 1790–1792.
SAMUEL ANDREWS, Printer and Publisher. 1. Frederick Craig and Company, 1790–1791. 2. Andrews, Craig and Brynberg, at the Post-Office, in Market-Street, 1790–1791. 3. Peter Brynberg and Samuel Andrews, 1791–1792.
PETER BRYNBERG, Printer and Publisher. 1. Frederick Craig and Company, 1790–1791. 2. Andrews, Craig and Brynberg, 1790–1791. 3. Peter Brynberg and Samuel Andrews, in Market-Street, 1791–1792.
FREDERICK CRAIG, Printer and Publisher. 1. Frederick Craig and Company, 1790–1791. 2. Andrews, Craig and Brynberg, 1790–1791.

PRINTING INSTITUTED IN
EAST FLORIDA, 1783, A. D.

ST. AUGUSTINE, 1783.

PRINTING INSTITUTED IN
GEORGIA, 1762, A. D.

AUGUSTA, 1785.
GREENBERRY HUGHES, Printer and Publisher, 1785–1786.
JOHN ERDMAN SMITH, Printer and Publisher. Printer to the State, 1786–1792.
SAVANNAH, 1762.
JAMES JOHNSTON, Printer and Publisher. James and Nicholas Johnston, Broughton-Street, 1790–1792.
NICHOLAS JOHNSTON, Printer. James and Nicholas Johnston, 1790–1792.

PRINTING INSTITUTED IN
KENTUCKY, 1787, A. D.

LEXINGTON, 1787.
JOHN BRADFORD, Printer and Publisher. At his Printing-Office, in Main-Street, 1790–92.

PRINTING INSTITUTED IN
DISTRICT OF MAINE, 1785, A. D.

FALMOUTH, 1785.
MACHIAS.
JAMES LYON, Author-Bookseller, 1791.
PORTLAND, 1786.
SAMUEL FREEMAN, Author-Bookseller, 1790.

BENJAMIN TITCOMB, JUNIOR, Printer and Publisher, 1790–1792.

THOMAS BAKER WAIT, Printer and Publisher. Opposite the Haymarket, 1790–1792.

PRINTING INSTITUTED IN

MARYLAND, 1726, A. D.

ANNAPOLIS, 1726.

FREDERICK GREEN, Printer and Publisher. 1. Frederick and Samuel Green, 1790–1792. 2. Frederick Green, Printer to the State, 1790–92.

SAMUEL GREEN, Printer. F. and S. Green, 1790–1792.

BALTIMORE, 1765.

JOHN ADAMS, Printer. Samuel and John Adams, 1790–1792.

SAMUEL ADAMS, Printer and Bookseller. Samuel and John Adams, in Market-Street, between South and Gay-Streets, 1790–1792.

JAMES ANGELL, Printer. Goddard and Angell, 1790–1792.

CHRISTIAN BAUM, Vender, 1792.

AMBROSE CLARK, Bookseller, 1791.

JOHN DALRUMPLE, Vender, 1792.

PHILIP EDWARDS, Printer and Publisher. 1. In Market-Street, seven doors west of Gay-Street, 1792. 2. At the new Printing-Office, in Market-Street, a few doors below Tripolet's Alley, and nearly opposite the Card Manufactory, 1792.

WILLIAM GODDARD, Printer and Publisher. W. Goddard and J. Angell, at their Printing-Office in Market-Street, 1790–1792.

DAVID GRAHAM, Printer and Publisher. At the new Printing-Office, in Calvert-Street, between Market-Street and the Court-House, 1791–92.

GEORGE HAGERTY, Stationer. John and George Hagerty, 1792.

JOHN HAGERTY, Stationer. John and George Hagerty, in Water-Street, 1792.

JOHN HAYES, Printer and Publisher. The corner of Market and Calvert-Streets, 1790–92.

— RICE, Bookseller. Rice and Company, 1792.

JOHN SCROGS, Vender, 1792.

NICHOLAS TSHUDY, Vender. In Market-Street, 1792.

MASON LOCKE WEEMS, Vender, 1792.

EASTON, 1790.

JAMES COWAN, Printer and Publisher, 1790–92.

ELIZABETH (HAGER's) TOWN, 1790.

STEWART HERBERT, Printer and Publisher, 1790–1792.

PETER HOEFLY, Vender, 1792.

FREDERICK TOWN, 1779.

MATTHIAS BÄRTGIS, Printer, Publisher and Bookseller. At his English and German Printing-Office, 1790–1792.

JACOB STEINER, Vender, 1792.

JOHN WINTER, Printer and Publisher. At his Printing-Office, in Patrick-Street, 1790–1792.

TALBOT COUNTY.

BENJAMIN M. WARD, Author-Bookseller. (At the place known as The Trap), 1792.

PRINTING INSTITUTED IN

MASSACHUSETTS, 1639, A. D.

ATTLEBOROUGH, 1777.

BOSTON, 1675.

THOMAS ADAMS, Printer. Printer to the honourable General Court of the Commonwealth of Massachusetts, at his Printing-Office, opposite the new Court-House, Court-Street, 1790–92.

EBENEZER TURELL ANDREWS, Printer. Thomas and Andrews, 1790–1792.

JOSEPH BELKNAP, Printer and Publisher. 1. J. Belknap and A. Young, at their Printing-Office, No. 34, Newbury-Street, 1791. 2. At the Apollo Press, north side of the State-House, State-Street, 1791–1792. 3. Belknap et Young, Rue de l' Etat, vis-à-vis la Banque-Nationale, 1792. 4. Belknap and Hall, at the Apollo Press, State-Street, 1792.

WILLIAM BILLINGS, Author-Bookseller, 1790.

JOHN BOYLE, Bookseller. In Marlborough-Street, 1790–1792.

JOSEPH BUMSTEAD, Printer. At his Printing-Office, No. 20 Union-Street, 1790–1792.

CHARLES CAMBRIDGE, Printer. 1. Near the Boston Stone, 1790. 2. J. White and C. Cambridge, near Charles-River Bridge, 1790–1792.

WILLIAM T. CLAP, Bookseller. No. 90 Newbury-Street, 1792.

NATHANIEL COVERLY, Printer, Publisher and Bookseller. 1. At the corner of Back-Street, leading to Charles-River Bridge, 1790. .2. At the Sign of the Grand-Turk, Newbury-Street, 1790–1792.

— DOYLE, Printer. Mills and Doyle, 1790.

BENJAMIN EDES, Printer and Publisher. 1. Benjamin Edes and Son, No. 7 State-Street, 1790–1792. 2. At the house next to Col. Colman's, in Kilby-Street, 1792.

BENJAMIN EDES, JUNIOR, Printer. B. Edes and Son, 1790–1792.

PETER EDES, Printer, 1792.

SAMUEL ETHERIDGE, Printer. Young and Etheridge, 1792.

JOHN EWING, Vender. At Mr. John Ewing's Grocery-Store. No. 42 Marlborough-Street, 1792.

JOSIAH FLAGG, Engraver, 1790.

JOHN FLEET, Printer. T. and J. Fleet, 1790–92.

THOMAS FLEET, Printer and Publisher. 1. T. and J. Fleet, at the Bible and Heart in Cornhill, 1790–1792. 2. Universitatis Typographorum, 1791–1792.

JOHN WEST FOLSOM, Printer and Bookseller. No. 30 Union-Street, 1790–1792.

EDMUND FREEMAN, Printer and Publisher. Opposite the north-east corner of the State-House [State-Street], 1790–1791.

JOHN GARDINER, Author-Bookseller, 1792.

BENJAMIN GUILD, Bookseller. At the Boston Bookstore, No. 59 [in] Cornhill, 1790–1792.

SAMUEL HALL, Printer and Bookseller. At his Printing-Office, No. 53 in Cornhill, 1790–92.

T. HALL, Printer. Belknap and Hall, 1792.

JOSEPH HOVEY, Bookseller. No. 39 Cornhill, 1790.

JOHN HOWEL, Printer and Publisher. Opposite the Court-House, in Court-Street, 1791.

BENJAMIN LARKIN, Bookseller. At Shakespeare's Head, No. 46 [in] Cornhill, 1790–1792.

EBENEZER LARKIN, JUNIOR, Bookseller. No. 50 Cornhill, 1790–1792.

— MILLS, Printer. Mills and Doyle, 1790.

JOHN NORMAN, Engraver, Printer and Bookseller. At his Office, No. 75 Newbury-Street, opposite the Sign of the Lamb, 1790–1792.

EDWARD-EVELETH POWARS, Printer and Publisher. Opposite the new Court-House, in Court-Street, 1790–1792.

BENJAMIN RUSSELL, Printer and Publisher. Near the State-House, in State-Street, 1790–1792.

EZEKIEL RUSSELL, Printer and Bookseller. In Essex-Street, near the stump of Liberty-tree, 1790–1792.

WILLIAM SELBY, Author-Bookseller, 1790.

ISAIAH THOMAS, Printer, Publisher and Bookseller. Isaiah Thomas and Ebenezer T. Andrews, at Faust's Statue, No. 45 Newbury-Street. 1790–1792.

JOSHUA THOMAS, Bookseller. Opposite the Treasury-Office, 1790.

DAVID WEST, Bookseller. No. 36 Marlborough-Street, 1790–1792.

JAMES WHITE, Printer and Bookseller. 1. In Court-Street, 1790. 2. J. White and C. Cambridge, near Charles-River Bridge, 1790–1792.

ALEXANDER YOUNG, Printer and Publisher. 1. Belknap and Young, 1791–1792. 2. Young and Etheridge, Market-Square, 1792. 3. Opposite the entrance of the Branch-Bank, State-Street, 1792.

CAMBRIDGE, 1639.

CHARLESTOWN, 1785.

CHELMSFORD, 1775.

CONCORD. 1776.

DANVERS, 1776.

GREENFIELD, 1792.

   THOMAS DICKMAN, Printer and Publisher, 1792.

HAVERHILL, 1790.

   PETER EDES, Printer and Bookseller, 1790.

MIDDLEBOROUGH, 1787.

NEW BEDFORD, 1792.

   JOHN SPOONER, Printer and Publisher. At his Office, corner of Water and Prospect Streets, 1792.

NEWBURY.

   JONATHAN PLUMER, Vender, 1790.

   EDMUND SAWYER, Bookseller, 1791.

NEWBURYPORT, 1773.

   WILLIAM HOYT, Bookseller, 1791.

   JOHN MYCALL, Printer and Publisher. In Merrimack-Street, a little below the Ferry-way, 1790–1792.

NORTHAMPTON, 1786.

   WILLIAM BUTLER, Printer and Publisher, 1790–1792.

PITTSFIELD, 1787.

   JOHN RUSSELL, Printer and Publisher. Russell & Storrs, at their Office a few rods west of the Meeting-House, 1787.

   ROGER STORRS, Printer and Publisher. 1. Russell & Storrs, 1787. 2. Roger Storrs, near the Meeting-House, 1788–1790.

PLYMOUTH, 1785.

REHOBOTH, 1776.

SALEM, 1768.

   WILLIAM CARLETON, Bookseller. 1. 1790–1791. 2. At his Shop, opposite the Rev. Mr. Price's Meeting-House, Main-Street, 1792. 3. At the Bible and Heart, 1792.

   THOMAS C. CUSHING, Printer and Publisher. 1. Dabney and Cushing, 1790. 2. Thomas C. Cushing, at his Printing-Office, No. 8 Paved [Main-] Street, near [corner] Court and Washington Streets, 1790–1792.

   JOHN DABNEY, Printer and Publisher. 1. Dabney and Cushing, in the Main-Street, 1790. 2. John Dabney, 1791

SPRINGFIELD, 1782.

   EDWARD GRAY, Printer, 1792.

   JAMES REED HUTCHINS, Printer and Publisher. At the corner of the entrance to the Court-House, 1792.

   EZRA WALDO WELD, Printer and Publisher. Opposite the Court-House, 1790–1792.

STERLING.

   M. SMITH, Vender, 1792.

   ROBERT BAILEY THOMAS, Author-Bookseller, 1790–1792.

STOCKBRIDGE, 1789.

   LORING ANDREWS, Printer and Publisher, 1790–1792.

TAUNTON.

   DANIEL BREWER, Bookseller, 1791–1792.

WATERTOWN, 1775.

   RICHARD EVERETT, Bookseller, 1790.

WORCESTER, 1775.
    ISAIAH THOMAS, Printer, Publisher, Bookseller, Stationer and Binder. 1. Isaiah Thomas, 1790–1792. 2. Isaiah Thomas and Leonard Worcester, 1792.
    LEONARD WORCESTER, Printer. Thomas and Worcester, 1792.

PRINTING INSTITUTED IN
NEW HAMPSHIRE, 1756, A. D.

CONCORD, 1789.
    GEORGE HOUGH, Printer and Publisher, 1790–92.
    ELIJAH RUSSELL, Printer and Publisher, 1792.
CONWAY.
    ZADOK KING, Vender. At his house, 1792.
DOVER, 1790.
    ELIPHALET LADD, Printer and Publisher. At his Printing-Office, near the Court-House, 1790–1792.
DUNBARTON.
    THOMAS BASSETT, Bookseller, 1791.
EXETER, 1775.
    JOHN LAMSON, Printer and Publisher, 1790.
    HENRY RANLET, Printer and Publisher. In the Main-Street, 1790–1792.
KEENE, 1787,
    JAMES DAVENPORT GRIFFITH, Printer and Publisher. In the Main-Street, 1790–1792.
PORTSMOUTH, 1756.
    DANIEL HUMPHREYS, Author-Bookseller, 1792.
    JOHN MELCHER, Printer and Publisher. 1. At his Office in Congress-Street, 1790. 2. At his Printing-Office, corner of Market-Street, 1790–1792.
    GEORGE JERRY OSBORNE, Printer and Publisher, 1790.
    GEORGE JERRY OSBORNE, JUNIOR, Printer, Publisher and Bookseller. 1. At his Office, Guttemberg's Head, Congress-Street, 1790–1791. 2. George and John Osborne, at the Spy Printing-Office, near the State-House, Guttemberg's Head, Congress-Street, 1791–1792.
    JOHN OSBORNE, Printer. 1. George and John Osborne, 1791–1792. 2. John Osborne, at the Spy Printing-Office, 1792.
    CHARLES PEIRCE, Bookseller. At the Columbian Book Store, No. 5 Daniel Street, 1791–92.

PRINTING INSTITUTED IN
NEW JERSEY, 1755, A. D.

BURLINGTON, 1765.
    DANIEL LAWRENCE, Printer. I. Neale and D. Lawrence, 1790–1791.
    ISAAC NEALE, Printer and Publisher. 1. I. Neale and D. Lawrence, nearly opposite James Sterling's Store, 1790–1791. 2. Isaac Neale, 1791–1792.

CHATHAM, 1779.
ELIZABETH TOWN, 1786.
    SHEPARD KOLLOCK, Printer and Publisher, 1790–1792.
NEW BRUNSWICK, 1783.
    SHELLY ARNETT, Printer and Publisher. Arnett and Blauvelt, 1792.
    ABRAHAM BLAUVELT, Printer and Publisher. 1. Abraham Blauvelt, 1790–1792. 2. Arnett and Blauvelt, 1792.
NEWARK, 1776.
    JOHN WOODS, Printer and Publisher, 1791–1792.
PRINCETON, 1785.
TRENTON, 1778.
    ISAAC COLLINS, Printer and Bookseller, 1790–92.
    JOHN MERSHON, Printer. Sherman and Mershon, 1792.
    GEORGE SHERMAN, Printer and Publisher. George Sherman and John Mershon, 1792.
WOODBRIDGE, 1755.

PRINTING INSTITUTED IN
NEW YORK, 1693, A. D.

ALBANY, 1771.
    JOHN ASPLUND, Vender, 1792.
    JOHN BARBER, Printer and Publisher. John Barber and Solomon Southwick, No. 48, north side of State-Street, 1792.
    ROBERT BARBER, Printer and Publisher. 1. Robert Barber and Company, No. 4, Maiden-Lane, four doors west of the Market, 1790. 2. No. 53, west side of Market-Street, opposite the Market, 1791.
    ELISHA CRANE, Bookseller, 1791.
    SOLOMON SOUTHWICK, Printer. 1. Robert Barber and Company, 1790–1791. 2. John Barber and Solomon Southwick, 1792.
    CHARLES R. WEBSTER, Printer and Publisher. 1. Charles R. and George Webster, at their Printing-Office, No. 46, (on the north side of) State-Street, corner of Middle-Alley [Middle-Lane], between the Dutch and English churches, 1790–1792.
    GEORGE WEBSTER, Printer. Charles R. and George Webster, 1790–1792.
CATSKILL-LANDING, 1792.
    MACKAY CROSWELL, Printer and Publisher. 1. M. Croswell and Company, 1792. 2. In the Chamber over Store of Noah Everest & Co., 1792.
FISHKILL, 1776.
GOSHEN, 1789.
    DAVID MANDEVILLE, Printer and Publisher. 1. Near the Court-House, 1789–1790. 2. David Mandeville and David M. Westcott, at the Academy, [near the Court-House], 1790–1792.
    DAVID M. WESTCOTT, Publisher. 1. Mandeville and Westcott, 1790–1792. 2. David M. Westcott, 1792.

HUDSON, 1785.
  ASHBEL STODDARD, Printer, Publisher, and Bookseller. Near the Market, 1790–1792.
KINGSTON, 1777.
  WILLIAM COPP, Printer. Nicholas Power and William Copp, 1792.
  NICHOLAS POWER, Printer and Publisher. Nicholas Power and William Copp, 1792.
LANSINGBURGH, 1787.
  JOHN BABCOCK, Printer and Publisher. Babcock and Hickock, corner of King and Hoosack-Streets, 1790.
  — HICKOCK, Printer. Babcock and Hickock, 1790.
  SILVESTER TIFFANY, Printer and Publisher. 1. At his Office over the Store of Mr. W. Bell, 1791–1792. 2. Silvester Tiffany, (a little south of Douglass' Tavern), 1791–1792. 3. Silvester Tiffany and William W. Wands, 1792.
  WILLIAM W. WANDS, Printer. Tiffany and Wands, 1792.
NEW YORK CITY, 1693.
  THOMAS ALLEN, Bookseller and Stationer. 1. Hodge, Allen and Campbell, and sold at their respective [several] Bookstores, 1790. 2. Thomas Allen, No. 16, Queen-Street, 1791. 3. No. 12, Queen-Street, 1792. 4. No. 186, Pearl-Street, 1792.
  EDWARD BERRY, Bookseller and Stationer. 1. Berry and Rogers, No. 35, Hanover-Square, 1790–1792. 2. Berry, Rogers and Berry, No. 35, Hanover-Square, 1792.
  JAMES BERRY, Bookseller. Berry, Rogers and Berry, 1792.
  BARTHOLOMEW BURGES, Author - Bookseller, 1790.
  JOHN BURGHER, Author-Bookseller, 1791.
  SAMUEL CAMPBELL, Bookseller. 1. Hodge, Allen and Campbell, and sold at their respective [several] Bookstores, 1790. 2. Hodge and Campbell, 1791–1792. 3. Samuel Campbell, No. 37, Hanover-Square, 1792.
  FRANCIS CHILDS, Printer and Publisher. 1. Francis Childs and John Swaine, No. 190, Water-Street, corner of King-Street, 1790. 2. Printers to the State of New York, No. 189 [190], Water-Street, near King-Street, 1790–1792. 3. Printers to the Congress of the United States, No. 190, Water-Street, corner of King-Street, 1790–1792. 4. No. 29 Water-Street, corner of King-Street, 1792.
  C. DAVIS, Bookseller. 1791.
  WILLIAM DURELL, Printer and Bookseller. 1. W. Durell and Company, 1790–1791. 2. W. Durell at his Book-Store and Printing-Office, No. 19, Queen-Street, near the Fly-Market, 1791–1792.

JOHN FENNO, Printer and Publisher. 1. No. 9, Maiden-Lane, near the Oswego-Market, 1790. 2. At his Office, No. 41, Broad-Street, near the Exchange, 1790.
HUGH GAINE, Printer, Bookseller and Stationer. At his Bookstore and Printing-Office, at the Bible, in Hanover-Square, 1790–1792.
BENJAMIN GOMEZ, Bookbinder and Stationer. No. 32, Maiden-Lane, 1792.
THOMAS GREENLEAF, Printer, Publisher and Bookseller. At the Printing-Office, No. 196, Water-Street, 1790–1792.
JOHN HARRISSON, Printer and Publisher. 1. Harrisson and Purdy, at their Printing-Office, No. 3, Peck-Slip, 1790–1791. 2. John Harrisson, at his Printing-Office, [at Yorick's Head] No. 3, Peck-Slip, 1791–1792.
ROBERT HODGE, Printer and Bookseller. 1. Hodge, Allen and Campbell, and sold at their respective [several] Book Stores, 1790. 2. Hodge and Campbell, 1791–1792. 3. Robert Hodge, No. 11, Water-Street, 1792.
THOMAS LLOYD, Stenographer and Author, 1790.
SAMUEL LOUDON, Printer and Publisher. No. 5, Water-Street, between the Coffee-House and Old-Slip, 1790–1791.
SAMUEL LOUDON, JUNIOR, Printer and Publisher. No. 5, Water-Street, between the Coffee-House and Old-Slip, 1792.
ARCHIBALD M'LEAN, Printer and Publisher. At his Printing-Office, Franklin's Head, No. 41. Hanover-Square, 1790–1792.
ANDREW MARSCHALK, Bookseller, 1791.
WILLIAM MORTON, Printer and Publisher. 1. At the Printing-Office, No. 231, Queen-Street, 1790–1791. 2. No. 55, King-Street, 1791–92.
BENJAMIN YOUNG PRIME, Author-Bookseller, 1791.
— PURDY, Printer. Harrisson and Purdy, 1790–1791.
JOHN REID, Bookseller, 1790–1792.
JOHN ROGERS, Bookseller. 1. Berry and Rogers, 1790–1792. 2. Berry, Rogers and Berry, 1792.
WILLIAM ROSS, Printer, 1790.
M. SMITH, Bookseller, 1791.
JOHN SWAINE, Printer. Childs and Swaine, 1790–1792.
JAMES SWORDS, Printer. T. and J. Swords, 1790–1792.
THOMAS SWORDS, Printer, Publisher and Bookseller. 1. T. and J. Swords, at their Printing-Office, No. 44, Crown-Street [near Smith-Street], 1790. 2. No. 167, William-Street, 1791. 3. No. 27, William-Street, 1791–1792.
POUGHKEEPSIE, 1777.
  NICHOLAS POWER, Printer and Publisher. Near the Court-House, 1790–1792.

SAG HARBOR, 1791.
DAVID FROTHINGHAM, Printer and Publisher. Near the Landing, 1791–1792.

PRINTING INSTITUTED IN
NORTH CAROLINA, 1751, A. D.

EDENTON, 1788.
ABRAHAM HODGE, Printer and Publisher. Hodge and Wills, Printers to the State, 1790–1792.
HENRY WILLS, Printer and Publisher. 1. Hodge and Wills, 1790–1792. 2. Henry Wills, 1792.
FAYETTEVILLE, 1787.
CALEB D. HOWARD, Printer. 1. Sibley and Howard, 1790. 2. Howard and Roulstone, 1790.
GEORGE ROULSTONE, Printer. 1. Howard and Roulstone, 1790. 2. George Roulstone, 1790–1791.
JOHN SIBLEY, Printer and Publisher. 1. Sibley and Howard, 1790. 2. John Sibley and Company, at Franklin's Head in Green-Street, 1790–1791.
HALIFAX, 1782.
ABRAHAM HODGE, Printer and Publisher. Joint-Printer to the State with H. Wills, 1792.
HILLSBOROUGH, 1788.
NEWBERN, 1751.
FRANÇOIS XAVIER MARTIN, Printer and Publisher, 1790–1792.
WILMINGTON, 1764.

PRINTING INSTITUTED IN
PENNSYLVANIA, 1685, A. D.

CARLISLE, 1785.
GEORGE KLINE, Printer and Publisher. 1. Kline and Reynolds, 1790. 2, George Kline, 1791–1792.
GEORGE REYNOLDS, Printer. Kline and Reynolds, 1790–1791.
CHAMBERSBURG, 1790.
WILLIAM DAVISON, Printer and Publisher, 1790–1792.
CHESTNUT HILL, 1763.
SAMUEL SAUR, Printer, Publisher and Bookseller. Buchdrucker auf Chesnut Hill, nahe bey dem 10ten Meilstein allwo die Readinger und Nordwelscher Strasse Zusammenkommen, 1790–92.
EPHRATA, 1745.
DER BRÜDERSCHAFT. Klosterpresse, 1790–1792.
FRIEDENSTHAL BEI BETHLEHEM, 1763.
GERMANTOWN, 1738.
MICHAEL BILLMEYER, Printer and Bookseller, 1790–1792.
JUSTUS FOX, Vender, 1792.
PETER LEIBERT, Printer and Bookseller. 1. Peter Leibert, 1790–1791. 2. Peter Leibert and Son, 1791. 3. Peter Leibert, 1792.

HARRISBURGH, 1789.
JOHN W. ALLEN, Printer and Publisher. 1. Allen and Wyeth, adjoining the Register's Office, 1792. 2. Mulberry-Street, opposite residence of Adam Boyd, esq. near the Bank, 1792.
T. ROBERTS, Printer and Publisher, 1790.
JOHN WYETH, Printer. Allen and Wyeth, 1792.
HOPE.
FREDERICK PETER, Vender, 1792.
LANCASTER, 1747.
JOHANN ALBRECHT, Printer, Publisher and Bookseller. 1. Albrecht und Lahn, in den Neuen Buchdruckerey, in der Queenstrasse, 1790. 2. Johann Albrecht und Company, in der Neuen Buchdruckerey, zwischen der Koenig und Dranien-Strasse in der Prinz-strasse, 1790–1791. 3. In der Neuen Buchdruckerey, in der Prinz-strasse, das Zweyte Haus, nordwärts vom Gesängniss, 1791–1792.
JACOB BAILEY, Printer and Bookseller, 1790–92.
WILLIAM DICKSON, Printer. In King-Street, 1792.
MATTHAEUS HEHL, Vender, 1792.
JACOB LAHN, Printer. Albrecht und Lahn, 1790.
NORTHUMBERLAND, 1792.
GEORGE SCHUSLER, Printer and Publisher, 1792.
OCTORARA, 1786.
PHILADELPHIA, 1685.
JOHN AITKEN, Printer and Bookseller, 1791.
ROBERT AITKEN, Printer and Bookseller. R. Aitken and Son, No. 22, [in] Market-Street, 1790–1792.
BENJAMIN FRANKLIN BACHE, Printer and Publisher. Up Franklin Court, in Market, between Third and Fourth-Streets, 1790–1792.
FRANCIS BAILEY, Printer and Bookseller. 1. At Yorick's Head, No. 116, [in] Market [High-] Street, 1790–1792. 2. On the south side of Market-Street, near Fourth-Street, at the Sign of Yorick's Head, 1791.
GODFREY BAKER, Bookseller. Godfrey Baker & Co., No. 59, Race-Street, 1792.
CLEMENT BIDDLE, Author-Bookseller, 1791.
THOMAS BRADFORD, Printer, Publisher and Bookseller. 1. At his Printing-Office, Laetitia-Court, 1790–1792. 2. No. 8, South Front-Street, 1791–1792.
ANDREW BROWN, Printer and Publisher. 1. At Washington's Head, Chestnut-Street, opposite the Post-Office, 1790. 2. At Washington's Head, in Chesnut-Street, near Front-Street, 1790–1792.
ROBERT CAMPBELL, Bookseller. 1. At his new Book and Stationery Store, on the west side [north-east corner] of Second-Street, below the Market, and five doors above Chesnut-Street, 1790. 2. Second-Street, No. 53 [54], the corner of Chesnut-Street, 1791–1792.

JOHN CAREY, Bookseller. 1. No. 112, Union-Street, 1791. 2. No. 26, Pear-Street, 1792.

MATHEW CAREY, Printer, Publisher and Bookseller. 1. Carey, Stewart and Company, No. 22, North Front-Street, 1790–1791. 2. From the Press of Mathew Carey, No. 118, Market-Street, 1791–1792.

FRANCIS CHILDS, Printer. 1. Childs and Swaine, at their Office No. 209. High-Street, near Fifth-Street, 1791–1792. 2. Francis Childs and John Swaine, Printers to the Congress of the United States, 1791–1792.

CHARLES [CARL] CIST, Printer, Publisher and Bookseller. 1. Carl Cist, in der Zweyten-Strasse, Num. 104, nah am Eck der Rehs-Strasse, 1790–1792. 2. No. 104, in Second-Street, near the corner of Race-Street, 1790–92.

DAVID C. CLAYPOOLE, Printer and Publisher. 1. Dunlap and Claypoole, 1790. 2. David C. Claypoole, at his Office, No. 2. South Third-Street, 1791–1792.

— COCHRAN, Printer. Stewart and Cochran, 1792.

JOSEPH CRUKSHANK, Printer, Publisher and Bookseller. 1. On the north side of Market-Street, between Second and [near] Third-Streets, 1790–1791. 2. No. 87 [91], High-Street, between Second and Third-Streets, near Sixth-Street, 1791–1792.

ALEXANDER JAMES DALLAS, Author-Bookseller, 1790.

JOHN DICKINS, Bookseller. 1. In [on] Fourth-Street, [east side] [No. 43] near the corner of Race-Street, 1790–1791. 2. No. 182, Race-Street, near Sixth-Street, 1791–1792.

THOMAS DOBSON, Printer and Bookseller. At the Stone-House, No. 41, Second-Street, between Market and Chesnut-Streets, 1790–92.

JOHN DUNLAP, Printer and Publisher. 1. John Dunlap and David C. Claypoole, on the south side of Market-Street, the third house east of Second-Street, 1790. 2. John Dunlap, at No. 48, Market-Street, opposite the Jersey-Market, 1791–1792.

JOHN FENNO, Printer and Publisher. 1. At his house, No. 69, Market- [High-] Street, north side between [a few doors above] Second and Third-Streets, 1790–1792.

WILLIAM GIBBONS, Printer. North Third-Street, No. 144, near Vine-Street, 1792.

Mrs. GRIFFITH, Vender, No. 417, South Front-Street, 1792

DAVID HALL, Printer and Publisher. Hall and Sellers, at the New Printing-Office, near the Market, [No. 51], Market-Street, 1790–1792.

PARRY HALL, Printer. No. 149, Chesnut-Street, near Fourth-Street, 1791–1792.

PELEG HALL, Printer. Prichard and Hall, 1790–1791.

EBENEZER HAZARD, Author-Bookseller, 1792.

TOBIAS HIRTE, Vender. No. 118, North Second-Street [next door to Widow Rasor], 1792.

READING HOWELL, Map - Publisher. No. 88, North-Fifth-Street, 1791–1792.

DANIEL HUMPHREYS, Printer. At the new Printing-Office in [No. 132, South] Front-Street, near the Drawbridge, 1790–1792.

ROBERT JACK, Author-Bookseller, 1790.

JOSEPH JAMES, Printer and Bookseller. 1. Joseph James, 1790. 2. James and Johnson, on the north side of Market-Street, between Third and Fourth-Streets, 1790–1791. 3. No. 147, High-Street, 1791.

BENJAMIN JOHNSON, Printer and Bookseller. 1. James and Johnson, 1790–1791. 2. Benjamin Johnson, No. 147, High [Market-] Street, 1792. 3. Johnson and Justice, at Franklin's Head, No. 41, Chesnut-Street, 1792.

WILLIAM JONES, Bookbinder and Bookseller. No. 73, Race-Street, 1791.

— JUSTICE, Printer. Johnson and Justice, 1792.

HEINRICH KÄMMERER, Printer. 1. No. 24, North Third-Street, 1792. 2. Steiner und Kämmerer, 1792.

THOMAS LANG, Printer and Bookseller. No. 21, Church-Alley, 1790–1792.

DANIEL LAWRENCE, Printer and Bookseller. No. 33 [78], North Fourth-Street, near Race-Street, 1792.

JOHN M'CULLOCH, Printer and Bookseller. In Third-Street, No. 1 [the third door] above [near] Market-Street, 1790–1792.

JOHN MACPHERSON, Author - Bookseller. No. 417, South Front-Street, 1792.

LEWIS NICOLAS, Author - Bookseller. At the Debtor's Apartment, 1791.

ELEAZER OSWALD, Printer. No. 156, [in] Market-Street, between Fourth and Fifth-Streets, 1790–1792.

VINCENT M. PELOSI, Publisher. At the Merchants and Exchange Coffee-House, 1791.

ZACHARIAH POULSON, JUNIOR, Printer and Publisher. 1. On the west side of Fourth-Street, between Market-Street and Arch-Street, 1790. 2. In Fourth-Street, near Market-Street, opposite the gate of the Friends' Burying Ground, 1790. 3. No. 30, North Fourth-Street, near the College [University], 1791–92.

WILLIAM PRICHARD, Bookseller and Auctioneer. Prichard and Hall, in Market-Street, between Front and Second-Streets, 1790–1791.

JOHN RALLING, Author-Bookseller, 1790.

CARL CHRISTOPH REICHE, Publisher. In der Vierten-Strasse, das naechste Haus und den sieben Sternen, und der Rees-Strassen Ecke, 1790–1791.

GEORGE REINHOLDT, Vender. No. 201. Market-Street, 1792.

HENRY RICE, Bookseller. 1. Rice and Company, 1790–1792. 2. H. and P. Rice, No. 50 Market-Street, 1792.

P. RICE, Bookseller. H. and P. Rice, 1792.

JACOB RITTER, Vender. In Front-Street, 3d door below Arch-Street, 1792.

DAVID SAUR, Bookseller, 1791.

THOMAS SEDDON, Printer and Bookseller. In Market-Street, between Front and Second-Streets, 1790.

WILLIAM SELLERS, Printer. Hall and Sellers, in Market-Street, 1790–1792.

SAMUEL HARRISON SMITH, Printer, 1791–1792.

WILLIAM SPOTSWOOD, Printer and Bookseller. 1. Front-Street, between Market and Chesnut-Streets, 1790–1792. 2. No. 69, Market-Street, near Second-Street, 1792.

MELCHIOR STEINER, Printer, Publisher and Bookseller. 1. Buchdrucker, in der Rees-Strasse, Zwischen der Zweyten-und Dritten-Strasse, No. 71, 1790–1792. 2. Steiner und Kämmerer, 1792.

PETER STEWART, Printer. 1. Carey, Stewart and Company, 1790. 2. Peter Stewart, No. 34, in Second, between Market and Chesnut-Streets, 1790–1791. 3. Stewart and Cochran, No. 34, South Second-Street, 1792.

ENOCH STORY, Printer and Bookseller. 1. In Third-Street, third door from Chesnut-Street, 1790. 2. In Second-Street, the east side, [five doors from [fifth door above] Arch-Street, the left hand upwards], 1790–1791. 3. Market-Street, between Fifth and Sixth-Streets (No. 209) north side, 1790. 4. In Fourth between Market and Chesnut-Streets, 1791. 5. Fourth-Street, (No. 36) nearly opposite the Indian Queen Tavern, 1792.

JOHN SWAINE, Printer. Childs & Swaine, 1791–92.

HENRY TAYLOR, Printer, 1790–1791.

BENJAMIN TOWNE, Bookseller. In Church-Alley, 1790.

WILLIAM WOODHOUSE, Bookseller. 1. In Front-Street, next door to the Coffee-House, 1790. 2. At the Bible, No. 6, South Front-Street, 1791–1792.

WILLIAM YOUNG, Printer, Bookseller and Stationer. No. 52, Second-Street, the corner of [Second and] Chesnut-Street, 1790–1792.

JOHN ZELLER, Printer and Bookseller. 1. Johann Zeller, 89 Race-Street, 1791. 2. John Zeller, at his Printing-Office, No. 89, Race-Street, five doors below Third-Street, 1791.

PITTSBURGH, 1786.

JOHN SCULL, Printer and Publisher. At his Printing-Office in Water-Street, near Comsby's Ferry, 1790–1792.

READING, 1789.

— BARTON, Printer and Publisher. Barton und Jungmann, 1790–1792.

GOTTLOB JUNGMANN, Printer. Barton und Jungmann, 1790–1792.

EDWARD ROSS, Vender, 1792.

YORK, 1777.

JOHN EDIE, Printer and Publisher, 1790–1792.

JOHN MORRIS, Vender, 1792.

ERNST SCHLOSSER, Vender, 1792.

PRINTING INSTITUTED IN
RHODE ISLAND, 1727, A. D.

NEWPORT, 1727.

HENRY BARBER, Printer and Publisher. At the foot of the Parade, 1790–1792.

PETER EDES, Printer and Publisher. On Thames-Street, 1790–1791.

JACOB RICHARDSON, Bookseller, 1790–1792.

PROVIDENCE, 1762.

ROBERT ADAM, Bookseller. At the head of the Long-Wharffe west side of the River, 1791.

JOHN CARTER, Printer and Publisher. At the Post-Office, near the State-House, 1790–1792.

JAMES GARDNER, Bookseller. Nearly opposite the Court-House, 1792.

BENNETT WHEELER, Printer and Publisher. 1. At his Office, on the west side of the River, 1790–1791. 2. Westminster-Street, 1790–1792. 3. At the Market-House Chamber, 1792.

WARREN, 1792.

NATHANIEL PHILLIPS, Printer and Publisher. At the Post-Office, 1792.

RICHARD LEE, Vender, 1792.

PRINTING INSTITUTED IN
SOUTH CAROLINA, 1732, A. D.

CHARLESTON, 1732.

THOMAS BARTHOLOMEW BOWEN, Printer and Publisher. No. 38, Bay, 1790–1792.

WILLIAM HAMMET, Author-Bookseller, 1792.

WILLIAM PRIMROSE HARRISON, Printer, 1791–1792.

JOHN M'IVER, JUNIOR, Printer. Markland and M'Iver, 1790–1792.

JOHN MARKLAND, Printer and Publisher. Markland and M'Iver, Printers to the city, No. 47, Bay, 1790–1792.

WILLIAM MASON, JUNIOR, Printer. Timothy and Mason, 1792.

JOHN MILLER, Printer and Publisher, 1790–92.

ANNE S. TIMOTHY, Printer and Publisher. Printer to the State, 1790–1792.

BENJAMIN FRANKLIN TIMOTHY, Printer and Publisher. Timothy and Mason, 1792.

WILLIAM P. YOUNG, Printer and Bookseller. Broad-Street, 1791–1792.

COLUMBIA, 1792.
D. CONSTABLE, Printer and Publisher, 1792.
GEORGETOWN, 1785.

PRINTING INSTITUTED IN
TENNESSEE, 1791, A. D.

KNOXVILLE, 1792.
GEORGE ROULSTONE, Printer and Publisher, 1792.
ROGERSVILLE, 1791.
GEORGE ROULSTONE, Printer and Publisher. Hawkins County Court-House, 1791–1792.

PRINTING INSTITUTED IN
VERMONT, 1778, A. D.

BENNINGTON, 1783.
ANTHONY HASWELL, Printer and Publisher. 1. Haswell and Russell, at their Office a few rods south of the Court-House, 1790. 2. Anthony Haswell, at his Office a few rods south of the Court-House, 1790–1792.
DAVID RUSSELL, Printer. Haswell and Russell. 1790.
DRESDEN, 1778.
POWNALBORO'.
A. NELSON, Vender, 1791.
RUTLAND, 1792.
ANTHONY HASWELL, Printer and Publisher. 1. At the south-west angle of the Court-House Square, 1792. 2. Printer for the State in the Western District at the Rutland Press, 1792.
WESTMINSTER, 1781.
WINDSOR, 1783.
JAMES REED HUTCHINS, Printer and Publisher. 1. Hutchins and Spooner, on the Main Street, 1791–1792. 2. James R. Hutchins, 1792.
ALDEN SPOONER, Printer and Publisher. 1. A. Spooner, 1790–1791. 2. Printer to the State of Vermont, 1790–1792. 3. Hutchins and Spooner, 1791–1792.

PRINTING INSTITUTED IN
VIRGINIA, 1730, A. D.

ALEXANDRIA, 1782.
— BOND, Printer. Hanson and Bond, 1790–92.
SAMUEL HANSON, Printer and Publisher. Hanson and Bond, 1790–1792.
ELLIS PRICE, Printer. Smith and Price, 1792.
JOHN SMITH, Printer and Publisher. John Smith and Ellis Price, at the east end of the Market-House, 1792.
CHARLOTTESVILLE, 1781.
FREDERICKSBURG, 1787.
TIMOTHY GREEN, Printer and Publisher, 1790–1792.

GEORGE TOWN, 1789.
M. DAY, Printer and Publisher. M. Day and W. Hancock, 1790–1791.
ALEXANDER DOYLE, Printer and Publisher, 1791–1792.
JAMES DOYLE, Printer and Publisher, 1792.
CHARLES FIERER, Printer and Publisher. 1. Charles Fierer, 1790. 2. Charles Fierer and Thomas W. Fosdick, 1790–1791.
THOMAS W. FOSDICK, Printer. Fierer and Fosdick, 1790–1791.
W. HANCOCK, Printer. Day and Hancock, 1790–1791.

MARTINSBURG, 1790.
NATHANIEL WILLIS, Printer and Publisher. At his Printing-Office, in Burke-Street, near the Court-House, 1790–1792.
NORFOLK, 1774.
DANIEL BAXTER, Printer and Publisher. 1. Prentis and Baxter, 1790–1792. 2. Baxter and Wilson, at their Office near the Town-Point, 1792.
WILLIAM DAVIS, Printer. Willett and Davis, 1792.
WILLIAM PRENTIS, Printer and Publisher. Prentis and Baxter, near Borough Tavern, 1790–1792.
CHARLES WILLETT, Printer and Publisher. C. Willett and W. Davis, near the Market, 1792.
THOMAS WILSON, Printer. Baxter and Wilson, 1792.
PETERSBURG, 1786.
WILLIAM PRENTIS, Printer and Publisher. 1790–1792.
RICHMOND, 1780.
JAMES CAREY, Printer. At his Printing-Office, near Shockœ Warehouse, 1792.
AUGUSTINE DAVIS, Printer and Publisher. Printer for the public, 1790–1792.
JOHN DIXON, Printer and Publisher. Printer to this Commonwealth, 1790–1792.
SIMON CREA McMAHON, Author-Bookseller, 1790.
THOMAS NICOLSON, Printer and Publisher. Two doors above the Eagle-Tavern, 1790–1792.
JOHN POPE, Author-Bookseller, 1792.
SHEPHERD'S TOWN, 1791.
NATHANIEL WILLIS, Printer, 1791.
WILLIAMSBURG, 1730.
WINCHESTER, 1787.
RICHARD BOWEN, Printer and Publisher. 1. Richard Bowen and Company, 1790–1792. 2. Richard Bowen, 1792.

END OF THE EIGHTH VOLUME.